Q: In an earlier version of Word, I cropped pictu dragging the handles. Why doesn't this work in Word 97?

A: This procedure has changed in Word 97. You now use the Crop button on the Picture toolbar to crop objects. Choose View, Toolbars, Picture to display the Picture toolbar. *See Chapter 13.*

Q: How can I use information from an Excel worksheet for my data source during a Word mail merge?

A: While in Mail Merge Helper, click on Get Data, Open Data Source. In the dialog box that appears, change the Files of Type selection to Excel, and locate the Excel worksheet. The Select Method option in the Open Data Source dialog box must be selected. Choose Open, and in the Confirm Data Source dialog box, make sure that the Microsoft Excel Worksheet via Converter option is selected. When you click on OK, you see an Open Worksheet dialog box where you can choose a worksheet or range of cells to use. *See Chapter 9.*

Q: What graphics file formats are built into Word 97?

A: Word 97 can read the following formats: Windows Bitmap (.bmp, .dib, .rel), Windows Enhanced Metafile (.emf), Windows Metafile (.wmf), JPEG File Interchange (.jpg), Portable Network Graphics (.png), and Macintosh PICT in Word's Mac version. *See Chapter 13.*

Q: If I save a Word 97 file in Word 7 format, will I lose any text formatting?

A: Some Word 97 features aren't supported in previous versions. Look out for embedded fonts, outline and numbered lists that use heading styles, bullet lists with more than one level of indentation, page borders, shaded characters, and animated, embossed, or engraved text. *See Chapter 3.*

Q: Is there something that will help me use my Word 97 documents in earlier versions of Word (I have Word 6 on my home computer)?

A: Copy the file Wrd97cnv.exe from the Word or Office 97 CD (it's in the ValuPack folder) to your hard drive where the earlier version of Word is installed. Double-click on it and the converter for Word 97 documents will be extracted and set up. *See Chapter 1.*

Q: When I run Spelling Checker in Mail Merge, Word tells me that it won't check text with "no proofing." What does this mean?

A: Word won't check any words that appear from merge fields. Select all the text in the merged document. Choose Tools, Language, Set Language. Select English (United States) and click on OK. This makes all text that results from a merge field into regular text; it will now be checked. *See Chapter 9.*

How to Order:

For information on quantity discounts contact the publisher: Prima Publishing, P.O. Box 1260BK, Rocklin, CA 95677-1260; (916) 632-4400. On your letterhead include information concerning the intended use of the books and the number of books you wish to purchase. For individual orders, turn to the back of this book for more information.

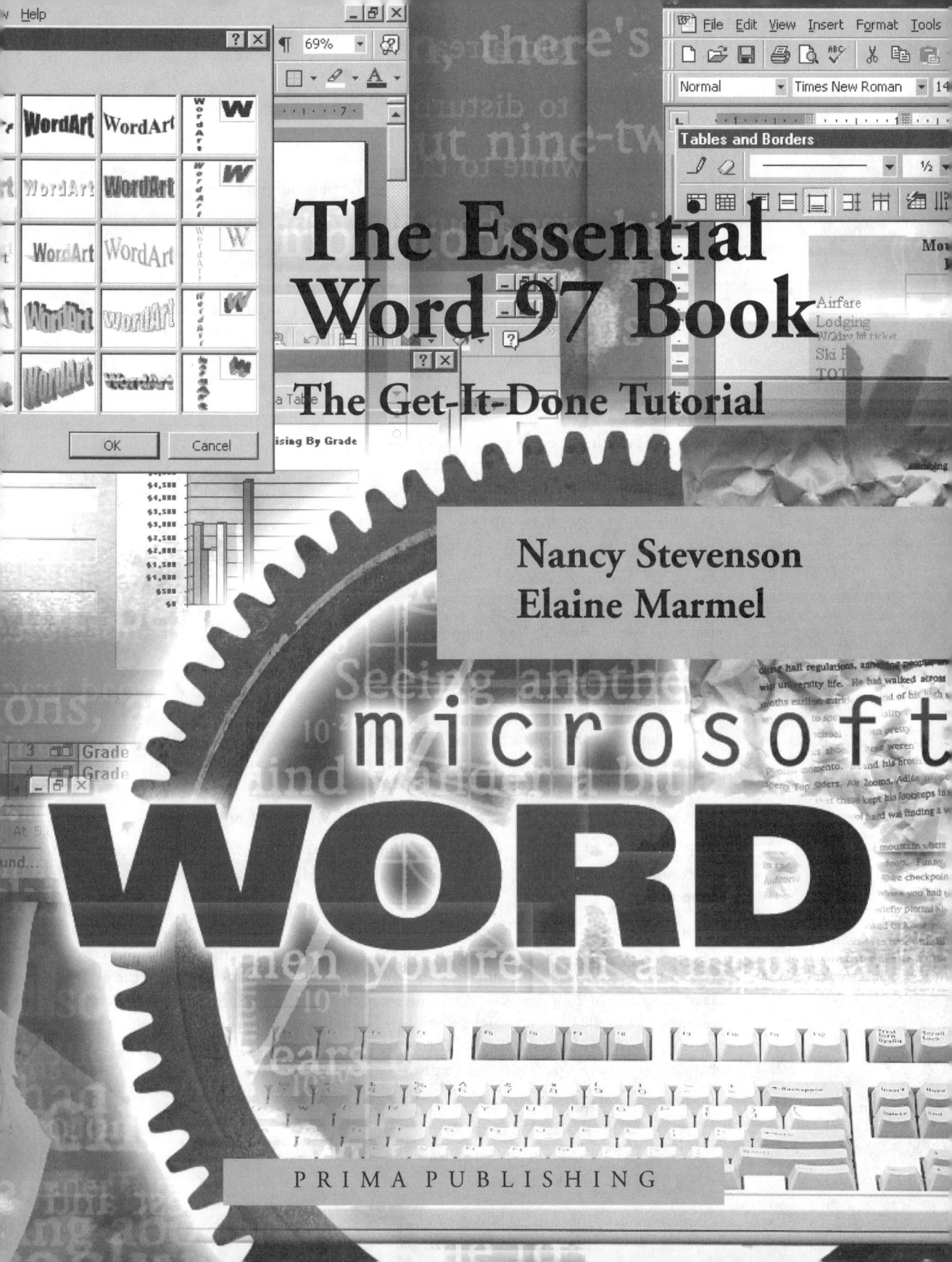

P is a registered trademark of Prima Publishing, a division of Prima Communications, Inc.

Prima Publishing is a registered trademark of Prima Communications, Inc.

Prima Publishing, Rocklin, California 95677.

© 1997 by Nancy Stevenson. All rights reserved. No part of this book may be reproduced or transmitted in any form or by any means, electronic or mechanical, including photocopying, recording, or by any information storage or retrieval system without written permission from Prima Publishing, except for the inclusion of brief quotations in a review.

Acquisitions Manager: Alan L. Harris
Managing Editor: Tad Ringo
Product Marketing Specialist: Julie Barton
Acquisitions Editor: Deborah F. Abshier
Assistant Acquisitions Editor: Jill Byus
Development Editor: Joyce Nielsen
Project Editor: Susan Christophersen
Editorial Coordinator: Stacie Drudge
Technical Reviewer: Diane Koers
Interior Layout: Michelle Worthington
Cover Designer: Vanessa Perez
Cover Illustration: Mike Tanamachi
Indexer: Sherry Massey

Prima Publishing and the author have attempted throughout this book to distinguish proprietary trademarks from descriptive terms by following the capitalization style used by the manufacturer.

Microsoft and Word 97 are registered trademarks of Microsoft Corporation.

INPORTANT: If you have problems installing or running Microsoft Word 97, notify Microsoft Corporation at (206) 635-7056. Prima Publishing cannot provide software support.

Information contained in this book has been obtained by Prima Publishing from sources believed to be reliable. However, because of the possibility of human or mechanical error by our sources, Prima Publishing, or others, the Publisher does not guarantee the accuracy, adequacy, or completeness of any information and is not responsible for any errors or omissions or the results obtained from use of such information. Readers should be particularly aware of the fact that the Internet is an ever-changing entity. Some facts may have changed since this book went to press.

ISBN: 0-7615-0427-3
Library of Congress Catalog Card Number: 97-65763
Printed in the United States of America
97 98 99 DD 10 9 8 7 6 5 4 3 2 1

This one's just for Lord G., and he knows who he is!

Acknowledgments

This book is the product of multiple talents. First, thanks to my co-author, Elaine Marmel, for her usual stellar and reliable job. Able acquisitions support was given by Jill Byus and Debbie Abshier, and as always, we couldn't have survived without it.

Our editors are all top flight: Joyce Nielson turned her expert eye to the organization and flow of the material; Susan Christophersen organized it all into real English; and Diane Koers spotted our technical faux pas.

And as always, to Prima, for providing the opportunity and for always maintaining a tough, but worthwhile, standard of excellence.

Nancy Stevenson

As Nancy said, this book is the product of multiple talents. My thanks to her for her creativity and her sense of humor (helps to keep things on an even keel). Also thanks to Debbie Abshier and Jill Byus for giving me the opportunity to write this book.

My thanks also to Joyce Nielsen, Susan Christophersen, and Diane Koers, who really added value to the book and made the review process easy and almost fun (author review is *never* fun, but this time it really came close, particularly when we laughed together over the way I compensated for memory brownouts).

Elaine Marmel

About the Authors

Nancy Stevenson is the author of more than a dozen computer books on topics ranging from presentation, spreadsheet, and word processing software to Web page design and online services. Formerly a Publishing Manager for Macmillan Publishing, she is currently a freelance writer and consultant. Nancy has taught technical writing at the university level as well as training computer users in hands-on workshops. She has been known to dabble in writing articles for national magazines and has penned an (as yet) unpublished mystery novel. She lives in Indianapolis with her husband, Graham, a patient and supportive soul.

Elaine Marmel is President of Marmel Enterprises, Inc., an organization specializing in technical writing and software training. Elaine spends most of her time writing and is the author of more than 20 books. Elaine also is a contributing editor for *Inside Peachtree for Windows*, a monthly magazine published about Peachtree for Windows, an accounting package. Elaine left her native Chicago for the warmer climes of Florida where she basks in the sun with her PC and her cats, Cato and Watson. Elaine also sings in the Toast of Tampa, an International Champion Sweet Adeline barbershop chorus.

Contents at a Glance

Introduction.................................... xxv

Part I	Creating Basic Documents 1
Chapter 1	A First Look at Word........................ 3
Chapter 2	Creating a Simple Letter.................... 29
Chapter 3	Building a Memo............................ 49
Chapter 4	Outlining a Sales Presentation.............. 73
Chapter 5	Finding Things in Your Document and Fixing Them....... 91
Chapter 6	Setting Up a Document for Printing.......... 113

Part II	Getting Visual 143
Chapter 7	Getting Visual with a Newsletter............ 145
Chapter 8	Crunching Numbers in a Business Report...... 179
Chapter 9	Using Mail Merge with a Sales Letter........ 221

Part III	Word Online 249
Chapter 10	Sending a Fax from Word.................... 251
Chapter 11	Exploring the Online World from Word....... 267
Chapter 12	Using Word to Publish a Corporate Web Page.. 291
Chapter 13	Creating a Multimedia Announcement.......... 321

Part IV — Making Word Work Your Way 347

Chapter 14	Creating a Collection Letter with Styles and Templates 349
Chapter 15	Automating Work with Fields and Macros 375
Chapter 16	Changing Your Word Environment 399

Part V — Using Word With Others 433

Chapter 17	Using the Master Document with a Client Proposal 435
Chapter 18	Working in a Group: A Department Report 457
	Glossary 475
	Index 483

Contents

Introduction xxv

Part I   Creating Basic Documents 1

Chapter 1   A First Look at Word 3

Opening Word 4
    Opening a New Document 4
    Making Use of Templates 5
Exploring the Word Environment 8
    Using Toolbars 8
    Doing Things Through Menus 10
    Exploring Word Views 12
Getting Around 15
    Discovering Document Map 15
    Using Select Browse Object 18
Getting Help 18
    Using the Contents and Index Feature 19
    The What's This? Feature 20
    Meet the Office Assistant 20
    Getting Word Help On the World Wide Web 22
Saving Documents 24
    Saving for the First Time 24
    Saving a File with a Different Name 26
    Exiting Word 26

Chapter 2	**Creating a Simple Letter** **29**

Entering Text 30
    Adding Text 31
    Inserting a Date 32
    Using AutoText 33
Selecting and Moving Text 36
    Selecting Text 36
    Deleting, Copying, and Moving Text .38
Applying Text Effects and Styles 41
    Using Simple Text Effects 41
    Applying Predefined Styles 42
Using Tabs 44
    Tab Types 44
    Setting and Removing Tabs 44

Chapter 3	**Building a Memo** **49**

Formatting Text 50
    Adjusting Text Font and Font Size 51
    Using Text Effects 54
    Adjusting Alignment 57
Working with Lists 59
    Adding Lists 59
    Adding Bulleted Lists 60
    Adding Numbered Lists 60
    Customizing Lists 63
Formatting Paragraphs 67
    Indenting Text 69

Chapter 4	**Outlining a Sales Presentation** **73**

Creating the Outline 74
    Entering Headings 75
    Promoting and Demoting Headings .76
    Adding Body Text 82

Contents

Using Outline View	84
Displaying Levels of Headings	84
Reorganizing an Outline	86
Deleting Headings	89

Chapter 5 Finding Things in Your Document and Fixing Them ... 91

Understanding AutoCorrect	92
How AutoCorrect Works	92
Seeing How AutoCorrect Works	93
Overriding an AutoCorrect Entry	95
Creating an AutoCorrect Entry	96
Using AutoFormat	97
Using Spelling and Grammar Check	98
Running Spelling and Grammar Check	99
Customizing How Spelling and Grammar Works	102
Using Custom Dictionaries	105
Finding the Right Word with Word's Thesaurus	106
Searching Through Your Document	107
Using Find and Replace	108
Getting There with Go To	111

Chapter 6 Setting Up a Document for Printing ... 113

Breaking a Document into Parts	114
Working with Headers and Footers	115
Adding Headers and Footers	115
Varying Headers and Footers within a Document	118
Changing Page Settings	122
Changing Margins	123
Changing Paper Size and Orientation	125
When the Paper Keeps Coming Out of the Wrong Tray...	127
Aligning Text on a Page	129
Using Line Numbers	131

Previewing Before Printing 134
Setting Up To Print 136
Printing a Single Envelope 137
Printing Labels 139

Part II Getting Visual 143

Chapter 7 Getting Visual with a Newsletter 145
Doing Things the Easy Way... 146
Newsletter Basics 148
Creating a Banner 150
Creating a Newsletter Using Text Boxes 155
   About Linking Text Boxes 160
   Typing in Text Boxes 163
   Formatting the Table of Contents Box 163
Creating a Newsletter Using Columns 165
   Inserting a Vertical Line Between Columns 169
   Balancing Text Between Columns .169
Adding Images to a Newsletter 171
   Working with Clip Art 171
   Drawing in Word 173
   Drawing Freehand 175

Chapter 8 Crunching Numbers in a Business Report 179
Inserting a Simple Table 180
   Inserting a Table 180
   Typing and Editing in a Table 181
   Summing Numbers in a Table 183
   Adding Rows or Columns 184
   Providing a Caption for a Table 185
   Merging Cells 187
   Deleting Rows, Columns, or Cells .188

Drawing a Complex Table 188
    Splitting Cells 190
    Erasing Row or Column Borders 191
    Adjusting Column Widths 193
Formatting a Table 197
    AutoFormatting a Table 197
    Aligning Tables on the Page 198
    Controlling the Direction of Text within Cells 199
    Aligning Information Horizontally within Table Cells 200
    Aligning Information Vertically within Table Cells 202
    Modifying Borders and Shading 203
Sorting Table Information 206
Working with Charts 208
    Inserting a Chart 208
    Moving a Chart 209
    Changing the Chart Type 211
    Sizing a Chart 212
    Changing Data in the Chart 213
    Adding a Title to a Chart 215
Connecting to an Excel or 1-2-3 Worksheet 216

Chapter 9   Using Mail Merge with a Sales Letter 221

Understanding the Merge Process 222
Building the Main Document 223
Working with Data Source Documents 228
    Using Data Stored in Personal Address Books 228
    Special Considerations When Creating Data Source Documents 229
    Working with Data Source Documents 229
    Editing a Data Source 234
Adding Fields to the Main Document 235
Merging 237
    Special Merging Options 237
    Performing the Merge 240
Customizing a Form Letter 243

Part III Word Online 249

Chapter 10 Sending a Fax from Word 251
Choosing a Fax Cover Sheet 252
Understanding How a Fax/Modem Works 253
Sending Your Fax 257
    Sending a Fax Cover Page Only 257
    Including a Document in a Fax Transmission 260
Using Microsoft Fax and Word 263
    Installing and Configuring Microsoft Fax 263
    Sending a Fax from Word with Microsoft Fax 265

Chapter 11 Exploring the Online World from Word 267
Working with Hyperlinks 268
    Using the Memo Wizard 268
    Inserting Hyperlinks 272
    Formatting Hyperlinks 273
    Using Hyperlinks 275
    Changing Hyperlinks 277
Sending E-Mail 278
Accessing the Web from Word 280
    Finding Out What's New from Microsoft .281
    Checking Out Microsoft's Free Stuff 281
    Getting Help Online 281
    Visiting the Microsoft Office Home Page 283
    Visiting the Microsoft Home Page 284
    Learning About the Web 284
    Microsoft Presents "Best of the Web" .284
    Searching the Web 285
    Creating a Web Site Hyperlink in a Word Document 287
    Printing a Web Page 288
    Downloading Information 288

Chapter 12 Using Word to Publish a Corporate Web Page ... 291

Web Page Design Issues ... 292
   Web Page Readability ... 292
   Web Page Speed ... 293
Creating a Web Page ... 293
   Using the Web Page Wizard ... 293
   Saving Your Web Page ... 295
   Word Features and Web Authoring ... 298
Modifying a Web Page ... 299
   Typing and Formatting Text ... 299
   Changing the Background Pattern ... 304
   Inserting a Line ... 305
   Using Scrolling Text ... 307
   Adding a Graphic to a Web Page ... 310
   Including a Background Sound ... 313
   About Using Charts on a Web Page ... 314
   Previewing a Web Page ... 314
Publishing Web Documents ... 317
Converting Word Documents to Web Documents ... 317

Chapter 13 Creating a Multimedia Announcement ... 321

Working with Photographs ... 322
   Inserting Photos in Documents ... 322
   Adjusting Brightness and Contrast ... 329
   Using Image Controls ... 332
Adding Sound ... 334
Animating Text ... 340
Adding Fill Effects ... 342

Part IV Making Word Work Your Way 347

Chapter 14 Creating a Collection Letter with Styles and Templates 349

Template and Style Basics 350
    Understanding Templates 350
    Understanding Styles 351
    Using Built-In Styles 353
Ways to Apply Styles 354
    Using Styles with Form Letters .355
    Automatically Formatting Documents 359
    Using the Style Gallery 361
Working with Templates 366
Modifying Templates 370
About Wizards... 372

Chapter 15 Automating Work with Fields and Macros 375

Field Code Basics 377
Manipulating Field Codes 383
Macro Basics 384
    Planning a Macro 384
    Understanding What Gets Recorded 385

Chapter 16 Changing Your Word Environment 399

Customizing Rules of Thumb 400
Working with Toolbars 400
Working with Menus 410
Toolbar and Menu Customization Options 424
Modifying the Office Assistant 424
Changing Word Options 426

Part V Using Word with Others 433

Chapter 17 Using the Master Document with a Client Proposal 435

Understanding Master Documents 436
Creating the Master Document 438
   Beginning a New Master Document 439
   Creating a Master Document Outline 440
Working with Subdocuments 441
   Creating Subdocuments 442
   Inserting a Word Document into a Master Document 444
   Moving Subdocuments Around 446
   Renaming a Subdocument 446
   Removing a Subdocument 447
   Combining Subdocuments 447
   Printing a Master Document 449
   Protecting Subdocuments 450
Finding Your Way Around a Master Document 451
   Adding a Table of Contents 451
   Inserting Cross References 453

Chapter 18 Working in a Group: A Department Report 457

Tracking Changes 458
   How Tracking Changes Works 458
   Accepting Revisions 463
   Comparing Documents 465
Creating Document Summaries 466
Routing Documents Online 467
   Creating a Routing Slip 469
   Sending the File 472

Glossary 475

Index 483

Hands On Topics

Accepting or rejecting changes to your report 464
Adding a background sound to a Web page 313
Adding a border 329
Adding a button to a toolbar 402
Adding a chart title 215
Adding a clip art image 171
Adding a command to a menu 411
Adding a header or footer to your document 117
Adding a macro to a menu 413
Adding a picture to a Web page 310
Adding a row to the top of a table 184
Adding a shortcut key to a menu item 418
Adding a table of contents to your proposal 451
Adding animated text to the document 340
Adding body text to a sales presentation 81
Adding numbered lists 60
Adding scrolling text 307
Adding text effects to memos 55
Adding text to your letter 31
Adding texture to your page 343
Adding word fields to customize a merge document 243
Adjusting heading levels in an outline 77
Adjusting text font and size in a memorandum 52

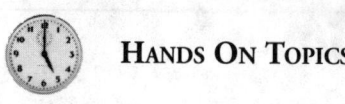 **Hands On Topics**

Aligning text vertically 129
Applying styles 42
AutoFormatting a simple table 197
Building a main document 224
Building the outline for your proposal 440
Centering a table between the left and right margins 198
Centering text horizontally in a cell 201
Changing a menu item's hot key 417
Changing the header or footer in a section 119
Changing the hyperlink's text 273
Changing the number of columns on a page 166
Changing the text on the Web page 300
Changing the Web page title 303
Changing the width of a column 193
Choosing an address book 228
Combining subdocuments in your proposal 448
Configuring Microsoft Fax 264
Controlling the direction of the text for the regions 199
Controlling wrapping 176
Converting an existing Word document to a Web document 318
Copying a Web address into a Word document 287
Creating a chart from a table 209
Creating a data source 229
Creating a memo with the Memo Wizard .269
Creating a new AutoText entry 33
Creating a routing slip for your report 469
Creating a single-celled first row 187
Creating a style by example 364
Creating a text box 156
Creating a Web page with the Web Page Wizard 294

Hands On Topics

Creating templates	367
Creating you own menu	420
Creating your own AutoCorrect entries	96
Creating your own toolbar	408
Customizing bullet styles	63
Customizing numbered lists	65
Customizing spelling and grammar functions	102
Deleting a row	188
Displaying a document summary	468
Displaying selected toolbars	401
Displaying the Style area	352
Displaying various levels of outline	84
Drawing the outline of a table	189
Editing in print preview	134
Entering headings for an outline	75
Erasing cell dividers	191
Finding and replacing things	109
Finding the perfect word with Thesaurus	106
Formatting a newsletter's table of contents	164
Formatting a text box	158
Indenting text in a memorandum	70
Inserting a cross-reference	454
Inserting a date	32
Inserting a date field in a form letter	357
Inserting a field code	379
Inserting a hyperlink into a memo	272
Inserting a line below a heading of a Web page	305
Inserting a numbered caption	379
Inserting a numbered sequence field	382
Inserting a photo	324

HANDS ON TOPICS

Inserting a section break 114
Inserting a simple table 180
Inserting a table in Word by linking to an Excel workbook 217
Inserting an existing document into a proposal 444
Inserting AutoText with the autoText toolbar 35
Inserting macro button fields 358
Inserting sound clips 335
Installing Microsoft Fax 263
Jumping to a linked document 275
Linking text boxes 161
Making a chart bigger 213
Merging selectively 239
Modifying scrolling text 309
Modifying styles 362
Modifying the border of an inside cell 205
Modifying the outside border of a table 203
Modifying the size of a graphic image on a Web page 311
Moving a chart 209
Moving and sizing a clip art image 172
Moving buttons around 404
Moving items around on a menu 416
Previewing a Word Web page in a Web browser 315
Printing a single envelope 137
Providing a caption for a table 186
Realigning and indenting text 300
Rearranging headings in a proposal 446
Recording a keyboard macro 394
Recording a macro 385
Recording a toolbar macro 388
Redistributing space across columns 194

Hands On Topics

Relinking headers and footers	120
Removing a button from a toolbar	406
Reorganizing a sales presentation outline	86
Resetting menus	420
Resetting toolbars	407
Resizing and cropping photos	326
Resizing text and changing text color	302
Running a macro	388
Running a spelling and grammar check	100
Running the keyboard macro	396
Running the Newsletter Wizard	146
Running the toolbar macro	393
Selecting text	37
Sending only a fax cover page	257
Setting paper size and orientation	126
Setting paragraph spacing	67
Setting up special headers	121
Setting up the merge	240
Setting up to be able to preview	366
Setting/removing tabs	45
Sharing styles between templates	371
Sorting a simple table	207
Sorting before merging	238
Splitting cells in a drawn table	190
Summing columns in a table	183
Supplying the volume and issue numbers	152
Suppressing line numbers	133
Tracking changes in a report	459
Turning headings into subdocuments	442
Using an existing data source document	233

Hands On Topics

Using AutoCorrect in an announcement 93
Using AutoShapes 173
Using drag and drop to move text 38
Using Master Document view 439
Using Sound Recorder 338
Using templates 368
Using text effects 41
Using WordArt for the banner text 150
Using WordMail to send a Word document 278
Vertically centering information in a complex table 202
Viewing a chart as a line chart 212
Viewing a Web page from inside Word 280
Working with line numbers 132
Working with lists 60
Working with selected text 38

Introduction

Essential things are things that you can't do without. Air and water fall into this category. Chocolate and true love are generally considered to fit the definition of essential. So, how does a book on Word for Windows qualify? Because this book is structured to give you exactly what you can't do without if you want to be successful with Word: clear, concise explanations of features grounded in real-world examples.

As you roam the aisles of bookstores these days, you'll find dozens of books on Word for Windows (some good, some not so good). Of course, we sincerely hope that you find this book to be one of the good ones. But we're sure that you will find it to be unusual. This book is based on the premise that mastering the complex and feature-rich software products of today doesn't require the abstract concepts and series of unrelated keystrokes that other books present. You need to see how to use Word to write a letter, to design a report, to create a newsletter, or to send a fax. That's what this book shows you. While you're creating these useful documents, you'll pick up just what you need to know about Word features so that you can tackle any word processing challenge that comes along. And we don't give you twenty different ways to do things; we give you the easiest method to get things done. If there are two equally easy methods, you'll be told about that option, but that's it.

Word for Windows probably will be the software with which you spend most of your computing time. This book gives you the information that you need to make the time both pleasant and productive.

Who Is This Book For?

This is an easy one: This book is for you if you want to learn the ins and outs of using Word for Windows. You probably have a computer, have used Windows software before, and own Word. But beyond that, few rules exist. You might have used an earlier version of Word and want to see what's new in this version of the software. Maybe you just want to get some ideas for how you can use Word to

Introduction

spruce up your documents. On the other hand, maybe you've never used Word before and need to learn all the basics. This book is for you.

Essential Word 97 for Windows isn't a typical reference book, because it's organized around the work you do, not the software features. Scan the table of contents and you'll see that almost every chapter is centered around a typical business document. You learn about how Word handles features such as tables and charts by generating a business report. You conquer drawing, columns, and inserting pictures by building a newsletter. You explore publishing on the World Wide Web by creating a company press release. This book is for people who understand that software features are useless if they don't help you get work done.

So, whether you're new to Word or consider yourself pretty handy with it, this book will help you become a better Word user. Along the way, we introduce you to the essential features of Word 97 for Windows—the latest, greatest version of the world's leading word processing software.

Overview of Contents

This book is divided into logical parts to help you easily find the type of procedure you're looking for.

Part I, "Creating Basic Documents," gives you your first look at the Word environment, including valuable help features. You'll build a simple letter, memo and outline, and in the process learn about adding and formatting text, working with lists and outlines, checking your document for spelling and other details, and saving your documents. The last chapter in this part gives details about printing your documents, including working with headers and footers, previewing before printing, and printing envelopes and labels.

Part II, "Getting Visual," is where you to use Word's clip art, table, and chart features. You'll design a newsletter, build a business report, and perform a customized mail merge using a sales letter.

Part III, "Word Online," shows you how to send a fax from Word, publish a press release to the World Wide Web, and even publish a corporate Web page using Word's Web Page Wizard. Finally, you'll have fun with several multimedia tools that can add sound and motion to your documents.

Part IV, "Making Word Work Your Way," is where you'll learn about customizing Word's styles, templates, toolbars, and menus so that you can truly make the software work like you do. You'll design custom templates for a collection letter, build simple macros, and make changes to toolbars and menus.

Introduction

Finally, Part V, "Using Word with Others," uses a client proposal and department report as models for writing documents in workgroups. Learn to make the most of Word's Master Document feature, track revisions by multiple users, and route documents to others online.

Conventions Used in This Book

To keep instructions clear and concise, we've followed some common conventions in this book. For starters, you can do almost everything in Word using either your mouse or keyboard commands—your choice. We've tried to give you the easiest way to get things done, but your preferences might differ from ours, so we occasionally provide alternative ways of performing commands. Table I-1 contains examples of instructions that you'll encounter throughout the book.

Table I-1 Conventions for Performing Actions in Word

Instruction	Meaning
Choose File, Open	Either type the underlined hot keys (F, O) or use your mouse pointer and click on the File menu to open it and select the Open command from it.
Press Alt+F	Hold down the Alt key on your keyboard and then press the F key simultaneously.
Press End, Home	Press the End key on your keyboard, release it, and then press the Home key.
Click on the Save button	Word tools are represented by buttons on a toolbar. Clicking on a button with your mouse pointer invokes the tool's function. The button name used in this book matches the name that appears when you point to a toolbar button.

Because you're building sample documents through much of this book, you'll be asked to enter (type) specific text. Text for you to enter will appear in **bold**. If we refer to text in a document, it will be shown in a `monospace` font to differentiate it. Whenever we introduce a new term or phrase, we *italicize* it so that you can be alert to the definition that will follow it. Also, clicking on the mouse refers to the left mouse button unless we specify to use the right one.

Although we build documents using specific text in these chapters, feel free to use your own documents instead. For example, if you have a letter already created in Word, and you want to use that document to practice the text-enhancement features discussed in Chapters 2 and 3, go ahead. It'll save you from typing our text, and will get you to work on your own documents right away. Remember: This is just practice. Simply perform the steps that we provide on a comparable element in your own document and you'll get similar results.

Special Elements

Did you notice at the end of the preceding section there was a Note about using your own documents? A Note is just one of the special elements used in this book to call your attention to something or provide a format for easy learning. Notes provide a bit more technical information about a feature or procedure. Here are some other special elements used in this book:

Hands On: Let Your Fingers Do The Working

To build our sample documents and practice Word features, we've included Hands On sections, which are specific step-by-step procedures for you to follow. (You'll occasionally see numbered steps outside of Hands On sections that also give a quick rundown of general procedures). Build our sample documents by using these steps, or perform the same steps on a document of your own, if you prefer.

Tips are little suggestions of other ways to get things done, or clever shortcuts or tricks for using Word.

INTRODUCTION   xxix

> ## Sidebars on the Side, Please
> To keep the essentials in the limelight, we've placed interesting background or additional facts about Word in sidebars. You can read them for a little more information, or breeze by them and still get the essential details. It's up to you. Most of the sidebars, however, are not only fascinating, but also make you a more well-rounded Word user.

> If you're in danger of making a mistake or losing information while performing a step, we warn you with a caution. We also tell you how to get out of trouble if you stumble.

Find It Online

The world is on the Net, so we've provided references to helpful or interesting Web sites that you might want to visit. Web addresses (called URLs) are listed like this:

    http://www.microsoft.com

We hope that you'll find *The Essential Word 97 for Windows Book* an essential part of your day-to-day productivity. Now it's time to get to work!

THIS FEATURE IS IN THE MARGINS TO LET YOU KNOW ABOUT RELATED INFORMATION ELSEWHERE IN THE BOOK.

microsoft WORD

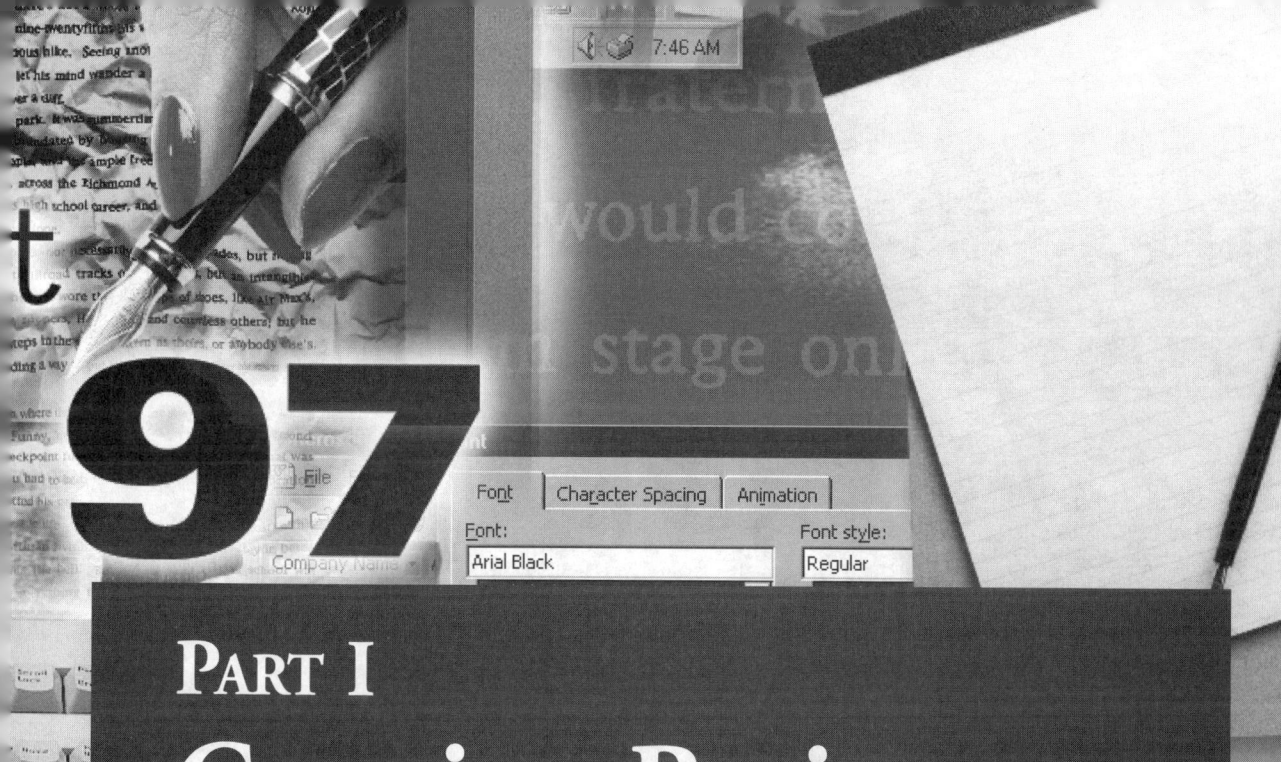

PART I
Creating Basic Documents

1 A First Look at Word 3
2 Creating a Simple Letter 29
3 Building a Memo 49
4 Outlining a Sales Presentation 73
5 Finding Things in Your Document
   and Fixing Them 91
6 Setting Up a Document for Printing 113

micros
WORD

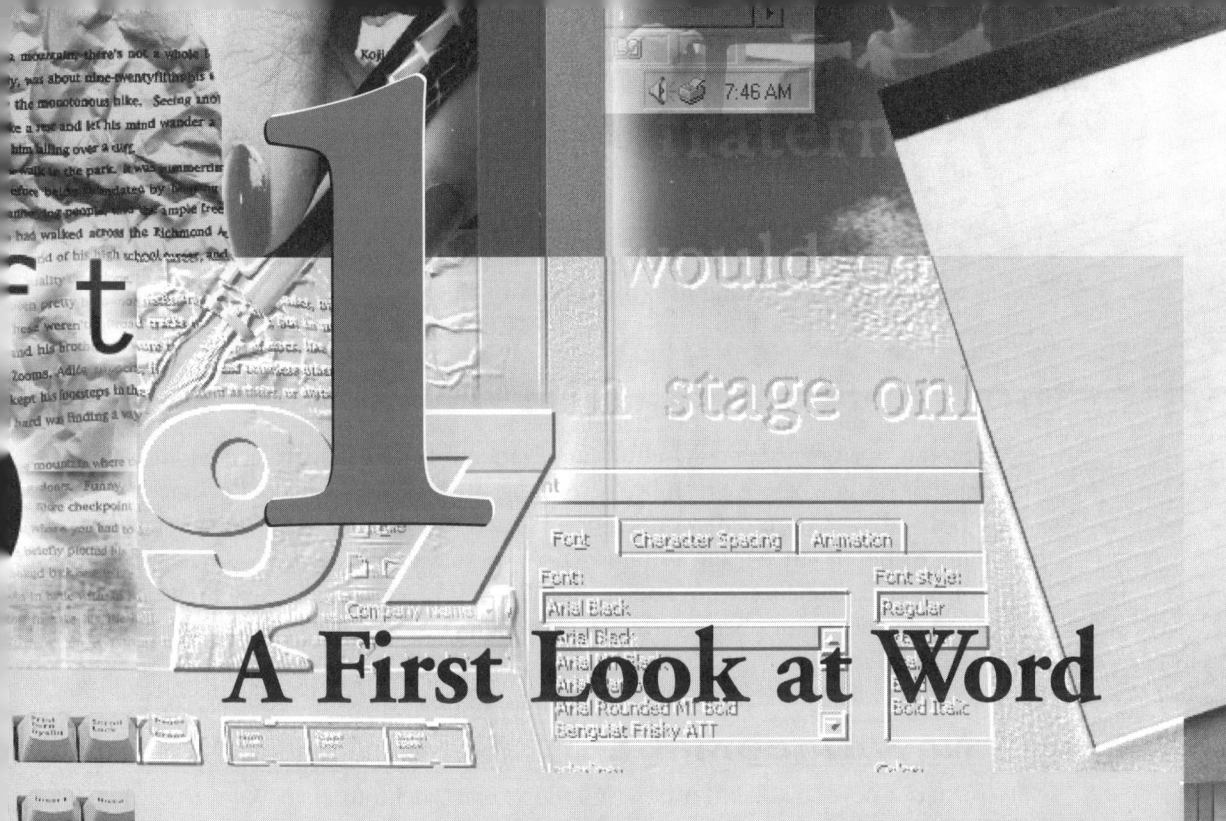

A First Look at Word

IN THIS CHAPTER

- **Toolbars**
- **Menus**
- **Getting Help**
- **Views**
- **Templates**
- **Opening and Saving Documents**

Word for Windows has become the most popular word processor in the world. That's because of an abundance of features and ease of use that would have astounded computer users of a decade or so ago. But even though Word is easy to use, the sheer number of features it offers means that you've got some learning to do.

PART I • CREATING BASIC DOCUMENTS

In this chapter, you'll receive your first glimpse of how Word uses toolbars and menus. You'll learn the mechanics of opening and saving documents, navigating around Word, and getting help in a variety of ways.

Opening Word

You can open Word for Windows in a variety of ways, and what you choose depends on how you want to begin working. If you have created a document in Word and want to resume working on it, locate that document file on your computer or floppy drive using Windows Explorer and double-click on the filename or icon. This launches Word and opens the file. If you want to begin a brand new Word document, or open existing Word documents, read the next section to see how to do that.

Opening a New Document

To start a new document, use the Windows Start menu to open Word from the Programs menu. Just click on Start to open the menu, select Programs, and then select Microsoft Word (see Figure 1.1).

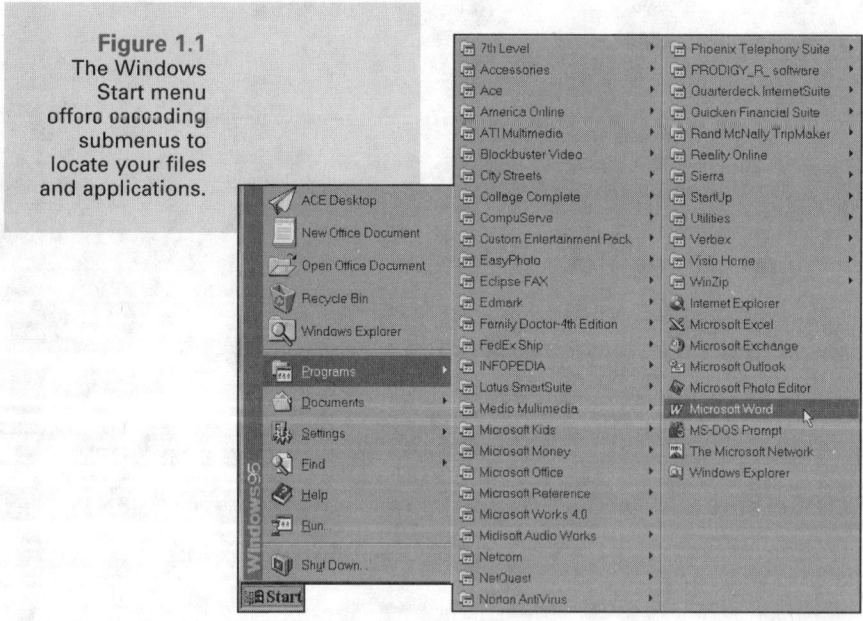

Figure 1.1
The Windows Start menu offers cascading submenus to locate your files and applications.

Note
Your Windows Programs menu will look unique because it shows the programs that you've loaded onto your computer. It will look similar, however, to the menu in the figure provided here.

You can also open Word by locating the Microsoft Word application file in the Microsoft Word of Office 97 folder on your hard drive and double-clicking on it.

Tip
You can easily create a shortcut to Word. Locate the Word application file in Windows Explorer and click on it with the right mouse button. From the shortcut menu that appears, choose Create Shortcut. A new Microsoft Word icon will appear in the Word folder. Click on this file and drag it onto your Windows desktop. Now, anytime you want to open Word, just double-click on this icon.

When you use any of these methods, Word will open to its main screen, as shown in the figure in the chapter opener. Word has several views (which you'll learn about shortly) and this figure shows Page Layout View; your program might open in Normal View. Whichever view opens, what you'll see is a new, blank document, temporarily named Document1. You can begin to work in this document right away, or choose to open a new document. Opening a new document gives you the ability to create a document based on a variety of built-in document templates.

Note
If you have installed Word as part of Microsoft Office 97, you have two other options: Select Start, Open Office Document or New Office Document; or, click on the Word icon on the Office Shortcut Bar.

Making Use of Templates

A template gives you a head start on building your Word document. *Templates* are files with certain formatting choices already made and saved for you, such as heading styles, text font, text size, and so on. Some templates, like the fax template

PART I • CREATING BASIC DOCUMENTS

> **YOU'LL LEARN MORE ABOUT STYLES IN CHAPTER 14.**

shown in Figure 1.2, provide design elements and placeholders for text. Others simply load some additional formatting styles that you can take advantage of in building your documents.

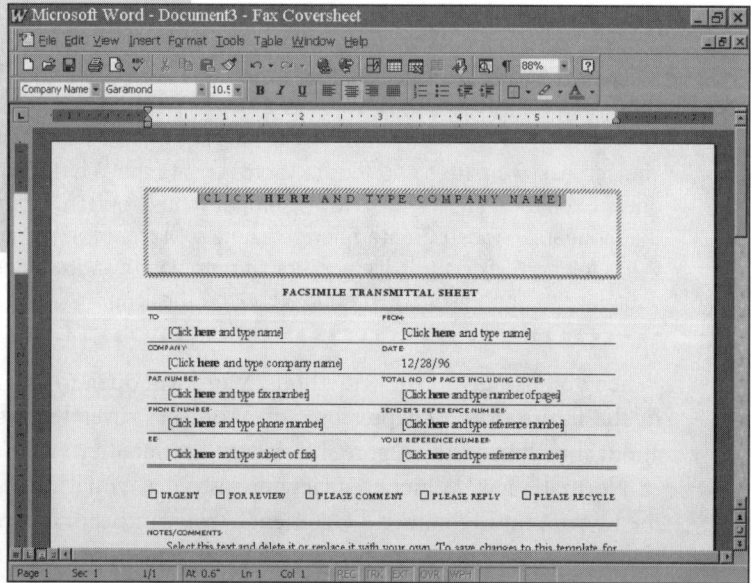

Figure 1.2
Templates offer the structure and formatting for common documents such as fax cover sheets, reports, and memos.

Get free templates from Microsoft at `http://www.microsoft.com/Office-FreeStuff/Word/`.

To open a new document from within Word, follow these steps:

1. Choose File, New. The New dialog box appears. Figure 1.3 shows the Reports tab of this dialog box.

Note

> **Dialog boxes in Word offer choices of ways to get things done; often they have tabs to place these choices into different logical categories. You make choices in dialog boxes using a variety of methods, which you'll see as you progress through this book. These methods include clicking in check boxes or on option buttons, selecting an item from a list, or entering text.**

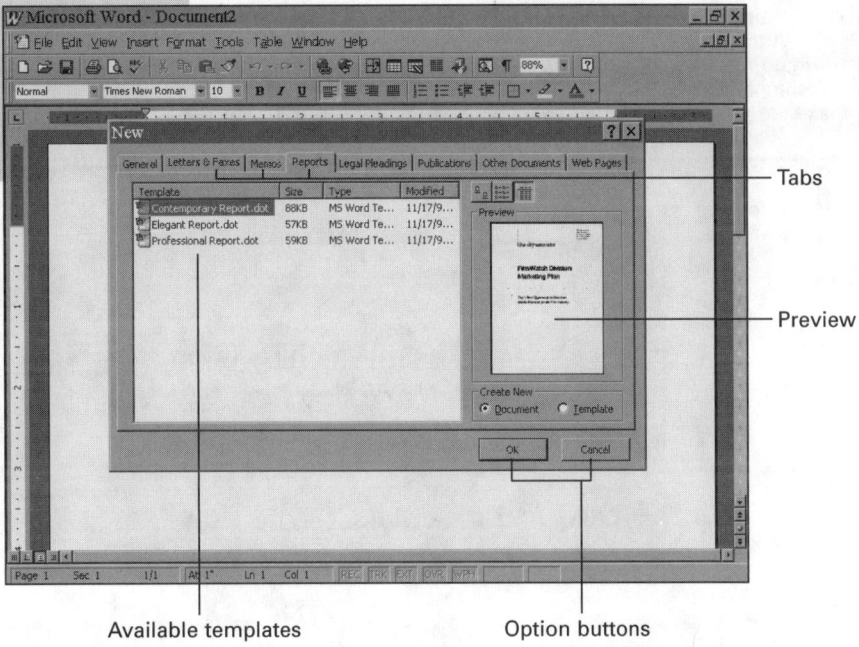

Figure 1.3 Select from different categories of templates in this dialog box.

2. Click on the Reports tab to select it. Several Report template files are stored here.
3. Click on the Contemporary Report template (a contemporary style of report). A preview of the template appears.
4. Make sure that the Document option button is selected, and click on OK.

> **If you open a template as a template rather than a document by selecting the Template option button in this dialog box, any changes that you make and save will change the template itself. The next time you want to base a document on that original template, you're out of luck!**

A new document based on the Contemporary Report template appears, as in Figure 1.4. It's temporarily named `Document 2 - Report`, because it's the second document that you've opened since you started Word. You can now make any changes that you like to the document, and save it or not—as you please.

Figure 1.4
Attractive formatting and sample text make templates valuable shortcuts to professional-looking documents.

Exploring the Word Environment

LEARN HOW TO CUSTOMIZE MENUS AND TOOLBARS IN CHAPTER 16.

It's time to take a moment to explore the Word neighborhood and get to know some of its most prominent residents: toolbars, menus, and views. A first glance shows that the Word screen is quite a busy place. The main area contains the document contents, and all around it are text menus and toolbar buttons used to do work with your document. And these aren't all the menus and toolbar buttons that you can display in Word; some of them don't appear until you're performing a task relevant to their function. The following sections, starting with toolbars, should familiarize you with these features.

Figure 1.5 shows the major features of the Word screen. In addition to the menu bar and toolbars, a title bar displays the name of the currently active document, scrollbars move around the document, a ruler helps you place things accurately on your page, buttons enable you to change from one Word view to another, and Windows control buttons help you manage the document and Word window. In addition, a status bar along the bottom of the Word screen gives you details about the page, section, line, and column where you're currently working.

Using Toolbars

By default, two toolbars are displayed on the Word screen: Standard, shown in Figure 1.5; and Formatting, shown in Figure 1.6.

CHAPTER 1 • A FIRST LOOK AT WORD   9

Figure 1.5
Here's the Word Environment with the Standard toolbar enlarged. The Standard toolbar helps you open, print, edit, save, and insert objects into your documents.

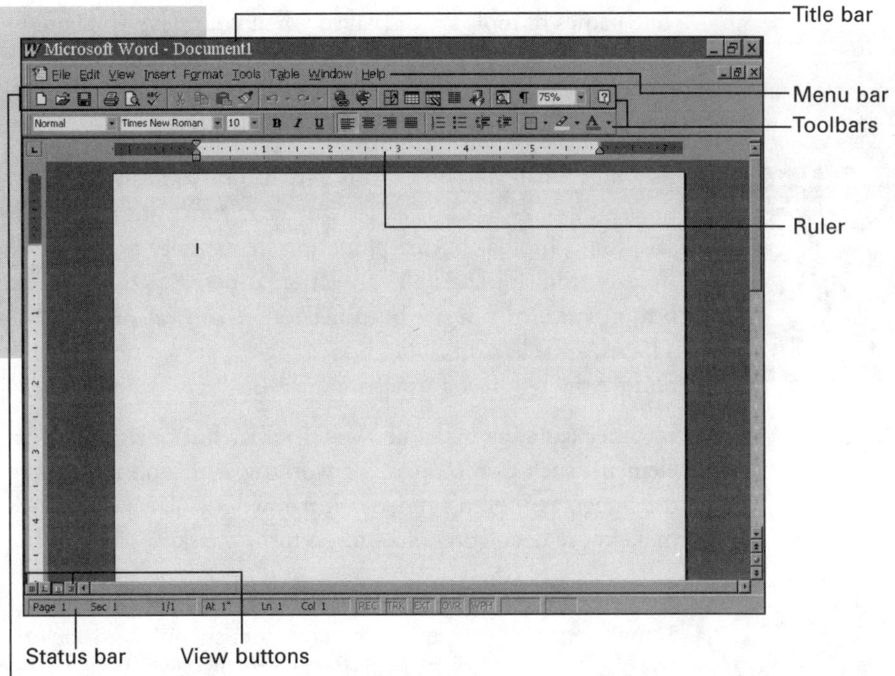

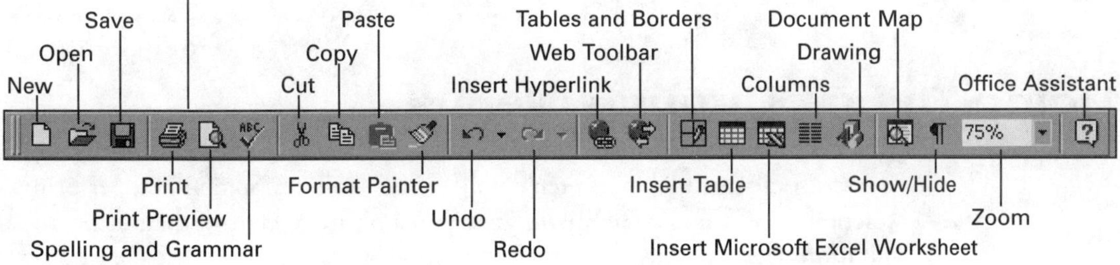

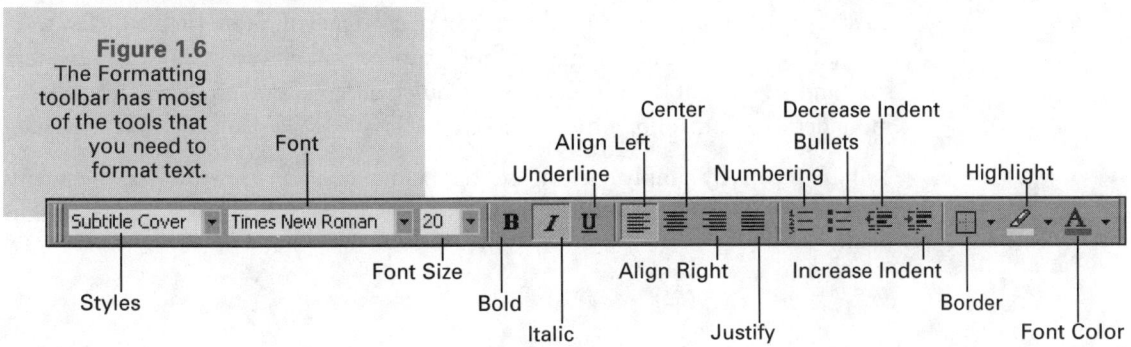

Figure 1.6
The Formatting toolbar has most of the tools that you need to format text.

The names of tools are displayed when you move your mouse pointer over them; these displays are called *ToolTips*, and they're a big help in learning the different tools available. Most of the tool names are self-explanatory, but you'll learn them best by using them in the chapters that follow.

> **SEE MORE ABOUT ADDING BUTTONS TO TOOLBARS IN CHAPTER 16.**

Basically, whatever you can do with a tool you can also do through a menu, but tools are a one-click option for initiating functions and commands, and can often save time. Toolbar buttons function in a variety of ways. When you click on the Bold button, for example, an action is performed on selected text. This type of button is called a *toggle* button because you can toggle its function off and on. That is, you click on Bold once to make selected text bold; click on Bold again to remove the boldface formatting.

In other cases, as with the Web Toolbar button, clicking on it displays another element, such as a toolbar for working with online documents. Still other buttons, such as Spelling and Grammar, will display a dialog box that enables you to make more detailed choices to perform a task.

> Some things that you can do through menus aren't available on toolbars by default. You can, however, add most menu commands as buttons to toolbars using the Customize feature.

Doing Things Through Menus

Although menu commands are related to the functions of toolbar buttons in most cases, some menu choices aren't available on toolbars. Sometimes, performing an action using a menu command gives you a bit more control than using a toolbar button does.

For example, you can click on the Italic button to italicize selected text, but if you select Format, Font, you get a dialog box that offers you more than a dozen text-formatting options, including italic, bold, superscript, all caps, colors for text, text size, and so on. Tools are shortcuts for quick actions, but often you'll want the more detailed control of a menu choice.

You use menus by simply clicking on the menu name on the menu bar. The menu drops down and often offers submenus for more specific choices, as shown in Figure 1.7.

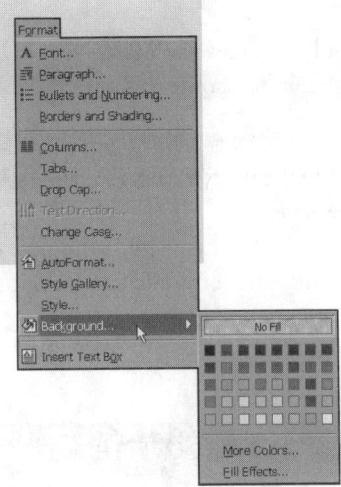

Figure 1.7
Some menu commands lead to more detailed menus or even color palettes, as with the F<u>o</u>rmat, Background command.

Making a menu selection can result in an action, such as when you select a background color from a submenu palette; but a menu selection most commonly displays a dialog box for making more specific choices to perform an action.

Table 1.1 gives a quick overview of what types of functions each menu on the Word menu bar contains.

Table 1.1 Word Menu Bar Functions

Menu	Overview of Functions
File	Opening, closing, saving, and printing files; choosing settings for your document pages
Edit	Selecting and editing text; finding text; going to specific places in your document
View	Changing among Word views; modifying the display size and toolbars; and working with headers and footers
Insert	Inserting fields, files, and hyperlinks into your document
Format	Applying a variety of format to text and objects
Tools	Proofing tools such as Spelling and Grammar, and AutoCorrect; Mail Merge and Macro functions; options to customize Word's performance
Table	Creating, formatting, and working with tables
Window	Displaying and arranging windows on-screen
Help	Word help files, including online help access

PART I • CREATING BASIC DOCUMENTS

Exploring Word Views

So far, you've been looking at only one view in Word—probably the Normal Layout view (unless you've changed it for some reason). Word has four standard views:

- *Normal view.* This is a general-purpose view in which you can enter and edit text in a simple layout.
- *Page Layout view* (see Figure 1.8). This view is the best one for seeing your page design and working with elements such as margins, pictures, columns, headers, and footers.

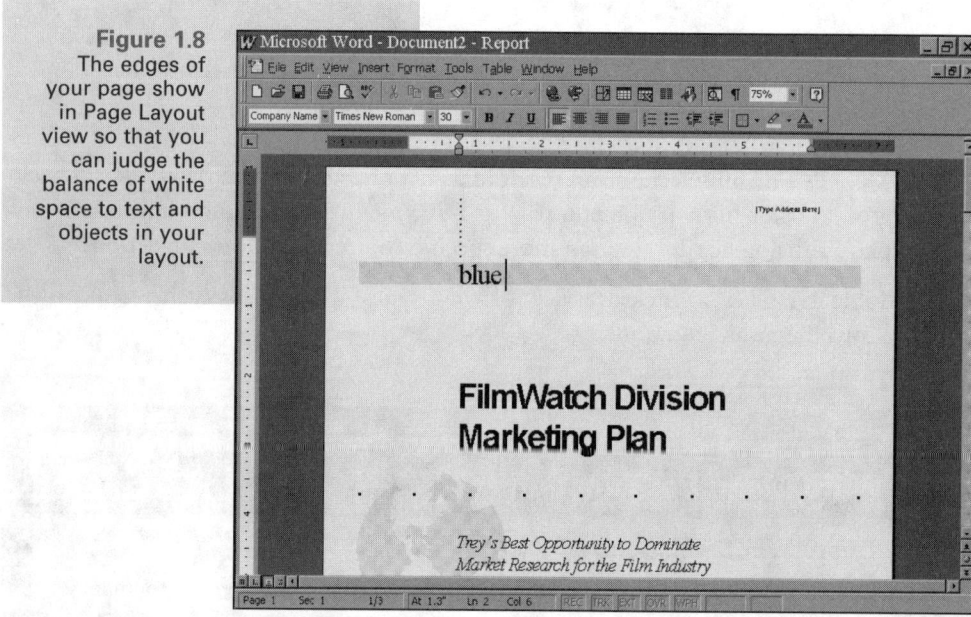

Figure 1.8
The edges of your page show in Page Layout view so that you can judge the balance of white space to text and objects in your layout.

- *Online Layout view.* This view is new to Word 97. If you're designing a document to be published on the World Wide Web, this view is useful because it mimics the way online documents are displayed (see Figure 1.9).

SEE CHAPTERS 11 AND 12 FOR MORE ABOUT DESIGNING ONLINE DOCUMENTS.

Figure 1.9 Online View gets rid of page breaks and displays material as a single page.

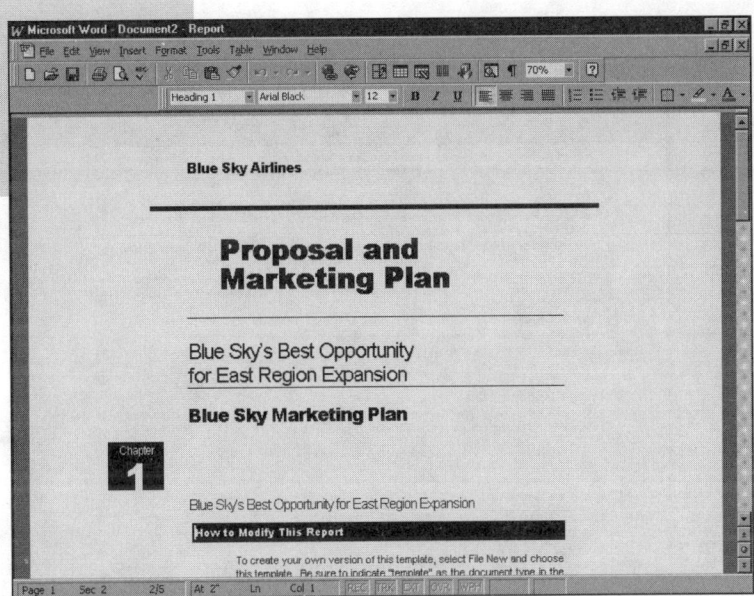

Note

When you access Online Layout view, the View buttons disappear from your screen. To move to any other view, select the <u>V</u>iew menu and choose the view you want by clicking on its name in the menu.

CHAPTER 4 COVERS THE OUTLINE VIEW IN MORE DETAIL.

- *Outline view* (see Figure 1.10). This is the view to use if you are focusing on the hierarchy of ideas and the flow of information in your document. It offers an expandable and collapsible view of text by heading levels.

Figure 1.10
A new toolbar appears when you enter Outline view, and plus and minus icons indicate whether levels of headings are displayed or hidden.

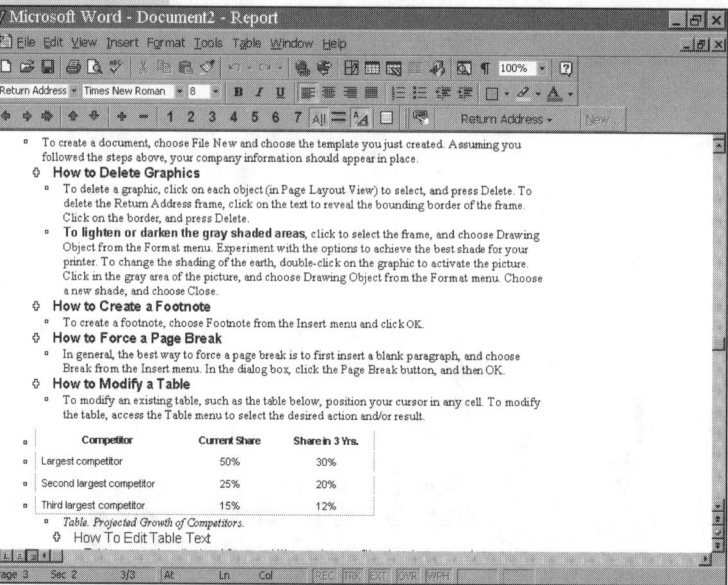

> You can also display a *Master Document view* through the View menu. This view is used in assembling larger documents from several smaller documents. Also, a Print Preview view is useful for seeing how documents will look before you print them on paper.

Note

SEE CHAPTER 17 FOR MORE ABOUT THE MASTER DOCUMENT VIEW. CHAPTER 6 EXPLORES PRINT PREVIEW IN MORE DETAIL.

You can change views using the *View buttons* near the lower-left corner of your Word screen (see Figure 1.11). You can also select the View menu and choose any view from among the commands there.

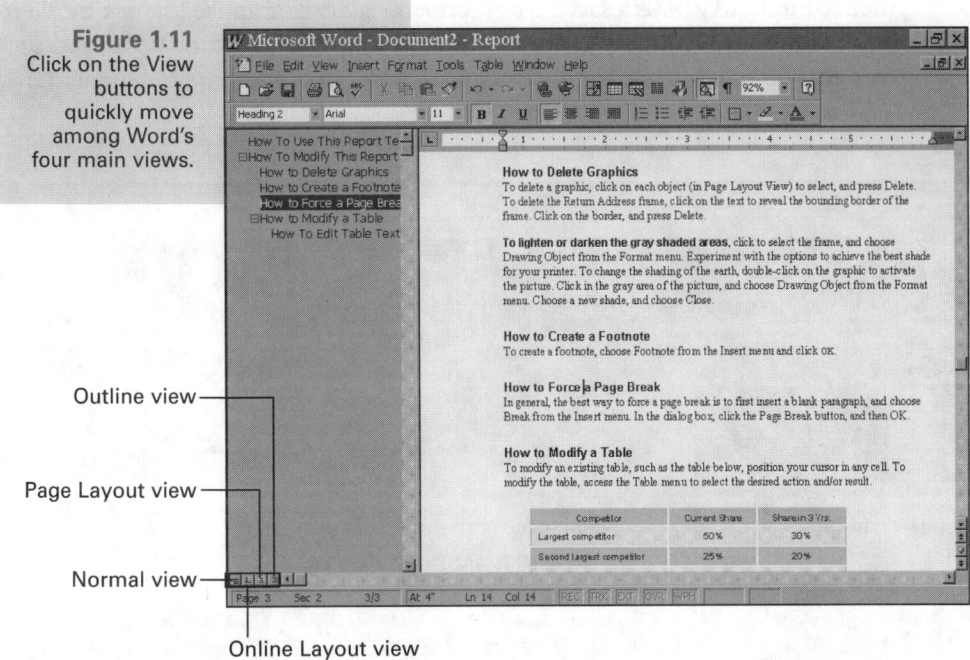

Figure 1.11 Click on the View buttons to quickly move among Word's four main views.

Outline view
Page Layout view
Normal view
Online Layout view

Getting Around

In this book, we assume that you've conquered Windows basics and know how to use scroll bars and keystroke functions such as [Pg Dn], [Pg Up], [Home], and [End] to move around a document on-screen. Word 97 offers some nice shortcuts for navigating through a document that are worth mentioning here, just in case you're not aware of them.

Discovering Document Map

The Document Map consists of a second pane along the left side of your Word screen containing the headings from the document (see Figure 1.12). This pane provides an outline of your document, and, it's a great way to keep track of your location and move around from topic to topic—especially with larger documents.

You can turn the Document Map on and off by clicking on the Document Map button on the Standard toolbar. Document Map works by displaying text that has any of Word's built-in heading styles (named Heading 1 through Heading 9) applied to it. (A *style* is a saved set of formats that can be applied to text by selecting it from the Style drop-down list on the Formatting toolbar). When you click on any heading displayed in the Document Map pane, your insertion point moves to that heading.

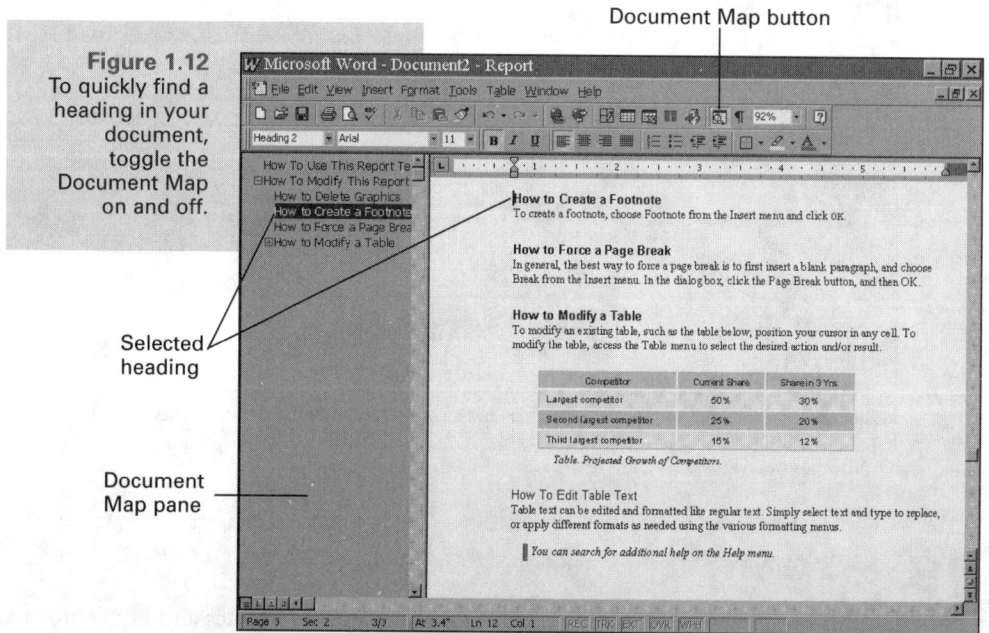

Figure 1.12 To quickly find a heading in your document, toggle the Document Map on and off.

You can choose to display different levels of headings in the Document Map. For example, to get an overview of major topics, you would collapse the lower level headings; to see all the subtopics in the document, you would expand all the levels. You can display heading levels two different ways. The first way involves the following steps:

1. Display the Document Map by clicking on the Document Map button.
2. In the Document Map pane, locate a heading with a small box containing a + or - sign to the left of it.
3. Click on a plus sign to display subheadings not currently shown. Click on a minus sign to hide subheadings that are currently showing.

The second way to display heading levels is to click on any heading with your right mouse button to see the shortcut menu in Figure 1.13. Select specific levels of headings that you would like to see from this menu.

CHAPTER 1 • A FIRST LOOK AT WORD   17

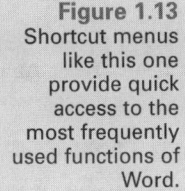

Figure 1.13
Shortcut menus like this one provide quick access to the most frequently used functions of Word.

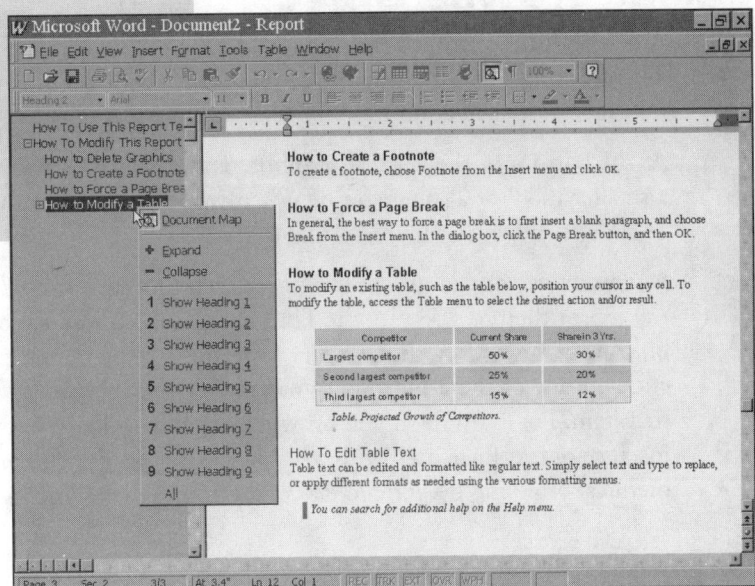

Document Map Tricks

Whenever we discover a neat new feature in software, we love to learn some clever tricks. Here are a few for the Document Map feature:

If you have the Microsoft Intellimouse that comes with some versions of Windows or Office, you can use it to work with the Document Map. Point to a heading with the mouse, press the [Shift] key, and move the wheel forward or back to expand or collapse headings.

Don't like the look of Document Map? You can change it by choosing Format, Style. In the Styles list, click on Document Map, and then click on the Modify button. Click on Format and make any changes that you like to the font, font size, or highlight color.

PART I • CREATING BASIC DOCUMENTS

Using Select Browse Object

> **THE SELECT BROWSE OBJECT FEATURE IS DISCUSSED IN DETAIL IN CHAPTER 5.**

A new feature controlled from the vertical scroll bar is called *Select Browse Object*. This feature provides a way of scanning through a document. It's worth a mention here as a navigation tool, however.

At the bottom of the vertical scroll bar is the Select Browse Object button, with a small symbol of a sphere on it. When you click this button, the pop-up palette of choices shown in Figure 1.14 appears.

As you move your mouse pointer over each tool, you should see a description at the top of the box. Besides the Find and Go To buttons, you can use the other buttons to browse by things such as heading, section, and page. Each time you click on one of these buttons, Word moves you forward to the next instance of that item. For example, if you browse by heading, the screen will display the next instance of text formatted with a heading style. In a document with a great many pictures, browsing by graphic takes you from one graphic to the next quickly.

Figure 1.14
The choices on this palette range from Find and Go To, to browsing by a number of criteria.

Getting Help

Word for Windows gets simpler to learn with each new version because of the added ease of use built into it. Features such as ToolTips to describe tool functions and shortcut menus to suggest likely actions make learning Word simpler. Sometimes, however, you just can't figure out what to do or how to use a feature. That's where Word Help comes in.

Tip

••
If you're an ex-WordPerfect user, be sure to check out the WordPerfect help feature. Select <u>H</u>elp, WordP<u>e</u>rfect Help to get explanations of how many WordPerfect functions relate to the same functions in Word.
••

Using the Contents and Index Feature

The Windows-like Help system allows you to look up Help topics in a simple index format, as shown in Figure 1.15. You get to this dialog box by selecting Help, Contents and then Index.

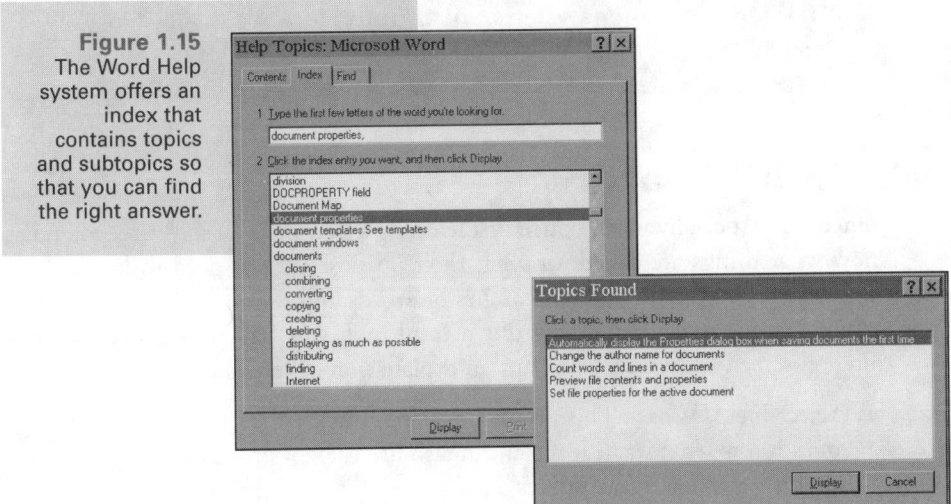

Figure 1.15 The Word Help system offers an index that contains topics and subtopics so that you can find the right answer.

Here you search for help using any of three methods:

- Choose a general topics on the Contents tab and move through various windows of subtopics by double-clicking on items of interest until you locate the information you need.

- Look through an Index by typing a term or phrase in a text box on the Index tab. This method uses a QuickPick system: you type a few letters and Word takes you to the area of the Index containing words that begin with those letters. In most cases, you don't even have to type a whole word to locate a topic.

- Use the Find tab to run a Help database search. Rather than search by categories of information, this method lets you search the Help system for words or phrases that might occur in the Help information itself. The first time that you use this feature, a Find Setup Wizard will walk you through the process and set up the database search.

PART I • CREATING BASIC DOCUMENTS

Note

A *wizard* is a feature of Microsoft software that takes you step by step through a process, asking you questions and having you fill in blanks. When you complete the simple steps, the wizard typically builds something based on your input. For example, the Newsletter Wizard produces a professional-looking newsletter, ready for you to enter specific stories and images.

The What's This? Feature

Sometimes, especially when you're first learning a new piece of software, you don't know what things are called, or what their purpose is. You need to know these things so that you can conduct searches by words and phrases. The What's This? feature answers that need. Using this helpful tool, you can simply point to anything on screen for which you want an explanation . Here's how it works:

1. Select Help, What's This? Your mouse pointer changes to an arrow with a question mark next to it. (You can also use the keystroke shortcut Shift+F1 to activate What's This?.)

2. Move the mouse pointer to the on-screen item that you want explained and click on it. A brief explanation, such as the one shown in Figure 1.16, appears.

3. Click anywhere outside of the description box to remove it from the screen.

Meet the Office Assistant

> CHAPTER 16 TELLS YOU ALL YOU NEED TO KNOW TO CUSTOMIZE THE OFFICE ASSISTANT.

The *Office Assistant* is an intriguing, sometimes annoying, little help feature new to Word 97 (see Figure 1.17). You can display the Office Assistant by clicking on the Office Assistant button on the Standard toolbar. Sometimes he'll appear all by himself when Word "senses" that you're having trouble getting something done (for example, if you repeatedly press a button for a feature that's inappropriate to where you are in the program at the time).

The idea behind Office Assistant is for you to simply type any question and click on the Search option button, at which point the Assistant will answer the question. The method used is known as a natural language interface, and in theory, it's great. But the Office Assistant is really just a database that searches for items that match terms used in your sentence. If you don't phrase the sentence just

Chapter 1 • A First Look at Word

right, you might not get the right answer. Still, for those who prefer to talk in complete sentences or who think in terms of what they want to do rather than feature names, Office Assistant can be of help.

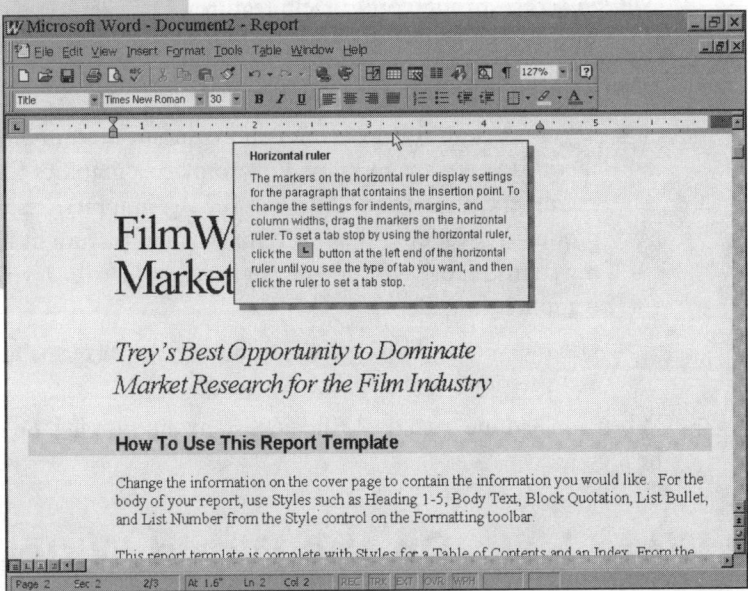

Figure 1.16
Use the terms in this explanation to look up more detailed information in the Contents and Index section of Word Help, if necessary.

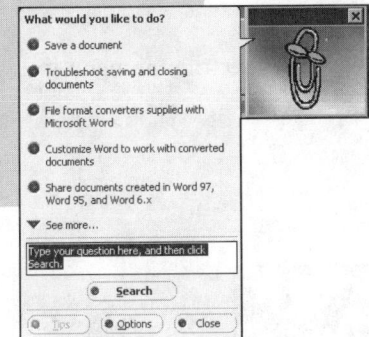

Figure 1.17
Ask this little guy anything; sometimes he gets it right, sometimes he doesn't.

Don't like the little paper clip character? You can customize Office Assistant to a variety of personalities, even Albert Einstein. Click on the Options button in the Office Assistant dialog box to access these customizing features.

PART I • CREATING BASIC DOCUMENTS

The feature is easy to use. Just click on the Office Assistant button and type your question; then, click on Search. You're typically offered several possible options for the type of task that you're performing. Click on the option button for the one that's closest to what you're trying to do and Office Assistant will display further levels of Help, eventually taking you into some of the same Help windows that you can access through other Help features. Here are some tips for phrasing your question for the greatest success:

- Keep your phrasing simple. Use verbs such as *do*, *is*, and *make*.
- Try to work in feature names and computer terminology if you know them. If you want to know how to place a graphics file in a document, for example, the question "How do I insert graphics?" is more likely to get a productive response than "I want to put a picture in the top-left corner of my status report." Although *put* is a simple verb, *insert* is standard computer lingo.
- Use the What's This? feature to find the right terms for items before you ask questions of the Office Assistant.

When you're done with the Office Assistant, simply click on the Close button and he'll go away.

Getting Word Help On the World Wide Web

The world is headed to the Internet and Microsoft is at the head of the pack. The new online help features that Microsoft added to its 97 range of products is a great way to get your online feet wet while getting up-to-the-minute help with Word 97.

Select Help, Microsoft on the Web to see the submenu in Figure 1.18.

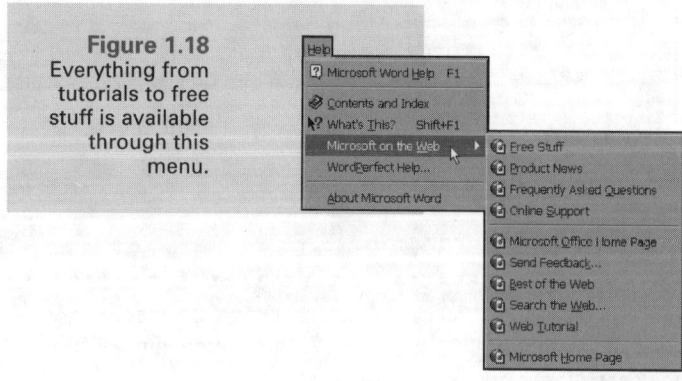

Figure 1.18
Everything from tutorials to free stuff is available through this menu.

CHAPTER 1 • A FIRST LOOK AT WORD 23

To use any of the elements on this menu, you need a modem and a connection to the Internet set up. If you haven't designated a default browser, Word may use Microsoft's Internet Explorer browser to take you to Microsoft's Web site (`http://www.microsoft.com`). For example, selecting Frequently Asked Questions takes you to the site `http://www.microsoft.com/MSWordSupport/content/faq/`, shown in Figure 1.19.

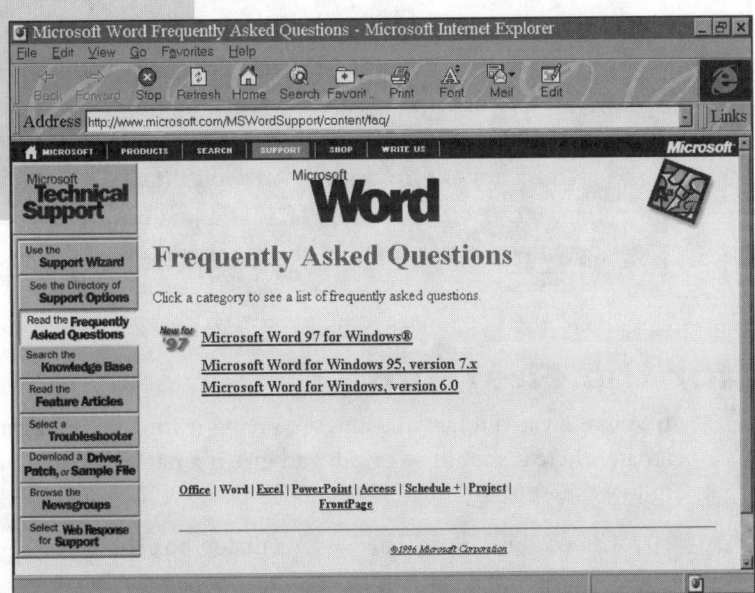

Figure 1.19
A world of up-to-date and even personal support is available in Word's support area.

If you need to modify Internet Explorer to use your Internet service provider, open the My Computer window, and double-click on the Dial-up Connections item..

You can get help from an actual technical support person by using the Online Support or Send Feedback choices to submit questions and get them answered by a Microsoft technical support person. Try the Web Tutorial option for an online, guided tour of Word features.

PART I • CREATING BASIC DOCUMENTS

Saving Documents

As any computer user knows, saving your work frequently is important. Nothing is worse than typing the first paragraph of the great American novel, only to have your brilliant words lost to a stray lightening storm or some obscure fatal error.

Note

Word has an automatic save feature that runs every few minutes to save a special recovered version of the current document in the case of a computer crash or program error. In that event, when you start Word again, the recovered document (the last automatically saved version of the document) should appear on-screen. Although it won't contain any changes that you made after the last automatic save, it will usually represent most of your work.

Saving for the First Time

If you've created a new file and are saving it for the first time, you'll have to designate where it should be saved, and give it a name. To save a file for the first time, follow these steps:

1. Choose File, Save. The Save As dialog box shown in Figure 1.20 appears.
2. Enter the file name in the File Name text box.

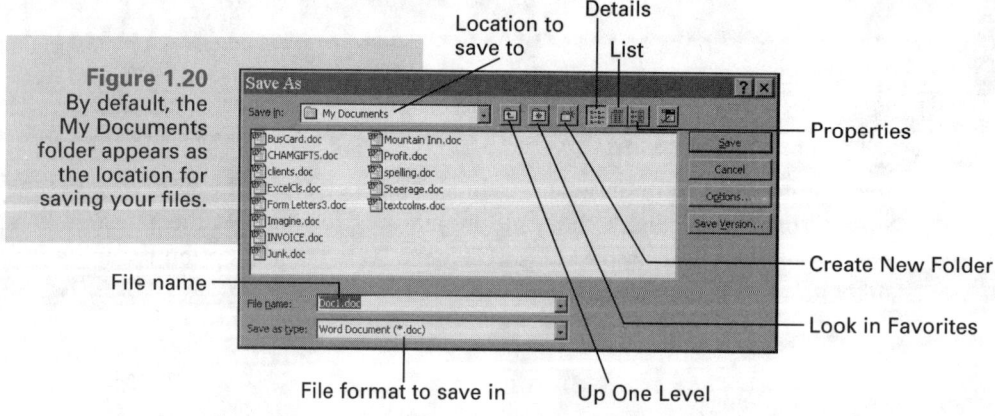

Figure 1.20
By default, the My Documents folder appears as the location for saving your files.

The file will be saved in Word 97 format by default, which provides a document extension of .DOC. If you'd like to save the file in another format—Word 2.0 or WordPerfect, for example—you can select those from the Save as Type drop-down list. Windows 95 will support long file names, so you're no longer limited to eight character names.

3. If you want to save the file in a different folder, you can browse the folders and files on your hard drive or disk drives by using the Save In drop-down list, or the Up One Level or Look in Favorites buttons. If you'd like to save the document to a folder that you haven't yet created, create it right here using the Create New Folder button.

You can change what information about files is displayed by using the List, Details, and Properties buttons in the Save As dialog box. The Properties choice, for example, shows details about documents in a separate pane, as shown in Figure 1.21.

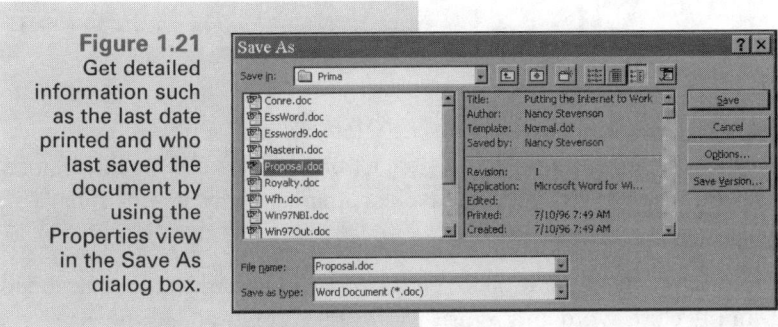

Figure 1.21
Get detailed information such as the last date printed and who last saved the document by using the Properties view in the Save As dialog box.

4. When you've found the proper location for the file and named it, click on Save to save the document.

Now that you've saved the file and given it a name, you can save it in the future by simply clicking on the Save button on the Standard toolbar, or by choosing File, Save. After a file has been saved initially, choosing File, Save saves the file without requiring you to open the Save As dialog box.

PART I • CREATING BASIC DOCUMENTS

Saving a File with a Different Name

LEARN MORE ABOUT SAVING A FILE AS AN HTML DOCUMENT IN CHAPTER 11.

Saving the same file with a new name is often convenient. For example, if you've written a client proposal and you'd like to use it as the basis for two different project documents, you can save it once and then save it a second time with a new name. To do this, have the document open in Word and then choose File, Save As. The Save As dialog box that you saw in the previous section (Figures 1.20 and 1.21) appears. Select the directory in which to put the file, and give the file a new name. Choose Save. You'll now have two identical files with different names.

Note

You can also save a file as an HTML document using the File, Save as HTML command. This creates a hypertext document that you can place on the World Wide Web, if you like.

Exiting Word

You can close Word by simply clicking on the Close control button in the upper-right hand corner of the window. If you prefer, you can also choose File, Close. Word will ask you whether you want to save documents, if any are open that you haven't saved.

If you have no unsaved documents open, performing either of the aforementioned actions will simply close Word and return you to the Windows desktop.

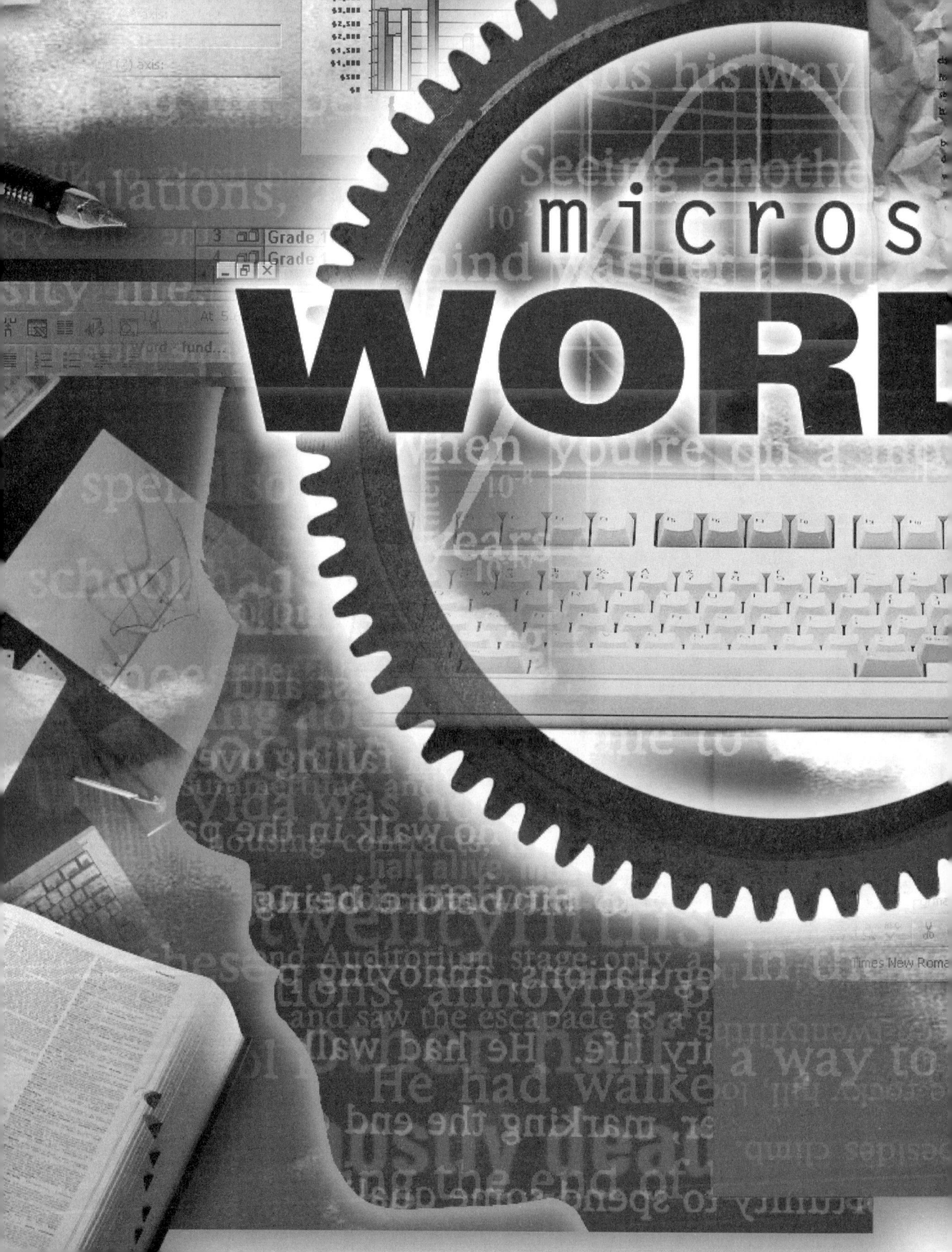

2
Creating a Simple Letter

IN THIS CHAPTER

- Entering Text
- Applying Text Styles
- Using Tabs
- Selecting Text

Word for Windows has become a sophisticated software product, which is part outliner, part drawing tool, part Web page publisher, and part workgroup document management tool. At heart, however, it is a word processor. The simple act of entering text and working with that text is one of the first and most essential skills you can learn.

30 Part I • Creating Basic Documents

In this chapter, you'll begin to build your first Word document. You will be entering text as well as selecting and applying simple styles to text. You'll also learn about the tab feature, which lets you manipulate the placement of text across the document page.

Entering Text

The first step in entering text is to open a new document. When you first open Word 97, a blank document appears based on the Blank Document template. (If you already have Word open and want to start a new, blank document, choose File, New, and click on the Blank Document item on the General tab. Click on OK to open the new file). Notice a blinking vertical line in the top-left corner of the new document. This is the insertion point, indicating where text will appear if you begin to type.

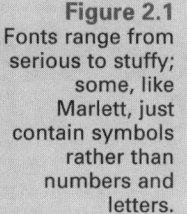

Changing text fonts is discussed in detail in Chapter 3.

This blank document is based on the Blank Document template, which applies a font called Times New Roman to text that you type. A *font* is a design family that gives the letters, numbers, and symbols a certain look. Some fonts are fancy, some resemble handwritten script, and some are a little more formal. You can see a few font varieties in Figure 2.1.

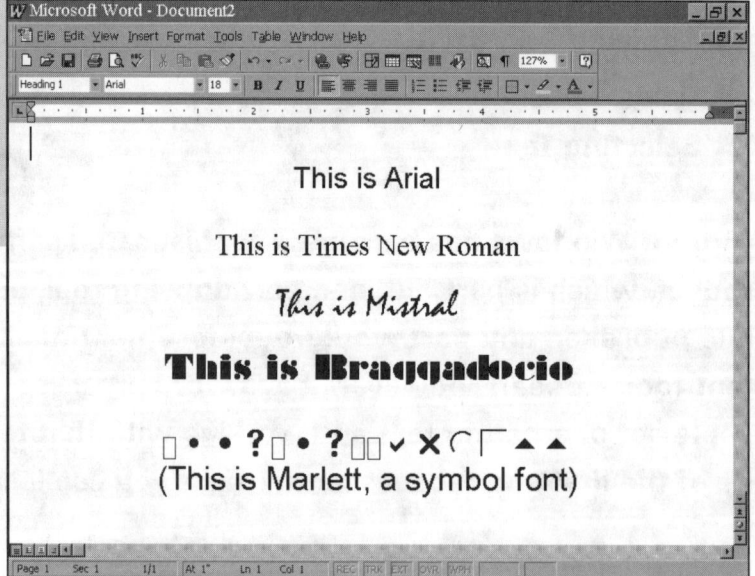

Figure 2.1
Fonts range from serious to stuffy; some, like Marlett, just contain symbols rather than numbers and letters.

CHAPTER 2 • CREATING A SIMPLE LETTER 31

Adding Text

The first step to building any kind of Word document is typically to enter the text: the words, numbers, and symbols that make up your message.

Hands On: Adding Text to Your Letter

Now you can start adding text to your Word document. Follow these steps to enter the return address for a letter:

> FOR DETAILS ABOUT FORMATTING THE SPACING OF LINES IN PARAGRAPHS SEE CHAPTER 3.

1. Type **Ms. Georgia Harrington**.
2. Press [Enter]. Pressing [Enter] places the insertion point at the beginning of the next line down.
3. Type **24 Barrow Street**.
4. Press [Enter] again.
5. Type **Tyrone, MD 44455**.
6. Press [Enter] five times. Your letter should now look like the one in Figure 2.2. To place blank lines between lines of text, you can simply press [Enter] several times.

Don't use the [Enter] key to create spacing between lines of text in your documents. If you want to double-space your text lines, for example, you can format the lines of your paragraphs to use double-spacing automatically.

When you're typing longer lines of text, as with paragraphs, you don't need to press [Enter] at the end of a line. Word uses a feature called *text wrapping* **that automatically returns your insertion point to the start of a new line when your text reaches the right margin. Press [Enter] only if you want to start a new paragraph or place a blank line in your document.**

PART I • CREATING BASIC DOCUMENTS

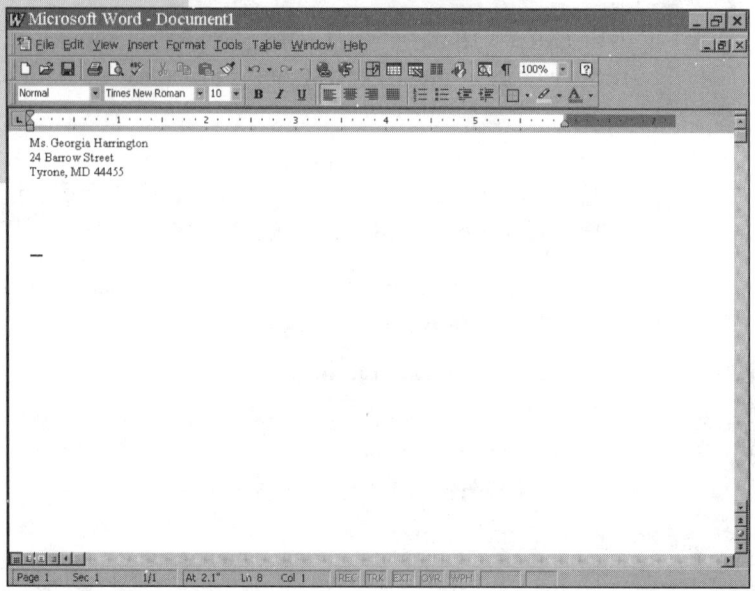

Figure 2.2
Notice that all text aligns to the left side of the document by default.

Inserting a Date

You'll be glad to know that you don't have to type all the text in a document; Word can do some of it for you. Common items such as the date or page numbers can be inserted on your page using a simple menu command.

Hands On: Inserting a Date

To quickly insert a date in your document, perform the steps that follow:

1. Choose Insert, Date and Time. The dialog box in Figure 2.3 appears.

Note

Notice that the date Word inserts in your document will be different than the one in these figures. The date inserted is the current date based on your computer calendar and clock at the moment you perform the insertion. We did this in 1996; your date will probably be 1997 or even 1998.

CHAPTER 2 • CREATING A SIMPLE LETTER   **33**

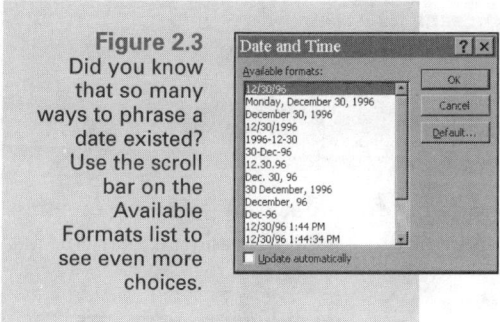

Figure 2.3
Did you know that so many ways to phrase a date existed? Use the scroll bar on the Available Formats list to see even more choices.

2. Click on the third date format down from the top to select it.

3. Click on OK to close the dialog box and place the date in your letter.

4. Press Enter three times to move down in your document (your insertion point should be on line 11 now; check the status bar at the bottom of your screen to confirm this).

If you want the date to reflect the current date every time you open the document, you can check the Update Automatically check box in the Date and Time dialog box.

Using AutoText

Another way to have Word enter text for you is to use a feature called *AutoText*. AutoText has some standard text items such as letter salutations and closings already built in. But you can also save text that you use often, such as people's addresses or a citation of a legal case, in AutoText. You can then instantly place that saved text in any document, with only a few steps.

Hands On: Creating a New AutoText Entry

You can create a new entry by choosing Insert, AutoText, AutoText and typing into a field in the dialog box that appears. You might find another way just as easy, though: type the text in your document, select it, and make it into an AutoText entry. Try this approach:

PART I • CREATING BASIC DOCUMENTS

1. Type the address that follows, pressing Enter after each line:

   Mr. Herbert Worth
   Worth Detective Agency
   54-A Spring Street
   Arlington, VA 54345

2. Click your mouse just before the *M* in Mr., and keeping your left mouse button depressed, drag over and down until the entire address that you just typed is highlighted on screen.

3. Choose <u>I</u>nsert, <u>A</u>utoText, <u>N</u>ew. The dialog box in Figure 2.4 appears.

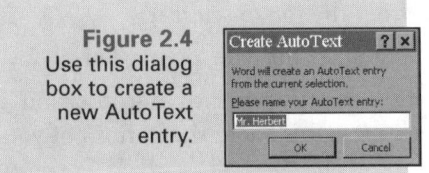

Figure 2.4
Use this dialog box to create a new AutoText entry.

4. Type **Mr. Worth** to change the name of the AutoText entry. You can name AutoText entries whatever you wish to make them easy for you to remember.

5. Click on OK.

6. When you return to your document, press the Backspace key on your keyboard to get rid of the address block for Mr. Worth, just so you can try out your new AutoText entry.

7. Type **Mr. Worth**; then, press F3.

The newly created AutoText entry is inserted in your document. Now that you've saved the entry, you can place it in documents again and again, anytime you like.

Using the AutoText Toolbar

An even faster way to insert AutoText is by using the AutoText toolbar. In the following procedure, you display the AutoText toolbar and insert two built-in Auto-Text entries into your document.

CHAPTER 2 • CREATING A SIMPLE LETTER **35**

> ### Hands On: Inserting AutoText into Your Letter with the AutoText Toolbar

To use the AutoText toolbar, follow these steps:

1. Press Enter twice to move two lines down from the inside address.
2. Choose View, Toolbars and click on AutoText from the submenu that appears. A new toolbar appears just beneath the Formatting toolbar at the top of your screen.
3. Click on the All Entries button on this new toolbar to see a drop-down list of AutoText choices. Move your mouse pointer down to the Reference Line item to display the submenu shown in Figure 2.5.

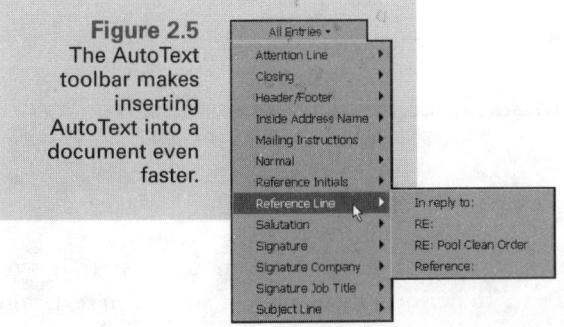

Figure 2.5
The AutoText toolbar makes inserting AutoText into a document even faster.

4. Click on the item in the submenu called `In reply to:`. The AutoText is inserted into your letter.
5. Press the spacebar once, and then type **Letter of August 23rd** to complete the reference line.
6. Now the letter needs a salutation. Press Enter twice.
7. Click on the All Entries button on the AutoText toolbar and select Salutation, To Whom It May Concern. The salutation AutoText is placed in your document. Your letter should now look like the one shown in Figure 2.6.

Some great uses for AutoText are the sometimes lengthy captions at the head of legal documents; your company mission statement; or paragraphs such as product descriptions that you use frequently in form letters to customers. In short, anything that you type frequently can be stored as AutoText and inserted easily.

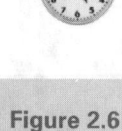

PART I • CREATING BASIC DOCUMENTS

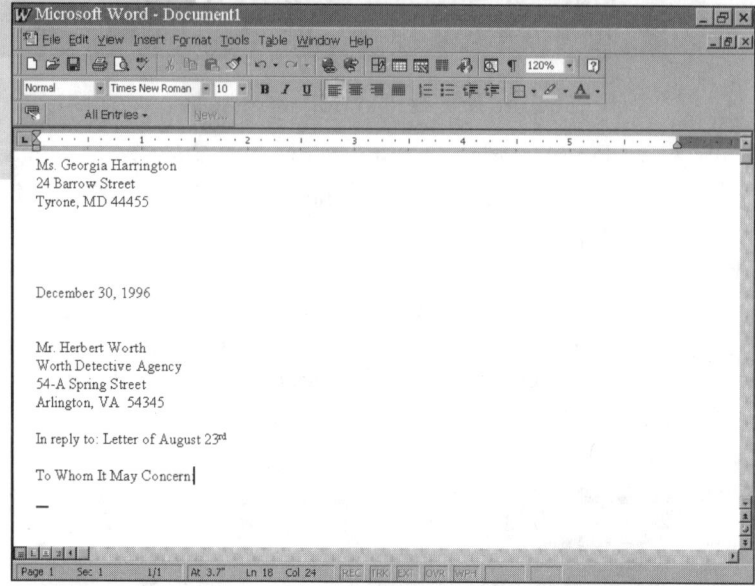

Figure 2.6
Build documents by inserting common phrases with the AutoText feature.

Selecting and Moving Text

Now that you've entered some text in a document, you can do many things to move around and modify that text. To perform these types of actions on text, you must select that text. Word has several ways to select items in documents, and if you've used other Windows software, you're probably familiar with some of those ways.

Selecting Text

You can choose from among three methods to select text:

- You can use your mouse to click and drag to highlight a selection.
- You can use the selection bar, an invisible area on the far left of your Word screen that allows you to select whole sentences, paragraphs, or the entire document.
- You can also use the Edit, Select All command to select all text.

To help you practice selecting text, finish entering the contents of this sample letter to match the text in Figure 2.7. Remember, you don't need to press [Enter] at the end of every line, but only at the end of each paragraph.

Chapter 2 • Creating a Simple Letter

Figure 2.7
Use the skills that you've just learned to complete this document.

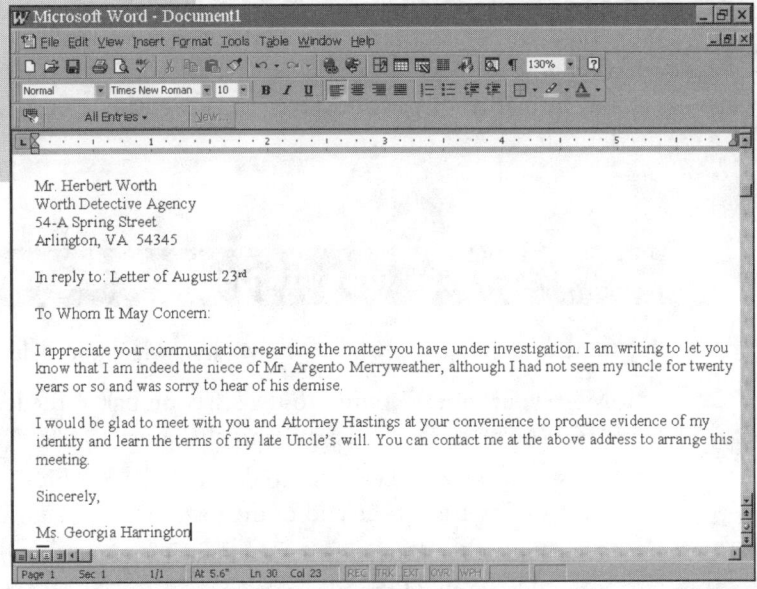

Hands On: Selecting Text

Follow this procedure to learn the various methods for selecting text:

1. Click to the left of the first letter of the second sentence in the first paragraph, and drag down to select the sentence. Clicking and dragging is most useful with selecting portions of paragraphs or sentences.
2. Click anywhere outside of the selected text to deselect it.
3. Move your mouse to the left of the first paragraph until the mouse pointer become a hollow, right-pointing arrow. When your mouse pointer arrow faces right, you know you're in the selection bar. The selection bar is useful for selecting chunks of text, such as lines or paragraphs. Click once to select the entire line to the right of the pointer.
4. Double-click to select the paragraph to the right of the pointer.
5. Press [Ctrl] and click once in the selection bar to select all the text in the document.
6. Click once anywhere in the document to deselect the selected text.
7. Choose Edit, Select All to select all text in the document. (You can also press [Ctrl]+[A] to do the same thing.)

Deleting, Copying, and Moving Text

Now that you've practiced various methods for selecting text, you can put the selection process to work. After you have selected text, you can delete it, move it, copy it, format it, or perform tasks such as creating AutoText, which you practiced earlier.

Hands On: Working with Selected Text in Your Letter

Try some of these tasks with text now. First, select and delete some text.

1. Move your mouse pointer to the selection bar to the left of the salutation (To Whom It May Concern:) and click once to select it.
2. Press Del on your keyboard to delete the text. This also deletes the return that you inserted at the end of the text.
3. Type **Dear Mr. Worth:** and press Enter to place a blank line between the new salutation and the first paragraph.

After you select text, you don't actually have to delete it to replace it with other text. Select the text and then just begin typing the new text; the old text is replaced automatically.

Now try moving selected text around your document. You can do this by dragging the text to where you want it. You can also use the cut-and-paste method. Cutting something places it in a temporary holding place called the Windows *Clipboard*; pasting places whatever is on that Clipboard into your document, effectively removing it from one location and placing it somewhere else.

Hands On: Using Drag and Drop to Move Text

Try moving some text using these steps:

1. Click and drag to select the phrase in the first sentence of the second paragraph, `learn the terms of my late Uncle's will`. (Don't select the period at the end!)

Chapter 2 • Creating a Simple Letter 39

2. Hold down the mouse button inside the selected text. Your mouse pointer becomes an arrow, a box, and a vertical line; the line in this pointer indicates where the text will move if you release the mouse, as shown in Figure 2.8.

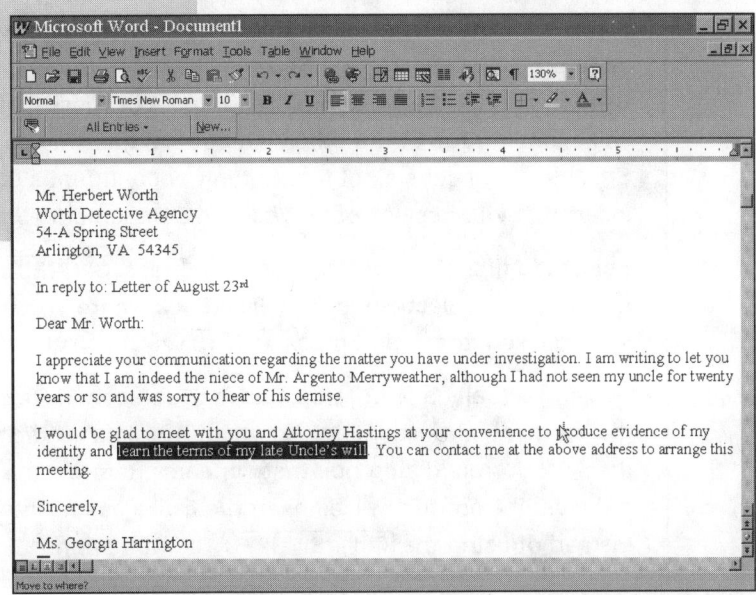

Figure 2.8 Let go of your mouse button now and your text will be placed where this vertical line indicates.

3. Drag the selected text to move it to an earlier point in the sentence, just after the phrase `at your convenience to`.
4. When the line portion of the pointer is at the correct place in the sentence, just before the phrase `produce evidence`, release your mouse button to place the text.
5. Select the word `and` at the end of the same sentence and click on the Cut button on the toolbar.
6. Move your insertion point just after the phrase `Uncle's will` in the same sentence, and click on the Paste button on the toolbar. The word is placed at this point in the sentence.

For more about cutting and copying among Office applications, read Microsoft's online reference material at `http://www.microsoft.com/officerefer-ence/getting results book`.

PART I • CREATING BASIC DOCUMENTS

Spiking Text

The Windows Clipboard holds only one selection at a time: anywhere from a single letter or number to pages of text. If you cut a second item, it replaces the first on the Clipboard. To remove more than one piece of text and save it ready to insert it elsewhere, you have to use a feature called *Spike*. The Spike is like those metal things that you used to find in offices; you placed papers or message slips on the spike, one on top of the other. (Of course, this was before e-mail!) The Spike lets you cut sets of text (often noncontiguous text), and then insert that whole stack of text back in a document at one time.

Select the first piece of text, and then press Ctrl+F3. Repeat this for as many text selections as you like. Click where you want to insert the set of spiked items, and press Ctrl+Shift+F3. All the text is inserted.

Spike is actually a feature of AutoText. To see what's on the Spike at the moment, choose Insert, Autotext, Autotext, and choose Spike in the AutoCorrect dialog box that appears. To insert the spiked text but not clear it from the Spike, insert the Spike as an AutoText entry, instead of using the Ctrl+Shift+F3 combination.

Copying text is much like cutting and pasting. You select the text, click on the Copy button on the toolbar, move your insertion point to the location where you'd like a copy of the text, and click on the Paste button. That's it!

•••

You can also select text, press Ctrl, and drag text. A copy appears in the new location.

•••

•••

You can find the menu commands for cutting, copying, and pasting on the Edit menu. Shortcut keystroke combinations for each are also listed there.

•••

CHAPTER 2 • CREATING A SIMPLE LETTER 41

Applying Text Effects and Styles

Selecting text also allows you to apply a variety of formatting effects, such as changing the font or font size or using different colors for text. These formatting options are explored in more detail in Chapter 3, but for now, try a few simple text effects to make your letter more visually attractive.

Using Simple Text Effects

The following exercise applies bold, italic, and underline effects, and uses a few simple built-in text styles.

Hands On: Using Text Effects in Your Letter

Three commonly used text effects, bold, italic, and underline, add emphasis to text. In fact, these effects are used so often that Word has buttons for each of them on the Formatting toolbar.

> YOU'LL LEARN MORE ABOUT MODIFYING FONTS AND USING SPECIAL EFFECTS IN CHAPTER 3.

1. Select the reference line, which begins `In reply to:`.
2. Click on the Bold button. The text becomes bold.
3. Click on the Italic button. The text is now bold and italic.
4. Click on the Underline button. Click anywhere outside of the text to deselect it, and the text now looks like that shown in Figure 2.9, with all three effects applied.

   You can use these buttons alone or in any combination. They are called *toggle* buttons, because you click on them once to apply an effect, and again to remove the effect, thereby toggling the effect on and off as you like.

5. Click on the Underline button again to remove the underline effect.

Tip

You can also apply these effects from the Font dialog box, which you open by choosing F̲ormat, F̲ont.

42 PART I • CREATING BASIC DOCUMENTS

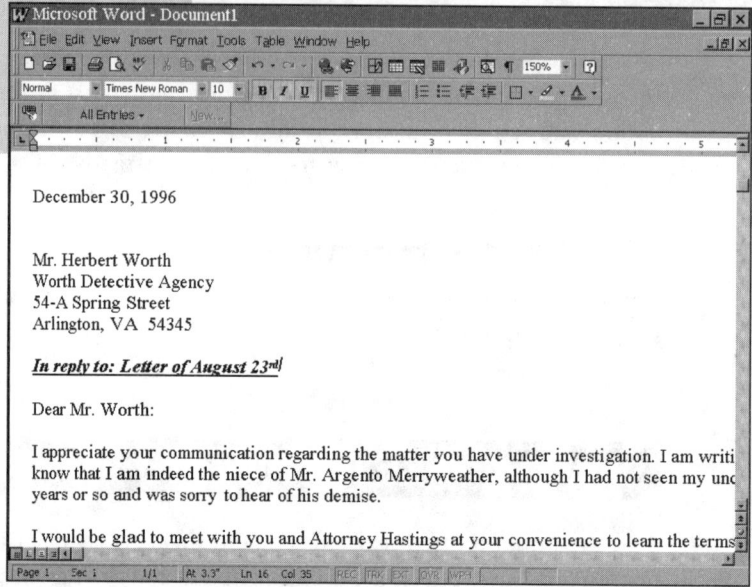

Figure 2.9
Bold, italic, and underline effects add emphasis to text.

Applying Predefined Styles

Word provides built-in styles that you can apply to text. Styles are predefined sets of formatting that may include elements such as font, font size, alignment, and even bold, italic, or underlining. You'll learn much more about using and even creating your own styles in Chapter 14, but you need at least a glimpse of how they work now.

Hands On: Applying Styles in a Letter

As an example of using a predefined style, apply a heading style to the return address from previous examples. This heading style gives the return address a little more distinction:

1. Select the return address at the top of the letter.
2. Find the Style button on the left end of the Formatting toolbar. Click on the arrow on the right side of the Style button. A drop-down list of styles appears, as shown in Figure 2.10.

CHAPTER 2 • CREATING A SIMPLE LETTER 43

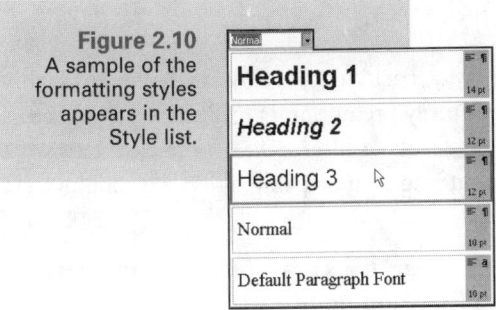

Figure 2.10
A sample of the formatting styles appears in the Style list.

3. Click on the choice named Heading 3. The new style is applied to your return address, as shown in Figure 2.11.

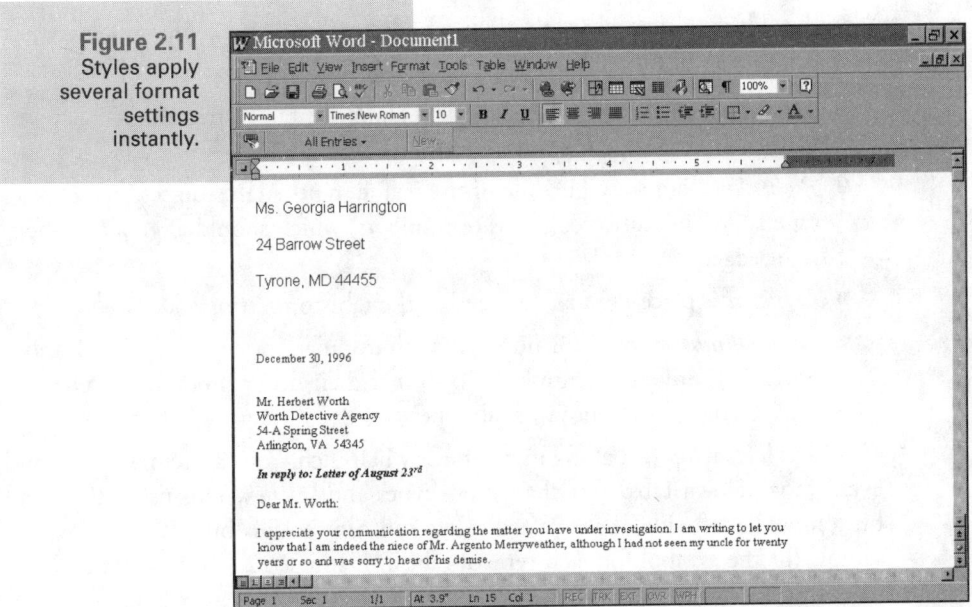

Figure 2.11
Styles apply several format settings instantly.

Notice that the style did more than just apply one format change, such as making text bold. This style, which is built into the Blank Document template, contains a new spacing setting between lines of text, the Arial font, and a 12-point font size. Different templates will have their own sets of styles attached, so you'll see more of them as you move through the chapters ahead.

Using Tabs

If you formerly used a typewriter, way back in the dark ages, you probably counted on tabs quite a bit. Tabs are simply preset points (called tab stops) across a page; you can move quickly to these points to insert text. In the past, tabs were used for placing an indent at the beginning of new paragraphs or arranging text in columns, as in a table of numbers.

The tab's golden days have faded, however, thanks to word processing features such as indenting for setting blocks of text in from the margin, or alignment to center text or tables to set data in nice, neat columns. Still, sometimes you just want to place one or two lines of text at a point across the page, and using tab stops is the easiest way to do so.

Tab Types

Word has four tab types: left tab, right tab, decimal tab, and center tab. Here is a brief description of each tab type:

- *Left tabs* align the left side of the text along the tab stop setting. This type is the common type for simple text.
- *Right tabs* align the right side of the text along the tab stop setting. This type is often used for columns of numbers, which should align along their right edge.
- *Center tabs* place the text centered at the tab stop setting.
- *Decimal tabs* are used for numbers with decimal points, such as 25.1 and 33.127. To line these numbers up so that their decimal points are all at the tab stop setting, use this tab type.

Word has left tabs preset along its ruler every half inch. You can remove these and even set your own tabs. You change tab types and set new tabs using the small button at the left side of the Word ruler. You can see this button, along with a sample for the symbol for each type of tab, in Figure 2.12. To display the Word ruler if it doesn't appear on-screen, choose View, Ruler.

Setting and Removing Tabs

You can use preset tabs, set new ones, and remove tab settings using the Tab button and ruler, or the Tabs dialog box.

CHAPTER 2 • CREATING A SIMPLE LETTER   45

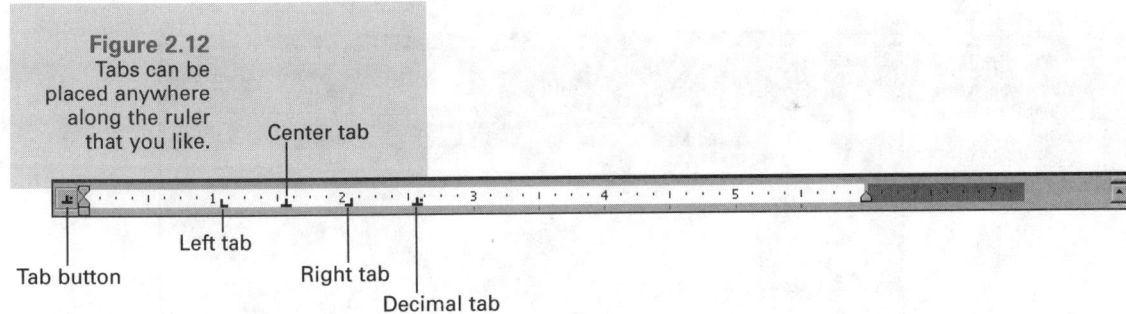

Figure 2.12
Tabs can be placed anywhere along the ruler that you like.

Hands On: Setting and Removing Tabs

You can practice using the tab button and ruler in the following procedure:

1. Place the insertion point before the reference line, which begins with the text `In reply to:`.
2. Press the Tab key on your keyboard. The text moves one-half inch to the right, which is the first preset tab stop.
3. Select the return address block at the top of the letter.
4. If the Tab button doesn't show the left tab symbol, click on it until you see the left tab symbol (an L shape).
5. Click on the ruler at the 2 1/2 inch mark. A left tab symbol should appear on the ruler. This action deletes any preset tabs up to that point, making the new tab stop the first stop along the page.
6. Click in front of the text `Ms. Georgia Harrington` to deselect the text.
7. Press [Tab]. The line of text moves to the new tab stop.
8. Repeat this with the other lines in the return address, until your return address looks like the one in Figure 2.13.

Caution

You must select text that you want to contain a tab setting before you set the tab. Be sure to deselect any text before pressing the [Tab] key, however. Pressing [Tab] when text is selected deletes that text.

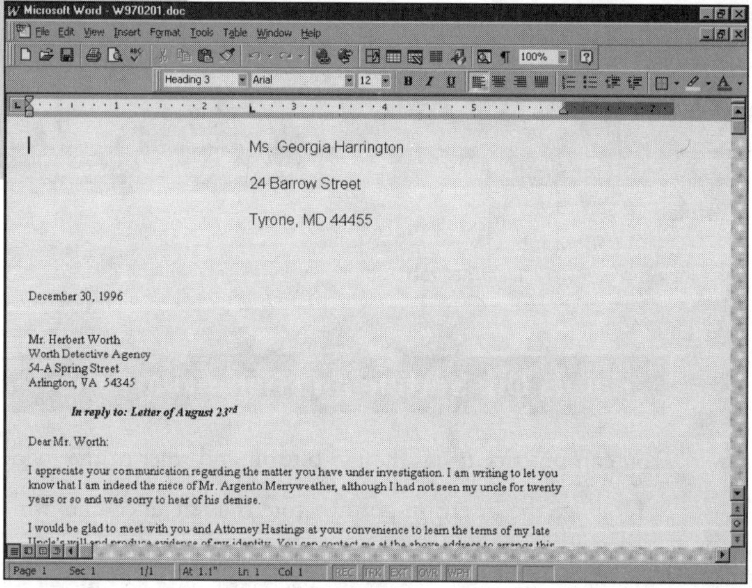

Figure 2.13 Text moves where you want it by using a single keystroke with tabs.

To remove a tab, you simply select the text where the tab is set, click on the tab symbol on the ruler, and drag it off the ruler.

You can also set and remove tabs using the Tab dialog box. You get there by selecting Format, Tabs. The dialog box in Figure 2.14 appears.

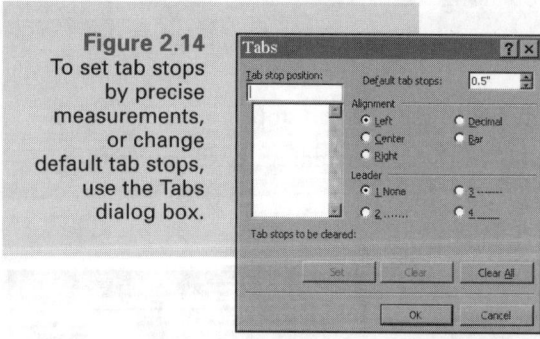

Figure 2.14 To set tab stops by precise measurements, or change default tab stops, use the Tabs dialog box.

Here's what you can do in the Tabs dialog box:

- Create a new tab stop by typing an exact measurement in inches in the Tab Stop Position text box, and then choosing Set.

CHAPTER 2 • CREATING A SIMPLE LETTER   47

- Align tabs (select the tab type) using the Alignment option buttons. The Bar option places a vertical line to indicate each tab stop on the ruler.
- Clear individual tabs or reset to original tab settings by choosing Clear All.
- Set leader characters.

Note

A leader character is a text element that fills the place between your insertion point when you pressed [Tab] and the tab stop. This is most often used to insert dots before page numbers in a table of contents. Leader characters help to guide the eye of someone reading across a page.

Here are a few last tips about setting tabs:

SEE MORE ABOUT TABS AND TABLES IN CHAPTER 8.

- To set a tab within a table cell, you must press [Ctrl]+[Tab] (pressing Tab moves you to the next cell in the table).
- You can move an existing tab stop by simply dragging it to a new location on the ruler.
- You can change the amount of spacing between the preset tab stops by choosing Format, Tabs and entering a new measurement in the Default Tab Stops box.

micros
WORD

Building a Memo

In This Chapter

- Formatting Text
- Formatting Paragraphs
- Aligning and Indenting Text
- Adding Bulleted and Numbered Lists

Typing text in a document is just the start. A great deal of what you do with documents to make them more professional looking relates to how you format and arrange that text on the page. Selecting the right type style (called a *font*), sizing the text, and arranging blocks of text on your page in appealing ways are foundations of what professional graphic designers do in designing documents. Now,

PART I • CREATING BASIC DOCUMENTS

with simple-to-use tools and even built-in designs, Word lets you create documents that are every bit as stylish and attractive as the professionals' documents.

Formatting Text

Text consists of the letters, numbers, and symbols that you type in a Word document. That text can be formatted to have a particular design style, or font, applied to it. Text can also be resized and styled in various ways to shift emphasis or to create a look for your document. That look makes a statement: elegant, informal, or businesslike, for example.

To begin this chapter, open a new Word document based on the Blank Document template and type the following text, also shown in the memorandum in Figure 3.1. Press Enter when you need to place extra space between lines as indicated, and use the preset tabs to place the text in the To/From/Date/Re block.

Memorandum

Arnold Toy Manufacturing
22 Arnold Drive
Poughkeepsie, NY 33456

To: Ms. Mary Anne Reynolds
From: Arnie Margolis
          Purchasing Manager
Date: December 27, 1996
Re: Order for Spring Hinges, P.O. Number 332-J779

To confirm our phone call today, I am placing an order for 20 cartons of your J-3X7 spring hinges, at a per unit price of $22.27 per carton. In addition, I would like catalogs sent to me for the following product lines:
1 inch plastic springs (TT-J78)
3 inch spring hinges (TJ-Y78)
Large spring clips (JT-L82)
Please remember that in order to receive prompt payment you must follow this three step billing process. Following this procedure will ensure timely payment.

Send a confirmation letter as soon as possible with our P.O. Number on it.
Send an invoice with the shipment.
Send a duplicate invoice directly to our accounting department.
Thank you again for your help with this order.

Figure 3.1
The default font for the Blank Document template is Times New Roman, 10 point.

Adjusting Text Font and Font Size

You have just entered the bare bones of a memorandum. Now you can start refining it by modifying the font size and changing which font is applied to the text.

Note

Although knowing how to perform all these formatting tasks is useful, Word has provided shortcuts to professional-looking documents. When you're done with this chapter, try opening some documents based on the Memo templates provided with Word; they contain formatting, alignment and even graphic elements to give you a head start on polished memos.

PART I • CREATING BASIC DOCUMENTS

Hands On: Adjusting Text Font and Size in a Memorandum

Most of the tools that you need to format text are found on the Formatting toolbar, so these steps begin with the Font and Font Size selections.

1. Select the word Memorandum at the top of your document.
2. On the Formatting toolbar, click on the arrow to the right of the Font drop-down list. You'll see a list of available fonts like the one in Figure 3.2. The fonts that you see may differ from those shown in the figure.

Figure 3.2
Many fonts are loaded as part of Word, but you can add other fonts from collections that you purchase.

3. Use the scroll bar on the Font list to locate Mistral. Click on Mistral and the new font is applied to selected text.

If, for some reason, you don't have Mistral available in your font list, just select another font; Desdemona or Howie's Funhouse are two interesting ones.

An easy way to view different fonts is to use the Font dialog box, rather than the Font drop-down list on the toolbar. The Font dialog box lets you preview the look of a font before you apply it.

4. Select the return address block (Arnold Toy Manufacturing and its address).
5. Choose F__o__rmat, __F__ont. The Font dialog box shown in Figure 3.3 appears.

You can also display the Font dialog box by right-clicking on selected text and choosing __F__ont from the shortcut menu that appears.

Chapter 3 • Building a Memo

Figure 3.3
The Font dialog box offers a central location to make many font formatting changes.

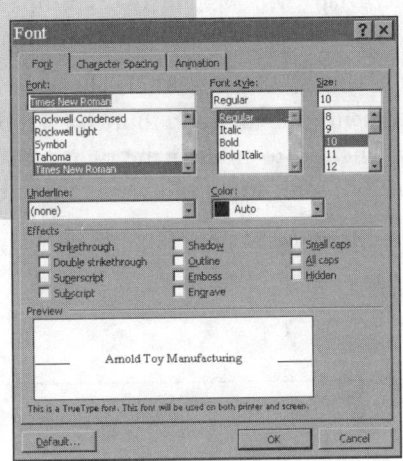

LEARN ABOUT ANIMATING TEXT IN CHAPTER 13.

The Font dialog box has three tabs for working with font formatting, spacing, and even the animation of text on the page Notice the Preview section on the Font tab, where you can see how any changes that you make will look before you apply them.

6. If it's not already the selected tab, select the Fo<u>n</u>t tab as shown in Figure 3.3.

7. Using the scroll bar of the <u>F</u>ont text box, locate Gill Sans. Click on Gill Sans and note the preview of the typeface in the Preview box.

8. Using the scroll bar in the <u>S</u>ize text box, change the font size to 16 points. Keep the dialog box open for the next procedure.

Tip

Font size is stated in *points*. A point is 1/72nd of an inch, so a 72-point line of text would be approximately 1 inch high. Different fonts aren't exactly proportional to each other, however, and some fonts at, say, 12 points, look smaller than others at the same size. Standard business documents typically use 10- or 12-point size for body text.

Word provides dozens of built-in fonts. Some of these are more informal looking (for example, Mistral or Howie's Funhouse). Others resemble more antique typefaces like those you see in older editions of books (such as Garamond and Baskerville). Still others are symbol fonts, which are made up of circles, squares, copyright symbols, mathematical symbols, and so on, rather than letters and

PART I • CREATING BASIC DOCUMENTS

numbers (Wingdings and Map Symbols are two examples of symbol fonts). Some, like Brush Script, even seem to resemble handwriting.

This variety of fonts helps you provide just the right tone for your correspondence. Templates for documents provide good font choices, but sometimes you'll want to select your own. The key to finding the right font is experimentation. Figure 3.4 gives you an idea of some fonts and ways to use them.

Find additional fonts from Microsoft at `http://www.microsoft.com/Office-FreeStuff/Word/`.

Figure 3.4
From brassy to beautiful, fonts make a statement about your document.

Notes to friends, party invitations, and announcements look great in Brush Script

Posters and flyers might benefit from the bold look of Impact

Formal correspondence and novels look great in Book Antiqua

Newsletter story headlines, report headings and invoices benefit from the clean look of Arial.

When it's time to just have fun, Braggadocio is a great choice.

Most business correspondence and reports use Times New Roman as a standard.

Using Text Effects

In the Font dialog box, you can do much more than just change your choice of font or font size. You can also add a variety of effects, from simple to fancy, to your text.

Word also has a built-in software program, called WordArt, for text enhancement.. You can use WordArt to apply even more special effects to text from a list of predefined choices. These snazzy effects range from making text curve to adding gradients, or appearing to make letters shrink into the distance.

CHAPTER 3 • BUILDING A MEMO   **55**

> YOU'LL LEARN MORE ABOUT WORDART IN CHAPTER 7.

Hands On: Adding Text Effects to a Memo

Besides the small caps effect that you're about to use, the Effects area of the Font dialog box offers quite a few choices. These range from simple effects, such as a shadow, to elegant effects such as engraving. Table 3.1, which follows this procedure, provides an overview of the effects available.

Follow these steps to add a small caps effect to text:

1. Click in the check box to apply the S<u>m</u>all Caps effect to the selected text.

You can choose to display or print hidden text. To display it, choose <u>T</u>ools, <u>O</u>ptions, and change the setting for hidden text on the View tab. To print hidden text, choose <u>T</u>ools, <u>O</u>ptions and change the setting on the Print tab.

2. Click on OK to apply your changes to the selected text.

Text formatting settings apply either to selected text, or, if no text is selected when you make the setting, to any text that you enter beginning where your insertion point is located and from now on in a document (until you make a new formatting choice).

Besides the font, font size, and the various text effects, you can also make changes to the font style (such as Bold, Italic), change the font color, or apply a variety of underlining styles to text.

Now make the following text changes, using either the toolbar buttons or the Font dialog box.

3. Change the font size of the word `Memorandum` to 36 points.
4. Make the subject line (beginning with `Re:`) Bold and Italic.
5. Click on OK to apply your changes.

Your memo should now look like Figure 3.5.

56 Part I • Creating Basic Documents

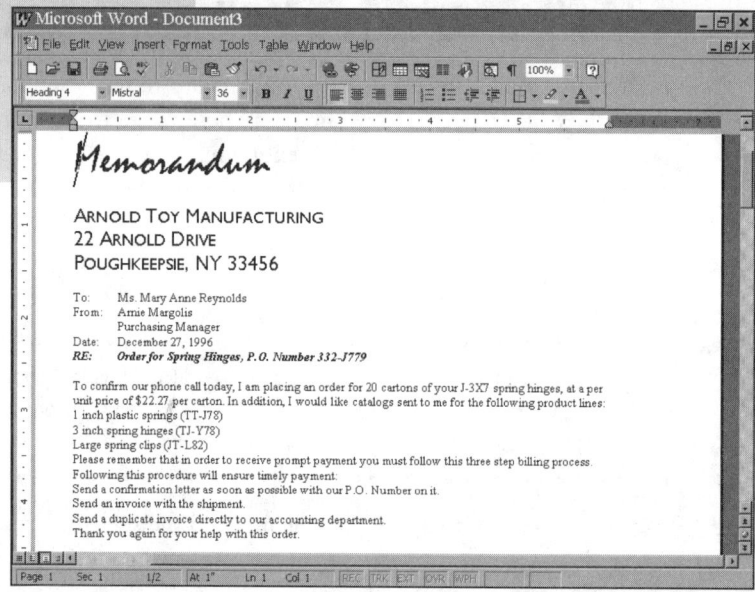

Figure 3.5
Your text is beginning to take shape with a few formatting steps.

Table 3.1 Word 97 Text Effects

Effect	Description
Strikethrough	Places a single line through text; useful to show suggested revisions to text
Double strikethrough	Places a double line through text
Superscript	Raises selected text two points above the baseline of normal text on a line
Subscript	Lowers selected text two points below the baseline of normal text on a line
Shadow	Applies a shading effect to text, making it seem to be casting a shadow
Outline	Shows the inner and outer edges of the text, looking like an outline of the letters
Emboss	Gives text the appearance of being raised lettering
Engrave	Makes text look as if it's pressed or etched into the page
Small Caps	Makes all letters uppercase and of the same reduced size
ALL CAPS	Makes all letters uppercase
(Hidden)	Keeps text from being displayed or printed

> ### How Much Is Enough?
>
> When you're presented with as many choices for formatting text as you are in Word 97, going overboard is easy to do. Overusing these formats can make a document look busy and unprofessional. A good rule of thumb is to not use more than three different fonts on a single page. Also, remember that styles such as bold and italic can make some fonts difficult to read. Used too often, these styles lose the effect of adding emphasis because you lose the element of contrast.
>
> Applying colors is easy using the Color drop-down list in the Font dialog box, but remember that colors are useless unless a document is printed on a color printer or viewed on-screen. The same advice about not overusing fonts and styles applies to color: it's the spice, not the main course.

Adjusting Alignment

Anyone who's the least bit organized knows that lining things up is a way of forcing visual order on our universe. You line up pens in a drawer, or line up garden tools on the left side of your garage and sports equipment on the right.

Aligning text to a location on a page fulfills similar desires for order and, in fact, has more logic to it than the way you've organized your garage.

By default, most text in a document is lined up to originate at the left margin because English reads from left to right. Headings for articles or report sections are often centered, however, so that they stand out. Numbers line up along their far-right digit, making their end points match. With the numbers 1,392 and 54, for example, the final numerals 2 and 4 line up when one appears on the line above the other.

In addition to the three distinct kinds of alignment just discussed (left, right, and centered), one more kind is also sometimes useful: justified. Justified text is more a matter of design preference than practical issues. Justified text is spaced out across a line so that both the right and left edges of the lines in a document look straight. This is different from the ragged look that left-aligned text creates on the right edge.

Figure 3.6 gives you an idea of what these four alignments do to a typical paragraph.

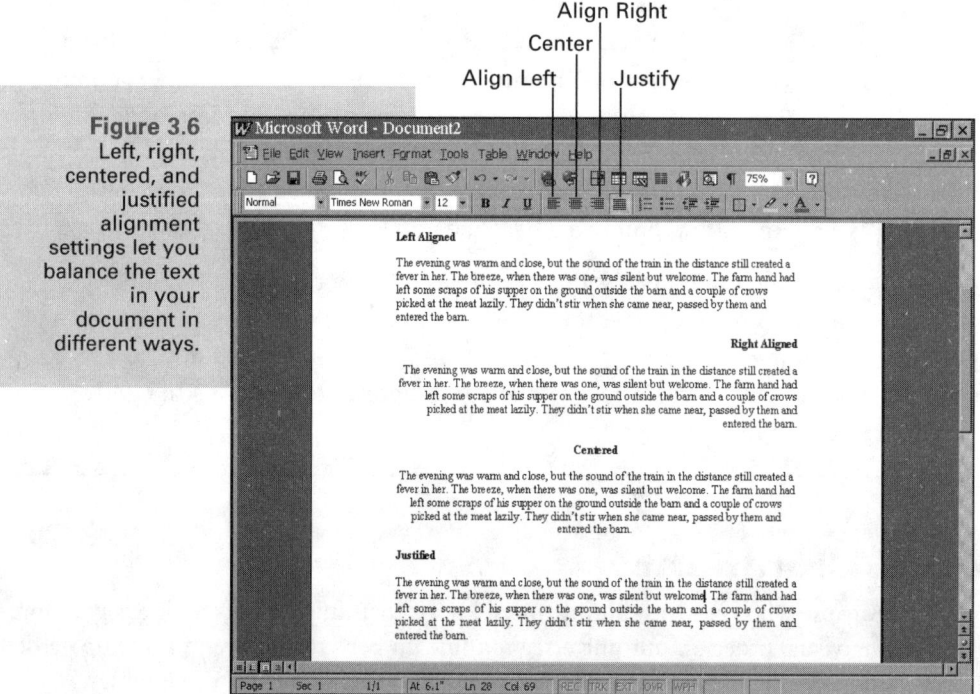

Figure 3.6 Left, right, centered, and justified alignment settings let you balance the text in your document in different ways.

Although there are general rules about how you use text alignment, such as numbers being right aligned and headings being centered, you can also use alignment simply to balance the text on your page to make it more visually organized and attractive. You can use alignment to balance elements of a document on the page in interesting ways.

Text that you enter into a Blank Document template is left aligned by default. You apply alignment to text by selecting the text and using one of the alignment buttons on the formatting toolbar, shown in Figure 3.6. Try that now with the sample memo.

1. Select the return address for Arnold Toy Manufacturing.
2. Click on the Align Right button.

    The text is moved to the right, balancing the large type for Memorandum on the page, as shown in Figure 3.7.

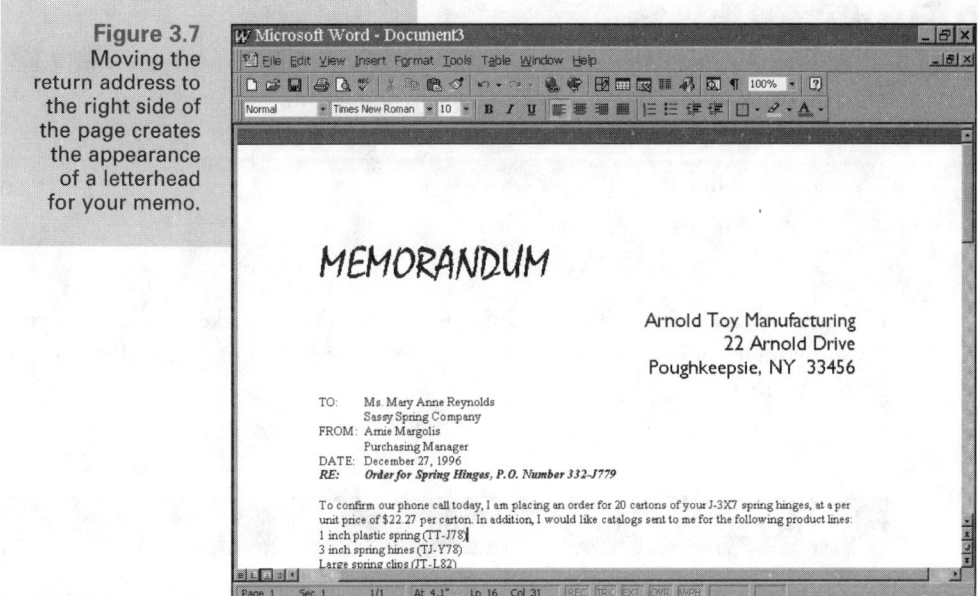

Figure 3.7 Moving the return address to the right side of the page creates the appearance of a letterhead for your memo.

Working with Lists

Another format that you can apply to text is a list format. Placing information in a list provides emphasis and makes it easy for a reader to scan quickly, as opposed to picking out that information in the prose.

Each line in a list is, technically speaking, a separate paragraph in Word. Word begins a new paragraph every time that you press (Enter). You can format these paragraphs of items with symbols or numbers preceding them to represent a list of items: key points, products, people, and so on.

Adding Lists

Word has two types of lists: bulleted and numbered. You use bulleted lists for sets of data with no particular (or equal) priority: a list of materials needed to assemble a stereo, or points that you'll be making in a report. Numbered lists have a priority or sequence involved; one item must be done or read before another, as in the numbered steps in the Hands On sections of this book.

Learning to use both kinds of lists in Word is a useful skill, allowing you to further organize information for readers of your documents and add visual appeal.

Adding Bulleted Lists

Typical bullets are solid black circles (the word comes from the French word *boullette*, meaning a small ball). You can use any letter, number, or symbol for a bullet, however:

- $ A dollar sign
- ß   An astrological symbol
- ➢   An arrow

In fact, you can use whatever symbols or text that Word makes available to you. To apply bullet points to a series of data, select it and then use the Bullets button on the Formatting toolbar.

Hands On: Working with Lists

In this Hands On exercise, you'll create bulleted lists. You'll work with different bullet styles shortly thereafter.

1. Select the list of springs followed by model numbers in parentheses in the memorandum, as shown in Figure 3.8.
2. Click on the Bullets button. The default round bullets appear at the beginning of each paragraph in the selected text.

Adding Numbered Lists

The process of applying the numbered list style to text is virtually identical to applying bullets.

Hands On: Adding Numbered Lists

Numbered lists are best to indicate a priority or sequence; use this feature for the three-step billing process mentioned in the memorandum.

1. Select the three-step billing process (the three lines beginning with the word *Send*) a little further down in the memo, as shown in Figure 3.9.
2. Click on the Numbering button on the toolbar. Word applies sequential numbers to each new paragraph in the selected text, as in Figure 3.9.

Figure 3.8
The selected text displays the default round bullet style.

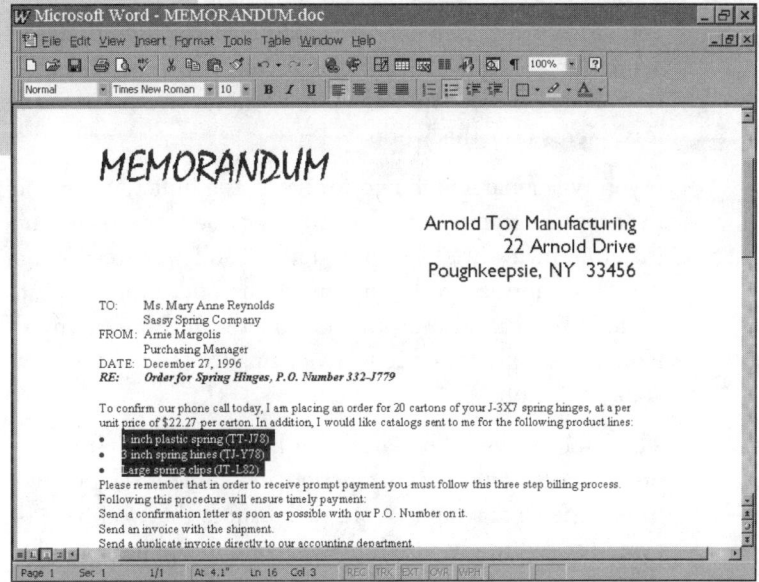

Figure 3.9
Both the Numbering and Bullet buttons are toggle buttons: click once to apply and again to remove the list style.

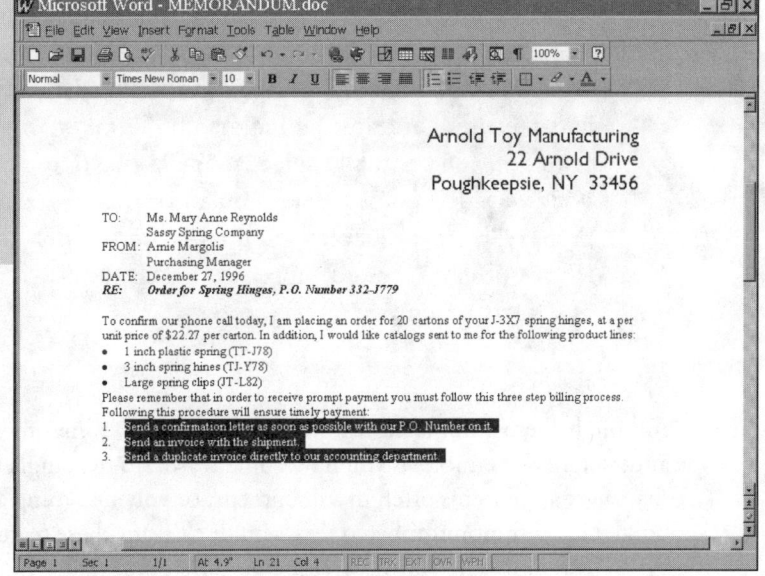

PART I • CREATING BASIC DOCUMENTS

Automating Lists

You didn't think that software could read your mind, did you? Well, think again. Word has a feature called AutoCorrect, which you'll learn more about in Chapter 5. AutoCorrect contains a setting that converts text into bulleted or numbered lists. Here's how this works.

If you type a paragraph and format it as a bullet, when you press [Enter] to create the next paragraph, Word assumes that you want to continue the bulleted list and therefore makes the next paragraph a bullet as well. Word continues under the same assumption until you remove the bullet format by clicking on the Bullets button. You can also go to the Bullets and Numbering dialog box and choose None, or simply press [Enter] twice in a row to move back to the normal style for your paragraph.

This process works similarly with numbered lists. If you type a number (1 or I) or a letter (a) followed by a period and some text, then when you press [Enter] to begin a new paragraph, Word will assume that you have begun building a numbered list. Word gives each new paragraph the next number in sequence. To stop this automatic formatting of a numbered list, you can either remove the numbered format on a new line, press the [Del] key to remove the automatically generated number, or press [Enter] twice.

Note

Notice that the preceding two figures show the text of the lists selected, but not the bullets and numbers preceding the text. You can't actually select these items. If you try to place your insertion point before a bullet or number, the insertion point will appear just before the text to the right of the bullet or number. There is a way to format these elements, however, which you'll see shortly.

Although these automated features can be helpful, sometimes they are downright annoying. For example, if you have some reason to use single bulleted items rather than a group of items often in a document, or you are typing a numbered list that's broken up with nonnumbered text, you don't want these features kicking in all the time. To remove the AutoCorrect feature that automates bullet and number formatting, choose Tools, AutoCorrect. Then, choose the Autoformat As You Type tab of this dialog box, shown in Figure 3.10.

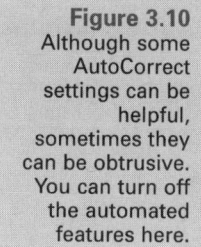
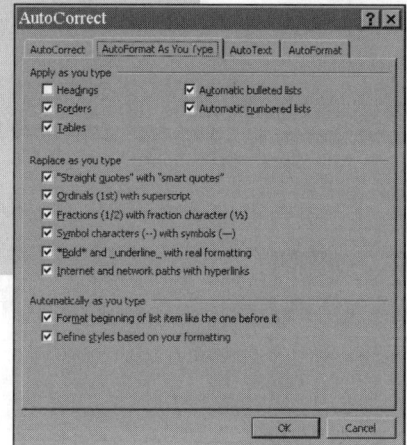

Figure 3.10 Although some AutoCorrect settings can be helpful, sometimes they can be obtrusive. You can turn off the automated features here.

Click in either the Automatic Bulleted Lists or Automatic Numbered Lists check boxes to turn off either feature. Click on OK to close the dialog box.

Customizing Lists

Changing the bullet or number to a different style, or applying common formatting such as increasing the size of these items, is easy. Before you modify a bullet or number style, you must either select the text of the list to modify all the lines simultaneously, or place your mouse pointer anywhere within a particular paragraph that you want to modify.

Customizing Bullet Styles

Now that you have created a bullet list, you can explore the ways Word allows you to customize the bullets themselves.

Hands On: Customizing the Styles of Your Bullets

The Bullets and Numbering dialog box allows you to do several things with bullets. If you want to remove bullets that have been applied previously, you can choose None. To choose one of the predefined alternate bullet styles displayed in this dialog box, just click on the preview of the style, such as a diamond or box shape, and then click on OK.

PART I • CREATING BASIC DOCUMENTS

You can also modify bullet styles in a number of ways beyond the preset styles, however. Try it now. You should select the three bullet points that you created, and then follow these steps:

1. Choose Format, Bullets and Numbering. The Bullets and Numbering dialog box appears with the Bulleted tab selected, as shown in Figure 3.11.

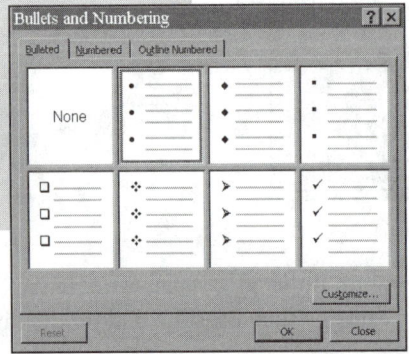

Figure 3.11
The Bullets and Numbering dialog box controls both types of lists from one location.

Tip

You can also select, or place your pointer in, text that you haven't yet turned into a bulleted list, choose Format, Bullets and Numbering, and apply bullets by using the choices in this dialog box rather than the buttons on the toolbar.

2. Click on the Customize button to open the Customize Bulleted List dialog box shown in Figure 3.12.

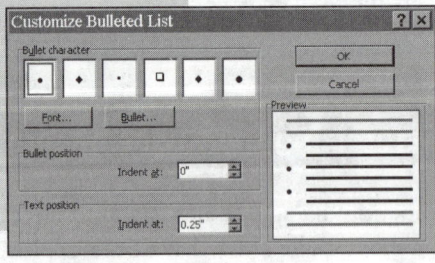

Figure 3.12
Use this dialog box to preview the changes that you've made in style and position of your text.

You can modify the position of bullets using the position settings in this dialog box. You can also make standard font formatting changes to the text of the bullets, such as resizing it or making it bold or a different color by clicking on the Font button here. Doing so takes you to the Font dialog box and offers you all the options that you've used before for formatting text.

3. To change the symbol used to indicate the bullet, click on the Bullet button. The dialog box shown in Figure 3.13 appears.

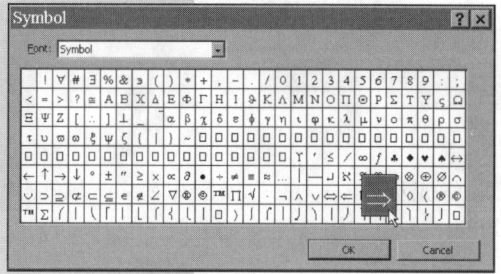

Figure 3.13 Symbols from mathematics, other alphabets such as Greek, arrows, and even smiley faces are available as bullet style choices.

You can choose from among several symbol typefaces by selecting from the Font drop-down list in the Symbol dialog box. You can also get a closer look at these tiny symbols by clicking on them one at a time. An enlarged image of the symbol appears when you do so.

4. With the Symbol font selected, click on the right-facing, hollow arrow in the preview window as shown in Figure 3.13.
5. Click on OK twice to close the Customize Bulleted List dialog box and apply the new bullet style.

Customizing Numbered Lists

You can also customize numbered lists to format the font used or to select different numbering styles. As with the bullets tab, some predefined numbering styles are available. But again, a broader range of choices is available if you choose to customize the numbered list style.

Hands On: Customizing Numbered Lists

Select the numbered list in the memo, and follow these steps:

1. Choose Format, Bullets and Numbering. The Bullets and Numbering dialog box appears, with the Numbered tab selected, as shown in Figure 3.14.

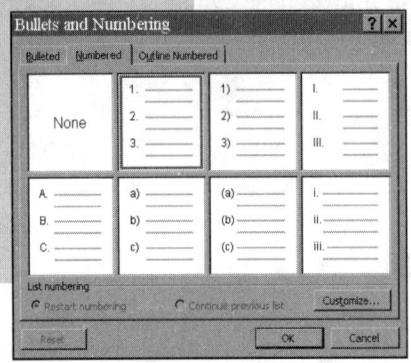

Figure 3.14 By selecting either a bulleted or numbered list before opening this dialog box, you'll open to the corresponding tab automatically.

2. Click on Customize to see the Customize Numbered List dialog box shown in Figure 3.15.

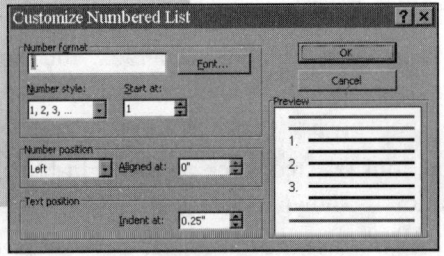

Figure 3.15 Determine just how your numbered list will appear using the settings in this dialog box.

You can get to the Font dialog box and make any standard text formatting changes to your numbers by clicking the Font button. If you want your numbers to be to aligned relative to the text, you can use the Number position and Text position settings to do so. If you want the numbers to begin at a number other than one (or a letter other than A, if you choose a letter style) modify this setting by using the arrows on the Start At box.

3. Open the Number Style drop-down list and choose the First, Second... style.
4. Click on OK. Word returns you to your document with the new style applied, as shown in Figure 3.16.

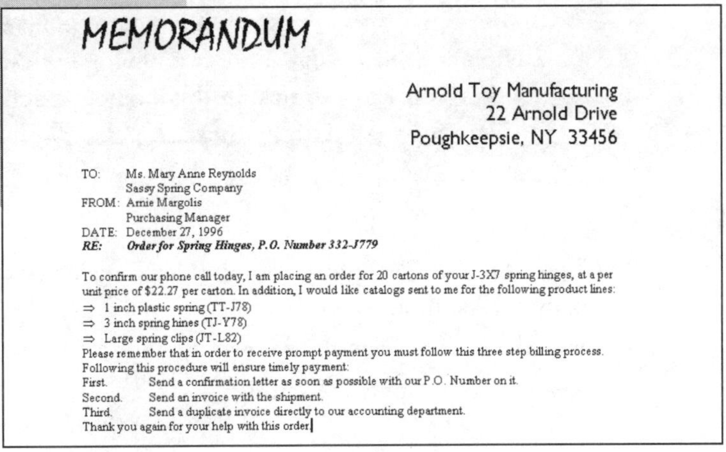

Chapter 3 • Building a Memo

Figure 3.16
Customize numbered lists to use letters, numbers, or even words before your text.

Formatting Paragraphs

As you learned in the preceding section on lists, in Word you create a new paragraph whenever you press [Enter]. Because text wraps automatically at the end of a sentence, you don't need to (and shouldn't!) press [Enter] until you reach the end of a paragraph, or unless you want to move to the beginning of a new line to place a table, bullet point, or other element there.

Most paragraphs in your document will consist of several sentences. Each item in a bulleted or numbered list is a paragraph, however, because a paragraph mark is automatically inserted at the end of each line in the list.

Formatting paragraphs deals mainly with issues of spacing: the spacing between the lines of the paragraph, between one paragraph and another, and from the document margins. In this section, you'll add paragraph spacing to the sample memo and modify indentation.

Hands On: Setting Paragraph Spacing

Word has two kinds of spacing for paragraphs: the space between each of the lines within a paragraph, and the space between each paragraph. Both settings are set from the same location.

1. Select all the text in the memo that falls after the return address (from the TO: line in the memo heading to the end).

68   Part I • Creating Basic Documents

Note

If you don't want to format multiple paragraphs, you can simply place your mouse pointer anywhere within the paragraph that you want to format (instead of selecting the paragraph) and proceed with the next step.

2. Choose F̲ormat, P̲aragraph. The Paragraph dialog box shown in Figure 3.17 appears.
3. Open the Li̲ne Spacing drop-down list and select 1.5 lines spacing.
4. Click on OK to apply the setting.

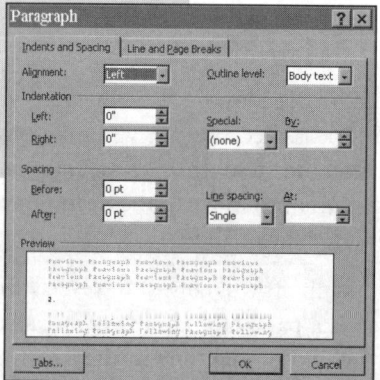

Figure 3.17
You can modify both indents and spacing in the Paragraph dialog box.

The Paragraph dialog box contains several spacing settings. If you change the B̲efore setting, you modify the spacing between this paragraph and the one that precedes it. If you change the Aft̲er setting, you adjust the space between this paragraph and the paragraph that follows it.

The Li̲ne Spacing setting adjusts the space between lines within the paragraph. For single, one and a half, and double spacing, you make the appropriate choice in the Li̲ne Spacing drop-down list and click on OK to apply it.

You may need to combine different type sizes within your paragraphs. The Li̲ne Spacing drop-down list contains settings to deal with this and other spacing issues. Those settings—At Least, Multiple, and Exactly—require that you also indicate an amount of space in the A̲t field. Here's how these settings work:

- *At Least* indicates a minimum line spacing but allows Word to adjust spacing to accommodate larger font sizes or inserted graphic objects that don't fit in the spacing indicated in the A̲t field.
- *Multiple* allows Word to increase or decrease spacing by a percentage rather than a point size. If you set the line spacing to Multiple and set the A̲t field to 3, you've set triple spacing.
- *Exactly* fixes the Li̲ne Spacing setting to the amount entered in the A̲t field. If you have larger font sizes within the paragraph and they aren't accommodated by the A̲t setting, tops and bottoms of the larger item may appear to be cut off, but the space between lines will remain even.

If you have a paragraph formatted to a Line spacing using Exactly and you insert clip art or another graphic object, the object is likely to appear with most of the object not visible. Adjusting the line spacing to At least will prevent this.

Indenting Text

Indenting involves placing lines of text relative to the left or right margin. Sometimes you'll indent whole paragraphs such as long quotes. Other times, you'll use initial indents so that all your paragraphs begin with the first line indented in one-half inch from the left margin. Indenting can offset important ideas or points, and draw attention to material in longer documents. It's also another way to add visual balance to the page.

You can deal with indenting text through the Paragraph dialog box (Figure 3.17) by simply choosing how far to indent selected text from the L̲eft or R̲ight margin. The simplest way to work with indents, however, is probably with Word's on-screen ruler. If the ruler is not displayed beneath the toolbars at the top of your screen, choose V̲iew, R̲uler to display it.

The ruler has three small tools along the edge of the left margin. Placed together, they look like a little hourglass; each of the tools, however does something different:

- The *First Line Indent* is the top triangle. It changes the indentation of the first line of a paragraph.
- The *Hanging Indent* is the bottom triangle. Moving this triangle keeps the first line of a paragraph where it was, but shifts the text following it to the

Part I • Creating Basic Documents

right or left of the left margin, depending on whether you drag it to the left or right.

- The *Left Indent* is the little box at the bottom of the hourglass. It will move all lines of a selected paragraph simultaneously.

Hands On: Indenting Text in a Memorandum

This memo example contains several opportunities to use indentation to organize information. Follow these steps:

1. Select the first paragraph in the memo, beginning with the words "To confirm."
2. Click on the First Line Indent marker on the ruler and drag it to the right one-half inch, as shown in Figure 3.18.

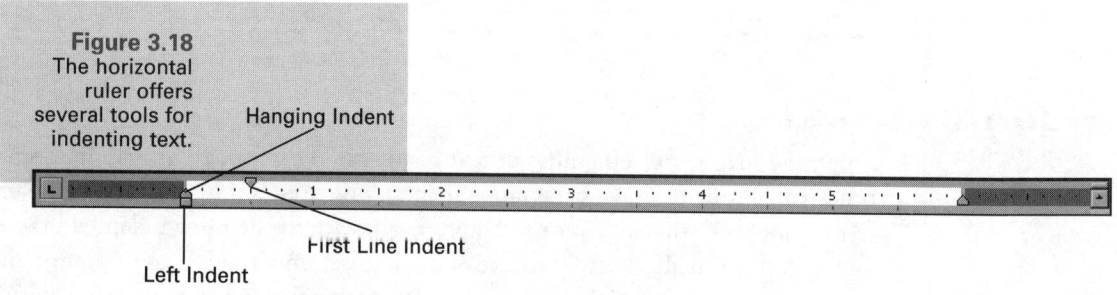

Figure 3.18 The horizontal ruler offers several tools for indenting text.

3. Select the bulleted list.
4. Drag the Left Indent marker to the one-inch mark on the ruler. The entire bulleted list indents.
5. Repeat Step 4 to indent the numbered list to the one-inch mark. Remember, if you have trouble dragging to a specific point on the ruler, you can always use the Paragraph dialog box to make precise settings.

You've now mastered using indent tools. Practice a little more while getting the rest of the memo in shape.

6. Select the second paragraph of the memo (beginning with the words "Please remember").

Chapter 3 • Building a Memo

71

7. Drag the First Line Indent marker in to the half-inch mark on the ruler.

8. Select the last line of the memo and repeat Step 7.

Your memo should now look like the one in Figure 3.19.

Figure 3.19
Text formatting, alignment, bulleted and numbered lists, and paragraph indenting all add to the clean look of this memo.

A great shortcut to indenting is to use the Increase Indent and Decrease Indent buttons on the Formatting toolbar. They move selected text in or out by 1/2-inch increments each time you use them.

micros
WORD

Outlining a Sales Presentation

IN THIS CHAPTER

- **Entering Headings**
- **Promoting and Demoting Headings**
- **Adding Body Text**
- **Displaying Levels of Headings**
- **Reorganizing an Outline**
- **Deleting Headings**

You probably create simple outlines in your head every day. You go to work (major topic); at work you attend a meeting, write a report, and make three phone calls (subtopics). After work, you go shopping (next major topic): you go to the grocery store, the department store, and the shoe store (subtopics), and so on. Word outlines organize these topics and subtopics with various levels of indentation.

This chapter shows you how to use the Outlining tools in Word to organize your thoughts, view various levels of detail, and turn it all into a polished document.

Creating the Outline

Word contains an Outline view that you turn on by using the View buttons at the lower-left corner of the screen (next to the vertical scroll bar) or by choosing View, Outline. When you open the Outline view in a blank document, you'll see a little bar that looks like a minus sign alongside your blinking insertion point and a special toolbar, shown in Figure 4.1. This toolbar allows you to display different levels of detail in the outline, and to reorganize the topics in your outline easily.

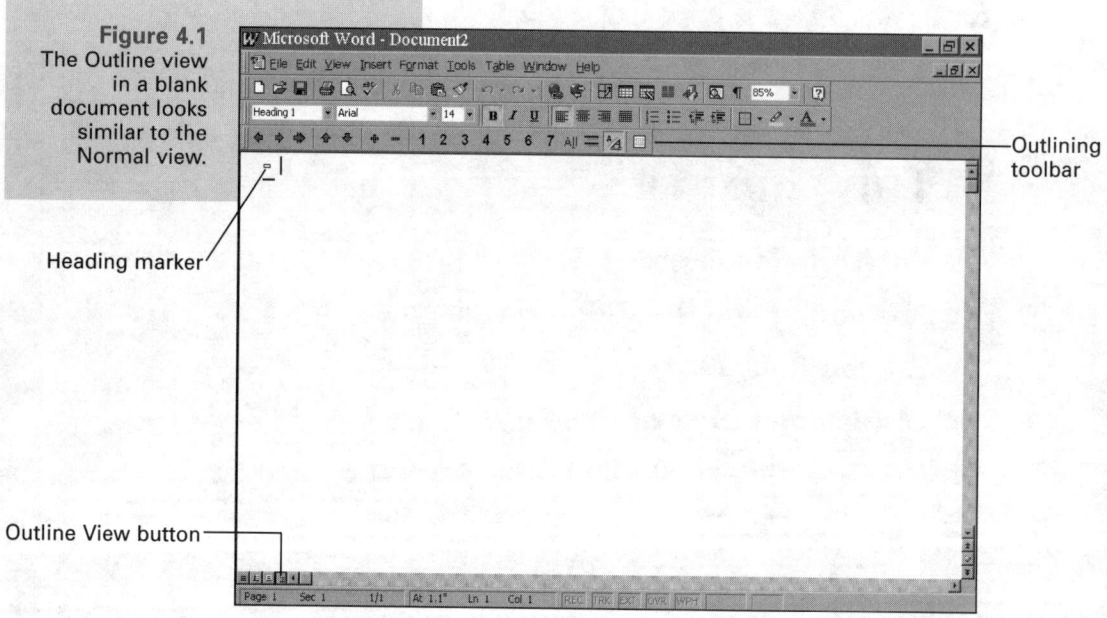

Figure 4.1
The Outline view in a blank document looks similar to the Normal view.

Heading marker

Outlining toolbar

Outline View button

Chapter 4 • Outlining a Sales Presentation

For more in-depth information about styles, see Chapter 14.

You can add text in other Word views and then switch to Outline view to see that text organized by heading levels based on heading styles that you've applied to the text. You can also enter text in another view and move to Outline view to promote and demote headings to levels of the outline. Or, you can begin building an outline in the Outline view itself by simply typing your document's major headings. As you indent those headings to various levels, Word automatically applies the corresponding heading style to the heading.

Note

Just a reminder: Chapter 2 briefly covered styles, which are predefined collections of formatting settings associated with templates. Styles can be applied to text. You can also create your own styles. Styles are applied using the Style drop-down list on the Formatting toolbar. Check this list of styles for the Blank Document template: it includes three heading styles that relate to outline levels.

Entering Headings

The first step in building your outline is to begin entering topics in Outline view. For this chapter, you'll build a sales presentation outline for a company called Andrews Metals.

Hands On: Entering Headings for an Outline

Before you begin these steps, open a new Word document based on the Blank Document template, and then switch to Outline view by clicking on the Outline view button.

1. Type the first heading: **Andrews Metals Sales Presentation**.
2. Press (Enter). A second heading marker appears.
3. Type the second heading: **Company History**.
4. Press (Enter).

5. Repeat steps 3 and 4 with the headings **Andrews' Reputation**, **Product Quality**, **Customer Service**, and **Summary**. Your outline should look like the one in Figure 4.2.

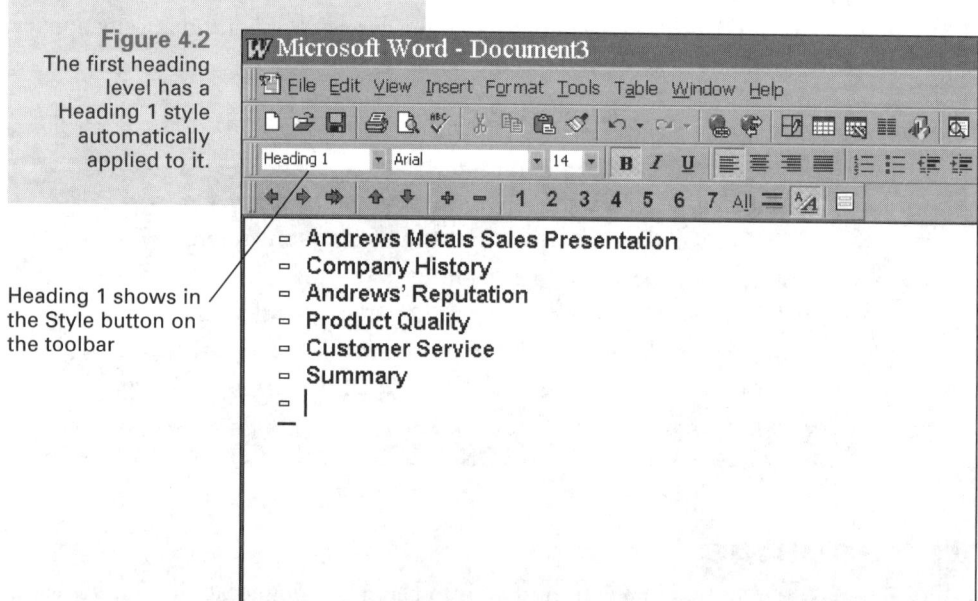

Figure 4.2 The first heading level has a Heading 1 style automatically applied to it.

Heading 1 shows in the Style button on the toolbar

You now have six headings at the same level in the document. The minus sign markers to the left of each indicates that no further headings (subtopics) appear underneath these headings. But because a document typically has an overall title (such as sales presentation) with major topics under that heading, you need to begin to organize things a bit to give your document structure.

Promoting and Demoting Headings

You can have many levels of headings in an outline (up to nine). The process of applying levels to headings is called either *demoting* or *promoting*, depending on whether you're moving a heading to a lower or higher level of detail. You can demote a heading to move in (indent) in the outline so that the heading becomes a lower-level subtopic. You can promote a heading (outdent) in the outline to become a higher level topic; however, you can't promote a heading any higher than Heading 1 level.

CHAPTER 4 • OUTLINING A SALES PRESENTATION 77

Hands On: Adjusting Heading Levels in an Outline

In this exercise, you can try promoting and demoting headings to see how this works. Understanding the tools on the Outlining toolbar, shown in Figure 4.3, will help you with this exercise. Many of these tools deal with options for displaying your outline in different ways, which we cover later.

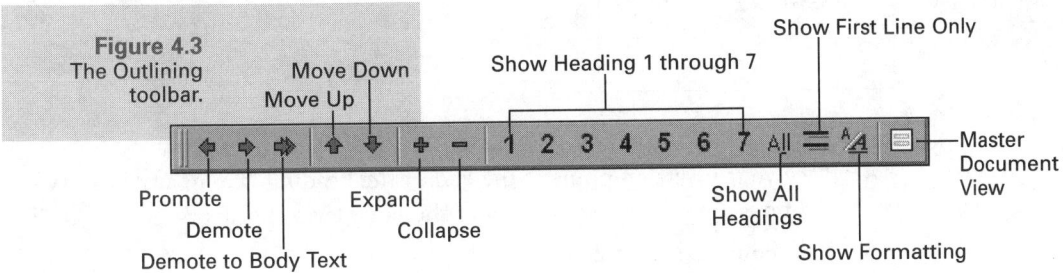

Figure 4.3
The Outlining toolbar.

1. Place your insertion point anywhere within the heading "Company History."
2. Click on the Demote button on the Outlining toolbar.

   Three things happen. The heading indents; the heading changes to a Heading 2 style (check the Style tool on the Formatting toolbar for the new style); and the marker to the left of the preceding heading has changed. When a heading has headings indented beneath it, the marker to its left will change to a plus sign, indicating that additional detail in the form of subheadings exists.

   To promote an indented heading back to a higher level, you simply use the Promote button, doing so repeatedly if necessary to bring it out to the correct level in the outline.

Tip

You can also press Tab to demote a heading, or press Shift+Tab to promote a heading.

3. Select the next four headings and click on the Demote button.

   Your outline should now look like the one in Figure 4.4. Now that you've got your major topics in place, you can add some subtopics and demote them to the appropriate level.

Figure 4.4
Your outline is beginning to take shape.

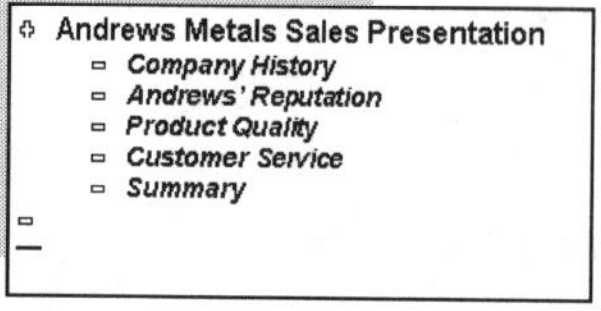

```
◇ Andrews Metals Sales Presentation
    □ Company History
    □ Andrews' Reputation
    □ Product Quality
    □ Customer Service
    □ Summary
```

4. Place your insertion point at the end of the heading "Company History" and press [Enter]. A new heading at the same level appears.
5. Type **Founded in 1926**.
6. With your insertion point still on the new heading line, click on the Demote button.

   The heading indents, and now has a Heading 3 style applied to it. In addition, the heading above it now displays a plus marker to show that it has subheadings underneath. Continue to build these subheadings by entering the new text shown in Figure 4.5.

   Here's a breakdown of how the headings that you've built in Outline view will relate to this finished document. The uppermost heading is the title of the document; the second-level headings represent the major headings in the document; the third-level headings consist of the first sentences of paragraphs within those topics.

7. Click on the Normal view button to see how your outline looks in Normal view (see Figure 4.6).
8. Click on the Outline view button to return to Outline view.

DOCUMENT MAP IS DISCUSSED IN CHAPTER 1.

Chapter 4 • Outlining a Sales Presentation

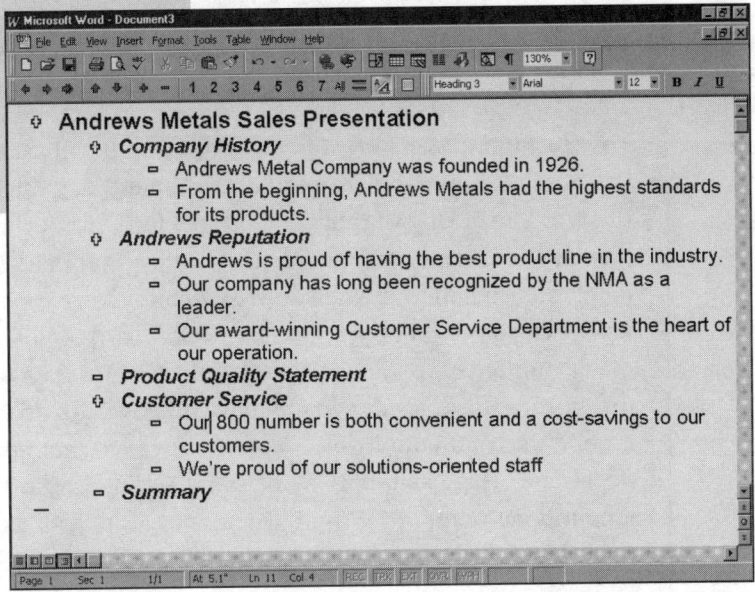

Figure 4.5
You can begin to see a sense of order and flow to ideas in the sales presentation document.

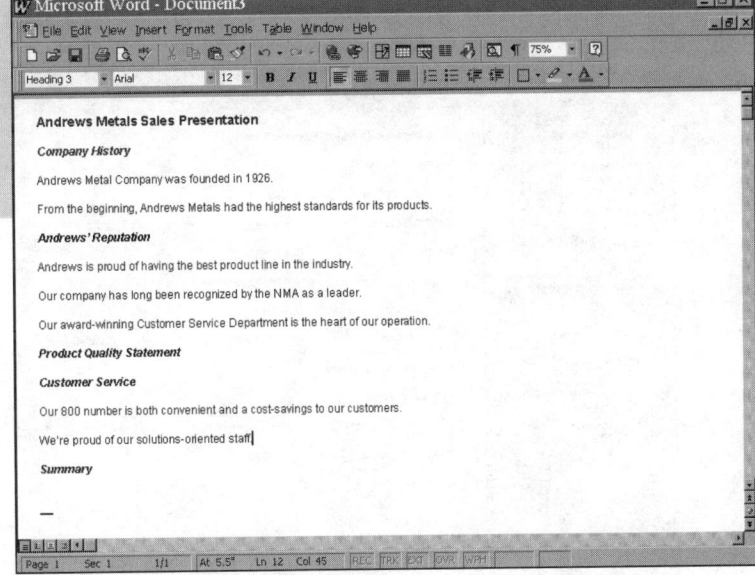

Figure 4.6
The special markers and indenting of the Outline view disappear when you move into other views.

How the Document Map Relates to Outlines

The Document Map, a feature new to Word 97, also reflects the outline structure that you've created. Document Map (also discussed in Chapter 2) is a kind of table of contents for your document; you can display the Document Map beside the document and use it to navigate your document by heading. Switch to Normal view and then click on the Document Map button on the Standard toolbar. You'll see how the Document Map view shows the outline structure side-by-side with the Normal view, as shown in Figure 4.7. Click on any heading in Document Map and your insertion point moves to that heading in the document. This is a great navigational and organizational tool in longer documents. To turn off Document Map, just click on the Document Map button on the toolbar once again.

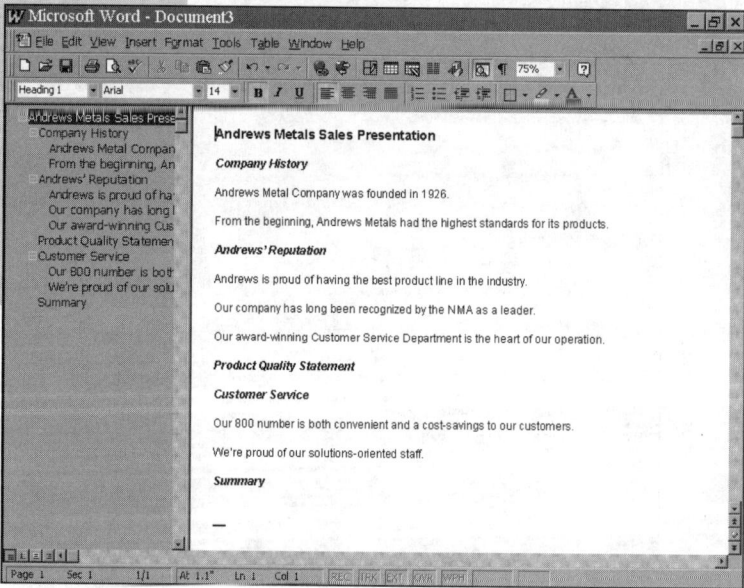

Figure 4.7
The Document Map feature is a view that's new to Word 97.

CHAPTER 4 • OUTLINING A SALES PRESENTATION **81**

Adding Body Text

All the headings that you create using the Demote button will continue to be created with heading styles. The buttons let you display levels range from 1 to 7, although you can actually create up to 9 heading levels. But you don't want the body text—the text that makes up the paragraphs of your presentation or report—to look like a heading, of course. Therefore, you need to demote the text to the body text style. You do this with another tool on the Outlining toolbar, the Demote to Body Text button.

> ### Hands On: Adding Body Text to the Sales Presentation

Follow these steps to make a heading into body text:

1. In the Outline view, place your insertion point at the end of the third heading down, the one beginning "Andrews Metal Company was founded...".

2. Press `Enter` and then type the following text:

    Harrison Andrews, a Scottish immigrant and engineer with degrees from Edinburgh University and Oxford, began the company. He started with a small factory in upper New York State, in the then small village of Poughkeepsie. Beginning with a formula for a high-tensile-strength iron still being used today, Andrews was soon supplying companies such as Amalgamated Construction and Otis Elevators with materials for a wide variety of metalworking needs.

3. With your insertion point still within this paragraph, click on the Demote to Body Text button on the Outlining toolbar.

    Your outline should now look like the one in Figure 4.8.

4. Switch to Normal view.

5. Click on the top heading and center it using the Center button on the Formatting toolbar.

    Any alignment changes that you make in other views won't affect the indentation of text in the Outline. Now that you have a document title centered at the top in Normal view, however, along with a paragraph of body text, you can begin to see how this outline can grow into a final report or presentation. You can also see how building a document in this way keeps your topics organized. Figure 4.9 shows the document in Normal view.

> **FOR AN EXPLANATION OF THE WAVY LINES THAT YOU SOMETIMES SEE IN TEXT, AS IN FIGURE 4.8, SEE CHAPTER 5'S DISCUSSION OF SPELL CHECK.**

> **CHECK OUT CHAPTER 3 FOR MORE INFORMATION ON PARAGRAPH FORMATTING.**

Figure 4.8
The relationship between a final document and your outline begins to shine through.

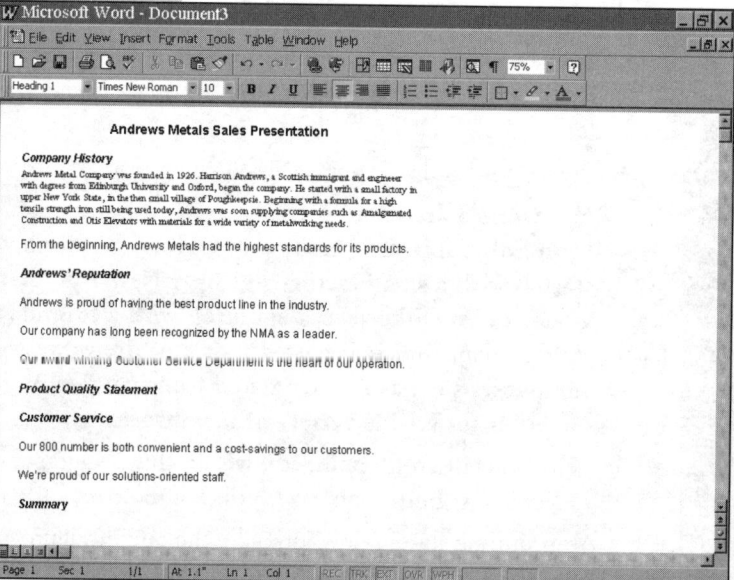

Figure 4.9
You can now complete the document by simply writing the text of the paragraphs as you've laid them out with topic sentences.

Note

If you press [Enter] to add extra spaces between the lines of your document in Normal view, each new paragraph created in this way will create new, blank headings in the Outline view. That's a good reason to use paragraph formatting to add space between paragraphs, instead of pressing [Enter] twice to put space between paragraphs.

6. Return to Outline view.
7. Complete the next paragraph (beginning with "From the beginning...") with this text:

   Andrews himself continued to work on new product development well into his '70s. On his death in 1972, a hand-picked team of management and metals fabrication professionals continued to run Andrews Metals with the same dedication to quality and improved products that the founder had insisted on.

8. Demote the paragraph that you just typed to body text.

Formatting and Outlines

You can apply any font formatting that you like to text in either Outline view or Normal view. Here's how formatting works:

- If you enter text in Outline view, that text will be assigned a heading style automatically, depending on its heading level. If you then stay in Outline view or switch to Normal or Page Layout view and change any formatting, your outline levels will remain intact, unless you apply a different heading style or the Normal style to the text. As long as you leave the text based on the heading style, no matter what formatting changes you make, the text will retain its heading level in the outline.

- If you enter text in Normal or Page Layout view, the default text style (called Normal) makes it body text. If you apply any of the heading styles (1, 2, 3) that are built into every Word template, you will see the text move to the corresponding heading level in the Outline view. Again, after that heading style is applied, you can make any formatting changes to the text that you wish and not change its level.

- Although you can use the Promote and Demote buttons to create heading levels in Outline view, you can also simply apply heading styles to text in Outline view to place the heading at a higher or lower level. (Using the Promote/Demote or Tab /Shift+Tab methods to do this is easier, though.)

Using Outline View

Now that you have several levels of headings in your document, you can begin to use some of the features of Outline view that help you see the details of your document from different perspectives, and to reorganize ideas and topics.

Displaying Levels of Headings

Sometimes you want to see just the upper-level headings in a document. For example, if you want to use the outline of a document as a speaker's guide to give an oral presentation, maybe just the major topics are needed, and not body text. The expanding and collapsing capabilities of Word outlining translate to the printed page when you display the Outline view before printing. Expand an outline and print it, and you get all the detail you've expanded in your printed copy. Collapse any portion of the outline, and that's how your outline document will print.

> **Hands On: Displaying Various Levels of the Sales Presentation Outline**

You can display just as much or as little detail as you like in Word's Outline view.

1. Click anywhere in the top heading of the outline.
2. Click on the Collapse button on the toolbar.

   This collapses the lowest level of the outline but leaves headings higher than that visible. Notice a wavy gray line, however, under the heading `Company History` in Figure 4.10. This indicates that some material is collapsed beneath this heading that isn't currently visible.

3. Click on the Collapse button one more time.

   Another level of detail disappears and more headings are underlined to indicate additional material that's no longer visible.

4. Click on the Expand button and the outline expands by one level of detail.

   You can move through the levels of detail one by one using the Expand and Collapse buttons. Or, you can take a few shortcuts.

5. With your insertion point still in the upper heading, click on the Show All Headings button. All levels of detail in the outline appear.

Chapter 4 • Outlining a Sales Presentation

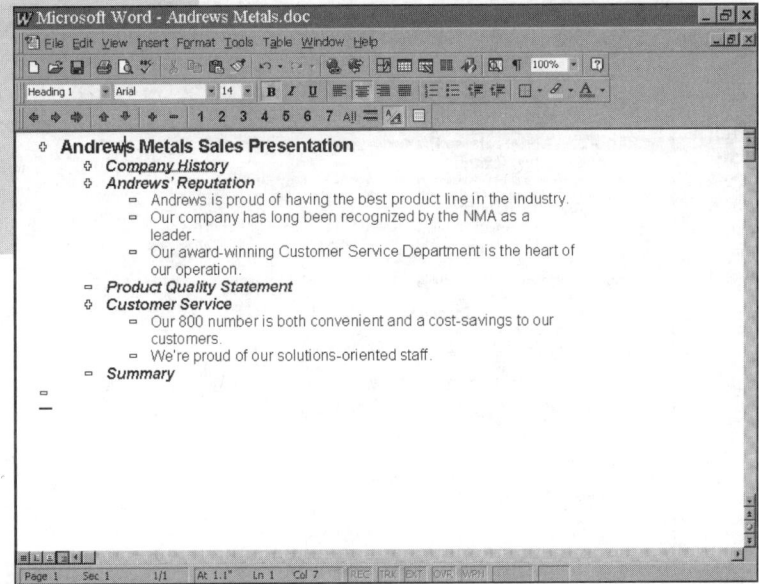

Figure 4.10 Plus signs tell you when a heading has detail beneath it which may or may not be displayed currently.

6. Click on the Show Heading 2 button.

   This quickly moves you to all heading levels up to the second-level headings. You can use any of the seven heading level buttons to open to the corresponding level of headings. This is much quicker than moving through the levels one by one using the Expand and Collapse buttons.

7. Click on the Show All Headings button.

8. Click on the Show First Line Only button.

This feature allows you to see just the first line of any body text (see Figure 4.11), so that in lengthier documents you don't have to scroll through pages of text to get a glimpse of the overall flow of things.

Note

Another good way to see more of your outline on a page is to hide the larger font formatting that is displayed by default. To do this, simply click on the Show Formatting button on the Outlining toolbar. To display the formatting again, click on the Show Formatting button again.

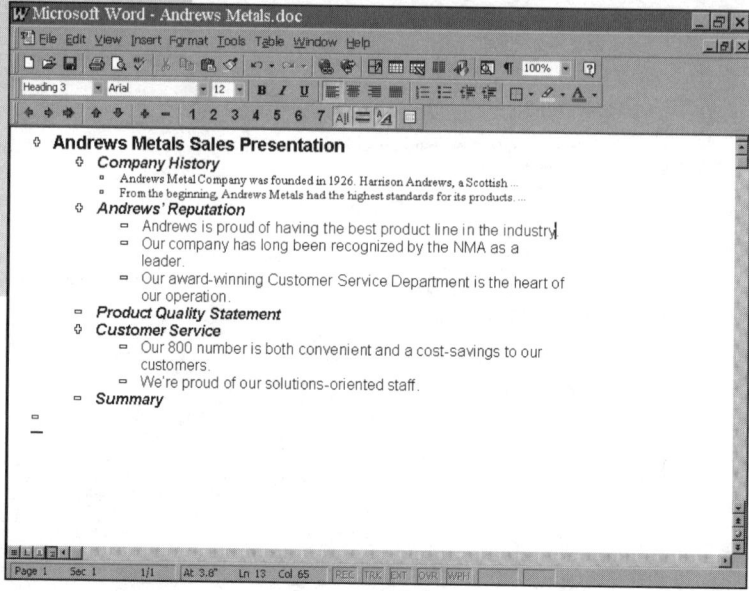

Figure 4.11 When you don't want whole paragraphs visible but you do want their lead sentences, Show First Line Only is a good Outline view display choice.

Notice that the First Line Only setting applies only to body text; multiple-line headings will be completely displayed.

Reorganizing an Outline

Will you type in all the points in a lengthy document in exactly the right order every time? Probably not. Writing anything, from a letter to a book, usually requires rethinking and reorganizing as you go along. A major topic becomes a minor topic. The first point becomes the last, and so on.

Hands On: Reorganizing a Sales Presentation Outline

Word's outlining features allow you to easily reorganize and modify an outline. You have a choice of using the click-and-drag method of moving headings, or using two buttons on the Outlining toolbar. Try both now.

CHAPTER 4 • OUTLINING A SALES PRESENTATION **87**

1. Select the heading `Product Quality Statement` by clicking in the selection bar to the left of it. (You can also simply click on a plus or minus marker to select a heading.)
2. Place your mouse pointer over the minus sign to the left of the heading until it becomes a four-headed arrow.
3. Click and drag the heading upward. As you do so, the pointer changes to an up- and down-pointing arrow, and a line appears across your page, with an arrow on it, as shown in Figure 4.12.

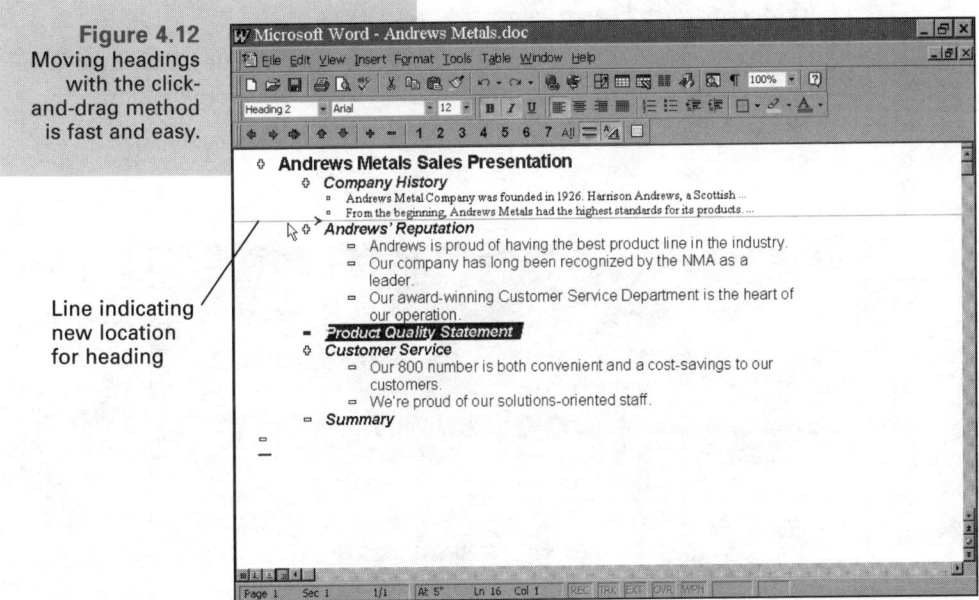

Figure 4.12
Moving headings with the click-and-drag method is fast and easy.

Line indicating new location for heading

4. When the line across the page is just above the heading `Andrews' Reputation`, release your mouse button. The heading moves to the new location.

 PART I • CREATING BASIC DOCUMENTS

Note

You can't move headings both to a new location and a new levels in the outline using this method. You must first drag the heading up or down, and then drag or promote or demote the heading to move it to a higher or lower level of the outline.

5. Select the third-level heading, beginning with "Our award-winning Customer Service Department..."
6. Click on the Move Down button. The heading moves down to the next spot at the same level, in this case moving down to become a subheading of the next level 2 heading, as shown in Figure 4.13.

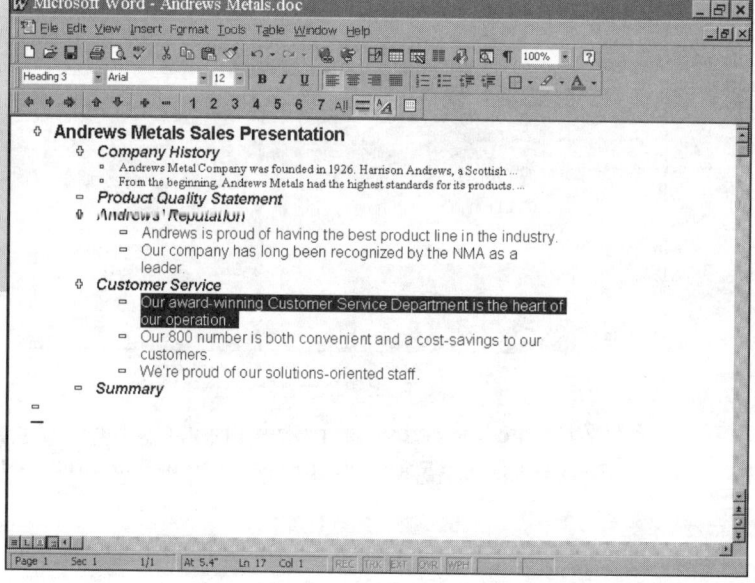

Figure 4.13
Headings move up or down but retain their level of indentation.

Tip

If you move a heading that contains subheadings or body text, the subheadings and body text will move right along with the heading.

Deleting Headings

One final matter to take care of before you leave this chapter: When you first created headings and pressed [Enter] after the last heading (Summary), you created a new, blank heading beneath it. Two easy ways exist to get rid of an unwanted heading:

- You can place the insertion point after the minus marker next to the blank heading, and then press [Backspace].
- Or, you can select the heading by clicking in the selection bar to its left and then pressing [Del].

micros
WORD

5

Finding Things in Your Document and Fixing Them

In This Chapter

- **Using Spelling and Grammar Check**
- **Understanding AutoCorrect**
- **Using Find, Replace, and Go To**

Getting your Word document out the door is a lot like leaving your own house in the morning. Most of us not only get dressed, slip on a pair of shoes, and grab our briefcase, but also check to make sure our tie is straight or that our hair is neatly combed. No matter that you've created a

PART I • CREATING BASIC DOCUMENTS

Word document full of big words dressed in pretty fonts: when it comes down to it, the details are what can make or break the look. When you've gone to the trouble of creating an attractive, organized document in Word, you shouldn't walk away from it without checking certain details. A little thing like a misspelled word, poor grammar, or a poor word choice can turn a thing of beauty into an embarrassment forever.

Word has several features designed to make you look good, including Spelling and Grammar Check, a built-in Thesaurus, and even a feature called AutoCorrect that fixes mistakes for you as you go along. In this chapter, you'll learn about how to fine-tune your document to help you sell your product, impress your boss, or inform the masses.

Understanding AutoCorrect

The first feature that we describe actually corrects mistakes or modifies entries as you type. *AutoCorrect* is perfect for those frequently misspelled words or typing errors. AutoCorrect can even replace one short set of letters with a different or longer phrase, saving you typing time.

How AutoCorrect Works

Most of us are creatures of habit: we make the same mistakes again and again (and not just in love). We do things like typing *teh* for *the*. We always misspell *accomodate* (hint: it has two m's). AutoCorrect is essentially a stored list of these common errors, along with the correct versions. When you type a word from the error list, AutoCorrect immediately replaces it with the correct version. Several of these common errors are already stored in AutoCorrect when you first install Word; however, you can add your own most common mistakes to AutoCorrect easily.

> FOR A LOOK AT ANOTHER FEATURE FOR AUTOMATING TEXT ENTRY, READ ABOUT AUTOTEXT IN CHAPTER 2.

But AutoCorrect isn't just about mistakes. AutoCorrect can also be used to convert one thing that's simple to type to another that's a little more involved. For example, if you often use the copyright symbol, you would typically have to change to a symbol typeface or use a number pad code (which you may or may not keep on the tip of your brain). With AutoCorrect, you just type **(c)** and Word converts it to the copyright symbol every time. You could also create your own AutoCorrect entry; for example, you can type your customer's initials and have AutoCorrect replace them with her full name and title. Using AutoCorrect this way saves you typing and helps to guard against typing errors and misspellings.

> **Caution:** A word of caution about AutoCorrect: Avoid using common letter combinations and actual words as AutoCorrect entries. The two letters *s* and *o* used to enter the company name Standard Outlets, for example, would replace the word *so* every time you type them, which is probably not what you'd intended.

A couple of things could happen when you begin to perform the following Hands On exercise. If you have default AutoCorrect settings on, which allow Word to correct as you type, you may find that you can't type certain words such as *acn* instead of *can*. AutoCorrect fixes them because they're built into its list of words. The replacement actually happens when you place a space following a word, type a period, or start a new paragraph (that's when Word knows that the entry is complete). If some default settings have somehow been changed, no corrections will be made as you type. You'll get to take a look at where this is all determined shortly.

Seeing How AutoCorrect Works

AutoCorrect is one of those features best appreciated in action. It can make your life easier by fixing problems before they even become problems. It can be annoying, however, if you don't know how it works.

> **Note:** If you have default settings for checking spelling and grammar as you type, you will also see several sets of wavy lines under your text in this memo. If these settings have been turned off, you won't have these lines. Red wavy lines indicate a potential spelling error; green lines indicate a possible grammar faux pas.

Hands On: Using AutoCorrect in an Announcement

Try using AutoCorrect to catch mistakes in a short but critical document, the announcement of a new company policy.

1. Type the short announcement shown in Figure 5.1.

PART I • CREATING BASIC DOCUMENTS

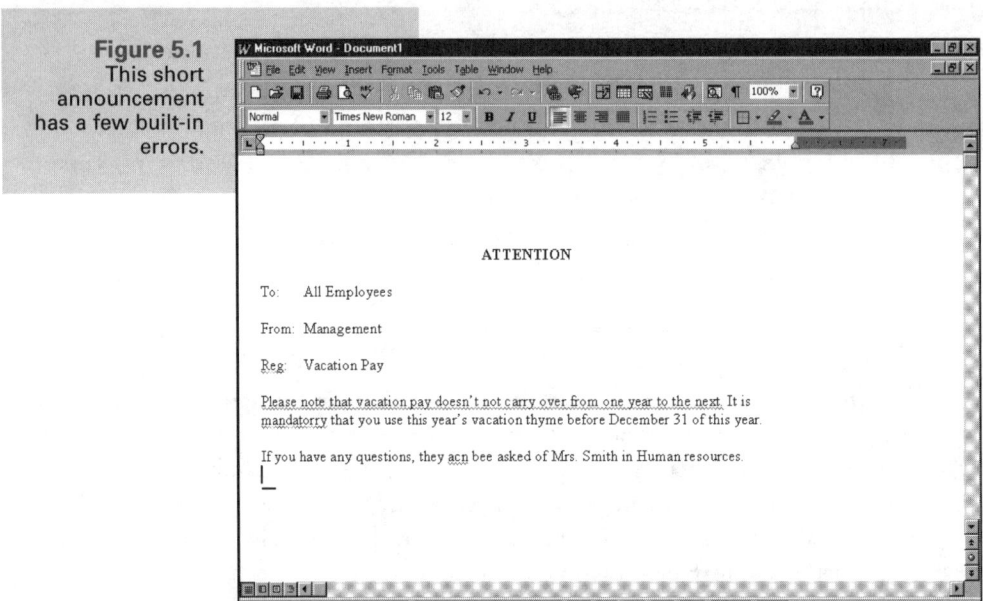

Figure 5.1
This short announcement has a few built-in errors.

2. Select Tools, AutoCorrect. The AutoCorrect dialog box in Figure 5.2 appears.

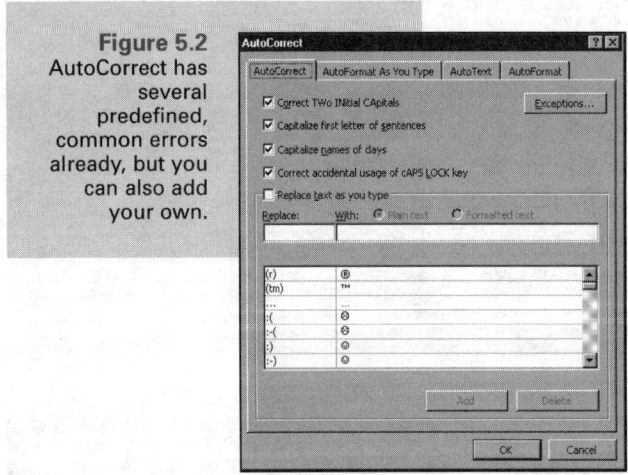

Figure 5.2
AutoCorrect has several predefined, common errors already, but you can also add your own.

3. Scroll down the list at the bottom of this dialog box (it's alphabetical) until you reach the entry for acn in the Replace column.
4. If it isn't checked, select the Replace Text As You Type check box.

Notice that this list consists not only of misspellings, but of common symbols such as trademarks and smiling faces, and even errors such as typing the words *and* and *the* without a space between them. The text in the Replace column in this dialog box is replaced with the text in the With column, as long as the check box above the list, Replace Text As You Type, is selected.

Besides simply replacing one entry with another, you can place general correction rules in force by selecting their check boxes in this dialog box. These include:

- **Correct TWo INitial CApitals.** If you have a tendency to capitalize the second letter of a word because you don't release the Shift key quickly enough after typing the first, this setting comes in handy. If you're typing a report on capitalization and want to show double-caps, however, turn this one off.

- **Capitalize First Letter of Sentences.** If you neglect to capitalize the first letter of sentences, Word will do it for you with this checked.

The Exceptions button in this dialog box defines certain exceptions to these capitalization rules. For example, if you type **apt.** or **a.** followed by a period, Word won't capitalize the words (figuring that they are the first letters in one-word sentences). Likewise, you can indicate exceptions to the initial caps rule here (if you belong to a club called HItech, for example, enter it here and Word won't correct the second capitalized letter.

- **Capitalize Names of Days.** Monday, Tuesday, Wednesday—you get it. These should always be capitalized, so let Word do it.

- **Correct Accidental Usage of cAPS LOCK key.** If you type part of a word with the Caps Lock feature activated (having pressed Caps Lock on your keyboard), Word changes the letters to lowercase and turns off Caps Lock. For example, try typing **tHIS**. It turns into *this* when you place a space after the word.

Overriding an AutoCorrect Entry

You can turn off the AutoCorrect feature by simply clearing the Replace Text as You Type check box in the AutoCorrect dialog box. You can also delete an AutoCorrect entry by selecting it from the list and clicking on the Delete button.

You won't always want to go through the effort of turning off the Replace Text as You Type feature, however, or deleting an AutoCorrect entry to enter one instance of AutoCorrect text. If you enter an AutoCorrect entry such as **(c)** and it turns into the copyright symbol, you can easily return it to the text you originally typed.

You can simply modify text that you've already entered and which AutoCorrect has replaced by moving your insertion point back there and editing it. As long as you don't press the spacebar after you correct the text, it won't change back.

Creating an AutoCorrect Entry

Now that you've seen how AutoCorrect entries are replaced and how to temporarily override them, it's time to learn how to create entries of your own.

Hands On: Creating Your Own AutoCorrect Entries

If the AutoCorrect dialog box isn't open, choose Tools, AutoCorrect to open it and then follow these steps to create a new AutoCorrect entry:

1. Place your insertion point in the Replace text box.
2. Type **Tank**.
3. Press Tab to move your insertion point to the With text box.
4. Type **Thank**. Remember that AutoCorrect are case sensitive, so capitalize appropriately.
5. Click on the Add button to add the entry to the list. It will appear in alphabetical order.

You can also create an AutoCorrect entry that replaces something with text that has unique formatting applied to it. Select the replacement word in your document (for example, your company name with a special font and color applied). Open the AutoCorrect dialog box. The selected text is already in the With text box. Select the Formatted Text option. Enter the word to be replaced by the selected text in the Replace text box, and click on Add to add the word to the AutoCorrect list. If you were to choose Plain Text, the text would take on whatever formatting is in effect in the paragraph where the word is located.

6. Click on OK to close the AutoCorrect dialog box.
7. Place your insertion point at the end of the last line in your document and press Enter.

Chapter 5 • Finding Things in Your Document and Fixing Them

8. Type **Tank you**. AutoCorrect replaces your entry with the words *Thank you*. But remember, if you're in the oil business or think that the word "tank" might crop up in your documents, go back and delete this particular AutoCorrect entry now!

Using AutoFormat

Another feature that will fine-tune things as you type is called *AutoFormat*. You may have noticed a couple of tabs on the AutoCorrect dialog box with the term AutoFormat in them. AutoFormat helps to ensure consistency in the way certain types of elements are handled by Word. For example, you can use AutoFormat to take a series of single lines that end in a return and automatically turn them into a bulleted list.

You get to the AutoFormat feature by selecting Tools, AutoCorrect. Then, select the AutoFormat As You Type tab, shown in Figure 5.3. You control AutoFormat by selecting or deselecting the items that you want with check boxes.

Note

Two AutoFormat tabs are actually available. Changes made on the AutoFormat As You Type tab control changes that are applied as you type a document. Formatting that you apply all at once (as with a template or style) is controlled on the AutoFormat tab of this dialog box.

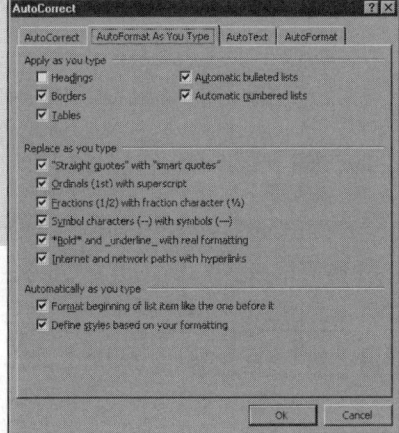

Figure 5.3
A plethora of check boxes provides the means to consistent formatting on this dialog box tab.

This dialog box is broken down into three sections:

- **Apply as You Type.** Applies certain formatting settings to text as you enter it. Test this by typing **1.** followed by text, and then press [Enter]. Now begin typing the next line. Word assumes that you just started a numbered list and therefore applies numbered list formatting. This formatting stays in effect until you turn it off using the Numbering button on the toolbar or the Bullets and Numbering command in the Format menu.
- **Replace as You Type.** Replaces certain entries with either another entry or an entry that's formatted differently. When you type the number **1** and the letters **st**, for example, Word superscripts the "st" in "1st" if that check box is selected. Another choice here replaces two hyphens with the more professional em dash.
- **Automatically as You Type.** Includes two check boxes: one to keep the beginning of lists consistent (so if you don't capitalize the first word in a first bulleted list item, none will be capitalized) and another to Define Styles Based on Your Formatting. This latter selection creates styles based on manual formatting that you apply to your paragraphs.

> SEE CHAPTER 14 FOR MORE ABOUT APPLYING STYLE TO YOUR TEXT.

Using Spelling and Grammar Check

Up to now, you've seen features that help prevent mistakes or inconsistencies as you create your document. But an important step after you've finished is often overlooked: doing a final check of spelling and grammar.

The Spelling and Grammar feature doesn't correct things as you go along (unless the misspelling is an AutoCorrect entry). Rather, if it's set up to do so, it places underlines to help you see your mistakes easily (unless you turn this feature off). Also, you can use the feature to take you through an item-by-item review of potential problems.

> **Tip**
> To see a list of suggested correct spellings for a word with a wavy red line under it, right-click on the word; suggestions and commands for a Spelling check are displayed on a shortcut menu.

Some important limitations to remember about this feature are as follows:

- **Spelling won't catch alternate spellings of words.** If you use *fair* or *fare*, it's all the same to Spelling because they are both correctly spelled words.

CHAPTER 5 • FINDING THINGS IN YOUR DOCUMENT AND FIXING THEM

- **Spelling won't verify the meanings of words.** Did you pay your bus fair? Was the judge's decision fare? Sounds fine to Word, but you've actually used the wrong words in both sentences.
- **Spelling won't catch a missing letter here and there as long as the incorrect word makes sense.** "If you right this sentence a night, Word is asleep a the wheel." Word knows that the word *right* is a real word, and that *a* is a word (though in both of these instances, it should be *at*). Similar problems crop up with words such as *the* instead of *they*, *a* instead of *an*, *to* instead of *too*, and so on.
- **Grammar mainly checks for things such as passive voice and run-on sentences.** It won't look for thoughts that could have been expressed more clearly, or phrasing that is not as elegant as you might wish. Those babies are up to you to find.

The bottom line with this feature is that you should use it, but also give your document a quick proofreading to make sure that you catch what Word doesn't.

If you need additional help with your grammar, check out the Azar grammar series at `http://www.phregents.com:80/azar2.html`.

Running Spelling and Grammar Check

You can run a Spelling and Grammar check at any time during the creation of a document and as many times as you like—for example, as you complete each draft for someone else's review. You should be sure to run this check every time that you complete a document, however. This feature will look for misspellings, sentences that appear to violate grammatical rules, and a few other patterns, such as a repeated word.

When you run a Spelling and Grammar check, you are presented with a couple of options. If the error encountered is in spelling, you're shown the misspelling and a list of suggestions for correct spelling. You then have the option to:

- <u>I</u>gnore the spelling
- Ignore All instances of this spelling
- <u>A</u>dd the word to your dictionary so that Word recognizes it in the future (useful for names of people and companies, as well as acronyms such as IBM)
- Highlight the correct spelling in the list of suggestions and <u>C</u>hange the word

PART I • CREATING BASIC DOCUMENTS

- Highlight the correct spelling in the list of suggestions and Change All instances of the word to the correct spelling
- Add the mistake and the correct replacement word to the AutoCorrect list of words

If the error is in grammar, the sentence is displayed and the type of grammatical rule that it violates is indicated. In some cases, Word will have a suggestion for correcting the problem; in others, it won't. You then have three options:

- Ignore the grammatical error
- Ignore All instances of this kind of error
- Go on to the Next Sentence

If you want to correct the error before proceeding, do so right in the Spelling and Grammar dialog box. The Change button then becomes available, so you can apply the correction to your document and then proceed with the Spelling and Grammar check.

If you don't want Word to check for grammar problems, remove the check mark from the Check Grammar check box in the Spelling and Grammar dialog box when it first appears.

Hands On: Running a Spelling and Grammar Check

To run a Spelling and Grammar check, follow these steps:

1. Choose Tools, Spelling and Grammar (or press F7 for a shortcut to this function). The dialog box in Figure 5.4 appears.

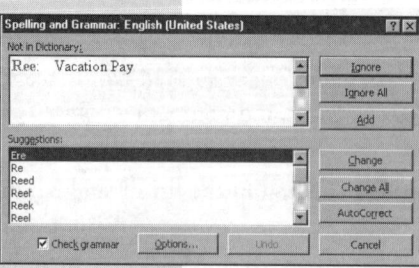

Figure 5.4 The first type of error that Word encounters, either a misspelling or grammatical mistake, is the kind it will present first.

CHAPTER 5 • FINDING THINGS IN YOUR DOCUMENT AND FIXING THEM 101

2. In the Suggestions list, select Re.
3. Choose <u>C</u>hange to change the word to the suggested spelling. The next problem is displayed, as shown in Figure 5.5.

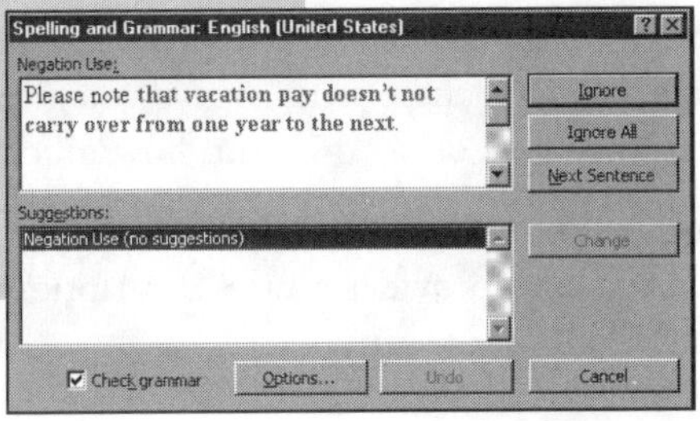

Figure 5.5
This time, Word has flagged a potential grammar problem.

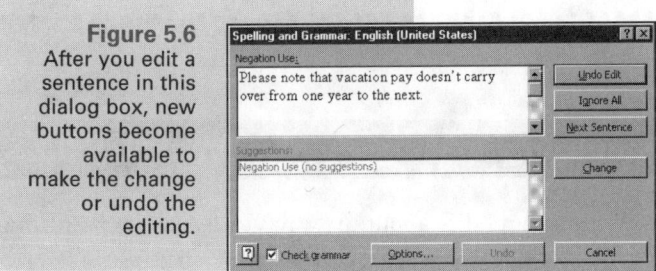

4. To correct the double negative in this sentence, select and then delete the word *not* in the sentence, as shown in the top half of this dialog box. The choices in the dialog box change, as in Figure 5.6.

Figure 5.6
After you edit a sentence in this dialog box, new buttons become available to make the change or undo the editing.

5. Choose <u>C</u>hange to make the change in your document.
6. In the next display, select the suggestion, *mandatory*, and click on <u>C</u>hange to correct the misspelling of *mandatorry*.

If you had AutoCorrect in effect when you created the document, you will not have any more problems to correct. If you didn't, you may get one more dialog box with the misspelling *acn* for *can*. Change it and you are returned to your document.

Notice that there are three more errors that Word didn't catch: *thyme* for *time*, *bee* for *be*, and the capitalization mistake in the department name *Human resources*.

These are the types of apparently correct items that Word can't make a judgment call on, and they are the reason that you should follow every Spelling and Grammar Check with your own proofreading pass.

Customizing How Spelling and Grammar Works

Word has several settings relating to how it checks for and flags potential spelling and grammar problems. Many of these settings give you greater control over how much Word is allowed to change on its own and how much is left up to you.

Again, the two areas of spelling and grammar have separate options. Table 5.1 lists the things you can change, and provides a brief description of how each change affects the Spelling and Grammar feature.

When checking different types of documents—for example, formal business documents versus personal notes to friends—you might want to explore the different writing style rules that Word offers. Click on the Settings button in the Spelling & Grammar tab of the Options dialog box to explore these. They use different rules of grammar for more formal or relaxed writing situations (such as allowing contractions in a more informal document).

Hands On: Customizing Spelling and Grammar Functions

Whatever you decide you want to modify about the way Word deals with Spelling and Grammar, you can follow this simple procedure to make changes:

1. Select Tools, Options.
2. Click on the Spelling & Grammar tab to bring it forward, as shown in Figure 5.7.

You can also get to this dialog box and tab by choosing the Options button in the Spelling and Grammar dialog box.

3. If there are any features you don't want active, remove the check mark from them. If there are features you do want active, select them.
4. To rerun the Spelling and Grammar check with the new settings, click on the Recheck Document button.
5. Click on OK to close the Options dialog box.

Chapter 5 • Finding Things in Your Document and Fixing Them

Table 5.1 Spelling and Grammar Options for Customization

Name of Option	What It Controls When Checked
Check spelling as you type	Turns on the feature that checks spelling as you type and places a wavy red line under misspelled words on screen
Hide spelling errors in this document that have been found	Hides the wavy red line indicating misspellings
Always suggest corrections	Word offers suggested correct spellings in the Spelling and Grammar dialog box
Suggest from main dictionary only	Word checks only its main dictionary, and not any open custom dictionaries, during the check
Ignore words in UPPERCASE	Words in all uppercase are not checked
Ignore words with numbers	Words with numbers in them are not checked
Ignore Internet and file addresses	Phrases structured like Internet addresses and file/directory locations will not be checked
Check grammar as you type	Turns on the feature that checks grammar as you type and places a wavy green line under grammar errors
Hide grammatical errors in this document	Hides the wavy green line indicating grammatical errors that have been found
Check grammar with spelling	Enables grammar checking in the Spelling and Grammar check function
Show readability statistics	Displays a list of statistics at the end of the check relating mainly to the use of passive voice and reader level

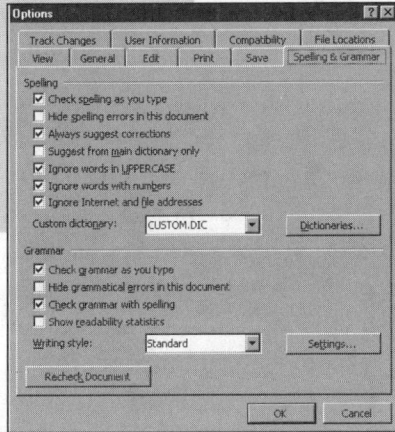

Figure 5.7
Both spelling and grammar are controlled from the same tab in the Options dialog box.

Readability Statistics: Just How Useful Are These?

Figure 5.8 shows the optional readability statistics that can be displayed at the end of a Spelling and Grammar check if you select that option.

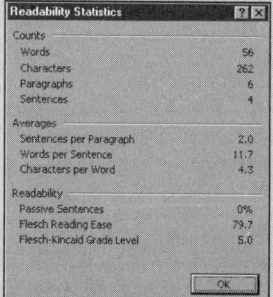

Figure 5.8
Some useful and some not-so-useful information is available in Readability Statistics.

The first section of this listing provides totals of various sorts of things in your document: words, characters, sentences, and paragraphs. This can be useful to writers who are paid by the word or aim for a document of a set number of words.

The second section provides averages, which are useful to see whether you have a tendency to write long or short sentences and use long or short words. If there were always a correlation between long sentences and run-on sentences, this would flag a problem with your writing style. It's perfectly possible to write long but well-constructed sentences, however.

The third section comes from readability measurements thought up by statisticians and academicians with too much time on their hands. They measure, mainly by incidence of passive voice, how readable your writing is. You get a score for ease of readability and are told what grade someone would have to pass in school in order to be able to read and understand your writing. The least useful of the three types of information, readability may prove more of a curiosity than an aide in your writing.

CHAPTER 5 • FINDING THINGS IN YOUR DOCUMENT AND FIXING THEM

Using Custom Dictionaries

If you want to use dictionaries other than the one built into Word—for example, a legal or medical dictionary—you can open them or even create your own from the Options dialog box that you've been using. Ready-made dictionaries are for sale from various companies for specialized interests or professions.

To open a dictionary from a disk or your hard drive, click on the <u>D</u>ictionaries button in the Options dialog box, Spelling and Grammar tab. You see the dialog box shown in Figure 5.9.

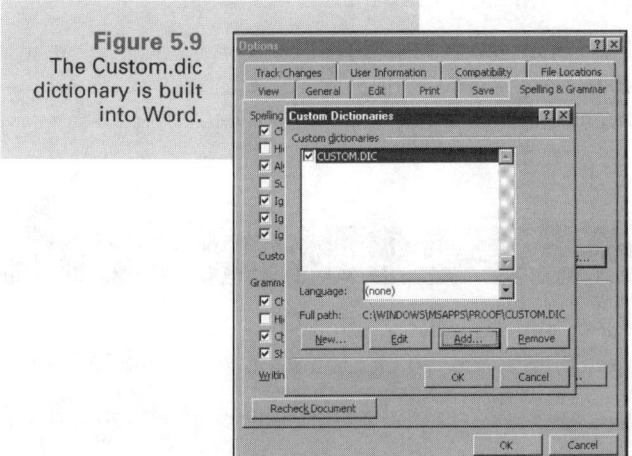

Figure 5.9
The Custom.dic dictionary is built into Word.

To add a dictionary, choose <u>A</u>dd. This displays an Open dialog box. Use the tools there to locate the file containing the dictionary on your hard drive or on a floppy or CD-ROM. Click on OK to add it to the open Custom <u>D</u>ictionaries list.

To create a new dictionary, choose <u>N</u>ew. You are presented with a dialog box where you can enter and save the name of your new dictionary. This new dictionary is simply a new Word file. You can type in any words that you want Word to recognize. This is very useful if your company uses a lot of terms of its own (acronyms for reports or procedures, for example). After you've entered words in your dictionary document, save it and Word will accept those spellings in the future.

To remove a dictionary, select it in the Custom <u>D</u>ictionaries list in the Custom Dictionaries dialog box and click on the <u>R</u>emove button.

PART I • CREATING BASIC DOCUMENTS

When you're done working with dictionaries, click on the OK button to close the Custom Dictionaries dialog box, and then click on OK to close the Options dialog box.

Finding the Right Word with Word's Thesaurus

A handy little feature in Word that's a snap to use is the built-in Thesaurus. You probably remember your Thesaurus from school: a compendium of synonyms that you could use to find just the right word for every occasion.

When you select a word and open the Thesaurus, Word offers a list of synonyms. If you like, you can look up further synonyms of words in the list, perhaps leading to a finer shade of meaning than the original list gave you.

Hands On: Finding the Perfect Word with Thesaurus

Word doesn't just offer words with a similar meaning. The Thesaurus feature can take you to many associated words, after you learn how to get around it:

1. Select the word *pay* in the body text of the short announcement that you created.
2. Select <u>T</u>ools, <u>L</u>anguage, <u>T</u>hesaurus (or use the shortcut Shift+F7). The dialog box similar to the one shown in Figure 5.10 appears. We've used this dialog box to search among layers of meaning so that we could call out some of the options that Thesaurus offers.

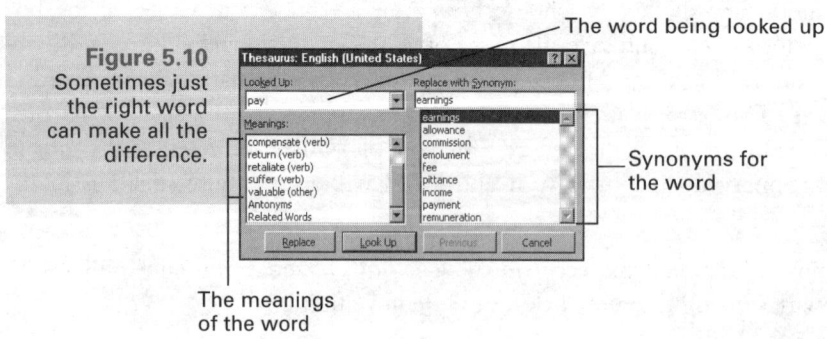

Figure 5.10 Sometimes just the right word can make all the difference.

3. Scroll down to the bottom of the list of M̲eanings for the word.

4. Click on the word *Antonyms*. This produces words with an opposite meaning (antonyms) rather than a similar meaning (synonyms), as in Figure 5.11.

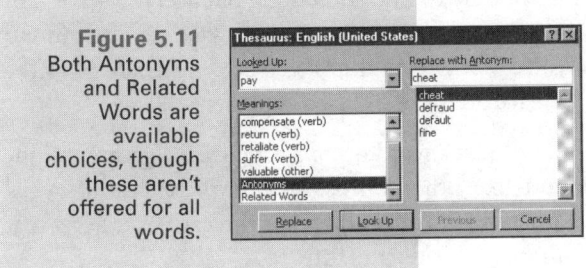

Figure 5.11 Both Antonyms and Related Words are available choices, though these aren't offered for all words.

5. Double-click on the word *pay* in the Loo̲ked Up text box to return to the synonym list for the original word.

6. Click on the word *payment* in the Replace with S̲ynonym list.

7. Click on L̲ook Up. This looks up the meaning and synonyms for the new word.

8. Click on the word *compensation* from the new list of synonyms that is displayed.

9. Click on R̲eplace to place the new word in your document and to close the Thesaurus dialog box.

Using the ability to move back and forth among synonyms, related words, and even words with an opposite meaning allows you to follow a train of words that may lead you to a better choice in the end.

Searching Through Your Document

One final skill that you'll probably need in polishing your document is the ability to easily find anything quickly and easily, and even replace one thing with another. For example, if you discover that you've put an old model number for a part throughout your document, you can just locate and replace all instances of that model number. Or, you might want to locate all the places in your report where you included Word tables so that you can verify the data in them. For these tasks, you'll use the Find and Replace, Go To, and Browse features of Word.

Using Find and Replace

Sometimes you just want to find a word in your document to check something. Did you remember to mention your boss's name in connection with a successful project? Did you include a reference to a publication in your bibliography? After you verify that this item is in your document, you're satisfied and you can forget it. But in many cases, you want not only to find something but also replace it. For example, if you spelled your client's name *Smith* in a proposal, and then found out that he spells it *Smythe*, you'd want to find and replace all instances of the name. That's why Find and Replace are so often used together.

Other times, you'll have to find not just a word or name, but text that has unique formatting or words that sound like other words. That's where Find's special search settings come in. Table 5.2 gives you a rundown of the various criteria that you can use in finding something in your document.

Table 5.2. Find Criteria

Criteria	Example of How It Restricts the Search
Match case	Finds instances of the word with the same upper- and lowercase usage (Match/Match, MATCH/MATCH, match/match)
Find whole words only	Finds only the whole word: *the* will find *the*, not *there*, *them*, or *their*
Use wildcards	If you enter **d?n**, Word finds *dan*, *don*, or *den*; if you enter **d*n**, Word finds *darken* and *deaden* (you will find many more wildcards through the Special feature)
Sounds like	Type **slick** and Word finds words such as *slug* or *slack*
Find all word forms speech	Finds various forms of speech and replaces with the correct form of
Format text	Matches formatting such as font, indentation, tabs, or highlighting on
Special	Locates various items such as em dashes, numbers, graphics, or line breaks

Chapter 5 • Finding Things in Your Document and Fixing Them

Hands On: Finding and Replacing Things

Try using Find and Replace to see just how narrowly Word lets you define a search in your document.

1. Choose Edit, Find. The Find and Replace dialog box shown in Figure 5.12 opens.

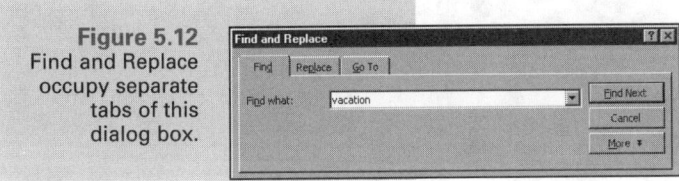

Figure 5.12 Find and Replace occupy separate tabs of this dialog box.

2. Type the word **vacation** in the Find What text box.
3. Click the More button to display the larger dialog box shown in Figure 5.13, which offers more options for searching, including a drop-down list that allows you to designate what format the text might have applied.

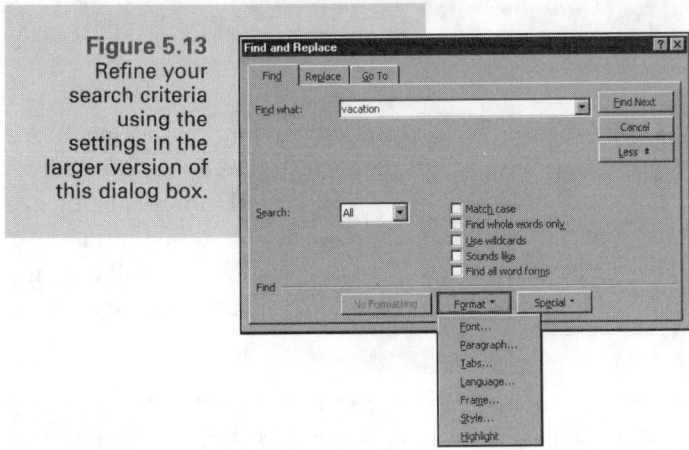

Figure 5.13 Refine your search criteria using the settings in the larger version of this dialog box.

4. Click on Find Next to find the word.
5. When Word highlights the word *vacation* in your document, click on the Replace tab (see Figure 5.14).

Part I • Creating Basic Documents

6. In the Replace With text box, type **holiday**.
7. Click on Replace to replace *vacation* with *holiday*.

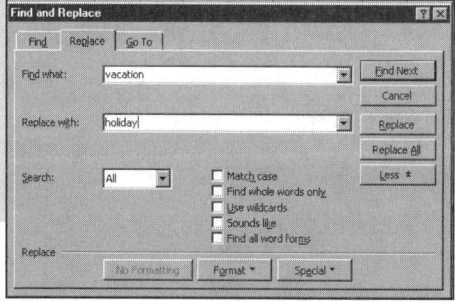

Figure 5.14
The Replace tab is where you enter the word you want instead of the one Word has found for you.

Note

If you locate something with the Find feature and want to go into your document to make an edit, just click in the document itself. The dialog box stays on-screen. The first click will select the item for which you searched; a second click will place your insertion point in the paragraph where the item is located. Make any edits you like, and then click on the Find Next button in the dialog box to proceed.

At this point, you can continue to find instances of the word by clicking on the Find Next button, replace every instance of the word in the document without checking each by clicking on Replace All, or click on Cancel to stop looking and then close the Find and Replace dialog box. If you continue to find instances of the word, when the last one has been located and dealt with, Word will display a message that it has checked the entire document. Click on OK to close the message and you're done.

Tip

Sometimes the larger version of the Find and Replace dialog box makes it hard to see found words highlighted in your document as the search progresses. If you want to go back to the smaller version of this dialog box at any time, click on the Less button.

CHAPTER 5 • FINDING THINGS IN YOUR DOCUMENT AND FIXING THEM 111

Getting There with Go To

DOCUMENT MAP ALSO HELPS YOU LOCATE ITEMS IN A DOCUMENT; IT'S COVERED IN CHAPTER 1.

The third tab of the Find and Replace dialog box is called Go To. This feature helps you quickly locate certain kinds of items in your document, such as footnotes, specific pages, or bookmarks. With the Find and Replace dialog box open, click on the Go To tab to see the tab shown in Figure 5.15.

You can go to a particular item in the Go To What list by selecting that item and then entering the criteria. For example, if you select Page, the text box is labeled Enter Page Number. Either type a number or, if you want to go to a page relative to the page you're on now (for example, jump 5 pages ahead or 20 pages back), enter a + or – before the number.

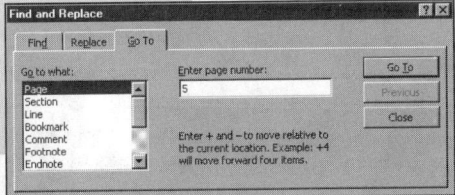

Figure 5.15
Want to jump 60 pages ahead? It's easy with the Go To feature.

Tip

Remember that you can also use your scroll bar to quickly go to a page or heading. The page number and heading are displayed next to the scroll box as you drag it up or down.

FOR MORE HELP FINDING THINGS, CHECK INTO WORD'S NEW SELECT BROWSE OBJECT FEATURE IN CHAPTER 1.

Use the other items in the Go To What list to go to instances of other types of elements, such as footnotes, tables, or even graphic objects.

micros
WORD

6

Setting Up a Document for Printing

In This Chapter

- Breaking a Document into Parts
- Adding Headers and Footers
- Changing Margins
- Changing Paper Size and Paper Orientation
- Aligning Text on the Page
- Previewing before Printing
- Selecting a Printer
- Specifying What to Print

As the world begins to move to a paperless environment, you may find more occasions when you don't need to print a document. But we're not there yet; most of the time, you still need to produce a nice-looking hard copy of most of your documents. Windows 95 controls printing in many ways; for example, you use Windows 95 to define the printer(s) to which you want to be able to print. Word controls many aspects of your document's actual appearance when you print it, however. In this chapter, you learn the basics of getting a document or a single envelope or label on paper.

Breaking a Document into Parts

By default, Word creates a "one-section" document. When your document contains only one section, all the page-related settings apply to the entire document. In some cases, however, you may want different settings for different parts of the document; for example, you may want to change margins for a portion of the document, or you may want different headers or footers to appear in different parts of the document. In these cases, you need to break your one-section document into multiple sections by inserting a section break. Then, you can establish different settings for each sections by simply placing the insertion point in the section that you want to affect and changing the setting that you want to change.

Word automatically inserts a section break for some page settings that you select; for example, Word automatically inserts section breaks when you change the number of columns on a page.

Hands On: Inserting a Section Break

To break a document into multiple sections, follow these steps:

1. Choose Insert, Break. Word displays the Break dialog box (see Figure 6.1).

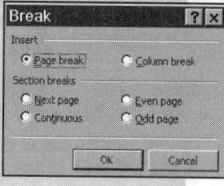

Figure 6.1 Use the Break dialog box to divide your document into multiple sections.

CHAPTER 6 • SETTING UP A DOCUMENT FOR PRINTING   115

2. From the options in the Section Breaks portion of the dialog box, specify the type of section break that you want to insert:
   - Next Page inserts a page break *and* a section break; the new section starts at the top of the next page.
   - Continuous inserts a section break at the insertion point; the new section starts on the same page at the insertion point.
   - Even Page inserts a section break and starts the next section on the next even-numbered page.
   - Odd Page inserts a section break and starts the next section on the next odd-numbered page.
3. Choose OK. Word inserts the section break you selected.

> **FOR MORE INFORMATION ON USING COLUMNS, SEE CHAPTER 7.**

Tip

You can insert a page break or divide your document into columns from the Break dialog box; however, you can quickly insert a page break by pressing Ctrl+Enter, and columns are established more easily using Word's Column command.

Working with Headers and Footers

You can use headers or footers to convey information about the document or your company. A *header* is information (text or a picture) that appears in the top margin of a document page; similarly, a *footer* is information that appears in the bottom margin of a document page. For example, a header or footer may contain the date and recipient in a letter, the date, volume number, and issue number of a newsletter, a chapter name, or a page number.

A sample header or footer might look like this:

07-15-97   The ABC Company   Page 1

Adding Headers and Footers

Headers and footers work exactly the same way in Word; the physical placement on the page is all that distinguishes between a header and a footer. To create a header or footer, choose View, Header and Footer. If you aren't working in Page Layout view, Word switches to Page Layout view, displays a pane where you enter header information, dims the text of your document so that you can't edit it, and displays the Header and Footer toolbar (see Figure 6.1). The Header and Footer toolbar aids you in creating your header or footer. Table 6.1 shows each button and its function, and if you pause the mouse pointer over each button, you'll see a ScreenTip that explains the button's function. All of the elements that you can insert from the Header and Footer toolbar (such as the date and the page number) will automatically update when you print the document.

At this point, you can simply type in the pane if you want (see Figure 6.2), and you can format the text that you enter in the same way you would format any text. The pane contains two predefined tabs to help you align header or footer text. If you simply start typing, whatever you type will appear aligned with the left margin of the page. If you press [Tab] once, the text that you subsequently type will center itself between the left and right margins. If you press [Tab] a second time, the text that you subsequently type will appear aligned with the right margin.

Table 6.1. Header and Footer Toolbar Buttons

Button	Function
Insert AutoText ▾	Insert AutoText entry
	Insert Page Number
	Insert Number of Pages
	Format Page Number
	Insert Date
	Insert Time
	Page Setup
	Show/Hide Document Text
	Same as Previous
	Switch Between Header and Footer
	Show Previous Section's Header/Footer
	Show Next Section's Header/Footer
Close	Close Header/Footer Pane

Chapter 6 • Setting Up a Document for Printing 117

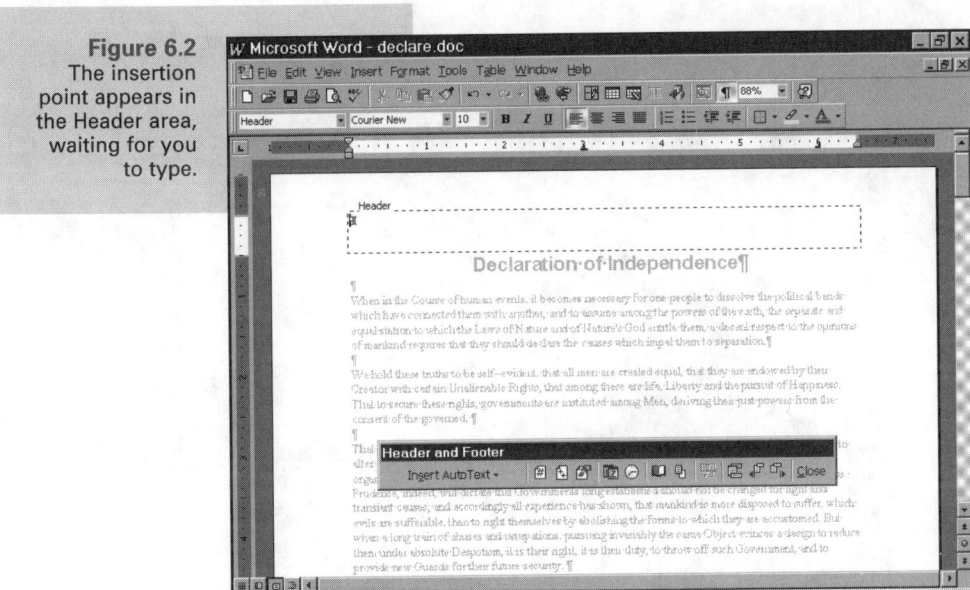

Figure 6.2
The insertion point appears in the Header area, waiting for you to type.

Hands On: Adding a Header or Footer

To add a header or footer to your document, follow these steps:

1. Choose View, Header and Footer.
2. Type and format the text of your header. Click on the Page Number, Number of Pages, Date, and/or Time buttons to quickly add those elements to your header.
3. Click on the Switch Between Header and Footer button to display the footer, and then type and format the footer just as you did the header (see step 2).
4. Click on Close or double-click on your document to close the header or footer pane and return to your document.

To quickly insert information in a header or footer, try using the Insert AutoText list box, which contains some standard information that typically appears in a header or footer (see Figure 6.3). To align a phrase with one of the predefined tab settings, first press Tab the requisite number of times and then open the list box and select a phrase.

Part I • Creating Basic Documents

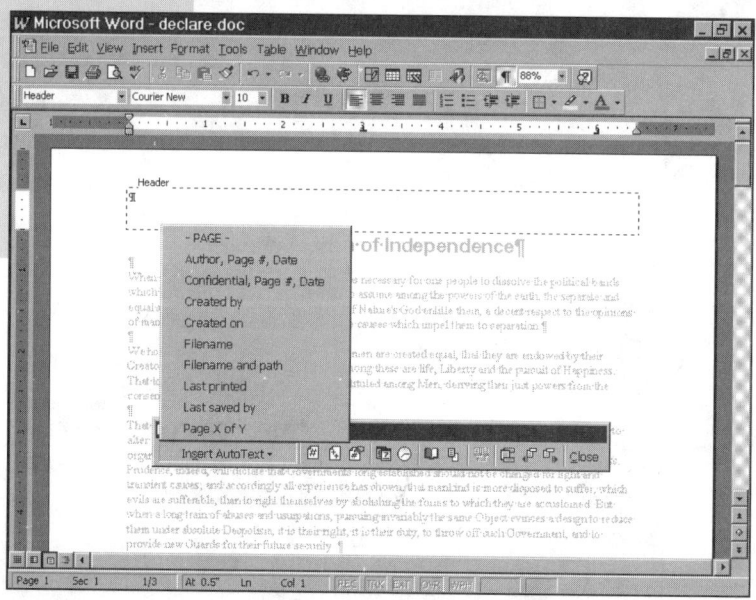

Figure 6.3
If you choose one of these phrases, Word will insert it in the Header or Footer box aligned with the insertion point.

Note

If you plan to choose a phrase that is separated by commas, *do not* press Tab before choosing the phrase, because Word automatically will align each portion of the phrase with one of the predefined tabs in the Header and Footer box. For example, if you do *not* press Tab and choose Confidential, Page #, Date, Word will place `Confidential` at the left margin, the current page number (preceded by the word `Page`) will appear centered, and today's date will align with the right margin. If you press Tab before selecting this phrase, a portion of your header or footer will fall outside the pane. If this occurs, you can easily correct this problem by deleting the tab at the beginning of the header or footer.

Varying Headers and Footers within a Document

Typically, a header or footer displays the same information on each page where it appears, but you do have some flexibility. You can use different headers and footers on odd and even pages. Or, you may want to use different headers and

Chapter 6 • Setting Up a Document for Printing

footers in different parts of your document. To create different headers or footers for different parts of your document, you insert section breaks to divide your document. Then you can vary the header and footer information in each section.

Using Different Headers or Footers for Different Sections

When you first create a document, Word assumes that the document is only one section; therefore, when you first create headers and footers, Word uses the same headers and footers throughout your document. If you divide a document into sections and subsequently create a header and footer, Word applies the same header and footer to all the sections in your document.

Suppose, however, that you want a different header or footer in a section; for example, you must go to that section and unlink the existing header or footer; then you must create the new header or footer. The new header or footer applies to the current section and to all following sections. Later, if you decide that you want your new header or footer to be the same as the previous header or footer, you can relink it.

Hands On: Changing the Header or Footer in a Section

For this exercise, assume that your document is already divided into multiple sections. To change the header or footer in one section and all subsequent sections, follow these steps:

1. Choose View, Header and Footer.
2. Click on the Show Next button. Word selects the header for the next section (see Figure 6.4). If you want to change the footer for the selected section, click on the Switch Between Header and Footer button instead.
3. To unlink the header or footer, click on the Same as Previous button. The `Same as Previous` line disappears from the top right of the header or footer editing pane.

You may have noticed that the Same as Previous button wasn't available in Figures 6.2 and 6.3. The button is available only when the document is divided into more than one section and you have displayed a header or footer in a section other than Section 1.

PART I • CREATING BASIC DOCUMENTS

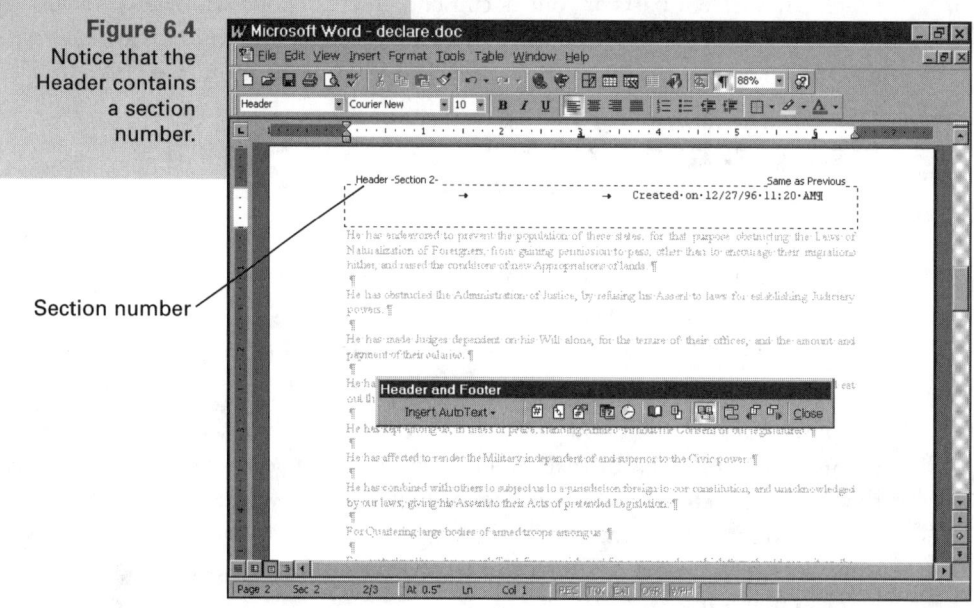

Figure 6.4
Notice that the Header contains a section number.

Section number

4. Create the new header or footer.
5. Click on the <u>C</u>lose button to close the Header and Footer toolbar and display your document.

Hands On: Relinking Headers and Footers

To relink a different header or footer to the previous header or footer, follow these steps:

1. Position the insertion point inside the section containing the header or footer that you want to relink.
2. Choose <u>V</u>iew, <u>H</u>eader and Footer. Word selects the header for the section in which you're located. If you want to change the footer for that section, click on the Switch Between Header and Footer button.
3. To relink the header or footer, click on the Same as Previous button. Word displays a message box asking whether you want to delete the header/footer and connect to the header/footer in the previous section.
4. Click on <u>Y</u>es.

5. Click on <u>C</u>lose to close the Header and Footer toolbar and display your document.

By relinking the header or footer to the previous header or footer, you change not only the current header or footer, but also those in all the following sections.

Creating First Page or Odd and Even Page Headers or Footers

In many cases, you may want a different header or footer to appear on the first page of a document, or you may want no header or footer to appear on the first page. Or, suppose that you want different headers and footers for the odd- and even-numbered pages in your document. For example, suppose that you're preparing a document that will be placed in a three-ring binder and each page will contain text on both sides of the page. In this case, your final product will contain facing pages, with odd-numbered pages appearing on the right side and even-numbered pages on the left side. You might want right-aligned headers on odd-numbered pages and left-aligned headers on even-numbered pages so that headers always appear on the outside edges of your document.

Hands On: Setting Up Special Headers

To set up special headers and footers for first pages, or odd and even pages in your document, follow these steps:

1. Choose <u>V</u>iew, <u>H</u>eader and Footer and click on the Show Previous or Show Next button to locate the section in which you want a different first-page header or footer.

2. Click on the Page Setup button to display the Page Setup dialog box and select the <u>L</u>ayout tab (see Figure 6.5).

3. In the Headers and Footers group, select Different <u>F</u>irst Page to create specific first page headers or footers, and then click on OK. The title of the header or footer editing pane for the section changes to `First Page Header` or `First Page Footer`.

   Or, in the Headers and Footers group, select Different <u>O</u>dd and Even and click on OK. Word retitles the header or footer editing box for the section you're in to `Even Page Header`, `Even Page Footer`, `Odd Page Header`, or `Odd Page Footer`.

PART I • CREATING BASIC DOCUMENTS

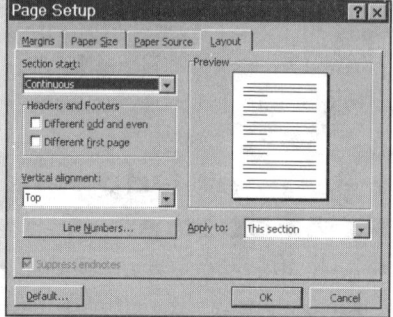

Figure 6.5
From the Layout tab of the Page Setup dialog box, you can create different first page or odd/even page headers and footers.

4. If you want a different header or footer on the first page or odd/even pages of the section, create it now.

5. Click on Close to display your document.

Note

Although you would expect these settings to apply to sections, Word's first-page headers and footers in fact apply to the whole document; that is, you can have a different first page header for the entire document, not for each section. Odd/even headers and footers do apply to each section, however; you can set up different odd-page and even-page headers and footers for different sections.

To remove first-page headers and footers from a section or document, clear the checks from the check boxes on the Layout tab of the Page Setup dialog box.

Changing Page Settings

Page settings in Word include a variety of formatting choices that affect the entire document. Page settings typically include margins, paper size and orientation, paper source, and text alignment on the page. By default, many page setup options, such as margins, headers and footers, and page numbers, apply to the entire document. Alternatively, you can apply these options to a designated section of text or from the position of the insertion point forward in your document.

It's important to remember, too, that page settings are stored with the individual document, which means that Word will *not* remember, from one document to the next, whether you have changed page settings such as margins or paper source. If you make a change, however, and you want that change to be permanent for all new documents that you create based on the Normal template, save your selections to the Normal template. In the Page Setup dialog box, which you'll see throughout this section, click on the Default button before you click on OK.

Changing Margins

> FOR INFORMATION ON MODIFYING A TEMPLATE, SEE CHAPTER 14.

Word's default margins are 1 inch at the top and bottom and 1.25 inches on the left and right. You can change the margins for the entire document or, if you divide the document into sections, for parts of the document. If you use different margin settings regularly, you can modify the Normal template so that they become the new defaults.

When you set margins, you also can establish facing pages and gutters for binding, set varying margins for different sections of your document, and apply your margin settings to the Normal template so that they become the new default settings.

To apply margin settings to your entire document, you locate the insertion point anywhere in the document when you set your margins. If you want to apply margins to only one part of your document, however, you must do one of the following three things before you set the margins:

- To apply margins to a selected portion of your text, select that text before you set the margins. If you apply margins to selected text, Word automatically inserts section breaks before and after the selected text.
- To apply margins to existing sections, first place the insertion point in the section, or select those sections whose margins you want to change.
- To apply margins from a specific point forward in your document, position the insertion point where you want the new margins to start, and then open the Apply to List box in the Page Setup dialog box and specify that the margins apply to the text from This Point Forward. If you apply margins from the insertion point forward, Word inserts a section break at the insertion point.

The easiest way to accurately change margin settings is to use the Page Setup dialog box. Choose File, Page Setup. In the Page Setup dialog box, select the Margins tab (see Figure 6.6).

PART I • CREATING BASIC DOCUMENTS

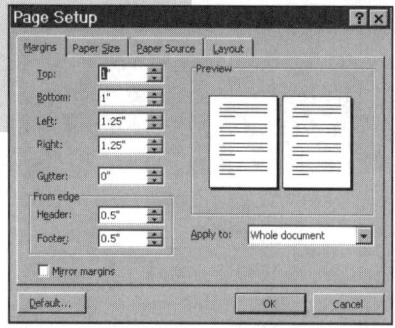

Figure 6.6
Use the Page Setup dialog box to set margins.

Tip

To quickly display the Page Setup dialog box, double-click anywhere in the gray part of the ruler. The tab of the dialog box that Word displays is the last tab you viewed.

To choose your Top, Bottom, Left, Right, and Gutter margins, type the amount of the margin or use the spinner (or press the up- or down-arrow key) to increase or decrease the margin setting by tenths of an inch. The Gutter setting controls the amount of extra spacing Word leaves on the binding edge of pages. Use this control to add space when you intend to bind a document. A gutter doesn't change your document's margins, but it does reduce the printing area. Gutters appear in the Preview box as a shaded area.

Note

As you select your margin settings, notice that the Preview box in the Page Setup dialog box shows you how a typical page with those settings will look.

To vary the margin settings in different parts of your document, the document must be divided into sections. Then, you use the Apply To list box in the Page Setup dialog box to apply margins to specific parts of a document. In the following table, you see the Apply To list box's available choices and the results of choosing an option. Note that "Selected Text" and "Selected Sections" will not be available unless you select text or a section before opening the Page Setup dialog box.

CHAPTER 6 • SETTING UP A DOCUMENT FOR PRINTING **125**

Option	Applies Margins to	When
This Section	Current section (No section break is inserted)	Insertion point is located within a section
Selected Sections	Multiple sections (No section breaks are inserted)	At least part of more than one section is selected
This Point Forward	Insertion point (Inserts new-page section break at insertion point)	Insertion point is where you want new margin to start
Selected Text	Selected text (Inserts new page section breaks at beginning and end of text)	Text is selected
Whole Document	Entire document (No section breaks inserted)	Insertion point is anywhere

•••

If you include sections with different margins in your document, remember that section breaks store all section settings. If you delete the section break, you'll lose the margin settings—margins will revert to the settings of the preceding section. If you accidentally delete a section break, choose Edit, Undo.

•••

The Mirror Margins check box helps you set up your document so that you can read it the same way you read books and magazines, where each page has printed material on both sides of the page. When you use mirrored margins, you no longer have left and right margins; instead, you have inside and outside margins. Mirrored margins work best in situations in which you plan to print your document on both sides of the paper and bind it together; you want wider margins on the inside than on the outside edges of such documents.

Changing Paper Size and Orientation

Word offers several predefined paper sizes, including letter and legal. If none of these sizes suits your needs, you can select a custom size instead and enter your

PART I • CREATING BASIC DOCUMENTS

own measurements. For example, you may set a custom paper size to create something smaller than usual, such as an invitation. You can select landscape (horizontal) orientation rather than the usual portrait (vertical) orientation to print "wider than usual" documents or to create a brochure or envelope.

Paper size and orientation settings apply to the current section, just like margin settings. If you haven't divided your document into sections, your settings apply to the whole document. If you select text to apply settings, Word inserts a new-page section break before and after the selection. If you apply settings to the insertion point forward, Word inserts a new-page section break at the insertion point's current position.

Hands On: Setting Paper Size and Orientation

To set paper size and orientation, follow these steps:

1. Select the text or section where you want to set paper size and orientation.
2. Choose File, Page Setup. In the Page Setup dialog box, select the Paper Size tab (see Figure 6.7).

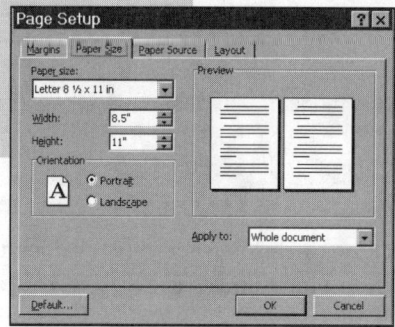

Figure 6.7
From this tab, you can choose a paper size and orientation.

3. From the Paper Size list, select a predefined paper size. In the Width and Height boxes, you can also type or select the width and height of your custom paper size.
4. For a vertical page, select Portrait from the Orientation group. Or, for a horizontal page, select Landscape from the Orientation group.

CHAPTER 6 • SETTING UP A DOCUMENT FOR PRINTING **127**

5. From the <u>A</u>pply To list, select the section to which you want to apply paper size and orientation settings. (For more information about the <u>A</u>pply To list, see the table in the "Changing Margins" section earlier in this chapter.)
6. Click on OK.

> If you set width and height for the page size, be sure that your printer can handle the paper size you specify. Some laser printers don't handle custom paper sizes well. Consult your printer manual for more information.

When the Paper Keeps Coming Out of the Wrong Tray...

Have you ever had one of those days when every time you print a document, the printer keeps flashing some silly message at you about inserting paper in the upper tray or some paper tray that you've never even seen? In cases like that, you need to set the paper source, which is the tray from which you want the printer to print.

Many printers have different trays from which paper can feed into the printer. Most laser printers, for example, have a default paper tray and a manual feed. You can specify that one section of your document be printed from the manual feed, whereas the rest of the document be printed from paper in the default paper tray. Some printers have two paper trays; you can specify that one section, such as the first page of a letter, be printed on letterhead in the first tray, whereas the remaining pages be printed on plain paper from the second tray.

As you can do with all page setup options, you can insert section breaks before you select paper source, or Word can insert section breaks for you. To select a paper source for your document, follow these steps:

1. Position the insertion point inside the section for which you want to set the paper source. (The change applies to the entire document unless the document has multiple sections.) You can also select the section for which you want to set the paper source. Or, position the insertion point where you want the new paper source to begin in your document.
2. Choose <u>F</u>ile, Page Set<u>u</u>p. In the Page Setup dialog box, select the <u>P</u>aper Source tab (see Figure 6.8). Be aware that the choices you see may be different from the ones in the figure; the choices available depend on the printer you use.

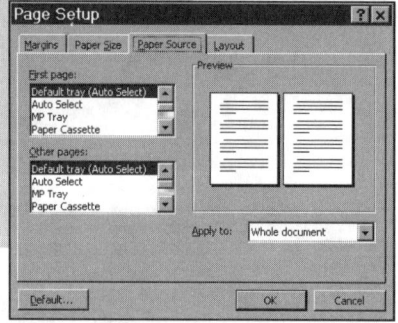

Figure 6.8
Use the Page Setup dialog box to print different sections of your document on paper from different paper trays.

3. From the First Page list, select the paper source for the first page of your document.
4. From the Other Pages list, select the paper source for the remaining pages of your document.
5. From the Apply To list, select the section to which you want to apply paper source settings (the list displays different options, depending on how much text is selected in the document). See the table in the Setting Margins section in this chapter for the meaning of the options in the Apply to list box.
6. Click on OK.

When you print a document with various paper sizes, orientations, or sources, your printer may pause at the end of each page and wait for you to indicate that it should continue. In some cases, you may need only to access the Print Manager and click on Resume. In other cases, you may need to press a button on the printer. Newer laser printers work well with varying paper sizes and orientations, but if you experience difficulties, check your printer manual.

If you want to apply your paper source selections to the Normal template so that they become the default settings, click on the Default button before you click on OK.

Be sure that you have installed the correct printer driver for your printer in Windows so that Word knows which paper trays your printer has available. Refer to your Windows book or printer manual for details.

CHAPTER 6 • SETTING UP A DOCUMENT FOR PRINTING 129

Aligning Text on a Page

Word usually aligns text vertically to the top margin in your document (see Figure 6.9). But you may want to align it differently—in the center of the page (see Figure 6.10) or justified on the page (see Figure 6.11).

If text fills each page, changing its vertical alignment does not make much difference; reserve this technique for pages that are not full or for sections that are less than a page in length. Text alignment applies to sections. If you haven't divided your document into sections, it applies to the entire document.

Hands On: Aligning Text Vertically

To vertically align text on the page, follow these steps:

1. Position the insertion point inside the section where you want to align text.
2. Choose File, Page Setup. The Page Setup dialog box appears. Click on the Layout tab.

Figure 6.9 By default, Word aligns text vertically at the top margin.

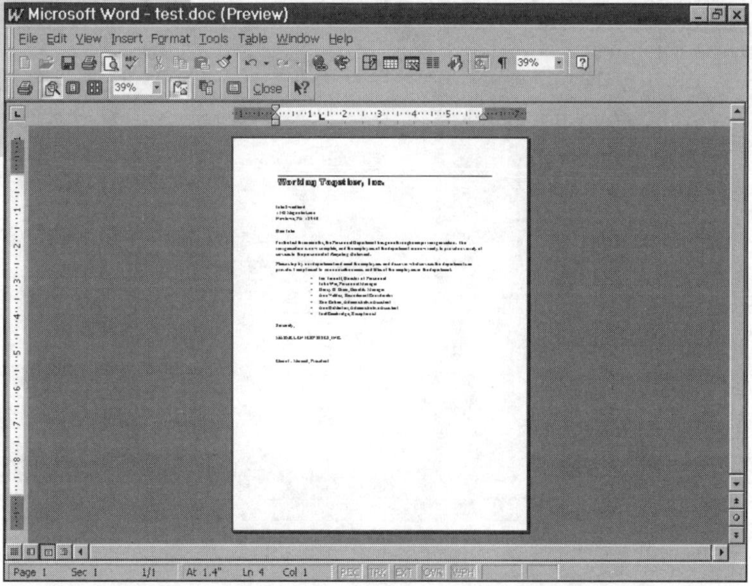

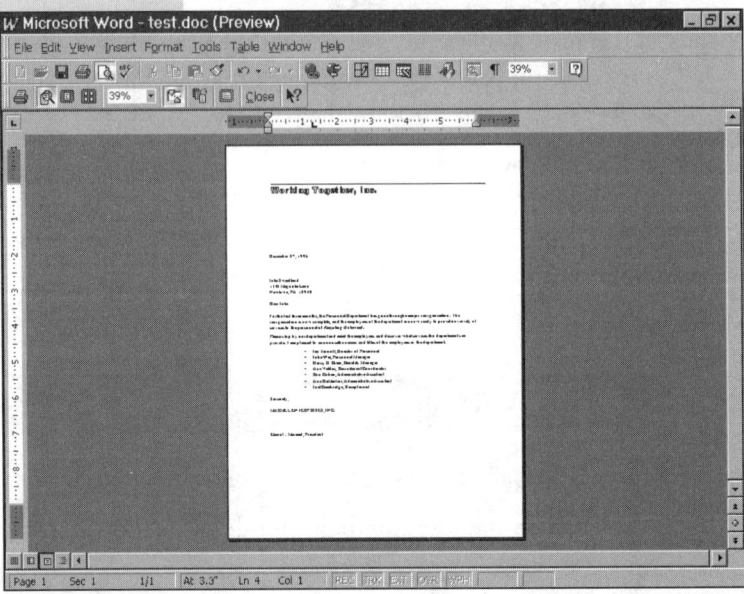

Figure 6.10 In some cases, particularly when using letterhead, centered vertical alignment is appropriate.

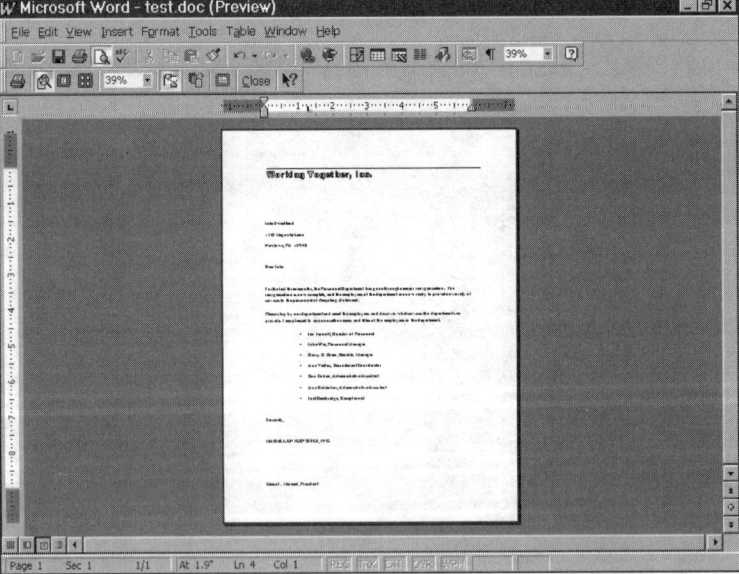

Figure 6.11 When you justify text on a page, the paragraphs on the page are spread evenly between the top and bottom margins.

3. In the Vertical Alignment list, select Center to center text on the page. You can also select Justify to spread paragraphs between the top and bottom margins on the page. Or, you can select Top to align text to the top margin (see Figure 6.12).
4. Click on OK.

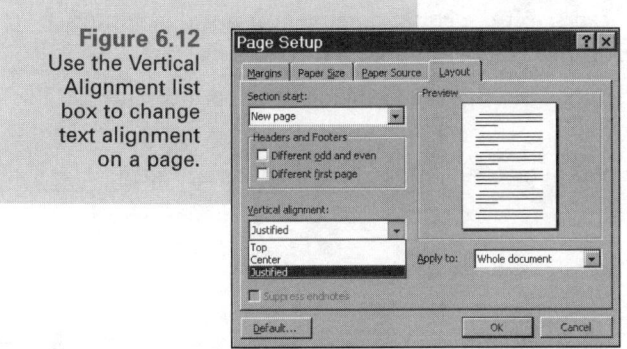

Figure 6.12
Use the Vertical Alignment list box to change text alignment on a page.

Using Line Numbers

If you plan to use a document for reference, you will help your readers if you number the line. Line numbering is common in a class that shares a document, or in legal briefs. In Word, you can number some or all of the lines in a document. If your document contains no section breaks, line numbers apply to the entire document. If your document contains sections, line numbers apply to the currently selected section. If you select text before you assign line numbers, Word places page section breaks before and after the selected text, isolating that text on a page (or pages) by itself. If you want to apply line numbers to an entire document that contains multiple sections, select the entire document before you apply the line numbers.

Numbers can start at 1 or some other number, and they can appear on each line or on only some lines. They can be continuous, or they can restart at each page or section. You can control the distance between text and the line numbers. You also can suppress line numbers for selected paragraphs.

Line numbers appear in the left margin of your page or to the left of text in columns. You can see line numbers on-screen in Page Layout view or in Print Preview or when you print the document.

Hands On: Working with Line Numbers

To add and format line numbers, follow these steps:

1. Position the insertion point inside the section containing lines you want to number. Position the insertion point anywhere inside a document that is not divided into sections. You can also select the text whose lines you want to number. Or, you can select the entire document if it is divided into sections and you want line numbering for all the sections.

2. Choose File, Page Setup. The Page Setup dialog box appears. Click on the Layout tab.

3. Click on Line Numbers. The Line Numbers dialog box appears (see Figure 6.13).

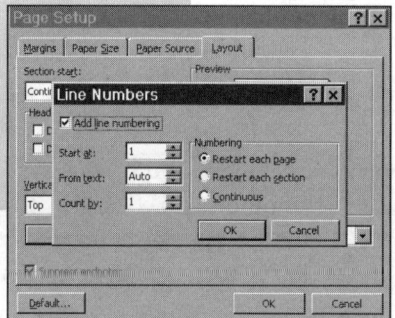

Figure 6.13 Use the Line Numbers dialog box to number the lines of your text for easy reference.

4. Choose Add Line Numbering.

5. Make changes to any of the following:
   - Choose Start At and type or select the starting line number.
   - Choose From Text and type the distance between the line numbers and text.
   - Choose Count By and type or select the increment by which you want lines to be numbered. Select 3, for example, if you want every third line numbered.

6. In the Numbering group, select any of the following:
   - Choose Restart Each Page for numbering to start over on each page.
   - Choose Restart Each Section to start over in each section.

Chapter 6 • Setting Up a Document for Printing

- Choose **C**ontinuous if you want line numbers to be consecutive throughout the document.

7. Click on OK. Click on OK again to close the Page Setup dialog box and return to your document, where you can see the line numbers (see Figure 6.14).

To remove line numbers, follow the preceding steps 1 through 4 and remove the check from the Add Line Numbering check box.

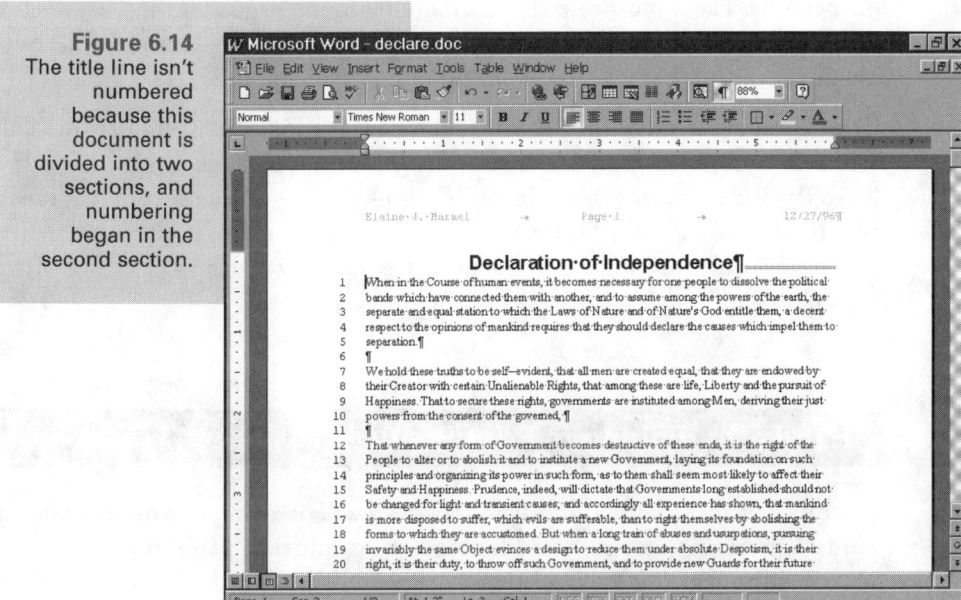

Figure 6.14
The title line isn't numbered because this document is divided into two sections, and numbering began in the second section.

Hands On: Suppressing Line Numbers

To suppress line numbers, follow these steps:

1. Select the paragraphs in which you don't want line numbers to appear.
2. Choose F**o**rmat, **P**aragraph. The Paragraph dialog box appears.
3. Click on the Lines and **P**age Breaks tab.
4. Choose **S**uppress Line Numbers.
5. Click on OK.

Previewing Before Printing

Although you can use Page Layout view to see how your document will look when you print it, Print Preview shows you the "bigger picture." Print Preview shrinks your document's text so that it is difficult to read, but shows you how the full page appears (see Figure 6.15). To display your document in Print Preview, click on the Print Preview button on the Standard toolbar, or choose File, Print Preview.

Notice the Print Preview toolbar that replaces the Formatting toolbar. You can use the Multiple Pages button to display more than one page at a time (see Figure 6.16). You can drag the page that appears in the bottom-right corner of the button down and to the right to display up to 24 pages at a time.

Other buttons on the Print Preview toolbar let you hide the menu bar (the Full Screen button), print your document (the Print button), hide or view the rulers (the View Ruler button), and attempt to shrink the size of your text so that it will all print on one page (the Shrink to Fit button). Click on the Close button to display your document in one of the standard Word views, such as Normal or Page Layout.

Hands On: Editing in Print Preview

You can edit in a limited way in Print Preview. For example, you can change words. You cannot, however, add footnotes or comments, perform a merge, create new documents, or open existing documents. To edit in Print Preview, follow these steps:

1. Make sure that the Magnifier button is selected (when you first display Print Preview, the button is selected; if you click on it, you deselect it).
2. Click anywhere on your document to enlarge the text so that you can see it.
3. Click on the Magnifier button to deselect it. You'll see an insertion point in your document. Edit as needed.
4. Click on the Magnifier button to select it again.
5. Click on the One Page button to display a full page of your document in Print Preview.

Chapter 6 • Setting Up a Document for Printing

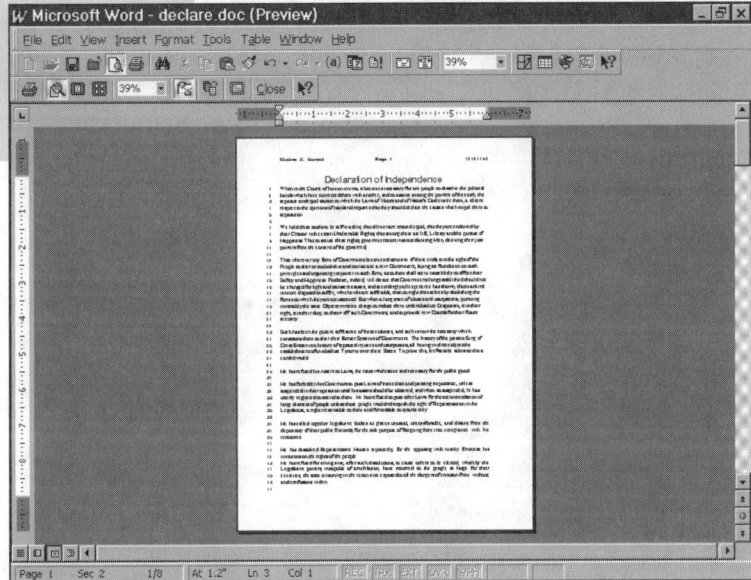

Figure 6.15
In Print Preview, you see a full page view of your document.

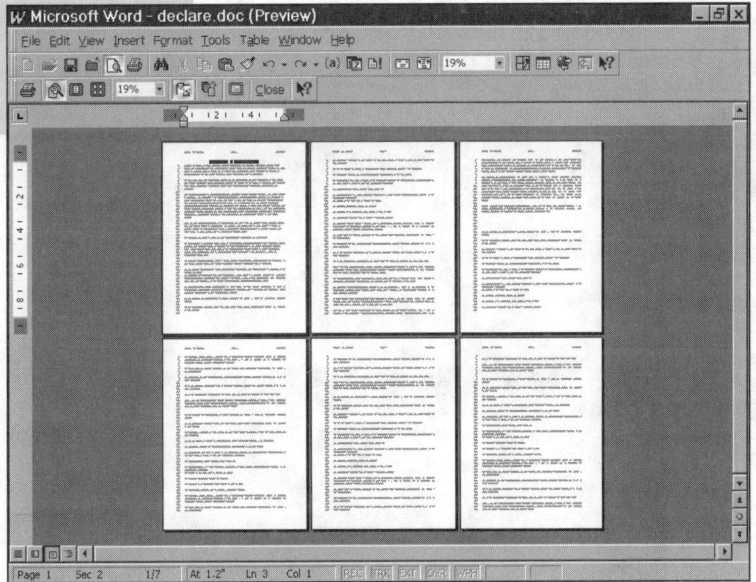

Figure 6.16
You can preview up to 24 pages at a time.

Part I • Creating Basic Documents

Setting Up To Print

Ready to get that document onto paper? The simplest way to print a document is to click on the Print button on the Standard toolbar. This method works best, however, if you want to print one copy of your document to the default printer. If you need to make any changes to those settings, you need to choose File, Print to display the Print dialog box (see Figure 6.17).

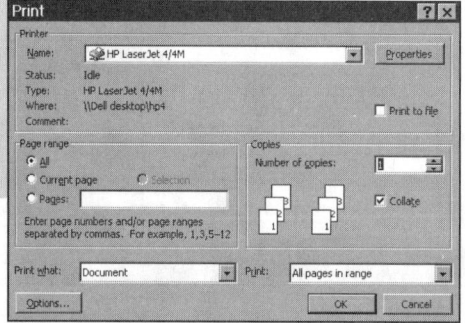

Figure 6.17
From the Print dialog box, you can select a printer and set other printing options.

For more information on faxing documents, see Chapter 10.

To select a printer, open the Name list box at the top of the Print dialog box (see Figure 6.18). All printers available to you for printing will appear in the list. Fax software sets up a "printer" when you install it, so, if you have installed fax software, you'll see a printer for your fax software in this list. Choose the printer to which you want to print. The Properties button next to the Name list controls the way the selected printer behaves; in most instances, you won't need to modify a printer's properties.

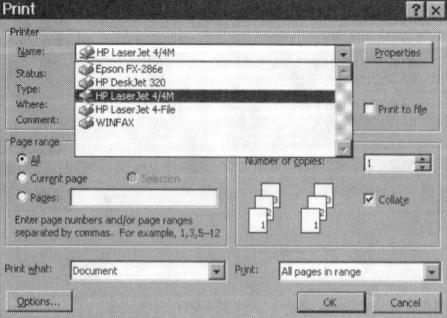

Figure 6.18
Select a printer from the Name list box.

CHAPTER 6 • SETTING UP A DOCUMENT FOR PRINTING   137

In the Page Range group, choose whether to print the entire document, the current page, or certain pages. You can print noncontiguous pages. Type, in the Pages text box, the pages that you want to print, separated by a comma or a semicolon. For example, typing **3–5; 6–9; 11** would tell Word to print pages 3 through 5, 6 through 9, and 11.

●●

If you select text before you open the Print dialog box, you will also be able to print just the Selection.

●●

In the Copies group, identify the number of copies that you want to print. If you choose to print more than one copy, placing a check in the Collate box will print one entire copy of your document before starting the next copy. If you choose not to collate, Word will print the correct number of copies of each page; for example, if you print three copies of the document and don't collate, Word will first print three copies of page 1 and then three copies of page 2, and so on.

From the Print What list box, you can choose to print your document or information about your document, such as the styles it contains. From the Print list box, you can choose to print all pages, odd pages, or even pages. To print your document, click on OK.

Printing a Single Envelope

FOR MORE INFORMATION ON USING THE MERGE FEATURE, SEE CHAPTER 9.

On many occasions, you may need to print an envelope to go with a letter you just typed. Using Word's Envelopes and Labels dialog box, you can easily prepare and print a single envelope. Note that, to print a large quantity of envelopes, you should use Word's merge feature.

Hands On: Printing a Single Envelope

If a letter already contains an address, Word will suggest that address to print on the envelope, saving you the task of retyping. To print a single envelope, follow these steps:

1. Choose Tools, Envelopes and Labels. Word displays the Envelopes tab of the Envelopes and Labels dialog box (see Figure 6.19).

Figure 6.19
If your document contains an address, it will appear selected in the dialog box.

Address in document

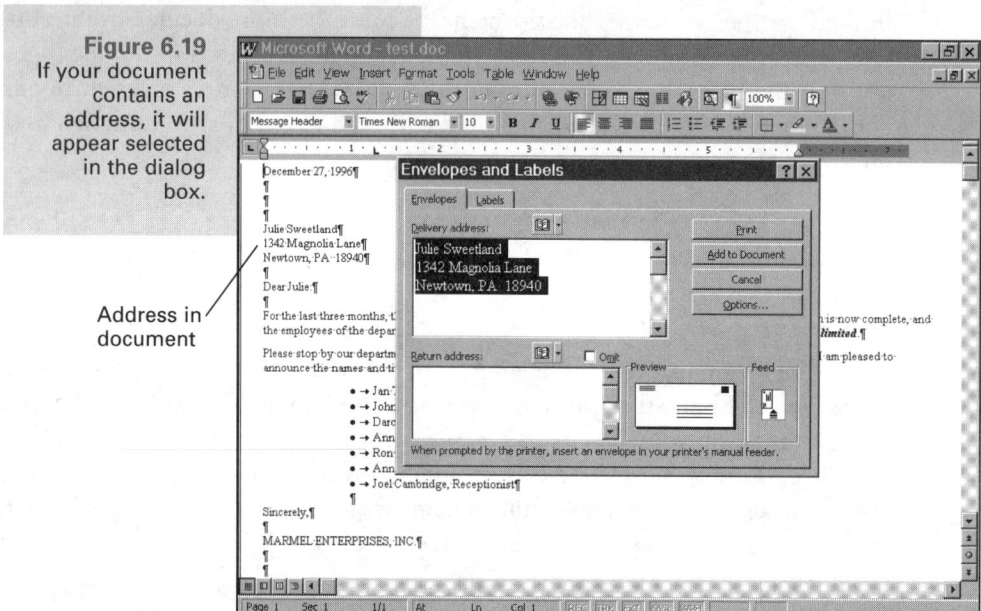

2. Click on the <u>P</u>rint button to print your envelope, or click on the <u>A</u>dd to Document button to place the envelope at the beginning of the document. If you place the envelope in the document, Word will also print the envelope when you print the document.

In the Envelopes and Labels dialog box, you can tell Word to use or omit a return address that you provide. If you remove the check from the O<u>m</u>it check box, you can type a return address in the <u>R</u>eturn Address box. If you click on the <u>O</u>ptions button, you can choose the envelope size (the default is a standard, #10 envelope), choose to use a delivery point barcode, a Facing Identification Mark (FIM for courtesy reply mail (both of the options are useful only for U.S. mail), and change the fonts for the Delivery address and the Return address, which default to the font you're using in your document.

Tip

You can print an envelope to an address stored in either your Microsoft Exchange or Outlook address book. Click on the Address button near the top of the dialog box to open your address book and select an addressee.

CHAPTER 6 • SETTING UP A DOCUMENT FOR PRINTING

> **Note**
>
> In many cases, particularly when using a laser printer, you'll need to manually feed the envelope through your printer. Check your printer manual for the correct method.

Printing Labels

Using the Labels tab of the Envelope and Labels dialog box, you can print a single label, or, if you're printing to a sheet of labels, you can print a full sheet of the same label. Be aware that you should use Word's merge feature to print many labels to different individuals.

Choose Tools, Envelopes and Labels and click on the Labels tab. As with envelopes, if your document already contains an address, Word will suggest that address for your label (see Figure 6.20). And, you can print a single label directly to the printer or create a new document that contains a full sheet of labels. The option buttons in the Print box determine whether you print a single label or a full sheet of labels. The type of label to which you are printing determines whether you can select the row and column to which to print the single label; typically, laser printer label sheets contain either two or three columns of labels.

> **Tip**
>
> You can print a label to an address stored in either your Microsoft Exchange or Outlook address book. Click on the Address button near the top of the dialog box to open your address book and select an addressee.

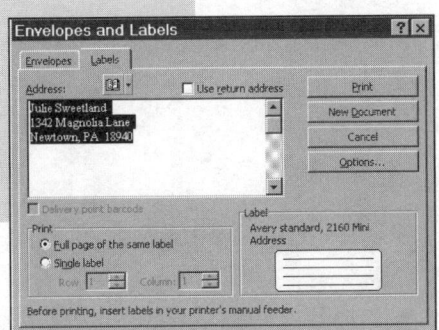

Figure 6.20
Use the Labels tab of the dialog box to print a single label or full sheet of the same label.

PART I • CREATING BASIC DOCUMENTS

To specify the type of label you are using, click on the Options button or on graphic that appears in the Label box and Word will display the Label Options dialog box (see Figure 6.21).

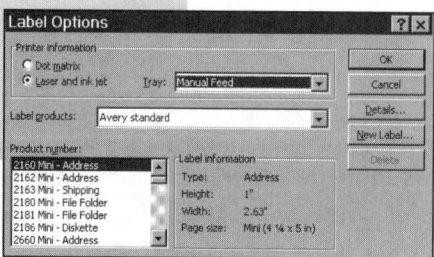

Figure 6.21
In this dialog box, specify the type of label you want to use.

Make sure that you select the correct type of printer—dot matrix or laser—at the top of the dialog box. Use the Label Products list box to select the manufacturer of your labels; Word supports hundreds of standard Avery and MACO labels. Find the product number in the list box at the bottom of the dialog box. When you finish, click on OK to redisplay the Envelopes and Labels dialog box. To print labels, choose Print. If you choose to create a new document containing labels, you can print those labels the same way you would print any document.

microsoft
WORD

PART II
Getting Visual

7 GETTING VISUAL WITH A NEWSLETTER 145
8 CRUNCHING NUMBERS IN A BUSINESS REPORT 179
9 USING MAIL MERGE WITH A SALES LETTER. 221

micros
WORD

7

Getting Visual with a Newsletter

IN THIS CHAPTER

- Newsletter Basics
- Creating a Banner
- Creating a Newsletter Using Text Boxes
- Creating a Newsletter Using Columns
- Adding Images to a Newsletter

Putting together a newsletter in Word will let you learn about several important features. Initially, we take a look at the Newsletter wizard. Then, we put together a newsletter without using the wizard; this way, you can learn how to work in newspaper-style columns and modify these columns to suit your needs. You'll also learn how to include various kinds of pictures in Word documents. We cover a new feature in Word 97, too—the text box. As you work through this chapter, feel free to save your newsletter document at any time.

Doing Things the Easy Way...

If you need to put together a newsletter and you don't have much time to spend on the project, the Newsletter wizard is for you. The wizard lets you choose from three different styles for your newsletter, and when the wizard completes, you have a five-page, three-column newsletter. You need to select and replace only the placeholder text that the wizard supplies.

Hands On: Running the Newsletter Wizard

To use the Newsletter Wizard, follow these steps:

1. Choose File, New.
2. Click on the Publications tab and select the Newsletter Wizard.
3. Click on OK. Word displays the first dialog box of the Newsletter Wizard (see Figure 7.1).

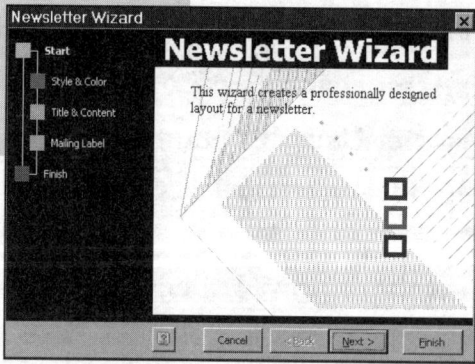

Figure 7.1
The opening dialog box for the Newsletter Wizard.

4. Click on Next to begin designing your newsletter. Word displays the Style and Content screen in the Newsletter Wizard (see Figure 7.2). For our sample newsletter, we chose the Elegant style and Black and White for the color.

CHAPTER 7 • GETTING VISUAL WITH A NEWSLETTER **147**

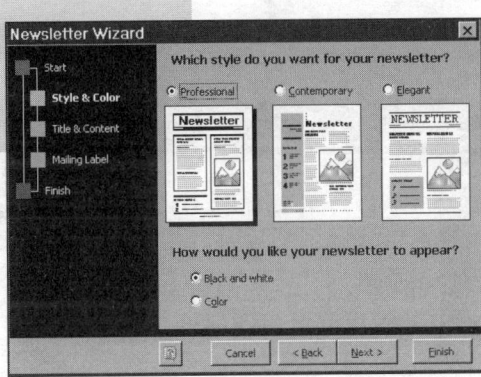

Figure 7.2
Select the style and color for your newsletter.

5. Click on <u>N</u>ext to continue designing your newsletter. Word displays the Title and Color screen of the Newsletter wizard (see Figure 7.3). We left the title as "Newsletter" and included the date, volume, and issue number.

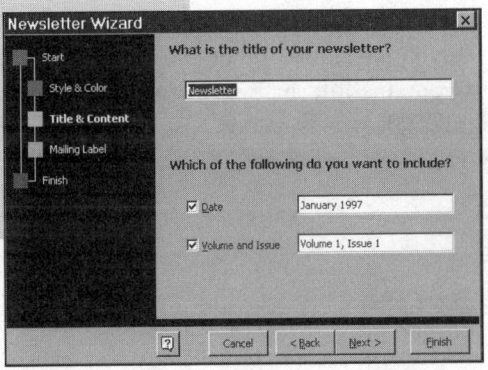

Figure 7.3
Provide a title and decide whether you want to print an issue date, and volume and issue numbers.

6. Click on <u>N</u>ext to specify whether you want to include an area for a mailing label on your newsletter. We chose to include a mailing label area.
7. Click on <u>N</u>ext to move to the last screen of the Newsletter Wizard, where you find that you have answered all the questions.
8. Click on <u>F</u>inish. After a brief delay, Word displays a skeleton for a newsletter on-screen. Figure 7.4 shows this screen in preview mode. You may also see the Office Assistant volunteering help.

Figure 7.4
A preview of Page 1 of the Newsletter in the Elegant style.

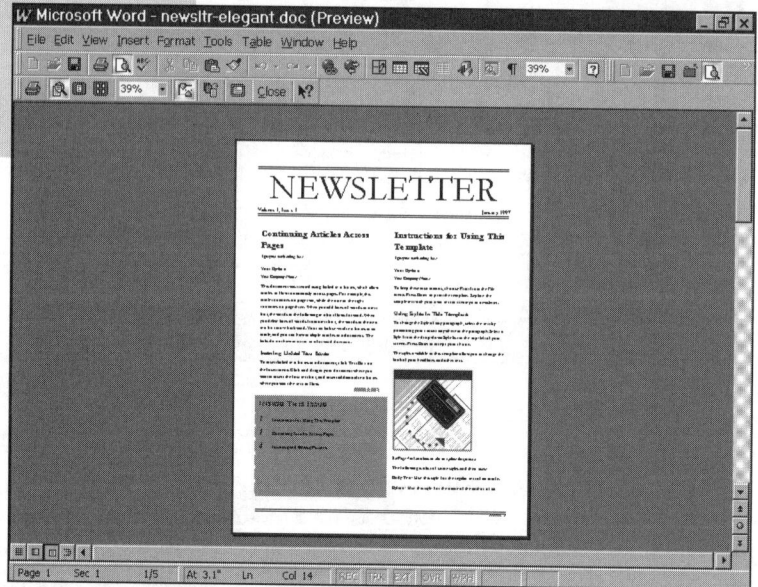

Using this skeleton, you select text and graphics and replace them with your own. The skeleton also contains information on using the elements included in the newsletter. In Figure 7.5, you see Page 1 of the Newsletter in the Professional style; and in Figure 7.6, you see Page 1 of the Newsletter in the Contemporary style.

Newsletter Basics

Although the Newsletter Wizard is a quick way to create a newsletter, it doesn't leave you with a lot of control. For example, what if you want to create a two-column newsletter? Or, what if you want most pages to contain three columns but one page would work best if it contained only two columns? As you move through the rest of this chapter, you'll learn how to create a newsletter from scratch. But before diving into the mechanics, we need to review some of the basic "desktop publishing" concepts that help make a good newsletter:

- Typically, the number of columns in your newsletter should remain consistent; you can, however, occasionally change the layout either because an article would work better in a different layout or to add visual interest. Do not use more than three columns on any page in a newsletter, however.

CHAPTER 7 • GETTING VISUAL WITH A NEWSLETTER 149

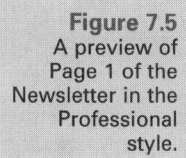

Figure 7.5
A preview of Page 1 of the Newsletter in the Professional style.

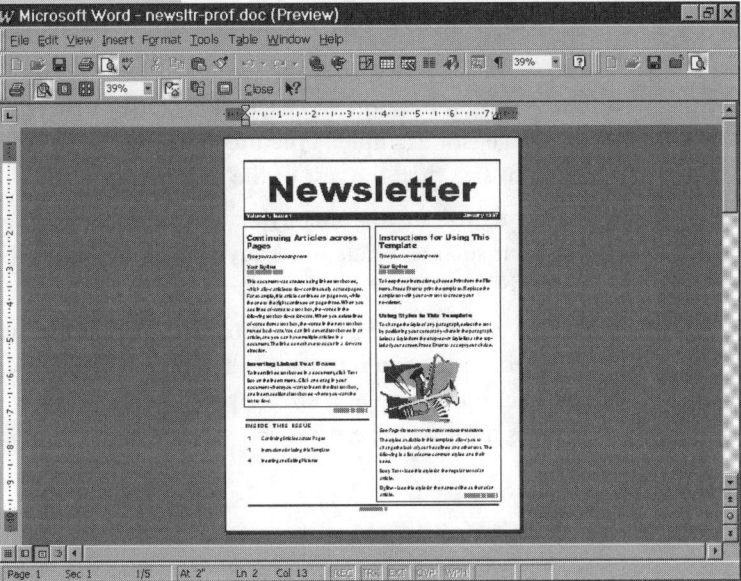

Figure 7.6
A preview of Page 1 of the Newsletter in the Contemporary style.

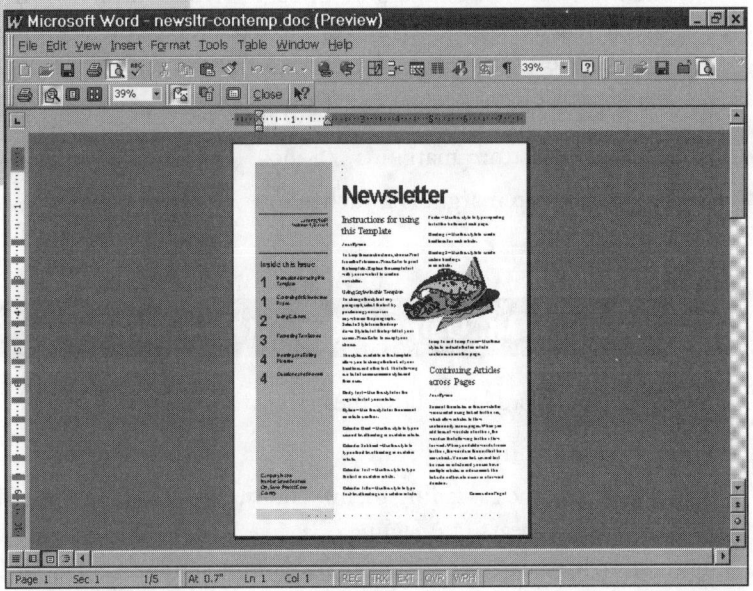

- Use a straight block style for paragraphs; don't indent the first line.
- Don't use justification; you'll create rivers of white space in your newsletter and make it more difficult to read.

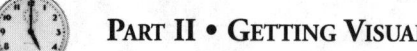

PART II • GETTING VISUAL

- Try not to overuse any one element; for example, if you draw lines between or around your columns, don't underline your headings.
- For variety, incorporate elements with different shading.
- Use graphics, but don't go overboard. One or two different visual elements on a page (for example, a picture and a text block shaded in gray or of a different size than the rest of the page) is sufficient.
- Don't mix too many fonts; typically, headlines should appear in a sans serif font such as Arial, and body text should appear in a serif font such as Times New Roman.
- A large part of achieving the visual effects that you want is trial and error, so expect to try and reject ideas before you settle on an appearance that you like. For example, if size or position aren't "right" the first time, make changes until you like what you see.

Creating a Banner

Start a new document by clicking on the New button on the Standard toolbar. Then, switch to Page Layout view, because many of the elements you use for a newsletter are accessible only in Page Layout view. We'll use WordArt and place the newsletter banner centered across the top of the document. Choose File, Page Setup, and click on the Margins tab. Set the document margins as follows:

- Left and right margins are .6 inch each
- The bottom margin is .75 inch
- The top margin is 2 inches

Hands On: Using WordArt for the Banner Text

To insert WordArt, follow these steps:

1. Choose Insert, Picture.
2. From the cascading menu, choose WordArt. The WordArt Gallery dialog box appears (see Figure 7.7).
3. Choose a style for your newsletter banner—we chose the style located on the second row, third from the left—and click on OK. Word displays the Edit WordArt Text dialog box (see Figure 7.8).

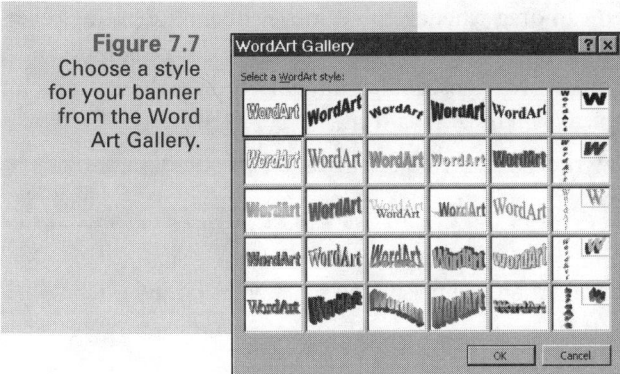

Figure 7.7 Choose a style for your banner from the Word Art Gallery.

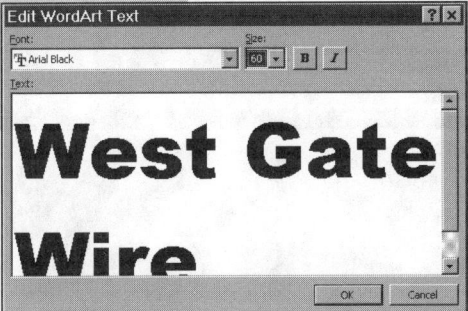

Figure 7.8 Type the text for the WordArt object.

4. Supply the text for the WordArt object and set a point size. Optionally, apply bold or italics. We typed the newsletter banner, **West Gate Wire**, and changed the point size to 54.

Note

> Because headlines look best in a sans serif font, be sure to select a font such as Arial or Arial Black.

5. Click on OK. Your WordArt object appears on-screen (see Figure 7.9).
6. We need to move the newsletter banner higher on the page. Because the object is already selected (you see white handles around it), use the mouse to drag the banner closer to the top of the page. You want to leave about a

PART II • GETTING VISUAL

3/4 inch margin. You can drag whenever you move the mouse pointer over the object and see a four-headed arrow. As you drag, you'll see a dotted outline representing the current position of the object; drop the object when the outline appears where you want it.

7. Click anywhere below the WordArt object to cancel its selection.

To better see the position of the banner on the page, click on the Print Preview button on the Standard toolbar. When you finish previewing, click on the Close button.

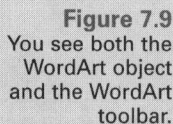

Figure 7.9
You see both the WordArt object and the WordArt toolbar.

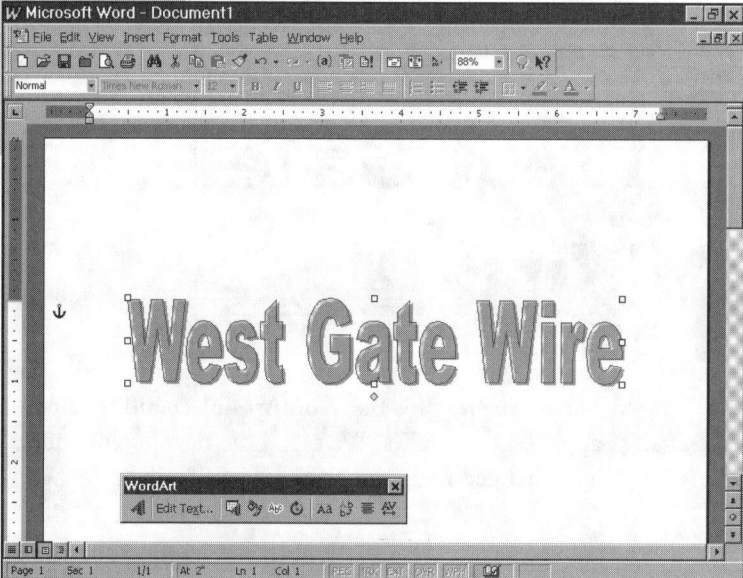

Hands On: Supplying the Volume and Issue Numbers

When we create the text information for the volume and issue numbers, we will also use Word's Border feature to provide a custom underline with a more elegant appearance than a typical underline. You can use borders (and shading) to provide special effects for any paragraph in any document. Later in this chapter, we use shading. To provide volume and issue numbers, follow these steps:

1. On the first line, at the left margin, set the font to the default font that you intend to use throughout the newsletter. Set the point size to an average point size. In the example, we chose Times New Roman 12 point.
2. Type the volume number and the issue number. We typed **Volume 4 Issue 6**.
3. To set a right-aligning tab, choose F*o*rmat T*a*bs to display the Tabs dialog box. Type **7.2** for the tab stop position, and set the alignment to *R*ight (see Figure 7.10).

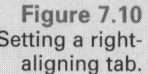
Figure 7.10
Setting a right-aligning tab.

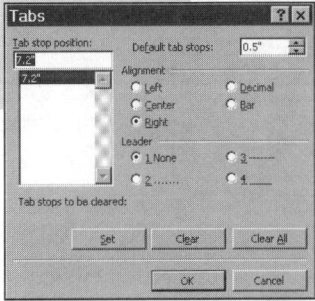

4. Click on OK and press the Tab key. Type the date for this issue of the newsletter (we typed **January, 1997**). Word will align the right edge of the date with the right tab that you set.
5. To set up a bottom border for the volume, issue, and date information, we actually place a top border on the line below the information. So, press Enter twice and then move the insertion point up one line.

The border that you're about to place will be attached to the first of the two paragraphs you just inserted. If you insert only one paragraph, Word will continue to attach the border to all subsequent paragraphs. You need one extra blank line below any paragraph to which to apply a border to ensure that the border applies *only* to that paragraph.

6. Choose F*o*rmat, *B*orders and Shading to display the Borders and Shading dialog box.
7. Choose the C*u*stom Setting and a line style that you want to appear underneath the volume, issue, and date information. We chose the ninth style in the St*y*le list.

PART II • GETTING VISUAL

8. On the Preview, you see borders on all sides. To remove the bottom and side borders, click on those borders or click on the buttons for the bottom and each side border (see Figure 7.11).

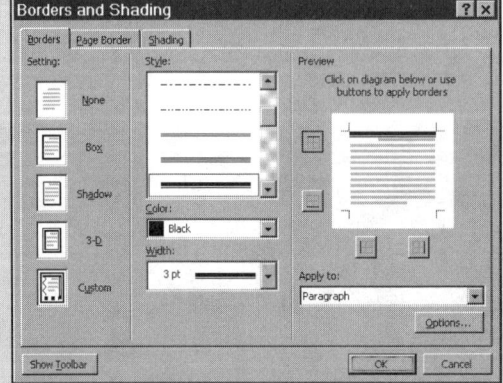

Figure 7.11
To set up a border for volume, issue, and date information, set up the Borders and Shading dialog box to place a top border on the line below the volume, issue, and date information.

9. Click on OK. The banner now contains the newsletter title as well as volume, issue, and date information (see Figure 7.12).

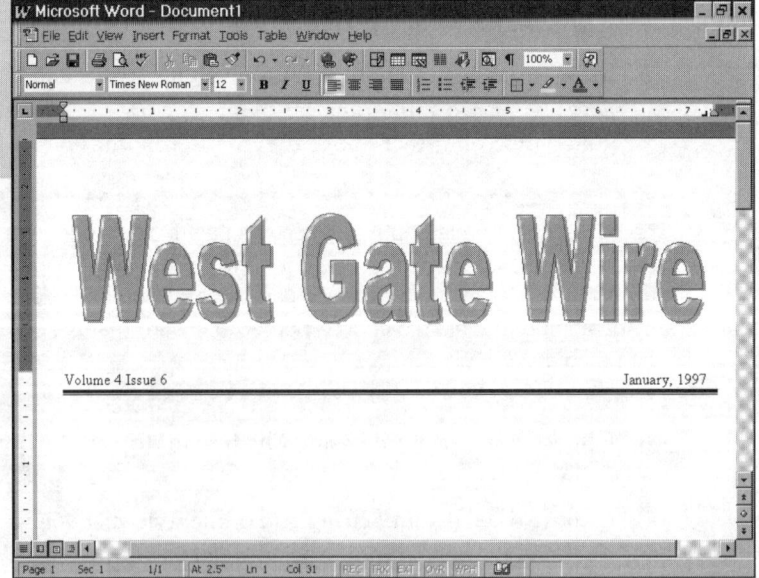

Figure 7.12
The top of the newsletter after adding volume, issue, and date information.

10. Insert a section break so that you can set separate margins for Page 1 and subsequent pages. Press the Down arrow once to move the insertion point down one line. Choose Insert, Break. In the Break dialog box, select Continuous from the Section breaks group and click on OK.

Each section can have its own set of margins. The top margin for Section 1 was 2 inches, but the top margin for Section 2 should be only 3/4 inch. Click in Section 2 (check the left edge of the status bar to make sure you're in Section 2), choose File, Page Setup, click on the Margin tab to change the top margin to .75 inch, and click on OK.

Creating a Newsletter Using Text Boxes

Most newsletters are formatted into two or three columns on a page. In Word, you have two ways to create a columnar layout, and the method that you choose depends on how you want the articles in your newsletter to flow. In a standard columnar flow, you type text down one column and then Word wraps to the top of the next column. We explore this method more later in the chapter.

Using text boxes, a new feature in Word 97, you can control the way articles flow in your newsletter. You can, for example, start more than one article on Page 1, and then have each article finish on some subsequent page of the newsletter. The text box, in most cases, replaces the frame in other versions of Word; by inserting text boxes and linking them, you can control the flow of text in your document.

Be aware that text box columns present some limitations. For example, you can include a graphic image inside a text box, but you cannot control the flow of text around the image. If your newsletter will rely heavily on graphics, you may prefer to use the standard columnar layout described later in this chapter.

Hands On: Creating a Text Box

To create a text box, follow these steps:

1. To make things easier, view nonprinting characters on-screen. Click on the Show/Hide button on the Toolbar or choose Tools, Options, and on the View tab in the Nonprinting Characters section, place a check in the All check box. Click on OK. Word displays tabs, paragraph marks, and spaces on-screen as well as optional hyphens and hidden text.
2. Press Enter once.
3. Choose Insert, Text Box. The mouse pointer changes to a crosshair.

If you display the Drawing toolbar, you'll find a button to insert a text box. To display the Drawing toolbar, click on the Drawing button that appears toward the right end of the Standard toolbar; it has geometric shapes on it.

4. Position the crosshair so that the intersection point appears where you want the upper-left corner of the text box to appear. We positioned the crosshair pointer at the upper-left corner of the last visible paragraph mark.
5. Drag down and to the right until the outline reaches the bottom margin of the page. Use the rulers to guide you while determining the right edge of the text box; make the text box approximately 2 inches wide.
6. Release the mouse button. Word inserts a text box (see Figure 7.13). If you scroll up, you'll see the insertion point.

If you don't get the text box sized exactly the way you want, place the insertion point in the column. Place the mouse pointer over a sizing handle—a small white box—on the edge of the text box. The mouse pointer changes to a two-headed arrow. Drag the handle to change the size of the text box. And, if you don't get the text box positioned exactly the way you want it, place the insertion point in the column. Place the mouse pointer over the outer edge of any portion of the text box. The mouse pointer changes to a four-headed arrow. Drag the text box to move it.

7. Click anywhere outside the text box and repeat Steps 3–6 for Column 2. Create a 2-inch wide text box that starts at the 2 1/2 inch mark on the horizontal ruler.

CHAPTER 7 • GETTING VISUAL WITH A NEWSLETTER   157

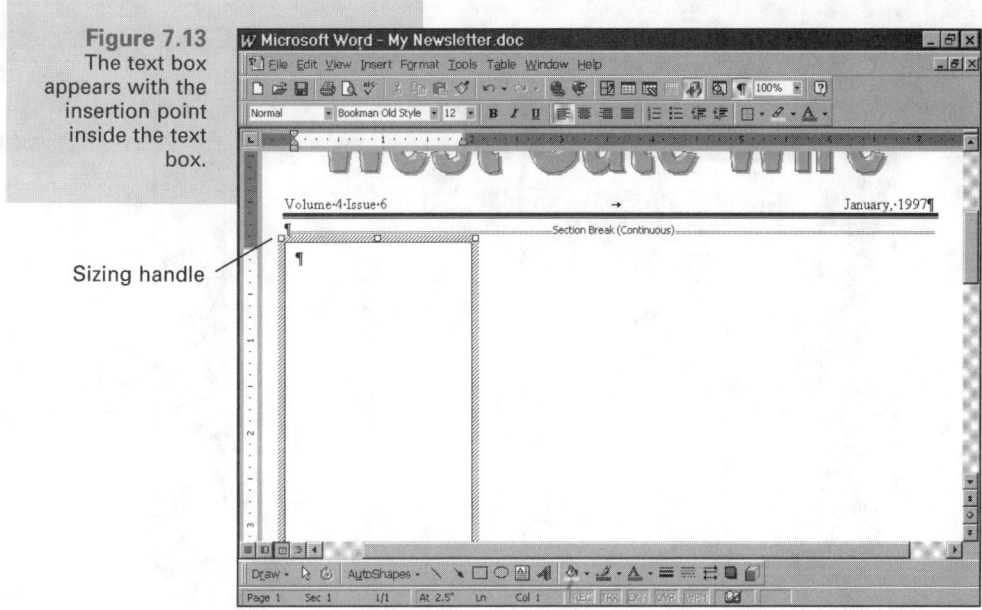

Figure 7.13
The text box appears with the insertion point inside the text box.

Sizing handle

8. For Column 3, insert two text boxes, each 2 inches wide. The first text box should fill approximately 2/3 of the column (we ended ours at the 4 1/2 inch mark on the vertical ruler). The second should fill the other 1/3 of the column.

9. Press Ctrl+End to move the insertion point to the end of the document.

10. Press Ctrl+Enter to insert a page break.

11. Repeat Steps 3–6 for each of the three columns on Page 2. When you finish, switch to Print Preview (use the button on the Standard toolbar or choose File, Print Preview). Your newsletter should look similar to the one in Figure 7.14.

Tip

In Step 2, you pressed Enter. The paragraph mark is useful if you need to insert text or graphics outside the text boxes. If you determine that you don't need these paragraph marks, you can delete them later.

PART II • GETTING VISUAL

Figure 7.14
The newsletter layout after inserting text boxes.

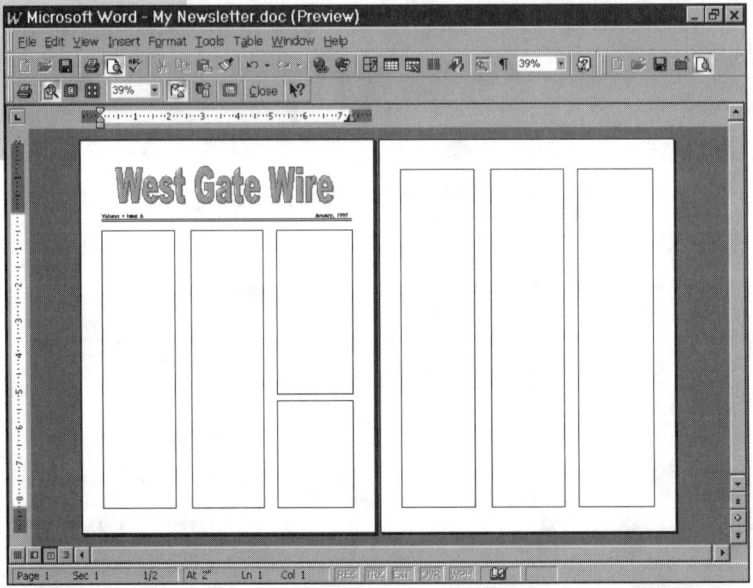

Hands On: Formatting a Text Box

As you just saw, text boxes appear surrounded by a border. You can change the appearance and behavior of text boxes.

1. Click anywhere inside the first text box to make sure that white handles and gray cross-hatching surround it.

2. Choose Format, Text Box. Word displays the Format Text Box dialog box. Click on the Colors and Lines tab.

3. Change the Fill Color to No Fill and the Line Color to No Line (see Figure 7.15).

4. Click on OK. On-screen, you may see a Page Break through the text box, and the border disappears. In Print Preview, the text box seems to disappear (see Figure 7.16).

5. Repeat this process for each text box except the smaller text box at the lower-right corner of Page 1.

Chapter 7 • Getting Visual with a Newsletter

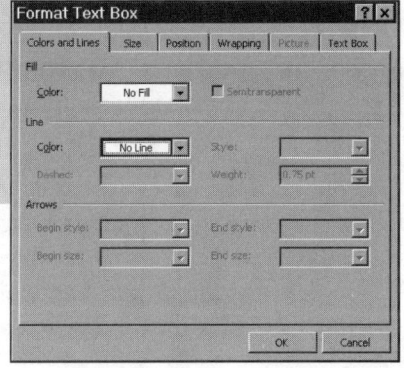

Figure 7.15
Remove the Fill Color and Line Color to effectively disguise the text boxes.

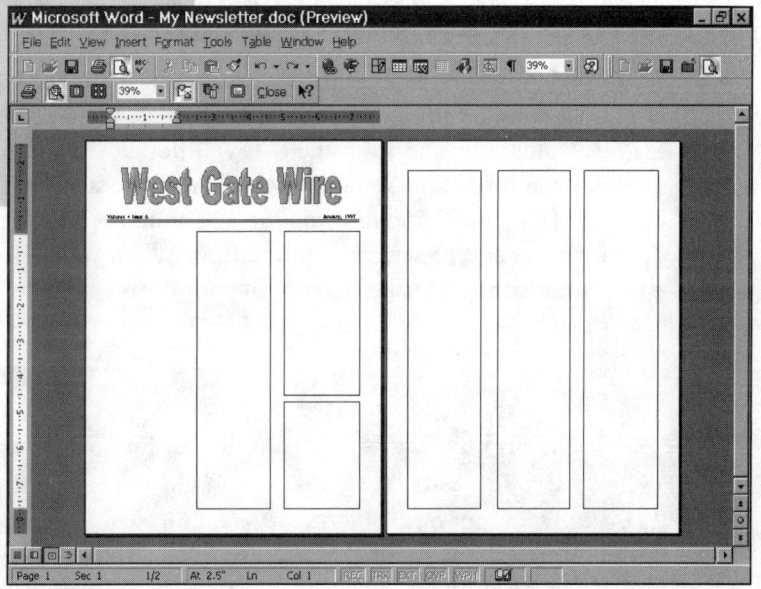

Figure 7.16
When you remove a text box's color and border, it seems to disappear in Print Preview.

You can quickly apply the same formatting to the text boxes by repeating your action. Click in a text box and then choose Edit, Repeat Format Drawing Object. Word will quickly apply the same formatting (removing the fill and line color) to the text box.

About Linking Text Boxes

To actually determine the flow of text in your document, you link text boxes. After text boxes are linked, you can type the text. As you type, Word will fill the first text box in the link. When the text box is full, additional text will flow to the second text box in the link.

The direction of the link is important, because you can, if you want, link "backward"; that is, you can link an item on Page 2 to an item on Page 1. In this case, the text will start on Page 2 and flow to Page 1—not terribly logical, but text box links allow you to do this. So, when creating a link, start with the text box where you want text to begin, and link to the text box where you want text to flow.

• •

To create links, text boxes must be empty. Also, links are a one-to-one relationship; that is, you cannot link one text box to two other text boxes.

• •

In our example, we will have two articles. The first article, "Personal Safety: Crime Fighting Strategies," will start on Page 1, Column 1. It will continue on Page 2, Column 1, and from there, it will flow to Page 2, Column 2, and then Page 2, Column 3. Our second article, "Current Issues for West Gate," will start on Page 1, Column 2 and flow to Page 1, Column 3, where it will end. See Figure 7.17 for a visual representation of the flow. When you finish creating links, you will not notice any visual difference in your document.

If you create a newsletter on your own, you may not know, at the time you start, the amount of text and the flow you want. You can link text boxes and later change the links by unlinking and relinking. You will still want to start by creating text boxes and creating links. As you're about to see, you can type directly into the text box. Or, if you have already typed the information in another document, you can open that document, select and copy the text, switch to your newsletter, click in a text box, and paste the text. If you have *not* linked text boxes and the text extends beyond the size of the box, you won't be able to see all the text.

Chapter 7 • Getting Visual with a Newsletter 161

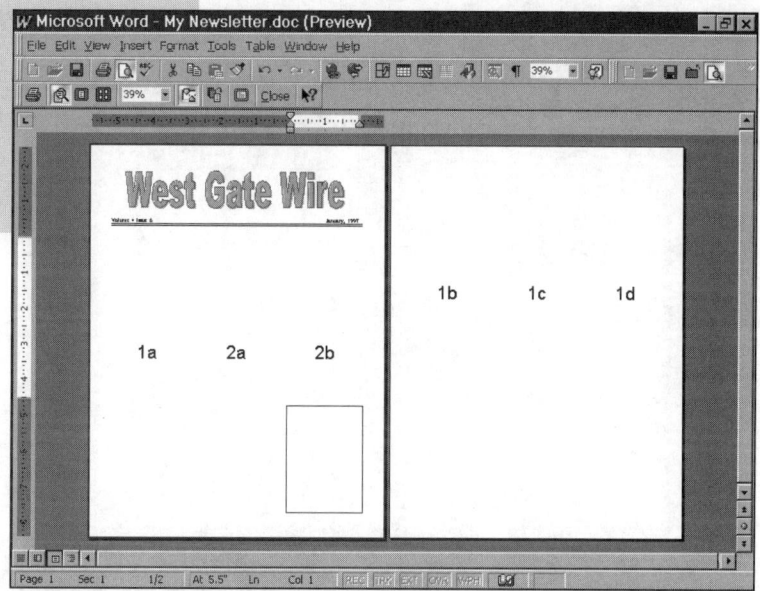

Figure 7.17
The numbers refer to the first or second article, whereas the letters provide the flow for that article.

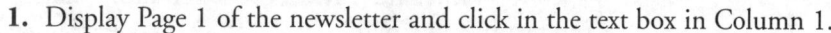

Hands On: Linking Text Boxes

To link text boxes, follow these steps.

1. Display Page 1 of the newsletter and click in the text box in Column 1.

Tip

If the Text Box toolbar already appears on-screen, skip step 2.

2. Choose View, Toolbars, and choose Text Box from the cascading menu that appears. Word displays the Text Box toolbar.
3. Click on the Create Text Box Link button on the Text Box toolbar.
4. Scroll until you see Page 2, Column 1—the column to which you want text to flow from Page 1, Column 1.
5. Slide the mouse pointer over Page 2, Column 1. The pointer changes to the shape of a pitcher pouring (see Figure 7.18).
6. Click anywhere in Column 1 on Page 2 to create the link.
7. Click on the Next Text Box button on the Text Box toolbar and Word will select the text box to which you created the link.

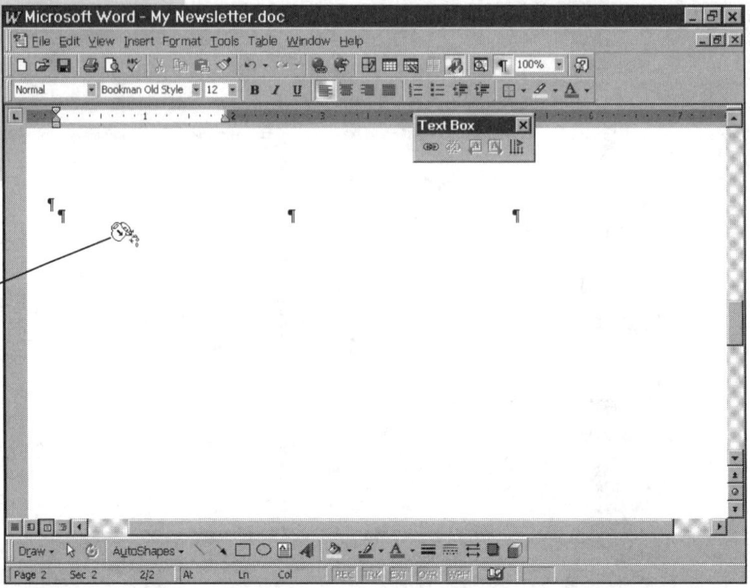

Figure 7.18
While creating a link, the mouse pointer changes to the shape of a pitcher.

Mouse pointer

8. Repeat steps 4–7 to link the text boxes for the first article. Follow the links listed in Table 7.1.
9. To link the two text boxes for the second article, click in Page 1, Column 2, click on the Create Text Box Link button, slide the mouse over to the top text box in Column 3 on Page 1, and click to create the link.
10. Close the Text Box toolbar by clicking on the X in the upper-right corner.

Table 7.1. Link Sample Newsletter Columns

Link this column	To this column
Page 2, Column 1	Page 2, Column 2
Page 2, Column 2	Page 2, Column 3
Page 1, Column 2	Page 1, top column in Column 3

Typing in Text Boxes

Start with an article title, and use a sans serif font such as Arial 16 point. Add boldface to the title. Your by-line should follow on the next line; use a serif font such as Times New Roman 10 point and add italics to your by-line. Type your article in a serif font such as Times New Roman 12 point. Click in the text box on Page 1, Column 1, and title the first article, **Personal Safety: Crime Fighting Strategies**, formatting the text as you work. Add your by-line if you want. Then, click in the text box on Page 1, Column 2, and title the second article **Current Issues for West Gate**. Again, format the text and add your by-line.

To see how text flow works with linked text boxes, you don't need to type any special text. So, we'll keep this simple. As the first sentence of the first article, type **This text is part of the first article.** Then, copy the sentence until you fill up Page 1 and the three columns on Page 2. We periodically created a paragraph by double-spacing, and periodically copied larger groups of sentences to make the process go faster.

For the second article, repeat this process using the sentence **This text appears in the second article.** This way, when the text flow created by the linked text boxes takes over, you'll be able to distinguish article 1 from article 2.

If you need to fill a space with sample text, you can type **=Rand()** and press Enter. Word will insert "The quick brown fox jumps over the lazy dog." You see three paragraphs and each will contain this sentence four times. This feature works only if you place a check in the Replace Text As You Type check box. Choose Tools, AutoCorrect, and click on the AutoCorrect tab.

In Figure 7.19, you see the article titles and the text flow of the newsletter. For ease of reading, We've temporarily turned off the display of nonprinting characters.

Formatting the Table of Contents Box

> **REFER TO CHAPTER 17 FOR MORE INFORMATION ON CREATING A TABLE OF CONTENTS.**

Most newsletters contain a small box on the front page that shows the articles in the newsletter and their page number. Sometimes, if the newsletter contains a large number of articles, the design might devote an entire column to the table of contents.

You can use Word's table of contents feature to insert fields that mark table of contents entries in your newsletter; in this chapter, we don't focus on that aspect of a table of contents. Instead, we format the box containing the table of contents entries to enhance its visual appeal.

Figure 7.19
Using linked text boxes, you can control the flow of text.

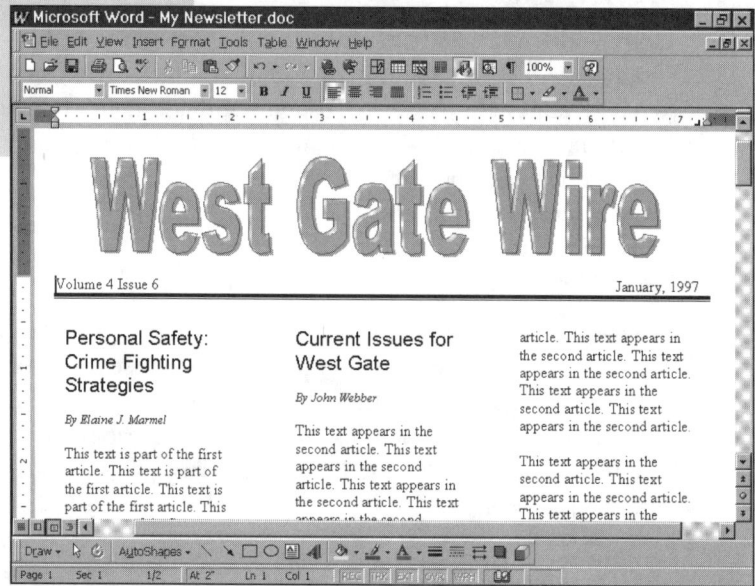

Hands On: Formatting the Newsletter's Table of Contents

1. Type the titles of three articles: **Personal Safety: Crime-Fighting Strategies**, **Current Issues for West Gate**, and **You'll Never Go Wrong with a Song** in Arial 12 point bold. We pressed (Enter) twice before the first title and between each title and (Tab) to include page numbers; the first two articles start on Page 1, and the last article starts on Page 3. Your spacing may not look exactly like the figure; just make the box attractive to your eye.

Note

You will be creating the third article later in this chapter.

2. Choose Format, Text Box. Word displays the Format Text Box dialog box.
3. Click on the Colors and Lines tab.
4. Set the Fill Color to Gray-25 percent (see Figure 7.20).

CHAPTER 7 • GETTING VISUAL WITH A NEWSLETTER **165**

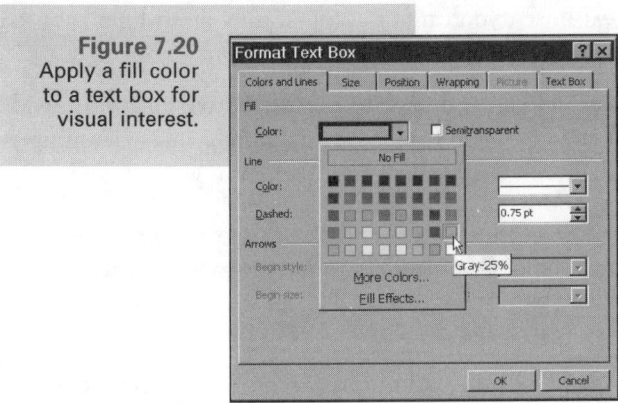

Figure 7.20
Apply a fill color to a text box for visual interest.

5. Click on OK. In Print Preview, your newsletter will look similar to the one in Figure 7.21.

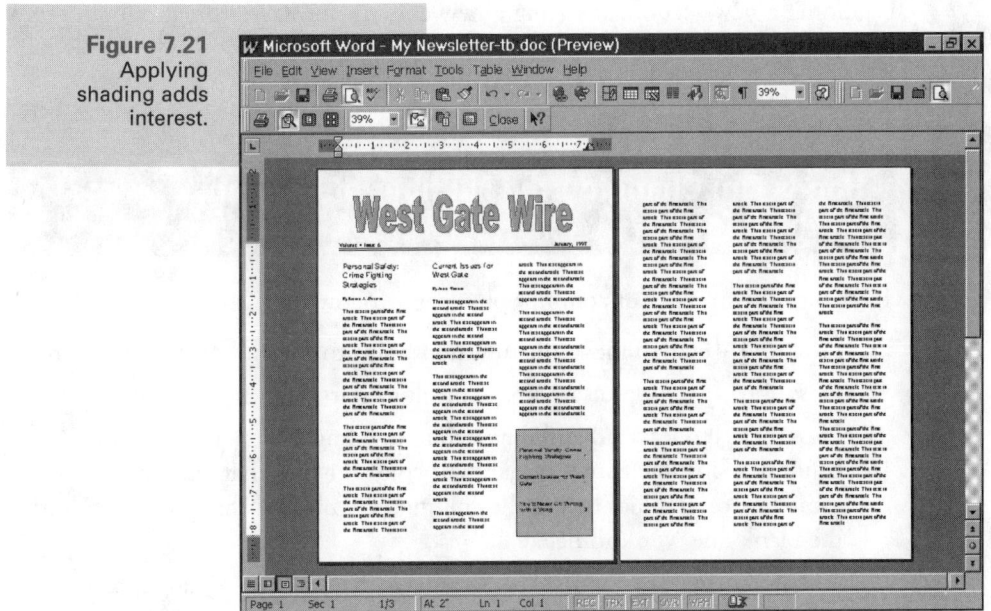

Figure 7.21
Applying shading adds interest.

Creating a Newsletter Using Columns

A Word document, by default, begins as a one-column document. So far, our newsletter is a one-column newsletter, and we've used text boxes to create the look of columns. The text box layout has some limitations, however: you cannot wrap

Part II • Getting Visual

text around graphics in text boxes, you cannot automatically insert lines between columns, and you cannot balance uneven columns of text.

To address these issues, we'll add a third page to our newsletter, and we'll divide it into three columns. When you switch from a one-column layout to a multiple-column layout, Word will automatically add a new section to your document.

•••
Text boxes and columns are not mutually exclusive; in fact, an excellent use of a text box is to create a sidebar that crosses over two columns of a three-column layout.
•••

As you saw earlier in the chapter, sections are simply parts of the document, and each section can have its own set of page formatting. In our example, Section 1 is only one column but it has a top margin of 2 inches. Section 2 is still one column, but it has a top margin of 3/4 inch. Section 3 will retain the 3/4 inch top margin, but it will contain three columns.

Sections can run continuously, or you can tell Word to insert a page break before beginning a new section. Inserting a new column format automatically inserts a continuous page break.

FOR MORE INFORMATION ON FORMATTING PAGES, SEE CHAPTER 9.

Hands On: Changing the Number of Columns on the Page

To change the number of columns on a page, follow these steps:

1. Press Ctrl+End to move the insertion point to the end of the document.
2. Press Ctrl+Enter to insert a page break to start Page 3.
3. Press Enter to leave a blank line before dividing the document into columns. This line comes in handy if you later find that you need to add some text or graphics before the columns; if you find that you don't need the blank line, you can delete it.
4. Choose Format, Columns. Word displays the Columns dialog box.
5. Choose the Number of Columns—we chose 3—and open the Apply To list box; then, choose This Point Forward (see Figure 7.22).
6. Click on OK to close the dialog box and apply your choices (see Figure 7.23).

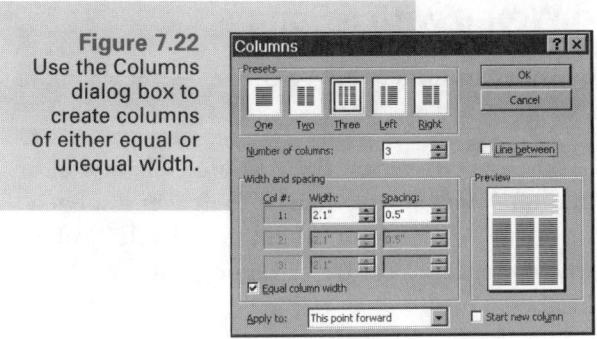

Figure 7.22
Use the Columns dialog box to create columns of either equal or unequal width.

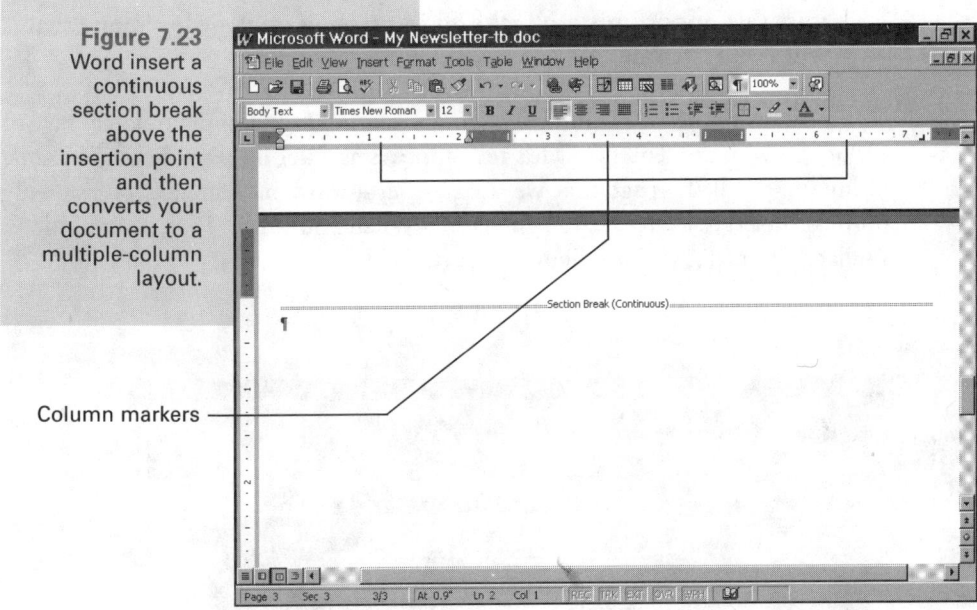

Figure 7.23
Word insert a continuous section break above the insertion point and then converts your document to a multiple-column layout.

Column markers

You add text to a columnar layout the same way that you add text in a text box layout or in any Word document. Just type. As you fill one column, Word will automatically wrap to the top of the next column.

We'll fill up part of Page 3 with a small article about singing valentines. Copy the text that you see in bold following this paragraph. We used Arial Bold, 16 point for the headline and Times New Roman, 12 point for the rest of the text.

PART II • GETTING VISUAL

You'll Never Go Wrong with a Song

This year, become someone's unforgettable Valentine—send a song to your special someone.

The Toast of Tampa Show Chorus, a past International Champion of Sweet Adelines International, will send a quartet to deliver a song, a card, and a box of chocolates, all for $50. Valentine deliveries will be taking place on Thursday evening, February 13, and all day on Friday, February 14.

To arrange for a singing Valentine to be delivered, contact June at 923-0849. Don't delay, because quartet availability is limited. Don't miss this opportunity to make an impression on your loved one that will last a lifetime.

Then, fill up the rest of Column 1, all of Column 2, and approximately half of Column 3 with the sentence, **This text appears as filler on page 3.** Use the same technique to fill the page that we used earlier—copy the sentence, occasionally pressing Enter twice to create paragraphs. When you finish, Page 3 should look similar in Print Preview to Figure 7.24.

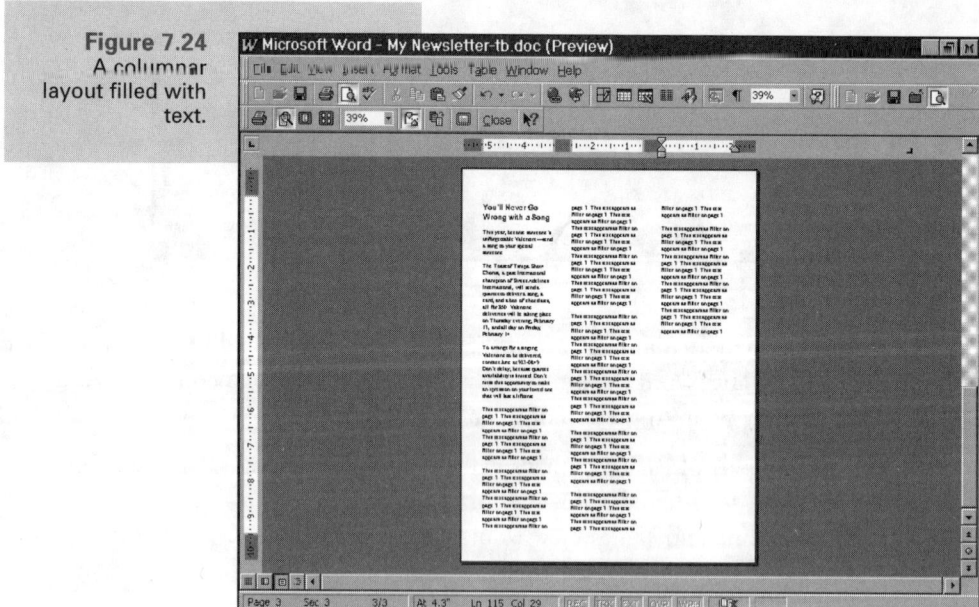

Figure 7.24
A columnar layout filled with text.

Inserting a Vertical Line Between Columns

To create visual interest, you can easily insert a vertical line between the columns of a columnar layout.

1. Place the insertion point anywhere in the section where you want a vertical line to appear between columns.
2. Choose Format, Columns.
3. In the Columns dialog box, click on the Line Between check box (see Figure 7.25).

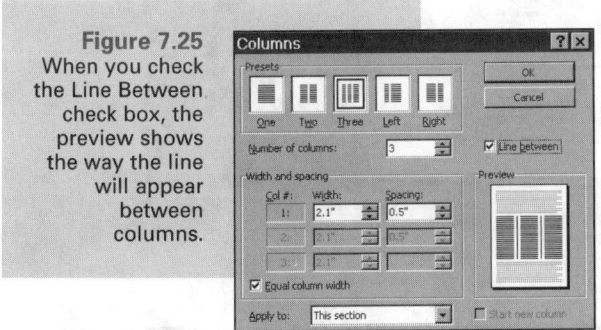

Figure 7.25
When you check the Line Between check box, the preview shows the way the line will appear between columns.

4. Click on OK. A vertical line appears between each column of the newsletter (see Figure 7.26).

Balancing Text Between Columns

In a column layout, on pages where text fills the page, Word automatically balances the text at the bottom of each column by lining up the last lines of each column. On pages where text doesn't fill the page, such as Page 3 in our newsletter, you might want to balance the text yourself so that all three columns on Page 3 end at the same approximate position on the vertical page. Use the Insert, Break command to insert a continuous section break at the end of the last column on the page where you want to balance text. Word resets the text on the page so that all columns contain the same amount of text (see Figure 7.27).

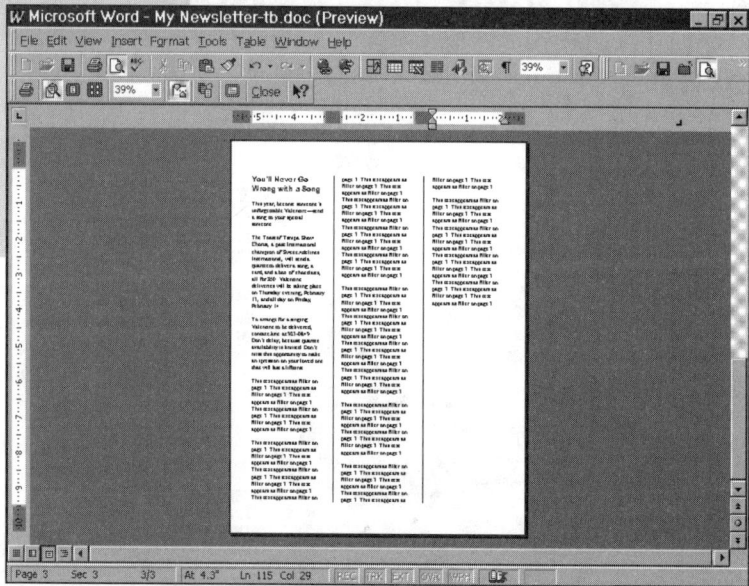

Figure 7.26
If you don't have a lot of other visual interest items, use vertical lines to enhance the visual appeal of your newsletter.

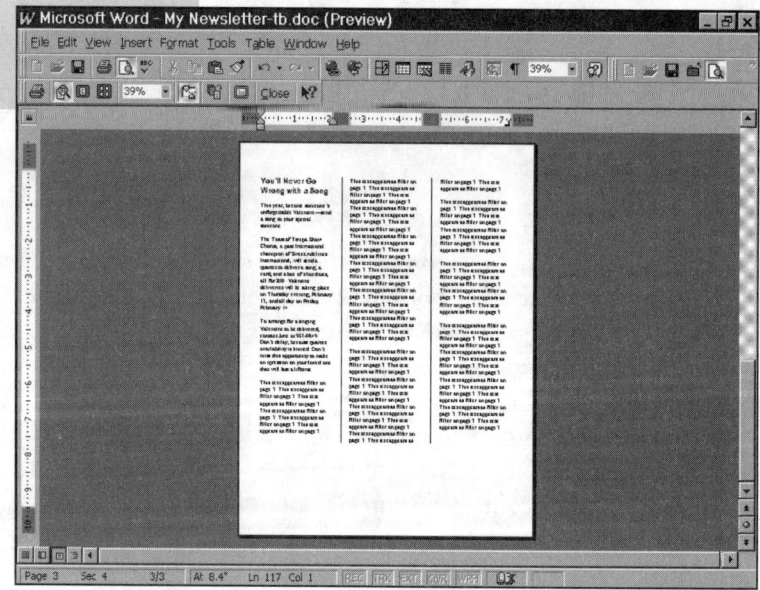

Figure 7.27
Balanced columns of text.

Adding Images to a Newsletter

Remember the old adage, "A picture is worth a thousand words"? It's particularly true in a newsletter. Pictures add visual interest and spice up what could otherwise be a boring layout.

In Word, you can add several different kinds of images to a document. You can use clip art, pictures, videos, AutoShapes, or you can draw freehand. In our scenario, a video would not be practical, but you add videos to documents the same way that you add pictures or clip art.

One important fact to remember: you can add images inside text boxes, but you cannot control the wrapping of the text in a text box. Therefore, if you plan to add images inside a text box, try to make them fill the column from side to side so that the lack of text wrapping is not so apparent. In this section, we focus on working with images in a columnar layout, where you have more control.

Working with Clip Art

A clip art image is an image that somebody else drew and saved in a computer file in one of several common formats. You insert clip art into a Word document usually to add visual interest or to enhance a story. You can buy clip art or you can download it from a variety of sources on any of the online services, the Internet, or private electronic bulletin boards. When you installed Word, some clip art was also installed; you'll find additional clip art on the CD that you used to install Word. To access all the clip art that came with Word, place your installation CD into your CD-ROM drive.

Note

If you did not purchase Word on a CD-ROM, additional clip art is not available.

Hands On: Adding a Clip Art Image

To insert a clip art image, follow these steps:

1. Place the insertion point at the location in your document where you want to insert a clip art image. In our example, add two more blank lines after

the first paragraph in the article about singing valentines and place the insertion point on the middle blank line.

2. (Optional) If you want to view the additional clip art available on the CD, insert the CD-ROM from which you installed Word.

3. Choose Insert, Picture. From the cascading menu, choose Clip Art. Word displays the Microsoft Clip Gallery 3.0 dialog box.

4. To find a particular category of image, use the list box on the left side of the dialog box. To find the image that we want to insert, choose Special Occasions. Then scroll down until you find the heart with wings (see Figure 7.28).

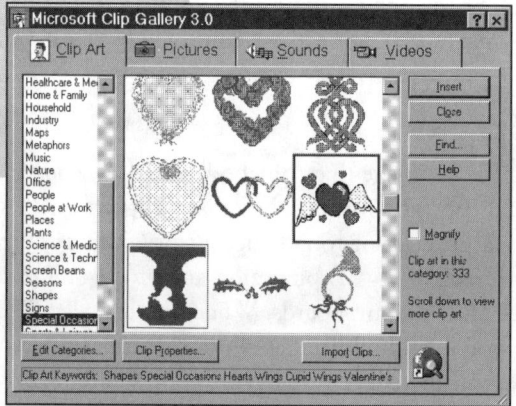

Figure 7.28
Images are organized by type and category in this dialog box.

5. Click on Insert. Word inserts the image in the document at the insertion point (see Figure 7.29).

Hands On: Moving and Sizing a Clip Art Image

To move or change the size of a clip art image, follow these steps:

1. In Page Layout view, click on the picture. Word places handles around the picture and displays the Picture toolbar.

2. Place the mouse pointer over the center of the picture and drag the picture to a new location. In the example, drag the heart to the middle of the second paragraph of the article.

CHAPTER 7 • GETTING VISUAL WITH A NEWSLETTER **173**

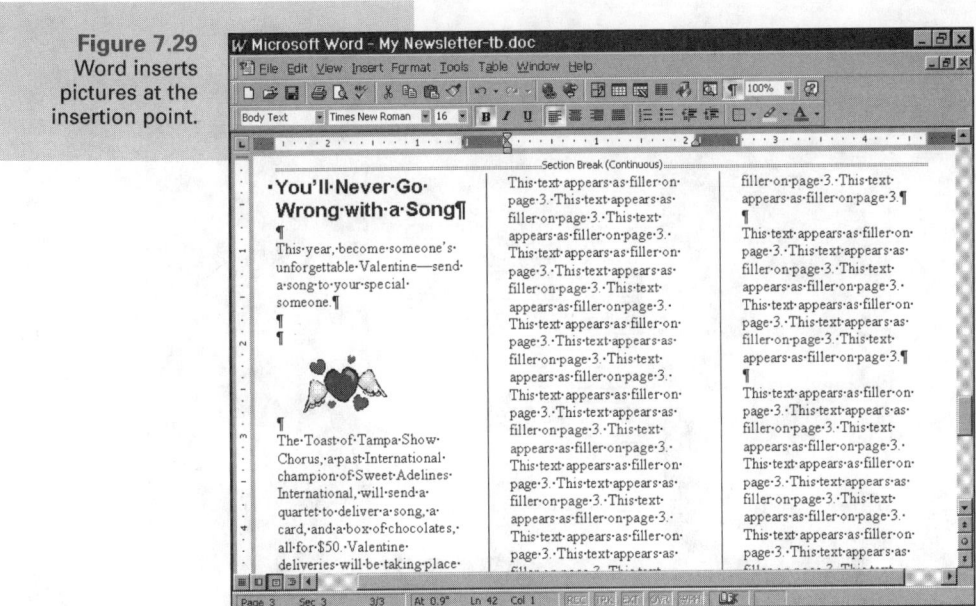

Figure 7.29 Word inserts pictures at the insertion point.

3. To change an image's size, place the mouse pointer over a handle until the point changes to a two-headed arrow. Then, drag the handle. To maintain scale, drag a corner. In our example, make the picture smaller (see Figure 7.30).

Drawing in Word

Using the Drawing toolbar, you can draw to add images to your documents. We know our limitations, so you won't be seeing any freehand drawings in this section. You will learn, however, to add an AutoShape. AutoShapes are a series of typical shapes that you might find of interest to use, such as stars or banners. Whether you draw freehand or insert an AutoShape, you also can apply shadows or three-dimensional effects to them. And, you can control the size, appearance, and style of lines and arrows as well as the line and fill color of all shapes.

Hands On: Using AutoShapes

To insert an AutoShape, follow these steps:

1. Make sure that the Drawing toolbar appears at the bottom of your screen. If it doesn't, click on the Drawing button on the Standard toolbar.

 PART II • GETTING VISUAL

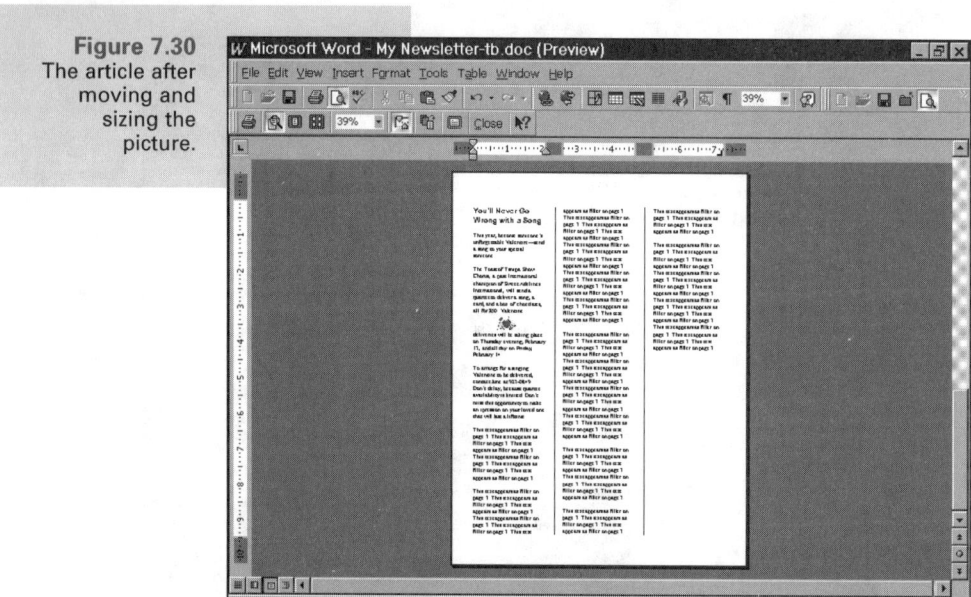

Figure 7.30
The article after moving and sizing the picture.

2. Click on the AutoShapes button on the Drawing toolbar. Word displays a pop-up list of the categories of AutoShapes available (see Figure 7.31).

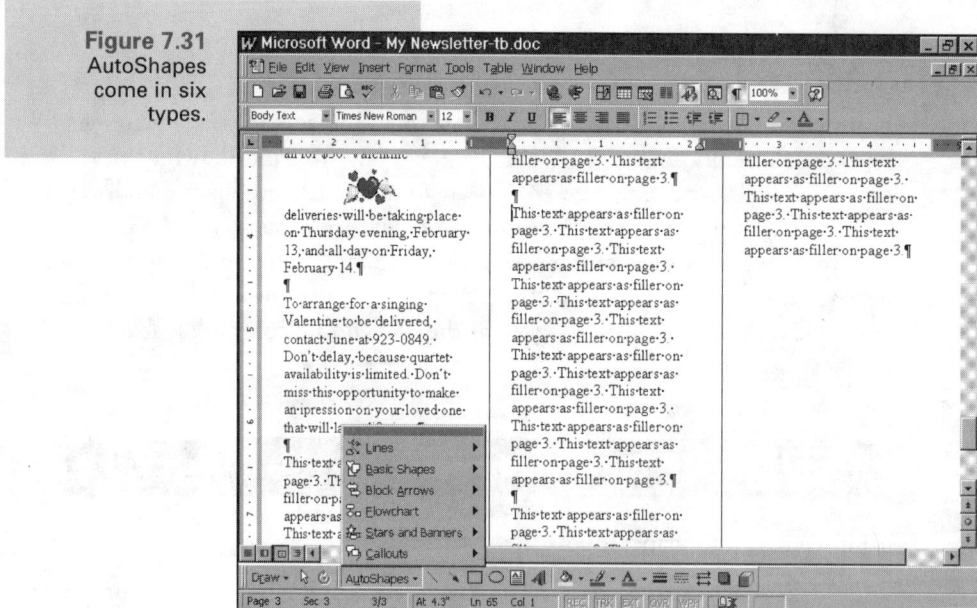

Figure 7.31
AutoShapes come in six types.

Chapter 7 • Getting Visual with a Newsletter

3. Highlight the type of AutoShape that you want to draw and choose an AutoShape. In the example, we highlighted Stars and Banners and chose the star in the upper-left corner of the palette—it's called Explosion.
4. Slide the mouse pointer to the location where you want the upper-left corner of the AutoShape to appear. The mouse pointer changes to a crosshair.
5. Drag down and to the right (we drew our AutoShape in the second column on Page 3). When you release the mouse button, you'll see an AutoShape (see Figure 7.32).

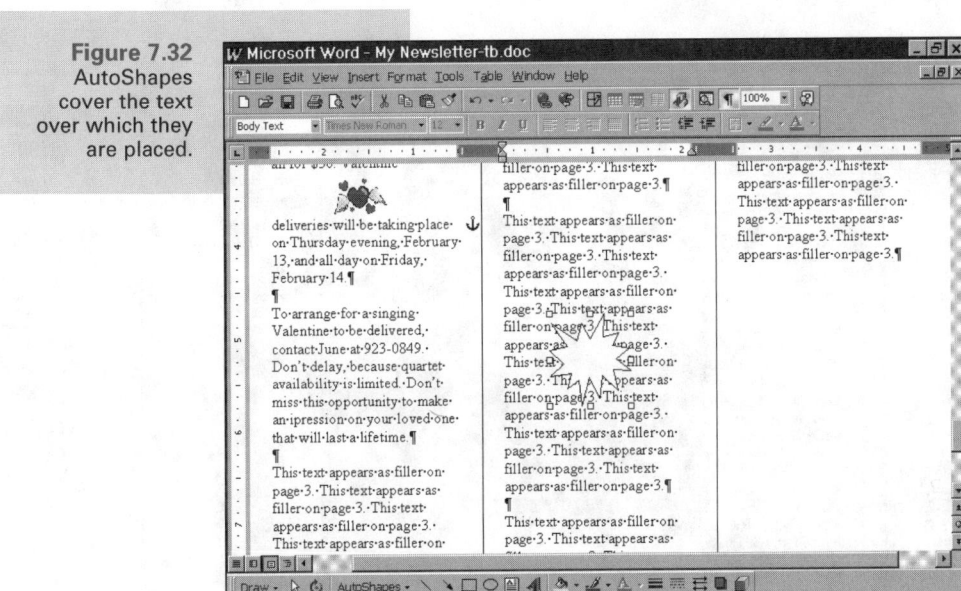

Figure 7.32 AutoShapes cover the text over which they are placed.

Drawing Freehand

As we said, we know our limitations. To draw freehand, use the Freehand drawing button on the Drawing toolbar. You'll find this button by clicking on the AutoShapes button, highlighting Lines, and choosing the button in the lower-right corner of the palette.

Tip

To delete any clip art image or AutoShape you have inserted, click on the object once to select it (handles appear around it). Then, press the Del key on your keyboard.

PART II • GETTING VISUAL

Hands On: Controlling Wrapping

As you just saw, text in a columnar layout wraps around pictures but is hidden by AutoShapes. You can control the way word wrapping behaves.

1. Click on the picture we inserted earlier.
2. Choose Format, Picture. Word displays the Format Picture dialog box.
3. Click on the Wrapping tab (see Figure 7.33). In Table 7.2, you'll find the meaning of the Wrapping Styles listed in the Format Picture dialog box. These wrapping styles are used for text boxes as well as pictures.

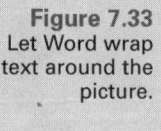

Figure 7.33
Let Word wrap text around the picture.

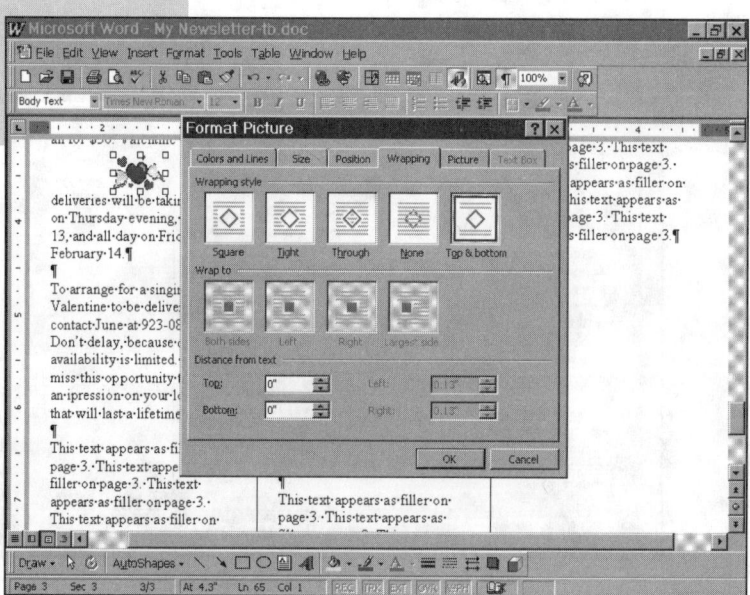

4. Choose Tight and then click on OK to see the results of wrapping (see Figure 7.34).

Chapter 7 • Getting Visual with a Newsletter 177

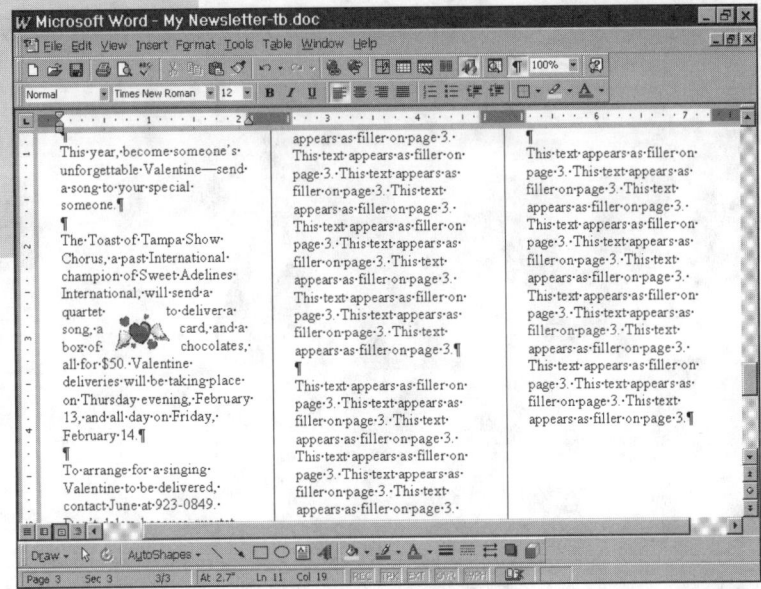

Figure 7.34
When you change the wrapping attributes to Tight, words wrap tightly around the picture.

Table 7.2. Wrapping Styles

Wrapping Style	Meaning
None	The object or text box hides any text or objects positioned underneath it
Square	Wraps text around all sides of the object or text box
Tight	Wraps text tightly around an object rather than the bounding box of an object
Through	Same as Tight, but wraps inside any parts of the object that are clear
Top and Bottom	Wraps text around the top and bottom of the object or text box, but not around the sides

micros
WORD

8

Crunching Numbers in a Business Report

In This Chapter

- Inserting Tables
- Drawing Complex Tables
- Formatting Tables
- Sorting Table Information
- Working with Charts
- Connecting to an Excel Worksheet

Good business reports include tables and charts as well as text. Tables help provide information that can be analyzed, and charts provide visual representations of numbers that can often make the old adage that a picture can be worth a thousand words true.

In this chapter, we build a simple business report (see figure on facing page) that includes text, tables, and a chart. Because Word provides a few different ways to place charts in documents, we include more than one table. The chart in the report will be prepared from the data in one of the tables. At any time during the chapter, feel free to save your document. We call it Business Report.doc.

Inserting a Simple Table

Simple tables are easiest to insert using either the Table menu commands or the Insert Table button on the Standard toolbar. What do we mean by "simple table"? A simple table is one that has a "standard" shape, allowing you to easily identify the number of rows and columns.

Before we actually insert a table, we need to start the report. Type the text that you see in bold following this paragraph; you'll insert your first table below that text. Make sure that you center the report title and subtitle. We used Times Roman 16 point Bold for the title, Times Roman 14 point Italic for the subtitle, and Times Roman 12 point for the paragraph text. Press Enter twice when you finish the paragraph.

Sales Analysis Comparison
1995 and 1996

Each year, Whirl Wind Surfers compares sales for the past two years. Generally, 1996 has been a good year, one in which most states in both regions have exceeded 1995 sales. As expected, Florida has remained our leader, with New York coming in second. In Table 1, you'll find an overview that compares 1995 and 1996 sales by state.

Inserting a Table

When you insert a table, Word places the table at the location of the insertion point.

Hands On: Inserting a Simple Table

To insert a table, follow these steps:

1. Click on the Insert Table button on the Standard toolbar. Word displays a grid below the button.

Chapter 8 • Crunching Numbers in a Business Report

2. Drag through the grid until you have highlighted the number of boxes that most closely matches the size of the table that you want to create. In our example, we highlighted 4 rows by 3 columns (see Figure 8.1).

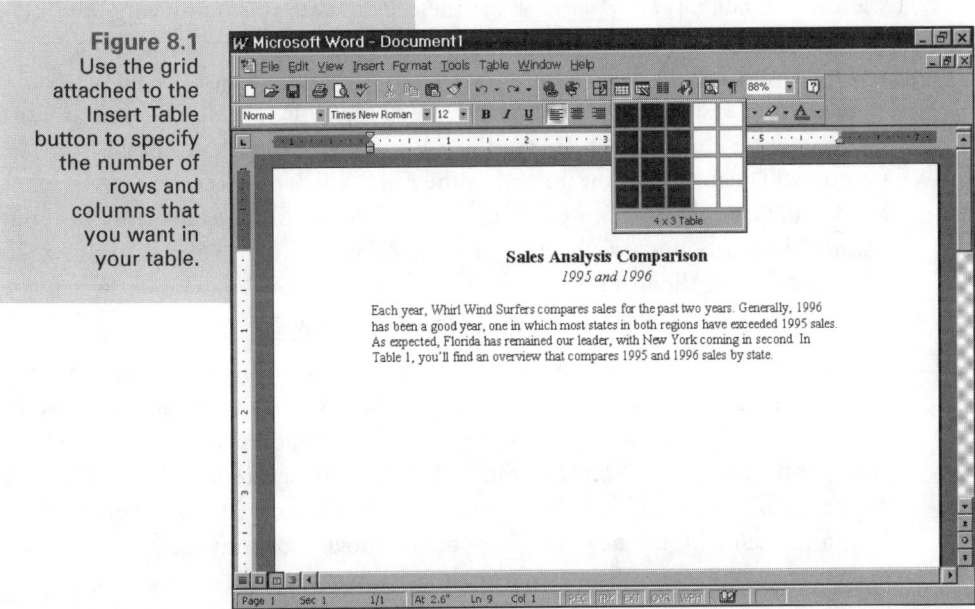

Figure 8.1
Use the grid attached to the Insert Table button to specify the number of rows and columns that you want in your table.

3. Click in the last highlighted cell. Word inserts a table in your document at the location of the insertion point.

You can add rows and columns to a table at any time, as you'll see later in this chapter.

Typing and Editing in a Table

If you know how to use Microsoft Excel, you know how to work in Word tables. Typing a table is just like typing a document in Word. You just type. A table consists of rows and columns, and the box at the intersection of a row and a column is called a *cell*. As in Microsoft Excel, columns are named with letters and rows are named with numbers; cells are named with the letter and number of the row and column at which they appear. The first cell in the table is called A1, and, on the same row, the second cell is called B1. The third cell in the second row is called

C2, and the last cell in the table is called C4. By the time you finish typing information into the table that we just created, the table will contain cells through C7, but B7 and C7 will be blank.

To move the insertion point from cell to cell, press the [Tab] key. To move backward in the table, press [Shift]+[Tab]. If the cell to which you're moving the insertion point already contains text, Word will select that text; you can replace the text by simply typing. When you press [Tab] while your cursor is in the last cell in a table, Word automatically adds a new row to the table. To select a cell, move the mouse pointer along the left side of the cell and inside the left cell boundary. The pointer will change to point up and to the right. Click to select the cell. To select a row, move the mouse pointer along the left edge of the first cell in the row, but *outside* the cell boundary. When you click, Word will select the entire row. To select a column, slide the mouse pointer to the top of the column. When the pointer changes to a black arrow pointing down, click.

You also can move and copy text in a table the same way that you move and copy text anywhere in a Word document. Select the text that you want to move or copy, and either drag the text (press [Ctrl] while you drag to copy) or use the Cut, Copy, and Paste buttons on the Standard toolbar. Be aware that, if you move or copy text to a table cell that already contains text, Word will replace the original text in the cell with the new text that you are moving or copying.

If you copy or cut table cells to another location in the document (not to a table), Word inserts the copied/cut information as new table cells, not plain text.

Type the information that follows into your table. Leave the totals blank; we'll let Word sum the numbers. Your document should look like the one in Figure 8.2 when you finish.

New York	1275	1395
Pennsylvania	953	1042
New Jersey	940	932
Florida	1524	1666
Georgia	1167	1277
Alabama	1147	1254
Total		

CHAPTER 8 • CRUNCHING NUMBERS IN A BUSINESS REPORT 183

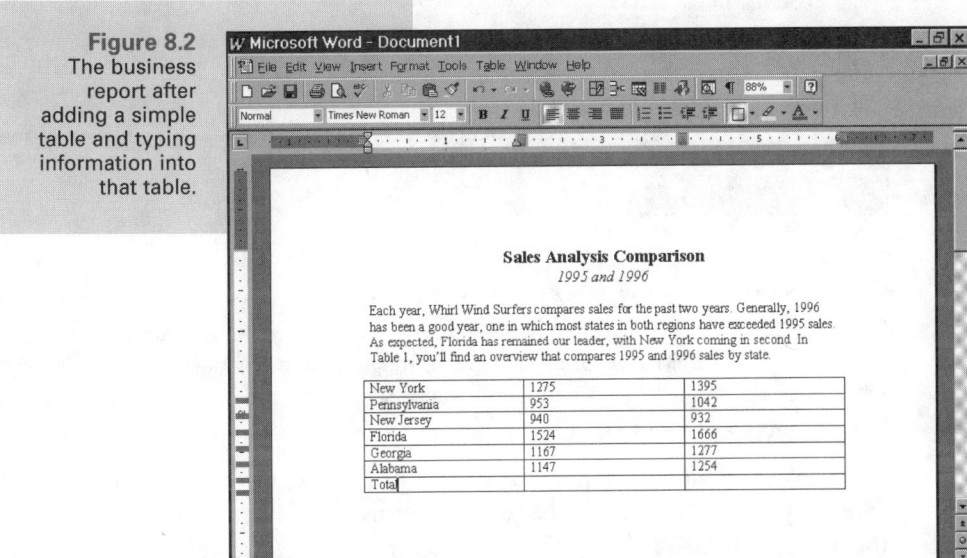

Figure 8.2
The business report after adding a simple table and typing information into that table.

Summing Numbers in a Table

If your table contains numeric data, as ours does, you can let Word add the columns or rows for you.

Hands On: Summing Columns in a Table

To sum numbers in a table column, follow these steps:

1. Place the insertion point in the cell where you want the sum to appear. In the example, we placed the insertion point in cell B7, the center cell in the last row.
2. Choose T_able, F_ormula. Word displays the Formula dialog box (see Figure 8.3).
3. The default formula sums the numbers that appear in cells above the insertion point. Because that's exactly what we want, click on OK. The sum appears.
4. Repeat Steps 1–3 for the last cell in the table.

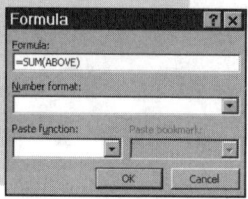

Figure 8.3
Use the Formula dialog box to tell Word to perform a mathematical calculation.

Tip

Formulas in Word also work just as they do in Excel. You could, for example, type the formula =**SUM(B1:B6)**. Unfortunately, formulas *do not* work as they do in Excel when you copy them; they do not automatically adjust for the new column or row.

If you place the insertion point anywhere in the text of the sum that you just entered, you'll notice that the background turns gray. When Word inserts a sum, the sum appears as a field in Word. You can think of *fields* as placeholders for text that might change. In this instance, if one of the numbers in the table changes, you can update the sum field and it will recalculate the sum of the column.

FOR MORE INFORMATION ON FIELDS, SEE CHAPTER 15.

In our case, however, we know that the numbers won't change; in fact, we don't want them to change. So, we'll convert the fields to actual numbers. Drag to select the field and press Ctrl+Shift+F9. Make sure that you select only the field and not the entire cell; you'll know that you selected the field if the rest of the cell's background remains white. If the background of the cell turns black, try again. To ensure that you select only the field, you might find it easier to select the field from right to left instead of left to right.

Adding Rows or Columns

Now we'll add a row at the top of the table that will contain column titles.

Hands On: Adding a Row to the Top of the Table

To add a row to the top of the table, follow these steps:

1. Place the insertion point anywhere in the first row of the table.
2. Choose T<u>a</u>ble, <u>I</u>nsert Rows. Word inserts a row above the row containing the insertion point and selects that row.

CHAPTER 8 • CRUNCHING NUMBERS IN A BUSINESS REPORT **185**

3. Press the left arrow key. In the new cell A1, type **State**. Press Tab to cell B1 and type **1995 Sales**. Press Tab to cell C1 and type **1996 Sales**. When you finish, your document should look like the one in Figure 8.4.

4. To bold the titles in the first row, select the entire row and click on the Bold button on the Formatting toolbar.

You might have noticed the Headings command on the Table menu. Use this command in long tables that extend over two or more pages to establish a row of column headings that you want to print on the second page and subsequent pages.

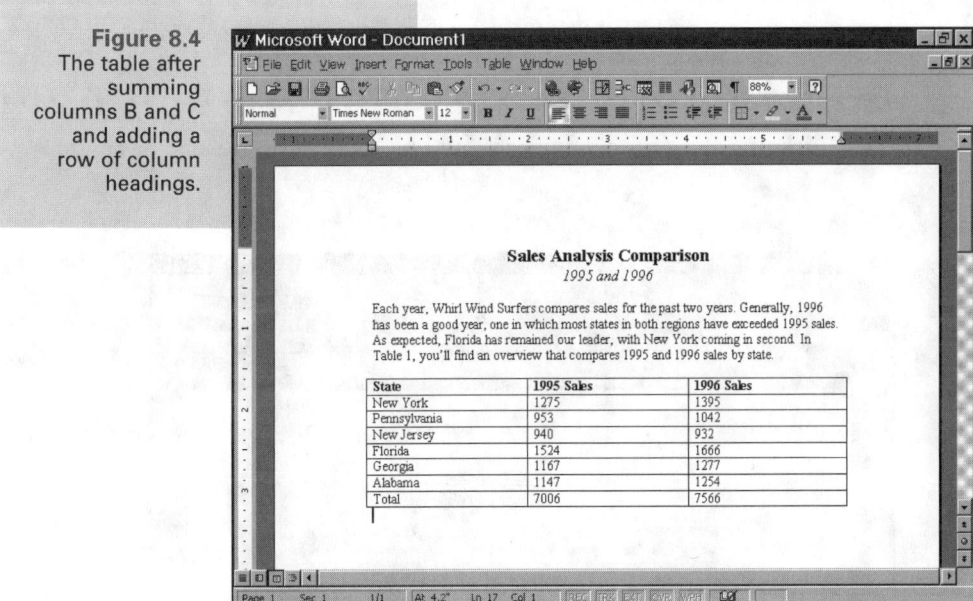

Figure 8.4
The table after summing columns B and C and adding a row of column headings.

Providing a Caption for a Table

To make sure that your readers understand what they're looking at, you should identify all tables, figures, charts, and so on in a document. One way to do this is to provide a caption.

PART II • GETTING VISUAL

Hands On: Providing a Caption for the First Table

To provide a caption for a table, follow these steps:

1. Place the insertion point anywhere in the table without selecting anything in the table.
2. Choose Insert, Caption. Word selects the table and displays the Caption dialog box.
3. Word suggests that the caption for the table should be `Table 1`. Add to the description by typing a period, a space, and **Annual Sales by State**.
4. Open the Position box and choose Below Selected Item.

> This list box will not be available if the insertion point did not appear in the table when you started these steps.

5. Click on OK. Your document should look similar to the one in Figure 8.5.

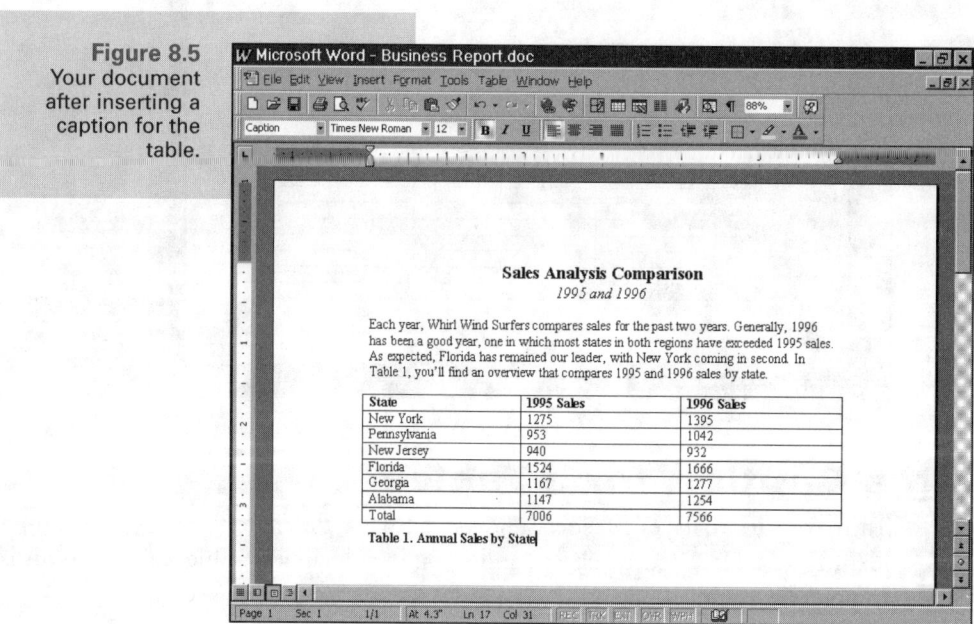

Figure 8.5
Your document after inserting a caption for the table.

CHAPTER 8 • CRUNCHING NUMBERS IN A BUSINESS REPORT **187**

Merging Cells

Another way to identify a table is to place the table's title in a row at the top of the table. If you want to try this method, you will want to add a row to the top of the table and then merge the cells of that row so that the row contains only one cell.

Hands On: Creating a Single-Celled First Row

To combine the cells of the first row into one cell, follow these steps:

1. Place the insertion point anywhere in the first row and choose Table, Insert Rows.
2. With the row still selected, reopen the Table menu and choose Merge Cells.
3. Click anywhere outside the selected row to cancel its selection. The first row in your table contains one long cell (see Figure 8.6).

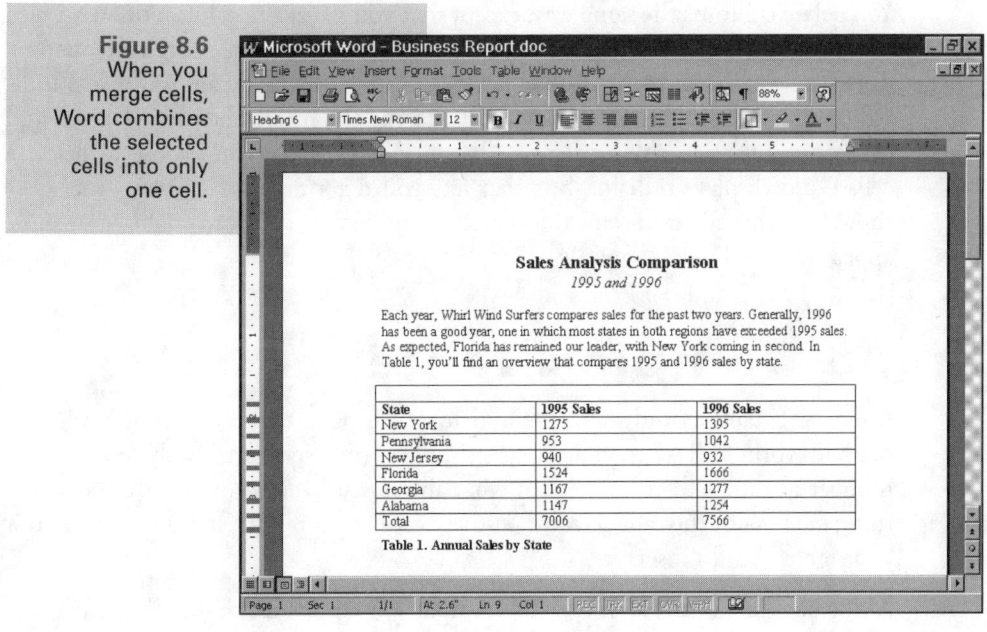

Figure 8.6
When you merge cells, Word combines the selected cells into only one cell.

> You can split cells (whether or not they were previously merged) by selecting the cell and then choosing Table, Split Cells. Word will let you decide how many rows and columns you want to create from the cell.

Deleting Rows, Columns, or Cells

Because we're going to use captions for our tables in this business report, we don't need the single-celled row at the top of the table.

Hands On: Deleting a Row

To delete a row in a table, follow these steps:

1. Select the row that you want to delete. In the example, select the merged cell in Row 1.
2. Choose Table, Delete Rows. Word deletes the row.

You delete columns the same way, except that you select the column in Step 1 and select the Delete Columns command in step 2. To delete an entire table, choose Table, Select Table; then, choose Table, Delete Rows. You can also delete individual cells by selecting them or simply placing the insertion point in a cell and then choosing the Table, Delete Cells command. When you choose to delete a cell, Word displays a dialog box that lets you determine which way other cells should be shifted. Be aware that deleting individual cells can make your table appear lopsided.

Drawing a Complex Table

Inserting a table is only one method for creating a table in Word. And, that method works well when your table is simple, with a standard, easily recognizable number of rows and columns. But what about cases when you want to do something fancy with the table layout? In these cases, you might find it easier to draw your table than to insert it.

At the bottom of the Sales Analysis Comparison report, make sure that one blank line appears below the caption that you inserted. Add the following text and press [Enter] twice when you finish.

CHAPTER 8 • CRUNCHING NUMBERS IN A BUSINESS REPORT 189

To provide a more accurate picture of sales, Table 2 shows you the breakdown for each state of each year's sales by quarter. You'll also see a breakdown and subtotal by region in Table 2.

Hands On: Drawing the Outline of a Table

To draw a table, follow these steps:

1. Click on the Tables and Borders button on the Standard toolbar. Word displays the Tables and Borders toolbar (see Figure 8.7).

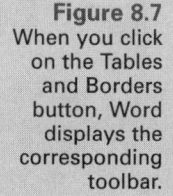

Figure 8.7
When you click on the Tables and Borders button, Word displays the corresponding toolbar.

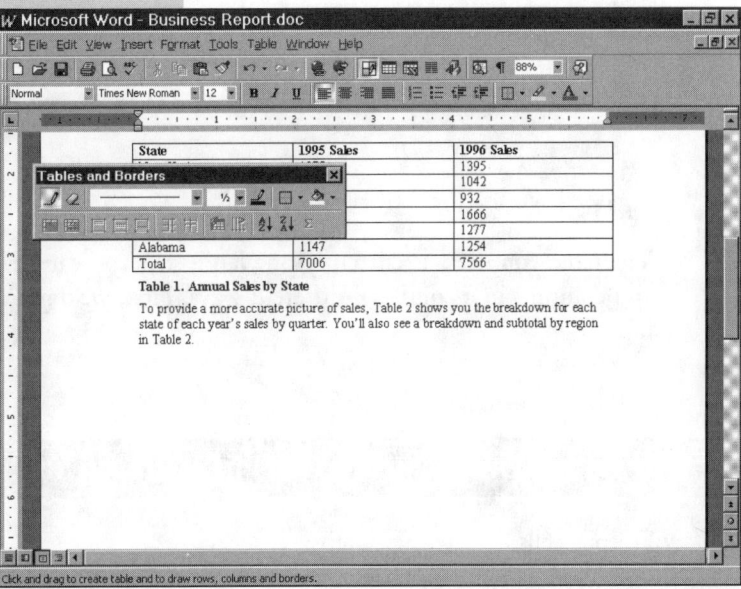

2. Move the mouse pointer to the bottom of the document text area and position it below the text at the left margin. The mouse pointer shape will be a pencil.

3. Drag the mouse pointer down and to the right margin until the outline that you see while dragging shows a rectangle approximately 6 inches wide by 3 inches long; use the horizontal and vertical rulers to guide you (see Figure 8.8). When you release the mouse button, the insertion point will appear inside the box you drew.

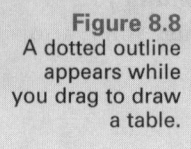

PART II • GETTING VISUAL

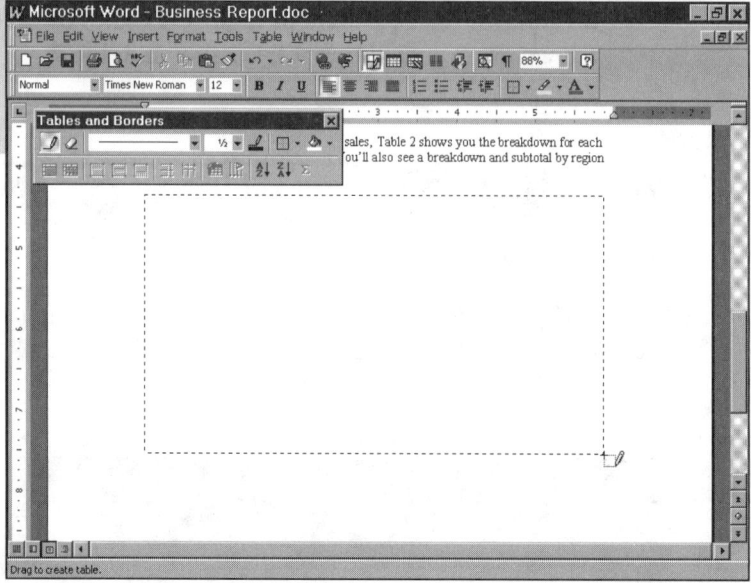

Figure 8.8
A dotted outline appears while you drag to draw a table.

Splitting Cells

The table you drew is currently one large cell. You can divide the cell into rows and columns in a couple of different ways. First, we'll get the basic layout of the table.

Hands On: Splitting Cells in a Drawn Table

To split cells, follow these steps:

1. Click on the Split Cells button on the Tables and Borders toolbar. It's on the bottom row of the toolbar, second from the left. Word displays the Split Cells dialog box (see Figure 8.9).
2. Set the number of columns to 10 and the number of rows to 11.
3. Click on OK. Word divides the cell into the specified number of rows and columns; they all appear selected on-screen. Click in any cell to cancel the selection.

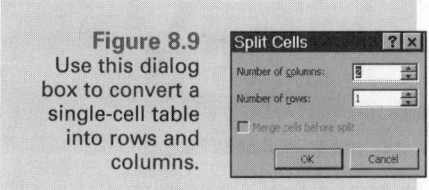

Figure 8.9 Use this dialog box to convert a single-cell table into rows and columns.

Erasing Row or Column Borders

After drawing the basic layout of the table, you use the Eraser button on the Tables and Borders toolbar to delete unwanted lines from the table.

Hands On: Erasing Cell Dividers

To erase cell boundaries, follow these steps:

1. Click on the Eraser button on the Tables and Borders toolbar. When you move the mouse into the table, the pointer shape changes to an eraser.
2. Drag along the line that you want to erase until the line is selected (see Figure 8.10).
3. When you release the mouse button, Word deletes the line.

If you erase the wrong line by mistake, use the Undo button on the Standard toolbar to restore it.

4. Repeat Steps 2 and 3 to erase lines until your table looks like the one in Figure 8.11.

You can add cell boundaries by drawing them, similar to the way you drew the table. Click on the Draw Table button on the Tables and Borders toolbar. Slide the mouse pointer onto the table to the location where you want to add a cell boundary. When the mouse pointer shape becomes a pencil, drag in the direction you want to add a boundary.

 **Part II • Getting Visual**

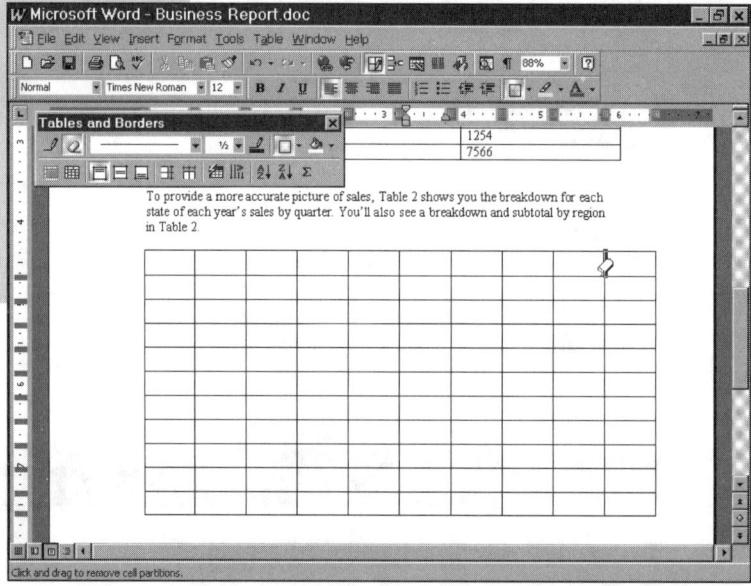

Figure 8.10
Dragging to erase a cell divider.

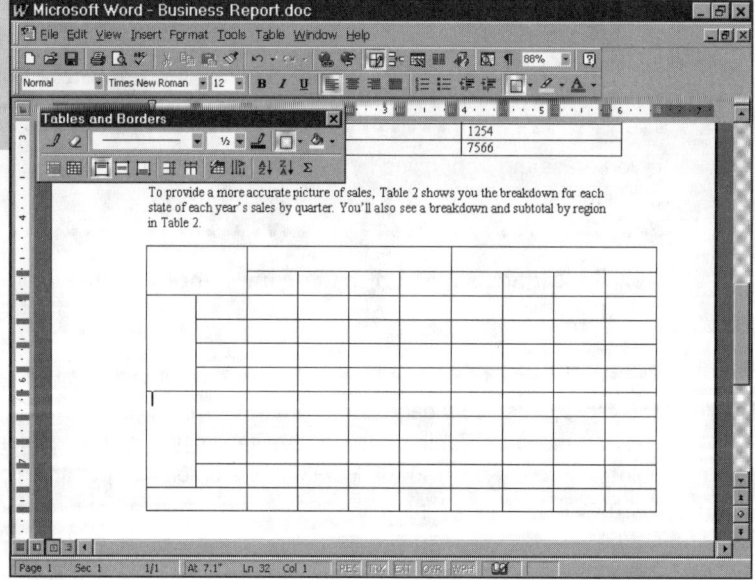

Figure 8.11
The table you drew after erasing cell boundaries.

CHAPTER 8 • CRUNCHING NUMBERS IN A BUSINESS REPORT 193

Adjusting Column Widths

You change column widths using the same technique whether you drew the table or inserted it. Make sure that neither the Draw Table button nor the Eraser button is selected; if necessary, click on one or the other to cancel its selection.

Hands On: Changing the Width of a Column

To change the width of a column, follow these steps:

1. Slide the mouse pointer onto the right boundary of the column whose width you want to adjust (see Figure 8.12).

You'll know that you turned off both the Draw Table button and the Eraser button by the shape of the mouse pointer when you slide it over the table. You should *not* see either a pencil or an eraser.

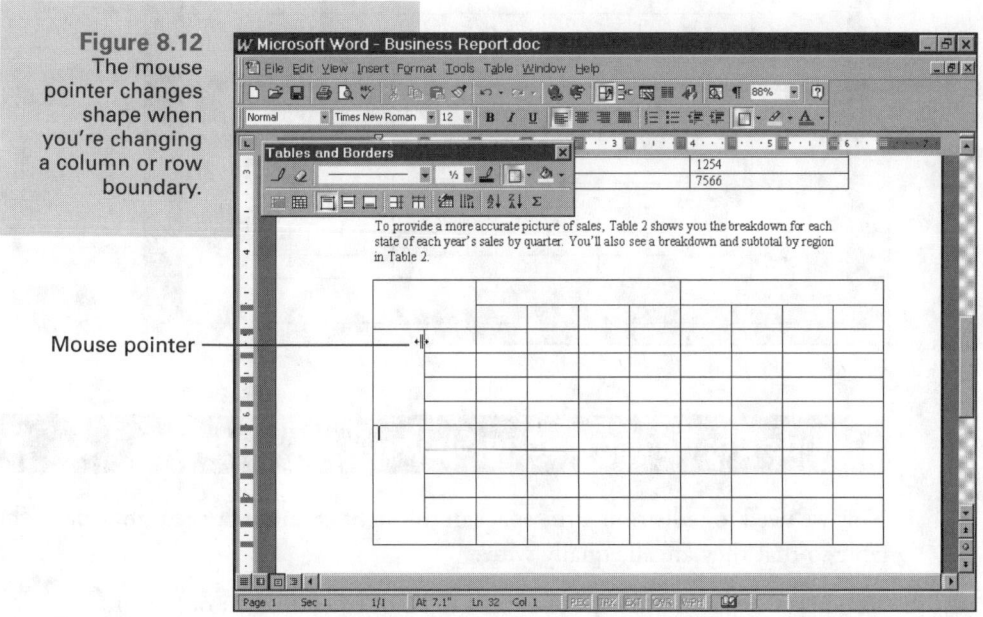

Figure 8.12 The mouse pointer changes shape when you're changing a column or row boundary.

Mouse pointer

PART II • GETTING VISUAL

2. Drag to the left to reduce the column's width. In our example, release the mouse pointer when you've dragged to divide the first column in half.

Dragging a column border to the left decreases the size of the column to the left and increases the size of the column to the right. Dragging a row border down increases the size of that row only; the rows below move down to increase the size of the entire table.

3. Repeat these steps to widen the second column. Drag its right boundary to the right to make it about 1/4 inch wider (see Figure 8.13).

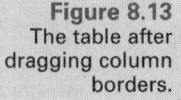

Figure 8.13
The table after dragging column borders.

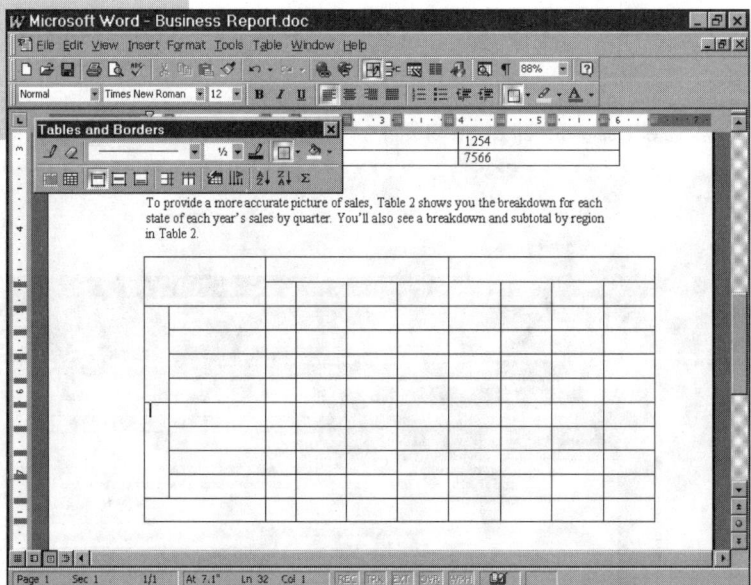

Hands On: Redistributing Space Across Columns

Now we need to redistribute the space in the eight columns at the right side of the table so that they are all equally wide.

1. Select the columns that you want to be of equal size. In our example, slide the mouse pointer over the top of the rightmost column and watch for the mouse pointer to change to a black arrow pointing down.

CHAPTER 8 • CRUNCHING NUMBERS IN A BUSINESS REPORT 195

2. Drag the mouse to the left. Word will select the columns, as you can see in Figure 8.14.

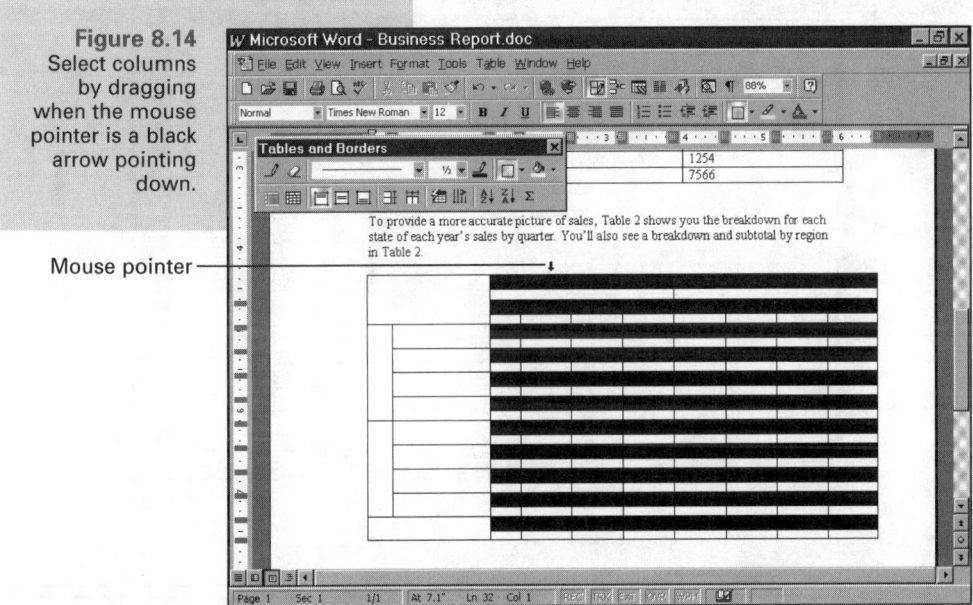

Figure 8.14
Select columns by dragging when the mouse pointer is a black arrow pointing down.

Mouse pointer

3. Click on the Distribute Columns Evenly button on the Tables and Borders toolbar. Word adjusts the selected cells (see Figure 8.15).

You need to put text into the table. Copy the information from the Sales Analysis Comparison that you entered earlier in the chapter into the table. Press Tab to move forward from cell to cell; press Shift+Tab to move backward. If you make a mistake while typing, correct it using the Undo button or the Backspace or Del keys. Make the years and the text in the first cell bold. Make the Region Total lines italic, and make the Company Total line both bold and italic. You can copy the numbers for the two regional totals and the company total, or you can use formulas. For each formula, choose Table, Formula. For the first regional total line, use the formula **=SUM(ABOVE)**. For the second regional total line, use **=SUM(C7:C9)**. Adjust this formula as you work across the row; the last formula in the row should be **=SUM(J7:J9)**. For the company total line, use the formula **=C6+C10**. Adjust the formula as you work across the row; the last formula in the row should be **=J6+J10**. Your table should look like Figure 8.16.

Figure 8.15
The Distribute Columns Evenly button distributes space to make columns equal in size.

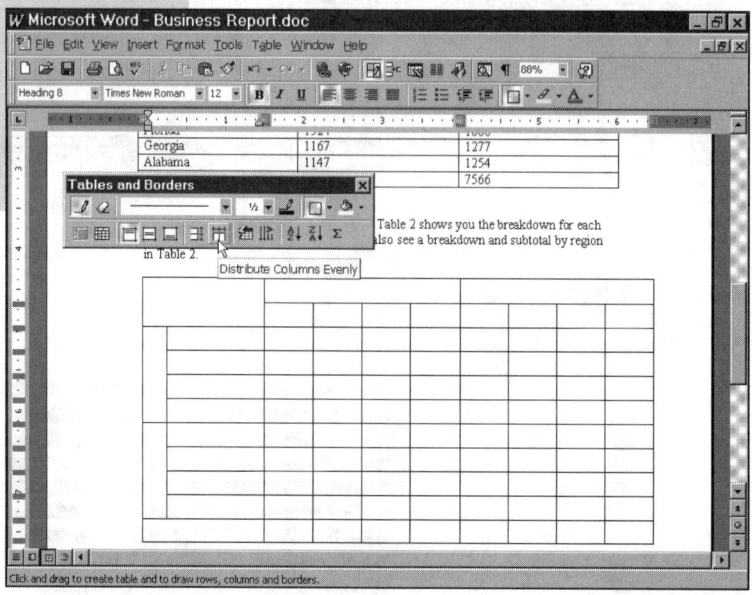

Figure 8.16
The table with text added.

Region and State		1995				1996			
		Q1	Q2	Q3	Q4	Q1	Q2	Q3	Q4
North	New York	320	310	302	343	352	326	323	394
	Pennsylvania	222	236	239	256	244	248	256	294
	New Jersey	243	240	225	232	235	239	230	228
	Region Total	785	786	766	831	831	813	809	916
South	Florida	334	380	392	418	367	399	419	481
	Georgia	267	290	299	311	294	305	320	358
	Alabama	276	280	289	302	304	294	309	347
	Region Total	877	950	980	1031	965	998	1048	1186
Company Total		1662	1736	1746	1862	1796	1811	1857	2102

CHAPTER 8 • CRUNCHING NUMBERS IN A BUSINESS REPORT   197

Formatting a Table

Now that you have information in both tables, it's time to make them more attractive. You can use one of two approaches (and we show you both): you can let Word automatically format a table, or you can manually apply formatting.

AutoFormatting a Table

You can quickly and easily produce some rather dramatic formatting effects by letting Word automatically format a table.

Hands On: AutoFormatting the Simple Table

To automatically apply formatting to a table, follow these steps:

1. Place the insertion point in any cell in the table that you want to format. In this example, we're formatting the first table we created, not the one we added most recently.
2. Choose Table, Table AutoFormat. Word displays the Table AutoFormat dialog box (see Figure 8.17).

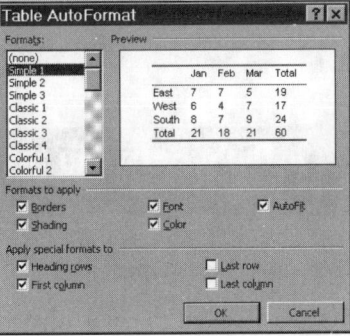

Figure 8.17 From this dialog box, choose the format that you want to apply to your table.

3. In the Formats list, select a format. Watch the Preview box to see a sample of the format. For the simple table, we chose 3D effects 1.
4. (Optional) If necessary, make changes to the check boxes at the bottom of the dialog box; in the example, we made no changes.
5. Click on OK. Word applies the format to the table (see Figure 8.18).

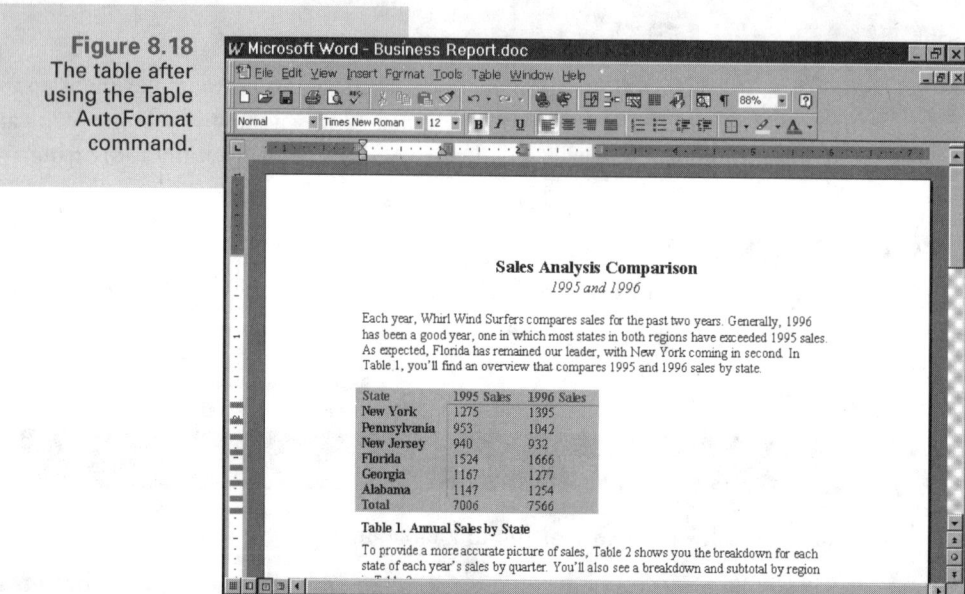

Figure 8.18
The table after using the Table AutoFormat command.

Aligning Tables on the Page

The automatic formatting that Word applied reduced the size of the cells in the table so that the table no longer fills the space between the left and right margins. With its present formatting, the table would look better if it were centered horizontally on the page.

Hands On: Centering a Table Between the Left and Right Margins

To center a table horizontally, follow these steps:

1. Place the insertion point in any cell in the table that you want to align.
2. Select the entire table by choosing Table, Select Table.
3. Click on the Center button on the Formatting toolbar; Word centers the table between the left and right margins (see Figure 8.19). Click anywhere on the page to cancel the selection of the table.

CHAPTER 8 • CRUNCHING NUMBERS IN A BUSINESS REPORT 199

Note

If you do *not* select the entire table, Word will not adjust the placement of the table on the page; instead, Word will center the contents of the selected cell(s) within those cells.

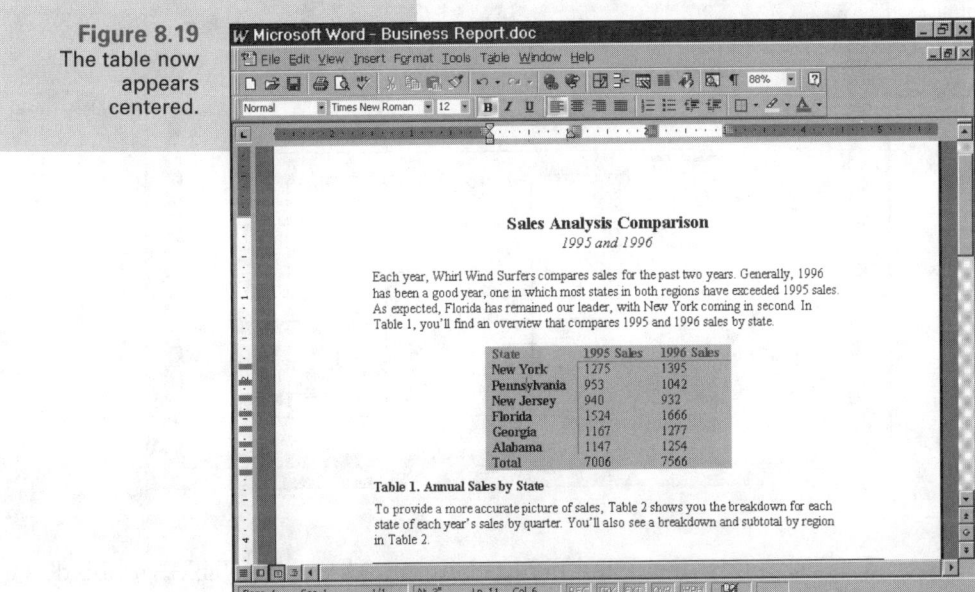

Figure 8.19
The table now appears centered.

Controlling the Direction of Text within Cells

In the more complex table that we created, we never identified the regions to which the states belong. When we type that text, it won't fit in the cells based on the size of the cells; instead of changing the cell size, we will change the direction of the text so that it appears vertically rather than horizontally within the cell.

Hands On: Controlling the Direction of the Text for the Regions

1. Click in the vertical blank cell immediately to the left of New York in the complex table, Table 2.

PART II • GETTING VISUAL

2. Type **North**, the region name for the first three states. Word inserts the text horizontally into the cell (see Figure 8.20).

Figure 8.20
Because of the shape of the cell, text doesn't fit in it horizontally.

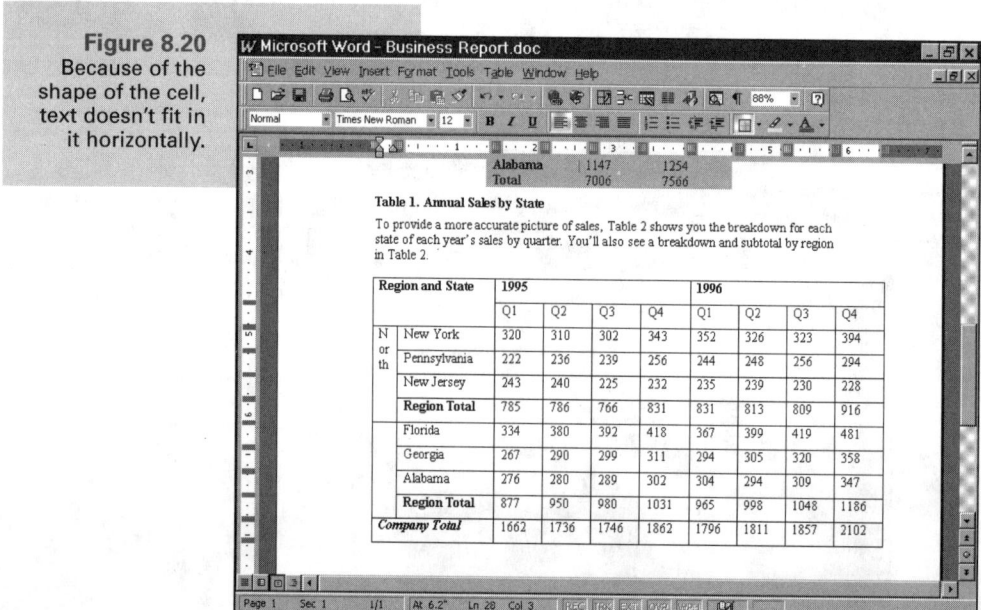

3. Click on the Tables and Borders button to display the Tables and Borders toolbar.

4. Click on the Change Text Direction button until the arrows on the button point to the right. Word changes the direction the text appears in the cell (see Figure 8.21).

5. Repeat these steps for the other narrow cell immediately below. The region name should be **South**.

Aligning Information Horizontally within Table Cells

In the complex table, Table 2, the titles in the table—years, quarters, and regions—would look better if they were centered within their cells.

CHAPTER 8 • CRUNCHING NUMBERS IN A BUSINESS REPORT **201**

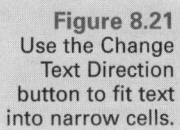

Figure 8.21
Use the Change Text Direction button to fit text into narrow cells.

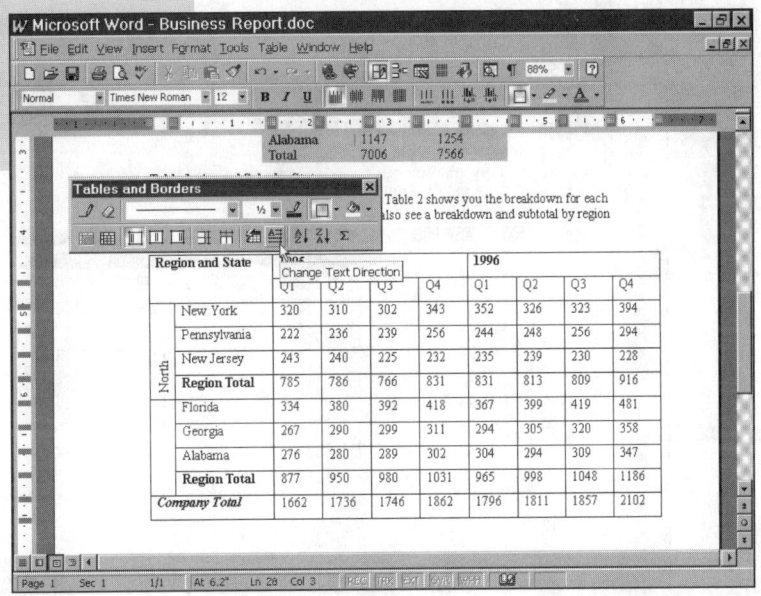

Hands On: Centering Text Horizontally in a Cell

To center text horizontally within cells, follow these steps:

1. Select all of Rows 1 and 2, including the title `Region and State`, the years, and the quarters.
2. Click on the Center button on the Formatting toolbar. Word centers the text within the selected cells (see Figure 8.22).

Tip

To center the text in a single cell, simply click in that cell and then click on the Center button on the Formatting toolbar.

3. Repeat these steps for the two narrow cells containing the region names.

Tip

You also can control text alignment within a cell from the Cell Height and Width dialog box. Select the cell and choose Table, Cell Height and Width.

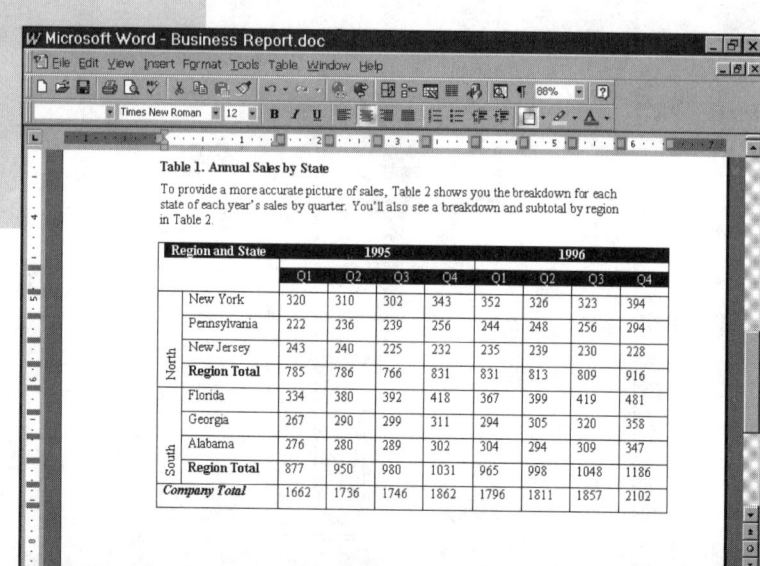

Figure 8.22
Use the buttons on the Formatting toolbar to align text horizontally within cells.

Aligning Information Vertically within Table Cells

You also can align text vertically within cells using the Tables and Borders toolbar.

Hands On: Vertically Centering the Information in the Complex Table

To center text vertically within cells, follow these steps:

1. Click anywhere in the complex table (Table 2) and choose Table, Select Table to select the entire table.
2. Click on the Tables and Borders button on the Standard toolbar to display the Tables and Borders toolbar.
3. Click on the Center Vertically button. Word centers all text in the table vertically within the cells of the table (see Figure 8.23).

CHAPTER 8 • CRUNCHING NUMBERS IN A BUSINESS REPORT

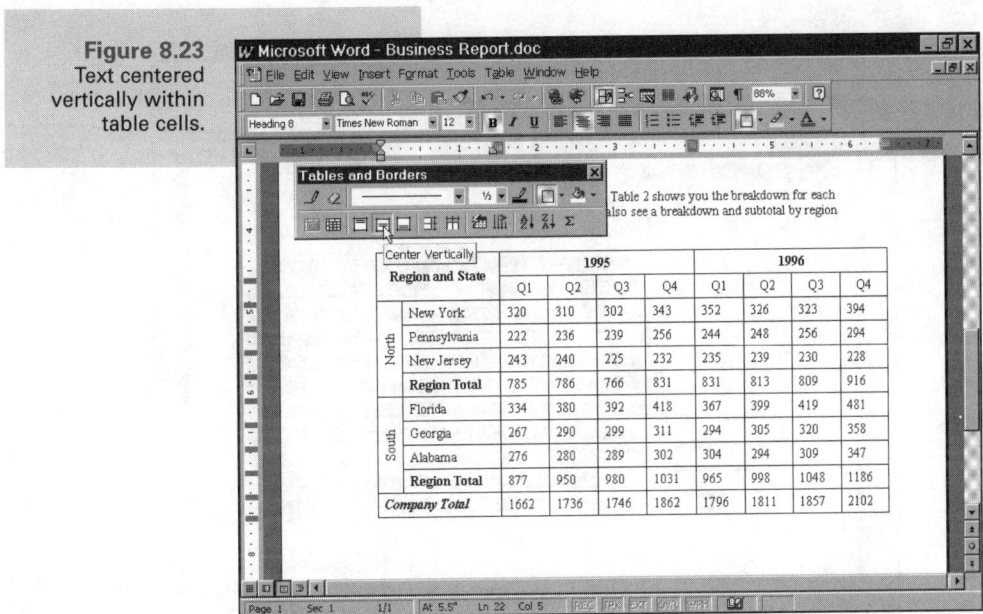

Figure 8.23
Text centered vertically within table cells.

Modifying Borders and Shading

Borders around and within a table can enhance its appearance and legibility.

Hands On: Modifying the Outside Border of the Table.

To modify the outside border of a table, follow these steps:

1. Click anywhere in the table and choose Table, Select Table to select the entire table.
2. If necessary, click on the Tables and Borders button on the Standard toolbar to display the Tables and Borders toolbar.
3. Open the line style list box and click on the border that you want to use to surround the entire table (see Figure 8.24).
4. Click on the Outside Border button and then click anywhere in the table. Word applies the line style that you selected to the outside border of the table (see Figure 8.25).

204 PART II • GETTING VISUAL

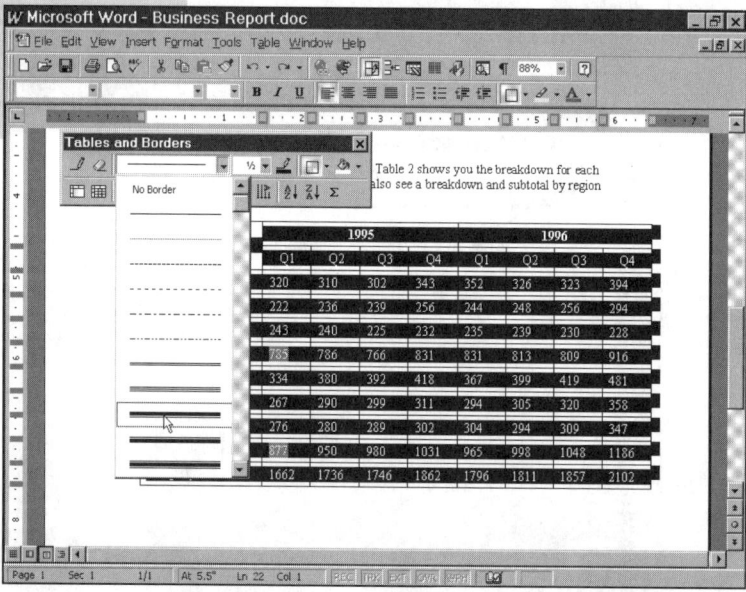

Figure 8.24
Choose a line style for the table's border.

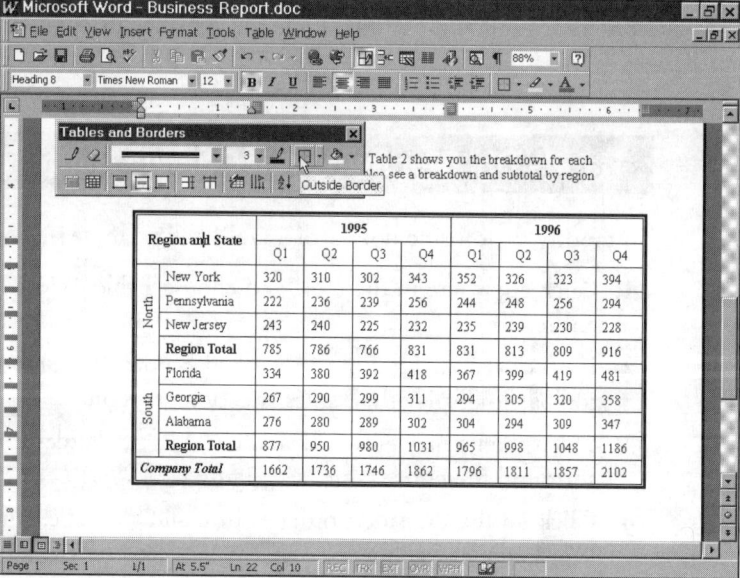

Figure 8.25
Use the Outside Borders button to apply the selected line style.

CHAPTER 8 • CRUNCHING NUMBERS IN A BUSINESS REPORT   205

Tip

You also can use the Borders and Shading dialog box to apply borders. Select the table and choose F*o*rmat, *B*orders and Shading.

Hands On: Modifying the Border of an Inside Cell

The distinction between the North and South Regions would be more clear if we made the border between them different from other cell borders in the table.

1. Select the first `Region Total` cell and all the cells in the rest of the row.
2. Open the Line Style list box on the Tables and Borders toolbar, and click on the border that you want to apply to the bottom of the selected cells. We chose a double line.
3. Click on the list box arrow next to the Outside Border button to display the borders to which you can apply the line style (see Figure 8.26).

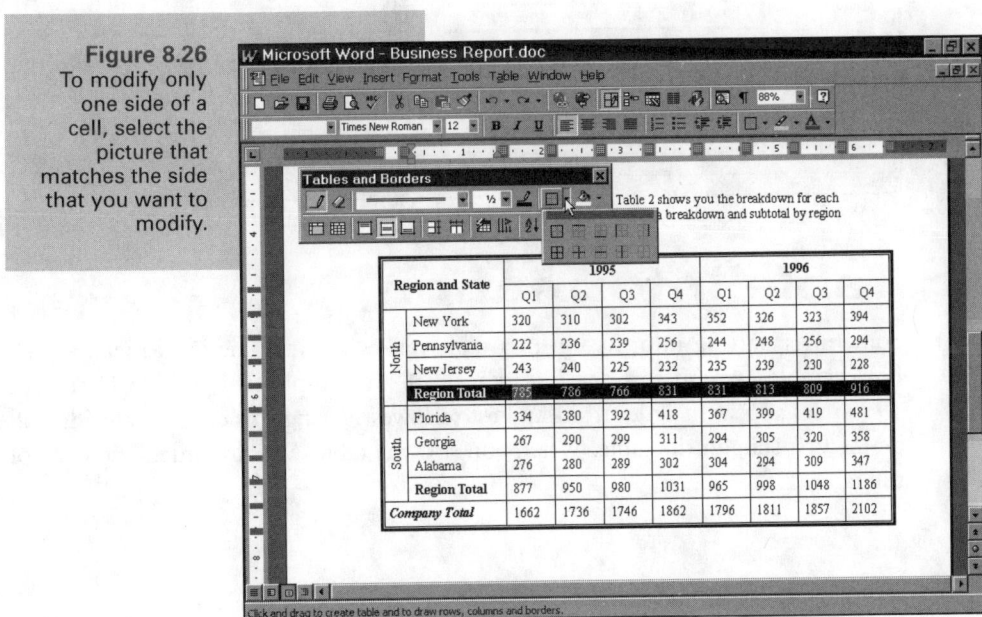

Figure 8.26
To modify only one side of a cell, select the picture that matches the side that you want to modify.

Part II • Getting Visual

4. Click on the middle picture in the top row to modify the bottom border of the selected cells. Word applies the border that you chose to the bottom of the selected cells.

5. Repeat these steps for the cell containing "North"; you still want to modify the bottom border even though the text flows in an unusual direction. When you finish, your document should look like the one in Figure 8.27.

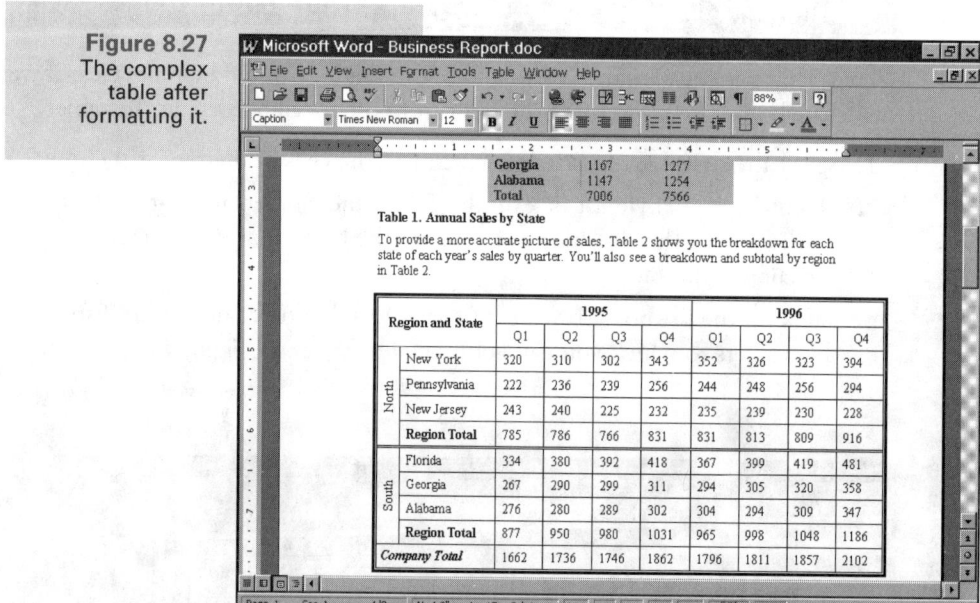

Figure 8.27 The complex table after formatting it.

Sorting Table Information

Sometimes, sorting information in a table makes the information easier to read. For example, we can sort the information in the simple table (Table 1) so that 1996 sales appear in order from highest to lowest. Using this criteria, Florida will be the first state in the table. When you sort the table, Word reorders the rows of the table.

CHAPTER 8 • CRUNCHING NUMBERS IN A BUSINESS REPORT **207**

Hands On: Sorting the Simple Table to Rank 1996 Sales

To sort information in a table, follow these steps:

1. Select the rows that you want to sort in the simple table (Table 1). Word will recognize a header row but not a total row; so, in the example, select all rows except the Total row.
2. Choose T<u>a</u>ble, <u>S</u>ort. Word displays the Sort dialog box (see Figure 8.28).

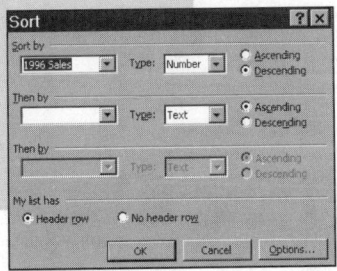

Figure 8.28 Use this dialog box to describe the way that you want to sort information in the table.

3. Open the <u>S</u>ort By list box and select 1996 Sales.
4. Select <u>D</u>escending to sort from highest to lowest.
5. (Optional) Use <u>T</u>hen By to set another sort to break ties if two cells have the same value.
6. Click on OK. Word sorts the table in order of 1996 Sales from highest to lowest (see Figure 8.29).

Tip

••

I aligned the second and third columns in the table to the right edge of the cells using the Align Right button on the Formatting toolbar.

••

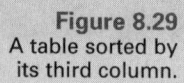

Figure 8.29
A table sorted by its third column.

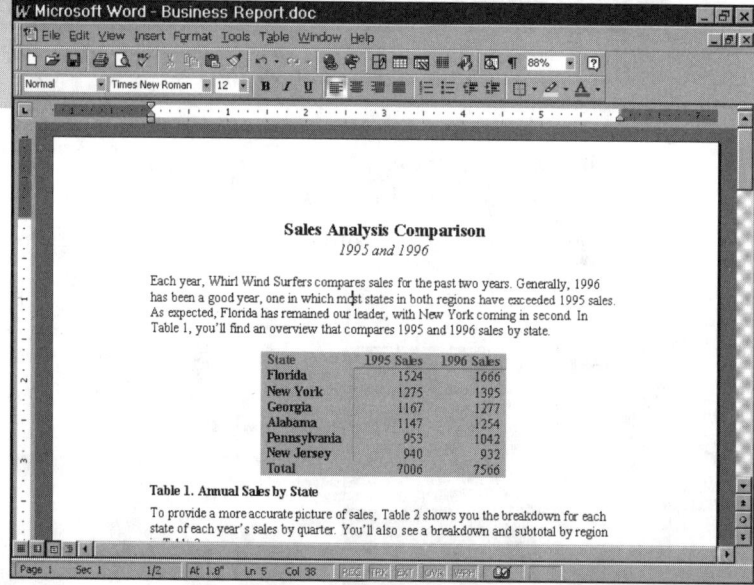

Working with Charts

The Chinese proverb says "A picture is worth a thousand words," so we'll create a visual representation of the simple table for our business report reader. You can graph the information in Table 1 right inside Word using an applet called Microsoft Graph. But before we begin to create the chart, we need to finish up Page 1.

To finish the complex table (Table 2), add a caption below it. Use the instructions found earlier in this chapter in the section titled "Providing a Caption for a Table", and the caption should read **Quarterly Breakdown of Sales by State and Region**. Then, add the following sentence at the end of Page 1: **To help clarify the trends, see the chart on the next page—it is a visual representation of the information in Table 1.** At this point, Word should insert a page break; if you don't see one, press Ctrl+Enter to start a new page.

Inserting a Chart

Now we're ready to chart the information in Table 1.

CHAPTER 8 • CRUNCHING NUMBERS IN A BUSINESS REPORT **209**

Hands On: Creating the Chart of Table 1

To create a chart from table information, follow these steps:

1. Press [Enter] once to add a new blank line that will appear below your chart. Then, press the Up arrow to place the insertion point back on the first line of Page 2.

This step allows you to later add text below the chart that you're about to insert.

2. Highlight the rows in the table that you want to chart; in the example, highlight all rows in the Table 1, the simple table, except the last row.

You rarely chart "totals" rows because the numbers aren't meaningful in a chart.

3. Choose Insert, Picture. From the cascading menu, choosing Chart. Microsoft Graph begins to work, and you'll see on-screen a worksheet window (called the Datasheet (you'll learn more about it later in this chapter) and a chart (see Figure 8.30). The black border around the chart indicates that you're working in Microsoft Graph, not Microsoft Word. Notice, also, that the menus and the toolbars at the top of the window have changed to Microsoft Graph's menus and toolbars.

Moving a Chart

As you noticed, Microsoft Graph inserts the chart immediately below the table. We want the chart on the second page, so we'll move it.

Hands On: Moving the Chart to the Second Page

To move a chart, follow these steps:

1. Close the Datasheet window by clicking on the Close box in the upper-right corner of the window.
2. Click anywhere in your document outside the chart to temporarily close Microsoft Graph; notice that Word's regular menus reappear.

Figure 8.30
Your document, immediately after graphing the information in Table 1.

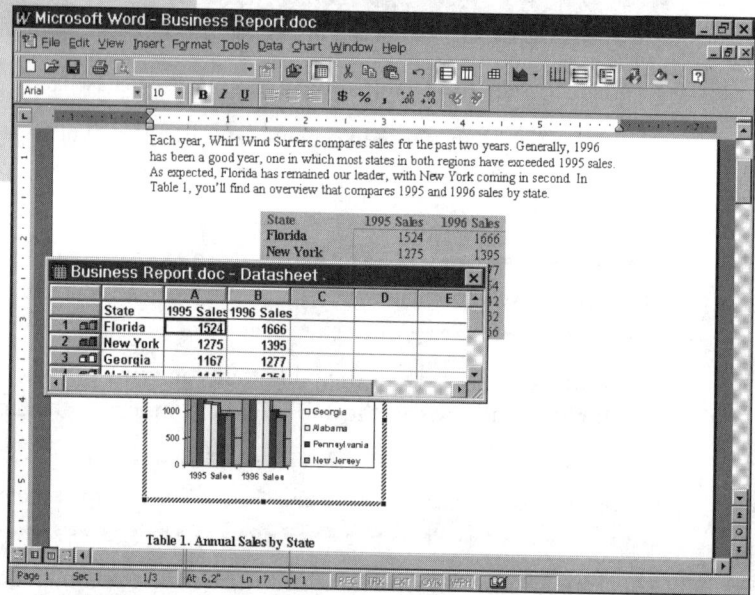

3. Click on the chart once. White handles appear around the chart (see Figure 8.31).

Figure 8.31
A chart object is selected in Word when white handles appear around it.

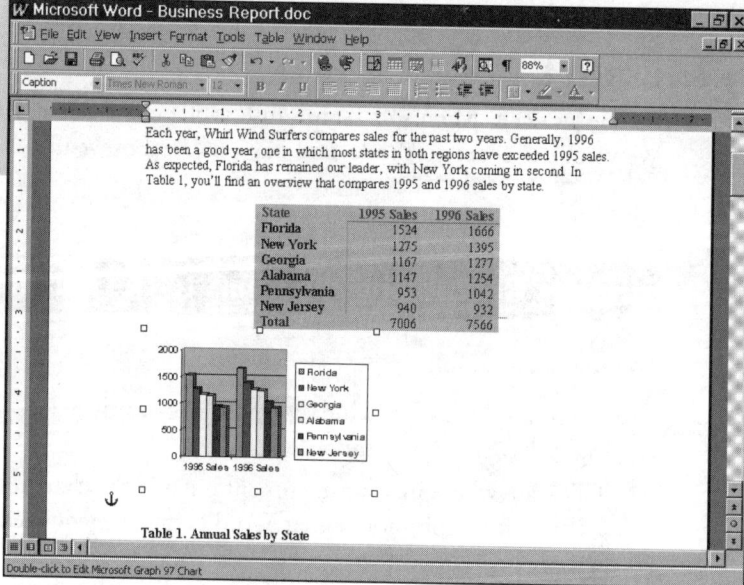

CHAPTER 8 • CRUNCHING NUMBERS IN A BUSINESS REPORT   211

4. Click on the Cut button on the Standard toolbar.
5. Microsoft Graph inserted an extra blank line between the table and the caption when it inserted the chart. Delete that line.
6. Press Ctrl+End to move to the end of the document, which should be near the top of Page 2.
7. Click on the Paste button on the Standard toolbar. Word reinserts the chart at the top of Page 2.
8. Slide the mouse pointer over the center of the chart until you see a four-headed arrow. Then drag the chart to the right until it appears centered between the left and right margins (see Figure 8.32).

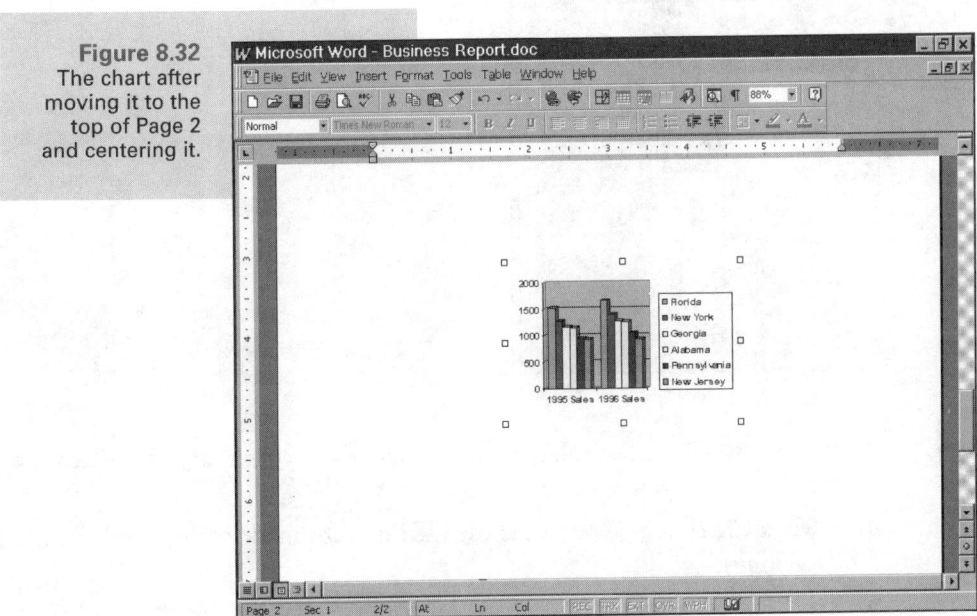

Figure 8.32
The chart after moving it to the top of Page 2 and centering it.

Changing the Chart Type

Suppose that you decide that you'd like to see what the chart would look like if you tried a different type of chart—a line chart, for example.

Hands On: Viewing the Chart as a Line Chart

To change the chart type, follow these steps:

1. Double-click on the chart to reopen Microsoft Graph. The datasheet also appears, but we don't need it right now, so close it using the Close button in the Datasheet window.

2. Choose Chart, Chart Type. Word displays the Chart Type dialog box (see Figure 8.33).

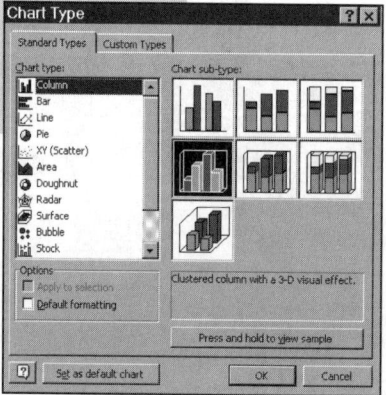

Figure 8.33 Select a new chart type for your chart.

3. In the Chart Type list, select Line. The chart subtypes change to match the chart type that you selected.

4. Select a Chart Sub-Type (we chose the line with markers displayed at each data point).

5. The Press and Hold to View Sample button allows you to preview your chart data in the new chart type without actually changing the chart (see Figure 8.34). Press and hold this button to see the preview, and then release the mouse button.

6. To retain the original chart type, click on Cancel in the dialog box.

Sizing a Chart

Now we'll enlarge the chart so that we can see it better.

CHAPTER 8 • CRUNCHING NUMBERS IN A BUSINESS REPORT **213**

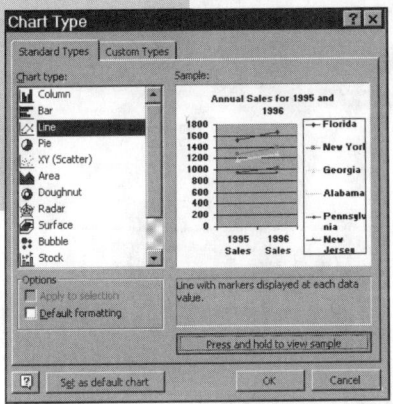

Figure 8.34
You can preview your data in a new chart type without actually changing your chart.

Hands On: Making the Chart Bigger

To resize the chart, follow these steps:

1. Slide the mouse pointer over the handle in the lower-right corner of the chart. The pointer shape changes to a two-headed arrow.
2. Drag the corner of the chart down and to the right so that the right side and the bottom are enlarged by approximately 1 inch each (see Figure 8.35).

You'll probably want to move the chart again to the left to re-center it between the left and right margins. Use the directions found earlier in this chapter in the section called "Moving a Chart."

Changing Data in the Chart

After you charted Table 1, suppose that you needed to change a number. Unfortunately, changing it in Table 1 does not fix the chart. Fortunately, you can use the Datasheet to make the change; Microsoft Graph will update the chart with any changes that you make in the Datasheet.

Double-click on the chart if it is not already active. To access the Datasheet, choose View, Datasheet. In Figure 8.36, we've enlarged the Datasheet window some and placed it below the chart so that you can compare the two.

214 PART II • GETTING VISUAL

Figure 8.35
Resizing a chart.

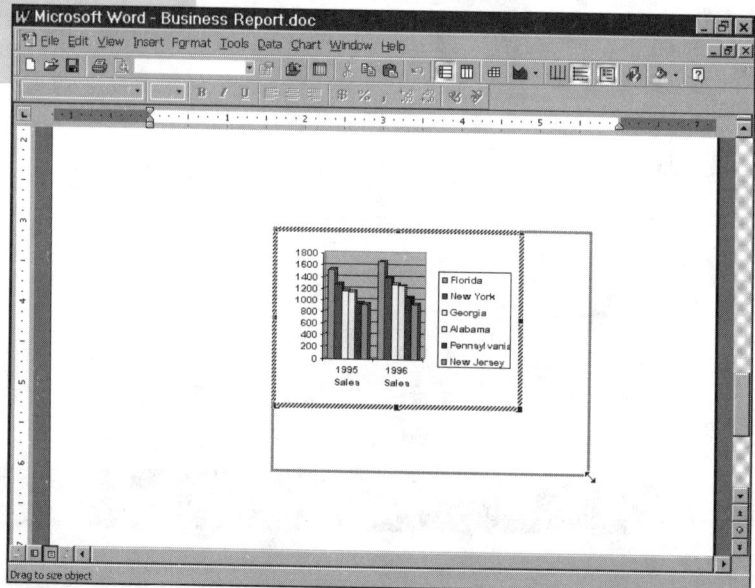

Figure 8.36
The Datasheet window showing the data that has been graphed in the chart.

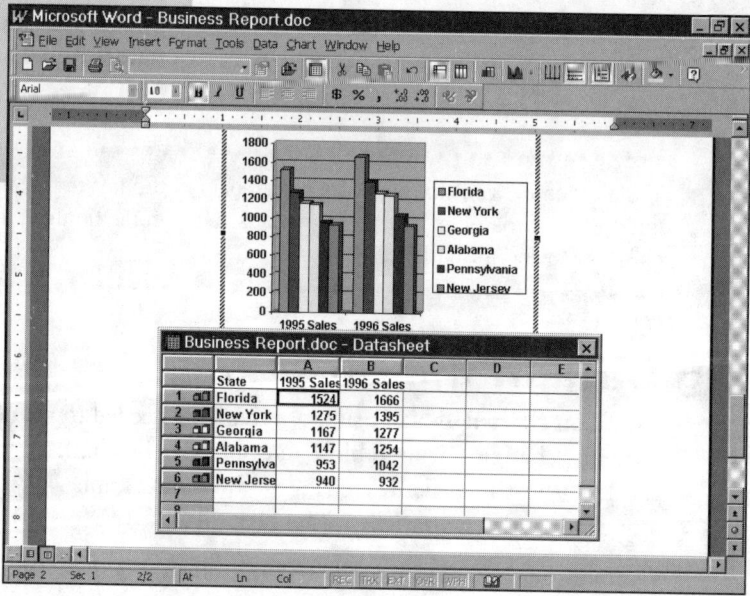

CHAPTER 8 • CRUNCHING NUMBERS IN A BUSINESS REPORT   215

Adding a Title to a Chart

The chart would be a lot more meaningful if it contained a title. We could either supply a caption, or we could use Microsoft Graph to supply a title. Because you already know how to insert a caption, we'll use Microsoft Graph.

Hands On: Adding a Chart Title

To add a title to a chart, follow these steps:

1. Choose Chart, Chart Options. You see the Chart Options dialog box (see Figure 8.37).

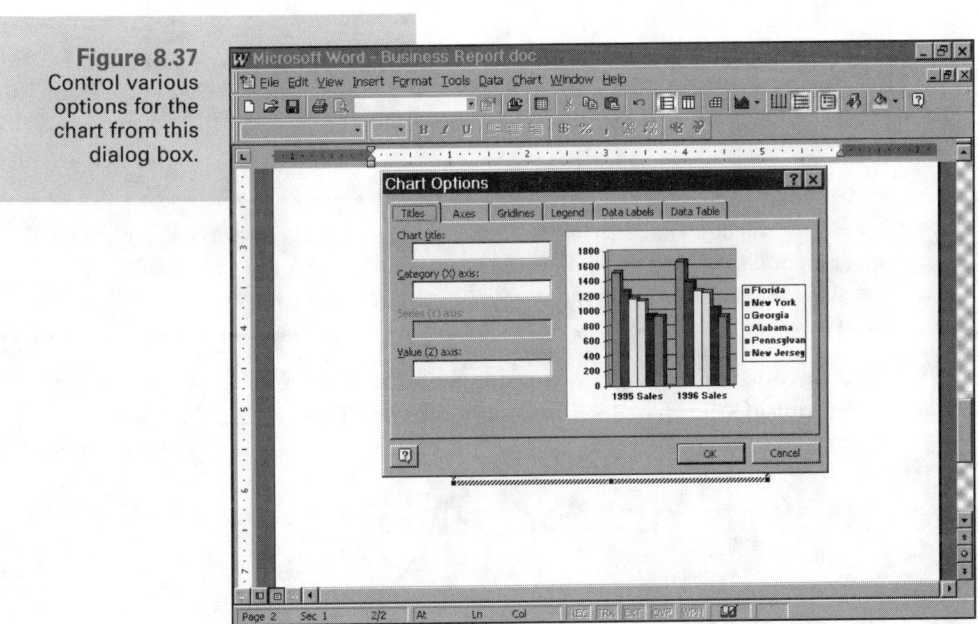

Figure 8.37 Control various options for the chart from this dialog box.

2. On the Titles tab, in the Chart Title text box, type the title that you want for the chart; I typed **Annual Sales for 1995 and 1996**.
3. Click on OK. The title appears on your chart (see Figure 8.38).

Figure 8.38
The chart after adding a title.

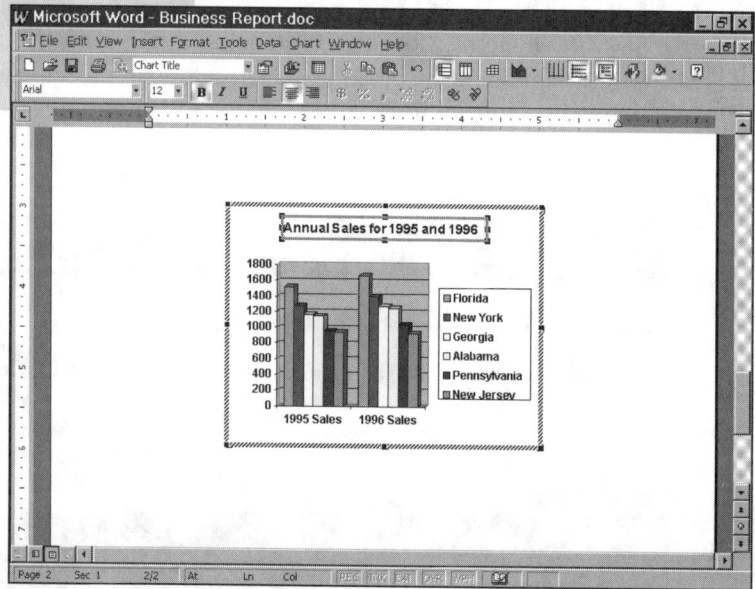

Notice the selection handles around the chart title. These handles *will not* appear if you are not displaying the Datasheet, but you can click on the title to select it. You can size the chart title the same way you size the chart.

Because you are now finished working with the chart, click anywhere in the document outside the chart to close Microsoft Graph and return to Word.

Connecting to an Excel or 1-2-3 Worksheet

The last way to place table information into Word is to connect to information in a worksheet. The information you'll read about in this section will work for both Excel and Lotus 1-2-3; to keep things simple, we refer only to Excel.

You actually have two ways to connect to information stored in Excel. Word distinguishes between them by calling them "Paste" and "Paste Link." What's the difference?

If you paste Excel information in Word that subsequently changes in Excel, the pasted information in Word *will not* be updated; you'll need to manually modify the information.

CHAPTER 8 • CRUNCHING NUMBERS IN A BUSINESS REPORT **217**

If you paste link Excel information to a Word document and the Excel information subsequently changes, the updates to the information *will* appear in your Word document.

Before you connect to information in a worksheet, you'll need to enter the following information into a new Excel workbook. When you save the workbook, name it **Sales Analysis table info.xls**. You can format the table in any way that you want in Excel; the formatting will carry over to Word.

Number of Salespeople		
	1995	1996
New York	5	5
Pennsylvania	3	3
New Jersey	3	3
Florida	5	6
Georgia	4	4
Alabama	3	4
Total	23	25

Switch back to Word using the Windows 95 Taskbar and press Ctrl+End to move to the bottom of the sample document in Word. Type the following paragraph. When you finish typing the paragraph, press Enter twice.

> You may have noticed, in Table 1, that New Jersey's sales are the only ones that didn't increase between 1995 and 1996; in fact, they decreased. In Table 2, you can see that New Jersey did not experience the same 4th quarter increase that other states experienced. We believe that Florida's and New York's success may be directly tied to the number of sales people they had each year; we believe that New Jersey's sales people could not adequately cover the territory. In Table 3, you see a comparison of the number of sales people each state had in each of the two years under study.

Hands On: Inserting a Table in Word by Linking to an Excel Workbook

To link Word to an Excel workbook, follow these steps:

1. Open Excel and open the workbook containing the information that you want to link to Word.

2. Select the information in Excel and click on the Copy button on Excel's Standard toolbar.
3. Use the Windows Taskbar to switch back to Word, leaving Excel open.
4. Choose Edit, Paste Special. Word displays the Paste Special dialog box (see Figure 8.39).

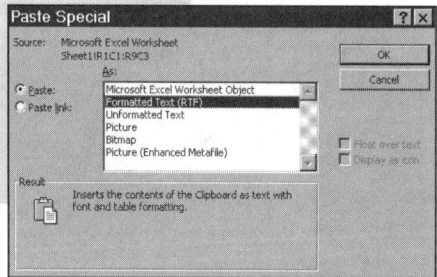

Figure 8.39
In this dialog box, you choose what you want to link and how you want to link it.

5. Word suggests that you paste the Excel worksheet information as formatted text—not an Excel workbook. If you accept these choices, your Word document will contain a copy of the information in the Excel worksheet that will appear as a table in Word. The copy *will not* be updated if anything in the Excel workbook changes. Select Paste Link to connect to the Excel workbook and have the Word document updated if the Excel information changes.

Note

If you choose to paste or paste link an Excel Object, you'll place a graphic object in your Word document. You will *not* be able to edit the object in Word; instead, if you double-click on the object, Excel will open and display the workbook.

6. Click on OK. The Excel information appears in your Word document (see Figure 8.40).

Because the information that you see in your Word document is a table, you can format the table in any of the ways you learned in this chapter. For example, in

CHAPTER 8 • CRUNCHING NUMBERS IN A BUSINESS REPORT

Figure 8.41, we widened the first column by dragging its right border. Then, we selected the entire table and centered it between the left and right margins. Last, we added a caption and centered it on the line below the table.

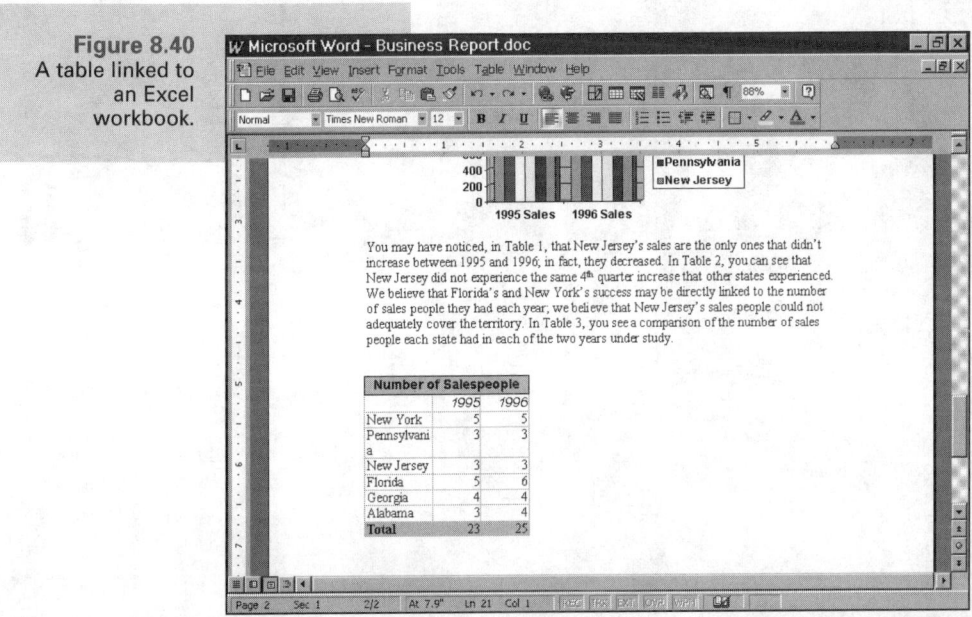

Figure 8.40
A table linked to an Excel workbook.

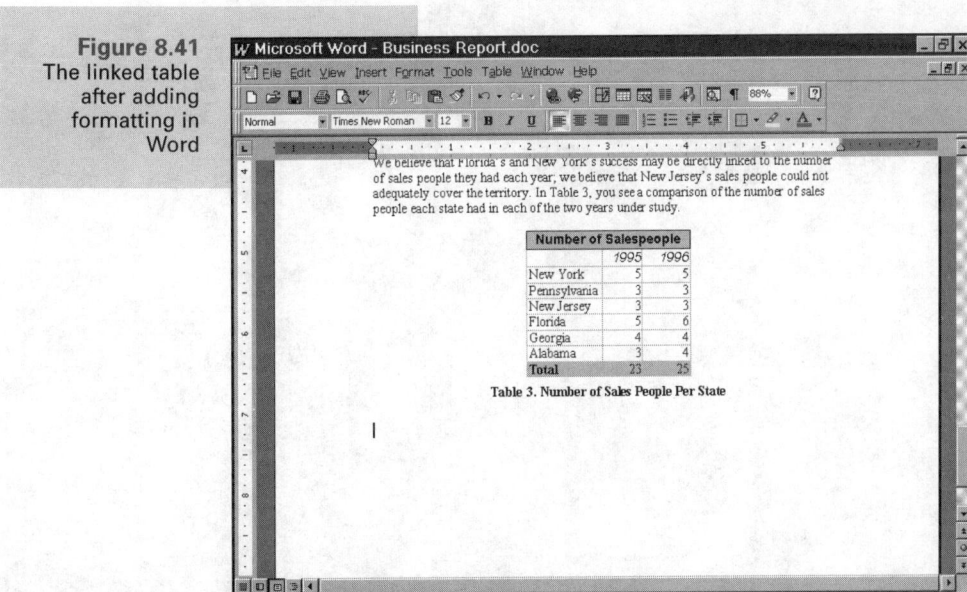

Figure 8.41
The linked table after adding formatting in Word

micros WORD

Using Mail Merge with a Sales Letter

In This Chapter

- Understanding the Merge Process
- Creating and Editing a Data Source Document
- Sorting a Merge
- Selectively Merging

Merging is the process of combining information contained in two different documents. The most common use of the merge function is to create a form letter. Typically, during the merge process, you combine names and addresses (stored in one document) with a letter that you want to send (stored in another document). In this chapter, we merge a list of customers with a sales letter. You'll see how to use the Mail Merge Helper, a Word tool that makes merging easier, to merge the information.

Understanding the Merge Process

To perform a merge, you need two documents: a *main document* and a *data source document*. You don't need to do a lot of planning before you start the merge process; basically, you need to figure out what information you need in each of these documents.

The content of the main document usually isn't too difficult to figure out. The main document contains information that doesn't change from letter to letter. If you're creating a form letter, the main document is the letter. The main document also contains *merge fields*, which identify where the information that changes should appear.

The data source is a little trickier, because it contains the information that *does* change from letter to letter. For a form letter that you're mailing to a list of people, the data source contains, at a minimum, names and addresses; however, it could also contain other information, depending on the letter that you're sending. A closer look at the data source document will help you better understand it.

The structure of the data source document is always the same. Word stores the information that you enter into the data source in a table; each row of the table represents a *merge record*, and each column represents a *merge field* (see Figure 9.1). The top row of the data source is called the *header record*, which contains the titles of the merge fields. The primary question that you need to answer when creating your data source is, "What merge fields should I include?"

Notice that we just told you that the main document contains merge fields and the columns in the data source also represent merge fields. Actually, these are the same merge fields. When you create a merge, you use the merge fields to tell Word *what* information needs to be combined from the data source, and *where* that information should appear in the main document.

Here comes the "Which came first, the chicken or the egg?" question of merging: What do you build first—the main document or the data source, because both require merge fields?

The solution: We will build our main document in two stages, and create the data source between Stage 1 and Stage 2. Here's our four-step process for merging:

CHAPTER 9 • USING MAIL MERGE WITH A SALES LETTER **223**

1. In Stage 1, we'll create a skeleton of the main document that contains all the unchanging information. Whenever we find a spot in the main document where changing information will appear, we'll simply type in a placeholder for a merge field, and simultaneously identify a field that must be included in the data source.
2. We'll use the information that we obtain from Stage 1 of building the main document to create the data source.
3. After creating the data source, we will return to the main document and replace our placeholders with merge fields.
4. Finally, we will merge.

Building the Main Document

As you know, the main document contains merge fields and all the information that will not change from letter to letter. During Stage 1 of building the main document, we will supply placeholder titles that represent merge fields at locations where information stored in the data source file should eventually appear.

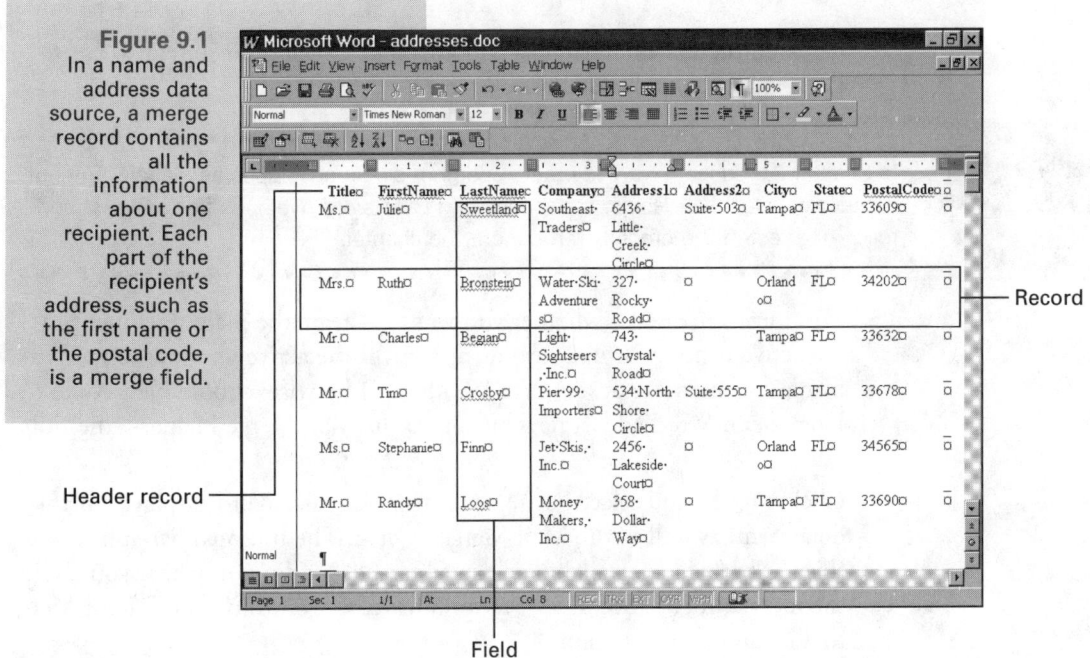

Figure 9.1
In a name and address data source, a merge record contains all the information about one recipient. Each part of the recipient's address, such as the first name or the postal code, is a merge field.

PART II • GETTING VISUAL

Hands On: The First Stage of Building a Main Document

To begin building a main document, follow these steps:

1. Choose <u>T</u>ools, Mail Me<u>r</u>ge. The Mail Merge Helper dialog box appears (see Figure 9.2).

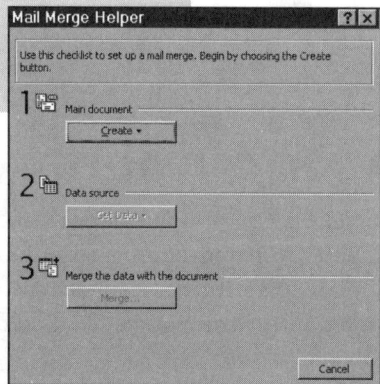

Figure 9.2 The Mail Merge Helper.

2. Click on the <u>C</u>reate button to choose a type of main document to create (see Figure 9.3). Choose Form <u>L</u>etters.

 *Tip*

• •

In Chapter 9, you learn how to create and print single envelopes and labels. To print multiple envelopes or labels, choose <u>M</u>ailing Labels or <u>E</u>nvelopes from this list and follow the rest of the process throughout the chapter.

• •

3. Word lets you choose whether you want to create the main document in the active window or in a new document. If the active window contains a blank document, choose <u>A</u>ctive Window. Otherwise, choose <u>N</u>ew Main Document. Word adds a new button to the Mail Merge Helper—the <u>E</u>dit button.

4. Click on <u>E</u>dit and select Form Letter from the list. Word displays a blank document, as well as the Mail Merge toolbar. The buttons that you see on this toolbar will be available or grayed out, depending on where you are in the merge process. See Table 9.1 for a list of the buttons on the Mail Merge toolbar and their functions.

CHAPTER 9 • USING MAIL MERGE WITH A SALES LETTER **225**

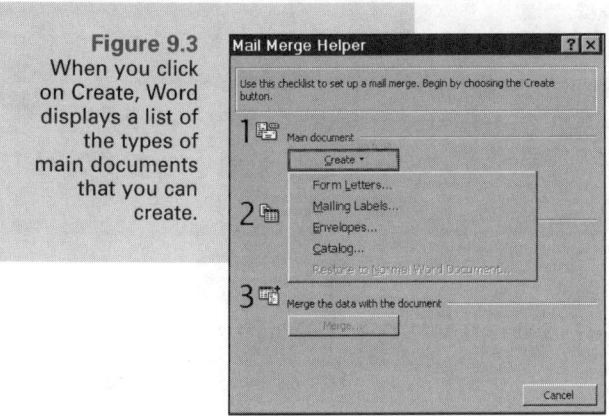

Figure 9.3
When you click on Create, Word displays a list of the types of main documents that you can create.

5. Type the main document, including placeholders, wherever information from the data source will eventually appear. Your letter should look similar to the one in Figure 9.4. The text for the letter also follows in bold, so that you can read it more easily.

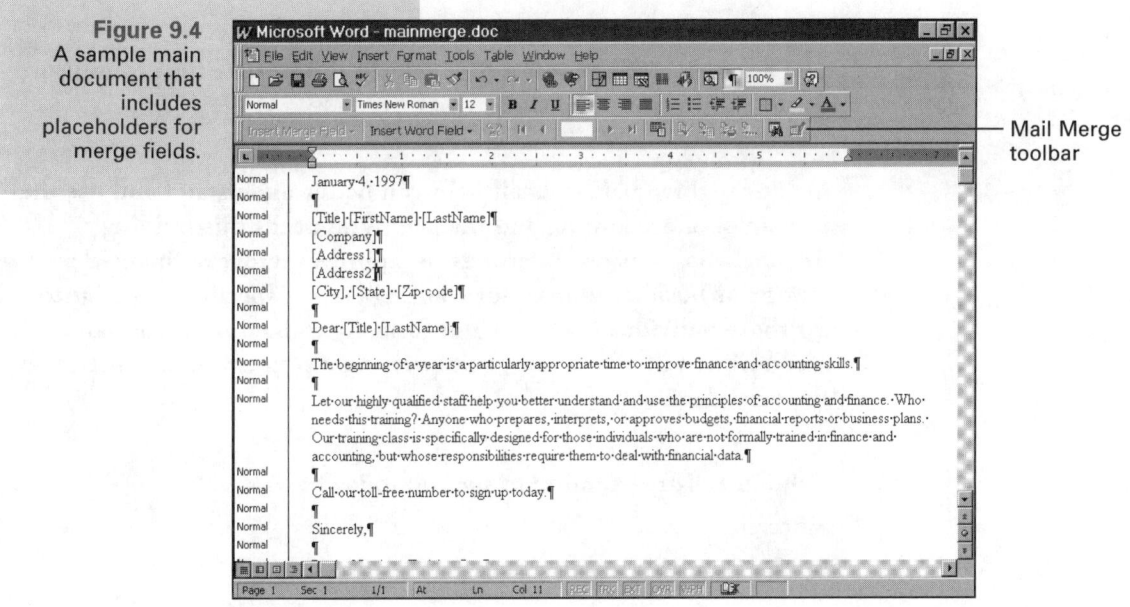

Figure 9.4
A sample main document that includes placeholders for merge fields.

Note: This text appears in the sample main document. Notice that we included spacing between placeholders (in the figure, the dots between the text represent spaces) just as if they were regular words. I also included punctuation such as the comma after [City].

Sample Text for a Mail Merge Document
January 4, 1997

[Title] [FirstName] [LastName]
[Company]
[Address]
[City], [State]   [ZIP code]

Dear [Title] [LastName]:

The beginning of a year is a particularly appropriate time to improve finance and accounting skills.

Let our highly qualified staff help you better understand and use the principles of accounting and finance. Who needs this training? Anyone who prepares, interprets, or approves budgets, financial reports or business plans. Our training class is specifically designed for those individuals who are not formally trained in finance and accounting, but whose responsibilities require them to deal with financial data.

Call our toll-free number to sign up today.
Sincerely,
By the Numbers Training, Inc.

Table 9.1 Mail Merge Buttons

Button	Button Name	Function
Insert Merge Field ▾	Insert Merge Field	Places a merge field in the main document
Insert Word Field ▾	Insert Word Field	Places a Word field in the main document to customize the document
	View Merged Data	Allows you to view the main document while including information from the data source
	First Record	Allows you to view the main document while including the first record in the data source
	Previous Record	Allows you to view the main document while including the previous record in the data source
	Go To Record	Allows you to specify a record in the data source to view in the main document
	Next Record	Allows you to view the main document while including the next record in the data source
	Last Record	Allows you to view the main document while including the last record in the data source
	Mail Merge Helper	Opens the Mail Merge Helper dialog box
	Check for Errors	Checks the merge for errors
	Merge to New Document	Performs the merge and places the results in a new document; each merged document makes up a page of the new document
	Merge to Printer	Performs the merge and prints the resulting merged pages.
	Mail Merge	Opens the Merge dialog box
	Find Record	Allows you to search for a particular record in the data source document
	Edit Data Source	Reopens the Data Form dialog box so that you can edit records in the data source document

Working with Data Source Documents

You learned earlier in this chapter that the data source contains the information that changes in each merged letter. In our example, the data source will contain name and address information. The data source can include other information; if, for example, your form letter concerns collections, you can include amounts due from customers in the data source document.

You can use address books that come with Microsoft programs as a data source, or you can create your own data source using the Mail Merge Helper. After you have created a data source document, you can use that document as your data source for any merge operation. When you set up the merge, Word attaches the data source document to the main document; that way, the two documents can share the merge fields.

Using Data Stored in Personal Address Books

Word 95 shipped with an internal address book called the Personal Address Book, in which you could store names and addresses that you used regularly. In Word 95, a tool to access this Personal Address Book appeared on the Standard toolbar. In Word 97, the tool disappeared from the Standard toolbar, but the functionality did not disappear from the program. The Personal Address Book is still available for use in the Envelopes and Labels dialog box (choose Tools, Envelopes and Labels), and you can merge the names and addresses stored in the Personal Address Book with a form letter or other merge document.

Word also lets you use names and addresses stored in address books of other Microsoft products such as Outlook or Schedule+.

Hands On: Choosing an Address Book

In any of these cases, you can choose an address book to serve as your data source by following these steps:

1. Choose Tools, Mail Merge or click on the Mail Merge Helper tool to reopen the Mail Merge Helper.
2. Click on Get Data to display a drop-down list of data sources.

Chapter 9 • Using Mail Merge with a Sales Letter

3. Choose Use Address Book. Word displays the Use Address Book dialog box that you see in Figure 9.5.
4. Select the address book you want to use and choose OK.

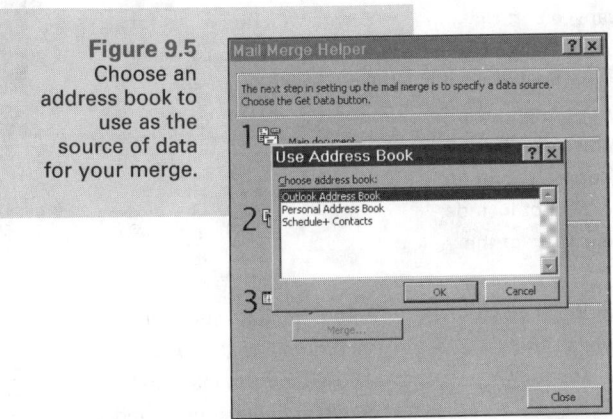

Figure 9.5 Choose an address book to use as the source of data for your merge.

Special Considerations When Creating Data Source Documents

Some special circumstances can affect the fields that you define in the data source document. In Table 9.2, you can find some examples of these circumstances and guidelines to follow in each case.

Working with Data Source Documents

Creating a data source document is a two-part process. First, you define the fields that will appear in the data source; then, you enter the actual data for each field. The Mail Merge Helper provides dialog boxes for each of these processes, and they appear one after the other.

Hands On: Creating a Data Source

You can create the fields for the data source file and add information to it by following these steps:

1. Choose Tools, Mail Merge or click on the Mail Merge Helper button on the Mail Merge toolbar. Word displays the Mail Merge Helper dialog box.

Table 9.2 Unusual Merging Situations

Issue	Example	Guideline
Do you need to sort your data?	You may want to sort mailing labels and/or envelopes by zip code, particularly if you are preparing a bulk mailing. In this case, be sure to create a separate field for the zip code. Do not include the zip code as part of the State field.	Create separate fields for any information by which you may want to sort.
Do some records contain more information than others?	Are some addresses two lines long while others are only one line long?	Create the data source to accommodate the longest record. You can leave fields blank in a data source, and blank fields will not necessarily create blank lines in the merge document.
Do you need to use similar information in different ways?	You may use the recipient's entire name and title in the inside address (for example, Ms. Mary Smith), but, later in the letter, address her directly (for example, Ms. Smith).	If you need to use the same information in more than one way, break the information up into separate fields; for example, create fields for Title, First Name, and Last Name.
Do you plan to use the data source document with more than one main document?	You might want to use a name and address data source for a form letter and to produce either mailing labels or envelopes.	You can selectively choose which fields will be merged into the main document; therefore, set up a single data source that includes all the information you think you will need for all uses of that data source.

2. Click on the Get Data button to display the drop-down menu and choose Create Data Source (see Figure 9.6).

CHAPTER 9 • USING MAIL MERGE WITH A SALES LETTER **231**

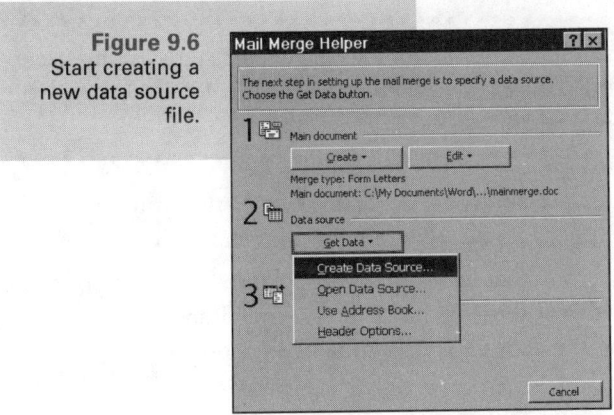

Figure 9.6
Start creating a new data source file.

3. Word displays the Create Data Source dialog box (see Figure 9.7), which you use to select fields that you want to appear in your data source document.

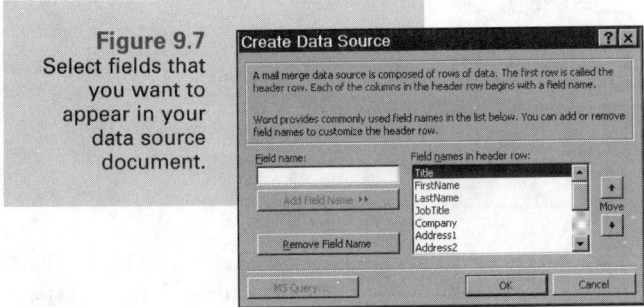

Figure 9.7
Select fields that you want to appear in your data source document.

4. Each field in the Field Names in Header Row list on the right will appear in the data source unless you highlight it and then click on Remove Field Name. If you need a field that doesn't appear, type it in the Field Name text box and then click on the Add Field Name button to add it to the list on the right. In our example, highlight and click on Remove Field Name for each of the following fields:

- JobTitle
- Country
- HomePhone
- WorkPhone

PART II • GETTING VISUAL

You can use the Move arrow buttons to reorder the field names in the list; the order is not critically important. In the dialog box where you actually enter data, Word will display the fields in the order that you select here.

5. Click on OK. Word displays the Save As dialog box so that you can save your data source document. Provide a file name and choose Save.

6. Word displays a dialog box that lets you choose to enter data into your data source document or add merge fields to your main document. We will continue creating the data source document, so choose Edit Data Source.

7. Word displays the Data Form dialog box that you can use to enter the information that should appear in your data source document (see Figure 9.8).

Figure 9.8
Use this form to enter data into your data source document.

8. Fill in the text boxes, pressing (Tab) to move from field to field as you type. If you don't have information for a particular field, such as Address 2, skip it. When you complete the form for the first record, click on Add New to add another record. When you have added all the information that you need to your data source, click on OK to redisplay the main document. The names and addresses that we included in the example data source appear in the following bold text.

Even if you have already attached a data source to a main document, you can create a new, different data source by simply following these steps again.

Sample Merge Data

This text is included in the sample document:

Ms. Julie Sweetland
Southeast Traders
6436 Little Creek Circle
Suite 503
Tampa, Fl 33609

Mrs. Ruth Bronstein
Water Ski Adventures
327 Rocky Road
Orlando, FL 34202

Mr. Charles Begian
Light Sightseers, Inc.
743 Crystal Road
Tampa, FL 33632

Mr. Tim Crosby
Pier 99 Importers
534 North Shore Circle
Suite 555
Tampa, FL 33678

Ms. Stephanie Finn
Jet Skis, Inc.
2456 Lakeside Court
Orlando, FL 34565

Mr. Randy Loos
Money Makers, Inc.
358 Dollar Way
Tampa, FL 33690

Hands On: Using an Existing Data Source Document

Suppose that you already created a data source file and it contains the information you need for a new merge. You don't need to recreate the data source file; you can attach it to a new main document. Follow these steps:

1. Open a new, blank document.

2. Create a new main document by choosing <u>T</u>ools, Mail Me<u>r</u>ge, <u>C</u>reate, and choose the type of document you want to create. Then, choose <u>A</u>ctive Window.

3. When Word redisplays the Mail Merge Helper, choose <u>G</u>et Data and then choose <u>O</u>pen Data Source. The Open Data Source dialog box appears; this dialog box looks and acts just like the Open dialog box. Find your data source file and choose <u>O</u>pen.

To attach a different data source to an existing main document, follow the same basic steps with the following exceptions. In Step 1, open the existing main document. In Step 2, Word will ask whether you want to change the document type of the existing main document or create a new main document. Because you chose the same type of main document that you originally created, the suggestion in the dialog box may look strange to you—it will suggest that you can change the existing main document from "form letters to form letters." Choose <u>C</u>hange Document Type.

Editing a Data Source

You can make changes to the information in the data source by redisplaying the Data Form. From the main document, click on the Edit Data Source button on the Mail Merge toolbar (last button on the right). Word redisplays the Data Form and displays in it the first record in your data source (see Figure 9.9).

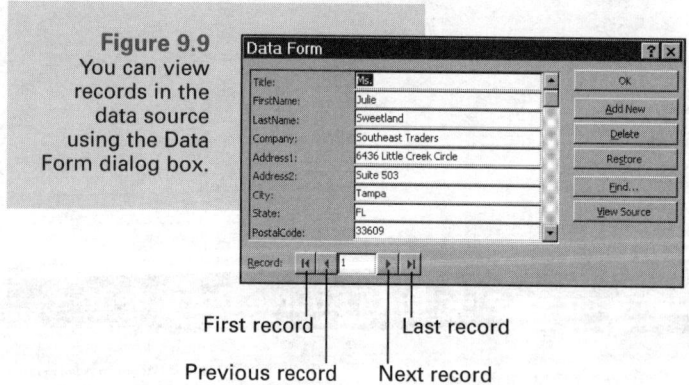

Figure 9.9 You can view records in the data source using the Data Form dialog box.

To view other records, click on the buttons at the bottom of the dialog box that move forward and backward through the data source. The leftmost button displays the first record in the data source, and the rightmost button displays the last record in the data source. The other two buttons move forward and backward one record at a time.

Click on the Delete button to delete a record, and use the Restore button to ignore changes that you may have made to the record you are viewing. Search for records by clicking on Find to display the Find in Field dialog box (see Figure 9.10). Supply the text that you want to search for in the Find what text box, and use the In field list box to identify the field Word should search for the text you specified.

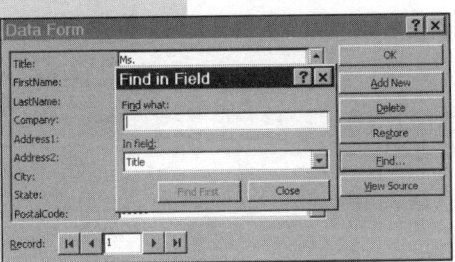

Figure 9.10
Using this dialog box, you can search for records by specifying information stored in a specific field.

The View Source button in the Data Form dialog box displays your data source in table format, the way Word stores it.

Adding Fields to the Main Document

On to Stage 2 of building the main document. It's time to insert real merge fields into the main document to replace the placeholders that we originally entered.

Hands On: The Second Stage of Building the Main Document

To finish building the main document, follow these steps:

1. In the main document, find the first placeholder that you entered.

Tip

You can use Word's Edit, Find command to search for the characters you used to identify each placeholder; in the example, we enclosed placeholders in square brackets ([]), so we can search for an opening square bracket ([).

2. Highlight the entire placeholder (see Figure 9.11).

PART II • GETTING VISUAL

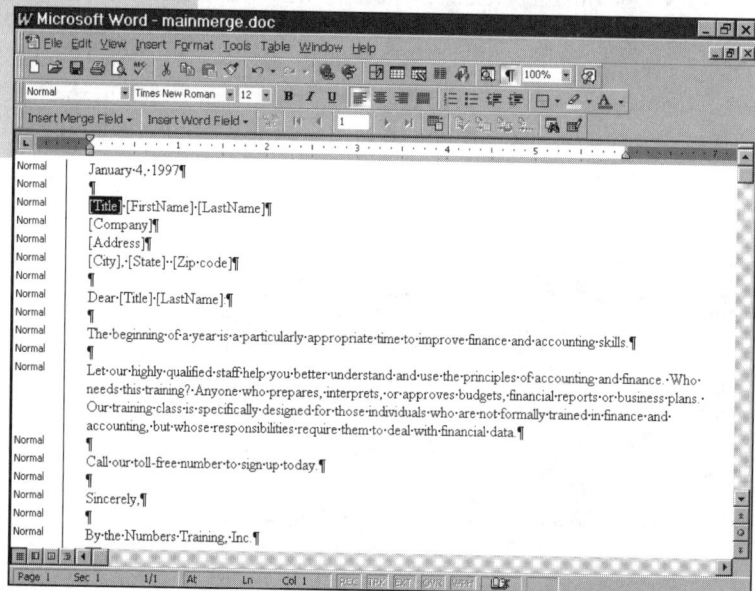

Figure 9.11 In the main document, select a merge field placeholder.

3. Click on the Insert Merge Field button on the Mail Merge toolbar (see Figure 9.12) to select the appropriate merge field from the list of merge fields available in the data source document.

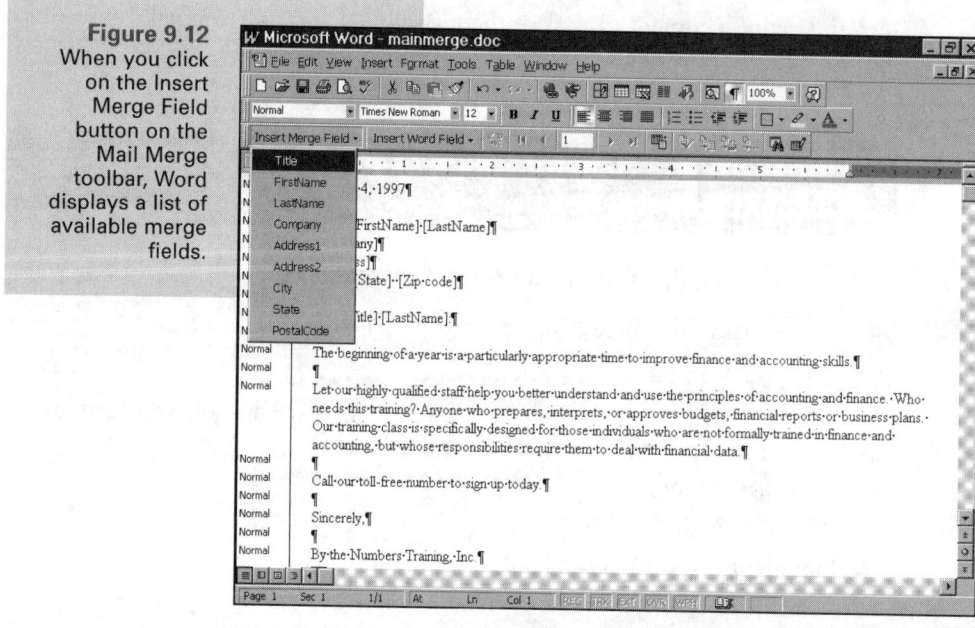

Figure 9.12 When you click on the Insert Merge Field button on the Mail Merge toolbar, Word displays a list of available merge fields.

CHAPTER 9 • USING MAIL MERGE WITH A SALES LETTER

4. Word replaces the highlighted placeholder with the merge field that you chose. The merge field is enclosed in angle brackets. Repeat Steps 2 and 3 for each placeholder in your main document. When you finish, your main document should look like the one in Figure 9.13.

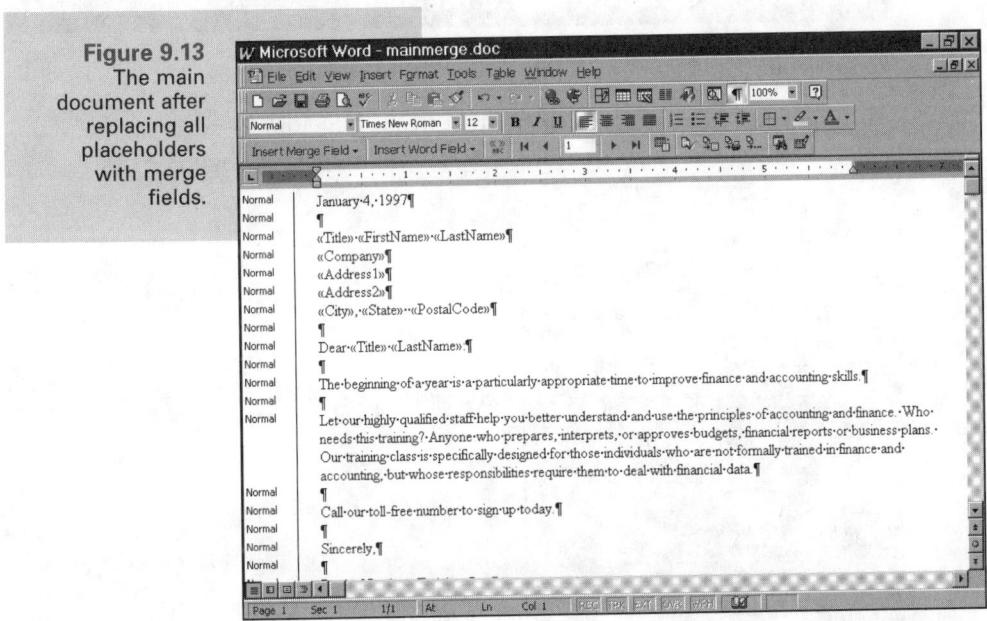

Figure 9.13
The main document after replacing all placeholders with merge fields.

Merging

At this point, you could simply merge your main document with your data source document. But, before we get to that, you should know about some special options available to you.

Special Merging Options

Before you merge, you can sort information so that, when you merge, the final products appear on-screen (and in print) in an order that you specified. Or, you can selectively merge so that you produce a mailing that goes to just some of the people in the file.

Sorting Merge Information

Sorting merge information is particularly useful if you plan to follow bulk mailing regulations and need to bundle all letters for a particular zip code. If you sort information by zip code, all letters for the same zip code will merge and print in a group; you'll save time because you won't need to sort manually after you print.

Hands On: Sorting Before Merging

To sort your data before merging, follow these steps:

1. Open the Mail Merge Helper either by clicking on its button on the Mail Merge toolbar or by choosing Tools, Mail Merge (see Figure 9.14).

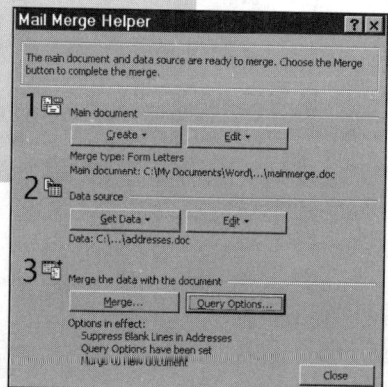

Figure 9.14 From the Mail Merge Helper, you can set sorting options for your merge.

2. Click on the Query Options button. Word displays the Query Options dialog box. Click on the Sort Records tab.

3. To set up a sort, open the Sort By list box and select a merge field by which you want to sort.

4. Click on either the Ascending or Descending option button to sort merged information from lowest to highest or from highest to lowest.

5. (Optional) Use the Then By list boxes to set additional sort fields if you want Word to break ties using another field. For example, in Figure 9.15, we've set up the merge so that records will sort in zip code order, and any duplicate zip codes will be sorted alphabetically by the last name of the recipient.

CHAPTER 9 • USING MAIL MERGE WITH A SALES LETTER **239**

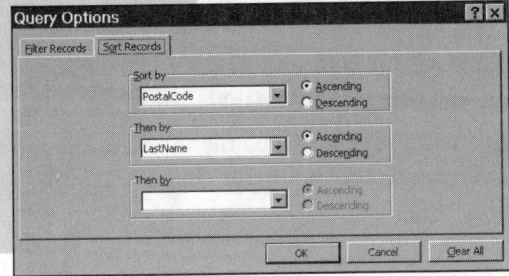

Figure 9.15
Use the Sort Records tab of the Query Options dialog box to produce merged documents in a specified order.

Selecting Records to Include in a Merge

Suppose that your data source file contains a large number of records, but you really want to mail to just some of the people in the file. For example, you may want to create letters for only single women.

Hands On: Merging Selectively

You can *filter* the data source so that Word merges only those records that match criteria you establish. Follow these steps:

1. Open the Mail Merge Helper either by clicking on its button on the Mail Merge toolbar or by choosing <u>T</u>ools, Mail Me<u>r</u>ge (see Figure 9.16).

2. Click on the <u>Q</u>uery Options button. Word displays the Query Options dialog box. Click on the <u>F</u>ilter Records tab.

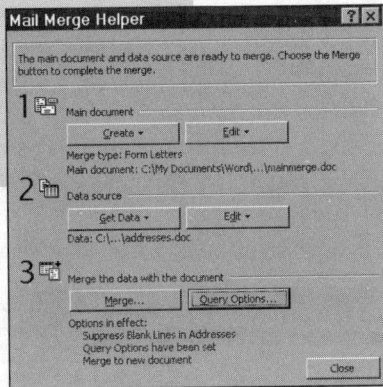

Figure 9.16
From the Mail Merge Helper, you can set selection options for your merge.

3. Open the first field list box and select a field that you want Word to use when selecting records. In the example, select Title.
4. Open the Comparison box and choose the operator that you want Word to use when selecting. In our example, select Equal to.
5. In the Compare To text box, type the information you want Word to use when selecting records to merge. In our example, type **Ms.** (see Figure 9.17).

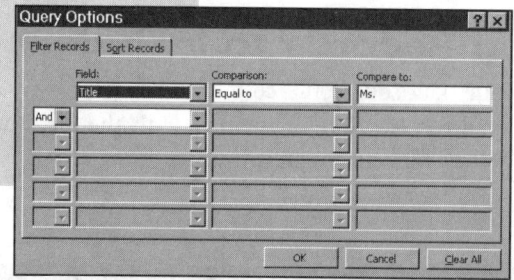

Figure 9.17 Filter criteria helps you selectively merge from the data source.

6. (Optional) Set up additional criteria for Word to use when selecting. You can set the second line (and subsequent lines) so that the other criteria you establish are used in addition to the first line (And) or as an alternative to the first line (Or). If you use And, you are limiting the selection more than if you choose Or; "And" means that *both* sets of criteria must be true before Word will select a record, whereas "Or" means that *either* set of criteria can be true and Word will select the record.
7. Click on OK to accept your filter criteria.

Performing the Merge

Using buttons on the Mail Merge toolbar, you can tell Word to perform the merge and send the output either directly to your printer or to a document. Using the Merge dialog box, however, gives you additional options to set. For example, you can merge to e-mail or fax. And you can specify a range of records to merge.

Hands On: Setting Up the Merge

To set up the merge and perform it, follow these steps:

Chapter 9 • Using Mail Merge with a Sales Letter

1. In the main document, click on the Mail Merge button on the Mail Merge toolbar, or choose Tools, Mail Merge, and then click on Merge. Word displays the Merge dialog box (see Figure 9.18).

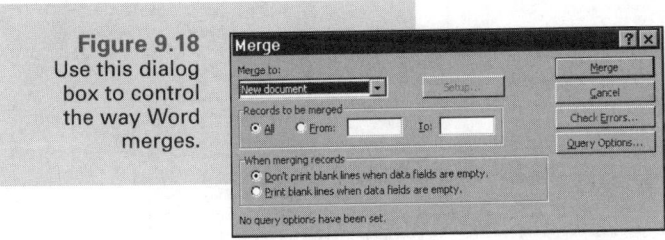

Figure 9.18
Use this dialog box to control the way Word merges.

2. From the Merge To list box (see Figure 9.19), choose where you want the merged documents to appear.

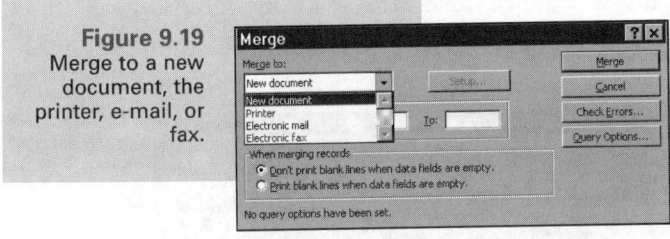

Figure 9.19
Merge to a new document, the printer, e-mail, or fax.

3. In the Records to be Merged box (refer to Figure 9.18), choose to merge all records that meet any filter criteria you set or specific record numbers.
4. In the When Merging Records box, tell Word how to handle blank lines.
5. Use the Query Options button to redisplay the Query Options dialog box.
6. Use the Check Errors button to have Word check the merge for errors before you actually merge. This is particularly helpful if your data source is large.
7. Choose Merge. Word merges according to your specifications. We set up the merge to appear in a new document (see Figure 9.20).

Perhaps the best view of the merged documents appears in Print Preview (see Figure 9.21).

> **You can learn more about Print Preview in Chapter 6.**

Figure 9.20
When you merge to a new document, Word places all merged documents in a new document, and separates each with a page break.

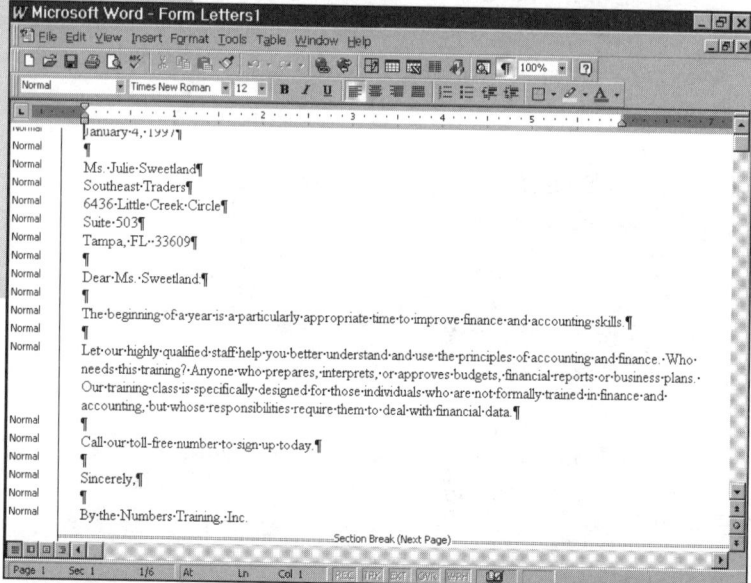

Figure 9.21
In this figure, you see 6 merged documents, but you can see up to 24 merged documents at one time in Print Preview.

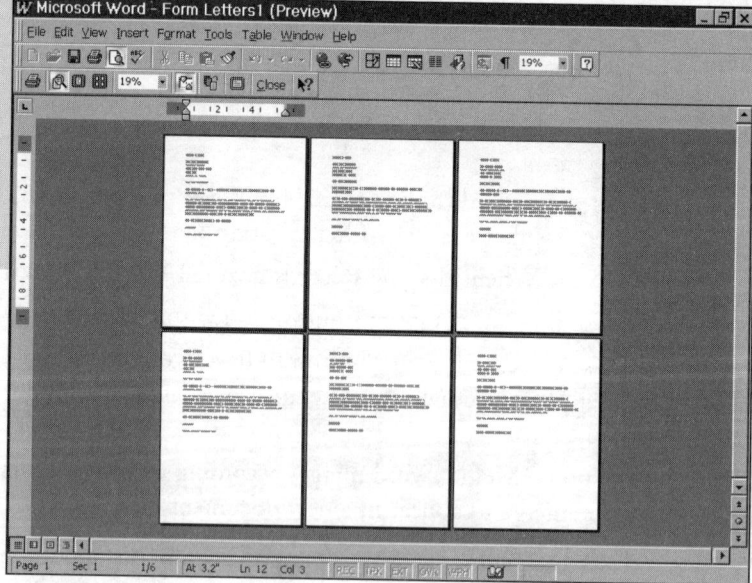

Customizing a Form Letter

You may have noticed the Insert Word Field button next to the Insert Merge Field button on the Mail Merge button. Using the Insert Word Field button, you can customize your form letter. Some of the fields, such as Ask, Fill-in, If...Then...Else..., and Set Bookmark, let you add information to your form letter. Other fields, such as Merge Record #, Merge Sequence #, Next Record, Next Record If, and Skip Record If help you control how data is merged.

Look at an example of how you can add information to a form letter using an If...Then...Else... field. In our example form letter, we informed the recipients about a class that we're offering—but we never told them when the class would be offered. Suppose that the class will be offered on different days in different cities. We can include an If...Then...Else... statement in the main document that will tell Word to print one date in letters to residents of Tampa, and another date in letters to residents of Orlando.

Hands On: Adding Word Fields to Customize a Merge Document

Follow these steps to add Word Fields to a merge document:

1. Position the insertion point in the main document where you want the customized information to appear. In our example, we positioned the insertion point at the end of the letter (see Figure 9.22).
2. Click on the Insert Word Field button on the Mail Merge toolbar and choose If...Then...Else... from the drop-down list (see Figure 9.23).
3. Word displays the Insert Word Field: IF dialog box (see Figure 9.24).
4. Use the three boxes at the top to set up the IF statement. For our statement, open the Field Name list box and choose City. Leave the Comparison at Equal to, and in the Compare To text box, type a value that would be valid in your merge (in our example, type **Tampa**).

244 PART II • GETTING VISUAL

Figure 9.22
Place the insertion point where you want the customized information to appear.

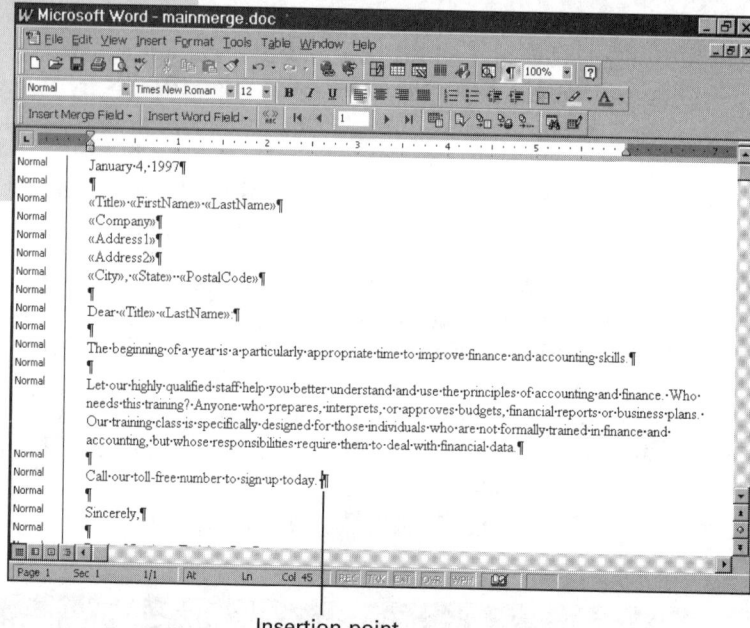

Insertion point

Figure 9.23
The Insert Word Field button on the Mail Merge toolbar provides a list of Word fields that you can use in a mail merge.

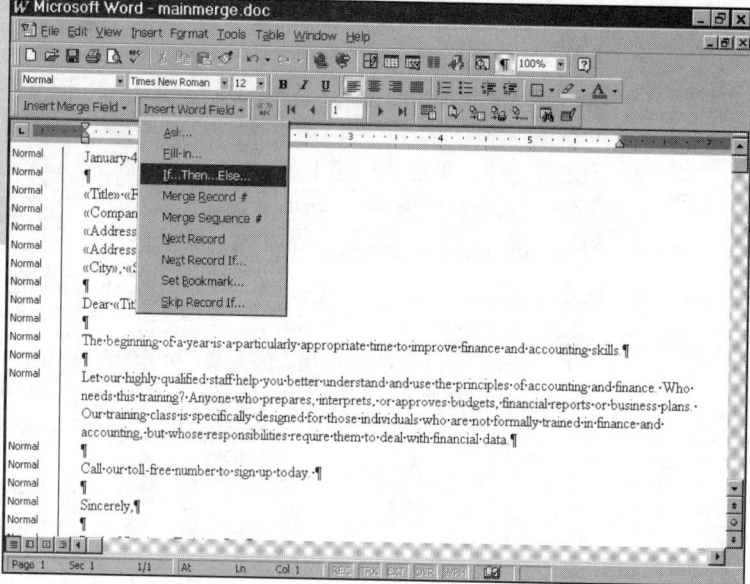

CHAPTER 9 • USING MAIL MERGE WITH A SALES LETTER   245

5. In the Insert This Text box, type the sentence(s) that you want Word to include if the conditions you just set are true; for our example, type the following: **Classes will be held on Tuesday, January 14, at 9:00 a.m. at our Tampa facility.**

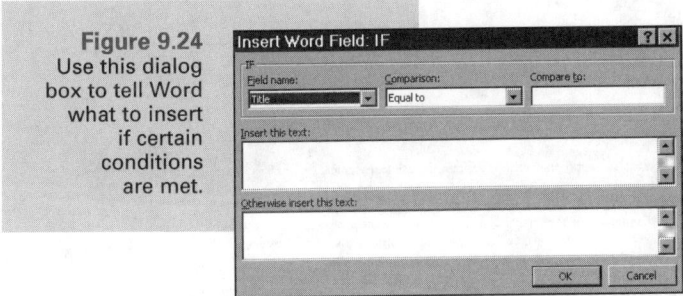

Figure 9.24
Use this dialog box to tell Word what to insert if certain conditions are met.

6. In the Otherwise Insert This Text box, type the sentence(s) that you want Word to include if the conditions you set are false; for our example, type the following: **Classes will be held on Thursday, January 16, at 9:00 a.m. at our Orlando facility.** Your dialog box should look like the one in Figure 9.25.

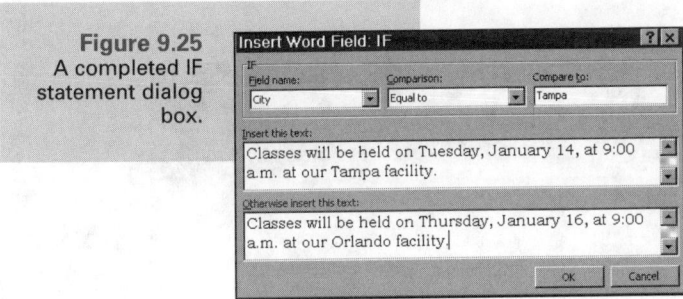

Figure 9.25
A completed IF statement dialog box.

7. Click on OK. Word inserts the first version of the IF statement into your document, but if you click anywhere in it, you'll notice that it has a gray background (see Figure 9.26). The gray background indicates that the statement is a field that will change from letter to letter.

Figure 9.26 A main document containing an IF statement.

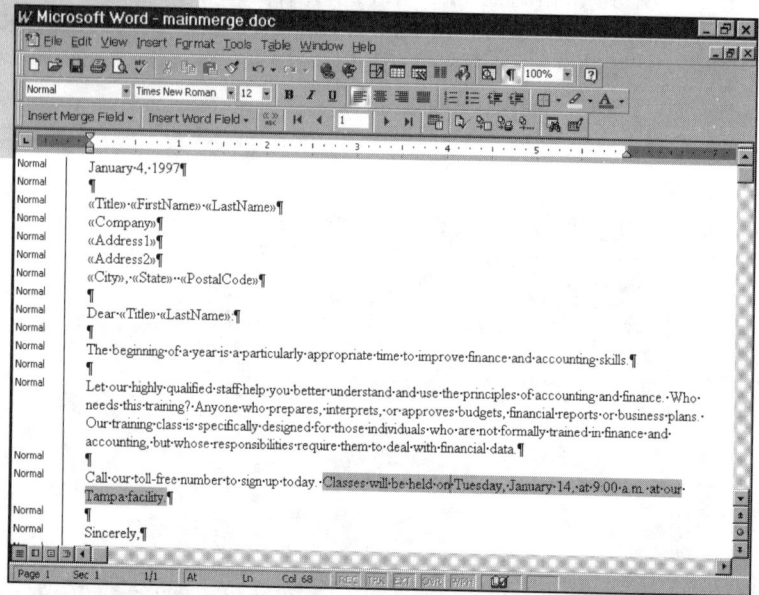

8. Merge your letters using the steps you followed earlier in this chapter. In our example, the first letter contains the class date for the Tampa facility (see Figure 9.27), and the second letter contains the class date for the Orlando facility (see Figure 9.28).

Figure 9.27 A recipient in Tampa sees the class date for Tampa.

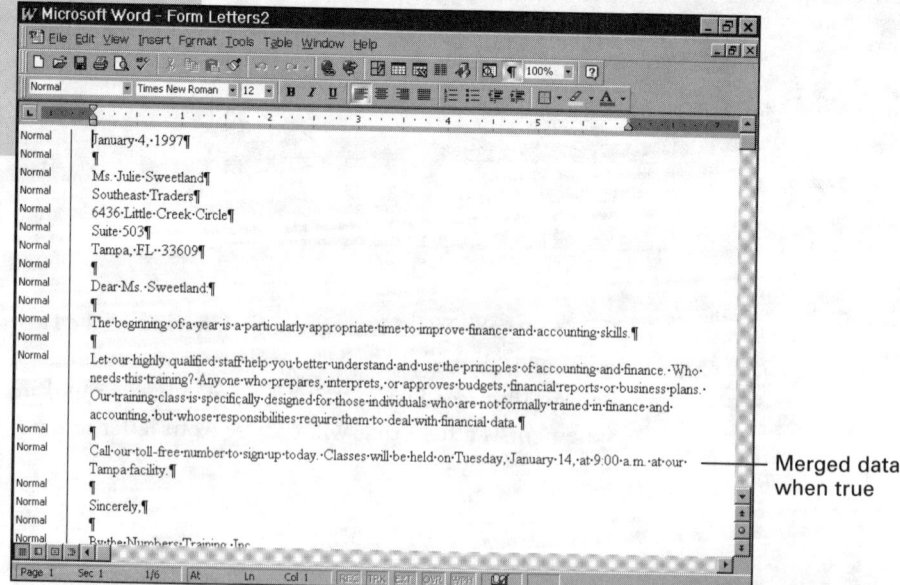

— Merged data when true

CHAPTER 9 • USING MAIL MERGE WITH A SALES LETTER

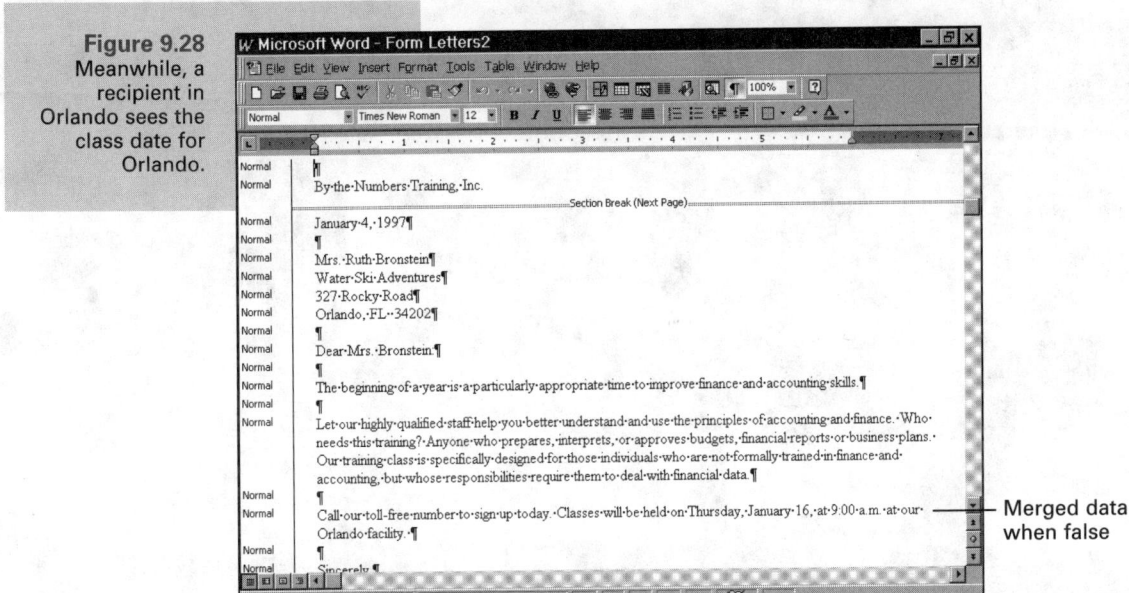

Figure 9.28 Meanwhile, a recipient in Orlando sees the class date for Orlando.

microsoft
WORD

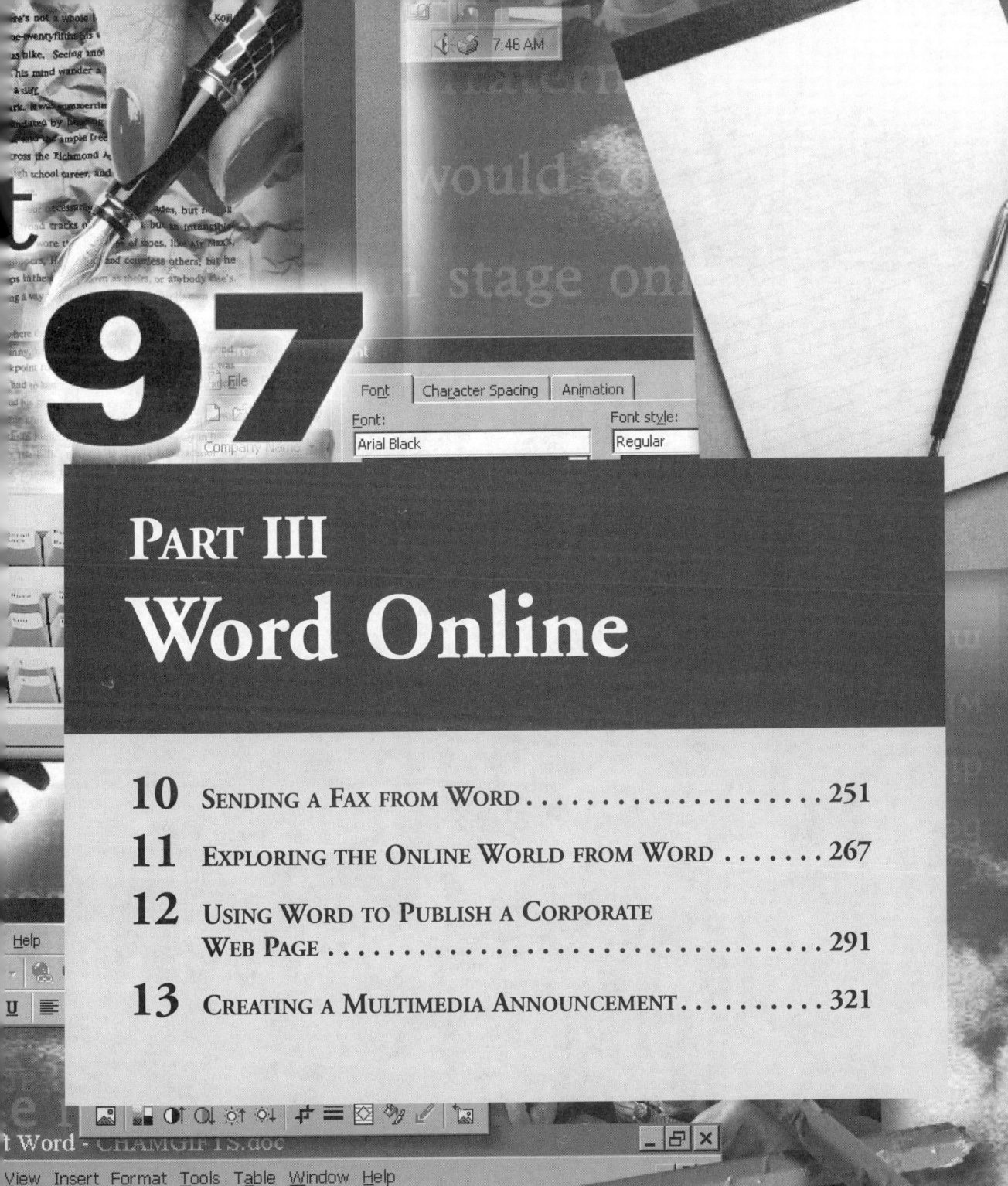

Part III
Word Online

10 Sending a Fax from Word 251

11 Exploring the Online World from Word 267

12 Using Word to Publish a Corporate Web Page 291

13 Creating a Multimedia Announcement 321

micros
WORD

10

Sending a Fax from Word

IN THIS CHAPTER

- Choosing a Fax Cover Sheet
- Working with a Fax/Modem
- Sending a Fax

As you know, the typical method of faxing involves feeding a printed document through a machine. Ordinarily, a fax transmission includes a cover sheet that identifies who is sending the document and how many pages the recipient can expect. Often, the cover sheet contains other instructions as well.

Word 97 supports this method of transmission by providing three different styles of cover sheets that you can fill out, print, and include with a fax that you send using a fax machine.

The advent of fax/modems, however, has changed the way people send faxes. People can now send documents directly from their computers, and receive faxed documents on their computers as well. Word 97 also supports this method of transmitting information by allowing you to send a fax while working in Word; you can still include a cover sheet, but you don't need a hard copy of it to send it.

In this chapter, you'll explore using Word to send a fax.

Choosing a Fax Cover Sheet

Word provides three different styles of cover sheets. The one you choose is a matter of personal preference. All are tastefully designed, and any one of them would represent you well to others (see Figures 10.1, 10.2, and 10.3).

Each of the documents shown in these three figures was created based on templates supplied by Microsoft. A *template* is a special kind of a Word document in which you store basic tools and elements that you use repeatedly to create other documents. For example, each fax cover sheet calls for the name, address, and phone number of the sender. That information can be stored in the template. Furthermore, each fax cover sheet calls for information such as a place to store the name of the fax recipient. That information is stored in the template. A template can also contain styles, formatting, and graphics that give the template a particular appearance. In the fax cover sheets, this information is used to create the different styles: Elegant, Contemporary, and Professional.

> **See Chapter 14 for more information on using and modifying templates.**

Every document that you create in Word is based on a template. Most documents are based on the Normal template, but fax cover sheets are based on one of the three fax templates.

One way to create a fax cover sheet is to start a new document based on one of the fax templates. As you'll see later in this chapter, however, using Word's Fax Wizard is easier. But before we discuss how to use the Fax Wizard, make sure that your modem is set up so that you can send (and receive) faxes using Word 97.

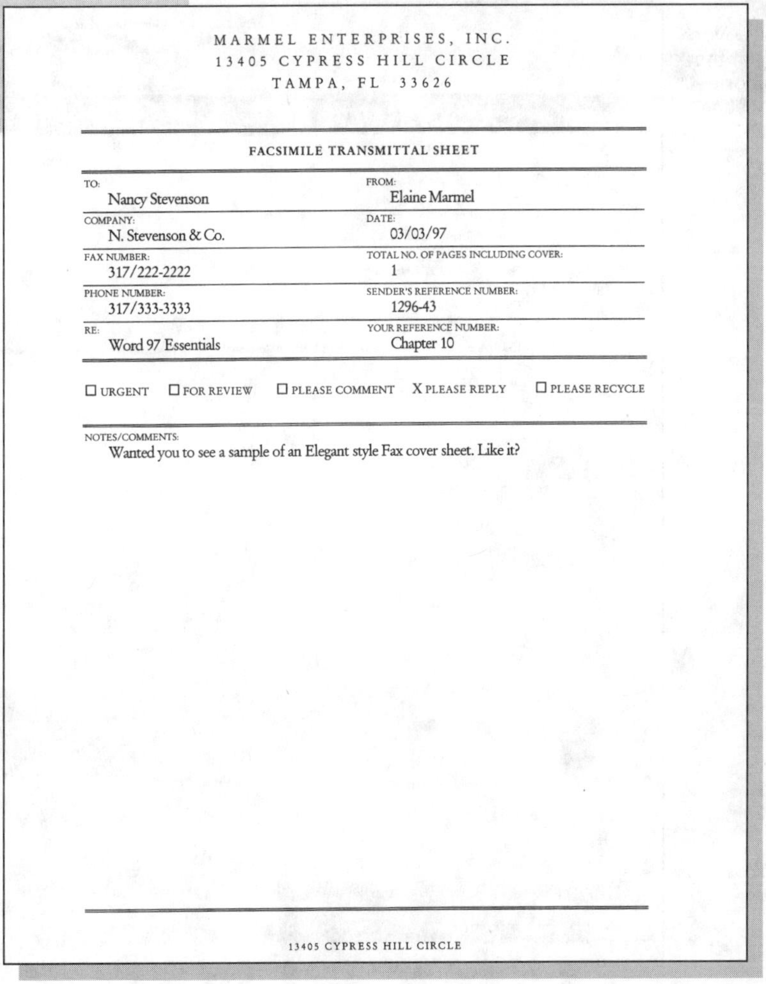

Figure 10.1
A fax cover sheet in the Elegant style.

Understanding How a Fax/Modem Works

Nowadays, nearly everybody knows how to send a fax using a fax machine. You get your "hard copies" together, prepare a cover sheet, place them in a fax machine, dial the recipient's phone number, and press Send. It's that simple and easy. Well, a fax/modem can be even easier. You don't need a hard copy of the document that you want to send, and your modem dials the recipient's phone number for you and automatically sends when the recipient answers.

Figure 10.2
A fax cover sheet in the Contemporary style.

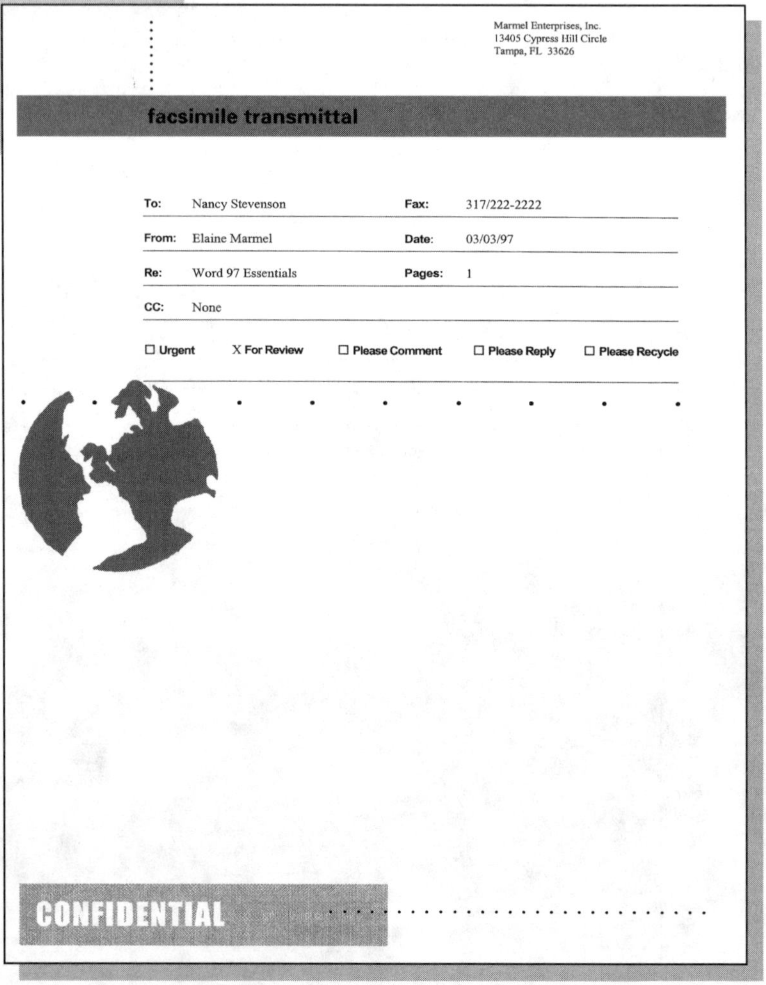

A *fax/modem* is an electronic device used to transmit data from one computer to another. A fax/modem can substitute for a fax machine if the information that you want to send consists of either the fax cover sheet only, or the fax cover sheet and a document stored on your computer.

CHAPTER 10 • SENDING A FAX FROM WORD **255**

Figure 10.3
A fax cover sheet in the Professional style.

13405 Cypress Hill Circle
Tampa, FL 33626
813/920-5555

Marmel Enterprises, Inc.

Fax

To:	Nancy Stevenson	**From:**	Elaine Marmel
Fax:	317-222-2222	**Pages:**	1
Phone:	317-333-3333	**Date:**	03/03/97
Re:	Word 97 Essentials	**CC:**	None

☐ Urgent   X **For Review**   ☐ **Please Comment**   ☐ **Please Reply**   ☐ **Please Recycle**

• **Comments:** Wanted you to see a sample of a Professional style Fax cover sheet. Like it?

Note

If you need to fax a document that *is not* stored on your computer, you must use a separate fax machine. You can, however, still create a fax cover sheet in Word and print that cover sheet to use when you send your fax.

Fax/modems can be installed in your computer (called *internal* fax/modems) or they can simply be attached to your computer (called *external* fax/modems). If your fax/modem is internal, you won't be able to see it, but you may be able to hear sounds such as a telephone dial tone and some electronic squealing and "bonging" noises when it is operating. If your fax/modem is external, you will see red lights flashing when the modem is operating, and you may also hear the modem.

If you have connected to the Internet or used any of the online services, such as America Online, CompuServe, or The Microsoft Network, then you have used a modem. And, as you probably realize, you used software with your modem that allowed you to interact with the modem. Just as you needed software to connect to the Internet or an online service, you also need software to use your modem to send a fax. Good news, here. Fax/modems typically come with such software. Two of the more popular programs are WinFax and QuickLink Fax.

If you don't have fax software, Windows 95 comes with an applet called Microsoft Fax that you can use in conjunction with Microsoft Exchange to send a fax. You'll see how to do that later in the chapter, using Microsoft Fax with Word to send a fax. But first, we cover the process of sending a Fax from Word using your fax modem and the software that came with it.

Install your fax software according to the manufacturer's instructions. After you install Fax software, you'll see how easy it is to use.

Fax software installs into the Windows environment as a printer. When you finish installing, check the Windows 95 Printers folder (click on the Start button, highlight Settings, and click on Printers) for a new printer listing (see Figure 10.4).

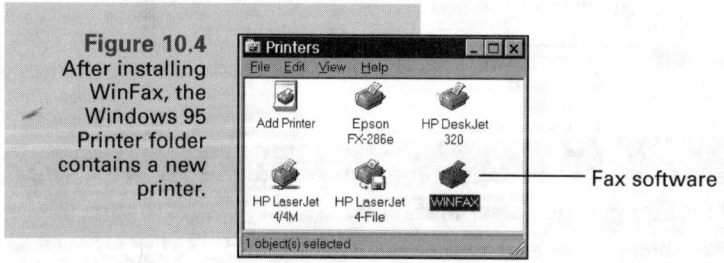

Figure 10.4
After installing WinFax, the Windows 95 Printer folder contains a new printer.

"Why a printer?", you might ask. Well, actually, a printer makes some sense, because a printer is an output device, and so is a fax/modem when you're sending a fax. So, to actually use your fax software in Word, you "print" to the fax modem, as you'll see in just a moment.

CHAPTER 10 • SENDING A FAX FROM WORD **257**

Sending Your Fax

Now it's time to send a fax. Typically, you'll send one of two kinds of faxes:

- One that includes just a cover sheet that also contains your message
- One that includes a cover sheet *and* one or more additional sheets

Sending a Fax Cover Page Only

Sometimes, you need to fax a brief message, and you can include that message right on the cover sheet. The easiest way to prepare and send a fax is to use the Fax Wizard. Wizards are "helpers" supplied with Microsoft products that walk you through a process.

Hands On: Sending Only A Fax Cover Page

To prepare and send a fax cover sheet, follow these steps in Word:

1. Choose File, Send To. From the cascading menu that appears, choose Fax Recipient. Word switches to Document 2 and starts the Fax Wizard (see Figure 10.5).

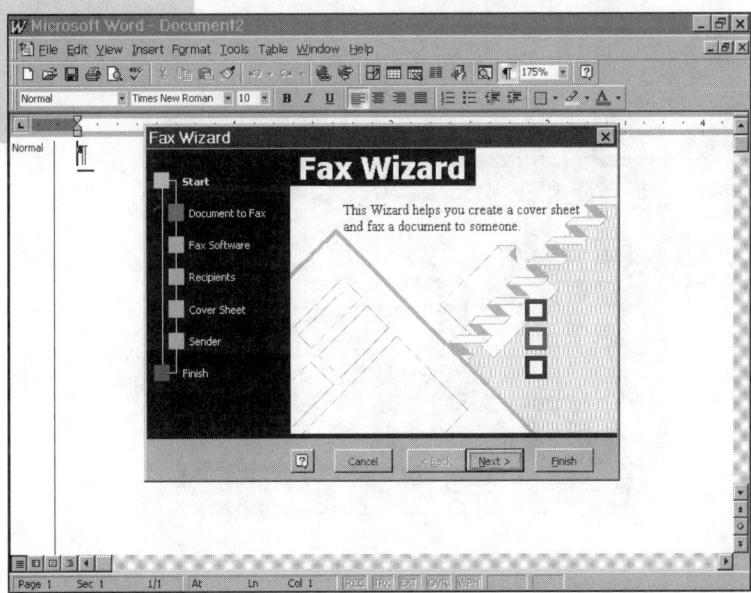

Figure 10.5 The opening screen of the Fax Wizard.

• •

From the opening wizard screen, you can click any of the choices on the left to go directly to that step, or you can let the wizard walk you through the process from beginning to end.

• •

2. Click on Next. The Fax Wizard asks you what you want to fax. Select "Just a cover sheet with a note" (see Figure 10.6).

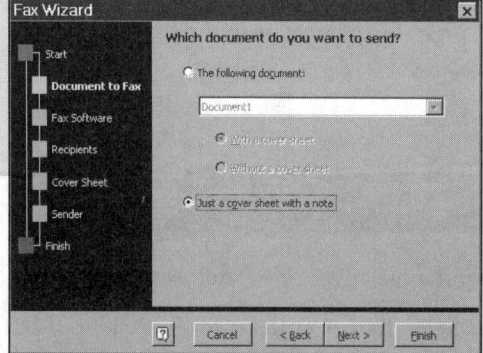

Figure 10.6
When you want to fax just a cover sheet, use the last option on this screen.

3. Click on Next. On this screen, identify your fax software by selecting the printer installed by your fax software from the list box. If you want to print your fax cover sheet so that you can send it using a fax machine, choose the last option (see Figure 10.7).

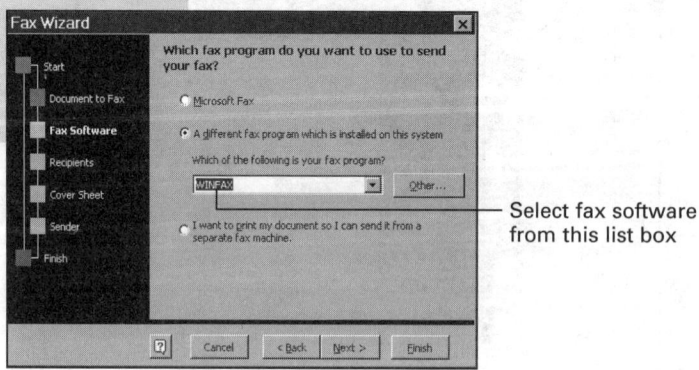

Figure 10.7
To select your fax software, use this list box.

Select fax software from this list box

CHAPTER 10 • SENDING A FAX FROM WORD 259

4. Click on <u>N</u>ext. Supply the name and fax number for the recipient(s) of the fax (see Figure 10.8). To use an address that you stored in your Microsoft Exchange or Microsoft Outlook address book, click on the <u>A</u>ddress Book button.

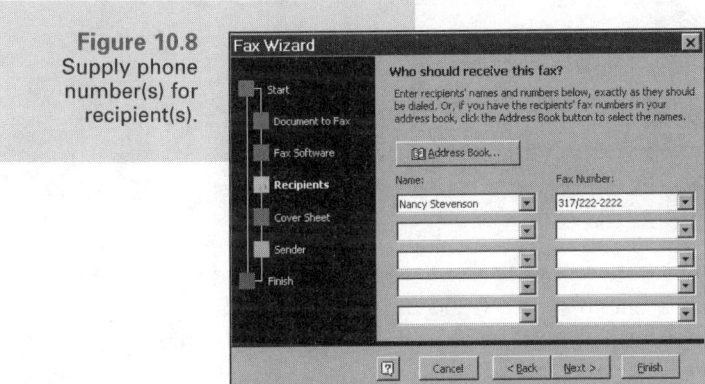

Figure 10.8
Supply phone number(s) for recipient(s).

5. Click on <u>N</u>ext. Choose a style for your fax cover sheet (see Figure 10.9). These are the same styles as those shown near the beginning of this chapter.

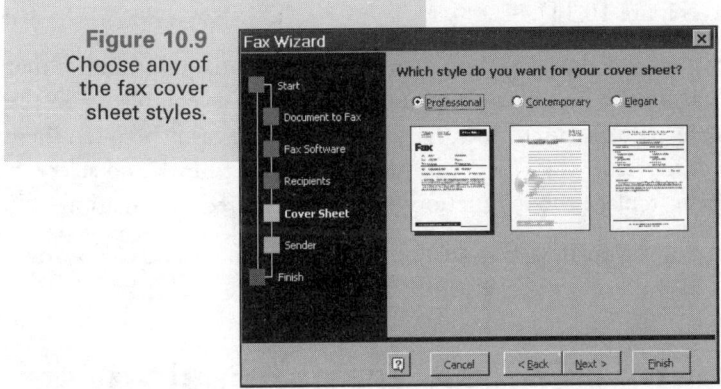

Figure 10.9
Choose any of the fax cover sheet styles.

6. Click on <u>N</u>ext. Supply information about yourself that you want to appear on the fax cover sheet (see Figure 10.10).

> YOU'LL LEARN ABOUT THE OPTIONS DIALOG BOX IN CHAPTER 16.

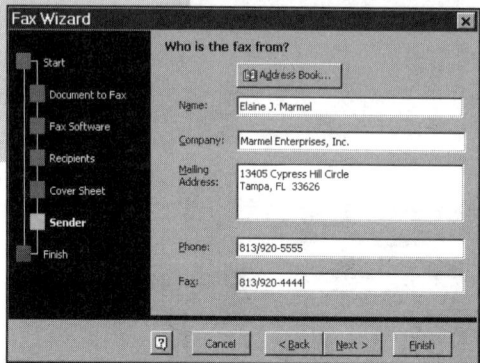

Figure 10.10
Supply sender information for the fax cover sheet.

By default, the address information in Figure 10.10 is blank. To avoid typing your address each time that you complete a fax cover sheet, store the information in the Options dialog box.

7. Click on Next. The Fax Wizard displays a final screen that tells you to rerun the Fax Wizard if you don't like the appearance of your cover sheet or if you have trouble faxing.

8. Click on Finish. Your cover sheet appears on-screen, along with the Office Assistant (see Figure 10.11).

As the Office Assistant explains, you should enter any additional information that you want to appear on the fax cover sheet. You may notice several places on the cover sheet that read [Click here and type...]. To move easily between these "Click Here" blocks, press F11. Word will jump to the next block and select it. You can then type to replace the instructions with the required information.

The next section shows you how to transmit both a document and a Fax cover sheet.

Including a Document in a Fax Transmission

The previous section covered how to use the Fax Wizard to prepare to send a fax, and you saw that the Fax Wizard also helps you set up a cover sheet. If you want to send more than just a cover sheet, you need to make only one change to the steps just described. Before you even start those steps, open the document that you want to send. Then, when you get to Step 2 from the previous section, the Fax Wizard will suggest that you send the open document (see Figure 10.12). Choose that option and continue with the rest of the steps in the previous section.

CHAPTER 10 • SENDING A FAX FROM WORD 261

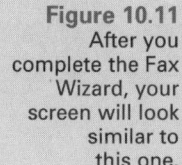

Figure 10.11
After you complete the Fax Wizard, your screen will look similar to this one.

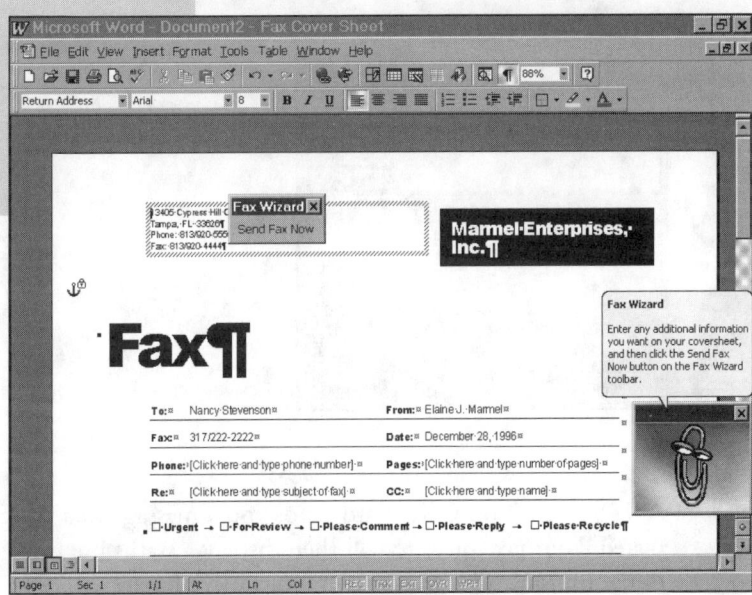

Figure 10.12
To include a document when you send a fax, open the document before you start the Fax Wizard. The title of the open document will then appear in the Fax Wizard.

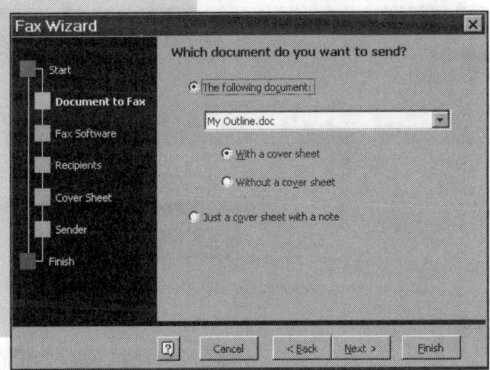

Although the Fax Wizard walks you through the process of creating a cover sheet, you still need to complete the minimum information that your fax software needs to actually send your fax. That is, you must supply, a second time, some of the same information that you supplied to the Fax Wizard. To send your fax, click on the Fax Wizard's Send Fax Now button. At this point, your fax software takes control, and you see a dialog box similar to the one in Figure 10.13.

Figure 10.13
You need to supply the minimum information required by your fax software. In our case, we will supply the recipient's name and phone number, and indicate that we've got an attachment to send.

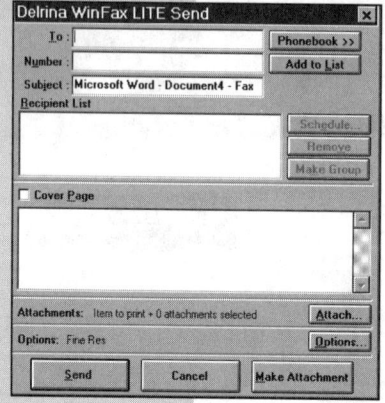

After you click on OK, Word sends you a message that the Fax Wizard has completed. Your fax software will then display a status box showing you the progress of the transmission until it is complete (see Figure 10.14).

Figure 10.14
While your fax software is transmitting, you'll see a box similar to this one.

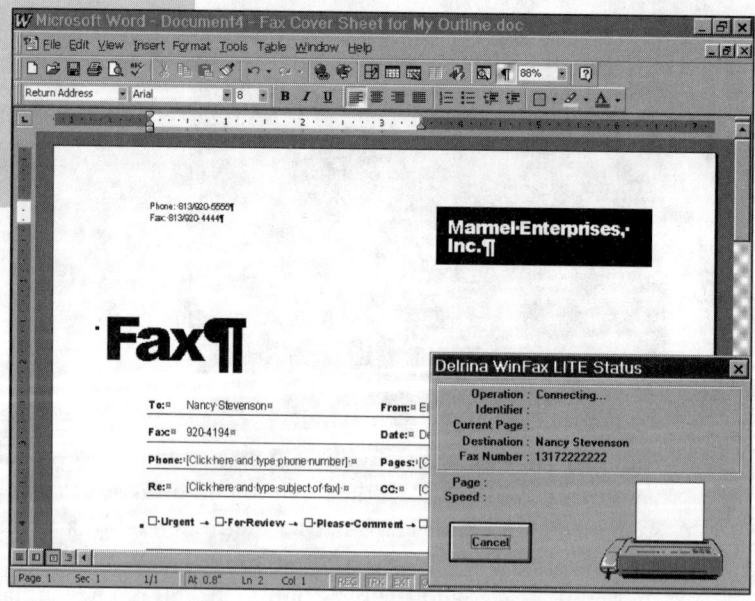

Using Microsoft Fax and Word

To use Microsoft Fax with Word, you need to first make sure that Microsoft Fax is installed and configured.

Installing and Configuring Microsoft Fax

First check to see whether Microsoft Fax is already installed. Click on Start, choose Programs, and then choose Accessories. Then look for a folder called "Fax." If you see that folder, Microsoft Fax is installed and needs only to be configured, which we'll walk through in a moment.

> ### Hands On: Installing Microsoft Fax

If you don't see a fax folder on the Accessories menu, then you must install Microsoft Fax. Follow these steps:

1. Click on the Start button, choose Settings, and choose Control Panel.
2. Double-click on Add/Remove Programs. When the Add/Remove Programs Properties box appears, click on the Windows Setup tab (see Figure 10.15).

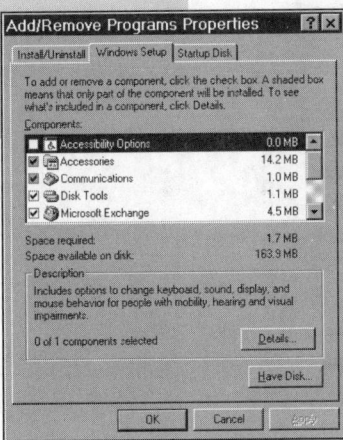

Figure 10.15 Install Windows 95 applets from this tab.

3. Scroll down until you find Microsoft Fax, place a check in its check box to select it, and click on the Apply button. One of two things will happen at this point: either Microsoft Fax will be installed, or you will be prompted to insert your Windows 95 setup disk. After you insert the disk and click on OK, Microsoft Fax will be installed.

Hands On: Configuring Microsoft Fax

Using Microsoft Fax takes some configuration. To configure Microsoft Fax, follow these steps:

1. Open the Control Panel. If you just finished installing Microsoft Fax, the Control Panel is already open. If you didn't need to install Microsoft Fax, then click on the Start button, choose Settings, and choose Control Panel.
2. Double-click on the Mail and Fax icons.
3. Check to see whether Microsoft Fax appears in the list. If it does, highlight it and click on Properties. If it doesn't appear, click on Add.
4. On the User tab, fill in your name and Fax number (see Figure 10.16).

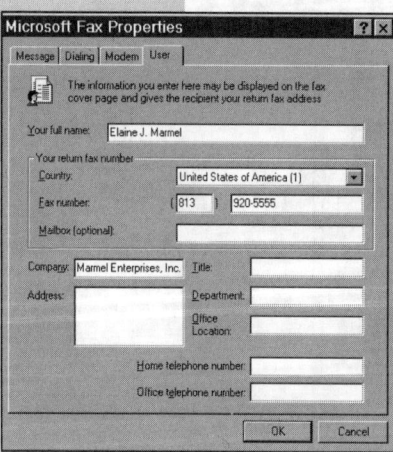

Figure 10.16
Fill in your name and Fax number. The rest is optional.

5. On the Message tab, remove the check mark from the Send Cover Page check box (see Figure 10.17).
6. Click on OK twice.

Now you're ready to send a fax from Word using Microsoft Fax.

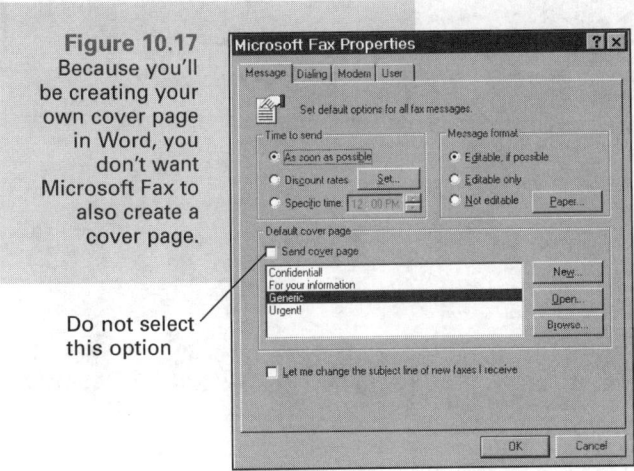

Figure 10.17
Because you'll be creating your own cover page in Word, you don't want Microsoft Fax to also create a cover page.

Do not select this option

Sending a Fax from Word with Microsoft Fax

Most of the process for sending a fax from Word is the same whether you use Microsoft Fax or software supplied with your fax/modem. Here are the differences when you use Microsoft Fax:

- On the second dialog box of the Fax Wizard you saw earlier in this chapter, choose Microsoft Fax (see Figure 10.18).

- When you click on the Send Fax Now button supplied by the Fax Wizard, you won't see an additional box where you supply information such as the recipient's name and phone number. Microsoft Fax will simply take over and start sending your fax.

- Microsoft Fax treats each document in Word as a separate fax. Therefore, if you attach a document to send using the Fax Wizard, Microsoft Fax will place two phone calls when you send your fax.

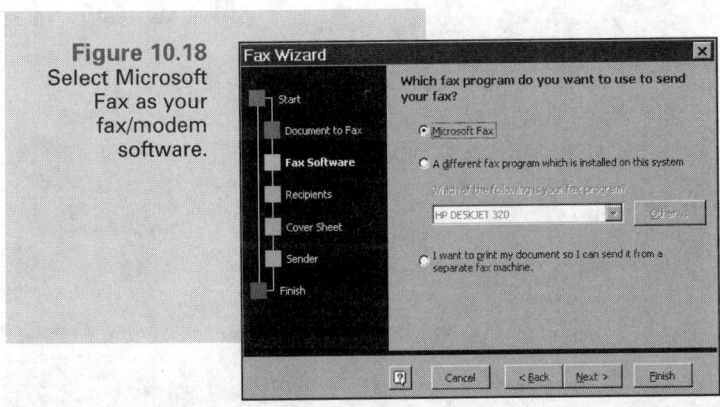

Figure 10.18
Select Microsoft Fax as your fax/modem software.

micros
WORD

11

Exploring the Online World from Word

IN THIS CHAPTER

- Working with Hyperlinks
- Sending E-Mail
- Accessing the Web from Word

Hyperlinks are new to Word 97. When you create a hyperlink, you create a way for a reader to jump from your current document to a location that you specify. Hyperlinks in a Word document can jump to another location in the same document, a different Word document on your hard drive, a different Office document on your hard drive, a document on your company's intranet, or even a page on the World Wide Web. In this chapter, you'll use the Memo wizard to build a memo (see figure on facing page) that includes hyperlinks to documents on your company's network as well as hyperlinks to Web pages. Then, you'll launch e-mail from inside Word and send the memo to a coworker.

In Word 95, your interaction with the online world was limited to sending e-mail from inside Word. Word 97 has expanded the capability to interact with the online world by providing the capability to access the Internet through the Internet Service Provider (ISP) of your choice. Without ever leaving Word, you can launch your Web browser and surf the Net.

In this chapter, you'll explore the Web pages that are directly accessible from Word; you'll visit two home pages—the Microsoft Home Page and the Microsoft Office Home Page—as well as visit pages that provide product news, online support, Frequently Asked Questions, free software, and the ability to search the Web. We even take at look at Microsoft's assessment of the best pages on the World Wide Web.

Working with Hyperlinks

Hyperlinks are interactive navigational tools. Using a hyperlink, you click in order to "jump" to another location in the same document, another Word document, an Office document, or even a Web page. Hyperlinks appear as text (usually blue and underlined) or graphics in your document, and they provide shortcuts to information.

When would you use a hyperlink? Suppose that you and a colleague are working on a report in which you are recommending the purchase of a new computer. While doing research for the report, you discover the Annual Sales Analysis report on your company's network. The sales analysis contains annual and quarterly sales data. You want to share this information with your colleague, so you create a memo and include a hyperlink to the document. You also want your colleague to check out two Internet sites that you discovered, so your memo also includes hyperlinks to those Web sites.

Using the Memo Wizard

Here we use Word's Memo Wizard to create the header information for the memo.

CHAPTER 11 • EXPLORING THE ONLINE WORLD FROM WORD 269

Hands On: Creating a Memo with the Memo Wizard

To use the Memo Wizard, follow these steps:

1. Choose File, New. From the New dialog box, click on the Memos tab.
2. Select the Memo Wizard and click on OK. The first of the Memo Wizard's dialog boxes appears.
3. Click on Next.
4. Choose the Contemporary style and click on Next.
5. For the Title (see Figure 11.1), type **Memo** and click on Next.

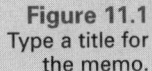
Figure 11.1
Type a title for the memo.

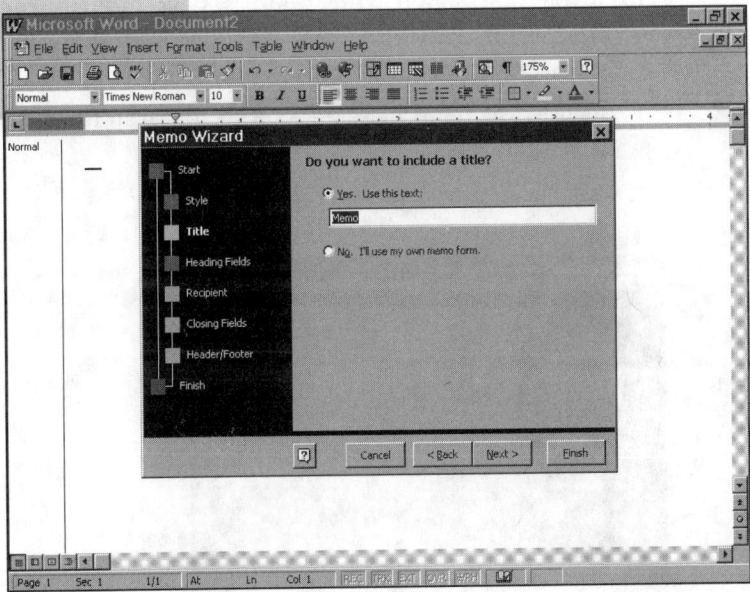

6. For the Heading Fields (see Figure 11.2), supply a date, your name, and a subject for the memo. We used the subject **Annual Sales Comparison Report**. Click on Next.
7. Supply recipients for the memo. If the recipients' addresses are stored in your address book, click on the Address Book button to copy them. Click on Next.

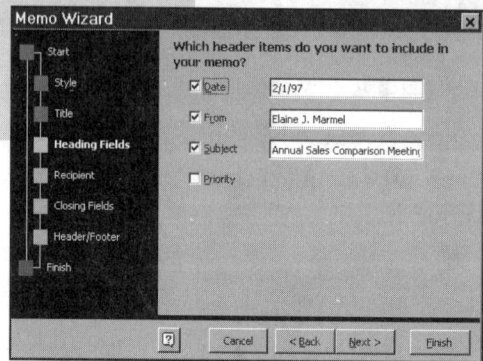

Figure 11.2 Supply Heading information for the memo.

8. If you want, supply writer's initials, typist's initials, enclosures, and attachments for your memo. We didn't include any of those in our example memo. Click on Next.

9. Identify the items that you want to appear in the memo's header and footer (see Figure 11.3).

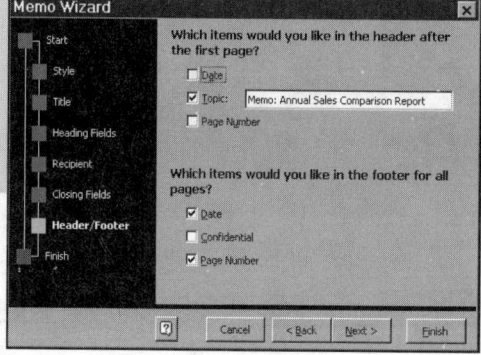

Figure 11.3 Identify the information that you want to appear in the memo's header and footer.

10. Click on Next and then click on Finish. The beginning of the memo appears on-screen (see Figure 11.4).

Tip

You may see the Office Assistant. You can close the window.

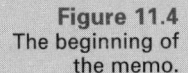

Figure 11.4
The beginning of the memo.

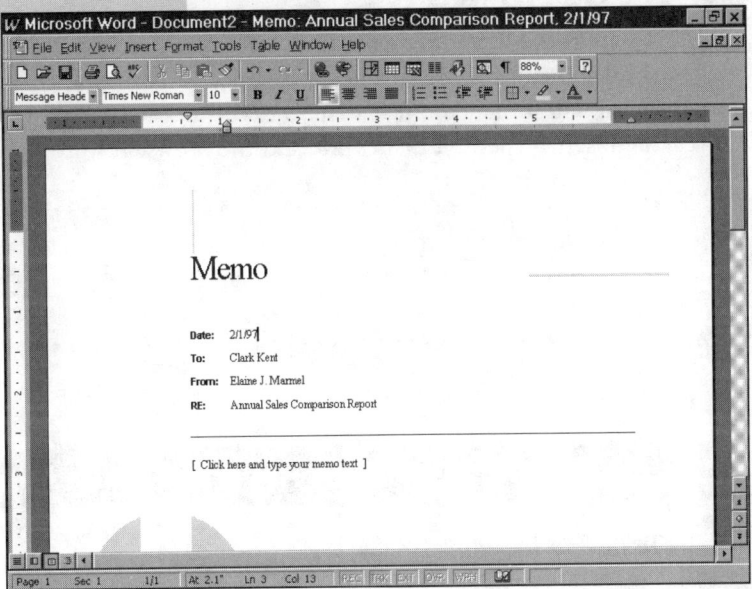

For more information on fields, see Chapter 15.

Now you will see how to enlarge the font for the text. Select all text below the title "Memo," open the Font Size list box on the Formatting toolbar, and click on 12. Now press F11. Pressing F11 moves the insertion point to the first place in the memo that requires text and selects the "Click here and type" block that appears. (Each "Click here and type" block is a field, and pressing F11 causes the insertion point to jump to the next field and select that field.) Type the body of the memo as it appears following this paragraph. Leave a space at the end of the typing and save your document. We called our example **Sales Comparison Memo**.

> While researching for our paper on the computer acquisition, I came upon the Sales Analysis Comparison for 1995 and 1996. It seems this report is prepared each year, and I thought we might be able to use some of the data in our proposal. Take a look at it and let me know what you think.

If you don't save your document, Word will prompt you to save it before inserting a hyperlink.

Inserting Hyperlinks

To insert the hyperlink, you must know the document's location (path name). If the document resides on a network drive, you can simply type the path name and Word will format the text that you type as a hyperlink. Otherwise, you can use the Insert Hyperlink dialog box and the browse feature to link to the file.

To jump to a different location in your document, you create a bookmark at the location to which you want to jump. You'll supply that bookmark name in the Insert Hyperlink dialog box.

FOR MORE INFORMATION ON BOOKMARKS, SEE CHAPTER 15.

Hands On: Inserting a Hyperlink into a Memo

To insert a hyperlink, follow these steps:

1. Leaving the insertion point where you want the hyperlink to appear, choose Insert, Hyperlink. Word displays the Insert Hyperlink dialog box (see Figure 11.5).

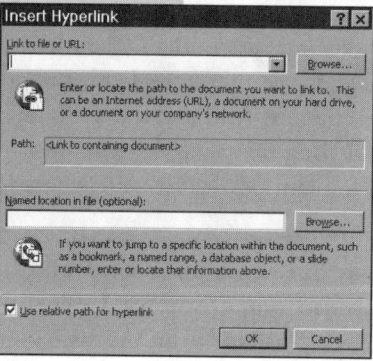

Figure 11.5
Use this dialog box to insert a hyperlink into a document.

2. In the Link to File or URL box, type the path to the document or use the Browse button to find the document.
3. Click on OK. Word inserts a hyperlink in your document (see Figure 11.6).

Figure 11.6
A hyperlink to another Word document.

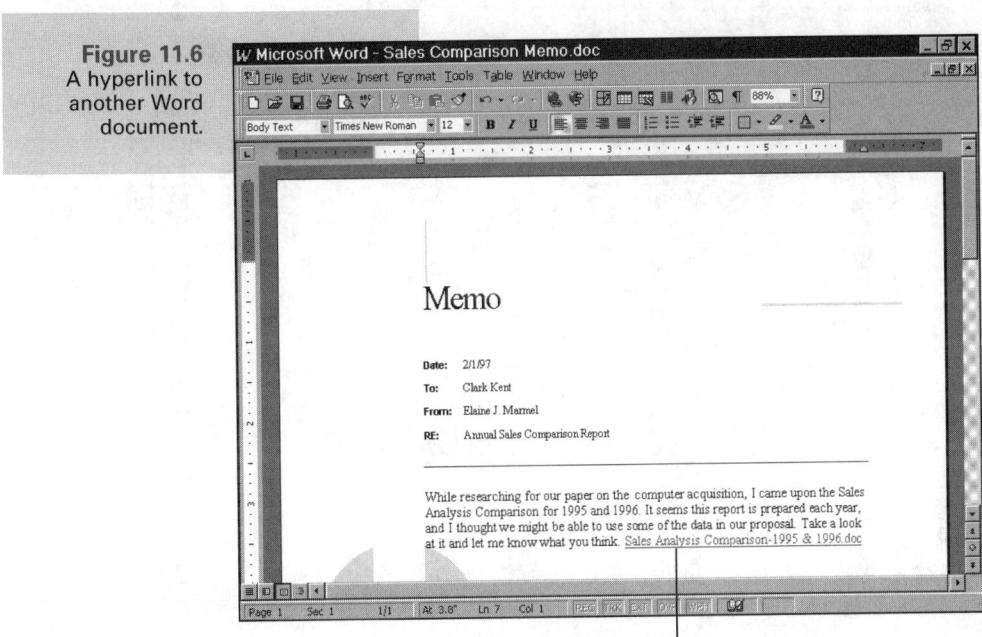

The hyperlink appears underlined

Formatting Hyperlinks

You can change the appearance of a hyperlink. You can even change the text that appears for the hyperlink.

Because clicking on the hyperlink will cause Word to open the linked document, you'll find it easiest to select the hyperlink text using the keyboard. Use arrow keys to position the insertion point, press [Shift]+[↑] to select a letter, or press [Ctrl]+[Shift]+[↑] to select a word.

Hands On: Changing the Hyperlink's Text

To format a hyperlink, follow these steps:

1. Use the arrow keys to position the insertion point at the beginning of the hyperlink.
2. Press and hold [Ctrl] and [Shift] and press the Right arrow key. Word selects the entire hyperlink (see Figure 11.7).

PART III • WORD ONLINE

Figure 11.7
The hyperlink after selecting it.

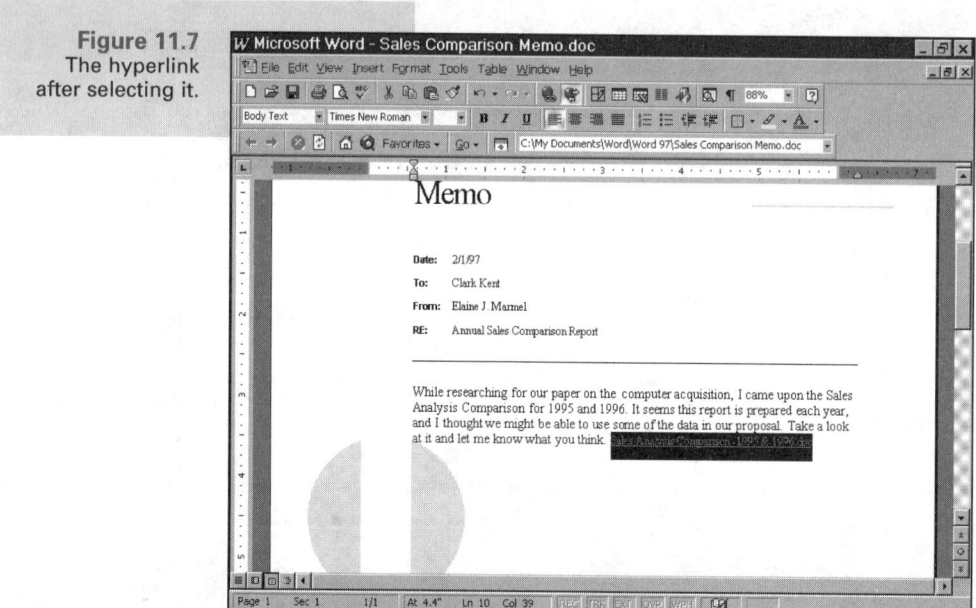

3. Type the text that you want to appear for the hyperlink. We typed **Click here to view Sales Analysis Comparison for 1995 and 1996.** Word changes the text for the hyperlink (see Figure 11.8).

Figure 11.8
The hyperlink after changing its text.

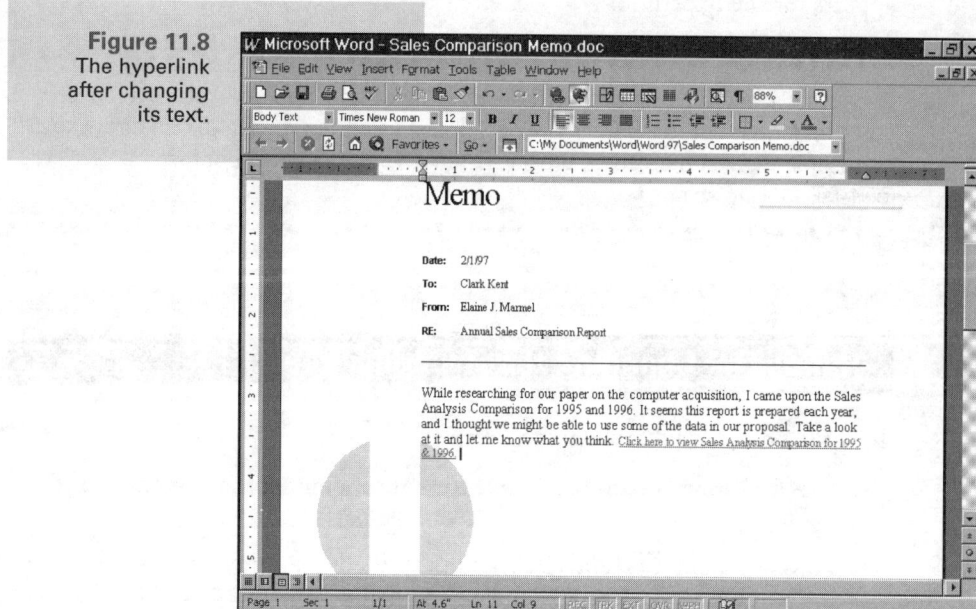

CHAPTER 11 • EXPLORING THE ONLINE WORLD FROM WORD 275

Using Hyperlinks

Now you can test the hyperlink.

Hands On: Jumping to a Linked Document

To use a hyperlink, follow these steps:

1. Move the mouse pointer over the hyperlink. The actual path to the hyperlink appears on-screen (see Figure 11.9).

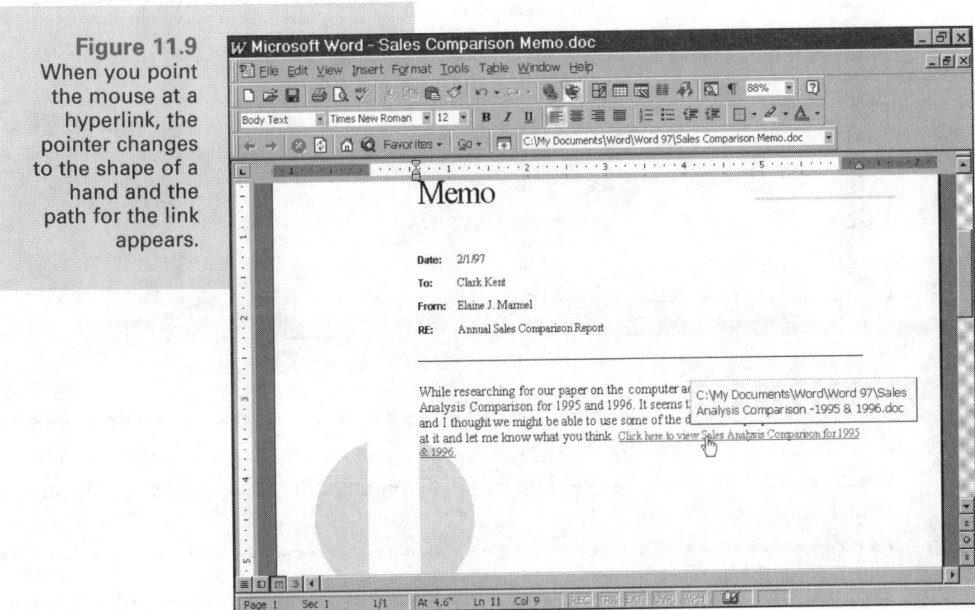

Figure 11.9
When you point the mouse at a hyperlink, the pointer changes to the shape of a hand and the path for the link appears.

2. Click on the hyperlink once. Word opens the linked document in a new window of its own (see Figure 11.10).

Notice that the Web toolbar appears at the top of the document below the Formatting toolbar. This toolbar closely resembles the toolbars that you see in Web browsers; you can use this toolbar to navigate between hyperlinks. Click on the Back button to return to the document containing the hyperlink. When you return to the original document, the hyperlink will appear in a new color (the default is purple), indicating that you have used the hyperlink. Also, the Forward button will be available. Click on it to redisplay the document to which the hyperlink jumps. When you finish with a document, you close it as usual. To hide the Web toolbar, click on the Web Toolbar button on the Standard toolbar.

Figure 11.10
The document that the hyperlink opened.

> If the document opened by the hyperlink *also* contains hyperlinks, you can jump to those just as you jumped to the first hyperlink. In this case, both the Forward and Back buttons will be available.

To finish the memo, include the text below and type the two hyperlinks that you see. Word will automatically format them; you won't need to insert them using the Insert Hyperlink dialog box. When you finish typing, your memo should look like the one in Figure 11.11. Save the memo.

> **Also, while browsing the Web, I found both Dell's and Gateway's Web sites—thought you might want to take a look at the pricing. I've included the URLs below.**
>
> **www.dell.com**
>
> **www.gateway2000.com**

Note

If Word doesn't recognize hyperlinks as you type them, you may have turned off some settings in the AutoCorrect dialog box. Choose Tools, AutoCorrect. On the AutoCorrect tab, make sure that you see a check in the Replace Text As You Type check box. Then, check both the AutoFormat As You Type tab and the AutoFormat tab, and make sure that you see a check in the Internet and Network Paths with Hyperlinks check box.

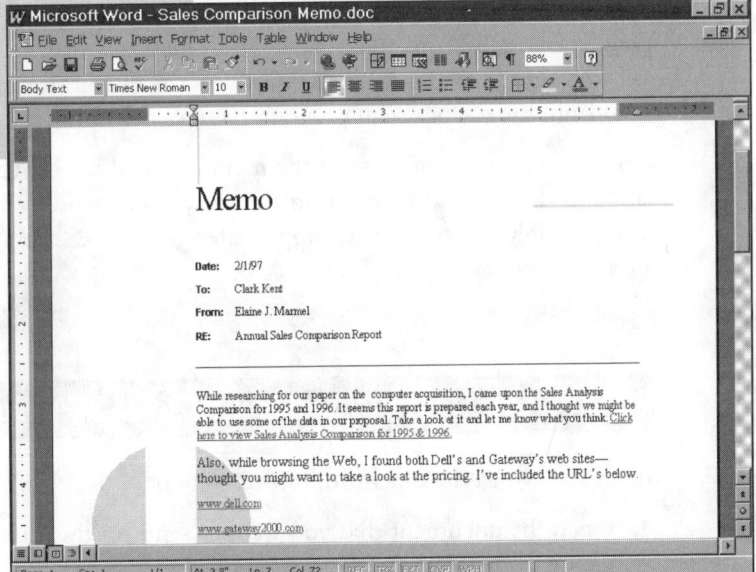

Figure 11.11
The completed memo includes additional hyperlinks.

Changing Hyperlinks

You can change the text for a hyperlink without changing the location to which the hyperlink jumps, as you saw when you formatted the hyperlink. But suppose that you want to change the actual location to which the hyperlink jumps? To change the hyperlink destination, right-click on the hyperlink, highlight Hyperlink on the shortcut menu, and, from the cascading menu, choose Edit Hyperlink. The Edit Hyperlink dialog box appears; it looks just like the Insert Hyperlink dialog box. Modify the hyperlink and click on OK.

> **Tip**
>
> Hyperlinks may stop working if the linked document is no longer located at the hyperlink destination. Changing the hyperlink should resolve this problem.

If the Hyperlink command doesn't appear on the shortcut menu, chances are good that you've got a typographical error in the hyperlink and Word is automatically checking for proofing errors. If you see a red wavy line below the hyperlink, you've got a typographical error. Resolve the error and you should see the Hyperlink command on the shortcut menu.

Sending E-Mail

When you install Word, WordMail is automatically installed. When you send e-mail from inside Word, WordMail delivers the e-mail message to your mail program; from there, your mail program handles delivering the message.

Suppose that you want to send the memo created in this chapter to a colleague via WordMail instead of printing the memo and sending it via "snail mail" (a term, probably not particularly appreciated by the U.S. Postal Service, that refers to traditional mail).

Hands On: Using WordMail to send a Word Document

To e-mail a Word document, follow these steps:

1. Open the document that you want to send (in this case, the Sales Comparison Memo).
2. Choose File, Send To. From the cascading menu, choose Mail Recipient. A WordMail window appears (after a brief delay), and the open document in Word appears as an icon in the message.

> **Note**
>
> You may be prompted for a Profile depending upon their system configuration.

CHAPTER 11 • EXPLORING THE ONLINE WORLD FROM WORD   **279**

Choose <u>R</u>outing Recipient (on the <u>F</u>ile, Sen<u>d</u> To menu) if you want the first recipient to send the document on to a subsequent recipient.

3. Address the mail message as you would address any mail message. Include any additional message text (see Figure 11.12). Format the message the same way you would format any Word document, using fonts, point sizes, character formatting, and so on.

You can even include a hyperlink in a WordMail message that you're sending to another user of Word 97. Remember, the hyperlink won't work unless the recipient is using Word 97.

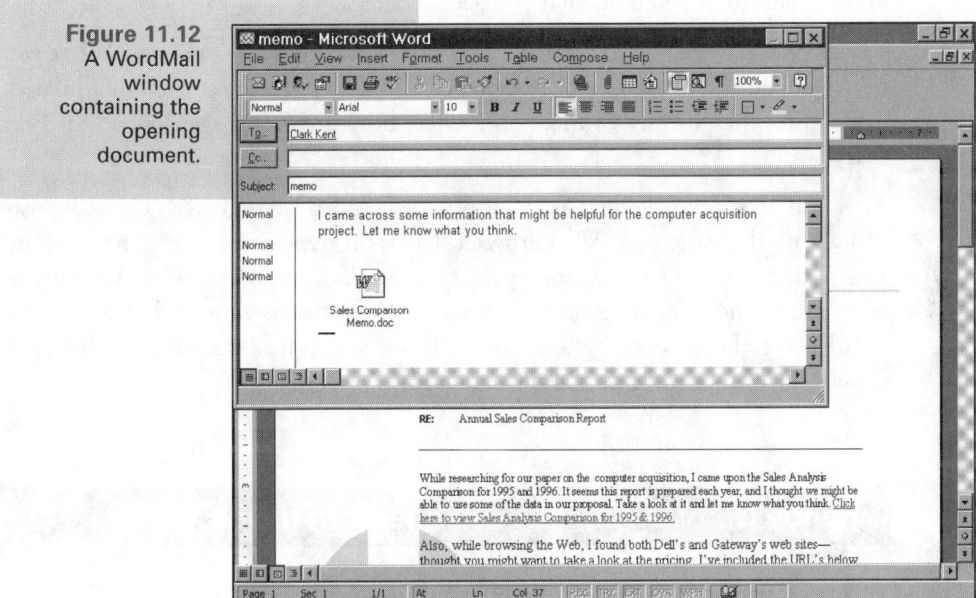

Figure 11.12
A WordMail window containing the opening document.

4. Send the message the way you would send any message in your mail program. The WordMail window closes and your original document reappears. Your mail program takes care of delivering the message.

Accessing the Web from Word

From inside Word, you can launch your Web browser and explore the Internet. You can visit both the Microsoft Office home page and the Microsoft home page. You'll find that Microsoft has free "stuff" available that you can download, and you can take advantage of Microsoft's Knowledge Base to help you resolve problems you might be encountering.

When you access the Web from inside Word, you actually launch your Web browser and use your Internet service provider to go online. One of the authors of this book uses The Microsoft Network as her Internet Service Provider, along with Internet Explorer 3.01 as her Web browser. What you see as you perform the steps in this chapter will depend on the Web browser and Internet Service Provider you use.

After your Web browser launches, you can navigate around the Web in the same way that you've always surfed the Web, using the buttons provided by your browser and the hyperlinks that you see on-screen.

The steps for accessing any of the Microsoft Web pages don't change. What you see when you access a page will change because Web pages are constantly updated. The figures that you see in this book reflect how the Web pages looked on February 1 and 2, 1997.

After you access the Web from inside Word, you can surf the Web the same way you always do using your Web browser. Click on hyperlinks or use the Forward and Back buttons to move from page to page. You can leave Word running as we've done, and you can switch back and forth between your Web browser and Word using the Windows 95 Taskbar. When you finish working on the Web, close your Web browser as you normally do.

Hands On: Viewing a Web Page from Inside Word

To view a Web page without leaving Word, follow these steps:

1. Choose Help, Microsoft on the Web.
2. From the cascading menu, choose the Web page that you want to view. You'll hear a lot of action on your hard disk, and you'll see your Web browser appear on top of Word.
3. Do whatever you need to do on-screen to sign onto the Web. The Web page that you chose will appear.

Finding Out What's New from Microsoft

It always pays to periodically check Microsoft's "What's New?" page; you may find out that a software update for a Microsoft program you use is available. Choose Help, Microsoft on the Web. From the cascading menu, choose Product News. When the Web page appears, it will look something like the one in Figure 11.13.

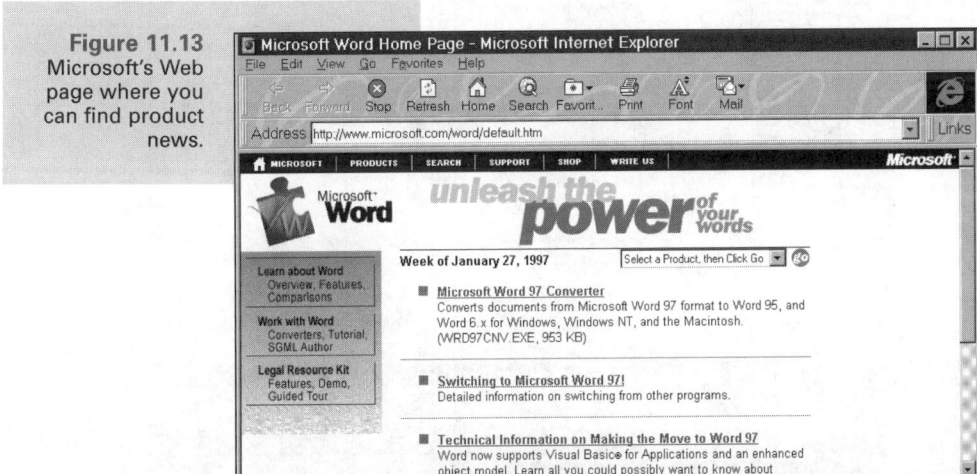

Figure 11.13 Microsoft's Web page where you can find product news.

Checking Out Microsoft's Free Stuff

Microsoft makes available many free items for you to use. For example, you can download templates and wizards to help you with common tasks in Word. To take a look at what's available, choose Help, Microsoft on the Web. From the cascading menu, choose Free Stuff. When the Web page appears, it will look something like the one in Figure 11.14.

Note that you initially see free stuff for Word, but you can use the list box on the left side of the window to select a product; Microsoft has free stuff available for all the Office products.

Getting Help Online

You can get help online in several different ways. First, you can choose Help, Microsoft on the Web. From the cascading menu, choose Frequently Asked Questions. You'll see a Web page that looks something like the one in Figure 11.15.

Figure 11.14
Microsoft's Web page where you can find free stuff.

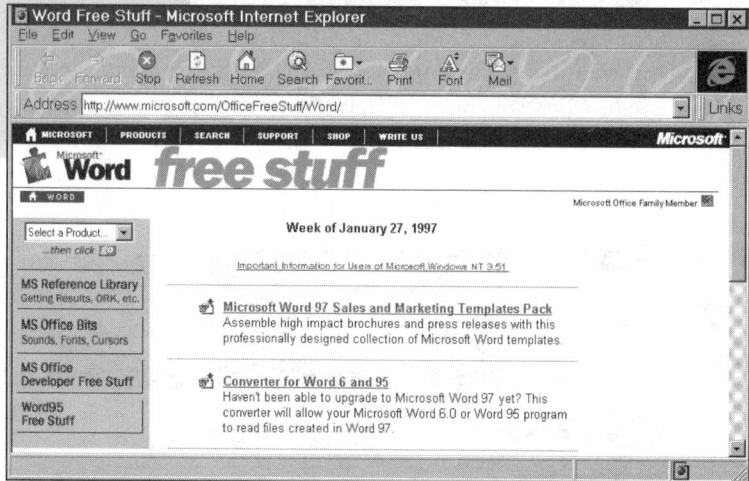

Figure 11.15
Microsoft's Web page where you can find answers to frequently asked questions.

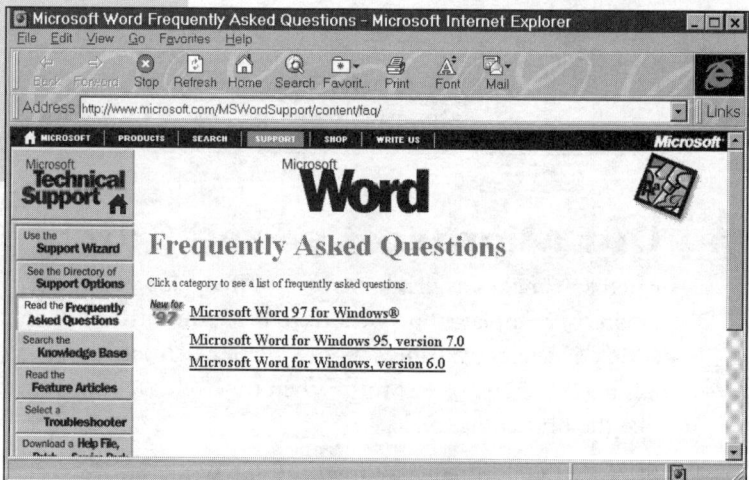

Alternatively, you can choose Help, Microsoft on the Web. From the cascading menu, choose Online Support. You'll see a Web page that looks something like the one in Figure 11.16.

CHAPTER 11 • EXPLORING THE ONLINE WORLD FROM WORD   283

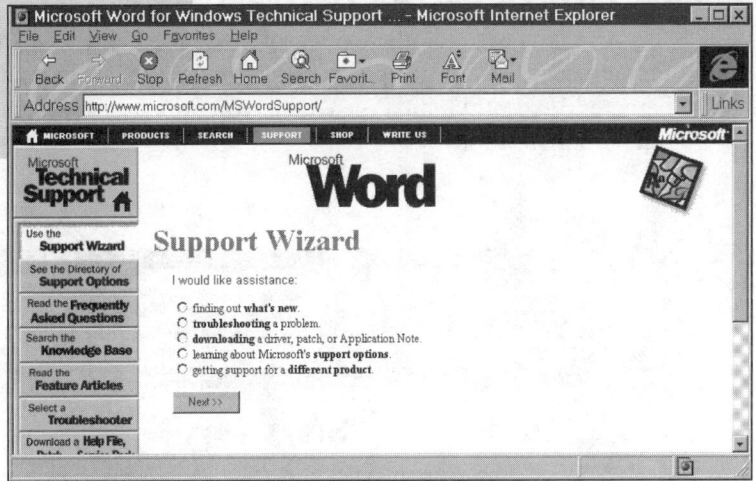

Figure 11.16
Microsoft's Web page where you can find the Support Wizard.

Visiting the Microsoft Office Home Page

For information specifically about Office, you can visit the Microsoft Office home page. Choose Help, Microsoft on the Web. From the cascading menu, choose Microsoft Office Home Page. You'll see a Web page that looks something like the one in Figure 11.17.

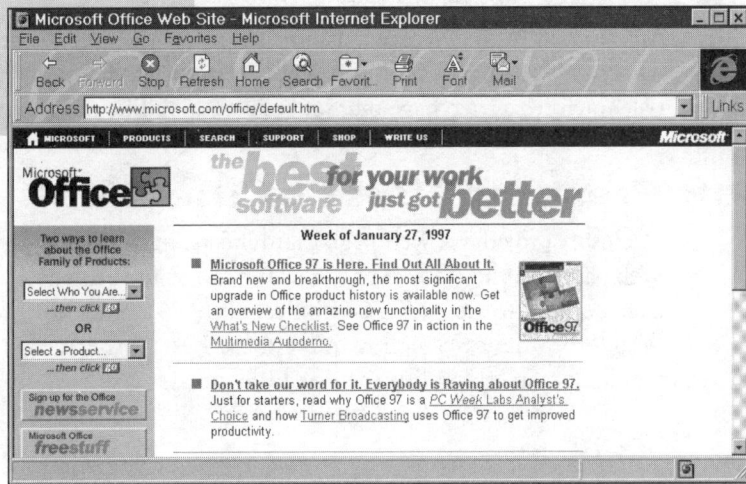

Figure 11.17
The Microsoft Office home page.

Visiting the Microsoft Home Page

If you're interested in other Microsoft products besides Office, visit the Microsoft home page. Choose Help, Microsoft on the Web. From the cascading menu, choose Microsoft Home Page. You'll see a Web page that looks something like the one in Figure 11.18.

Figure 11.18
The Microsoft home page.

Learning About the Web

Are you new to the Web? Want some help? Use the Web Tutorial provided in Word. Choose Help, Microsoft on the Web. From the cascading menu, choose Web Tutorial. You'll see a Web page that looks something like the one in Figure 11.19.

Microsoft Presents "Best of the Web"

Microsoft provides a Web page that reflects, in the opinion of Microsoft, the best Web pages on the Web. If you're in the mood to surf, check out this page and use its hyperlinks to view Microsoft's Best of the Web. Choose Help, Microsoft on the Web. From the cascading menu, choose Best of the Web. You'll see a Web page that looks something like the one in Figure 11.20.

CHAPTER 11 • EXPLORING THE ONLINE WORLD FROM WORD **285**

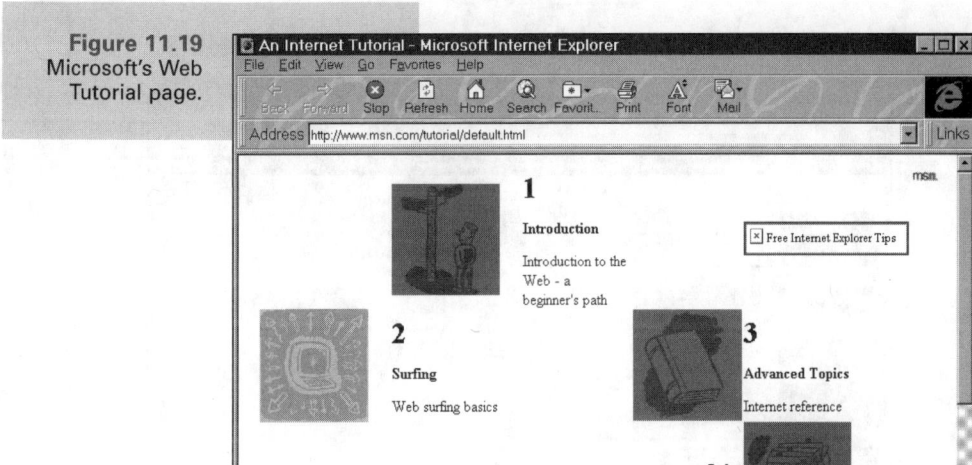

Figure 11.19
Microsoft's Web Tutorial page.

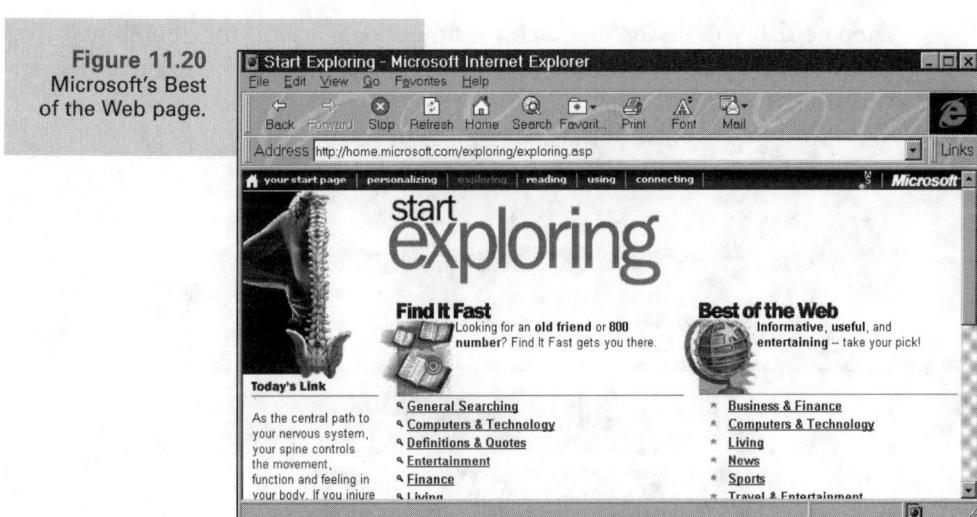

Figure 11.20
Microsoft's Best of the Web page.

Searching the Web

You may have used the Search button on your Web browser. Microsoft has its own search page where you have access to all the popular Internet search engines. Choose Help, Microsoft on the Web. From the cascading menu, choose Search the Web. You'll see a Web page that looks something like the one in Figure 11.21.

Figure 11.21
Microsoft's Search page.

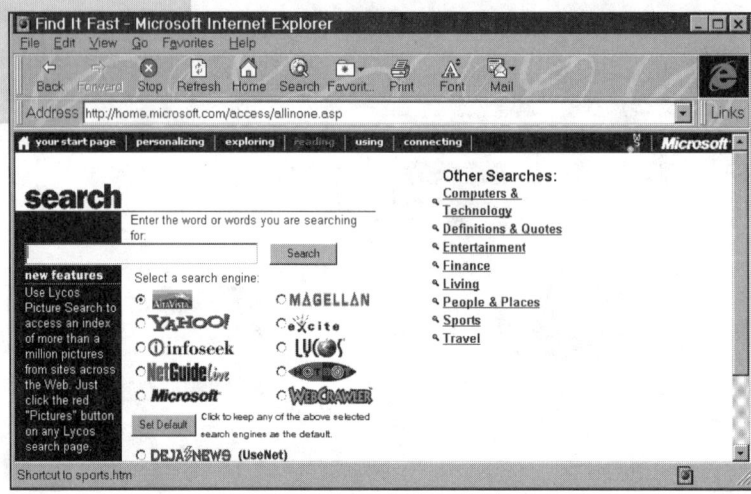

Suppose that you decide to search for other books from Prima Publishing. You would type **"Prima Publishing"** (include the quotation marks) in the search text box, choose a search engine (we chose AltaVista) and click on the Search button. You'd see a page similar to the one in Figure 11.22.

Figure 11.22
The results of having searched for Prima Publishing.

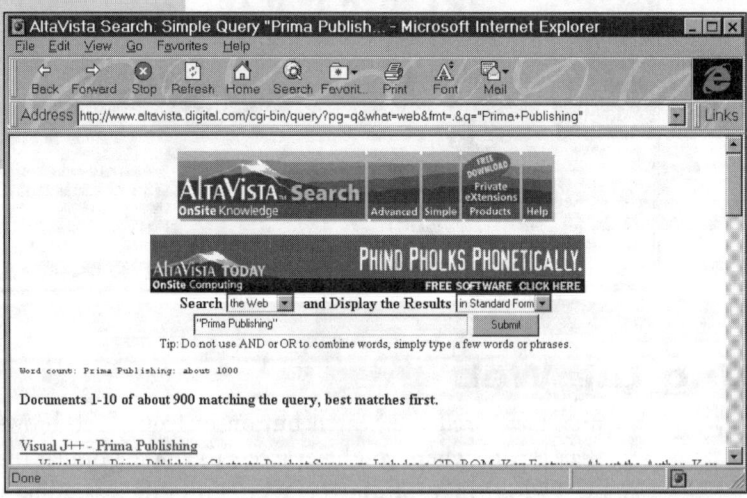

Note

If you don't use quotation marks, you search for all individual occurrences of either "Prima" or "Publishing" and your search results will include a much larger selection of choices. Larger selections from search results can be good, but sometimes, they can be overwhelming. To narrow a search, you enclose the words in quotation marks so that the search engine searches only for those two words together, not individually.

You would then use one of the hyperlinks displayed and jump to another Web page.

Creating a Web Site Hyperlink in a Word Document

Suppose that, in your travels, you find a Web page that would be relevant in a Word document you are preparing. You already learned that you can simply type the Web address into your document, but you also can copy the address into your document directly from the Web site. We jumped to Prima Publishing's Other Books page in the search that we performed in the last section.

Hands On: Copying a Web Address into a Word Document

To create a hyperlink from a web site in a Word document, follow these steps:

1. Open the Word document that will contain the hyperlink to the Web page.
2. On the Web, navigate to the page you want to link to your Word document.
3. Select the URL (Universal Resource Locator) information, which is the Web site's address. Right-click to display a shortcut menu, and click on Copy to place the URL on the Clipboard (see Figure 11.23).
4. Use the Windows 95 Taskbar to switch to Word.

PART III • WORD ONLINE

Figure 11.23
Copying a URL.

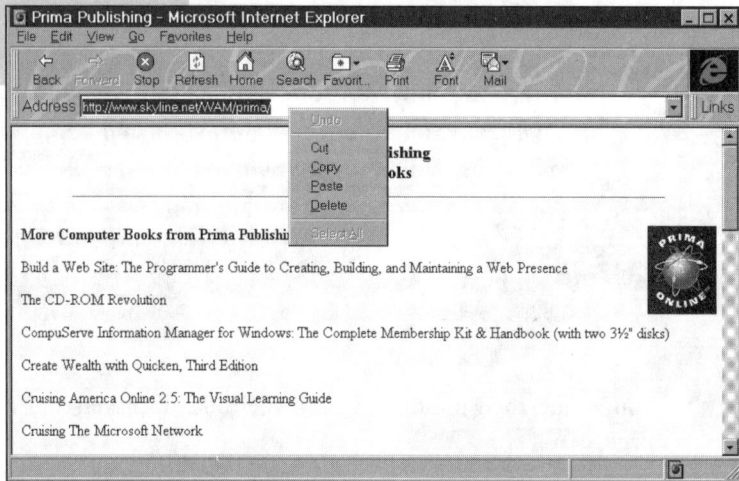

5. Position the insertion point where you want the hyperlink to appear, and click on the Paste button on the Standard toolbar.

6. When you type a space or a period, or when you press [Enter], Word will format the text as a hyperlink.

If you add a Web page to your Favorites list in your Web browser, you'll also find that Web page available in the Favorites list on Word's Web toolbar.

Printing a Web Page

You can print any Web page you see; simply view the Web page in your browser and click on the Web browser's Print button or choose File, Print in the Web browser.

Downloading Information

Suppose that, as you were browsing through the Frequently Asked Questions, you found an answer to a question that you want to pass along to coworkers. You can copy a hyperlink to the page and send it to them via e-mail, or you can download the document and send the actual document to them. The steps for this process may vary slightly from Web browser to Web browser, but the method is basically the same.

CHAPTER 11 • EXPLORING THE ONLINE WORLD FROM WORD **289**

Hands On: Downloading Information from the Web Using Internet Explorer 3.01

FOR MORE INFORMATION ON HTML FORMAT, SEE CHAPTER 12.

To download information, follow these steps:

1. Navigate to a document on the Web that you want to download.
2. Choose File, Save As File. The Save As dialog box appears.
3. Navigate to the location where you want to store the document and supply a filename. You can save the document as an HTML document or as plain text.

•••

Tip

Word 97 can read HTML format, so you will be able to open the document in Word 97. Otherwise, save the document as plain text.

•••

4. Click on Save.

micros
WORD

12

Using Word to Publish a Corporate Web Page

In This Chapter

- Web Page Design Issues
- Creating a Web Page
- Modifying a Web Page
- Publishing Web Documents
- Converting Word Documents to Web Documents

Word 97 makes creating a Web page that you can then publish on the World Wide Web very easy. You can actually create Web pages in two different ways: you can use a wizard or template, or you can convert an existing Word document to Web page format—known as HTML. Using either of these methods, you'll notice that Word customizes

PART III • WORD ONLINE

the menus and toolbars to provide you with Web page authoring tools and features.

HTML stands for *HyperText Markup Language*, which is a system of placing tags in a document that refer to graphics and formatting. To view the actual graphics and formatting, you typically use a Web browser. HTML tags can be very complicated to create manually; Word 97 creates them for you.

To create a Web page, you will need to make sure, however, that you have installed the Web page authoring components of Word. Open the File menu and look to see whether the Save as HTML command appears. If it does not, you have not installed Web page authoring components. You need to rerun the Word setup program, choose Custom Install, and place a check in the Web Page Authoring (HTML) check box.

In this chapter, we show you how to create a Web page using the Web Page Wizard that comes with Word (see figure on facing page), which supplies suggested backgrounds and layouts. If you want more control over the design, you can, instead, create a Web page using the Blank Web Page template.

Web Page Design Issues

Before you jump into creating a Web page, you should consider some design issues such as the readability of your page and the speed with which it loads. Readability is important if you expect to get your message across; speed is important if you expect impatient Web surfers to give you a chance to get your message across.

Web Page Readability

Text on Web pages should be easy to read. Choose a fairly standard serif font, such as Times New Roman, for paragraph text; and choose a fairly standard sans serif font, such as Arial, for headings. Make sure that any background you add to your Web page doesn't interfere with the readability of your text.

Evaluate the content of your Web page from an organizational perspective. Well-organized pages will get your ideas across to your reader quickly. For information that appears in two columns, consider using Word tables as a layout tool for Web

Chapter 12 • Using Word to Publish a Corporate Web Page

page information. You can either draw or insert the table. As you'll learn later in this chapter, HTML format does not support certain formatting, and newspaper columns is one of those formats. But you can use tables to arrange text and graphics. You may notice some differences about tables on Web pages; for example, tables do not have borders when you insert them on Web pages, but you can add borders.

As you plan your Web page, be aware that Web pages can look different in different Web browsers because features that may appear on a Web page may *not* be supported in all browsers. If you plan to use an advanced technique, such as an inline video, test the feature on as many browsers as you can to make sure that your viewers don't miss any critical information if their browser doesn't support that feature.

Web Page Speed

Try to design Web pages that load quickly. Studies have shown that Web surfers lose patience with Web pages that take longer than 20 seconds to load. Large graphic images are often the culprit that slows down viewing a Web page, so try to keep the size of graphic images down to about 20,000 bytes each. And be aware that some browsers contain features that allow the surfer to turn off viewing graphics and videos altogether. In Word, you can specify alternative text that will appear in place of graphic images; that way, any readers who have turned off viewing graphics won't miss your message.

Creating a Web Page

You can create a Web page in one of two ways: from scratch, or by converting an existing Word document. We start here by creating a brand new Web page. If you're creative, you can use the Blank Web Page template; if you're like us, you'll use the Web Page Wizard.

Using the Web Page Wizard

The easiest way to create a Web page—and get some help with design ideas—is to use the Web Page Wizard to walk you through choosing a layout and a background that you can then modify.

Hands On: Creating a Web Page with the Web Page Wizard

To use the Web Page Wizard to create a Web page, follow these steps:

1. Choose File, New.
2. In the New dialog box, click on the Web Pages tab.
3. Choose the Web Page Wizard and click on OK. Word starts a new document, and the Web Page Wizard suggests a layout (see Figure 12.1).

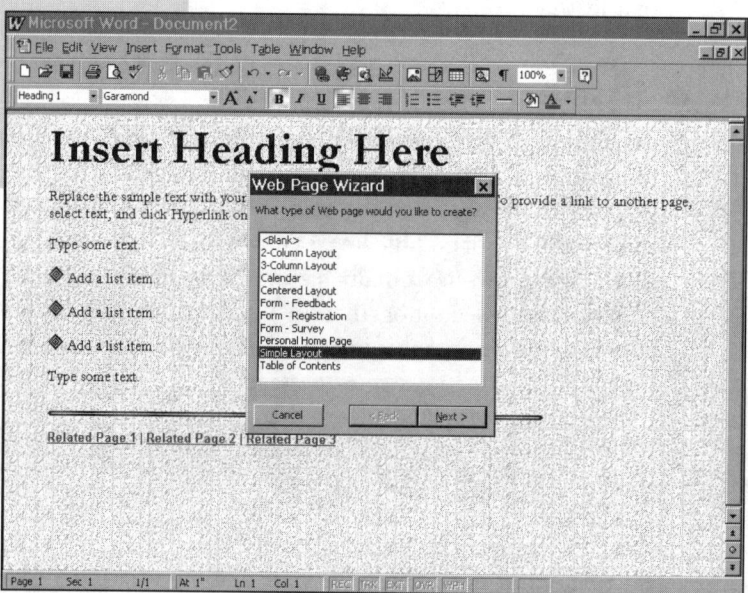

Figure 12.1
From this dialog box, choose the layout that you want for your Web page.

4. Choose a layout. As you highlight each layout, the document in the background changes to show you the layout. We chose Centered Layout.
5. Click on Next. The Web Page Wizard asks you to select a style for the Web page (see Figure 12.2).
6. Choose a style (we chose Professional in our example) and then click on Finish. Word displays the skeleton Web page on-screen (see Figure 12.3).

Chapter 12 • Using Word to Publish a Corporate Web Page

295

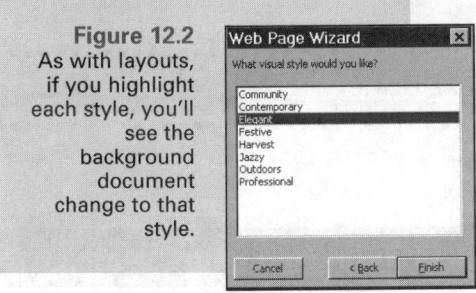

Figure 12.2
As with layouts, if you highlight each style, you'll see the background document change to that style.

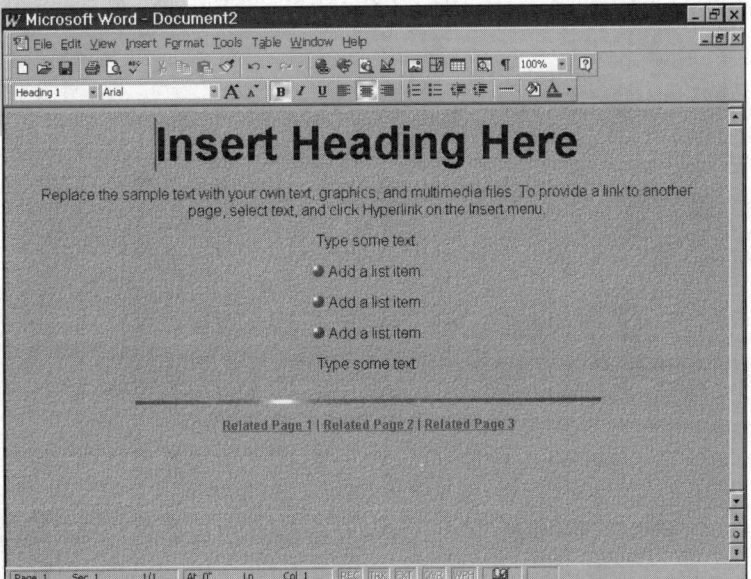

Figure 12.3
The results of running the Web Page Wizard.

Saving Your Web Page

When you save a Web page that you create, you actually save several different files; each element of the Web page (graphic images, bullets, lines, and so on) is saved separately. Each of the Web page files will be saved to the same folder. Keeping all the files for a Web page together becomes important when it's time to publish the Web page; you'll need to make sure then that you publish all the files.

When you save a Web page, therefore, you should save it to its own folder. The next exercise shows you how to create a new folder inside the Word folder, which is inside the My Documents folder.

PART III • WORD ONLINE

Periodically save your Web page as you work on it.

Hands On: Saving the Files of Your Web Page

To save your Web page and its associated files, follow these steps:

1. Choose File, Save. Word displays the Save As dialog box (see Figure 12.4).

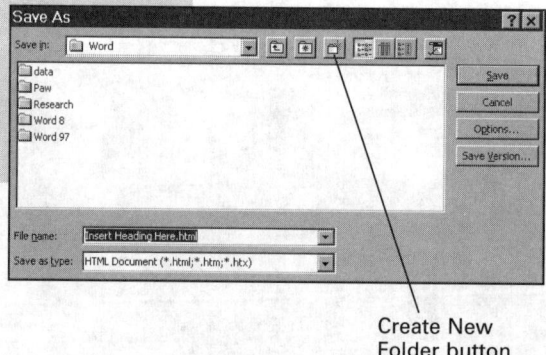

Figure 12.4 Use this dialog box to create a new folder and save your Web page in it.

Create New Folder button

2. (Optional) If the current folder is not where you typically store documents, navigate to that folder or the folder inside which you want to store Web documents.

3. Click on the Create New Folder button. Word displays the New Folder dialog box.

4. Type a name for the new folder (ours is called **Web Page Files**) and click on OK. The new folder appears in the Save As dialog box (see Figure 12.5).

5. Double-click on the new folder to open it.

6. In the File Name text box, type the name for your Web page. Because we're terribly creative, we called ours **New Web Page**.

CHAPTER 12 • USING WORD TO PUBLISH A CORPORATE WEB PAGE 297

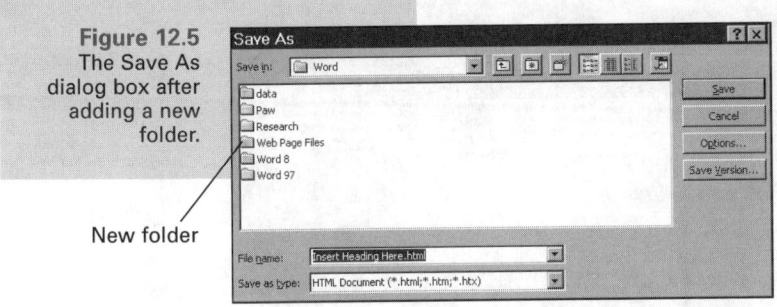

Figure 12.5
The Save As dialog box after adding a new folder.

New folder

Note If you aren't using a 32-bit browser, you may run into trouble if you use long filenames when you save your Web page files. We suggest that you use the latest version of the 32-bit browser of your choice.

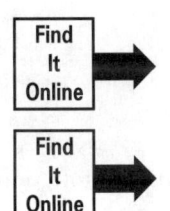

Find It Online

To download the latest version of Internet Explorer, go to:

```
http://www.microsoft.com/ie/download/
```

Find It Online

To download the latest version of Netscape Navigator, go to:

```
http://www.netscape.com/cgi-bin/123.cgi
```

7. Click on <u>S</u>ave. Word saves the Web page and its associated files. The title that you supplied for the Web page appears in the title bar of the Web page document.

If you close Word before you finish working on the Web page, you'll later need to reopen the Web page. You reopen the Web page using basically the same method that you would use to reopen any Word document. Navigate to the folder containing your Web page and display; then, in the Files of <u>T</u>ype list box, select All Files (*.*). Choose your Web page document. If you can see document name extensions, you'll see .html as the file's extension (see Figure 12.6).

Tip If you close your Web page before you create hyperlinks, the hyperlink formatting that you see in Figure 12.3 will not appear when you reopen the document; the formatting will reappear when you create real hyperlinks.

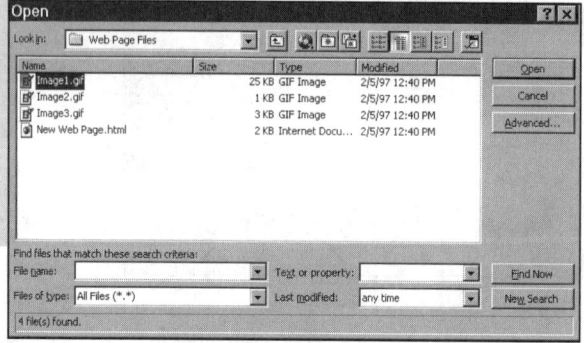

Figure 12.6
Notice that the folder containing your Web page also contains other files that were created when you saved the Web page.

Word Features and Web Authoring

Although a Web page looks like other Word documents, it does vary in some ways. In particular, some Word features change or simply are not available during Web authoring. The following Word features are not supported by HTML and therefore are not available during Web authoring:

- Newspaper columns
- Comments
- Revision marks
- Highlighting
- Font enhancements: emboss, engrave, all caps, small caps, shadow, double strikethrough, outline
- The flow of paragraphs and the spacing before and after paragraphs
- Tabs
- Margins
- Page numbering
- Page borders
- Headers and footers
- Endnotes and footnotes
- Cross references
- Master documents
- Tables of contents, authorities, and indexes
- Versions
- Mail merge

Table 12.1 shows the Word features that change during Web authoring, along with a description of how they change.

Table 12.1 Word Features

Feature	Change
Animated text	This feature uses scrolling text.
Font sizes	HTML uses different font sizes that do not correspond specifically to point sizes. You can change font sizes in a Web page, and Word will display text in sizes ranging from 9–36 points.
Underlining effects	Special underlining effects, such as dotted underline, are not available.
Ruler	The ruler doesn't appear by default. You can display it, however, by sliding the mouse pointer into the thin gray area immediately below the Formatting toolbar.
Equations, charts, and objects	HTML converts all objects to graphic images; therefore, you cannot update any data in them without recreating them.
Drawing objects	These objects are not available on the Drawing toolbar, but they are available from the Insert menu as picture objects.

Modifying a Web Page

Now that the Web Page Wizard has supplied a skeleton Web page, we need to make changes to it.

Typing and Formatting Text

The Web Page Wizard supplies "dummy" text where you should supply real text. You change the text on a Web page document the same way that you change text in any Word document.

Hands On: Changing the Text on the Web Page

To change text on a Web page, follow these steps:

1. Select the headline and type **Western Hemisphere Pools**.
2. Select the text immediately below the headline and type a second headline: **The Southeast's Premiere Pool Construction and Service Company**.
3. Select the first occurrence of the phrase `Type some text` and replace it by typing **We specialize in:**
4. Select the first `Add a list item` text and replace it by typing **New Pool Construction**.
5. Select the second `Add a list item` text and replace it by typing **Pool Repairs**.
6. Select the third `Add a list item` text and replace it by typing **Pool Cleaning and Servicing**.
7. Select the second occurrence of the phrase `Type some text` and replace it by typing **For more information, check out our other pages by clicking below.**
8. Select `Related Page 1` and replace it by typing **Read Our Company History**.
9. Select `Related Page 2` and replace it by typing **Purchase Supplies**.
10. Select `Related Page 3` and replace it by typing **Provide Feedback**. When you finish typing, your Web document should look like the one in Figure 12.7.

Hands On: Realigning and Indenting Text

Now, realign the bullets, which look strange centered.

1. Select the three bullets and their text.
2. Click on the Align Left button on the Standard toolbar.
3. Click on the Increase Indent button on the Standard toolbar until the bullets seem to appear in the middle of your screen. The number of times that you'll need to click depends on the display resolution you are using. Remember, we're using the Increase Indent button because HTML doesn't support tab settings.

CHAPTER 12 • USING WORD TO PUBLISH A CORPORATE WEB PAGE **301**

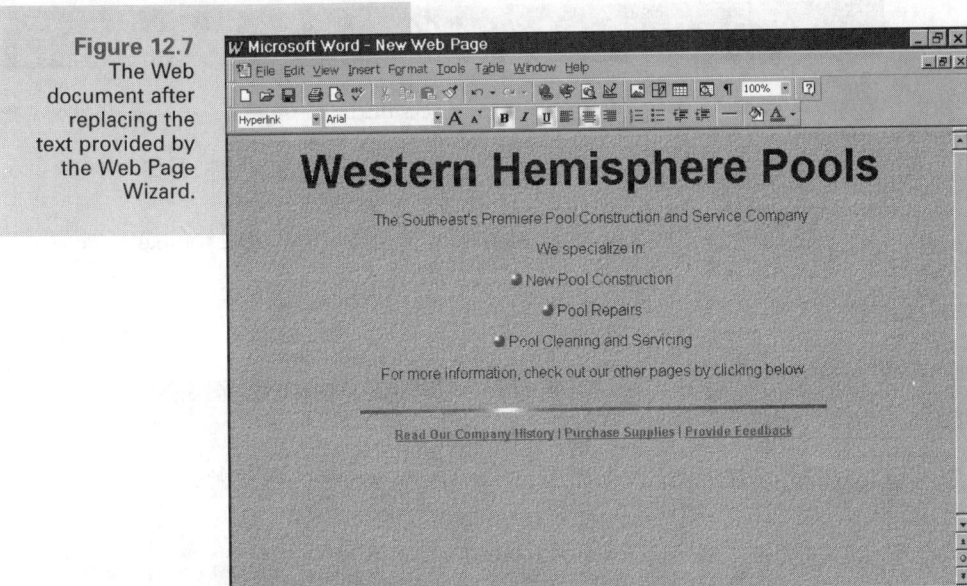

Figure 12.7
The Web document after replacing the text provided by the Web Page Wizard.

4. Click anywhere to cancel the selection. Your Web document should look like the one in Figure 12.8.

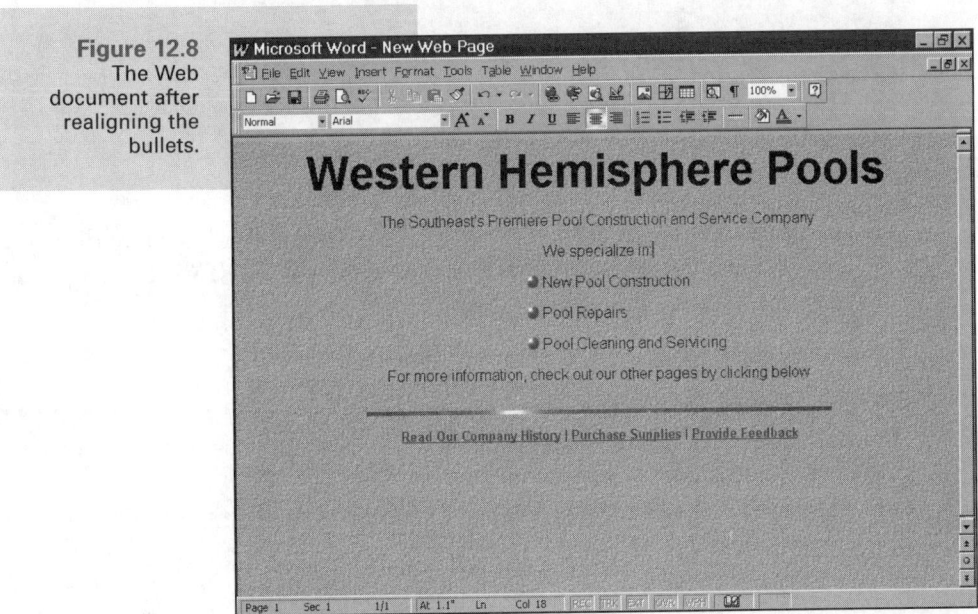

Figure 12.8
The Web document after realigning the bullets.

PART III • WORD ONLINE

Hands On: Resizing Text and Changing Text Color

Now, resize and change the color of the second headline.

1. Select the second headline, which reads `The Southeast's Premiere Pool Construction and Service Company`.
2. Click on the Increase Font Size button on the Standard toolbar once (see Figure 12.9).

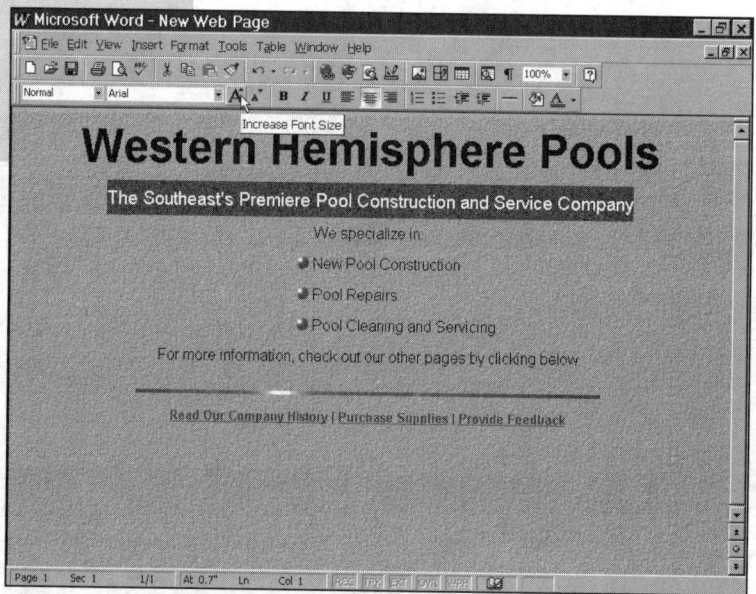

Figure 12.9
The Web page after increasing the size of the second headline.

3. Click on the list box at the right edge of the Font Color button to display a color palette (see Figure 12.10) and choose the color red. Word changes the color of the second headline to red.
4. Click anywhere on-screen to cancel the selection of the text.

Tip

On the Format menu, you'll find a Text Colors command. This command will control the color of all text on the page, not just selected text.

CHAPTER 12 • USING WORD TO PUBLISH A CORPORATE WEB PAGE 303

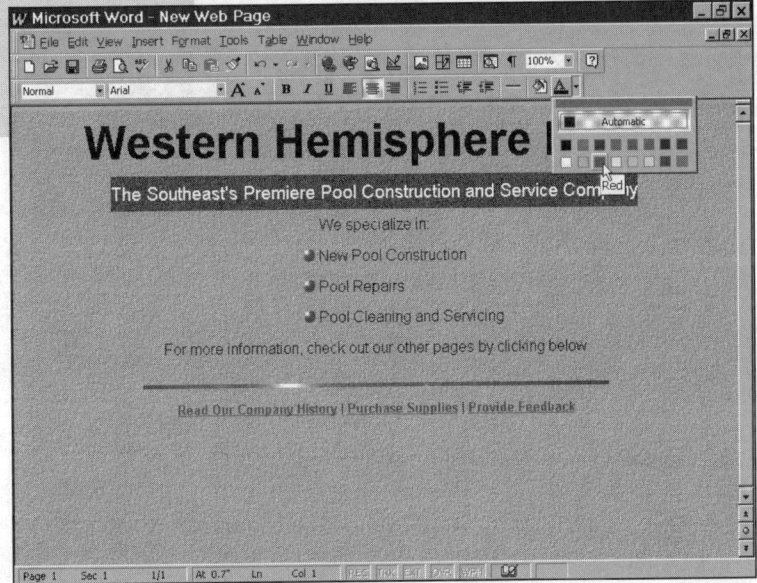

Figure 12.10
Changing the color of selected text.

Hands On: Changing the Web Page Title

Now change the title of the Web page so that it is more meaningful to Web page viewers.

1. Choose File, Properties.
2. In the Title text box, type the title that you want to appear in the title bar of the Web page. This is the title that viewers will see; we named our Web page **Western Hemisphere Pools**.
3. Click on OK. Word changes the title that appears in the title bar of the Web page (see Figure 12.11).

Figure 12.11
The Web page with the title bar that viewers will see.

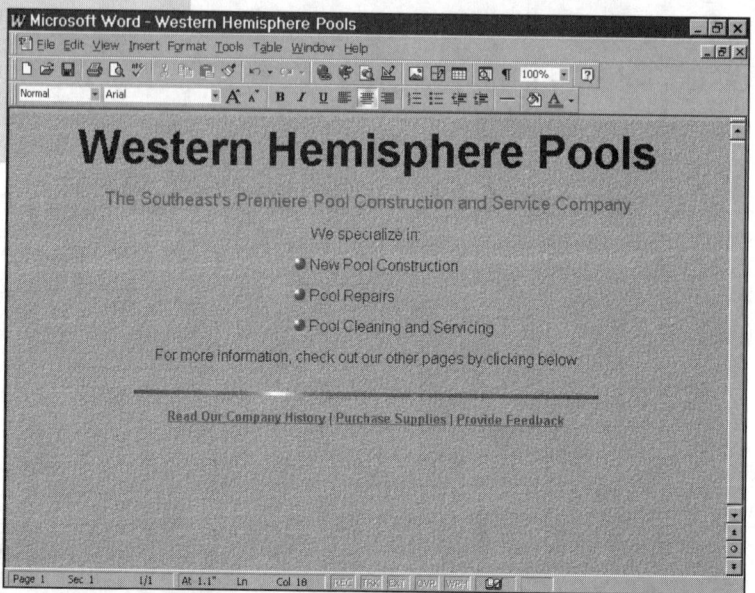

Note

If you don't save your Web page until after you change the title bar, Word will suggest the first few words that appear on the Web page as the title for the title bar. Similarly, Word will suggest the same words for the filename under which you save the Web page. Because we saved before renaming the Web page, the title that we just created appears only in the title bar; the filename of the Web page remains what we named it.

Changing the Background Pattern

The background pattern of the Web page is making the text somewhat difficult to read.

Chapter 12 • Using Word to Publish a Corporate Web Page

Hands On: Changing the Background Texture of a Web Page

To change the appearance of the background of the Web page, follow these steps:

1. Choose F<u>o</u>rmat, Bac<u>k</u>ground. From the cascading menu, choose <u>F</u>ill Effects. Word displays the Fill Effects dialog box (see Figure 12.12).

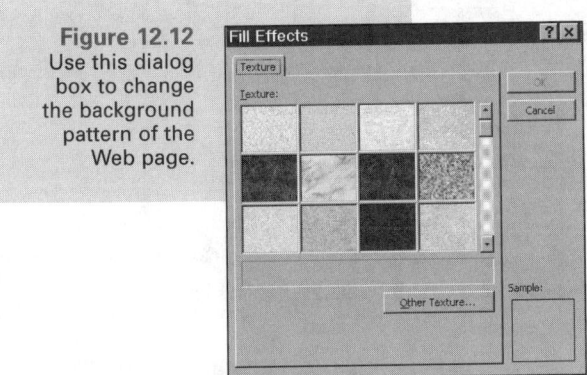

Figure 12.12 Use this dialog box to change the background pattern of the Web page.

2. Select a new background pattern for the Web page (we chose the second sample from the left in the second row) and click on OK. Word changes the background of the Web page (see Figure 12.13).

Inserting a Line

Lines provide simple, attractive graphics on Web pages.

Hands On: Inserting a Line Below the Second Heading of the Web Page

To add a line to a Web page, follow these steps:

1. Position the insertion point at the beginning of the line containing the text `We specialize in`.

306 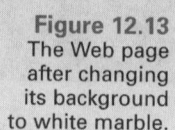 Part III • Word Online

Figure 12.13
The Web page after changing its background to white marble.

2. Choose Insert, Horizontal Line. Word displays the Horizontal Line dialog box (see Figure 12.14).

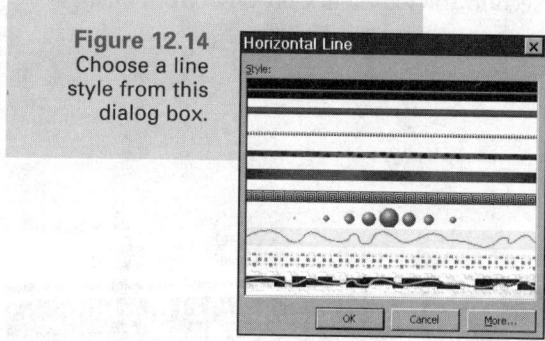

Figure 12.14
Choose a line style from this dialog box.

3. Choose a line style (we chose the last one in the box) and click on OK. Word inserts the line above the insertion point (see Figure 12.15).

CHAPTER 12 • USING WORD TO PUBLISH A CORPORATE WEB PAGE **307**

Figure 12.15
The Web page after inserting a line.

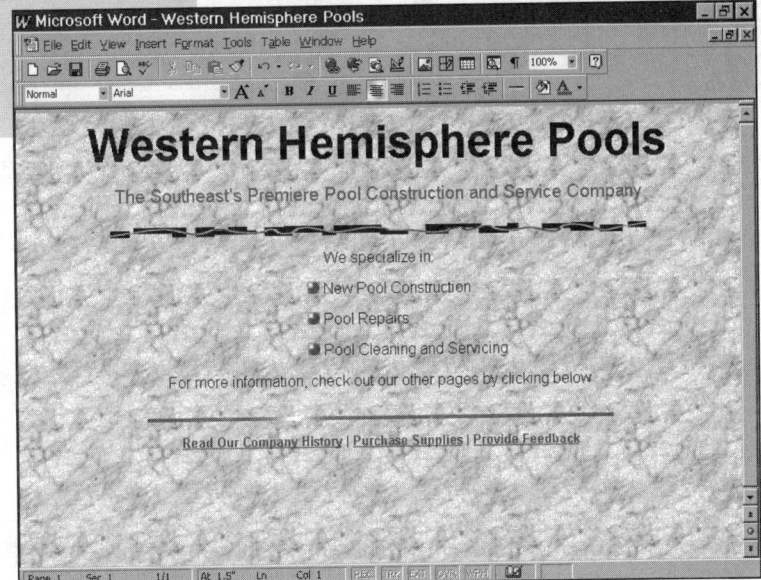

Using Scrolling Text

Scrolling text on a Web page provides quite a dramatic effect. Unfortunately, not all Web browsers support scrolling text. Any surfer who happens to be using a browser that doesn't support scrolling text will see regular text.

Hands On: Adding Scrolling Text

To add scrolling text to a web page, follow these steps:

1. Word will insert scrolling text above the insertion point; place the insertion point at the beginning of the line containing the text `We specialize in` and press Enter to create a blank line for the scrolling text. Press the Up arrow once to place the insertion point on the blank line.

2. Choose Insert, Scrolling Text. Word displays the Scrolling Text dialog box (see Figure 12.16).

3. Change the direction that text scrolls by opening the Direction list box and choosing Right.

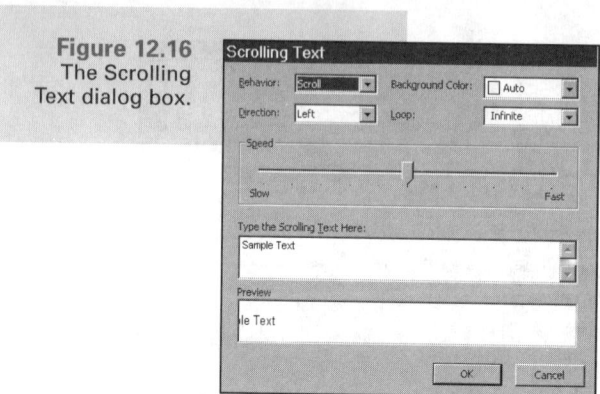

Figure 12.16
The Scrolling Text dialog box.

4. In the Type the Scrolling Text Here text box, replace the words Sample text with the text that you want to appear. We typed **Welcome to Our Home Page**.

5. Click on OK. Word displays scrolling text on your Web page (see Figure 12.17).

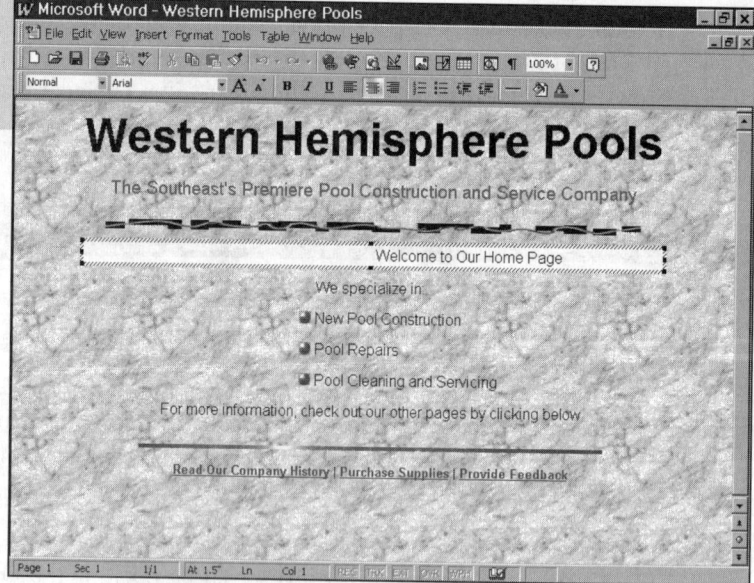

Figure 12.17
Word displays the scrolling text in a graphic box.

CHAPTER 12 • USING WORD TO PUBLISH A CORPORATE WEB PAGE   309

> **Tip**
> If you make a mistake or decide that you want to delete the scrolling text, make sure that the object is selected (black handles appear around it as in Figure 12.17) and choose Edit, Clear.

Hands On: Modifying Scrolling Text

You can change the appearance of scrolling text.

1. With scrolling text selected (black handles appear around it), click on the Bold button on the Formatting toolbar. Word bolds the scrolling text.

2. To change the background color of the scrolling text, reopen the Scrolling Text dialog box by choosing Insert, Scrolling Text.

3. Open the Background Color list box and select a background color from the list (see Figure 12.18). We chose Gray-50%. A sample will appear in the Preview box.

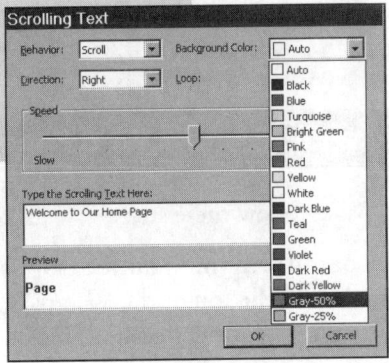

Figure 12.18 Choosing a background color for scrolling text.

4. Click on OK to apply your choice, and click anywhere on the home page to cancel the selection of the scrolling text. Your Web page should resemble the one in Figure 12.19.

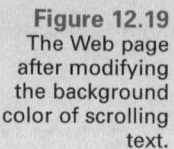

PART III • WORD ONLINE

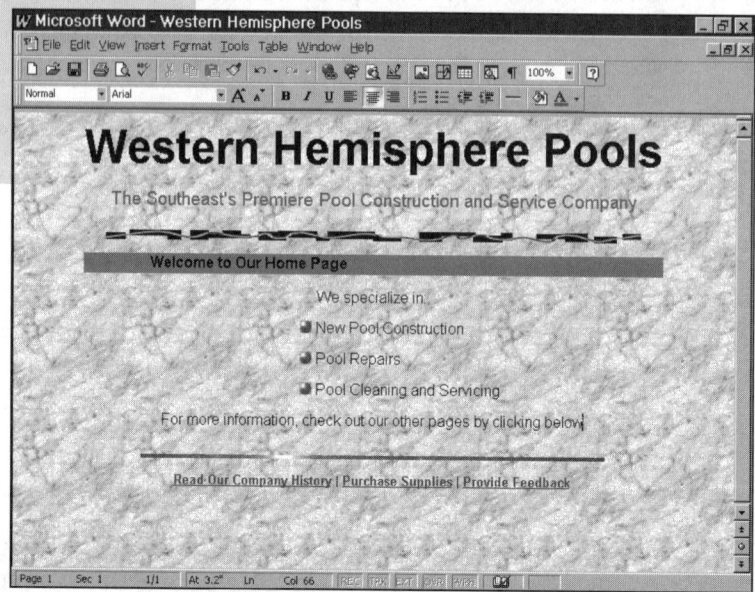

Figure 12.19
The Web page after modifying the background color of scrolling text.

Adding a Graphic to a Web Page

Web pages usually include some graphics, just to create visual interest.

Hands On: Adding a Picture to a Web Page

To add a picture to a Web page, follow these steps:

1. Position the insertion point where you want the graphic to appear. In the example, create a blank line at the top of the Web page by positioning the insertion point at the beginning of the first headline and pressing Enter once. Then, press the Up arrow key to move the insertion point onto the blank line.

Tip

Some clip art is installed automatically when you install Word; if you have Office, you'll find additional clip art on the Office CD. Insert the Office CD before completing Step 2 to view all the clip art available.

CHAPTER 12 • USING WORD TO PUBLISH A CORPORATE WEB PAGE **311**

2. Choose Insert, Picture. From the cascading menu that appears, choose Clip Art. Word displays the Microsoft Clip Gallery 3.0 dialog box (see Figure 12.20).

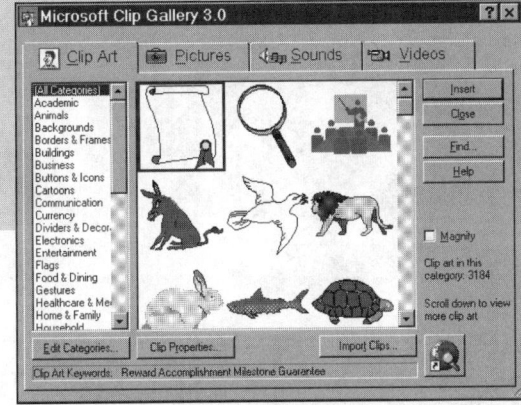

Figure 12.20 Choose an image to insert on the Web page. You can choose a clip art image, a picture, or a video.

3. From the appropriate tab (Clip Art, Pictures, or Videos), choose an image. We chose the World Globe (Western Hemisphere).

•••

If you know the kind of clip art, picture, or video that you want to insert, choose it from the list on the left. In the example, we chose Maps.

•••

4. Click on Insert. Word inserts the image on your Web page (see Figure 12.21).

Hands On: Modifying the Size of the Graphic Image on the Web Page

The globe is much larger than we actually want it to be, so we will reduce its size.

1. Click on the graphic image so that handles surround it.
2. Move the mouse pointer over the lower-right corner handle until the pointer changes to a two-headed arrow pointing diagonally.

312 Part III • Word Online

Figure 12.21
The image Word inserts is large because the font size at the insertion point was large.

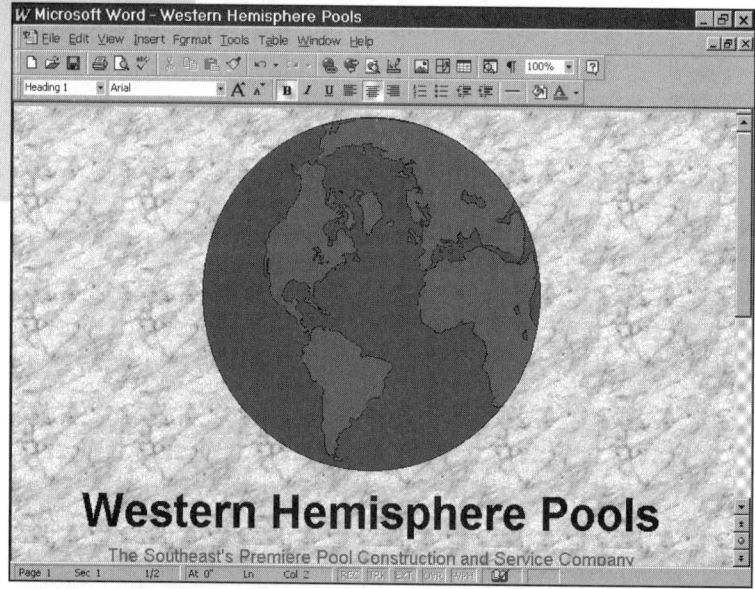

3. Drag the mouse up and to the left (see Figure 12.22) until it appears to be the size you want. As you drag, the mouse pointer changes to a plus sign.

Figure 12.22
Resizing the image.

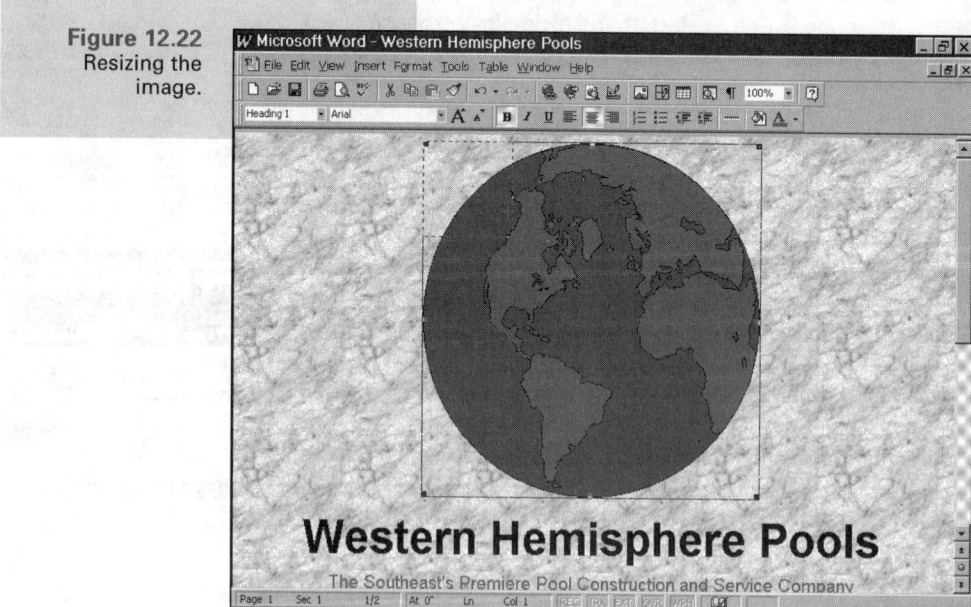

CHAPTER 12 • USING WORD TO PUBLISH A CORPORATE WEB PAGE **313**

4. When you release the mouse button, Word resizes the image and repositions it so that it is centered horizontally on the page. If necessary, repeat these steps until you are satisfied with the size of the image. we resized the image until we could see all the text on the Web page (see Figure 12.23). Again, what you see will depend on your monitor size and your display resolution.

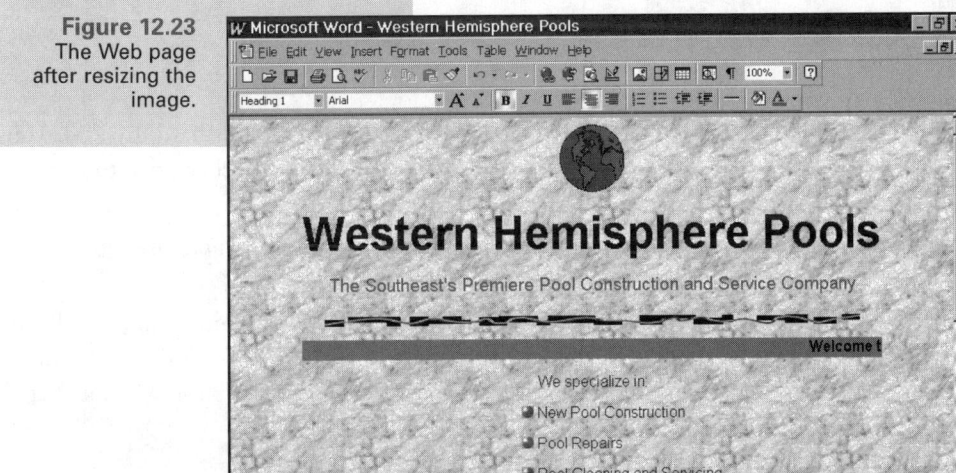

Figure 12.23
The Web page after resizing the image.

Including a Background Sound

You can have a background sound play when someone views your Web page; background sounds don't slow Web browsers because they load and begin to play while the Web is loading and, if a surfer switches to another Web page, the sound stops.

Hands On: Adding a Background Sound to a Web Page

To add a background sound to a Web page, follow these steps:

1. Choose Insert, Background Sound.

2. From the cascading menu, choose Properties. Word displays the Background Sound dialog box (see Figure 12.24).

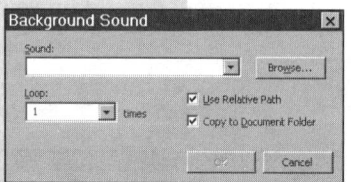

Figure 12.24
Use this dialog box to assign a background sound to your Web page.

3. Click on Browse to see a list of sounds available on your hard drive for you to attach to your Web page. If necessary, switch to another drive to find a sound.
4. Select a sound (we selected Beethoven's "Für Elise") and choose Open to redisplay the Background Sound dialog box.
5. Click on OK to assign the sound. It will begin to play, and will play all the way through once until it finishes. In the future, the sound will play only when you open the Web page or, after you publish the page, when a Web surfer views your page.

To stop the sound from playing, choose Insert, Background Sound. From the cascading menu, choose Stop. To change the sound, reopen the Background Sound dialog box and find a new sound to apply.

About Using Charts on a Web Page

When you save a Web page, you save a document in HTML format. Suppose that your Web page includes a chart. That chart is considered an object, and HTML format converts all objects to graphic images. Therefore, you cannot update any data in a chart without recreating it. If you know that you'll need to update a chart, save a copy of your Web page as a Word document. When you need to update the chart, open the Word document and update the chart. Then, resave the document as a Web page using the instructions that you'll find later in this chapter for converting a Word document to a Web document.

Previewing a Web Page

So far, you've viewed your Web document in Word. Now you'll preview it using a Web browser.

Chapter 12 • Using Word to Publish a Corporate Web Page 315

Hands On: Previewing a Word Web Page in a Web Browser

To use a browser to preview a Web page that you've created in Word, follow these steps:

1. Save your Web document in HTML format.
2. While viewing your Web document, click on the Web Page Preview button on the Standard toolbar (see Figure 12.25).
3. Your Web browser appears on-screen and displays your Web page (see Figure 12.26).

Notice that spacing changes from Word to your Web browser. To move the bullets over more to the right, switch back to Word, select the bullets, and click on the Increase Indent button on the Standard toolbar. To switch back to Word, use the Windows 95 Taskbar. Save the Web document in Word and preview again by clicking on the Web Page Preview button again. We found that we needed to indent only once more to create an appealing image in the Web browser (see Figure 12.27). And if you can't see everything on one page that you want the Web surfer to see, you might consider changing the spacing between lines.

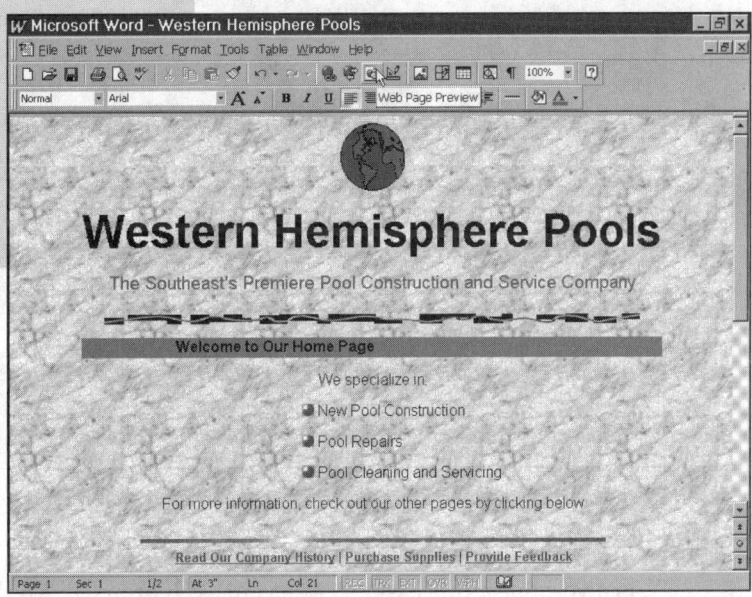

Figure 12.25 Click on the Web Page Preview button to preview the appearance of your Web page in a Web browser.

Figure 12.26
The Word Web page in a Web browser.

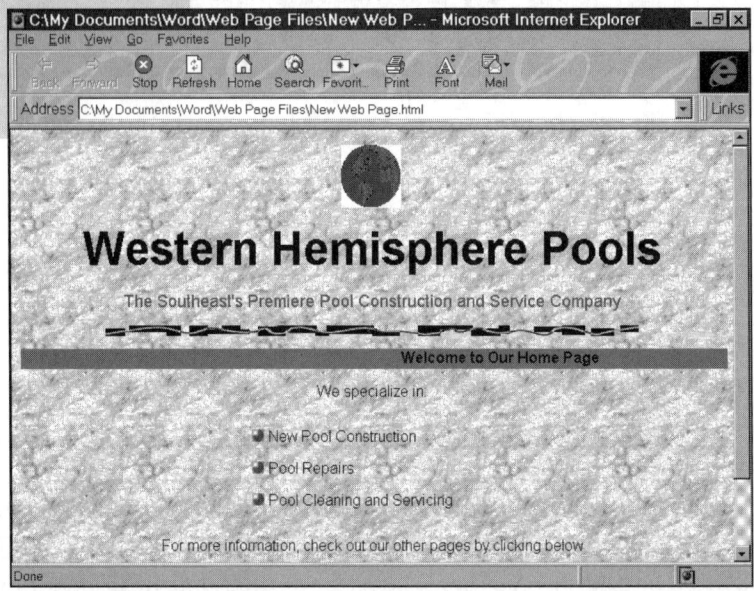

Figure 12.27
The Web document after adjusting it for the Web browser.

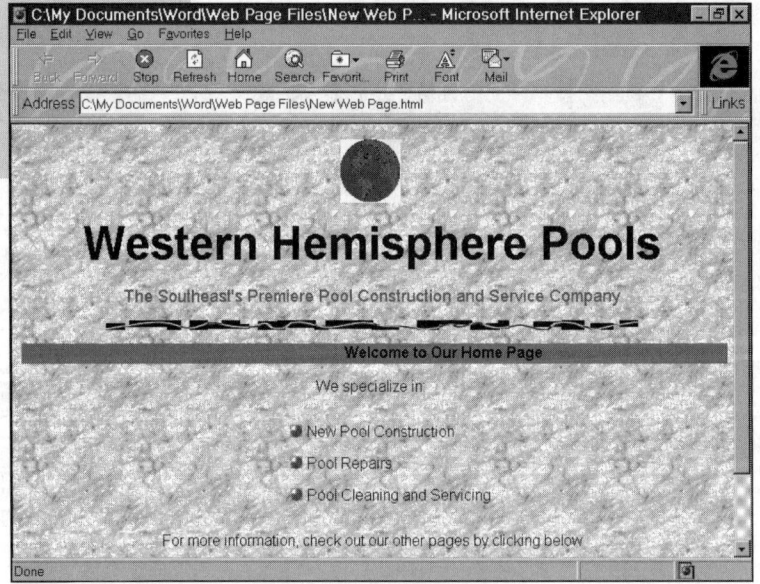

When you finish previewing, close your Web browser. Word and your Web document in Word will reappear.

CHAPTER 12 • USING WORD TO PUBLISH A CORPORATE WEB PAGE **317**

> **TO MORE INFORMATION ON HYPERLINKS, SEE CHAPTER 11.**

At this point, you would create other Web pages for each of the three hyperlinks that you intend to add at the bottom of this Web page. Then, you would add hyperlinks using the directions that you found in Chapter 11. We're going to skip this process, because it would repeat what you've already learned in this chapter and in Chapter 11.

Publishing Web Documents

You've already learned how to save a Web document; now the question is, "How do I get my Web page out there so that others can see it?"

If you're publishing your Web pages on a network, you need to save your Web pages and their related files (the graphics, lines, bullets, and so on) in a place on the network to which everyone has access.

If your company has an intranet based on Internet protocols, you may need to copy your Web pages and their related files to a Web server. Talk to your network administrator and find out what you need to do.

If you want to publish your Web pages on the World Wide Web, you can either act as your own Web server or you can locate an Internet Service Provider (ISP) that also allows you to display your Web pages. To act as your own Web server, you need to install Web server software such as Personal Web Server, which is available on the Office 97 ValuPack, or Microsoft Internet Information Server, which will act as an advanced Web server. If you choose to act as your own Web server, remember that your Web page will be available only as long as your computer is turned on; further, the speed of your computer will play a role in the speed of the presentation of your Web page to Web surfers.

Converting Word Documents to Web Documents

Throughout this chapter, we used the Web Page Wizard to create a Web page. But suppose that you have information in a regular Word document that you would like to publish as a Web page. Do you need to recreate it using the Web Page Wizard? No. You simply need to save the document in HTML format. Remember, however, that some standard Word features are not available in HTML format, so your document may lose some of its formatting during the conversion. You'll need to preview it after converting it to see what converted correctly.

Hands On: Converting an Existing Word Document to a Web Document

To convert a Word document into a Web document, follow these steps:

1. Open the Word file that you want to publish as a Web page.
2. Choose File, Save As HTML. Word displays the Save As HTML dialog box. This dialog box looks just like the Save As dialog box.
3. Word suggests that you rename your document by using its existing name but attaching an extension of HTML; further, the Save as Type that Word suggests is HTML Document. If necessary, change the document name and the location where you want to save the document.
4. Click on Save. Your document is now saved in HTML format, suitable for viewing on the Web.

If you have access to the Internet and you have access rights to an FTP site that supports saving files, you can save documents to the Internet using the File, Save As command. These files *are not* in HTML format, but they can be downloaded by others to use as standard files.

micros
WORD

13
Creating a Multimedia Announcement

In This Chapter

- Working with Photographs
- Adding Sound
- Animating Text
- Adding Fill Effects

Multimedia is quite simply the combination of various media such as sound, photographs, and animation. Multimedia is what makes the World Wide Web go round, what glues your kids to their screens playing computer games through the night, and what makes computers a central tool in making business presentations. Why should your word processor be left out of this sensory revolution? It shouldn't.

PART III • WORD ONLINE

Word can take advantage of many multimedia materials. Your customer can experience these effects by opening your Word document on his or her computer, or the effects can be incorporated into documents that you publish on the Web (see Chapters 11 and 12 for more about Web publishing). In this chapter you are introduced to four features that can add pizzazz to your pages: photographs, sound, animated text, and exciting textures for your page background.

Working with Photographs

Photos can be used in a variety of ways. You can place photos in documents, such as a newsletter, and that document can be printed in greyscale tones on a black-and-white printer to quite nice effect. Or, you can print on a color printer, or even pass your Word file on to a printing company and have it reproduce the colors in the picture more exactly.

You can get your hands on photos to use in Word documents in a couple of ways. There are collections of photos on CD such as the Kodak Photo CD. When you purchase such a collection, you have the right to use it in certain ways; different collections grant you different rights, so read the fine print carefully.

You can also download photos that you find online, but be careful: unless you get specific permission to reproduce such a photo, you could be violating a copyright. Finally, you can take a photograph that you shot or that you have the rights to and, using scanning equipment, scan it into a computer file.

Note You can also take negatives from photos to certain companies that do photo processing and ask to have your pictures put on CD for you. CDs can typically hold around 100 photos or more.

Where you get the photo is up to you. The process of placing it in your Word document is delightfully easy, however.

Inserting Photos in Documents

Inserting a photograph into a Word document is just like inserting any other file. Word has certain filters available to deal with this process. Here's a list of filters available with Word; if one you need wasn't installed when you installed Word, you can run Word setup again to load it on your computer:

- .eps   Encapsulated Postscript
- .pcx   PC Paintbrush file
- .tif   Tagged Image format
- .pcd   Kodak Photo CD
- .gif   Graphics Interchange Format

You don't need a separate filter for the .bmp (Windows Bitmap), .jpg (Joint Photographic Experts Group), or .wmf (Windows Metafile) formats; Word handles them fine on its own.

To place a picture in a document, you'll be using the Insert Picture dialog box shown in Figure 13.1. This is similar to other Insert and Open dialog boxes that you've seen in Word, where you can use the Look in text box and buttons adjacent to it to locate files on your hard, floppy, or CD drives. The Search the Web button here can be especially useful when looking for multimedia files online. When you locate and click on a file, a preview of it appears.

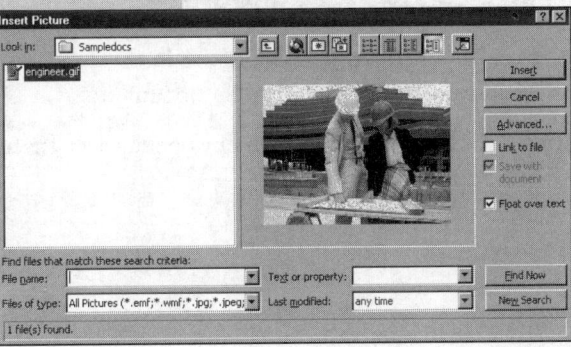

Figure 13.1
By default, Word searches for all picture files.

Three check boxes on the right of this dialog box are especially useful when working with photographs:

- Float over text imports the file as a drawing object, so that you can use various drawing tools to place the photo on your page and layer it with other drawing objects. If you remove the check mark from this check box, the photo is brought in within your paragraph and treated as text.

PART III • WORD ONLINE

> **FOR MORE ABOUT HOW LINKING WORKS, SEE CHAPTER 7.**

- **Link to file** allows you to establish a link to the original file, so that any changes to that file are updated in your document (as long as the original file is available to Word when you next open this document). If you place a check mark here, the third check box, Save with document, becomes available.

- **Save with document**, when checked, indicates that you want a copy of this file embedded in your document and saved with it. If you want to keep your Word file size smaller, remove this check mark. Then, the photo won't be saved with the Word file; rather, when you next open it, Word will retrieve the file from its original location once again.

Tip

A great way to find multimedia files to use in your documents is to use the Microsoft on the Web section of the Word Help menu. Select Free Stuff from this menu and you'll be taken to the Microsoft Web site, where you can search for photos, sound, and even animation files.

Hands On: Inserting a Photo

After you have obtained a photo file to use in this exercise, you're ready to begin. Follow these steps to insert a photo in a document:

1. With a new, blank Word document open, select Insert, Picture, From File, as shown in Figure 13.2.

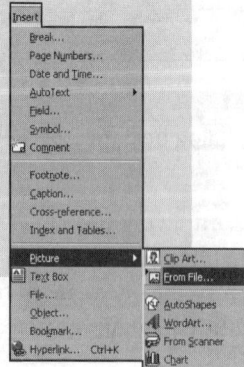

Figure 13.2
Notice that you could choose From Scanner from this cascading menu if you wanted to use a scanned photographic image.

Chapter 13 • Creating a Multimedia Announcement 325

2. In the Insert Image dialog box shown in Figure 13.3, locate a photographic image, and click on it to see a preview.

3. Choose Insert to proceed. If you are importing an image from a Kodak Photo CD collection, the dialog box in Figure 13.3 appears.

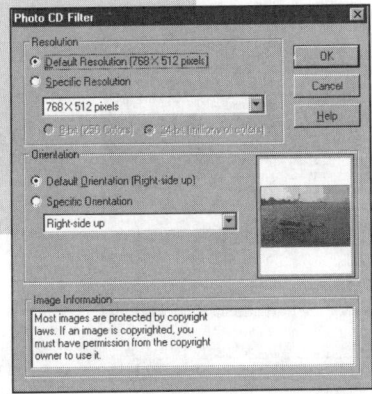

Figure 13.3
This is where you can manipulate how a Kodak Photo CD photo file is brought into Word.

Note

Computer file resolution deals with how many dots per inch (dpi) your printer produces; the higher the resolution, the more dots on the paper and the crisper your printed image. In a photograph, resolution has to do with pixels: just as with dots per inch for a printer, the more pixels in a photograph image, the darker and crisper the image appears. This dialog box allows you to manipulate the resolution of images brought in from Kodak photo collections, and default settings are usually correct. If you are bringing in any other kind of image, you won't even see this dialog box.

4. If you see the dialog box in Figure 13.3, click on OK to proceed. Otherwise, your image should now be inserted on your page, as in Figure 13.4.

A centralized listing of photography Web sites can be found at:

```
http://www.american-photo.com/cool/photogs.htm
```

Part III • Word Online

Figure 13.4
The image may appear larger than you wish, but don't worry: you can resize it easily.

Hands On: Resizing and Cropping Photos

When the image is in your document, you can use the Picture toolbar and simple resizing techniques to modify it.

1. Click on the picture. Eight handles appear around the edges of the picture, and the Picture Toolbar shown in Figure 13.5 appears.

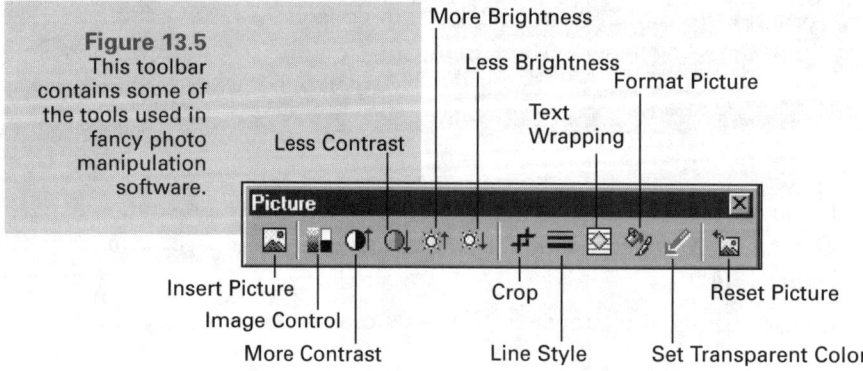

Figure 13.5
This toolbar contains some of the tools used in fancy photo manipulation software.

Chapter 13 • Creating a Multimedia Announcement

2. Click on the top-right handle; your mouse pointer becomes a two-headed arrow. Drag toward the center of the photo, about an inch. A dashed line will appear as you drag, showing you the new size of the photo, as in Figure 13.6.

Figure 13.6 Drag a corner handle to resize while retaining original proportions; use a handle on the sides, top, or bottom to resize without retaining proportions.

Dashed line indicating new photo dimensions

3. Click on the Crop tool on the Picture toolbar.

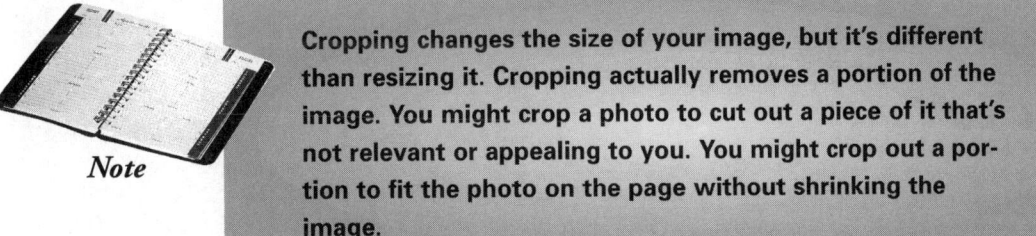

Note

Cropping changes the size of your image, but it's different than resizing it. Cropping actually removes a portion of the image. You might crop a photo to cut out a piece of it that's not relevant or appealing to you. You might crop out a portion to fit the photo on the page without shrinking the image.

4. Click on the top-right handle and drag. Crosshairs appear at each corner of the image, as in Figure 13.7.

Figure 13.7
The cropping tool is selected on the toolbar; you must click on it again to turn it off.

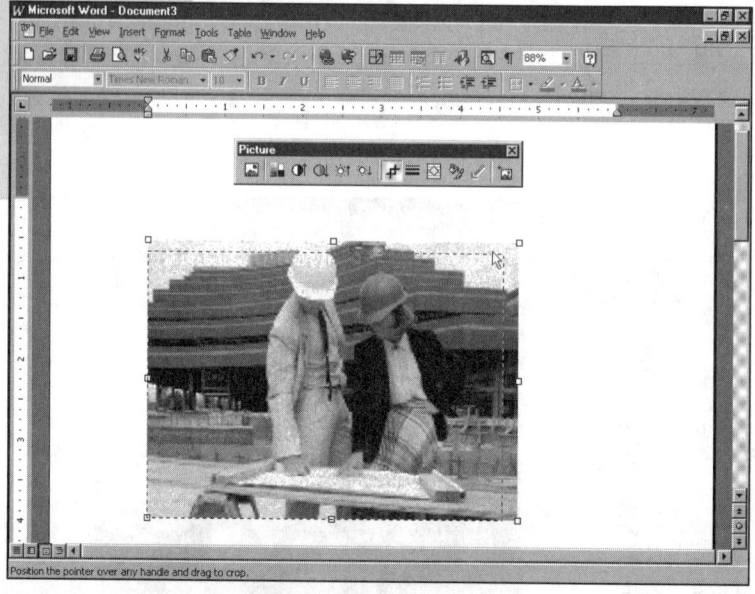

5. When you've dragged a small amount (say 1/2 inch), click and release your mouse button.

6. Click on the Crop tool to turn it off.

You can also use the Format Picture dialog box to crop a picture to exact measurements. To do so, click on the Format Picture button on the Picture Toolbar and then enter a measurement on the Picture tab of the Format Picture dialog box, shown in Figure 13.8.

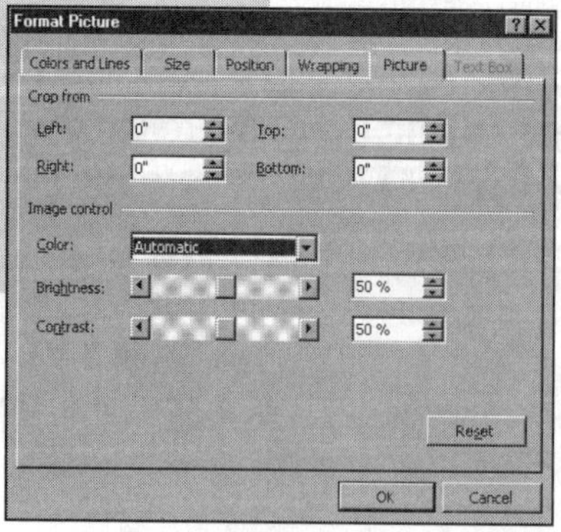

Figure 13.8
Select the Picture tab and type exact measurements for cropping here.

> **Hands On: Adding a Border**

The Format Picture feature also allows you to add a border to your picture. Borders help to set off a picture or add definition to its edges if it fades toward the outer edges.

1. Click on the Format Picture button on the Picture Toolbar. The Format Picture dialog box appears.
2. Select the Colors and Lines tab to see the panel shown in Figure 13.9.

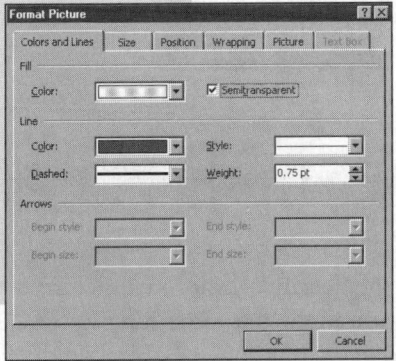

Figure 13.9 The six tabs of the Format Picture dialog box allow you to manipulate your picture in many ways that are also offered through the Picture toolbar.

3. In the Line section of this panel, open the Color drop-down list and select black.
4. Make sure that the Style selection has a thin line style in it.
5. You can modify the weight of the line with the Weight selector; select .75 using the Up and Down arrows here.
6. Click on OK to apply the line border to your picture, as shown in Figure 13.10.

Adjusting Brightness and Contrast

One of the keys to making photographs work in Word documents is being able to adjust the image so that it prints clearly, whether you're using a low-end, black-and-white printer or a sophisticated color printer. To adjust the image, you can start by modifying your picture using two tools: brightness and contrast. You can modify these by using the four tools on the Picture toolbar: More Contrast, Less Contrast, More Brightness, and Less Brightness. You can click on these tools repeatedly to add more or less of any effect.

Figure 13.10
A border can add definition to your photographic image.

Contrast has to do with the density of color in a picture, also referred to as *saturation*. The higher the saturation, the more intense the colors appear. Because showing the effect of higher saturation in a black-and-white book is difficult, you'll have to play with that setting yourself to see what happens at higher contrast settings on your computer screen. If you lower the contrast as shown in Figure 13.11, however, you can see how the picture seems to become less distinct.

Brightness is an adjustment to how much black and white an image has. The more brightness, the more white an image has; the less brightness, the more black in the image. Figure 13.12 shows our image with more brightness added; that is, more white, and therefore a faded-looking image.

On the other hand, too little brightness, which leaves mainly black and little white in the image, can make your photo too dark, as in Figure 13.13.

If you think that the photo you inserted could benefit from these adjustments, use the Brightness and Contrast tools now to make modifications.

Tip

If you make changes and decide you don't like them after all, you can use the Reset button on the Picture toolbar to return to the original image; all changes you made will be lost, however, including resizing, cropping, and adding borders.

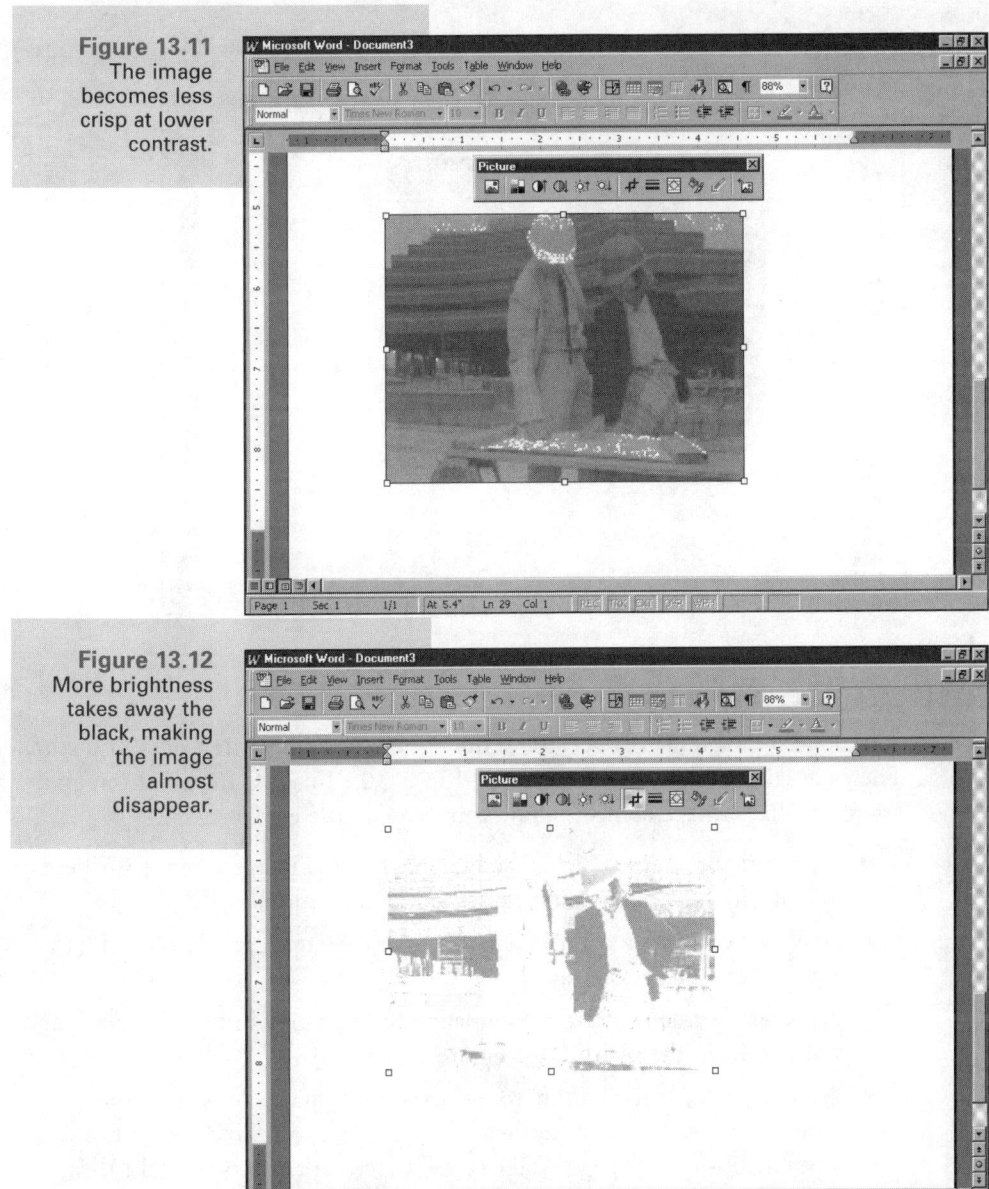

Figure 13.11
The image becomes less crisp at lower contrast.

Figure 13.12
More brightness takes away the black, making the image almost disappear.

Figure 13.13
Too little brightness can eventually make your photo appear solid black.

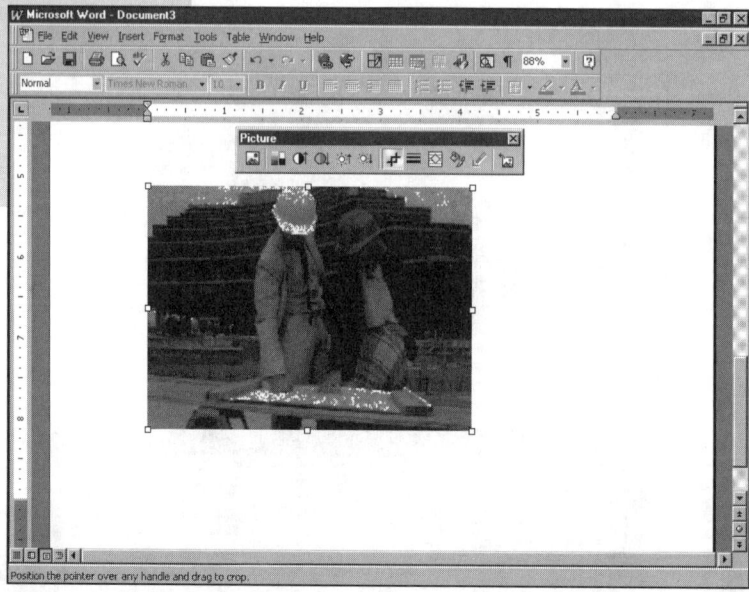

Using Image Controls

You can also use built-in effects to set the brightness and contrast of your picture. These are called *image controls*, accessed through the Image Control button on the Picture toolbar. Image controls allow you to apply these effects:

- Automatic provides automatic adjustment of the image when it is inserted to make it as clear as possible based on its resolution.
- Grayscale converts a color image to a grayscale image, replacing colors with various shades of gray.
- Black and White posterizes the image, using no gray but simply black and white to form the picture (see Figure 13.14).
- Watermark fades the picture to a background image. This resembles watermarks used on fine stationary: a faded image behind the text or other items on your page. You can use watermark effects to make the picture a sort of background or wallpaper for your document (see Figure 13.15).

For this example, you can leave the setting at Automatic.

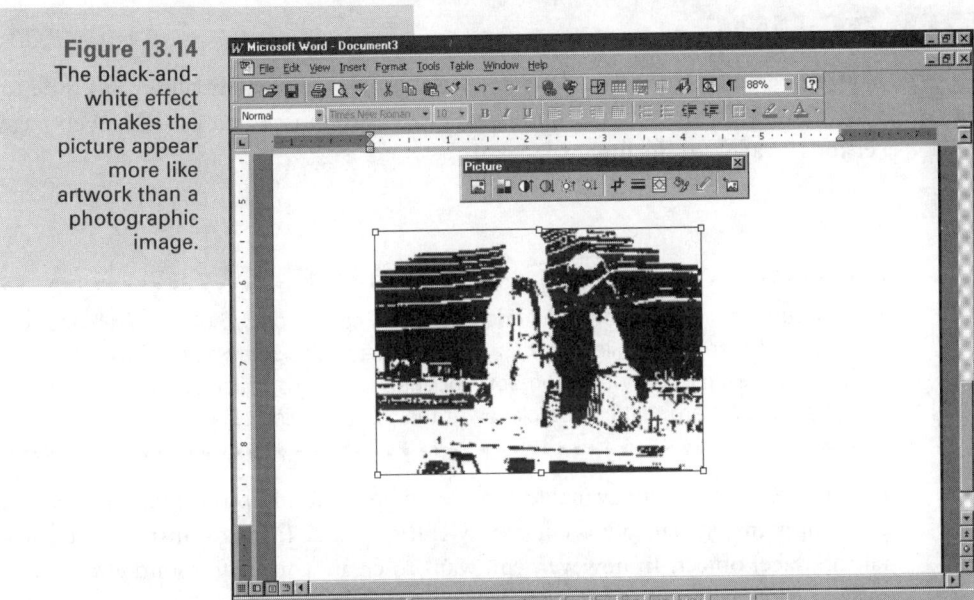

Figure 13.14
The black-and-white effect makes the picture appear more like artwork than a photographic image.

Figure 13.15
Notice how the Watermark effect resembles the image with more brightness applied, as in Figure 13.12.

Adding Sound

SEE CHAPTER 12 FOR MORE ABOUT WEB PAGE DESIGN.

Now that you have the visual element of your announcement all set, it's time to add sound to it. Sound and animation effects are most often used on Web page versions of a Word document.

Tip

You can turn your document into a document that can be placed on the Web at any time by simply selecting File, Save as HTML. For a Web page, you can insert background sounds that play when someone opens your page, or use sound clips like the one you'll insert here that can be played at the viewer's discretion.

If you have a sound clip available as a file on your CD, floppy, or hard drive, you can simply insert that sound clip as a MIDI sequence (Musical Instrument Digital Interface) object. If, however, you want to create your own sound effects, you can use Microsoft's Sound Recorder, built right into Windows.

Note

> To use sounds, you must have a sound card installed in your computer and speakers attached to or built into the computer. Most computers today come with a sound card (usually Sound Blaster); if you hear little bleeps and chimes go off as you perform various functions in Word, you're all set. You can check whether you have a sound card, however, by selecting the Windows Start menu, Settings, Control Panel. From the Control Panel window, choose System, and click on the Properties tab. Look in the Device Manager list to see whether a sound card is installed.

Find It Online

Visit the Creative Labs Web site to learn more about Sound Blaster soundcards at

```
http://www.reserve.co.uk/www.public/catalogue/
soundcards.html
```

CHAPTER 13 • CREATING A MULTIMEDIA ANNOUNCEMENT **335**

> ### Hands On: Inserting Sound Clips

Several sound clips come with Windows 95; you'll use one of those to add sound to this sample document.

1. Choose <u>I</u>nsert, <u>O</u>bject. The Object dialog box shown in Figure 13.16 appears.

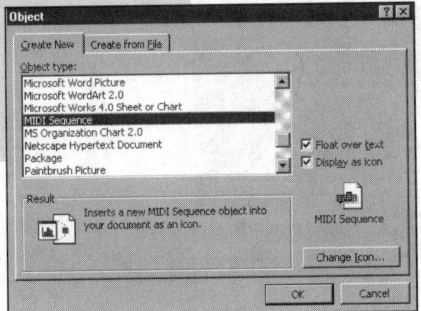

Figure 13.16
MIDI is a standard sound format commonly used.

2. Select MIDI Sequence in the Object Type list.
3. Place a check mark in the Display as icon check box. This will place a small MIDI Sequence icon on your page, which, when double-clicked, plays back the sound clip.
4. Click on OK. The MIDI Sequence panel displays, as in Figure 13.17, ready for you to open a sound file.
5. Select <u>F</u>ile, <u>O</u>pen to open a sound clip file. The dialog box shown in Figure 13.18 appears.
6. If the Media folder contents shown in the preceding figure don't appear, use the Look in text box and other tools in this dialog box to locate the Windows directory and Media folder.
7. Select Bach's *Brandenburg Concerto* No. 3.rmi (notice that MIDI files come in both .rmi and .mid formats).
8. Choose <u>O</u>pen to open the file. The MIDI Sequence panel should now look like the one shown in Figure 13.19, with the name of the *Brandenburg Concerto* across the top and the control buttons available to you.

336 Part III • Word Online

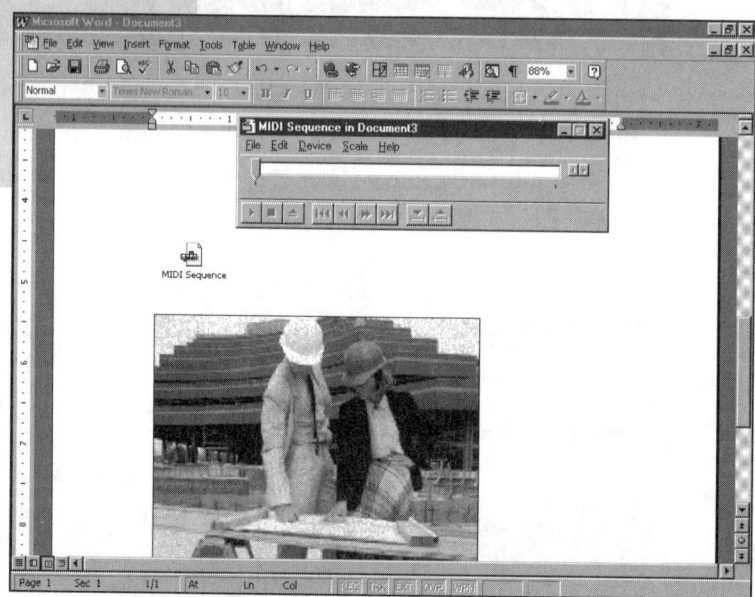

Figure 13.17
These menus and buttons help control how your sound clip plays back.

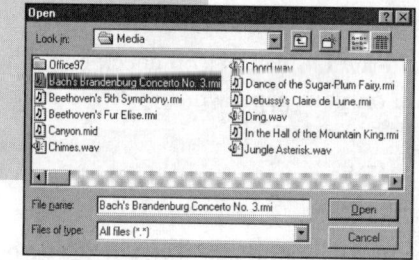

Figure 13.18
By default, this dialog box should point you to the Windows Media folder.

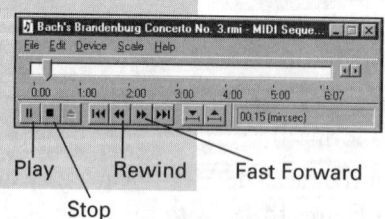

Figure 13.19
The interface of most sound software is much like your favorite tape recorder.

9. Click on the Play button to hear the selection. (Pretty impressive, huh?) Notice that the little marker in the middle moves to the left, showing the progress of the playback relative to its total length.

CHAPTER 13 • CREATING A MULTIMEDIA ANNOUNCEMENT

10. This clip lasts more than six minutes. Let it play to the end or, if you tire of it, press the Stop button.
11. Choose Device, Volume Control. The Volume Control panel shown in Figure 13.20 appears.

Note

The Volume Control panel will include balance and volume controls for all the sound devices installed on your computer. You can elect not to display any one of these by choosing Options, Properties in this dialog box, and then removing the check mark from that device.

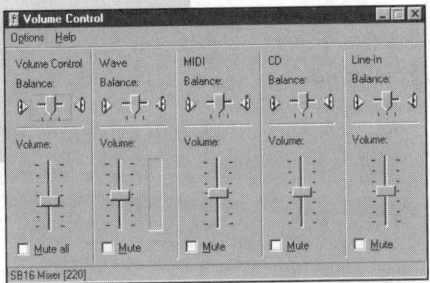

Figure 13.20 Little "handles" let you adjust volume up or down.

12. Adjust the Volume Control of the MIDI selection by clicking on the little image of a handle and dragging it up or down to raise or lower the volume. If you wanted to modify the balance of sound between left and right speakers, you could do that with the Balance control.
13. Click on the Close button to close this panel.
14. Click anywhere outside of the MIDI Sequence panel to remove it from your screen and return to your document.
15. Double-click on the MIDI Sequence icon; the sound clip plays.

Tip

To stop playback of a sound on your page, press [Alt]+[Tab]. The MIDI Sequence panel becomes available and you can use the Stop button to halt playback. You can also stop playback by right-clicking on the MIDI Sequence icon and selecting MIDI Sequence Object, Edit.

PART III • WORD ONLINE

Hands On: Using Sound Recorder

Perhaps you'd like to record your own sounds to add to your Word document. You can do that easily using the Windows Sound Recorder. You must open the Sound Recorder separately, use it to record a sound file, and then copy that file into your Word document. Here's how it works.

1. Minimize the Word window.
2. Choose the Windows Start menu, <u>P</u>rograms, Accessories. From the side menu that appears, choose Multimedia, Sound Recorder. The Sound Recorder panel appears, as shown in Figure 13.21.

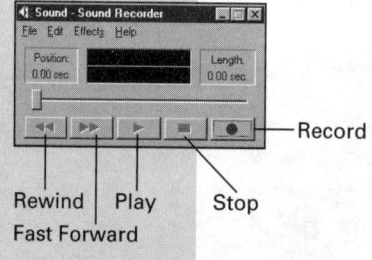

Figure 13.21 When you play back a sound clip, the thin white line in the middle will begin to oscillate to reflect spikes and valleys of the sound.

Note

The Sound Recorder program has similarities to the MIDI Sequence program. The program has Play, Stop, Rewind, and Fast Forward buttons. While you're playing back a sound clip, a marker moves to the right to show you its progress. But one very important additional button here, Record, is what you use to record your own sound files. Also, if you don't have a built-in microphone in your computer, you need to attach one to your computer to make this exercise work.

3. Now it's time to record a sound. Click on the Record button and speak this into the microphone this: "Announcing Bennett Engineering's new consulting program." If you want to use a phrase more appropriate to the photo you inserted, feel free to modify this.
4. Click on the Stop button to stop recording.

CHAPTER 13 • CREATING A MULTIMEDIA ANNOUNCEMENT

339

Note

If you didn't do so well in your recording, don't worry. You can simply click on the Rewind button and start again. If you want to hear how your recording sounds, use the Play button to listen to it. When it's just right, proceed with the next step.

5. Choose Edit, Copy.
6. From the Windows taskbar, maximize the Word window.
7. Choose Edit, Paste. A sound icon like the one in Figure 13.22 appears.

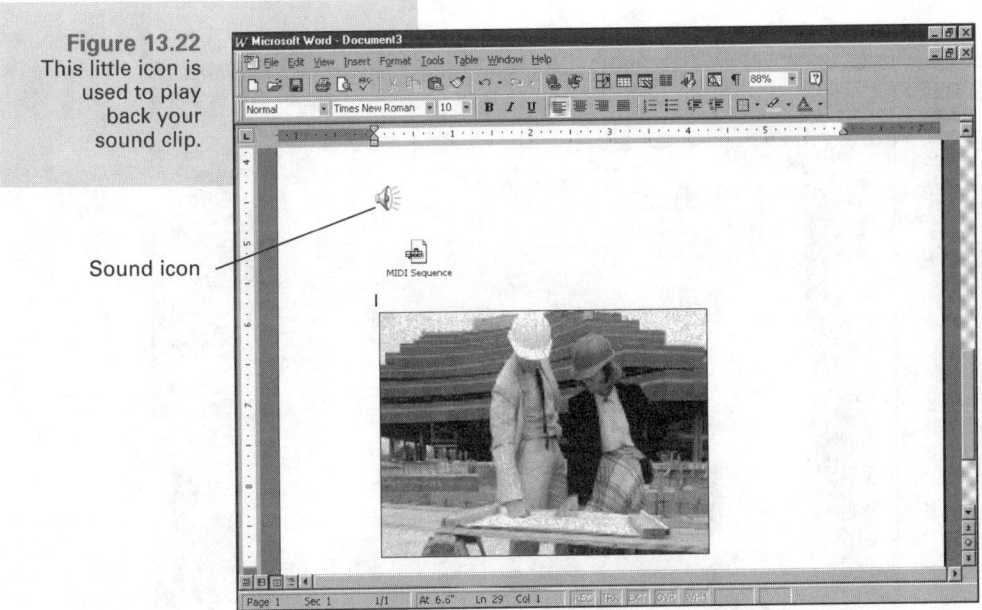

Figure 13.22
This little icon is used to play back your sound clip.

Sound icon

8. Double-click on the icon to hear your recording played back.

You can also open existing sound clips from Sound Recorder, copy them, and paste them into your Word document if you like.

PART III • WORD ONLINE

Animating Text

Now that you have sound and a photo in your announcement, you'll add some text and then animate that text to add motion to the document.

Hands On: Adding Animated Text to the Document

1. Place the insertion point above the Sound Recorder sound clip icon and type **Announcing**.
2. Place your insertion point before the MIDI Sequence icon and type **An elegant solution to your engineering needs.** (See Figure 13.23.)

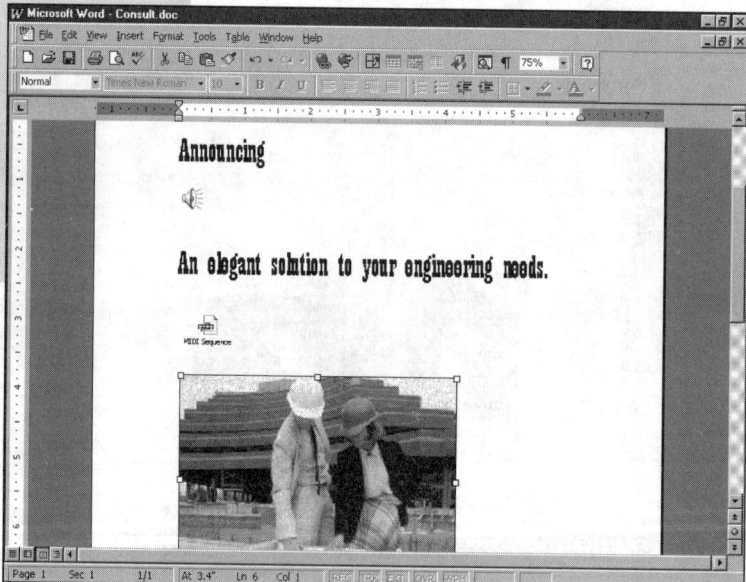

Figure 13.23
If necessary, you can click on the sound clip icons and drag them up or down on the page to achieve this placement of text.

3. Select the text Announcing.
4. Choose F̲ormat, ̲Font.
5. Click on the An̲imation tab of the Font dialog box, shown in Figure 13.24.

Chapter 13 • Creating a Multimedia Announcement

Applying an animation effect to text is simply a matter of selecting one from the Animations list. When you do so, the style will preview in this dialog box. The animations range from marquee style light effects to shimmering (the text seems to shudder on the screen) and a flashing background. Of course, these animation effects will have impact only when your document is viewed on a Web page or as an on-screen document.. They will print, however, as you can see in the preview of the Sparkle Text effect in Figure 13.24; it seems to throw confetti shapes all around the text.

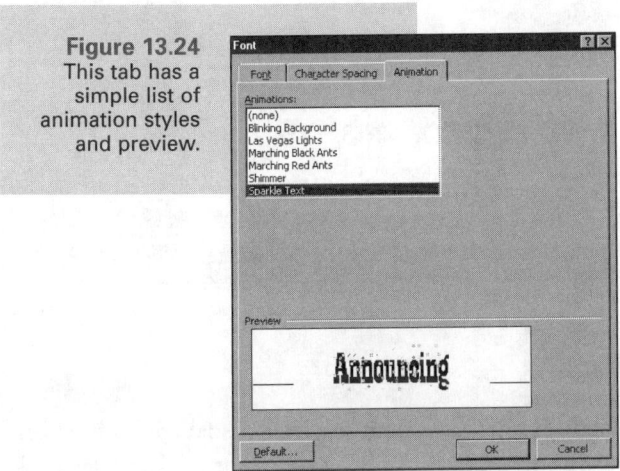

Figure 13.24
This tab has a simple list of animation styles and preview.

Tip

As with any other special effect, animation should be used sparingly and for emphasis. Remember that the animation will repeat continuously, and this can be distracting if someone is trying to read a lot of text on the page. Animate a single word or one short phrase on your page rather than long paragraphs of text.

6. Choose the Sparkle Text effect and click on OK. Your text now appears as shown in Figure 13.25.

PART III • WORD ONLINE

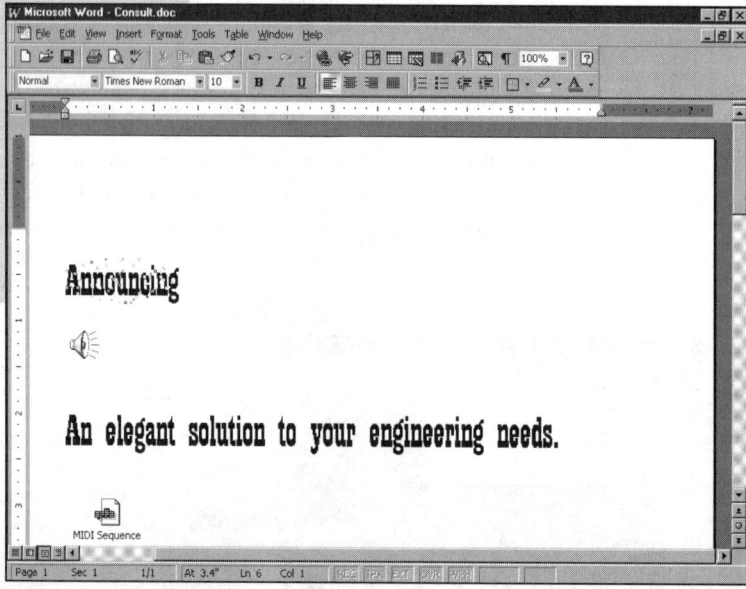

Figure 13.25
The keyword on this page is Announcing, and the animated effect draws the reader's attention to the sound clip announcement right below.

Adding Fill Effects

One final effect that you'll add to this document to give it visual appeal is a background for the entire page. You can simply apply a solid color to your page background, but there's a lot more that you can do with Fill Effects:

- Gradients produce the effect of light coming from a source to give a glow to a one- or two-color background.
- Patterns place lines in your background that form patterns such as pinstripes, thatching, or brick work.
- Textures are predefined backgrounds that resemble materials from granite and burlap to wood and marble.
- Pictures can be inserted as the background of your page. If you preferred, for example, to have the photograph that you inserted form the background of your page rather than fitting in a defined space, you could place it as a Background picture effect.

Hands On: Adding Texture to Your Page

All of the background effects are added using pretty much the same methods that you'll use to add texture to this document.

1. Select F*o*rmat, Bac*k*ground. A side menu appears with a palette of solid color choices and two other choices: *M*ore Colors or *F*ill Effects.
2. Select *F*ill Effects.
3. When the Fill Effects dialog box appears, click on the Texture tab, shown in Figure 13.26.

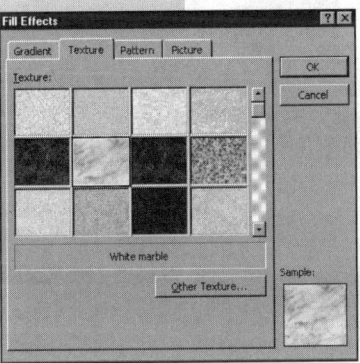

Figure 13.26 You can even import textured backgrounds by selecting Other Texture and using a graphics file for your background.

4. Click on the effect called Granite (the one in the second row down, on the far right). When you select an effect, its name is displayed below the texture palette and a Sample is displayed.
5. Click on OK to apply the background.

Your announcement, complete with sound, photo, animated text, and a textured background now looks like the one in Figure 13.27.

When using backgrounds (and especially textures), be careful that the texture doesn't conflict so much with your text that it becomes hard to read. Although you can print documents with textured backgrounds to nice effect as well as viewing the background on a Web page, for example, some look nicer in print than others. Compare Figure 13.27 with Figure 13.28, for example. This background (Canvas) and a different font (Baskerville) not only make it easier to read the text, but this combination gives a different feel to the whole announcement.

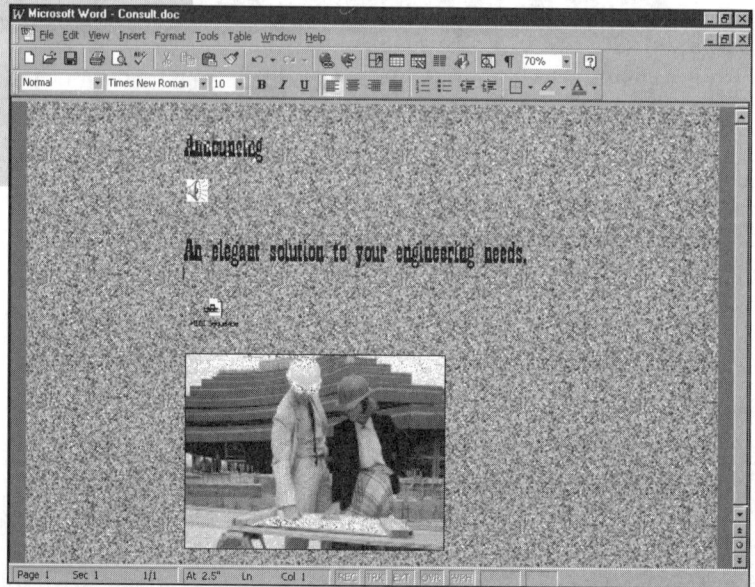

Figure 13.27
The strong texture of granite adds an elegance to your document.

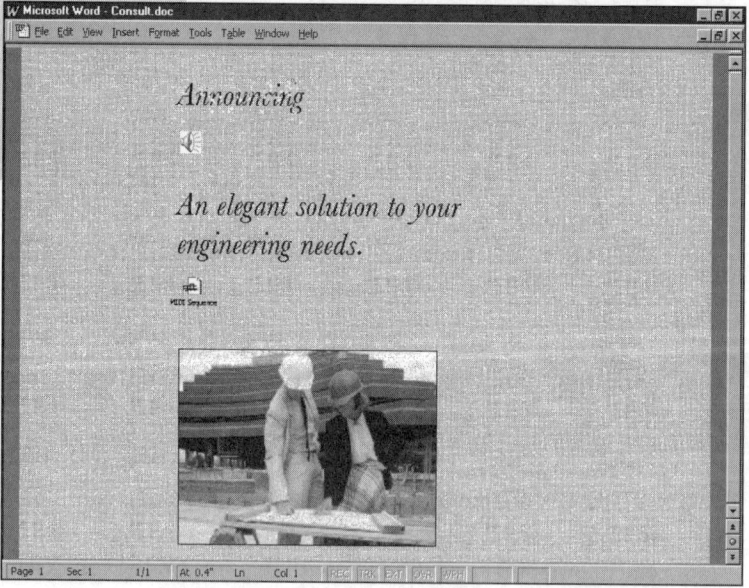

Figure 13.28
Play around with backgrounds and fonts to get ones that are complementary.

PART IV
Making Word Work Your Way

14	CREATING A COLLECTION LETTER WITH STYLES AND TEMPLATES	349
15	AUTOMATING WORK WITH FIELDS AND MACROS	375
16	CHANGING YOUR WORD ENVIRONMENT	399

micros
WORD

14

Creating a Collection Letter with Styles and Templates

IN THIS CHAPTER

- **Template and Style Basics**
- **Ways to Apply Styles**
- **Working with Templates**
- **Modifying Templates**

Styles, templates, and wizards save you time by automating repetitive tasks. Styles and templates are features available to you in Word that you can use to define settings for documents, paragraphs, and words that you can reuse.

Templates store document settings, and styles store settings for paragraphs and words. You use at least one style and one template every time you start Word. Document1, which appears when you start Word, is based on the Normal template, which is designed for general use. Word always assigns the Normal style, a basic style, to the first paragraph. We talk more about the Normal template and the Normal style throughout this chapter.

> FOR MORE EXAMPLES ON USING WIZARDS, SEE CHAPTER 7, CHAPTER 11, AND CHAPTER 12.

For example, in this chapter, you'll create a template for a standard collection letter that you might send. Some information in a collection letter doesn't change; think of it as "boilerplate." Other information, however, such as the amount the recipient owes, does change. In this chapter, you'll create a typical collection letter that includes styles, and you'll save that letter as a template so that you can use it over and over again. Your collection letter will include prompts for the information that changes so that you can complete a collection letter quickly and easily.

Although you've seen wizards used in other places in this book, you'll also learn more about them in this chapter.

Template and Style Basics

Before you get into working with both templates and styles, you need a basic understanding of each, particularly because they work together.

Understanding Templates

Use *templates* to save layouts for documents that you create on a regular basis. When you create documents in Word, they are always based on a template. Think of a template as a foundation document. Whenever you create a document, you choose a template on which to base the document; the document then has access to all the settings contained in the template. A template contains settings that apply to the whole document, such as margins and vertical page layout. It also contains macros, autotext, toolbars, and *styles*, which save the settings for paragraph and character formatting that you use on a regular basis.

Word comes with several predefined templates and each contains predefined styles; you can modify both the templates and the styles, and you can create your own templates and styles. One particular template and one particular style deserve special mention. These are the Normal template and the Normal style.

Every time you start Word, you open a document based on the Normal template. The Normal template is intended for general use and contains some basic settings. Pages are a standard 8 1/2 by 11 inches in size, with a portrait orientation and 1-inch margins at the top and bottom of the page. Left and right margins are 1 1/4 inches each. The Normal template is a *global* template; that is, any settings available in it are also available to all documents, not just documents based on the Normal template. You can therefore access settings stored in the Normal template and use them in any document you create, even if your document is *not* based on the Normal template, but is using a different one.

The Normal style is a paragraph style, intended for general use in a document. In the Normal template, the Normal style's settings are the following:

- A font and a font size that depends on your printer (the most common font is 10-point Times New Roman)
- Left-alignment
- Single-spacing

You can change any and all of these settings, and you'll learn how later in this chapter. You will find the Normal style in every template, but don't be fooled: the Normal style can have different characteristics in different templates. Suppose that you have two different templates, and each contains the Normal style. In the first template, the Normal style might use a Times Roman font, whereas in the second template, the Normal style might use an Arial font.

Understanding Styles

Use *styles* to save the formatting settings that you use on a regular basis. Word lets you define two different types of styles: paragraph and character. Character formats include settings that affect single words, such as bold, italics, or underlining. You'll find the available character formats in the Font dialog box.

Paragraph formats include settings that affect an entire paragraph, such as line spacing and indentation, as well as character formats. Yes, you can apply character formats to an entire paragraph. So, then the obvious question becomes, "How do I know whether I'm applying a character format or a paragraph format?"

Take the simplest case to answer the question: place the insertion point in any word in a paragraph of a document—do not select any text—and apply a format. Under these conditions, Word applies formats based on the location of the insertion point. You have applied a character format if only the word containing the insertion point is affected. If, however, the entire paragraph is affected, you have applied a paragraph format.

Paragraph formats are most useful when you want to reuse settings that you establish for a certain type of paragraph. Suppose, for example, that you want all numbered paragraphs to be indented one-half inch from the margin, and you also want the distance between the number and its text to be one-half inch. You can save these settings in a style so that you can simply apply the style whenever you create a numbered paragraph; you won't need to format each numbered paragraph.

Character formats are most useful when you regularly switch between different kinds of character formatting. The most common character formats—bold, italics, and single underline—have predefined shortcut keys and also appear on the Formatting toolbar. Suppose that your work requires you to regularly switch between two fonts within the same paragraph, however. You could create a character style for the font that you use less often. The font that you use more often would be the default font for the paragraph style.

Hands On: Displaying the Style Area

The style in effect at the insertion point appears in the Style box on the Formatting toolbar; for example, you may have noticed the Normal style, which is the default style that Word assigns. If you use styles a great deal, as we do, you may want to display the Style area, which will appear at the left side of the screen when you work in Normal view. Note that you won't see the Style area in any view *except* the Normal view.

1. Switch to Normal view (use either the buttons on the status bar or choose View, Normal).
2. Choose Tools, Options. Word displays the View tab of the Options dialog box.

   (Optional) Place a check in the All check box in the Nonprinting characters section to view, on-screen, characters such as tabs and spaces.
3. Set the Style Area Width at the lower-left corner of the dialog box to be approximately one-half inch (see Figure 14.1).
4. Click on OK. Word redisplays the current document with the Style Area visible (see Figure 14.2).

Tip

When the Style Area is visible, you can use it to select an entire paragraph. Move the mouse pointer into the Style Area next to the paragraph that you want to select. When the pointer changes to an arrow pointing up and to the right, click. Word selects the entire paragraph.

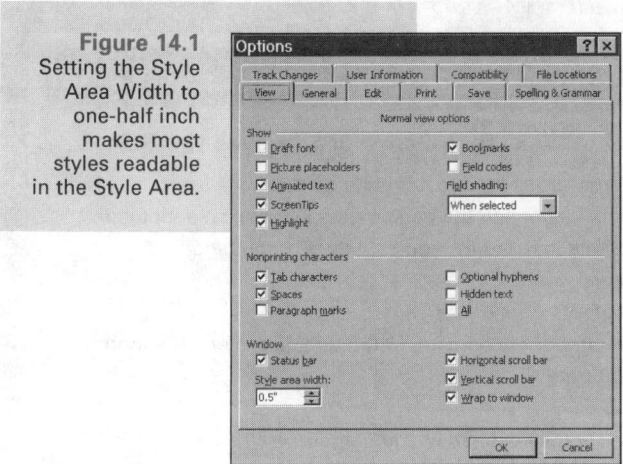

Figure 14.1
Setting the Style Area Width to one-half inch makes most styles readable in the Style Area.

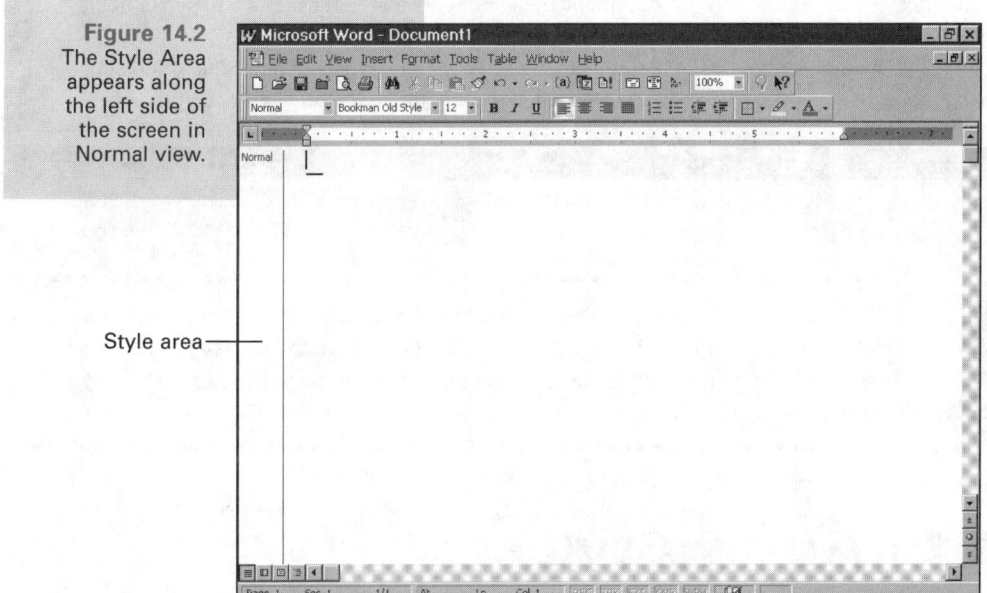

Figure 14.2
The Style Area appears along the left side of the screen in Normal view.

Style area

Using Built-In Styles

In addition to the Normal style, Word comes with some other styles referred to as the *built-in styles*. In earlier versions of Word, these styles were also called *standard styles*. Word uses these styles automatically under certain circumstances. For example, when you create an envelope, Word automatically uses the Envelope Address style for the delivery address and the Envelope Return style for the return address. See Table 14.1 for a list of the most common built-in styles.

Table 14.1. Built-In Styles

Built-In Style	Type of Text to which Word Applies the Style
Annotation Text	Comments inserted to annotate a document
Annotation Reference	Initials identifying the person who inserted an annotation
Caption	Captions inserted for figures, tables, or equations
Footer	Footers
Footnote or Endnote Text	A footnote or endnote
Footnote or Endnote Reference	The number or character in the text that refers to a footnote or endnote
Header	Headers
Index 1–Index 9	Index entries defined in a document
Line Number	Automatic line numbers added using the Page Setup command
Page Number	Automatic page numbers inserted using the Page Numbers command
TOC 1–TOC 9, Table of Authorities, Table of Figures	Entries in tables of contents, tables of authorities, and similar tables created using the Index And Tables command

Word also contains some built-in HTML styles that apply formatting supported by HTML on Web pages. These styles work a little differently, however; changes you make to them will not be saved and will be converted only if the formatting is HTML-supported.

Ways to Apply Styles

In Word, you can apply styles using one of three methods:

- You can let Word automatically format your document. This feature is turned on by default when you install Word. For example, if you type a number followed by a period, hyphen, close parenthesis or greater than sign (>), a space or tab, and text, Word will convert the text to a numbered list.

CHAPTER 14 • CREATING A COLLECTION LETTER 355

- You can switch templates and reformat your document using the Style Gallery, where you can preview the results of changing to another template.
- You can create styles and manually apply them.

In both the first and second cases, you can reformat a document relatively quickly and painlessly. The disadvantage, however, is that you have little control over the selection of styles.

Using Styles with Form Letters

To practice applying styles using these methods, we need a document. In this exercise, we create the collection letter that you see in Figure 14.3. The text for the letter appears on the next page so that you can easily copy it. Please type it exactly as you see it, including dollar signs ($) that appear in front of words. Later, we're going to save this document as a template, but if you fear losing the data and don't want to risk having to reenter it, you can save the document just as you usually would.

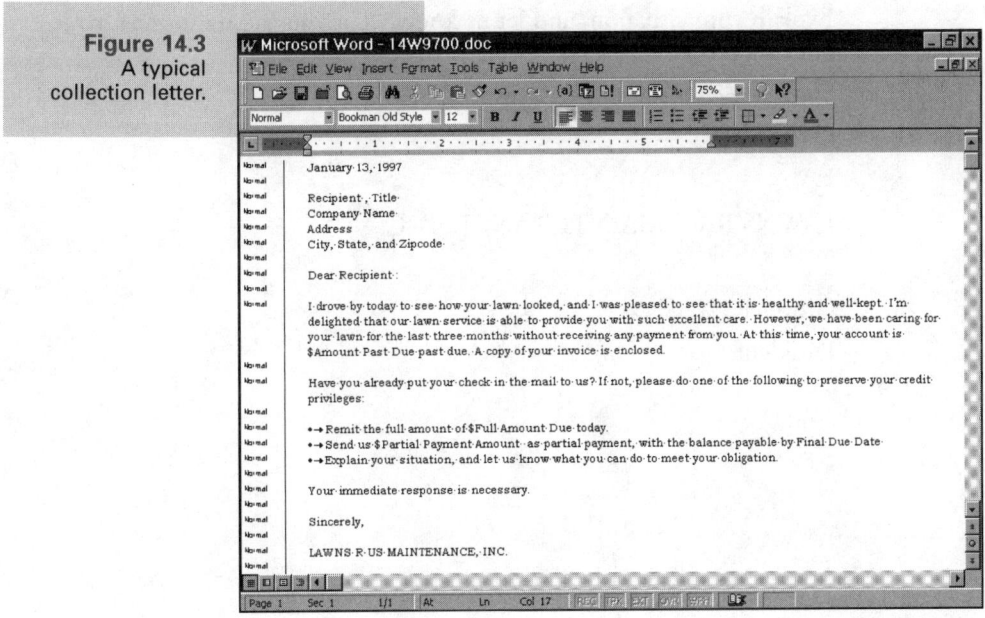

Figure 14.3
A typical collection letter.

February 1, 1997

Recipient , Title

Company Name

Address

City, State, and Zipcode

Dear **Recipient**:

I drove by today to see how your lawn looked, and I was pleased to see that it is healthy and well kept. I'm delighted that our lawn service is able to provide you with such excellent care. However, we have been caring for your lawn for the last three months without receiving any payment from you. At this time, your account is $**Amount Past Due**. A copy of your invoice is enclosed.

Have you already put your check in the mail to us? If not, please do one of the following to preserve your credit privileges:

Remit the full amount of $**Full Amount Due** today.

Send us $**Partial Payment Amount** as partial payment, with the balance payable by **Final Due Date**

Explain your situation, and let us know what you can do to meet your obligation.

Your immediate response is necessary.

Sincerely,

LAWNS R US MAINTENANCE, INC.

Grover R. Weedless
President

Chapter 14 • Creating a Collection Letter   357

Our form letter contains two types of fields, and all the fields in the form letter appear in boldface type in the sidebar. The first is a date field and the second is a macro button field. We use a date field to ensure that, each time we use the form letter, it displays "today's date". Each of the other bold entries in the sidebar is actually a macro button field. Macro buttons can actually run macros, but they also have a special property: you can jump from one macro button field to the next by pressing F11. When you fill in a form letter later, these macro buttons entries will help you to quickly jump from place to place in the document to supply the information that changes from letter to letter. The following steps result in inserting a date field.

Hands On: Inserting a Date Field in a Form Letter

Place the insertion point in the document at the location where you want the field to appear (in our case, at the top of the document).

1. Choose Insert, Field. Word displays the Field dialog box.
2. Choose Date and Time in the Categories list, and then choose Date in the Field Names list (see Figure 14.4).

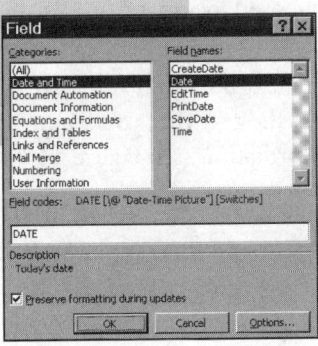

Figure 14.4
Selecting the Today's date field.

3. Click on the Options button to select a format for the date (see Figure 14.5).
4. Click on Add to Field to add the format.
5. Click on OK to redisplay the Field dialog box.
6. Click on OK to insert the field.

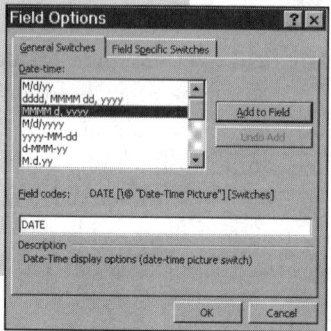

Figure 14.5
MMMM d, yyy inserts a date formatted to display the full month, a single-digit day if appropriate, and four characters for the year.

Hands On: Inserting Macro Button Fields

Macro buttons in Word can actually run a macro, but in our case, we're simply using them as placeholders that let you quickly fill in the changing information in the form letter. To insert any of the macro buttons into the form letter, follow these steps:

1. Place the insertion point in the letter where you want a "Click here" field to appear.
2. Choose Insert, Field. Word displays the Field dialog box.
3. From the Categories list, choose Document Automation. From the Field Names list, choose MacroButton.
4. Click at the right end of the text box toward the bottom of the dialog and type **NoMacro**, a space, and the text that you want to appear in the form letter to prompt you for information (see Figure 14.6).

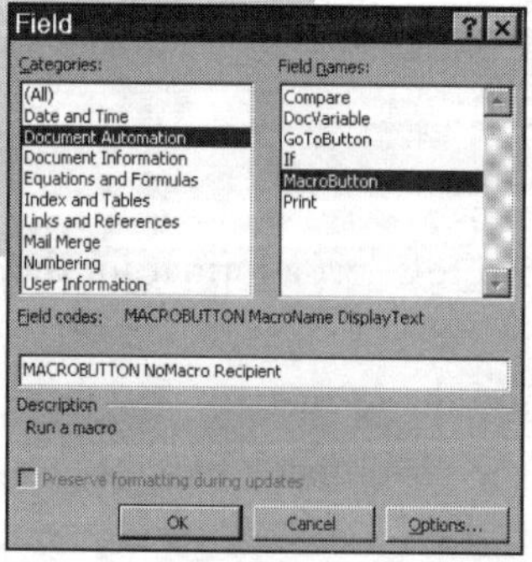

Figure 14.6
Add text for a prompt to the Macro Button field.

Chapter 14 • Creating a Collection Letter

5. Click on OK. Word inserts a macro button field in your document with the text that you provided as a prompt.
6. Repeat Steps 1–5 for each field that you need to insert in the form letter.

Automatically Formatting Documents

If you like Word's automatic formatting features, you need go no further. Just type and let Word automatically format your document. You may not want Word to automatically format your document while you type, however; you may prefer to let Word review your entire document and suggest formatting changes that you can accept or reject. You can turn off some or all of the automatic formatting that Word performs. To do so, choose Tools, AutoCorrect (see Figures 14.7 and 14.8).

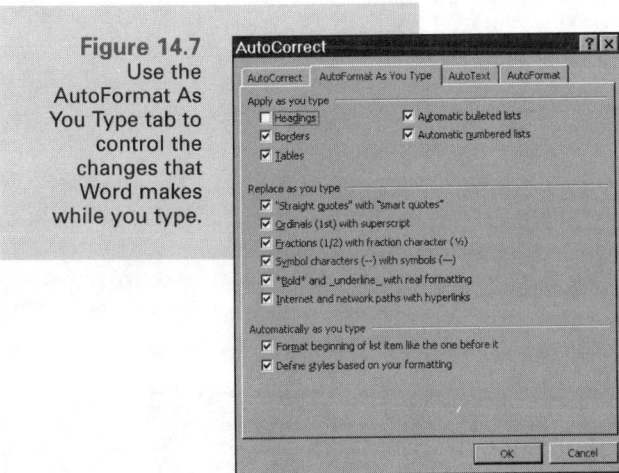

Figure 14.7
Use the AutoFormat As You Type tab to control the changes that Word makes while you type.

To let Word suggest formatting changes, choose Format, AutoFormat. In the AutoFormat dialog box (see Figure 14.9), choose to review changes and select a document type that Word should use while formatting.

Tip

••
If you choose AutoFormat now, Word makes changes but does not let you review and accept or reject them.
••

After automatically formatting, you'll see the changes to your document and a dialog box in which you can review each change and accept or reject it, or accept or reject all changes (see Figure 14.10). Because of the information we cover in the rest of this chapter, reject all changes.

Figure 14.8
Use the AutoFormat tab to control the changes that Word makes when it automatically formats your document.

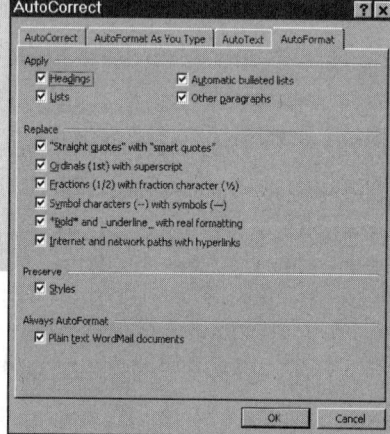

Figure 14.9
Use this dialog box to automatically format a document in one step.

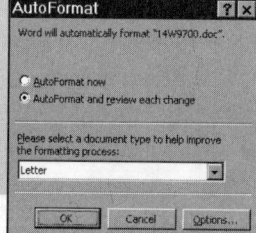

Figure 14.10
Word lets you review formatting changes and accept or reject them.

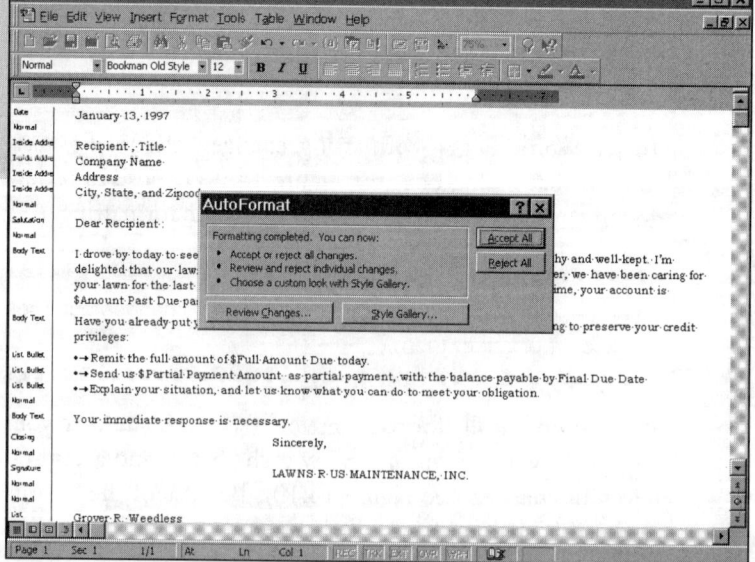

Using the Style Gallery

You can also preview what your document would look like if you switched to another template and used its styles. Choose Format, Style Gallery to display the Style Gallery dialog box. In Figures 14.11 and 14.12, you can see the collection letter formatted using two different templates. Because we're just looking at examples, don't choose either of these templates; when you finish viewing, click on the Cancel button to close the dialog box.

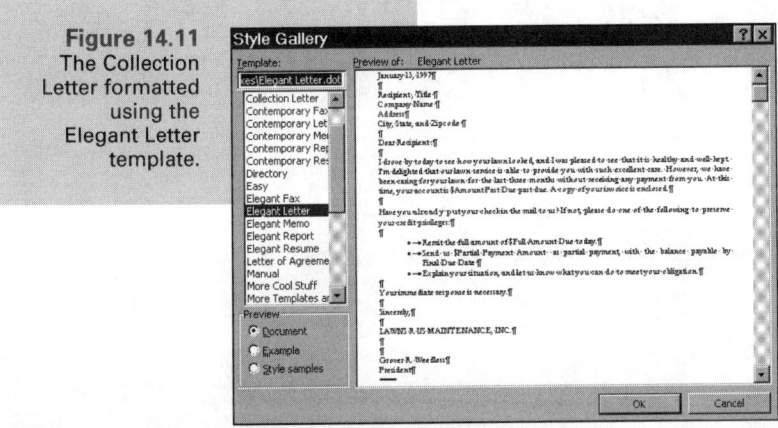

Figure 14.11
The Collection Letter formatted using the Elegant Letter template.

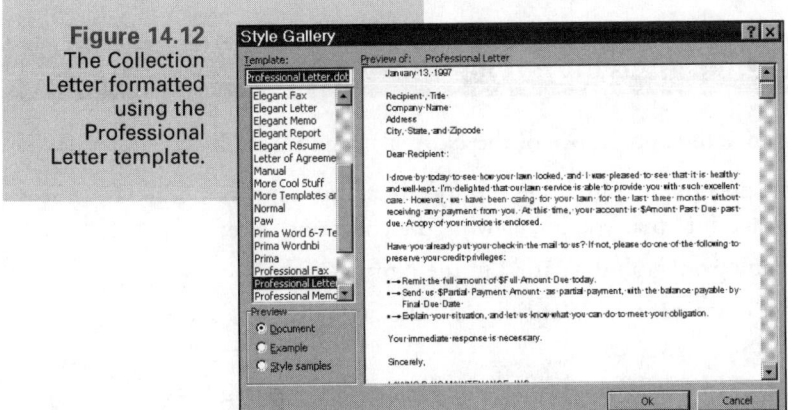

Figure 14.12
The Collection Letter formatted using the Professional Letter template.

Place the insertion point in the paragraph whose style you want to change, or select the paragraphs whose styles you want to change. In the example, select the paragraphs where the recipient's address will appear.

Open the Style list on the Formatting toolbar and choose the style that you want to apply (see Figure 14.13). On your screen, you may not see all the styles that appear in the figure.

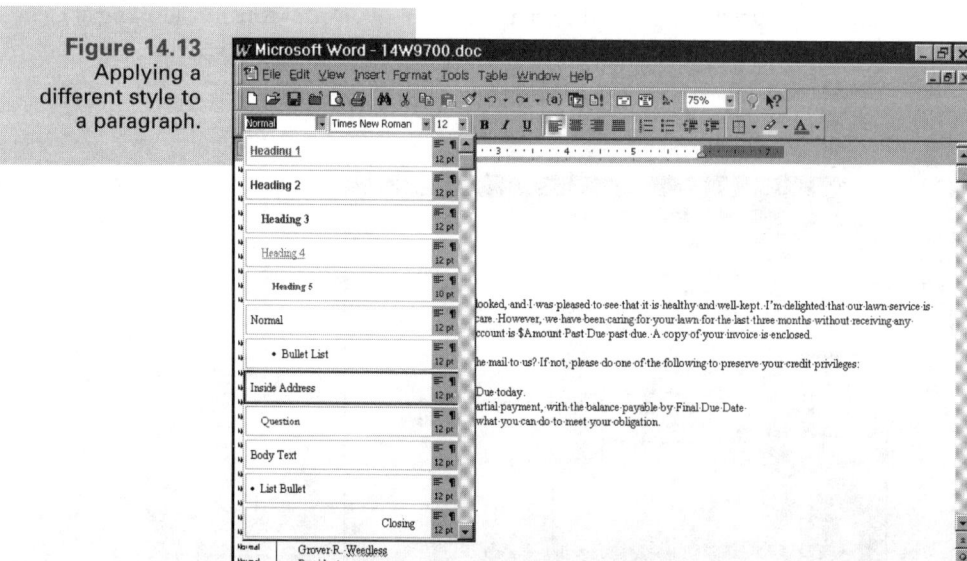

Figure 14.13 Applying a different style to a paragraph.

Hands On: Modifying Styles

Here we change the appearance of the Normal style in our Collection letter.

1. Open a document containing the style that you want to modify. In this case, make sure that you are viewing the collection letter.
2. Select any paragraph formatted in the Normal style.
3. Choose Format, Style. Word displays the Style dialog box (see Figure 14.14).
4. Click on Modify. Word displays the Modify Style dialog box.
5. Click on the Format button to display a pop-up list of items that you can modify for the style (see Figure 14.15).
6. Choose Font. Word displays the Font dialog box. Choose the font that you want; for our example, choose Times New Roman 12 point.
7. Click on OK. Word redisplays the Modify Style dialog box.

CHAPTER 14 • CREATING A COLLECTION LETTER   **363**

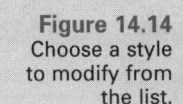

Figure 14.14
Choose a style to modify from the list.

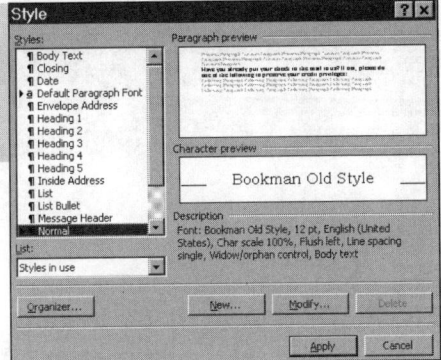

Figure 14.15
Choose the feature that you want to modify.

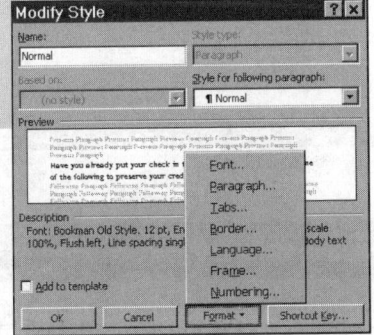

8. (Optional) Select the <u>A</u>dd to Template check box if you want all new documents based on the current template to use the settings that you just selected.

9. (Optional) Select the A<u>u</u>tomatically update check box if you want Word to redefine this style whenever you add manual formatting to it. For example, if you check this box and then select text in the document and change the font using the Formatting toolbar, Word would change the selected text and all other text formatted in the style of the selected text.

10. Click on OK. Word redisplays the Style dialog box.

11. Choose <u>A</u>pply. Word modifies all text in your document formatted in the style that you just modified; in our example, all text in the Normal style now appears in Times New Roman 12 point (see Figure 14.16).

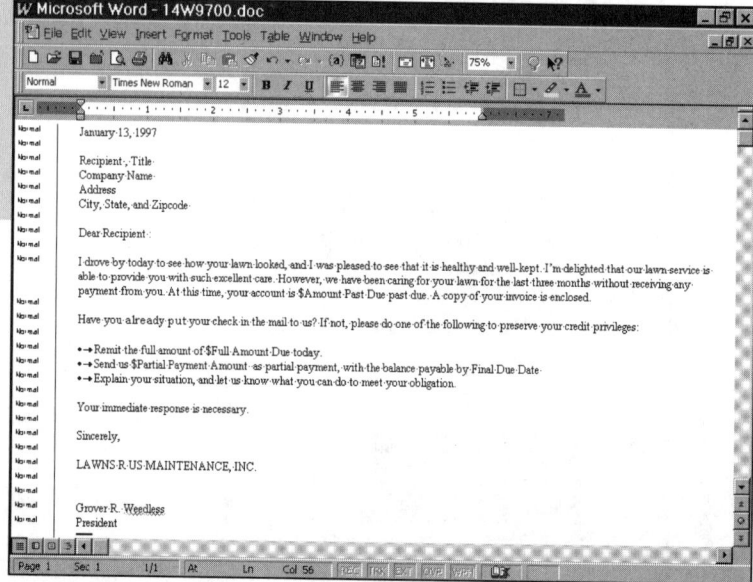

Figure 14.16
The collection letter after changing the font of the Normal style to Times New Roman 12 point.

Hands On: Creating a Style By Example

The easiest way to create a new style is to format a paragraph until it looks the way you want, and then to store those settings in a style. Follow these steps to create a Bullet List style for the collection letter that indents bullets one-half inch from the left margin:

1. Select text in your document that most closely matches the style that you want to create. In our example, select the three bulleted items near the bottom of the letter.
2. Make the formatting change that you want to make; in our example, click on the Increase Indent button on the Formatting toolbar twice.
3. Click in the Style text box on the Formatting toolbar so that the name of the current style—Normal, in our case—appears selected (see Figure 14.17).
4. Type the name of the new style—in our example, call it Bullet List—and press [Enter]. Word changes the name of the style in the Style Area to the new style's name (see Figure 14.18).

Chapter 14 • Creating a Collection Letter

365

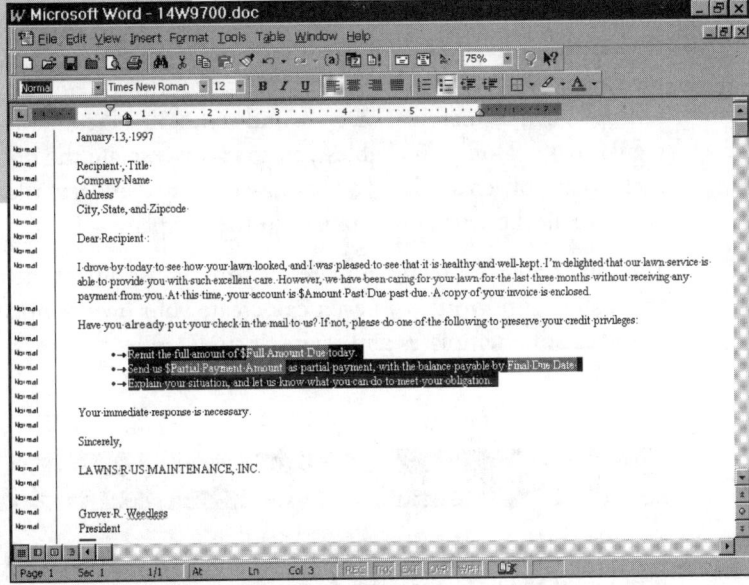

Figure 14.17 After applying the formatting that you want, select the name of the current style.

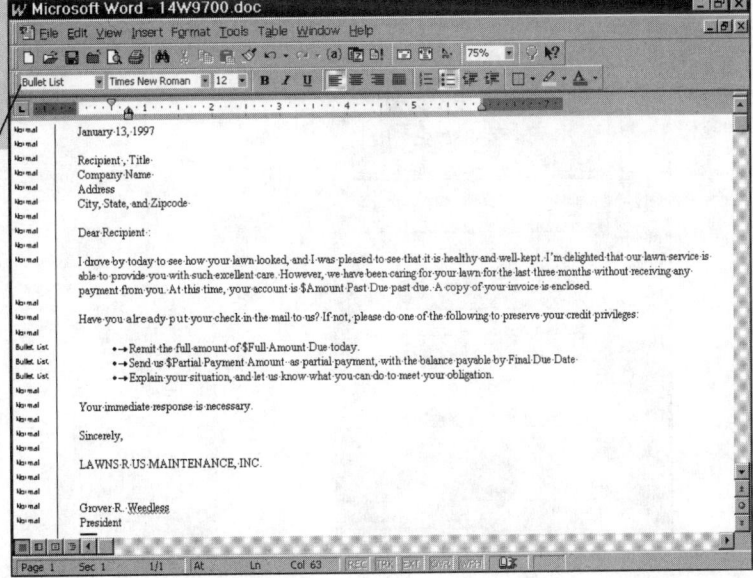

Figure 14.18 Word creates a new style with the formatting that you applied.

Bullet List style

Working with Templates

As you learned earlier, *templates* store document settings, and styles store settings for paragraphs and words. You can create your own templates to save layouts and settings, such as margins, macros, and styles, for documents that you create on a regular basis. Doing so enables you to easily recreate the document. Every document that you create in Word is based on a template; the document then has access to all the settings contained in the template.

You can create your own templates or you can use any of the predefined templates that come with Word. You even can create your own template by modifying one of the existing templates and saving it under a new name.

Hands On: Setting Up to Be Able to Preview

You can tell Word to allow you to preview a template before you actually choose it to use as the basis for your document.

1. Choose File, Properties. Word displays the Properties dialog box for the current document (see Figure 14.19).

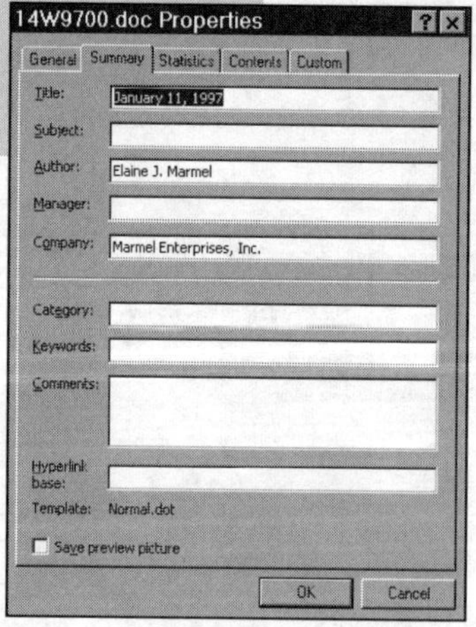

Figure 14.19 The Properties dialog box.

2. Select the Save Preview Picture check box at the bottom of the Summary tab.
3. Click on OK.

CHAPTER 14 • CREATING A COLLECTION LETTER 367

Hands On: Creating Templates

Creating a template is an easy matter: you simply save a document as a template. Here we save the collection letter as a template.

Remember, any text that you type and save as a template will appear each time you open a new document based on the template.

1. Choose File, Save As. Word displays the Save As dialog box.
2. Open the Save As Type list box and choose Document Template (see Figure 14.20). Word should automatically switch to the folder in which templates are typically stored.

Figure 14.20
Use the Save As dialog box to create a template.

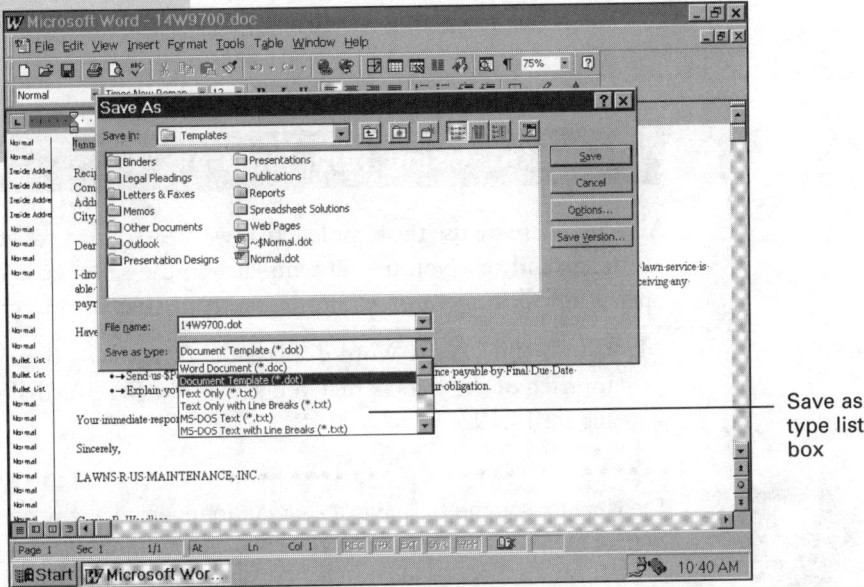

The folders that you see inside the Templates folder may be different from the ones that you see in the picture, because you can organize your templates into any set of folders you want.

PART IV • MAKING WORD WORK YOUR WAY

Tip

If you don't see the Templates folder in the Save In list, open the Save In list and navigate to the folder where Word stores your templates. If you installed your software into default folders and you're using Microsoft Office, you'll find a Templates folder inside the Microsoft Office folder. If you're using Word, you'll find a Templates folder inside the Winword folder.

3. You'll see several folders that help organize your templates into categories. Double-click on the Letters & Faxes folder to open it.

4. If you previously saved the open document, Word suggests the existing name for the document, but changes the extension to .dot. Change the name to anything you want to name the template. We call the one in our example "Collection Letter." You don't need to add the .dot; Word will automatically add it for you.

5. Click on Save. Word saves your template; on-screen, your document name in the title bar shows the name that you provided for the template.

6. Close the template by choosing File, Close.

Hands On: Using Templates

Although here we use the template that we created for a collection letter, you need to understand that you use all templates in the same way. Follow these steps to open a new document based on the template that you select.

1. Choose File, New. Word displays the New dialog box, which contains tabs for each of the folders that you saw in the Save As dialog box in the Figure 14.19.

Tip

The New tool on the toolbar is a shortcut for opening a new document based on the Normal template. Choosing File, New and choosing the Blank Document that appears on the General tab of the New dialog box is the same as clicking on the New tool.

2. Click on the tab containing the template that you want to use; in our example, click on the Letters & Faxes tab.

3. Highlight the template on which you want to base a document; in our example, highlight the Collection Letter template (see Figure 14.21).

Chapter 14 • Creating a Collection Letter

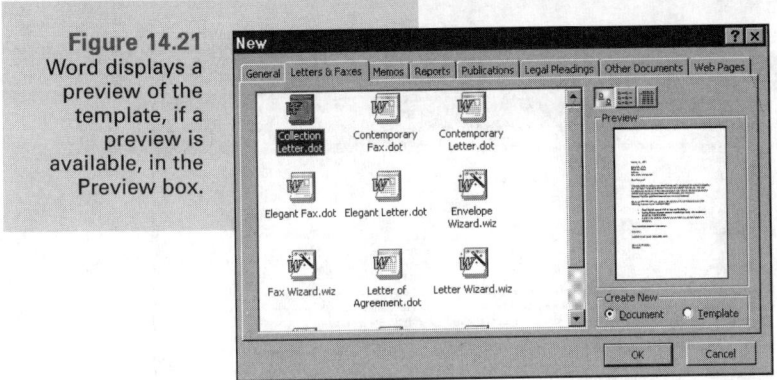

Figure 14.21
Word displays a preview of the template, if a preview is available, in the Preview box.

4. Click on OK. Word displays a new document on-screen, based on the template you selected. If that template contained text, as our example did, you'll see the text on-screen (see Figure 14.22).

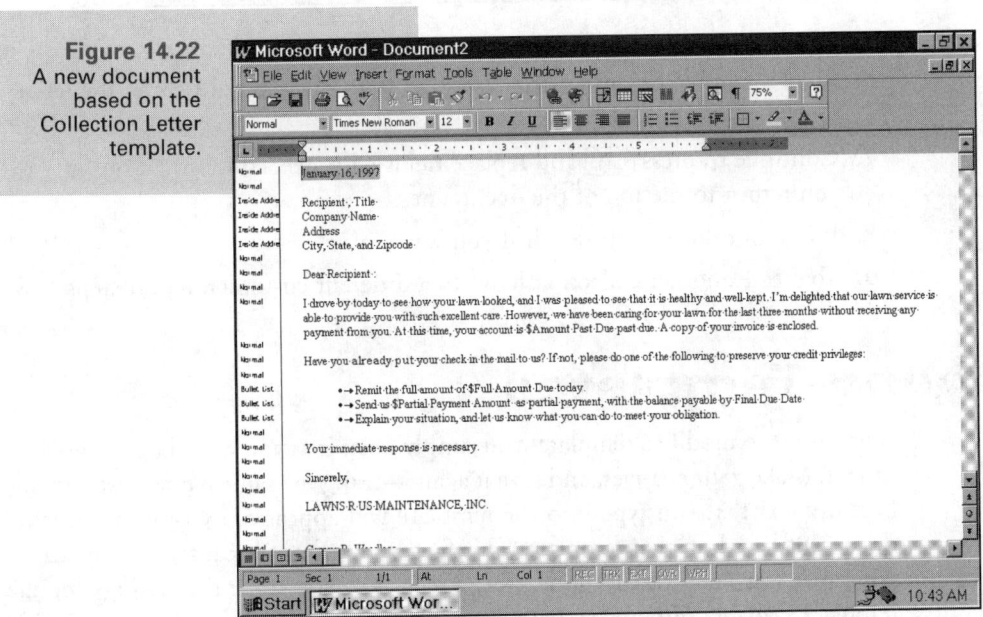

Figure 14.22
A new document based on the Collection Letter template.

5. To fill in the information needed for the Collection Letter, press F11. Word jumps to the first field and selects it. In this case, you don't want to modify the first field—the date—so press F11 again. Word jumps to the next field and selects it (see Figure 14.23).

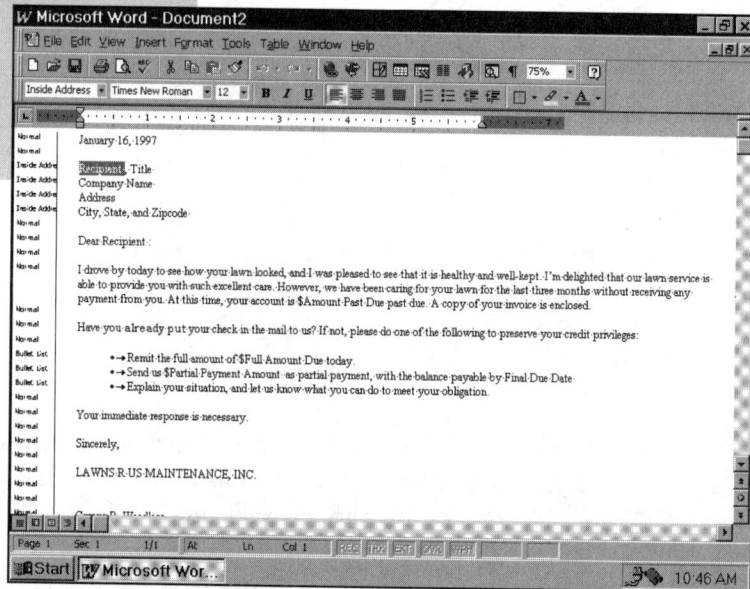

Figure 14.23
When you press F11, Word jumps to and selects the next field in the document.

6. Type the information needed. Word replaces the selected field in the letter with the text that you type.

7. Continue to press F11 and replace fields with needed information until you return to the top of the document.

8. Print your document; save it if you want.

9. To create another collection letter to a different customer, repeat steps 1–8.

Modifying Templates

If you want to modify a template, you simply open it as you would open any document. Make your changes, and save it again—using the same name. Just remember: any text that you type into the template will appear every time you open a document based on that template. This fact is important because, in some cases, you don't want any text to appear on-screen, but you want the settings for the template available. When you want to display a blank document that uses specific settings, be careful not to save any text on-screen when you resave the template.

To open the template, use the File, Open command to display the Open dialog box. Using the Look In list box, navigate to the folder inside Templates folder

Chapter 14 • Creating a Collection Letter

containing the template that you want to open. Change Files of Type list box at the bottom of the Open dialog box so that Document Templates (*.dot) appears. Highlight the template that you want to modify and choose Open.

Hands On: Sharing Styles Between Templates

Suppose that you created a style and stored it in a specific template. Later, you discovered that you'd like that style to be available in another template—and therefore have documents based on that template. You do not need to recreate the style. Instead, you can use Word's Organizer to copy the style (and macros, autotext and toolbars) between templates.

1. Choose Tools, Templates and Add-Ins. Word displays the Templates and Add-ins dialog box.

2. Click on the Organizer button. Word displays the Organizer dialog box (see Figure 14.24). The left side of the box displays elements available in the current document; the right side of the box displays elements available in the Normal template.

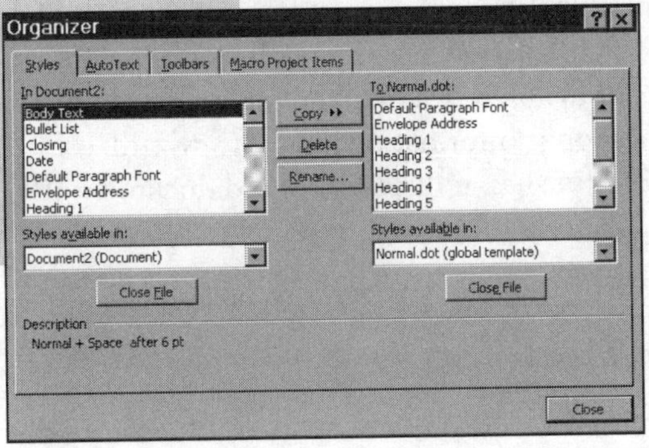

Figure 14.24 Using the Organizer dialog box, you can share elements between templates.

3. Click on the tab containing the element that you want to copy; in our example, display the Styles tab.

4. (Optional) If you want to copy an element to or from a template that doesn't appear in the Organizer dialog box, use the Close File buttons that appear below the list boxes on each side of the dialog box to close the current document and/or the Normal template. When you click on one of

these Close File buttons, the elements disappear from the list, and the Close File button becomes an Open File button. Click on Open File, and Word displays the contents of the Templates folder. Navigate until you find the template you want use, and open it.

It doesn't matter which side of the box displays the template or document from which you want to copy; the buttons in the middle will change direction as needed, as you'll see in a moment.

5. In either list, highlight the element that you want to copy; in our example, highlight the Bullet List style.
6. Click on the Copy button. The element appears in the other list.
7. Click on the Close button at the bottom of the Organizer dialog box to close it.

About Wizards...

Wizards walk you through completing common tasks. In Chapter 7, we used the Newsletter wizard to set up a newsletter. Word's wizards are stored with templates; to use a wizard, you choose the File, New command, click on the tab in the New dialog box containing the wizard that you want to use, highlight the wizard, and click on OK. What happens next depends on the wizard you selected. Typically, you see a series of dialog boxes that ask you questions about the task you want to complete; you supply information that the wizard uses to complete the task. When the wizard finishes, it displays a Word document that uses the information you supplied.

Word ships with the following wizards to help you:

- Envelope Wizard
- Fax Wizard
- Letter Wizard
- Mailing Label Wizard
- Memo Wizard
- Newsletter Wizard
- Legal Pleading Wizard
- Resume Wizard
- Web Page Wizard

Chapter 14 • Creating a Collection Letter

In addition to these wizards, you can find additional wizards and templates in two other locations:

- On the Microsoft Office 97 CD, look in the ValuPack folder for a folder called Template. Open that folder and choose Word.
- If you have access to the World Wide Web, you'll find additional wizards and templates on the Microsoft Office Web Site. To easily find these additional wizards and templates, open Word's Help menu and choose Microsoft on the Web. Then, click on Free Stuff.

> **For more information on accessing Microsoft's Web site, see Chapter 11.**

micros
WORD

15

Automating Work with Fields and Macros

In This Chapter

- Field Code Basics
- Manipulating Field Codes
- Macro Basics

As you work in Word, you'll find a variety of tasks that you do on a regular basis. Some of these are simple, such as opening and saving documents. But some can be more complex. Suppose, for example, that you often create reports that include many figures, and your figures are numbered, like the ones in this book. Further, before a figure appears in your report, you refer to the figure some place in the text. Keeping track of the correct "next figure number" to type can waste a lot of your time. Now double that time loss when you consider that you need to keep track of both the next figure number and the next text reference to the figure. You can automate tasks like this one by using fields and macros, and then Word will track and insert the figure numbers and references to figure numbers for you.

Field codes are hidden codes that you insert by using commands from the Insert menu or by typing. You typically see, on-screen and in print, the results of fields, such as dates, page numbers, or figure numbers. You can, however, see and print the actual code for a field. Word contains more than 60 types of field codes that you can use, for example, to track numbers, as our example showed, or build a table of contents, or insert a date in a document. The beauty of field codes is that they change as necessary. For example, a date field code inserts "today's date". If you open the document tomorrow and update the field, the date will change to be tomorrow's date.

Think of *macros* as mini-programs that you create to automate a multistep process in Word. The beauty of a macro is that you quickly complete all the steps in your multistep process with only one keystroke or click. The easiest way to create a macro is to let Word record the keystrokes of the process as you perform it. Prior to Word 97, Word wrote macros in WordBasic, its own macro programming language; starting with Word 97, Word uses the Visual Basic for Applications programming language to write macros. You can edit macros you create if you learn Visual Basic.

Note
Word 97 automatically converts macros written in WordBasic to Visual Basic so that you can use macros written in previous versions of Word.

The basic premise in this chapter is that you're creating a report that includes a standard header, symbols, figure numbers and references to those figure numbers. You'll first learn about field codes and how to use them, including Word's caption feature, which uses sequence number fields to track figure numbers. Then, you'll learn how to create three different macros, and set up each so that you run it in a different way. One macro inserts a header. The second macro inserts a symbol that you use frequently. The third macro inserts a separate sequence number field code that you can use to track figure number references.

CHAPTER 15 • AUTOMATING WORK WITH FIELDS AND MACROS 377

Field Code Basics

A field is a code, but most of the time you see the results of the field, which look like regular text. In Figure 15.1, you see the main merge document that we created in Chapter 8; it contains field codes, but you see field results. In Figure 15.2, you see the same document displaying field codes, not results.

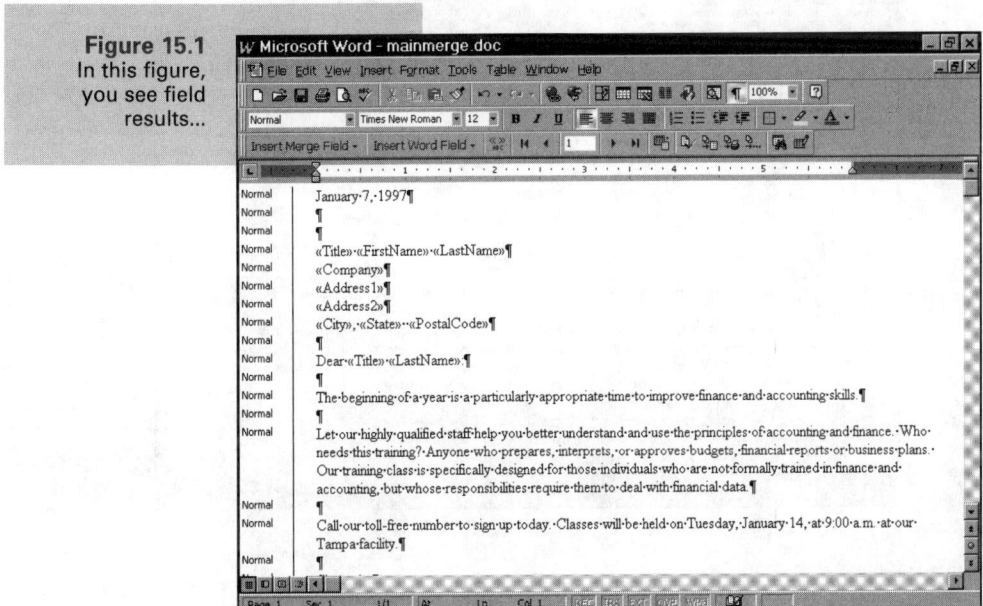

Figure 15.1
In this figure, you see field results...

The information displayed by a field can change. For example, a date field code inserts "today's date". The date that actually appears in the document depends on the system date of your computer. Most fields do not update automatically to show you the most current result. You must update fields manually or take an action that updates fields, such as printing or merging. You'll learn how to manually update fields later in this chapter.

Fields contain three parts:

- Field characters
- The field code
- Switches

Field characters are braces that define the beginning and end of the field. You cannot type these braces; Word automatically inserts them when you insert a field or choose a menu command that inserts a field. The *field code* defines the type of action the field performs. *Switches* are arguments that control the action or appearance of some fields. If a switch contains more than one word, the switch usually must be enclosed in quotation marks (" ").

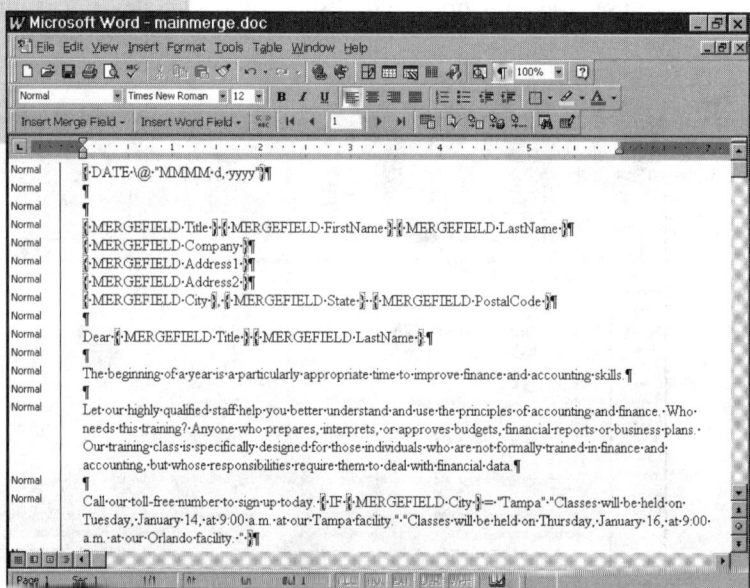

Figure 15.2
...but in this figure, you see the field codes.

A field that displays the current date in a format such as `September 12, 1997`, may look like the following:

    {DATE \@ "MMMM d, yyyy" * MERGEFORMAT}

where the braces ({ and }) are field characters, `DATE` is the field code, and `\@ "MMMM d, yyyy" \* MERGEFORMAT` is the switch.

Typically, you'll enter a field code using the Insert, Field command. But you'll also find that you have inserted a field when you choose one of several other commands:

Edit, Paste Special, Paste Link

Insert, Page Numbers

Insert, Comment

Insert, Date and Time (if you also check the Update Automatically check box)

Insert, Form Field

Chapter 15 • Automating Work with Fields and Macros

Insert, Cap<u>t</u>ion

<u>I</u>nsert, Cross-<u>R</u>eference

<u>I</u>nsert, Inde<u>x</u> and Tables

Hands On: Inserting a Field Code

To insert a field code, follow these steps:

1. Place the insertion point in the document at the location where you want to see the field result.
2. Choose <u>I</u>nsert, Fi<u>e</u>ld. Word displays the Field dialog box (see Figure 15.3).

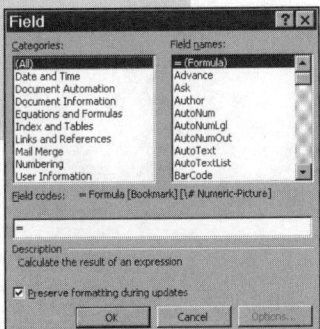

Figure 15.3
Use the Field dialog box to insert a field.

3. Select the type of field that you want from the <u>C</u>ategories list, or select All. We insert the document author's name in this exercise, so select Document Information.
4. Select a field code from the Field <u>N</u>ames list. In our example, select Author.
5. Click on OK. Word inserts the results of the field (in our case, `Elaine J. Marmel`) in your document (see Figure 15.4).

Hands On: Inserting a Numbered Caption

You can insert captions for figures, tables, and equations using the <u>I</u>nsert <u>C</u>aption command. In this case, Word uses a sequence number field. We insert two figure captions and one table caption in this example, and then view the fields (as opposed to the results) so that you can see the way Word handles sequence number fields.

1. Select the object for which you want to provide a caption, or place the insertion point where you want the caption to appear in your document.
2. Choose Insert, Caption. Word displays the Caption dialog box (see Figure 15.5).

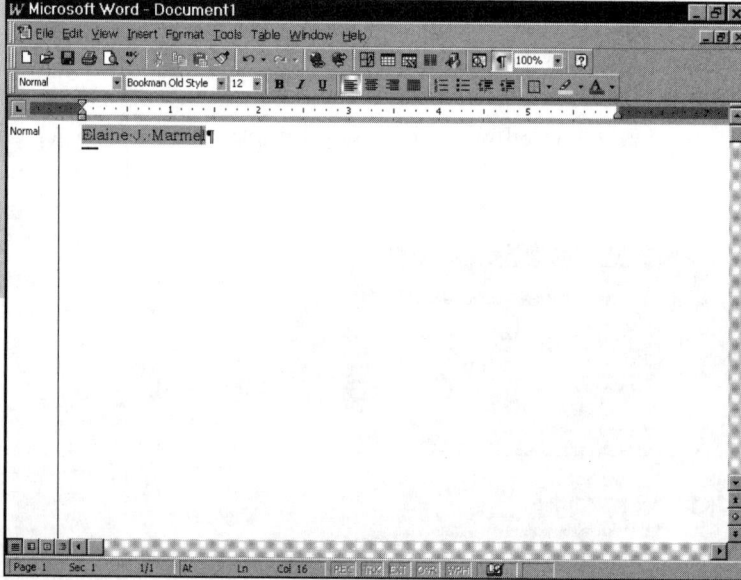

Figure 15.4
If you place the insertion point anywhere in text created by a field, you'll see a gray background, indicating that the text is a field result.

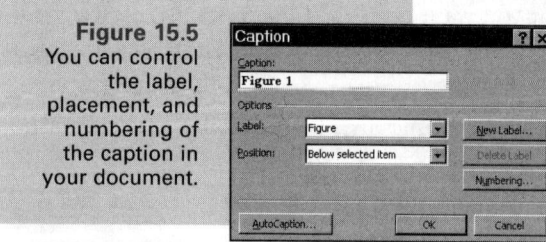

Figure 15.5
You can control the label, placement, and numbering of the caption in your document.

Tip

You also can tell Word to automatically caption certain items, such as Excel worksheets and charts, if they appear in your document.

3. Click on OK. Word inserts a label, Figure 1, in your document.

CHAPTER 15 • AUTOMATING WORK WITH FIELDS AND MACROS 381

Repeat these steps one more time, and Word inserts Figure 2 into your document. Repeat these steps a third time, but open the Label list box and choose Table. When you click on OK, Word inserts Table 1 into your document (see Figure 15.6).

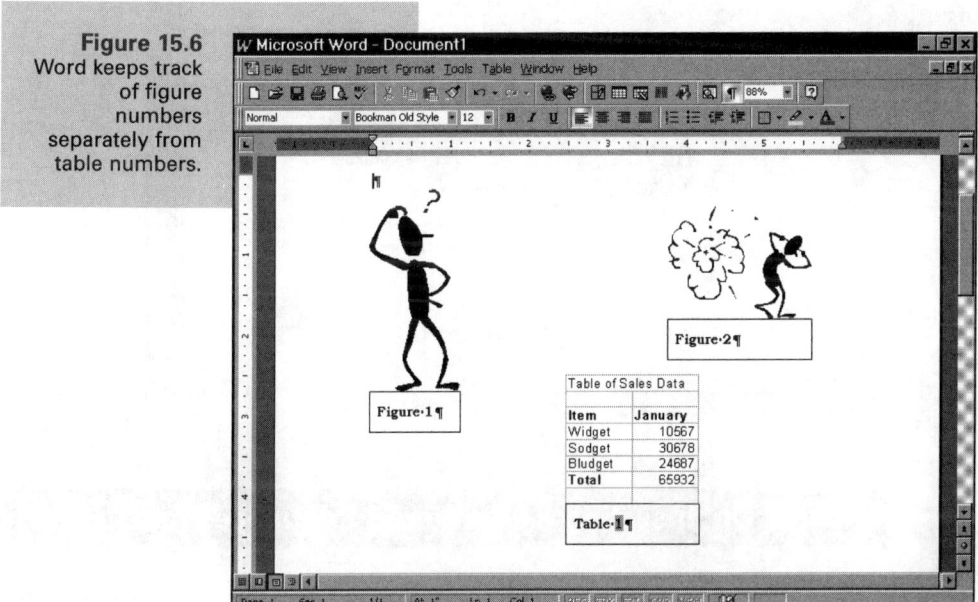

Figure 15.6
Word keeps track of figure numbers separately from table numbers.

Now, press Alt+F9 to see how Word tracks figure numbers separately from table numbers (see Figure 15.7). The field code, SEQ, uses a bookmark named Figure for figure numbers, and another bookmark named Table for table numbers. *Bookmarks* are useful for marking a location in a document or text to which you want to refer. Using this technique, Word can track as many different sets of sequential numbers as you want.

Tip

• •
You can use bookmarks to mark a location in a document while you are editing so that you can easily return to that location later. Position the insertion point at the location you want to mark and choose Insert, Bookmark. Type a name for the bookmark in the dialog box that appears and click on Add. To return to the location you marked, choose Edit, Go To. In the dialog box that appears, type the name of the bookmark and click on Go To. Then, click on Close to close the dialog box.
• •

Figure 15.7
When you display the field code instead of its result, you can see the difference between the figure field code and the table field code.

Hands On: Inserting a Numbered Sequence Field

The Caption feature takes care of numbering figures, tables, and equations that appear in your document, but how do you refer to the same figure, table, or equation in the text of your document? That is, how do you let Word track the numbers when you're typing along and you need to type, "Refer to Figure 1 for more information"? You create your own SEQ field with its own bookmark.

1. Place the insertion point in the document at the location where you want to see the field result.
2. Choose Insert, Field. Word displays the Field dialog box.
3. From the Categories list, choose Numbering.
4. From the Field Names list, choose Seq.
5. Click in the text box where SEQ appears and type the name of the bookmark that you want to use. In our example, we type **reference** (see Figure 15.8).
6. Click on OK. Word inserts the results of the field—1.

The next time you repeat these steps, Word will insert 2. This approach is functional, but tedious; later in this chapter, we write a macro to automate inserting this sequence number field.

Figure 15.8
Supply a word that represents a bookmark for a sequence number field.

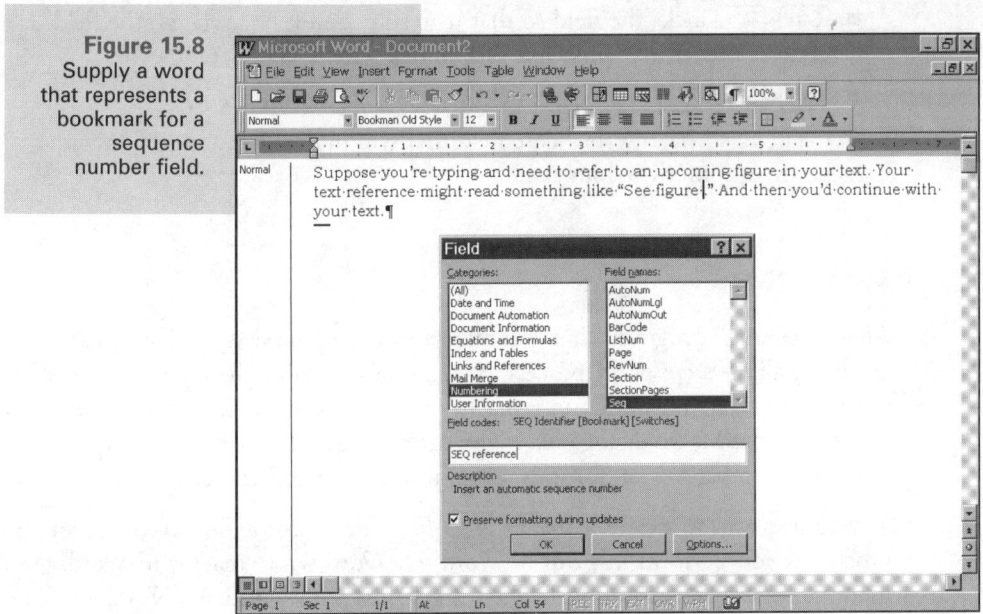

Manipulating Field Codes

Following are some commonly used shortcut keys and their purpose:

- **F9** updates fields that you have selected.
- **Shift+F9** toggles your view of the selected field codes between the code and its result.
- **Alt+F9** toggles your view of all fields in the document between the code and its result.

A few field codes, such as {xe} (index entry), {tc} (table of contents entry), and {rd} (referenced document) do not display because they are formatted automatically as hidden text. To display them, choose Tools, Options, and, on the View tab, place a check in the Hidden text check box.

- **Ctrl+Shift+F9** converts a field code to regular text, permanently replacing the code with its last result.
- **F11** moves to and selects the next field in the document.
- **Shift+F11** moves to and selects the previous field in the document.

- Ctrl+F11 locks the field so that its result cannot be updated; the field code, however, remains. You can unlock a field to update it.
- Ctrl+Shift+F11 unlocks a field so that you can update it.
- Alt+Shift+D inserts a date field that will update in conjunction with your computer's system clock.

Macro Basics

Macros are small programs that automate a multistep process in Word. Instead of executing all the steps of the process, you run the macro and it executes all the steps of the process. If you don't run a macro often, you can simply create it and then run it from the Macro dialog box. If you use the macro frequently, you might want to create a toolbar button for it or assign it to a keyboard combination.

The easiest way to create a macro is to let Word record the keystrokes of the process as you perform it. Prior to Word 97, Word wrote macros in WordBasic, its own macro programming language; starting with Word 97, Word uses the Visual Basic for Applications programming language to write macros. You can edit macros that you create if you learn Visual Basic. In this section, we go through the basics of creating a macro and then you'll actually create three different macros.

Planning a Macro

> **SEE CHAPTER 14 FOR MORE INFORMATION ON COPYING MACROS BETWEEN TEMPLATES.**

When you save a macro, Word stores the macro in a template, and you can choose the template in which Word stores the macro. If you store the macro in the Normal template, the macro will be available in all documents, regardless of the template upon which they are based. If you store the macro in any other template, the macro will be available only when you're working in a document based on that template. To choose a template for the macro, don't open the template (the .DOT file); simply open a document based on the template.

Note

> Suppose that you initially decide to store the macro in one template and later decide that you would have been better off to have stored it in another template. Don't worry—you don't need to recreate the macro. You can copy macros between templates, as discussed in Chapter 14.

Chapter 15 • Automating Work with Fields and Macros

Before you actually record a macro, you might want to practice the procedure you plan to record so that you know the order in which you want to select items or choose commands. For example, if you select text and then run a macro, the macros operates on items that you select manually. If, however, you run the macro and *then* select text, the macro will always try to operate on the same selected text.

Understanding What Gets Recorded

While you record a macro, Word works pretty much as you would expect it to work; for example, you can select text or move around your document using the Go To dialog box or using keyboard shortcuts such as Ctrl+Home or Ctrl+End to move to the beginning or the end of the document. You'll find, however, that mouse actions are limited while recording a macro; you can choose menu commands using the mouse, but you cannot select text or move within the document using the mouse.

If you open a dialog box while recording a macro, Word will record the settings for all options in the dialog box *if you click on OK*. For dialog boxes that contain tabs (such as Format, Paragraph), Word records the settings of the tab that you are viewing when you click on OK. If you want to save the settings for more than one tab in a dialog box, you must, while recording the macro, open the dialog box as many times as necessary to display each tab that you want to record, and click on OK while viewing that tab.

Be aware that some commands, such as Table, Show Gridlines, toggle between on and off, but the Word records a single statement in the macro to execute the command. That means that the macro will simply switch the current state when you run it; if gridlines are hidden, the macro will cause them to be displayed, but if gridlines are displayed, the macro will cause them to be hidden.

Hands On: Recording a Macro

The first four steps that follow start recording the macro. Steps 5–8 are the steps that the macro records. These steps will change for you as you record macros of your own. The last step completes the recording process.

1. Choose Tools, Macro, Record New Macro.

>
>
> To begin recording a new macro, you can double-click on the REC symbol that you see on the status bar at the bottom of the Word screen. It appears gray when no macro is being recording, and changes to black after you start recording.

2. In the Record Macro dialog box that appears, type a name for your macro. The name can be descriptive and as long as you like; it cannot contain any spaces and it must begin with a character. Call this macro InsertSymbol (see Figure 15.9). Also, open the Store Macro In list box and choose a template in which to store the macro.

3. In the Description box, add to or replace the existing description with a description of what the macro does.

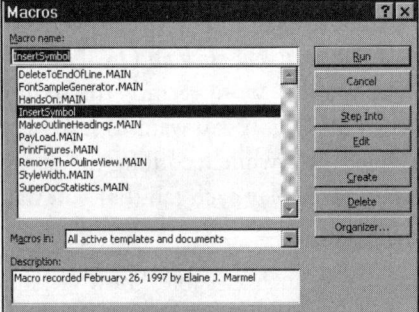

Figure 15.9
Describe your macro in this dialog box.

4. Click on OK. Word displays the Macro toolbar, which contains only two buttons: Stop Recording and Pause Recording. In addition, the mouse pointer changes to include an icon for a cassette tape (see Figure 15.10).

5. Choose Insert, Symbol. The Symbol dialog box appears.

6. Find and click on the symbol that you want the macro to insert in your document.

7. Choose Insert. Word inserts the symbol in your document (see Figure 15.11).

8. Choose Close to close the Symbol dialog box.

9. Click on the Stop Recording tool on the Macro toolbar. The Macro toolbar disappears, REC in the status bar returns to gray, and the mouse pointer returns to normal.

CHAPTER 15 • AUTOMATING WORK WITH FIELDS AND MACROS

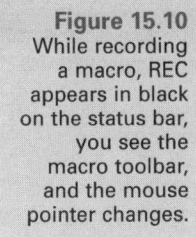

Figure 15.10
While recording a macro, REC appears in black on the status bar, you see the macro toolbar, and the mouse pointer changes.

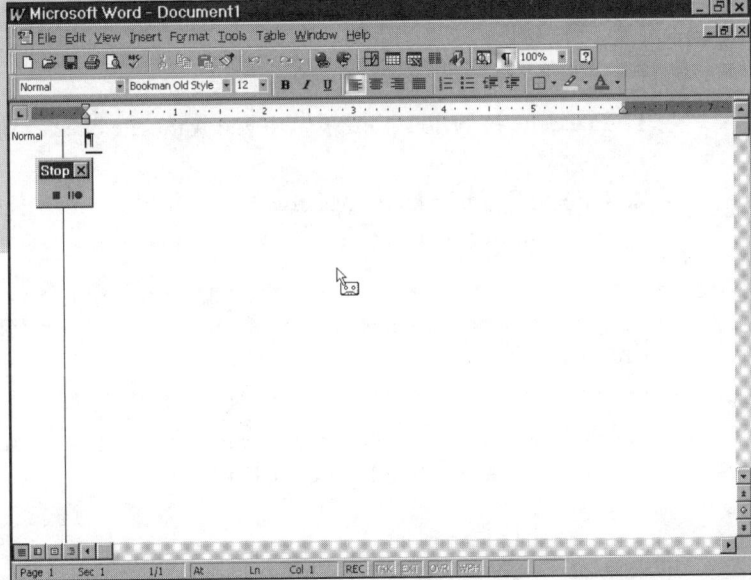

Figure 15.11
During macro recording, Word inserts the symbol just as it would if you were not recording a macro.

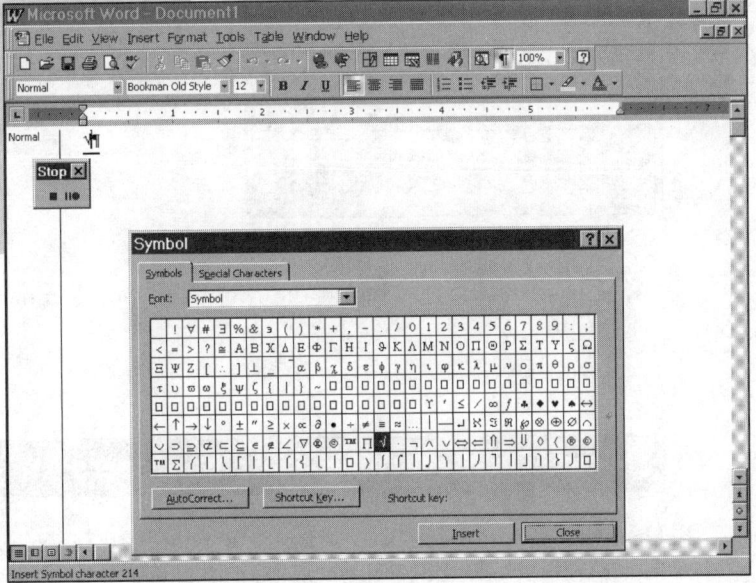

PART IV • MAKING WORD WORK YOUR WAY

Hands On: Running the Macro

To run a macro, follow these steps:

1. Place the insertion point where you want the check mark symbol to appear.
2. Choose <u>T</u>ools, <u>M</u>acro, <u>M</u>acros. Word displays the Macro dialog box, which lists all available macros.

All the macros with names ending in .MAIN were created in prior versions of Word. Word 97 converted them to Visual Basic.

3. Highlight the macro that you created; you'll see its description in the Description box (see Figure 15.12).

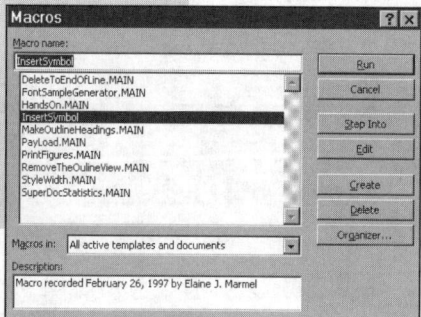

Figure 15.12
When you highlight a macro, Word displays its description in the Description box.

4. Choose <u>R</u>un. Word inserts the symbol in your document at the insertion point.

Hands On: Recording a Toolbar Macro

Here we create a macro that inserts a standardized footer into a document. The footer will include the author's name, the date, and the page number. In the first 8 steps, we assign this macro to a toolbar button. Then, we record the macro.

1. Double-click on REC on the status bar to begin recording a macro.

CHAPTER 15 • AUTOMATING WORK WITH FIELDS AND MACROS **389**

2. In the Record Macro dialog box that appears, supply a name and description for the macro, and decide where to store the macro (see Figure 15.13).

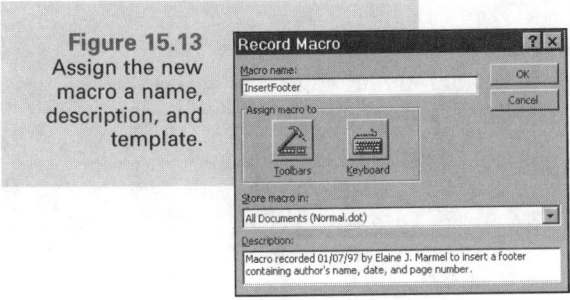

Figure 15.13
Assign the new macro a name, description, and template.

3. Click on the Toolbars button in the middle of the dialog box. Word displays the Customize dialog box (see Figure 15.14).

Note

The Office Assistant may appear in order to offer you help assigning your macro to a toolbar button.

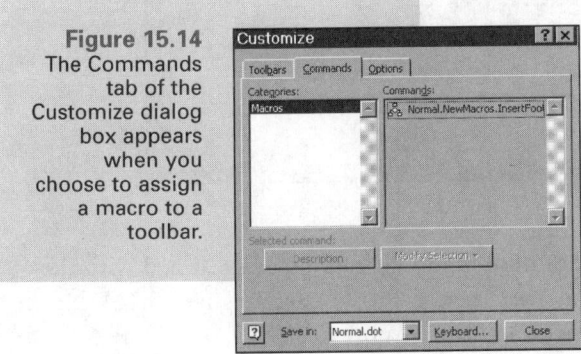

Figure 15.14
The Commands tab of the Customize dialog box appears when you choose to assign a macro to a toolbar.

4. From the Commands column, drag the button to the location on any toolbar where you want the button to appear. As you drag the macro to a toolbar, the mouse pointer changes to include a small rectangle. As you

move the insertion point onto a toolbar, Word will display a large insertion point on the toolbar, indicating that Word will place the macro, when you drop it, to the right of that insertion point (see Figure 15.15).

Note

If you want to place the button on a toolbar not currently displayed, click on the Tool<u>b</u>ars tab and place a check in the box to the left of the toolbar name. Word will display that toolbar. Then, switch back to the Commands tab and perform step 4.

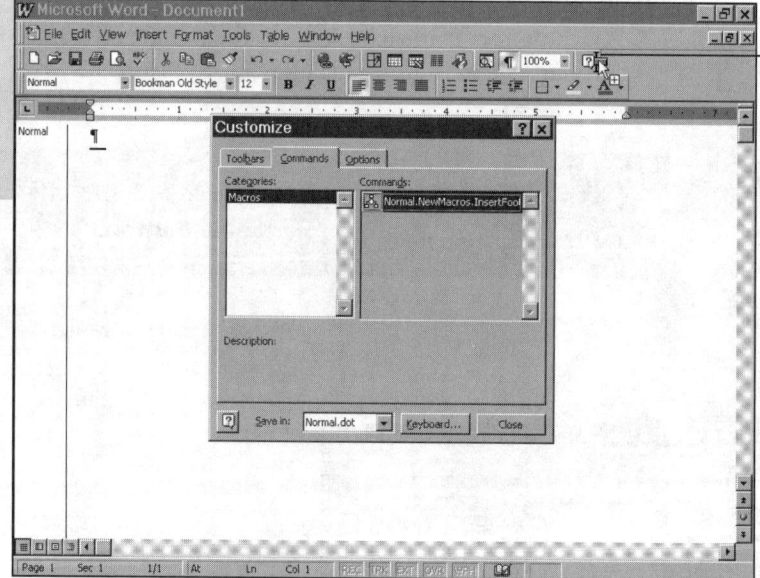

Figure 15.15
When you see the large insertion point on a toolbar, you can drop the macro.

5. When you drop the macro onto the toolbar, it appears selected with the name that you saw in the Customize dialog box (see Figure 15.16). Notice also that the Modify Selection button is now available.
6. Click on <u>M</u>odify Selection. A pop-up list box appears (see Figure 15.17).
7. To change the text name for the button, click in the Name text box and modify the name. You can include spaces in the name. As soon as you choose another command, the change you made appears on the toolbar.

CHAPTER 15 • AUTOMATING WORK WITH FIELDS AND MACROS **391**

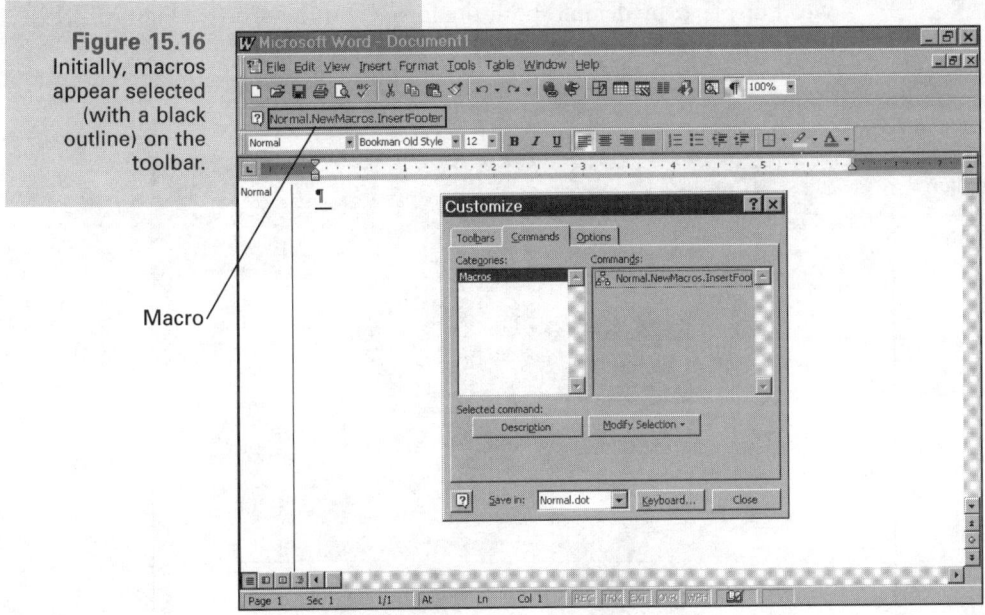

Figure 15.16
Initially, macros appear selected (with a black outline) on the toolbar.

Macro

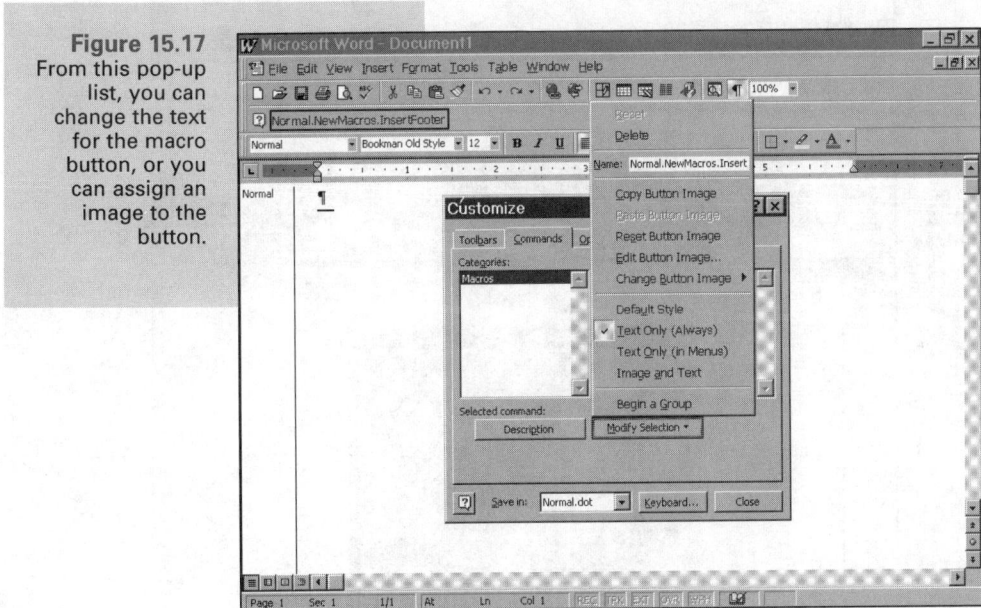

Figure 15.17
From this pop-up list, you can change the text for the macro button, or you can assign an image to the button.

8. If you want to use an image for the button, highlight Change Button Image to see available images (see Figure 15.18). If you choose an image,

PART IV • MAKING WORD WORK YOUR WAY

Word displays, by default, both the image and the text (see Figure 15.19). When you finish, click on Close.

Figure 15.18
You can assign an image to a macro button.

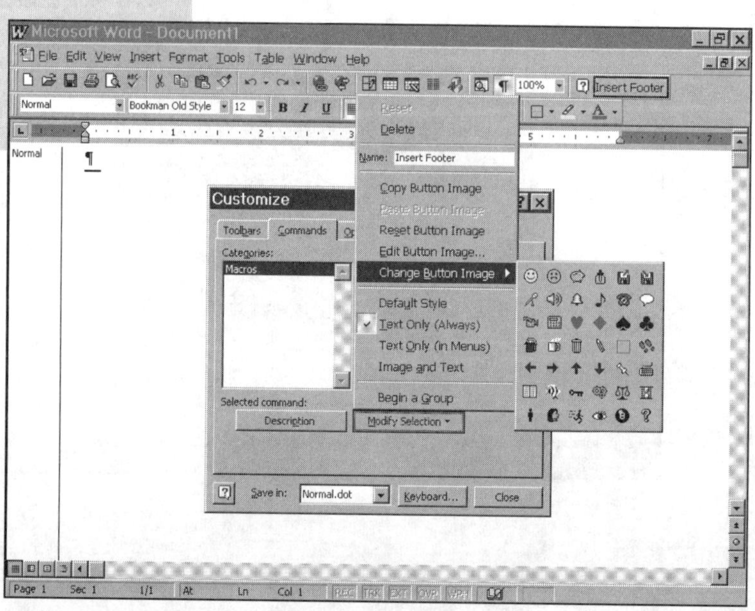

Figure 15.19
If you assign an image to a macro button, Word displays both the image and the text.

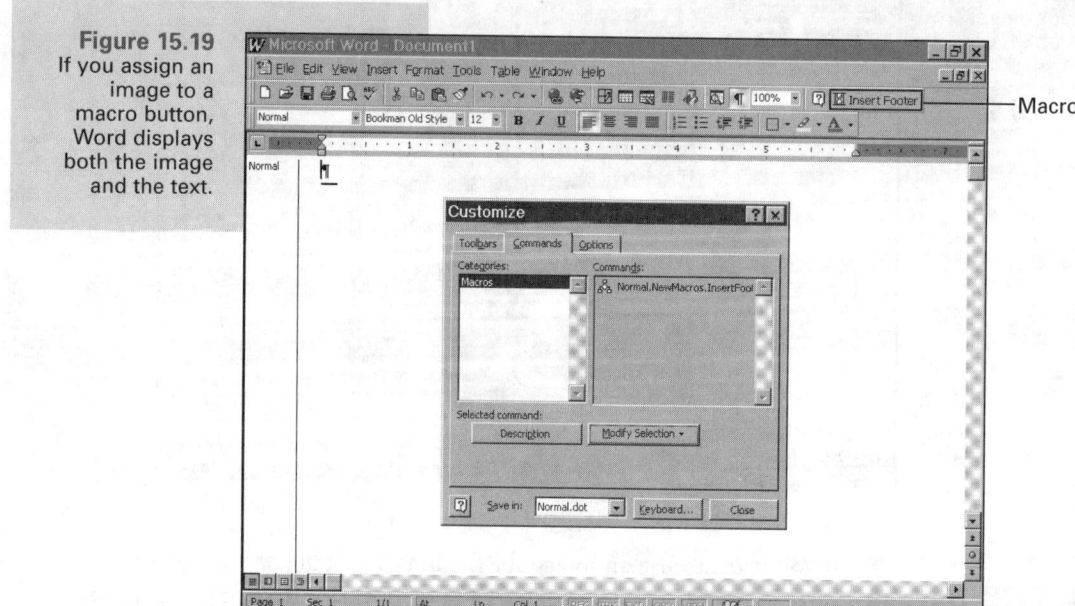

CHAPTER 15 • AUTOMATING WORK WITH FIELDS AND MACROS **393**

Tip

To display the button only on the toolbar, reopen the Modify Selection list box and choose Default Style.

9. Choose View, Header and Footer. From the Header and Footer toolbar, click on Switch Between Header and Footer.
10. Click on the Insert AutoText button and choose Author, Page #, Date (see Figure 15.20).

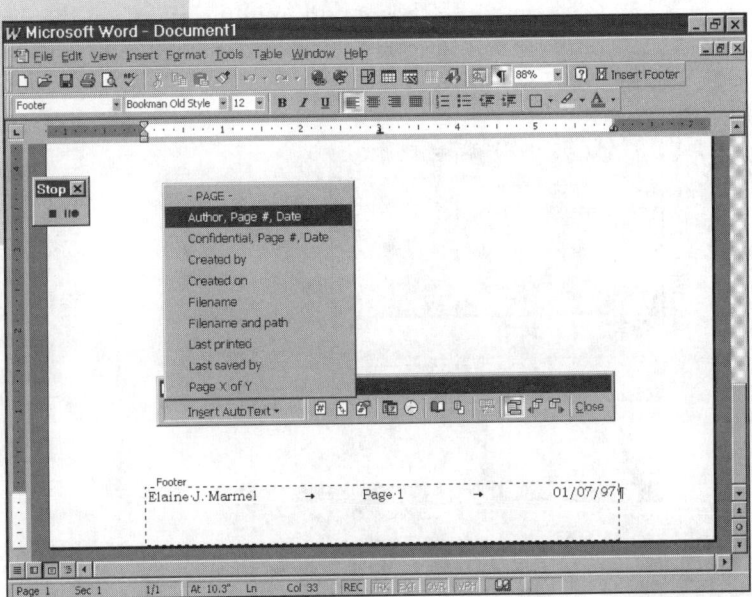

Figure 15.20
Use the Insert AutoText button to insert the information that you want to appear in the footer.

11. Click on Close to close the Header and Footer toolbar.
12. Click on Stop Recording to finish the macro.

Hands On: Running the Toolbar Macro

To run a toolbar macro, follow these steps:

1. Open a new document based on the template containing the macro that inserts a footer.
2. Click on the toolbar button you created. Word inserts the footer stored in your macro.

PART IV • MAKING WORD WORK YOUR WAY

Hands On: Recording a Keyboard Macro

Earlier in this chapter, you learned how to insert a sequence number field code that you can use to keep track of references to figure numbers. Now you can see how to create a macro to insert the sequence number and assign it to a keyboard combination. Steps 1–5 set up the macro and assign it to a keyboard shortcut.

1. Double-click on REC on the status bar to begin recording a macro.
2. In the Record Macro dialog box that appears, supply a name and description for the macro, and decide where to store the macro (see Figure 15.21).
3. Click on the Keyboard button in the middle of the dialog box. Word displays the Customize Keyboard dialog box (see Figure 15.22).

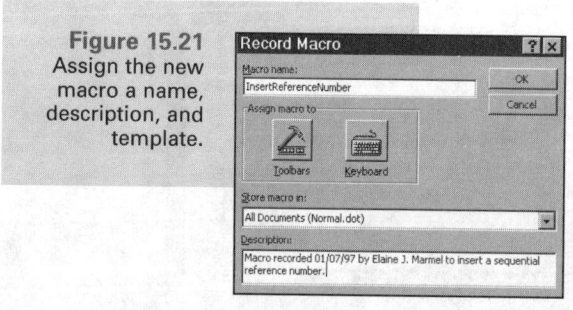

Figure 15.21 Assign the new macro a name, description, and template.

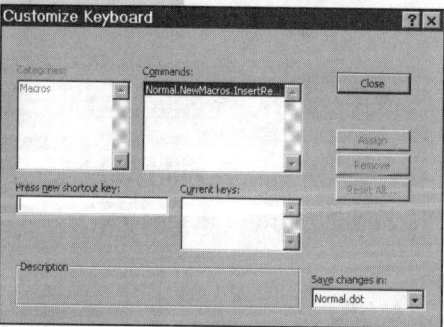

Figure 15.22 The insertion point appears in the Press New Shortcut Key box.

4. Press the combination of keys that you would like to use to play the macro. Typically, you'll want to press [Alt] and some other key on the keyboard—most preassigned Word shortcut keys do not include the [Alt] key. In our example, we pressed [Alt]+[R], for "reference number" (see Figure 15.23).

CHAPTER 15 • AUTOMATING WORK WITH FIELDS AND MACROS **395**

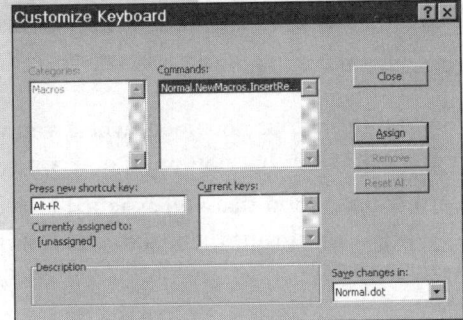

Figure 15.23
If the key combination that you select is available, Word indicates that it is currently unassigned.

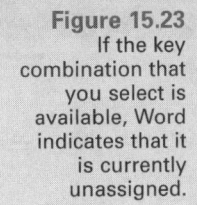

> **Tip**
>
> If the key combination that you select is already assigned, Word will display its assignment in place of "[unassigned]". Backspace and try a different combination.

5. Click on <u>A</u>ssign and then Close. Now begin recording the macro.
6. Choose on <u>I</u>nsert, <u>F</u>ield.
7. In the Field dialog box, choose Numbering from the <u>C</u>ategories list and Seq from the Field <u>N</u>ames list.
8. Add the identifier, such as "reference" (see Figure 15.24).
9. Click on OK, and then click on Stop Recording on the Macro toolbar.

Figure 15.24
Selecting the SEQ field.

Hands On: Running the Keyboard Macro

To run a keyboard macro, follow these steps:

1. Place the insertion point in your document where you want the sequence number to appear. Make sure that no text or object is selected.
2. Press the keyboard combination that you assigned to the macro; in our example, press Alt+R. Word runs the macro and inserts a sequence number in your document.

micros
WORD

16

Changing Your Word Environment

In This Chapter

- Working with Toolbars
- Working with Menus
- Toolbar and Menu Customization Options
- Modifying the Office Assistant
- Changing Word Options

As you work in Word, you'll find things that you wish you could do; for example, maybe you wish you could have a tool on a toolbar that closed documents for you so that you wouldn't need to use the File, Close command. Well, you can change your Word environment to suit the way you work. You can customize toolbars, menus, and add keyboard shortcuts to menu commands. In fact, you can create your own toolbars and menus. You even can customize the way the Office Assistant appears and functions.

Customizing Rules of Thumb

When you modify an existing toolbar or create one of your own, you have some choices about where Word stores the changes you make. And it's important to understand these choices; otherwise, you'll run into unexpected situations; for example, you might think that you "lost" an existing Word shortcut, or perhaps tools don't appear on the toolbar anymore.

The choice you need to make before you make a change involves choosing a template in which to store customized toolbars, menus, and shortcut keys. You can store the changes that you make in either the Normal template or in another template. If you store changes in the Normal template, those changes are available in all documents, whether the document is based on the Normal template or on another template. When you store a customized feature in any template other than the Normal template, however, those changes and features are available only in documents based on that template. If you happen to accidentally create conflicts—suppose, for example, that you accidentally assign the same keyboard shortcut to two different commands—Word follows a rule of precedence to resolve the conflicts: Word uses features stored in other templates before it uses features stored in the Normal template.

> **FOR MORE INFORMATION ON TEMPLATES, SEE CHAPTER 14.**

So, if you want a modification that you make to be available in every document you create, open a document based on the Normal template before you customize. If you want the modification to be available only to documents based on a certain template, open a document based on that template before you customize.

Working with Toolbars

You can decide what toolbars appear when you start Word. You can customize existing toolbars or, if you want, you can create your own toolbar. You can add buttons on toolbars, and you can change the location of a button on a toolbar. If you modify one of the toolbars that comes with Word, you can reset the toolbar so that it reappears the way it was before you modified it.

You also can create your own toolbar. You might decide, for example, that you don't use most of the buttons on the Standard toolbar, so you don't want to display that toolbar. Instead, you'd like to display just some of the buttons on the

Chapter 16 • Changing Your Word Environment 401

Standard toolbar and also display buttons that don't currently appear on the Standard toolbar.

Most of the work you do customizing toolbars happens in the Customize dialog box, except for controlling which toolbars appear on-screen at all times.

Hands On: Displaying Selected Toolbars

To display selected toolbars, follow these steps:

> Most of Word's toolbars are context-sensitive; that is, they will appear when you start a process that uses them. Remember how the Merge toolbar appeared when you set up a merge? Typically, you don't need to display, all the time, toolbars other than the Standard and Formatting toolbars.

1. Choose View, Toolbars. A cascading list of available toolbars appears (see Figure 16.1).

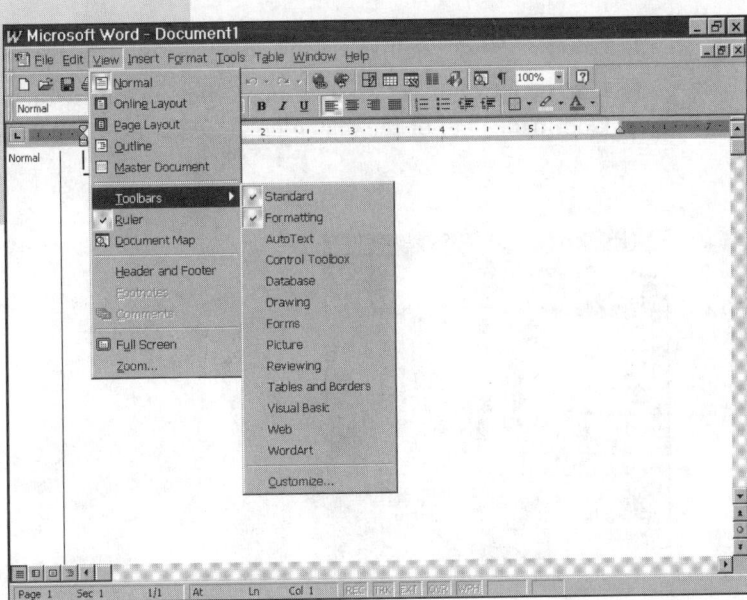

Figure 16.1
If a check appears to the left of a toolbar, that toolbar appears on-screen.

PART IV • MAKING WORD WORK YOUR WAY

2. Display any toolbar that currently doesn't appear on-screen by choosing it. Word will display the toolbar, and the next time you display the list, you'll see a check to the left of the toolbar's name. Similarly, hide any toolbar that currently appears on-screen by choosing it. Word will hide the toolbar, and the next time you display the list, you won't see a check to the left of the toolbar's name.

Hands On: Adding a Button to a Toolbar

Suppose that you want to add a button to the Standard toolbar that executes the File, Close command.

Tip

To change any toolbar, that toolbar must appear on-screen. If the toolbar that you want to modify doesn't appear on-screen, select it from the View, Toolbar menu.

1. Open a document based on the template in which you want to store the new toolbar button. If you want the new toolbar button available to all new documents, view Document1, which is based on the Normal template.
2. Choose View, Toolbars. A cascading list of available toolbars appears.
3. Choose Customize. Word displays the Customize dialog box. Choose the Commands tab of the dialog box (see Figure 16.2).

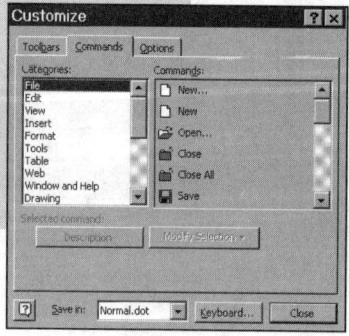

Figure 16.2
When the Customize dialog box is open, you can modify toolbars displayed on-screen.

4. From the Categories list on the left, highlight the category related to the toolbar button that you want to add. In our example, highlight File.

CHAPTER 16 • CHANGING YOUR WORD ENVIRONMENT **403**

5. In the Comman<u>d</u>s list on the right, find the command that you want to add—in our example, the Close command. If you're not sure of a command's purpose, highlight it in the list and then click on the Description button (see Figure 16.3).

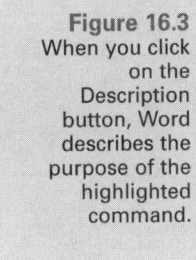

Figure 16.3
When you click on the Description button, Word describes the purpose of the highlighted command.

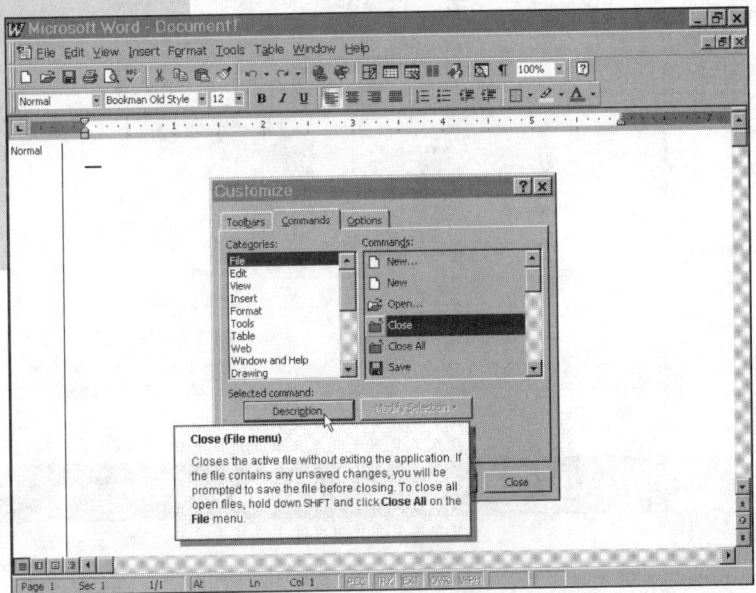

6. Drag the command out of Customize dialog box and onto the toolbar where you want it to appear (see Figure 16.4). While you drag, the mouse pointer changes to include a button and a plus sign.

7. Drop the button when you find the correct location. In our example, place the button between the Open button and the Save button.

8. (Optional) If you opened a document based on a different template and you want to save the change to that template, open the Save in list box at the bottom of the Customize dialog box and select that template.

9. Choose Close to close the Customize dialog box.

Tip

• •
Test your change. Close Word and then reopen it. If you stored your change in the Normal template, you should see the modified toolbar. If you stored your change in another template, open a new document based on that template.
• •

 PART IV • MAKING WORD WORK YOUR WAY

Figure 16.4
When the mouse pointer is positioned in the toolbar, you'll see a large insertion point at the location where the button will appear.

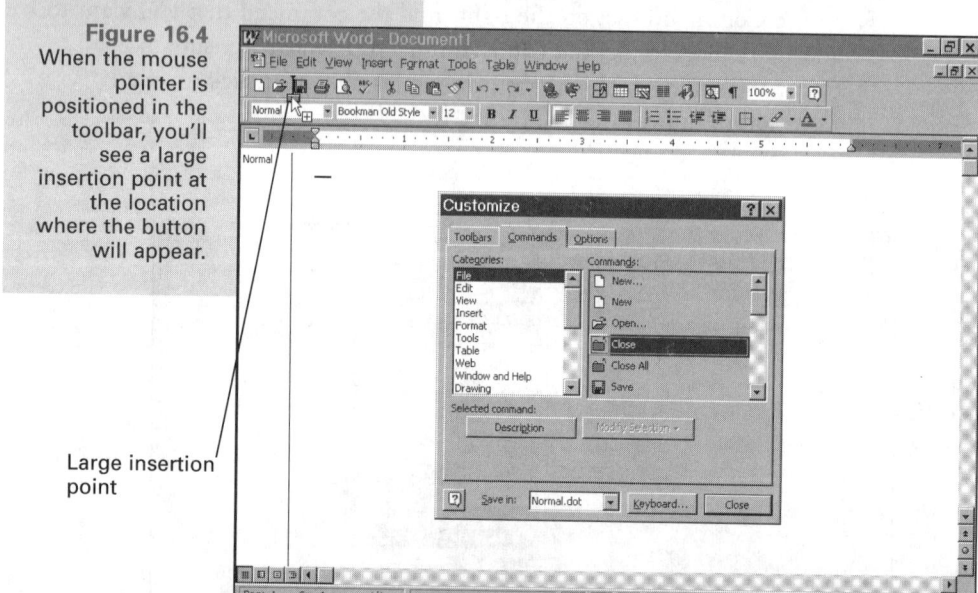

Large insertion point

Hands On: Moving Buttons Around

Suppose that you want to change the position of the Close button so that it appears between the Save and the Print button.

 *Tip*
Remember, to make a change to a toolbar, that toolbar must appear on-screen. If the toolbar that you want to modify doesn't appear on-screen, choose View, Toolbar and select it from the cascading menu.

1. Open a document based on the template in which you want to store the changes to a toolbar. If you want the changes to the toolbar available to all new documents, view Document1, which is based on the Normal template.
2. Choose View, Toolbars. A cascading list of available toolbars appears.
3. Choose Customize. Word displays the Customize dialog box (see Figure 16.5).
4. Drag the button on the toolbar to its new location. When you click on the button that you intend to move, Word selects it by placing a dark black border around it. While you drag, the mouse pointer changes to include a button and a plus sign (see Figure 16.6).

CHAPTER 16 • CHANGING YOUR WORD ENVIRONMENT **405**

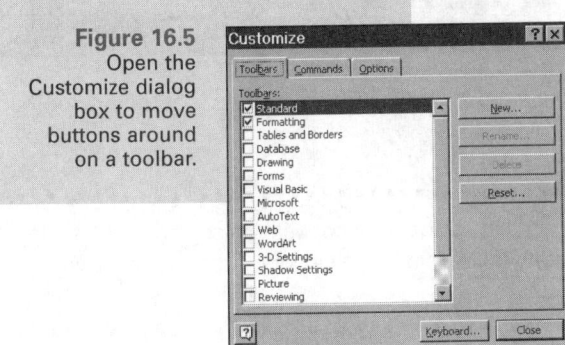

Figure 16.5
Open the Customize dialog box to move buttons around on a toolbar.

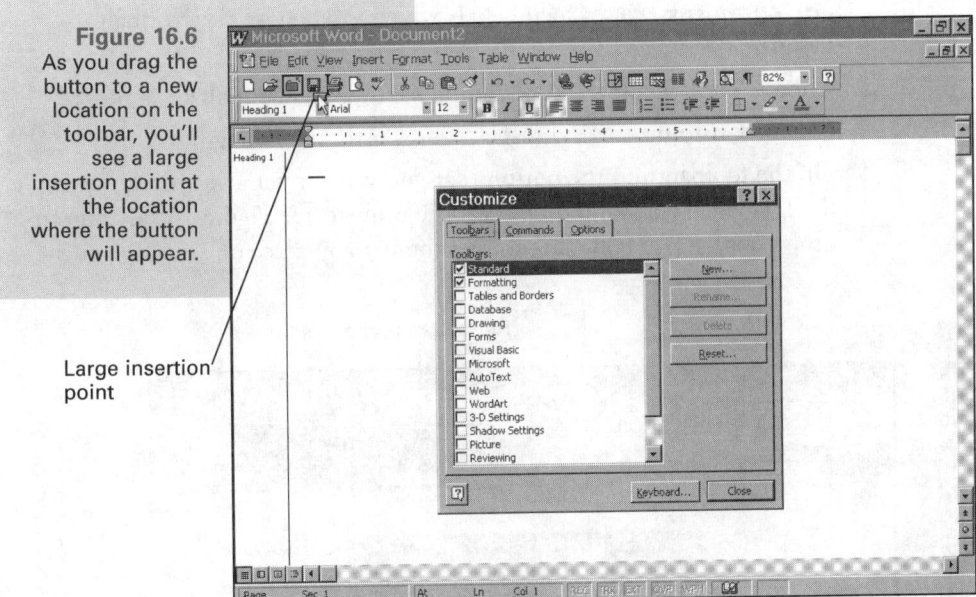

Figure 16.6
As you drag the button to a new location on the toolbar, you'll see a large insertion point at the location where the button will appear.

Large insertion point

5. Drop the button at the correct location. In our example, place the button between the Save button and the Print button.

6. (Optional) If you opened a document based on a different template and you want to save the change to that template, open the Save in list box at the bottom of the Customize dialog box and select that template.

7. Choose Close to close the Customize dialog box.

PART IV • MAKING WORD WORK YOUR WAY

Hands On: Removing a Button From a Toolbar

Suppose that you want remove the Drawing button from the Standard toolbar because you rarely draw.

To remove a button from a toolbar, that toolbar must appear on-screen. If the toolbar doesn't appear on-screen, choose View, Toolbar and select it from the cascading menu.

1. Open a document based on the template in which you want to store the changes to a toolbar. If you want the changes to the toolbar available to all new documents, view Document1, which is based on the Normal template.
2. Choose View, Toolbars. A cascading list of available toolbars appears.
3. Choose Customize. Word displays the Customize dialog box.
4. On the toolbar, find the button that you want to remove—in our example, the Drawing tool—and drag it off the toolbar (see Figure 16.7). You can drop a tool you're removing from a toolbar any place on your document.

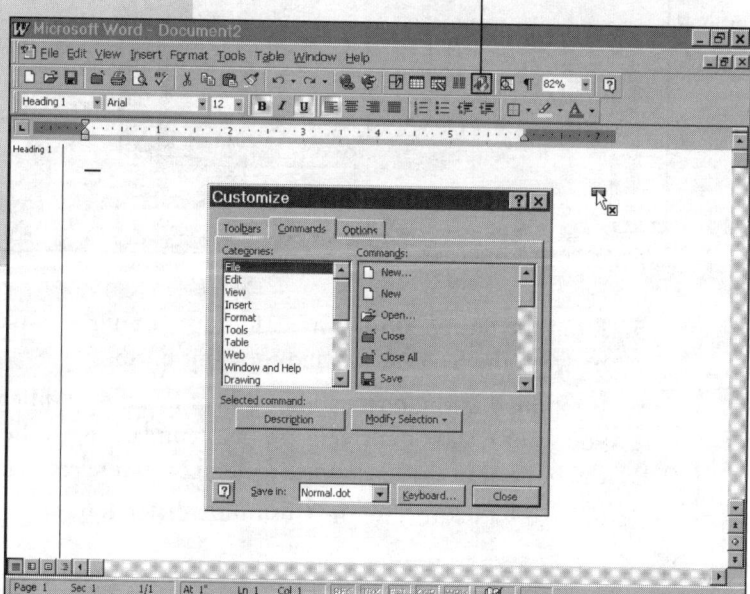

Figure 16.7
As you drag, the button that you chose to remove will be selected on the toolbar and the mouse pointer shape will change.

CHAPTER 16 • CHANGING YOUR WORD ENVIRONMENT **407**

5. (Optional) If you opened a document based on a different template and you want to save the change to that template, open the Save in list box at the bottom of the Customize dialog box and select that template.

6. Choose Close to close the Customize dialog box.

Hands On: Resetting Toolbars

Suppose you decide that you don't like the changes you made to a toolbar and you want to restore the toolbar to its original appearance.

1. Open a document based on the template whose toolbars you want to reset.
2. Choose View, Toolbars. A cascading list of available toolbars appears.
3. Choose Customize. When Word displays the Customize dialog box, click on the Toolbars tab.
4. Highlight the toolbar that you want to restore to its original appearance and click on the Reset button. Word displays the Reset Toolbar dialog box (see Figure 16.8).

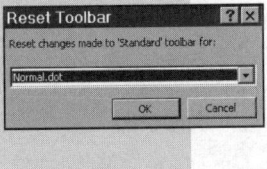

Figure 16.8
Use the Reset Toolbar dialog box to restore a toolbar to its original factory settings.

Note

Depending on the way you set up Windows 95, you may not see the .dot extension.

5. From the list box, choose a template containing toolbars that you would like to reset to their original appearance.
6. Click on OK to close the Reset Toolbar dialog box. Word will reset toolbars.
7. Choose Close.

PART IV • MAKING WORD WORK YOUR WAY

Hands On: Creating Your Own Toolbar

Suppose that you decide that you don't need most of the tools on the Standard toolbar, but you'd like to see some of them as well as a collection of tools that execute commands you use regularly.

1. Open a document based on the template in which you want to store the new toolbar you're going to create.
2. Choose View, Toolbars. A cascading list of available toolbars appears.
3. Choose Customize. When Word displays the Customize dialog box, click on the Toolbars tab.
4. Click on the New button. Word displays the New Toolbar dialog box (see Figure 16.9).

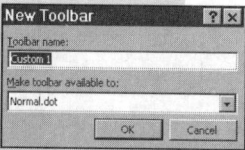

Figure 16.9
Use this dialog box to begin creating a new toolbar.

5. In the Toolbar Name box, type the name that you want to give to your custom toolbar. We call ours **Elaine**.
6. From the Make Toolbar Available To list box, choose a template in which to store the toolbar.

Tip

Your new toolbar will be available only in documents based on this template. If you choose the Normal template, your new toolbar will be available in all documents.

7. Click on OK. Word places an empty toolbar, whose name you can't read at the moment, on your screen (see Figure 16.10).
8. Click on the Commands tab of the Customize dialog box.
9. Using the drag-and-drop techniques described earlier in this chapter in "Hands On: Add a Button to a Toolbar," drag and drop buttons onto the toolbar. The buttons on the Elaine toolbar are listed in Table 16.1.
10. To create divisions on the toolbar, find the tool that you want to appear to the right of the division and drag it slightly to the right. On the Elaine toolbar, we created divisions between the Print and Find tools and between the Redo tool and the Envelope tool (see Figure 16.11).

Chapter 16 • Changing Your Word Environment

409

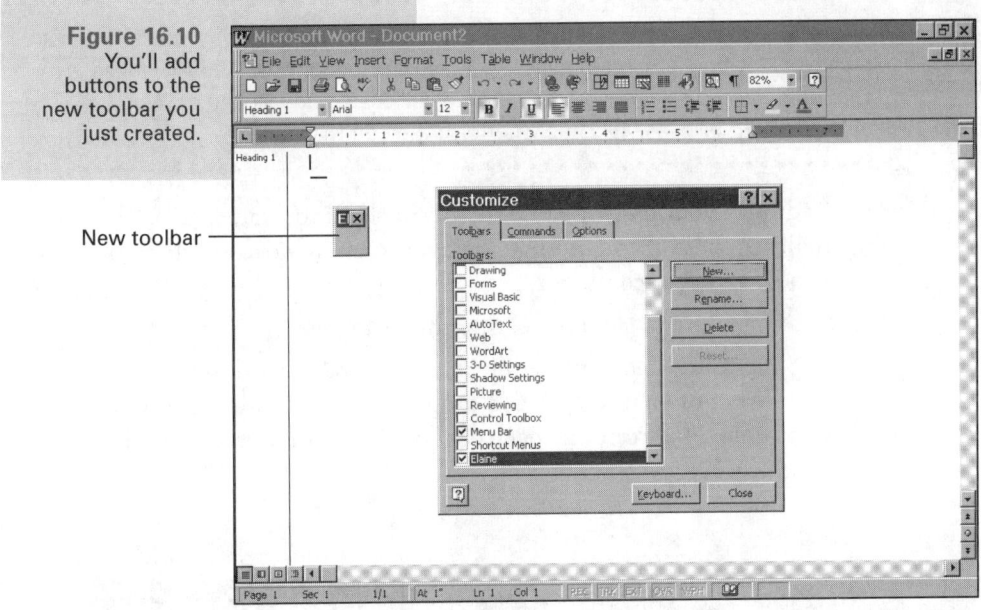

Figure 16.10
You'll add buttons to the new toolbar you just created.

New toolbar

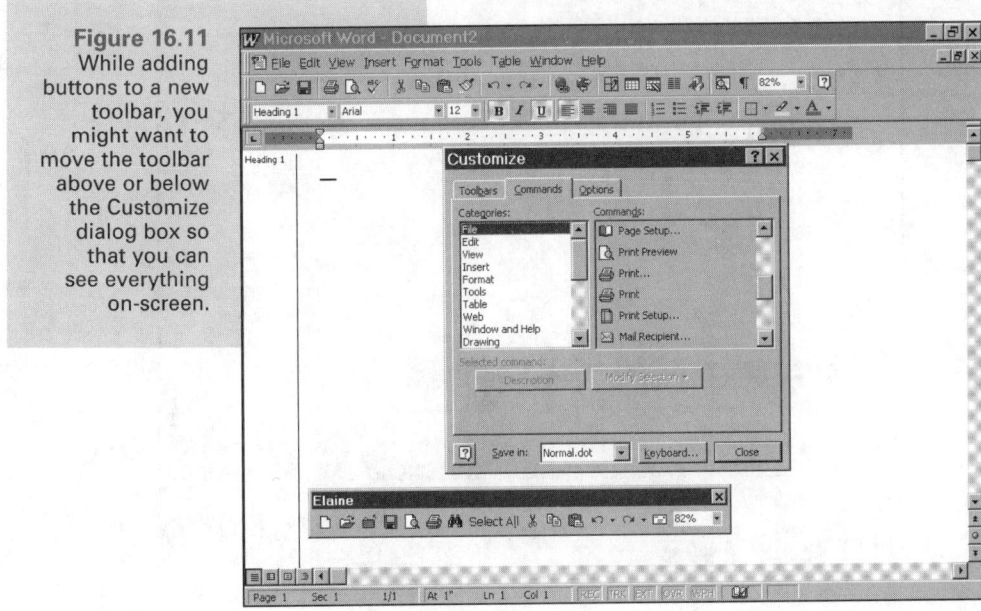

Figure 16.11
While adding buttons to a new toolbar, you might want to move the toolbar above or below the Customize dialog box so that you can see everything on-screen.

Part IV • Making Word Work Your Way

You might notice, in the Commands portion of the dialog box, what looks like multiple versions of the same command, such as Print... and Print. Actually, these are different commands. The version that includes ellipses (...) will open a dialog box. The version without ellipses will simply perform the command.

11. To display your toolbar and hide the Standard toolbar, click on the Toolbars tab in the Customize dialog box and remove the check from the Standard toolbar check box.

12. Click on Close to close the Customize dialog box.

13. To place your toolbar where the Standard toolbar used to appear, drag the title bar of your toolbar and drop it when the outline for your toolbar is positioned between the menus and the Formatting toolbar (see Figure 16.12).

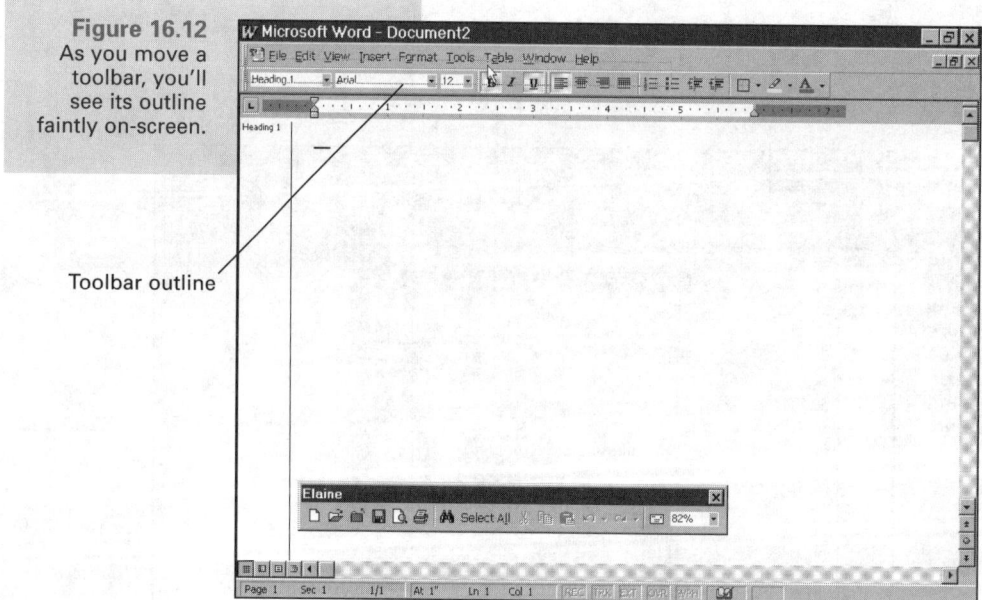

Figure 16.12 As you move a toolbar, you'll see its outline faintly on-screen.

Working with Menus

In addition to modifying toolbars, you can modify menus or create your own menus. The same storage rules apply: If you save a menu change to the Normal template, it will be available in all documents, but if you save a menu change to a different template, it will be available only to documents based on that template.

Table 16.1. Tools on the Elaine Toolbar

Tool	Category	Command
New	File	New
Open	File	Open
Close	File	Close
Save	File	Save
Print Preview	File	Print Preview
Print	File	Print
Find	Edit	Find
Select All	Edit	Select All
Cut	Edit	Cut
Copy	Edit	Copy
Paste	Edit	Paste
Undo	Edit	Undo
Redo	Edit	Redo
Envelopes and Labels	Tools	Envelopes and Labels
Zoom	View	Zoom

You can add commands or macros to menus. When we're talking in a global sense, we'll refer to both commands and macros as menu *items*. You can change the location of a menu item on its menu. If you modify one of the menus that comes with Word, you can reset the menu so that it appears, once again, the way it did before you modified it. You also can create your own menu; you might decide, for example, that you use a set of seven or eight commands consistently, and it would be easier for you if they all appeared on the same menu.

As with toolbars, most of the work you do customizing menus happens in the Customize dialog box.

Hands On: Adding a Command to a Menu

Suppose that you want to add a command to the File menu that closes all open documents.

1. Open a document based on the template in which you want to store the new menu command. If you want the new menu command available to

all new documents, view Document1, which is based on the Normal template.

2. Choose Tools, Customize. Word displays the Customize dialog box—the same dialog box that you accessed earlier from the View, Toolbars cascading menu. Choose the Commands tab of the dialog box (see Figure 16.13).

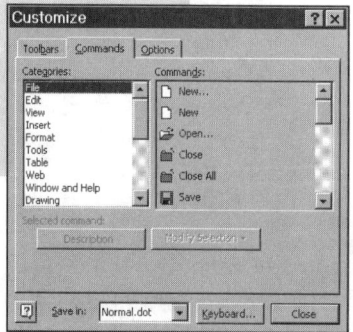

Figure 16.13
When the Customize dialog box is open, you can modify menus.

3. From the Categories list on the left, highlight the category related to the menu command that you want to add. In our example, highlight File.

4. In the Commands list on the right, find the command that you want to add (in our example, the Close All command). If you're not sure of a command's purpose, highlight it in the list and then click on the Description button.

5. Click to open the menu on which you want to place the command (in our example, open the File menu).

6. Drag the command out of the Customize dialog box and onto the menu where you want it to appear (see Figure 16.14). While you drag, the mouse pointer changes to include a button and a plus sign.

7. Drop the command in the correct location. In our example, place the command immediately below the Close command.

The menu will remain open until you close the Customize dialog box.

8. (Optional) If you opened a document based on a different template and you want to save the change to that template, open the Save in list box at the bottom of the Customize dialog box and select that template.

CHAPTER 16 • CHANGING YOUR WORD ENVIRONMENT **413**

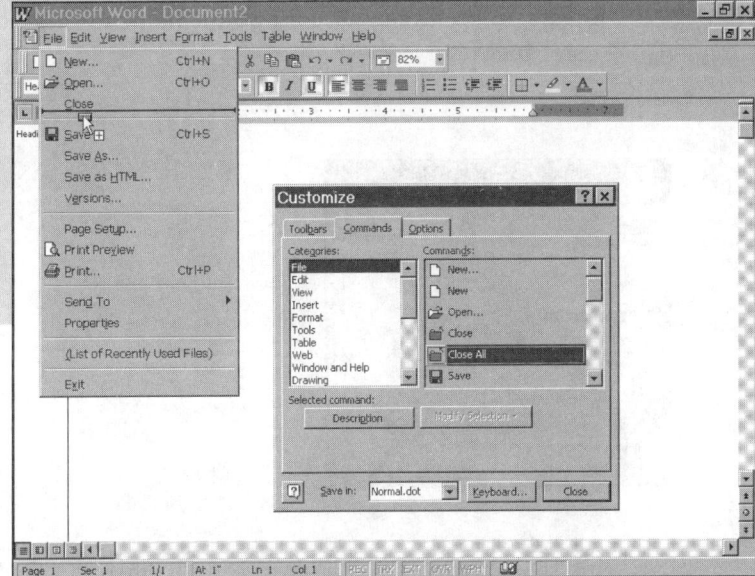

Figure 16.14
When the mouse pointer is positioned on the menu, you'll see a large horizontal insertion point at the location where the command will appear.

9. Choose Close to close the Customize dialog box.

As with toolbars, you can test your change. Close Word and then reopen it. Then, open the menu that you modified. If you stored your change in the Normal template, you should see the modified menu. If you stored your change in another template, open a new document based on that template.

Hands On: Adding a Macro to a Menu

Adding a macro to a menu is basically the same process as adding a command to a menu, but you may want to change the name of a macro when you add it to a menu, because Word supplies its Visual Basic name.

1. Open a document based on the template containing the macro that you want to add to a menu.
2. Choose Tools, Customize. Word displays the Customize dialog box. Click on the Commands tab of the dialog box.

3. From the Categories list on the left, highlight the Macro category. Word displays, in the Commands list on the right, any available macros (see Figure 16.15).

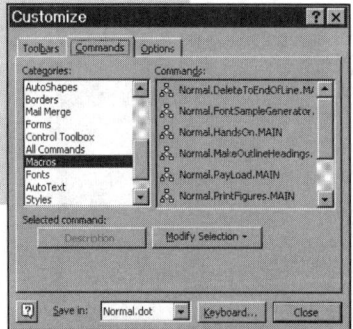

Figure 16.15
When you select the Macro category, Word displays available macros in the Commands list.

4. Find the macro that you want to add to a menu in the Comman_d_s list on the right.
5. Click to open the menu on which you want to place the macro (in our example, the _E_dit menu).
6. Drag the command out of Customize dialog box and onto the menu where you want it to appear (we place the macro at the bottom of the Edit menu). While you drag, the mouse pointer changes to include a button and a plus sign.
7. To change the macro's name on the menu, right-click the macro on the menu (see Figure 16.16).
8. Choose the Name command on the menu (you can edit the text in the box so that the name of the command becomes anything you want). Press Enter when you finish editing. We changed the name to Macro: Hands On (see Figure 16.17).
9. (Optional) If you opened a document based on a different template and you want to save the change to that template, open the Save in list box at the bottom of the Customize dialog box and select that template.
10. Choose Close to close the Customize dialog box.

CHAPTER 16 • CHANGING YOUR WORD ENVIRONMENT **415**

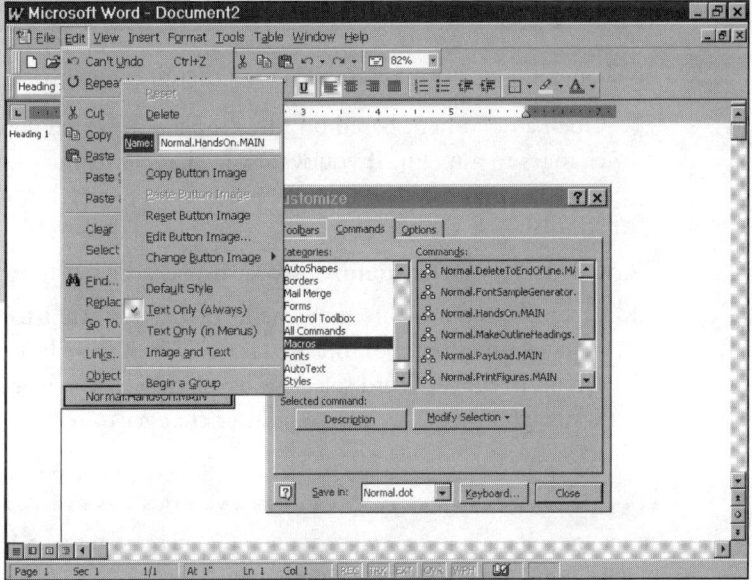

Figure 16.16
From the shortcut menu, you can modify the appearance of any menu command, not just a macro menu command.

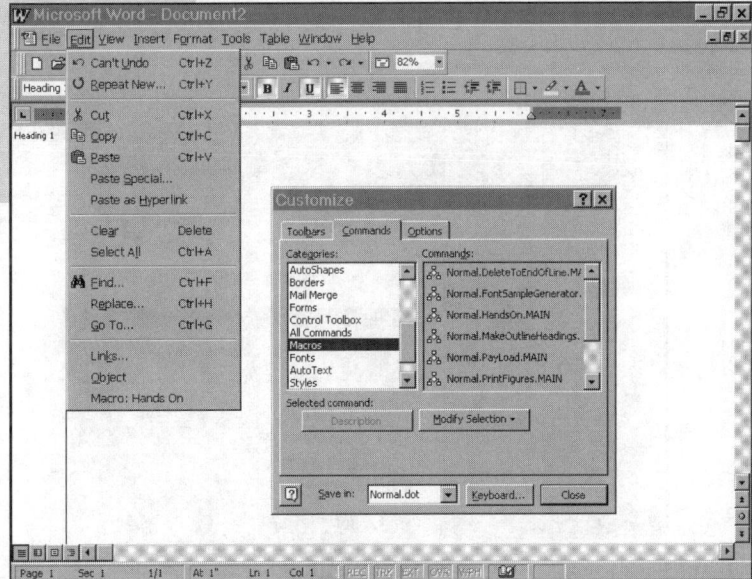

Figure 16.17
Use the Name command on the shortcut menu to rename a macro or command on a menu.

PART IV • MAKING WORD WORK YOUR WAY

Hands On: Moving Items Around on a Menu

To change the position of an item on a menu, follow these steps:

1. Open a document based on the template in which you want to store the changes to a menu. If you want the changes to the menu available to all new documents, view Document1, which is based on the Normal template.

2. Choose Tools, Customize. Word displays the Customize dialog box.

3. Open the menu containing the item that you want to move and drag the item to a new location on the menu. When you click on the item that you intend to move, Word selects it by placing a dark black border around it. While you drag, the mouse pointer changes to include a button and a plus sign.

> **Tip**
>
> To move a menu item to a different menu, you must remove the item from the first menu and then add it to the second menu.

4. Drop the item at the correct location. In our example, place the Close All command above the Close command (see Figure 16.18).

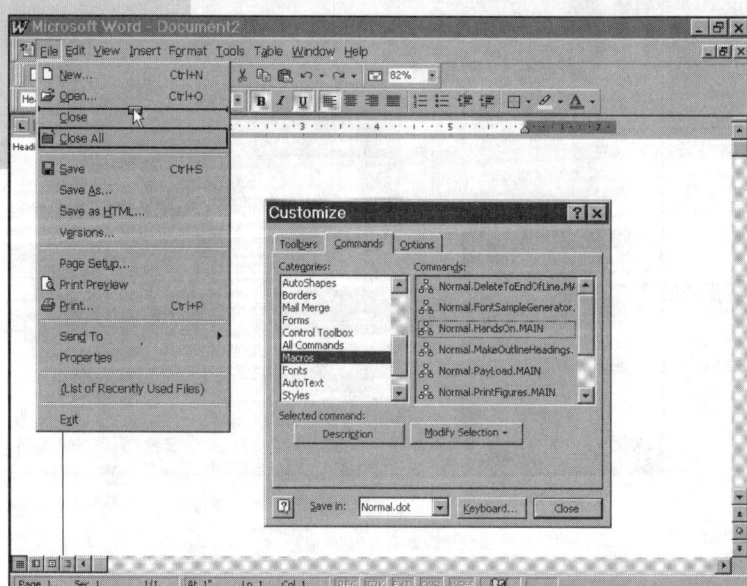

Figure 16.18
As you move a menu command, the mouse pointer changes.

Chapter 16 • Changing Your Word Environment

5. (Optional) If you opened a document based on a different template and you want to save the change to that template, open the Save in list box at the bottom of the Customize dialog box and choose that template.

6. Choose Close to close the Customize dialog box.

Hands On: Changing a Menu Item's Hot Key

When you add a command to a menu, Word will try to assign a hot key to the command (an underlined letter that you can press to choose the command). You can, however, cause conflicts; for example, when we added the Close All command to the File menu, Word assigned it a hot key letter of C. But the Close command already had a hot key letter of C. In this exercise, we assign a new hot key letter to the Close All command. We're using L because no other command on the File menu uses L as its hot key.

1. Open a document based on the template in which you want to store the changes to a menu. If you want the changes to the menu available to all new documents, view Document1, which is based on the Normal template.

2. Choose Tools, Customize. Word displays the Customize dialog box.

3. Open the menu containing the command whose hot key you want to change. Right-click the command on the menu to display the shortcut menu.

4. Choose the Name command on the menu. Move the ampersand (&) so that it appears immediately before the letter that you want Word to use as the hot key, and press Enter when you finish. In our example, we moved the ampersand so that it appears between the *C* and the *l* in *Close* (see Figure 16.19).

5. (Optional) If you opened a document based on a different template and you want to save the change to that template, open the Save in list box at the bottom of the Customize dialog box and choose that template.

6. Choose Close to close the Customize dialog box.

You can remove a menu item from a menu if the Customize dialog box is open. Choose Tools, Customize. Then, open the menu containing the item that you want to remove. Drag the item anywhere onto your document.

Part IV • Making Word Work Your Way

Figure 16.19
Move the ampersand to change the hot key letter.

Hands On: Adding a Shortcut Key to a Menu Item

Suppose that you want to add a keyboard shortcut to the File, Close. Follow these steps:

1. Open a document based on the template in which you want to store the changes to a menu. If you want the changes to the menu available to all new documents, view Document1, which is based on the Normal template.
2. Choose Tools, Customize. Word displays the Customize dialog box.
3. Click on the Keyboard button to display the Customize Keyboard dialog box (see Figure 16.20).
4. From the Categories list on the left, highlight the category containing the menu item for which you want to add a keyboard shortcut. In our example, highlight File.
5. In the Commands list on the right, highlight the command for which you want to add a keyboard shortcut (in our example, choose the File, Close command). A description of the item's function will appear at the bottom of the box.
6. Click in the Press New Shortcut Key box and press the keyboard combination that you want to use for this command. Word will indicate

CHAPTER 16 • CHANGING YOUR WORD ENVIRONMENT **419**

whether that shortcut is already assigned to another command or whether it's available (see Figure 16.21).

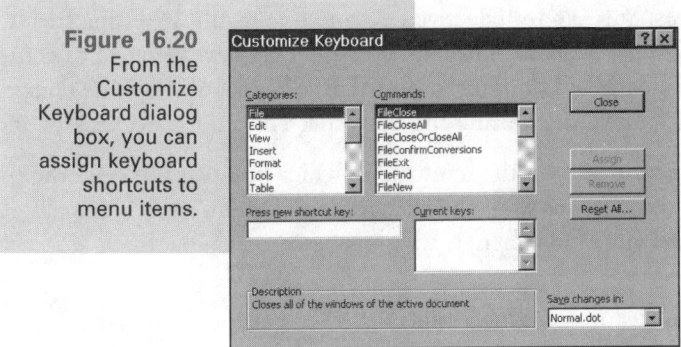

Figure 16.20
From the Customize Keyboard dialog box, you can assign keyboard shortcuts to menu items.

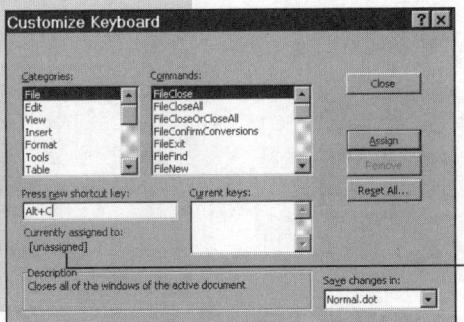

Figure 16.21
After you press a key combination, Word indicates, immediately below the Press New Shortcut Key box, whether the combination is in use or available.

— Status of selected shortcut combination

You'll find that most Alt key combinations are available. To print a copy of key assignments, choose File, Print. In the Print dialog box, open the Print What list box and choose Key Assignments.

7. Choose Assign and then Close to assign the key combination and close the Customize Keyboard dialog box.

8. Choose Close to close the Customize dialog box.

To remove a keyboard shortcut combination, follow these steps, but in Step 6, highlight the existing key combination in the Current Keys list box. In Step 7, choose Remove.

Hands On: Resetting Menus

It's important to understand that, when you reset menus, you are resetting *all* changes to *all* menus. You cannot selectively restore one menu. Resetting menus *does not*, however, affect keyboard shortcuts that you may have assigned to commands that appeared on Word's original menu. Those keyboard shortcuts remain in effect unless you remove them using the steps covered in the previous section.

1. Open a document based on the template in which you want to store the changes to a menu. If you want the changes to the menu available to all new documents, view Document1, which is based on the Normal template.
2. Choose Tools, Customize. Word displays the Customize dialog box.
3. Click on the Toolbars tab and highlight Menu Bar (see Figure 16.22).

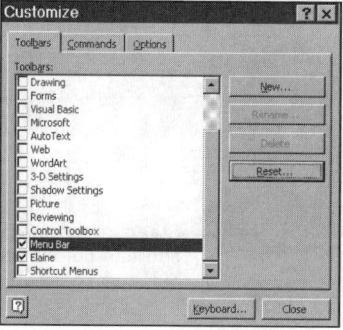

Figure 16.22
To reset menus, highlight Menu Bar in the Toolbar list.

4. Choose Reset. Word displays the Reset Toolbars dialog box and suggests that changes to the Menu Bar toolbar be reset for the Normal template. If you opened a document based on a different template, open the list box and select that template.
5. Click on OK to reset the menus and redisplay the Customize dialog box; choose Close to close the Customize dialog box.

Hands On: Creating Your Own Menu

To create your own menu, follow these steps:

1. Open a document based on the template in which you want to store the changes to a menu. If you want the changes to the menu available to all new documents, view Document1, which is based on the Normal template.
2. Choose Tools, Customize. Word displays the Customize dialog box. Choose the Commands tab.
3. Scroll down to the end of the Categories list and highlight New Menu (see Figure 16.23).

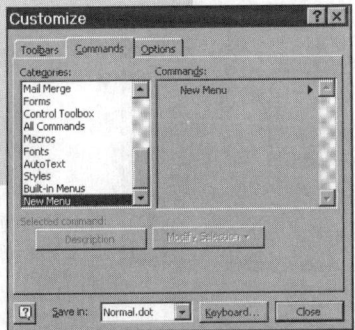

Figure 16.23
To create your own menu, choose New Menu from the Categories list.

4. Drag the New Menu choice that appears in the Commands list to the location on the menu bar, and drop it where you want your new menu to appear. While you drag, the mouse pointer changes to include a button and a plus sign. When you move the mouse pointer into the menu bar, you'll see a vertical insertion point at the location where the new menu will appear. In this example, we placed the new menu between the Table menu and the Window menu.
5. Rename the new menu by right-clicking on it on the menu bar, choosing Name, and typing a new name for it. To include a hot key letter, include an ampersand immediately before the hot key letter. Press [Enter] when you finish naming the menu. We named our example menu "Elaine" and included an ampersand between the first two letters (see Figure 16.24).
6. To add commands to your menu, highlight a category in the Categories list on the right. From the Commands list, drag a command onto your menu. As you drag, the mouse pointer again changes to include a button and a plus sign. Move the mouse pointer in the menu bar on your menu; you'll see a small gray square below your menu. Move the vertical insertion point

422 PART IV • MAKING WORD WORK YOUR WAY

into that small gray square and drop the command to add it to the menu (see Figure 16.25).

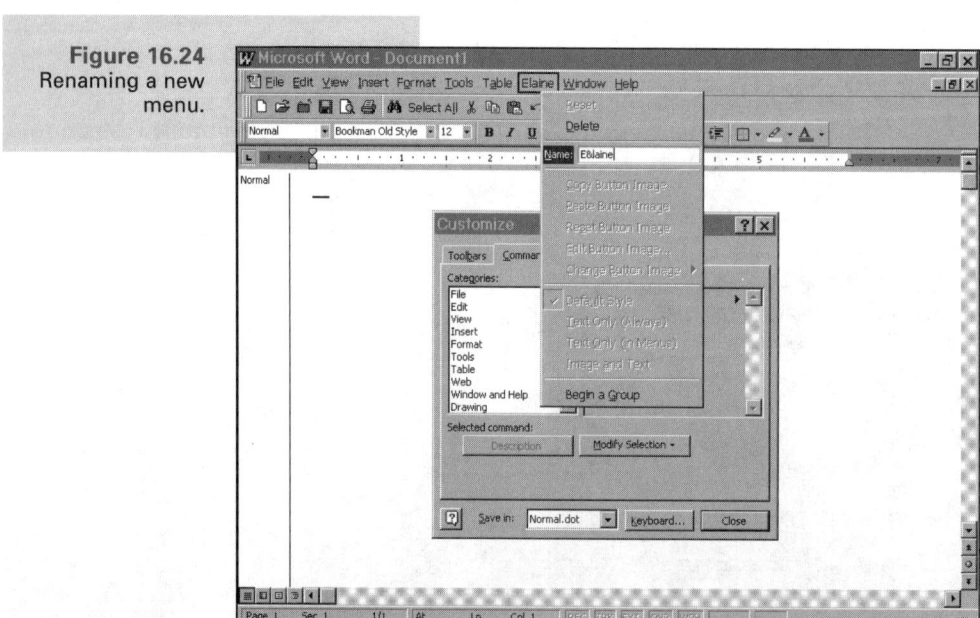

Figure 16.24
Renaming a new menu.

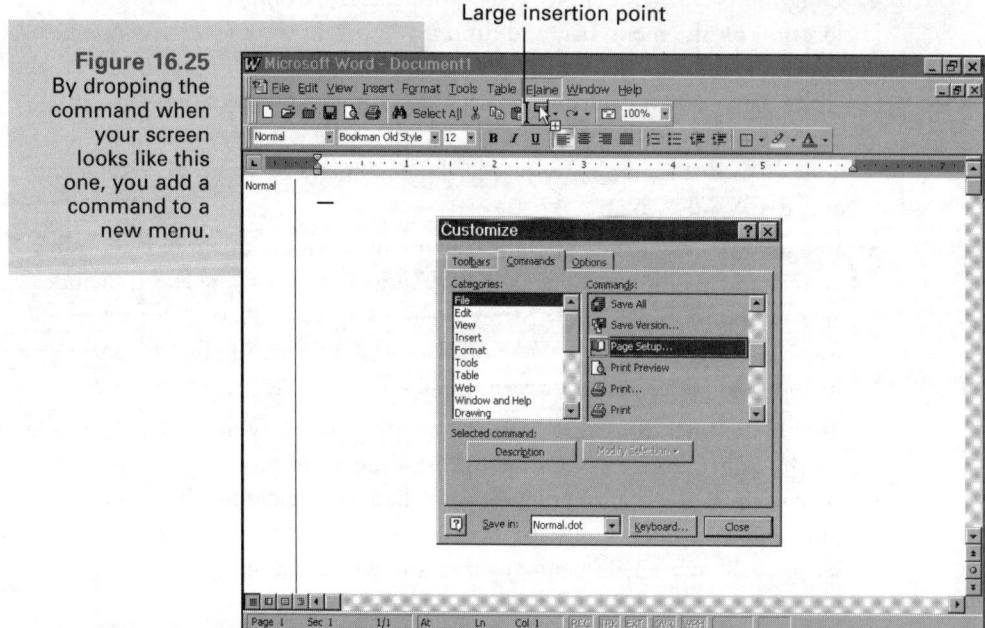

Figure 16.25
By dropping the command when your screen looks like this one, you add a command to a new menu.

CHAPTER 16 • CHANGING YOUR WORD ENVIRONMENT **423**

7. Repeat Step 6 for each command that you want on your menu. Whenever a command already appears on your menu, Word changes the vertical insertion point to a horizontal insertion point so that you can identify a command's location on the menu.

8. To group commands on the menu, select the first command of the group on the menu and right-click. From the shortcut menu, choose Begin a Group (see Figure 16.26). Repeat this step to end the group by selecting the first command that you want to appear outside the group.

Figure 16.26
To group commands, use the Begin a Group command.

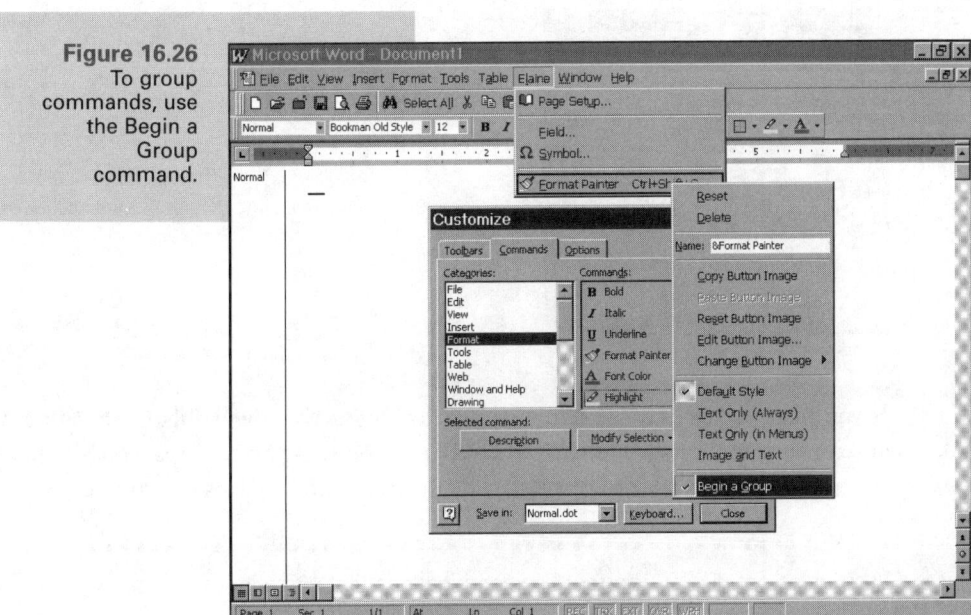

9. (Optional) If you opened a document based on a different template and you want to save the change to that template, open the Save in list box at the bottom of the Customize dialog box and select that template.

10. Choose Close to close the Customize dialog box.

Tip

To remove a command from your custom menu, display the Customize dialog box by choosing Tools, Customize. Then, open the custom menu you created and drag the item anywhere onto your document.. To remove your entire custom menu, open the Customize dialog box. Then, drag the menu off the menu bar.

PART IV • MAKING WORD WORK YOUR WAY

Toolbar and Menu Customization Options

You can customize the way the toolbars look, whether you see ScreenTips when you point at a toolbar button, the information contained in the ScreenTip, and the way menus behave. Open the Customize dialog box and click on the Options tab (see Figure 16.27).

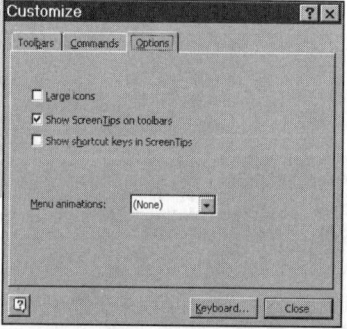

Figure 16.27
Use the Options tab to control appearance and behavior of toolbars and menus.

If you place a check in the Large Icons check box, Word will enlarge the appearance of each tool on each displayed toolbar. If you show ScreenTips, you also have the option of having Word display shortcut keys in Screen Tips (see Figure 16.28).

Tip

••
Word does not display shortcut key combinations that you added.
••

Modifying the Office Assistant

The Office Assistant is a cartoon-like help tool (see Figure 16.29) that you can display by clicking on the Office Assistant tool at the right edge of the Standard toolbar or by opening the Help menu and choosing Microsoft Word Help. You can control the appearance and behavior of the Office Assistant. Click on Options to display the Office Assistant dialog box (see Figure 16.30).

In the Assistant Capabilities section, you control what the Office Assistant does. In the Show Tips About section, you control what kind of help the Office Assistant tries to provide. In the Other Tip Options section, you control how much

Chapter 16 • Changing Your Word Environment

help the Office Assistant provides—and you can reset the Office Assistant's tips so that you will see tips you have already seen once.

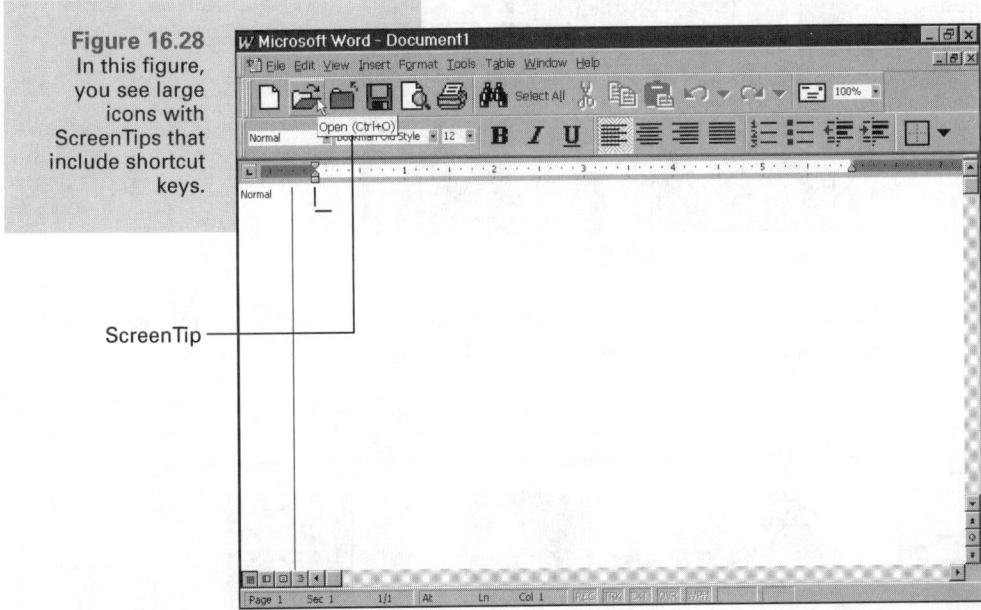

Figure 16.28 In this figure, you see large icons with ScreenTips that include shortcut keys.

ScreenTip

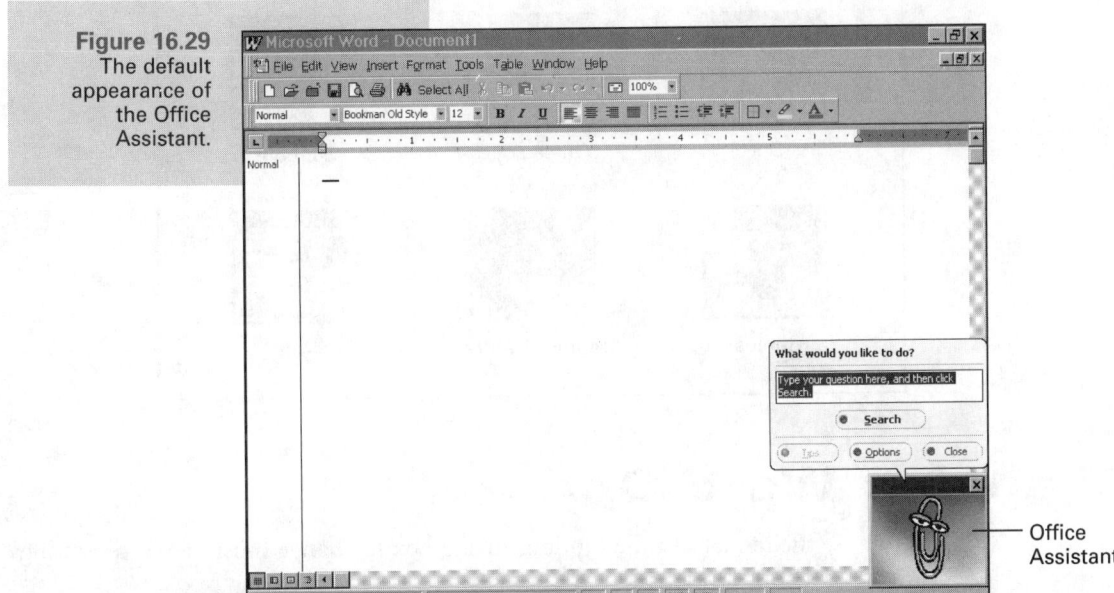

Figure 16.29 The default appearance of the Office Assistant.

Office Assistant

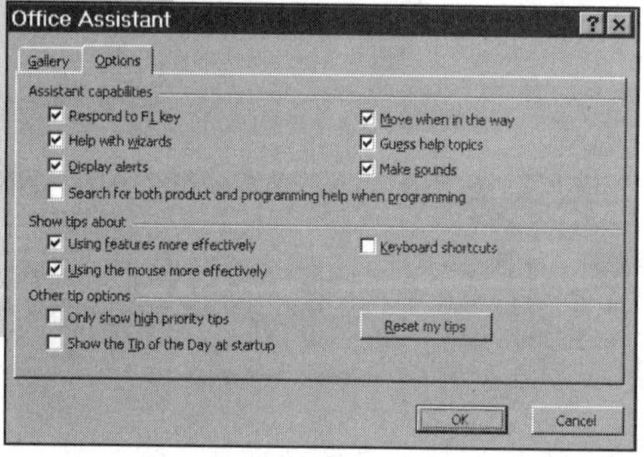

PART IV • MAKING WORD WORK YOUR WAY

Figure 16.30
From the Options tab of the Office Assistant dialog box, you can control the behavior of the Office Assistant.

On the Gallery tab, you can control the appearance of the Office Assistant. You can choose from any of the assistants that you see in Figure 16.31.

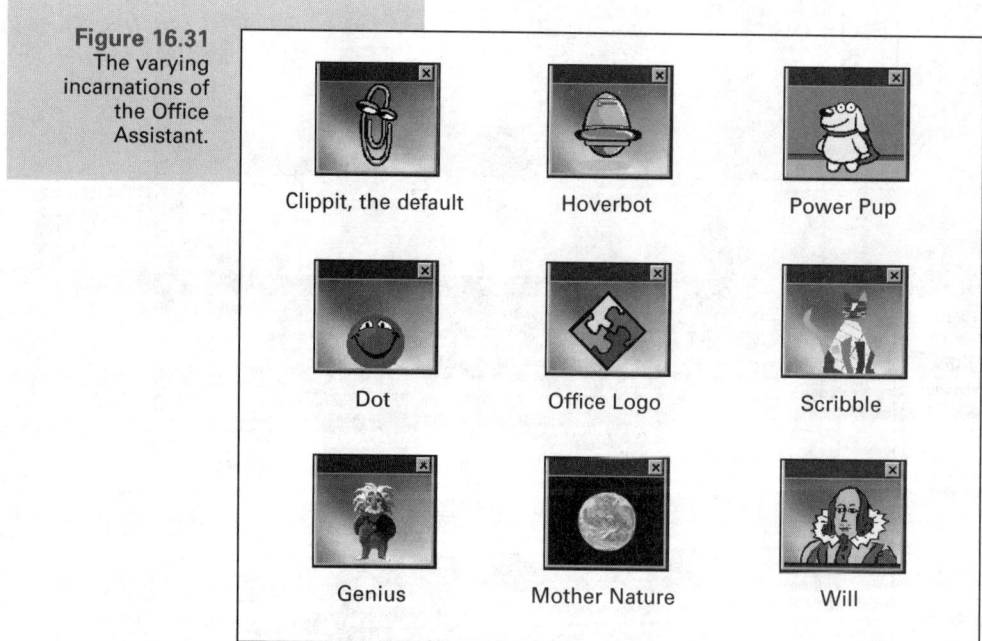

Figure 16.31
The varying incarnations of the Office Assistant.

Changing Word Options

You use the ten tabs in the Options dialog box to change most of Word's settings (choose Tools, Options).

CHAPTER 16 • CHANGING YOUR WORD ENVIRONMENT   427

The View tab (see Figure 16.32) controls the appearance of your screen. The choices on this tab change for each of Word's different views (Normal, Page Layout, Outline, and Online Layout).

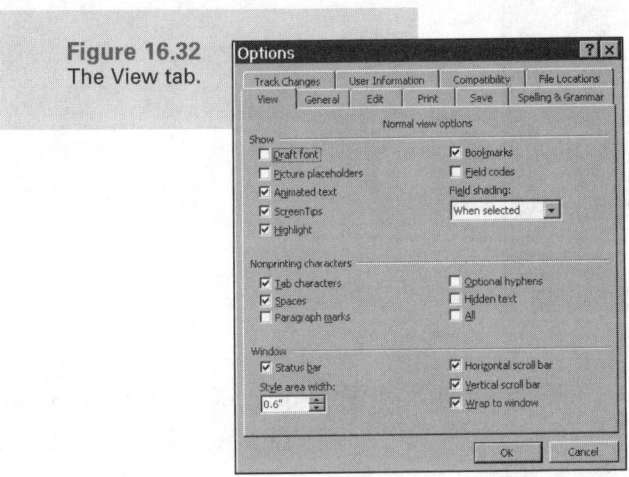

Figure 16.32
The View tab.

The General tab (see Figure 16.33) controls general options such as background colors and repagination.

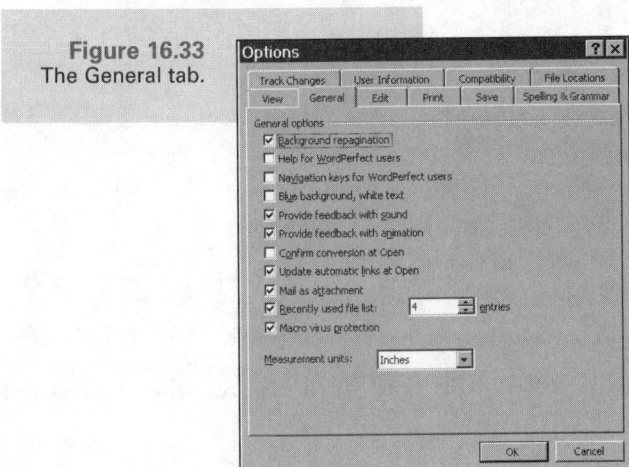

Figure 16.33
The General tab.

The Edit tab (see Figure 16.34) controls editing behavior such as whether typing replaces a selection and whether drag-and-drop editing is available.

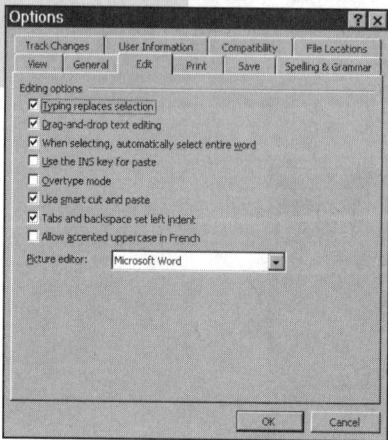

Figure 16.34
The Edit tab.

The Print tab (see Figure 16.35) controls how Word behaves when you print as well as what will print.

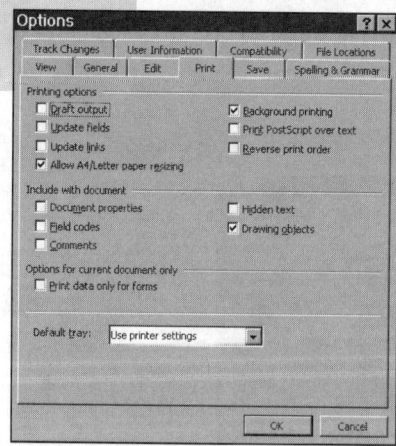

Figure 16.35
The Print tab.

The Save tab (see Figure 16.36) controls how Word behaves when you save a document.

The Spelling and Grammar tab (see Figure 16.37) controls how Word behaves during spelling and grammar checking. These options are available only if you installed the Spelling Checker and the Grammar checker.

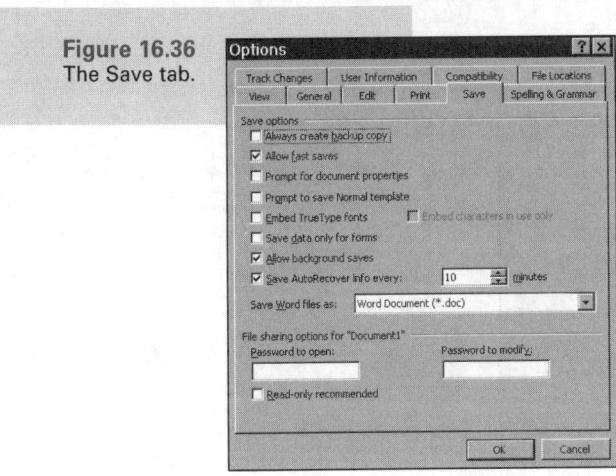

Figure 16.36
The Save tab.

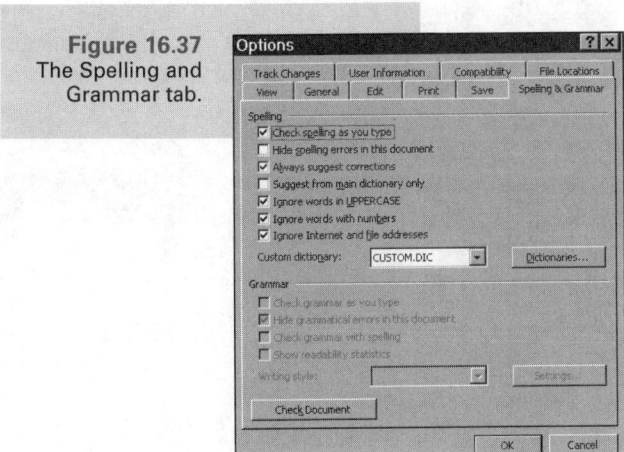

Figure 16.37
The Spelling and Grammar tab.

On the Track Changes tab (see Figure 16.38), you can designate the markings that Word uses when tracking document revisions.

On the User Information tab (see Figure 16.39), you can supply information about yourself that Word will use in envelope and label addresses and in field codes.

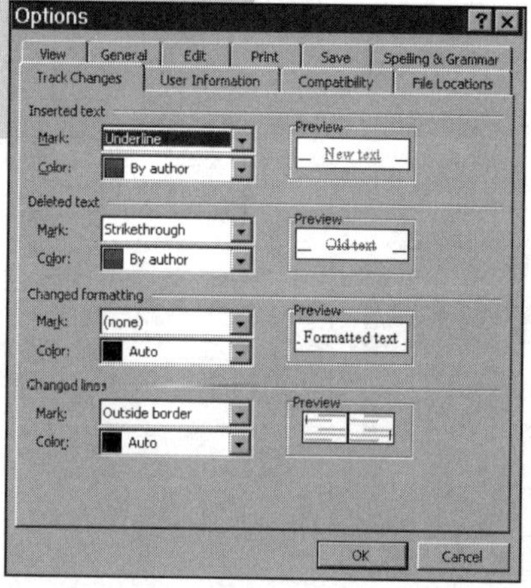

Figure 16.38
The Track Changes tab.

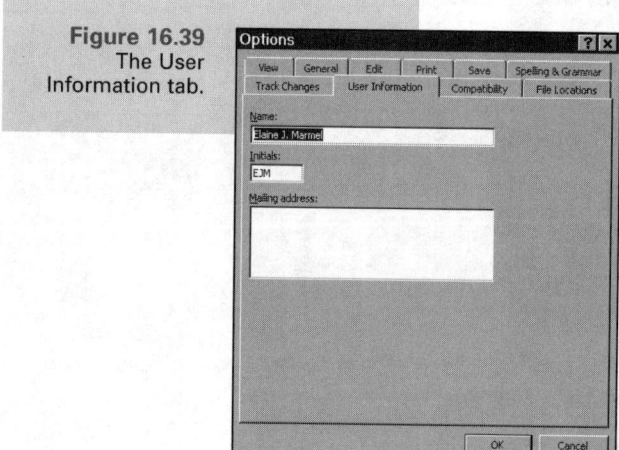

Figure 16.39
The User Information tab.

On the Compatibility tab (see Figure 16.40), you can control how Word behaves when opening documents created in other programs.

From the File Locations tab (see Figure 16.41), you can control the folders Word uses by default. For example, set your Documents folder so that Word knows where to look when opening and saving documents.

Chapter 16 • Changing Your Word Environment

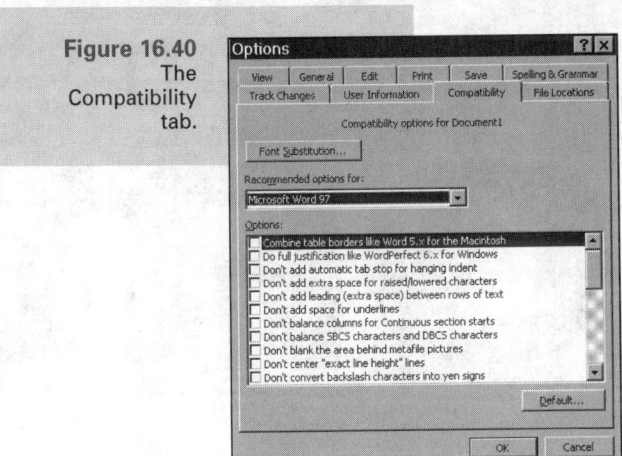

Figure 16.40
The Compatibility tab.

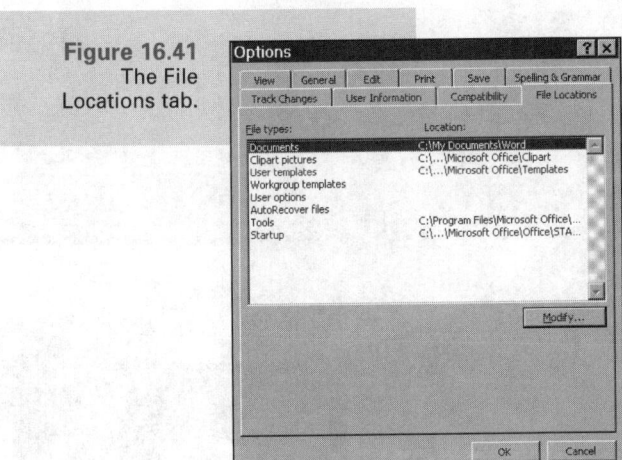

Figure 16.41
The File Locations tab.

microsoft WORD

Part V
Using Word with Others

17 Using the Master Document with a Client Proposal 435

18 Working in a Group: A Department Report 457

micros
WORD

Chapter 17

Using the Master Document with a Client Proposal

IN THIS CHAPTER

- **Understanding Master Documents**
- **Creating the Master Document**
- **Working with Subdocuments**
- **Adding a Table of Contents**
- **Inserting Cross References**

In today's business world, a lot of things are done by committee: designing a new ad campaign, launching a new research project, or creating a client proposal, for example.

Computers linked together in networks allow many people access to the same documents. This can be a great way to get everybody's input. But it can also be a nightmare; duplicated effort, topics not covered, and lost document versions aren't uncommon. Think of too many cooks in your kitchen, and then make it digital.

Word's Master Document feature solves many of those potential problems by offering a system of organization for the various pieces of a larger document. Master documents offer access to those pieces in an efficient way and give you the means to protect the contents so that only the appropriate person can make changes. (The committee meetings are still up to you, though).

Understanding Master Documents

Here's how master documents work. You create one document in a Master Document View, which looks something like Word's Outline View (see Figure 17.1).

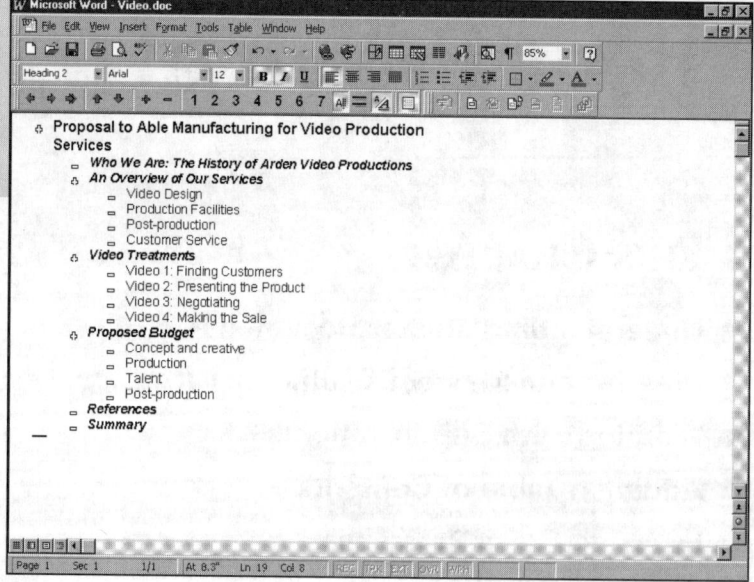

Figure 17.1
Start your master document by building a simple outline in Master Document View.

You can designate one level of headings in the document to use as subdocuments (Word actually bases the subdocuments on that heading style for the whole document). When you make a heading into a subdocument, Word creates and saves such a separate document and places a hyperlink in the master document (see Figure 17.2). Anyone in your workgroup can open that separate file and work on it.

CHAPTER 17 • USING THE MASTER DOCUMENT 437

Figure 17.2
When you make a heading into a subdocument, it displays as a hyperlink, ready for you to jump to it with a few clicks of your mouse.

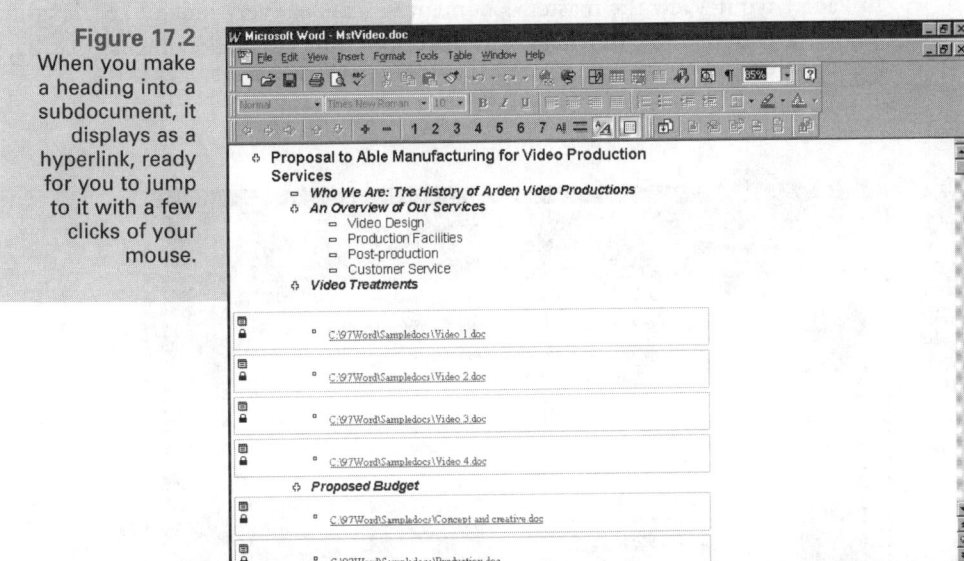

When anyone opens the master document, any working changes to subdocuments are reflected in the master document (see Figure 17.3). You can easily expand or collapse the subdocument text to get the best perspective on your document.

Figure 17.3
Work with document text in subdocuments and see it reflected in the master document.

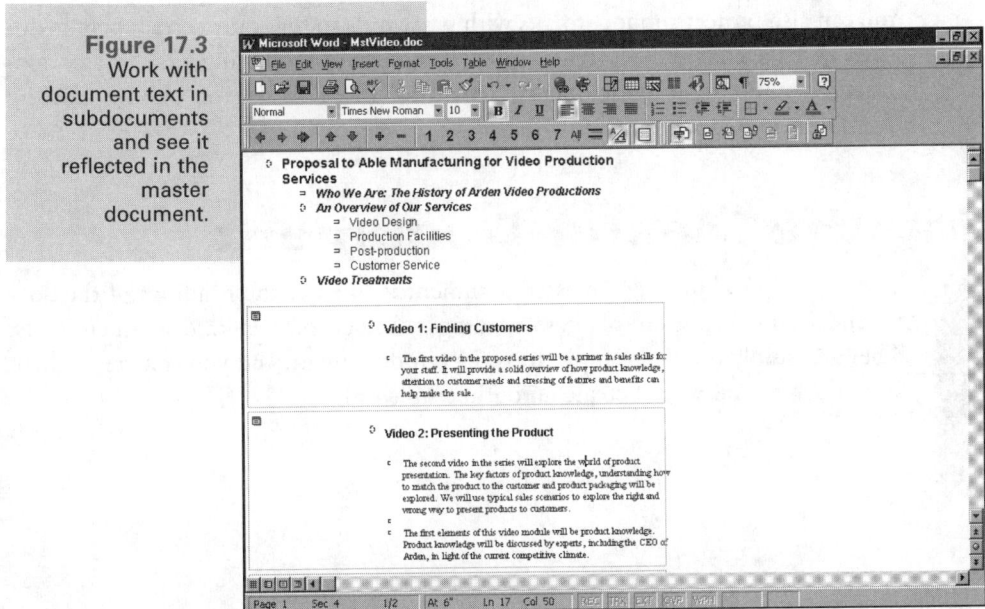

PART V • USING WORD WITH OTHERS

In Page Layout View the master document will appear very much like a lengthy report, with report headings actually corresponding to subdocuments (see Figure 17.4).

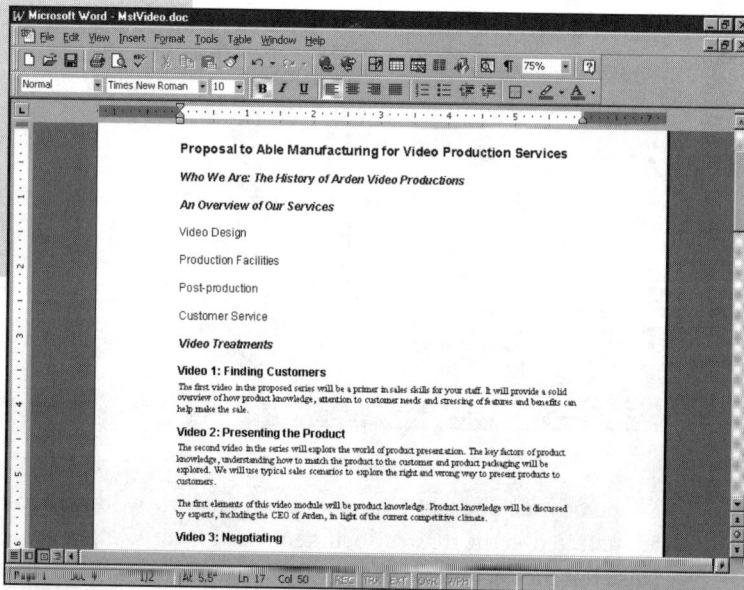

Figure 17.4
The pieces of a master document come together automatically to create professional-looking reports and proposals.

You can also protect subdocuments with passwords so that only certain people can actually make changes. Word also offers flexibility in modifying your master document, combining subdocuments, renaming them, and even adding existing Word documents as subdocuments.

Creating the Master Document

LEARN MORE ABOUT OUTLINING IN WORD IN CHAPTER 4.

The first step to building a master document is to enter the headings of the document. Many, if not all, of these headings will become separate subdocuments. They are simply the major topic areas of your document, and you can create them very much as you would create an outline in Word.

Beginning a New Master Document

In this chapter, you'll build a master document for a proposal from a video company to a manufacturing company to produce a series of sales videos.

Hands On: Using Master Document View

Before you type the actual headings of this proposal, you need to get to know Master Document View.

1. Open Word.
2. Choose File, New and open a new document based on the Blank Document template.
3. Choose View, Master Document. The Master Document View appears, displaying the toolbar shown in Figure 17.5.

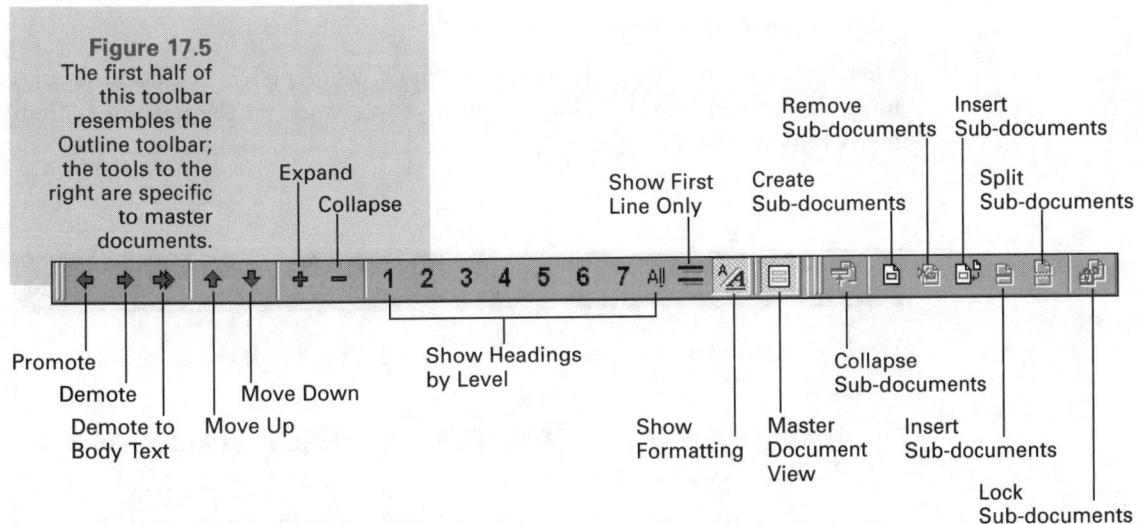

Figure 17.5
The first half of this toolbar resembles the Outline toolbar; the tools to the right are specific to master documents.

4. At the minus symbol where your insertion point is blinking, type the first heading: **Proposal to Able Manufacturing for Video Production Services**.
5. Press Enter. The insertion point moves down a line, and a new minus symbol appears, reading to enter a new heading at the same level.

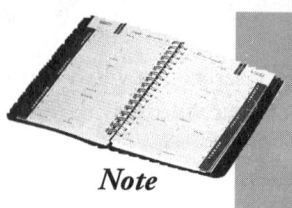

Note: Notice that the headings have the Heading 1 style applied automatically. Master Documents use heading styles to create subdocuments. These heading styles, with their fonts, text effects, and font size settings, also make your document look well designed when you switch to Page Layout view.

Creating a Master Document Outline

At this point, you can continue to enter headings, using the outlining tools to promote and demote headings to various levels of detail as you go. One important thing to keep in mind about the levels of different headings in your outline relative to master documents: when you create your first subdocument from a heading, you are telling Word that only headings at this level (1, 2, or 3, for example) will be made into subdocuments. Not all headings at that level automatically become subdocuments; you must specifically make a heading into a subdocument for that to happen. Any document that you do turn into a subdocument, however, will have to be at that same level.

Therefore, thinking through which headings will represent subdocuments is important as you build the outline. Will people work on the document from major topics, or by subtopic?

Hands On: Building the Outline for Your Proposal

You begin your master document by simply typing in headings, as in the following steps:

1. Type the second heading: **Who We Are: The History of Arden Video Productions**.
2. Click on the Demote button on the Master Document toolbar. The heading indents on level.
3. Press [Enter].
4. Type the next heading: **An Overview of Our Services**. This is automatically placed at the level of the heading that preceded it, so you don't have to demote it.
5. Press [Enter].
6. Type the next heading: **Video Design**.

CHAPTER 17 • USING THE MASTER DOCUMENT

7. Click on the Demote button to indent this heading one level.
8. Continue repeating these steps to create the outline shown in Figure 17.6. Use Demote and Promote buttons to organize headings; for example, when you reach the next major topic (Video Treatments), use the Promote button to move it up one level.

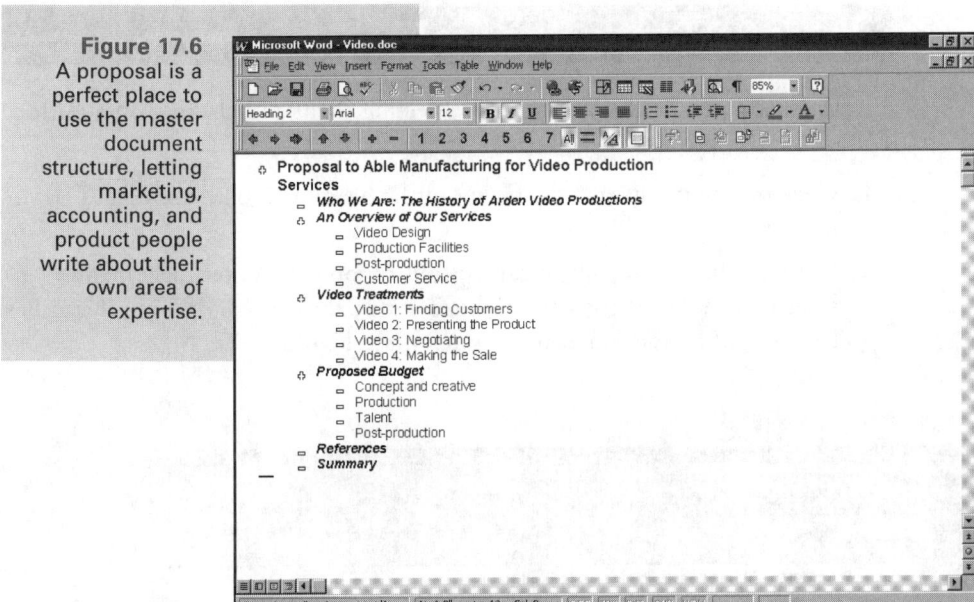

Figure 17.6
A proposal is a perfect place to use the master document structure, letting marketing, accounting, and product people write about their own area of expertise.

Working with Subdocuments

Now that you have the basic structure of your document, it's time to designate certain headings as subdocuments. You can even take an existing Word document and insert it as a subdocument, if you like. After you've created subdocuments, you can manipulate them: move them, rename them, or even combine them as you like.

Notice the outline structure of the master document in Figure 17.6. Plus signs indicate headings that have subheadings beneath them. Minus signs indicate headings with no subheadings below. You can use the outlining tools on the Master Document toolbar to display different levels of detail. Click on the Show Heading 1 to show only headings at that level; Show Heading 2 to show the next level, and son on. Use the Show All Headings button to see the full outline of your master document. For the purpose of the next step, be sure that all headings are showing in your outline.

 PART V • USING WORD WITH OTHERS

Creating Subdocuments

It's time to begin working with subdocuments. Keep in mind that the first heading you designate as a subheading will determine the heading level for all subdocuments.

Hands On: Turning Headings into Subdocuments

Creating subdocuments is as simple as selecting them and clicking on a button. Follow these steps to do so:

1. Click on the minus sign to the left of the heading `Video Design` to select it.

2. Click on the Create Sub-document button on the Master Document toolbar. The heading is now outlined with a thin line, indicating that it has been set off as a separate subdocument (see Figure 17.7).

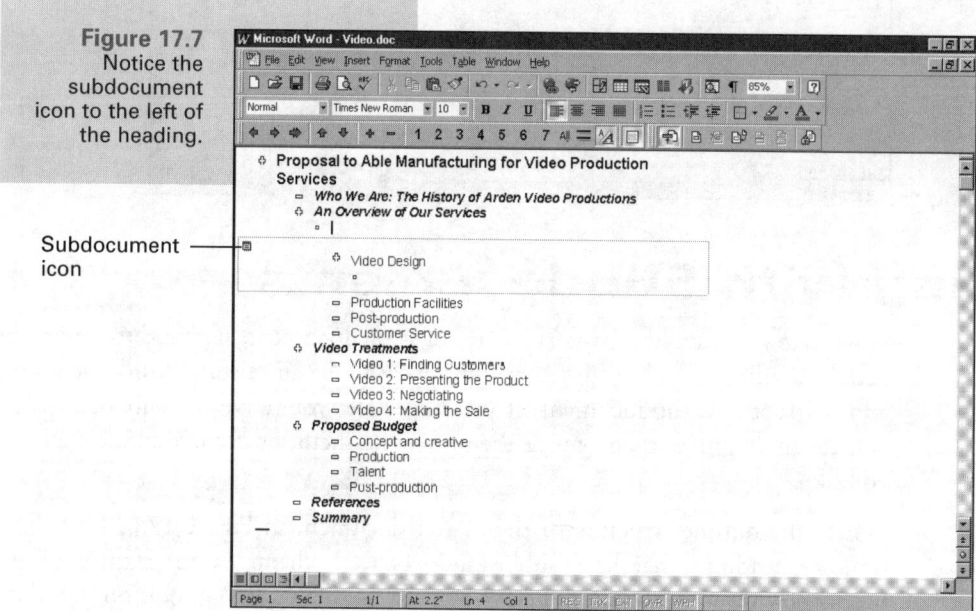

Figure 17.7
Notice the subdocument icon to the left of the heading.

Subdocument icon

3. Choose File, Save, and in the dialog box that appears, name the master document **Video.doc**.

CHAPTER 17 • USING THE MASTER DOCUMENT **443**

4. Save the document by clicking on OK in the Save As dialog box. When you return to the document, the subdocument has also been saved. Now if you close the document and then open it again, the subdocument heading has turned into a hyperlink address, as shown in Figure 17.8.

Whenever you insert or create a subdocument in a master document, saving the document is important so that the new document and connections to it can be established. The subdocument will be saved in the same directory and folder as the master document.

Figure 17.8
The Heading is used as the new document's name.

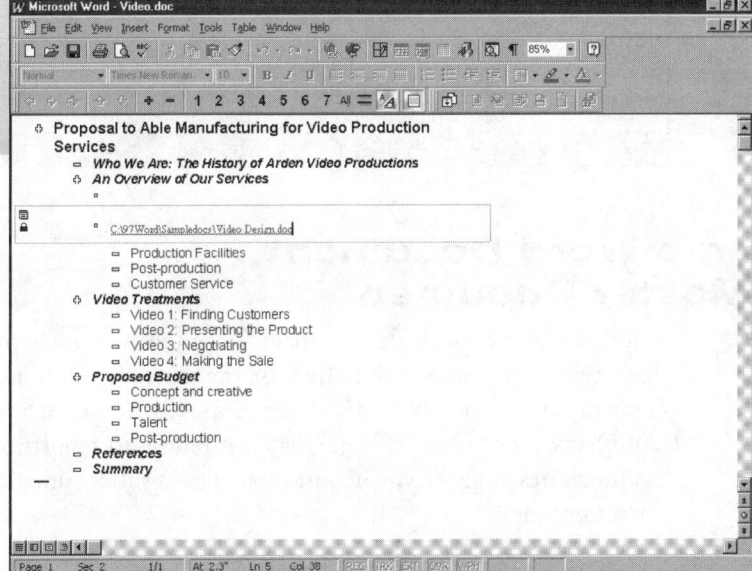

5. Double-click on the hyperlink to open the subdocument, shown in Figure 17.9.

6. Save the document, and then close it by double-clicking on the Close control button in the top-right corner of your screen. You are returned to the master document.

Word has created this subdocument, and if you were to close the master document and go out to the directory where it was saved to, you would see the new subdocument listed as well as the master document.

PART V • USING WORD WITH OTHERS

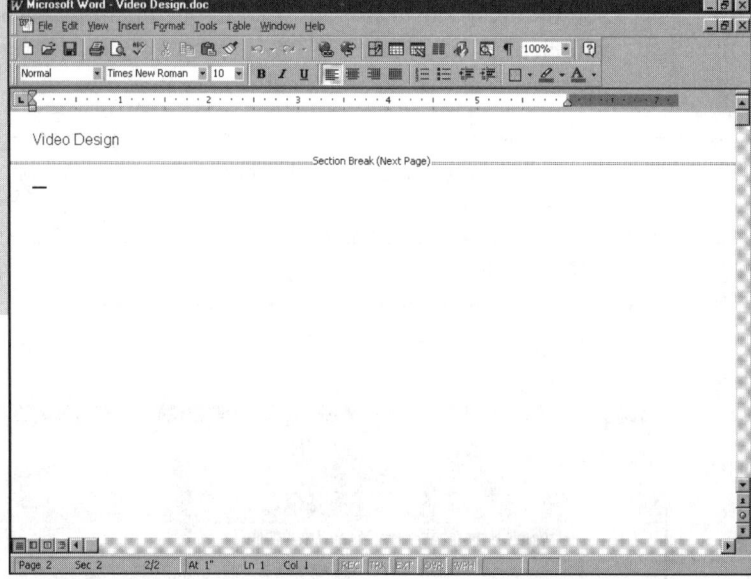

Figure 17.9
The heading appears at the top of your subdocument, followed by a section break. Begin typing text following the break and it will be formatted as body text.

Inserting a Word Document into a Master Document

You may already have a document in Word that you'd like to include in a master document. For example, you often use the same pieces of information about your company and its products in all your proposals. You may have a document called "An Overview of Our Services" that you plug into reports, proposals, and product brochures. Why retype it? Just insert it as a subdocument in your master document outline.

Hands On: Inserting an Existing Document into the Proposal

Follow these steps to place any Word document that already exists into your master document:

1. Place the insertion point at the end of the heading References and press Enter.
2. Click on the Insert Subdocument button on the Master Document toolbar. The Insert Subdocument dialog box shown in Figure 17.10 appears.

CHAPTER 17 • USING THE MASTER DOCUMENT 445

Note

If the Insert Subdocument button isn't available, you may need to click on the Expand Subdocuments button to open your outline up all the way. After you do, the Insert Subdocument button becomes available.

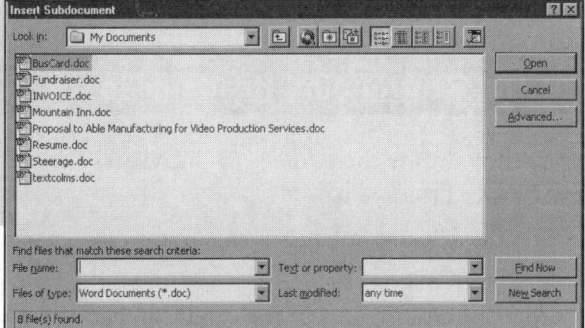

Figure 17.10 Locate the document that you want to insert using the buttons and text boxes in this dialog box.

3. Locate a Word file that you have on a floppy or your hard disk and choose **O**pen to place it in your master document.

The new subdocument appears, preceded by a section break in the master document. If you now click on the Collapse Subdocuments button, the heading will be displayed as a hyperlink to the document that you inserted.

Note

Documents that you insert in a master document may have their own formatting applied. They will take on the formatting of the master document when displayed in master document. What if you want to modify their formatting, however? You can do that by opening the subdocument and making changes there.

Moving Subdocuments Around

After you have created headings and subdocuments in your master document, you may want to reorganize them. This works very much the same as in the Outline View of Word with one exception. By default, when you create a subdocument from an existing file and save it in the master document, it's locked, or protected from modification within the master document. This is indicated by a small lock icon to its left in the master document view. To rearrange any inserted subdocument that is locked (which they are by default), you must first unlock it.

> **Hands On: Rearranging Headings in the Proposal**
>
> 1. If you're not already there, move to the Master Document View (choose View, Master Document).
> 2. Click on the Expand Subdocuments button to expand the outline, if it's not already expanded.
> 3. Place your insertion point in the subdocument called Video Design.
> 4. Click on the Lock Document button on the master document toolbar to unlock the document. The small lock icon disappears.
> 5. Click on the document icon on the far left of the subdocument area and drag the document down. As you do, a gray line will appear (see Figure 17.11).
> 6. When the gray line is in position between the Post-production and Customer Services headings, release the mouse button to place the subdocument.

Renaming a Subdocument

The headings in your documents are used as the filenames for your subdocuments. That may be fine, or you may want to rename a subdocument so that your workgroup can locate subdocuments in a directory more easily.

To rename a subdocument, simply open the document, either by double-clicking the hyperlink to it in the master document or using the File, Open commands from Word to open it as you would any other document. Then simply choose File, Save As, and save the document with a new name. Be sure, however, to then save the master document so that the link to the new file name is updated in the master document.

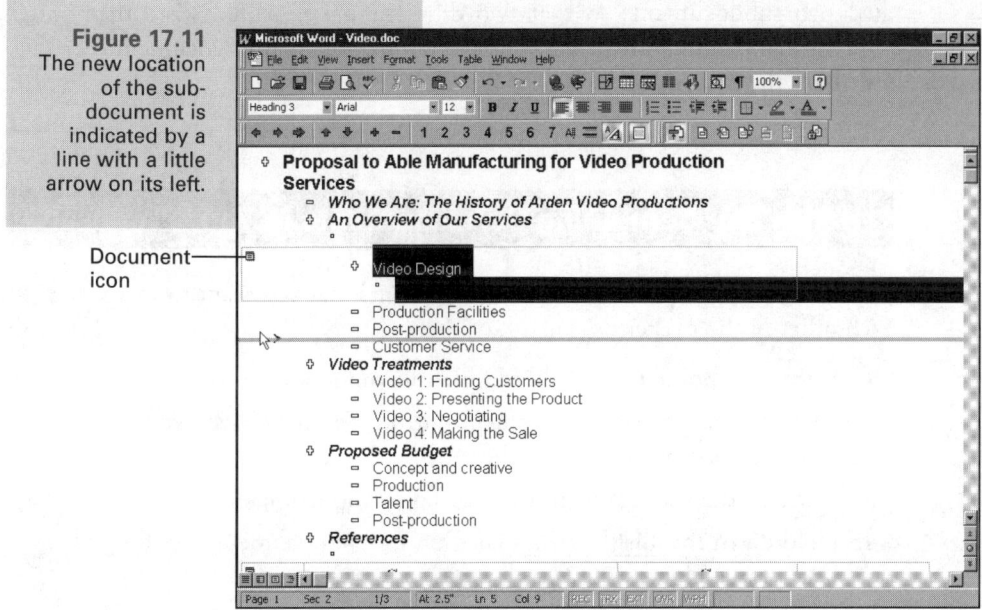

Figure 17.11
The new location of the subdocument is indicated by a line with a little arrow on its left.

Document icon

If you rename a subdocument, the original file still exists. If you don't need it anymore, go in and delete the file to keep your directory from getting cluttered with files that you don't need.

Removing a Subdocument

If you decide not to include a subdocument in your master document, you can do so easily. When you delete the subdocument, however, the file itself is not deleted. The connection to the master document is simply gone. Going to the proper directory and deleting the file itself if you no longer need it is a good idea. This does two things: it reduces clutter on your computer or network, and it prevents a workgroup member from working on that document by mistake.

To delete a subdocument from the Master Document View, you simply click on the subdocument icon to select it, and then press Del.

Combining Subdocuments

Sometimes as a larger document grows, you'll discover that what you thought were two distinct topics actually work well as one topic. Or, you might have cre-

PART V • USING WORD WITH OTHERS

ated two subdocuments so that two different people could write them, after which you'll combine them into one section in your master document. For this, you'll use the Merge Subdocument feature.

Hands On: Combining Subdocuments in Your Proposal

Your first step is to place the two subdocuments that you want to merge next to each other in the master document.

1. Place your pointer on the heading Post-Production.
2. Click on the Create Subdocument button. You now have two subdocuments next to each other.
3. Click on the subdocument icon for Post-Production.
4. Hold down the [Shift] key and click on the subdocument icon for Video Design (see Figure 17.12).

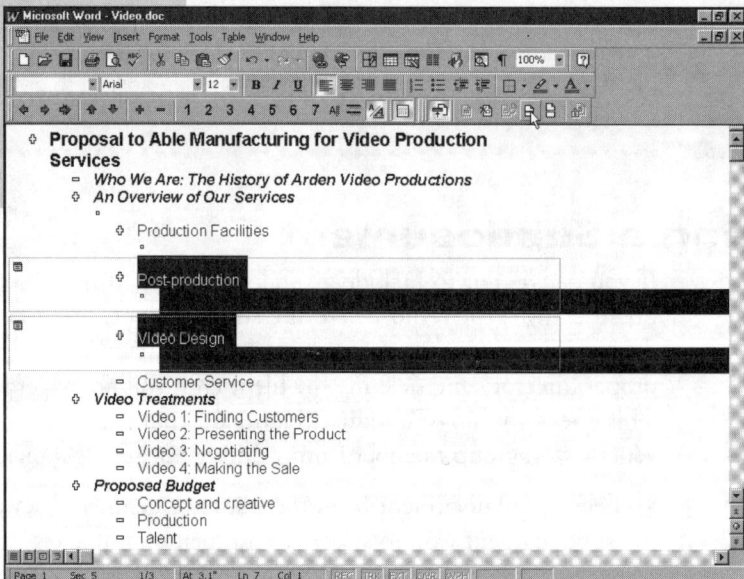

Figure 17.12
To combine subdocuments, you must place them next to each other in your outline.

5. Click on the Merge Subdocuments button on the Master Document toolbar. The two documents form one subdocument (see Figure 17.13).

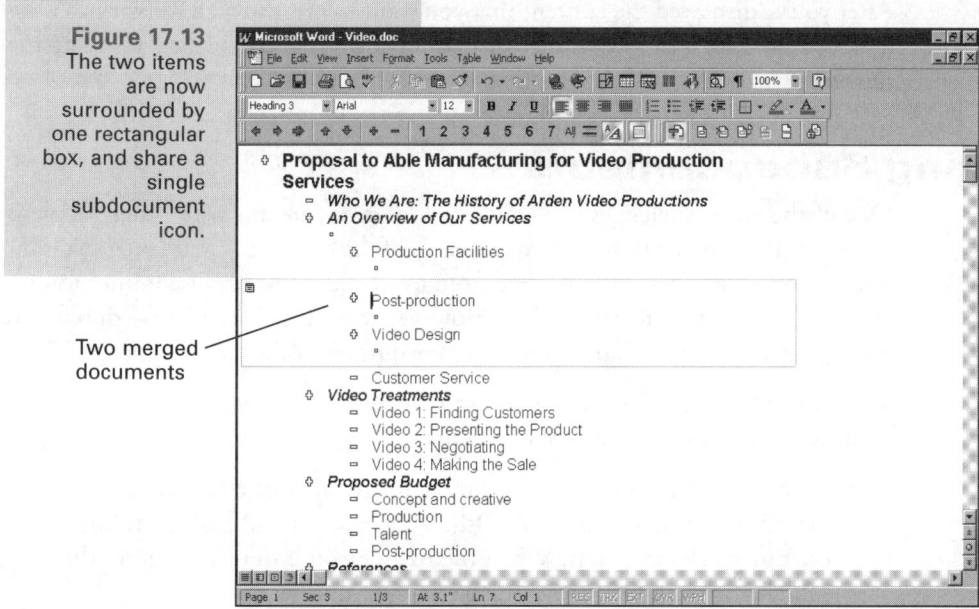

Figure 17.13
The two items are now surrounded by one rectangular box, and share a single subdocument icon.

Two merged documents

Note

> When you combine subdocuments, the first subdocument that you select before merging them is the file into which the contents of the other documents will be inserted. The other subdocument file or files will still exist, however. Once again, if you don't need them as separate files, delete them to save space and keep your directories in order.

Printing a Master Document

When you create a master document, Word gives some flexibility in what elements of it you can print. Sometimes you may want to print only the upper-level topics in your document, and other times you will want to print all the details, including whatever body text has been inserted in each subdocument.

Determining what will print is simply a matter of using the tools in Master Document View to expand or collapse the master document. For example, if you want to print the entire document, click on the Expand Subdocuments button to display all the subdocument text, and use the heading level buttons to determine what level of headings will show. To print just upper-level headings, click on the Collapse Subdocuments button (this is the toggle version for the Expand Subdocuments button) and choose to display only Level 1 headings.

After you've displayed the content that you want to print, switch to Normal View and choose <u>F</u>ile, <u>P</u>rint. Use the settings in the Print dialog box to print the document.

Protecting Subdocuments

One of the great challenges of working on large documents with other people is to be sure that no one is messing with pieces of the document that you don't want anyone to touch. This is often done from overzealousness or miscommunication about who is responsible for what. However it occurs, it can cause duplicated effort, lost content, and not a few angry encounters at the water cooler.

Word provides a few features to ensure that not just anybody can poke around your master document and subdocuments.

- If one person is working on a subdocument, anyone else is effectively locked out of that document. Others can open it and look at it, but they can't make changes to it. When the first person is done and closes the subdocument, it becomes available to everyone again.

- You can assign passwords to documents so that only those who know the password can either open or modify them. You do this by choosing <u>F</u>ile, Save <u>A</u>s, and then click on the Options button in the Save As dialog box. The Save options dialog box appears, as shown in Figure 17.14. You can assign a password to open or modify the document, or make the entire document read-only by selecting the <u>R</u>ead-only Recommended check box. This setting will only alert the reader that it's wise not to make changes to the document; however, once he or she has read and accepted that warning dialog box, the file is editable. When you're done making settings, click on OK to return to the Save As dialog box and save the file.

A little advice about passwords. Don't make them so simple that anyone could guess them. Don't use your name, your department number, or anything obvious. Do make them complicated enough that no one could easily stumble across them. Combinations of numbers and letters work best (such as BT3270J); the more random, the better.

Finally, protect passwords by instructing the members of your workgroup not to give them out to anyone. If they must—for example, because one is out sick and somebody else needs to work on that person's portion of the document—have the absent person let you know when he or she returns so you can change the password. In any case, advise your co-workers to change their passwords on a regular basis just to be really safe.

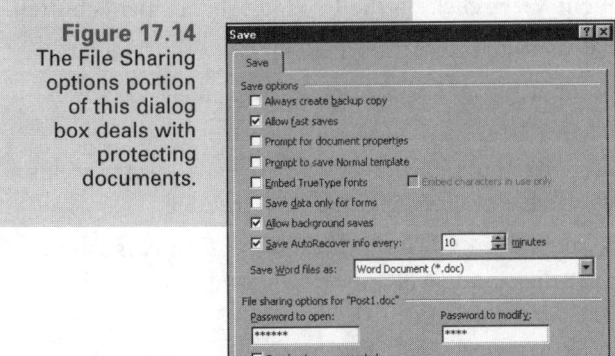

Figure 17.14
The File Sharing options portion of this dialog box deals with protecting documents.

Finding Your Way Around a Master Document

Master documents are typically larger documents, sometimes more than 100 pages or more in their final form. It's useful to the readers of such documents to be able to find things in them easily. Two tools are particularly useful to your readers: a table of contents that helps them locate topics by page number; and cross references to relevant information elsewhere in the document.

Adding a Table of Contents

Word can instantly generate tables of contents based on its built-in heading styles, or other styles that you create and apply to headings. The key to use this feature is being consistent in how you use these styles. You can designate, for instance, that all headings with the heading 1 style appear in your table of contents, but no others. Or, you can have all headings with Heading 1, and Heading 2 styles included in the table of contents, and have all the Heading 2s indented so that the reader can see the subtopic structure more easily. You can generate tables of contents with or without associated page numbers.

Hands On: Add a Table of Contents to Your Proposal

If you've used Word's standard styles for headings, generating a table of contents is simple to do by following these steps:

PART V • USING WORD WITH OTHERS

1. From Master Document View, click on the Expand subdocuments button.
2. Choose View, Normal to switch to the Normal View.
3. Place the insertion point at the end of the document and choose Insert, Break, or simply press Ctrl+Enter.
4. When the Break dialog box appears, click on OK to place a page break so that you can begin your table of contents on a separate page.
5. Choose Insert, Index and Tables. Click on the Table of Contents tab to make the active tab; the dialog box will appear as shown in Figure 17.15.

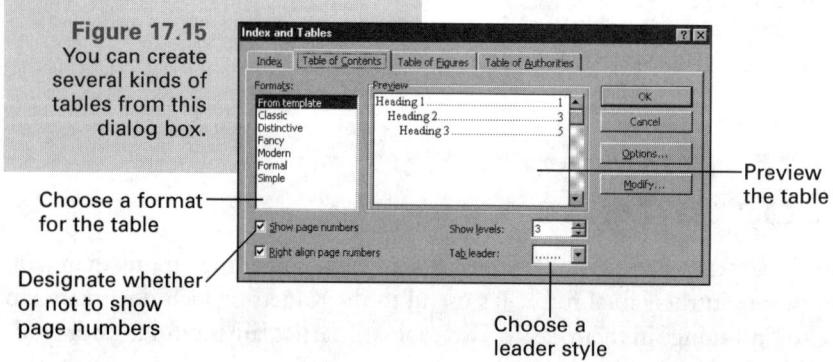

Figure 17.15
You can create several kinds of tables from this dialog box.

Choose a format for the table

Designate whether or not to show page numbers

Preview the table

Choose a leader style

By default, Word used Heading 1, 2, and 3 styles for the levels of the table of contents. If you wanted to change this, you could click the Options button in this dialog box. You will see the Heading 1, 2, and 3 styles checked, at three levels of indentation. If you wished to use your own heading styles on which to base the table of contents, you could place level numbers next to different headings, as shown in Figure 17.16.

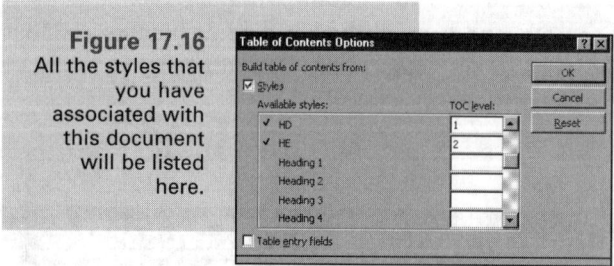

Figure 17.16
All the styles that you have associated with this document will be listed here.

6. In the Index and Tables dialog box, select the Distinctive format from the Formats list.

CHAPTER 17 • USING THE MASTER DOCUMENT **453**

7. Click on OK to insert the table. It will look something like the table in Figure 17.17; depending on the document that you inserted as a subdocument, page numbers may differ.

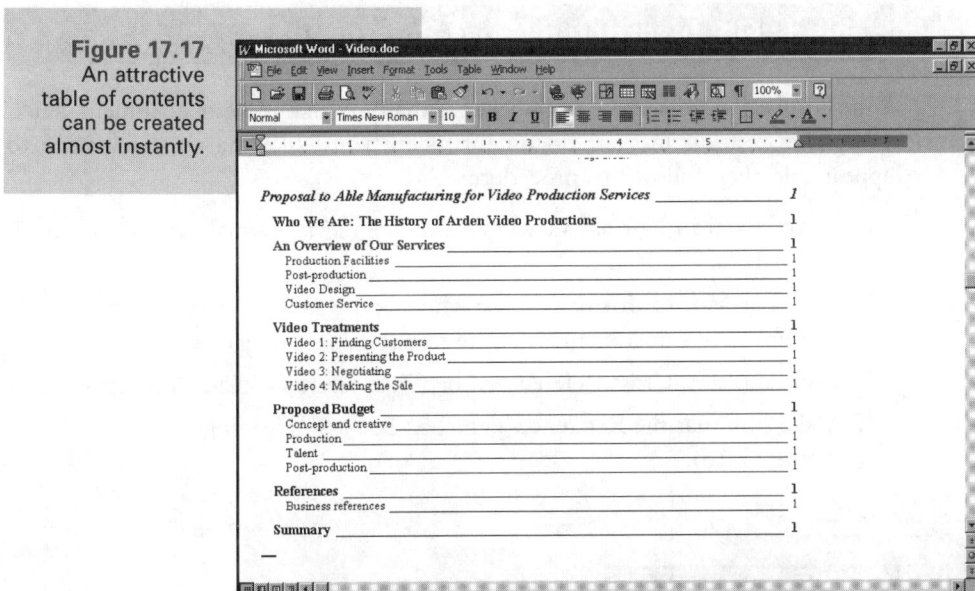

Figure 17.17
An attractive table of contents can be created almost instantly.

From the Index and Tables dialog box, you can choose to show or not to show page numbers. If you show them, you can choose to have different styles of leaders (which are the line or series of dots that extends from the end of each heading to the page number to help the reader's eye follow across). You can also change the default setting of showing three levels of heading to more or less. The longer the document, the more valuable the table of contents is to help your reader find his way around.

Tip

An Index, Table of Figures, or Table of Authorities can be generated in a similar way, using the same dialog box.

Inserting Cross References

Cross references help your reader find information related to or providing background for a point in your document. They are a sort of internal roadmap, allowing your readers to find their way around to information that interests them.

Inserting cross references is simple. You can insert a reference to a heading, a page number, or simply the direction to look above or below the current text.

Hands On: Inserting a Cross Reference

You can place a cross reference anywhere that you like in your document. First, go to the location in your document where you'd like the cross reference to appear, and then follow this procedure:

1. If you're not in Normal View, move there (<u>V</u>iew, <u>N</u>ormal, or click on the Normal View button).
2. Type **For More Information see** where you want the cross reference to appear in your document. (Be sure to put a space after "see").
3. Choose <u>I</u>nsert, Cross-<u>R</u>eference. The Cross-reference dialog box appears.
4. Make sure that the Reference <u>T</u>ype text box says Heading (see Figure 17.18).

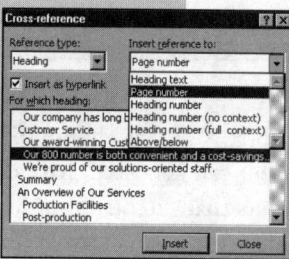

Figure 17.18
Select a heading and the kind of reference that you want to make here.

5. Open the Insert <u>R</u>eference To drop-down list, as shown in Figure 17.18, and select Heading Text. Notice that you can also select the page number, or just the statement Above or Below.
6. Select the heading Production Facilities in the For <u>W</u>hich Heading list.
7. Click on Insert. When you're done, click on Close to close the dialog box.

CHAPTER 17 • USING THE MASTER DOCUMENT 455

> FOR MORE ABOUT HYPERLINKS, SEE CHAPTER 11.

The reference to the other heading is inserted. If you wish, you can now type the word Page and a space, and then add the page number to the reference. You might want to type a comma, and then insert the cross-reference above or below. If you choose the latter, Word will pick the appropriate one, based on this heading's relative position to the cross-reference heading.

Note

Notice that by default, the Insert as Hyperlink check box is selected in the Cross-reference dialog box. You can remove this check mark, but if you leave the setting, the person reading this document on-screen can immediately jump to that section of the document by just clicking on the cross reference itself.

microsoft WORD

Chapter 18
Working in a Group: A Department Report

In This Chapter

- Tracking Changes
- Creating Document Summaries
- Routing Documents Online

Workgroups are a fact of today's business world. Whether you're joined by expertise, corporate structure such as a department, or interest, building documents with others can be a challenging experience. In the previous chapter, you learned how master documents can be used to allow each member of a workgroup to work on his or her own piece of a document. Then, those pieces can be easily brought together. But another work style exists. In this

PART V • USING WORD WITH OTHERS

scenario, several people work on the same piece of a document, with one writing a draft, another editing it, a third adding comments, and a fourth incorporating the changes, for example.

Being able to follow these revisions in a logical way, route the document from person to person, and summarize the final document are all tools for effective workgroup writing. Those are the features that we cover in this final chapter.

Tracking Changes

Whether each member of a writing team is adding text, editing existing text, or just adding comments about the text, a logical way of tracking those layers of input is vitally important.

> TO LEARN ABOUT PROTECTING DOCUMENTS WITH MULTIPLE USERS, SEE CHAPTER 17.

In olden days (before computers), creative but ultimately ineffective methods were used to track document changes. These ranged from different colors of pens for each person's input to hundreds of little sticky notes tacked onto dog-eared pages. One pen running out of ink or one sticky note fluttering away on the breeze could be disastrous. Word offers a far superior system of tracking changes either on-screen or in print. Word can even compare one version of a document with another and highlight the differences for you. When you're done reviewing changes, you can incorporate them all in seconds.

How Tracking Changes Works

Word's revision tracking feature will indicate changes in a document in a few ways:

- Deleted text will be formatted with strikethrough.
- New text will be underlined and will appear in a color. If you have a few people making revisions, each person's revisions will appear in a different color.
- A vertical line will appear in the margin next to paragraphs with changes.
- New to this version of Word is a small text box that appears when you pass your mouse pointer over revised text. This text tells you the change, who made it, and the date (for example, `Deleted by Nancy Stevenson, 1/23/97`).

You need to keep a few variations in mind. Changes made to revisions (for example, if you make a spelling mistake as you enter a revision, and then correct it) aren't indicated as revisions. Only changes to the original text are marked as revisions.

If you delete a selection and move it elsewhere in the document, the deleted original will have strikethrough formatting, but the moved copy will appear as entirely new text wherever you move it in the document. This can be the only confusing feature of tracking. If someone makes a change to a paragraph, for example, either before or after moving it, the changes won't be shown because it looks like entirely new text.

Hands On: Tracking Changes in a Report

1. Choose File, New.
2. In the New dialog box, click on the Reports tab, shown in Figure 18.1.

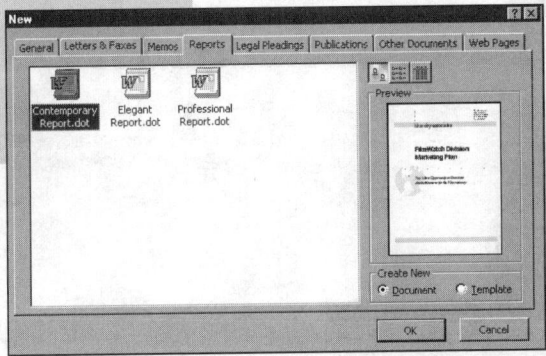

Figure 18.1 Word has three styles of report templates to choose from.

3. Select the Contemporary Report template and click on OK. A report titled "FilmWatch Division Marketing Plan," shown in multiple page display in Print Preview in Figure 18.2, appears.
4. Choose Tools, Track Changes. From the submenu that appears (see Figure 18.3), choose Highlight Changes.
5. The Highlight Changes dialog box appears (see Figure 18.4). This dialog box has three settings:
    - Track changes while editing turns on and off the tracking feature.
    - Highlight changes on screen lets you see marks indicating changes on your screen as you work.
    - Highlight changes in printed document shows revision marks, including new text as gray and underlined in black-and-white documents.

Figure 18.2
This report has sample text that describes how to develop a report in Word.

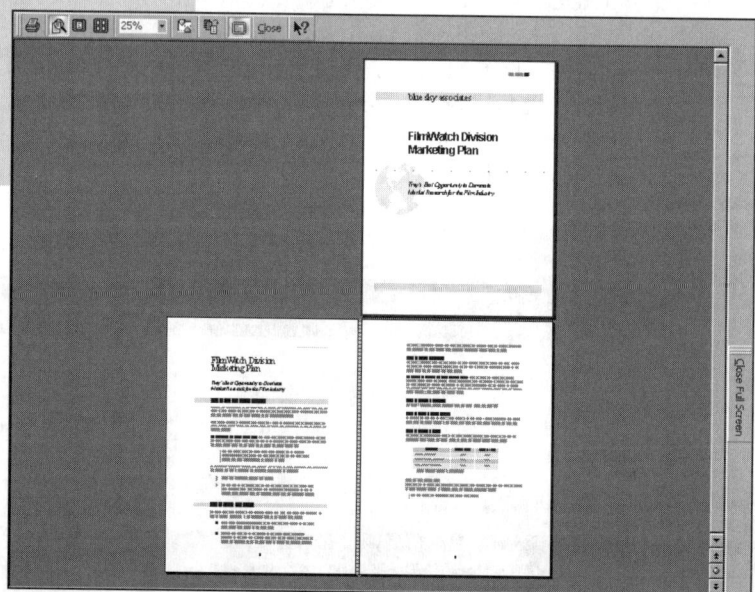

Figure 18.3
The Track Changes menu has three choices. The first two deal with tracking changes, the third with comparing one document with another.

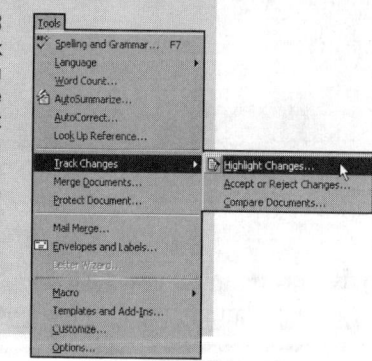

Figure 18.4
Three check boxes control the tracking function.

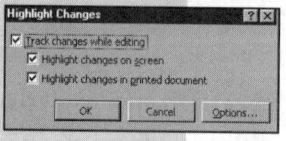

CHAPTER 18 • WORKING IN A GROUP: A DEPARTMENT REPORT   461

> **Tip**
>
> If you want to modify what colors or marks are used to indicate revisions, click on the Options tab in the Highlight Changes dialog box and select new ones.

6. Select the check box for <u>T</u>rack Changes While Editing to turn on the feature.
7. Click on OK to close the dialog box and return to your document.
8. On the first page of the document, delete the word `Trey's` and type **Today's**, as shown in Figure 18.5.

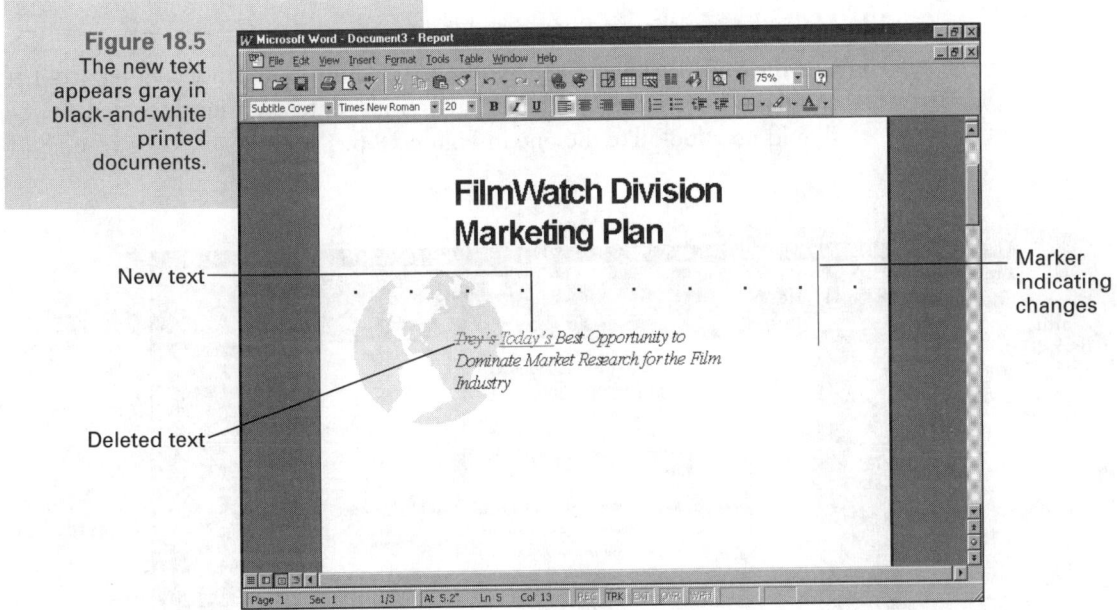

Figure 18.5
The new text appears gray in black-and-white printed documents.

New text
Deleted text
Marker indicating changes

9. Move to the next page and change `Trey's` to **Today's** again in the subheading.

> **Tip**
>
> If you have multiple instances of something to be changed, you can use Find and Replace to make edits simultaneously. All changes made this way will be tracked.

10. Replace the heading `How to Use This Report Template` with the heading **How We Compare to the Competition**.

462 PART V • USING WORD WITH OTHERS

11. Beneath the second paragraph, insert this comment: **Joe, shouldn't we add something about company history here? Marsha.**

Note

You might want to designate a text style for comments or create a new one. Then, if you should want to get rid of just comments but leave edits in, you can use Find to locate all text with that style and delete it quickly. Also, doing this makes comments easier to spot for your readers.

12. Make the text that you just typed Italic.
13. Cut the fourth paragraph (beginning "In addition to producing reports") and paste it after the comment that you just entered. Your document should now look like the one in Figure 18.6.

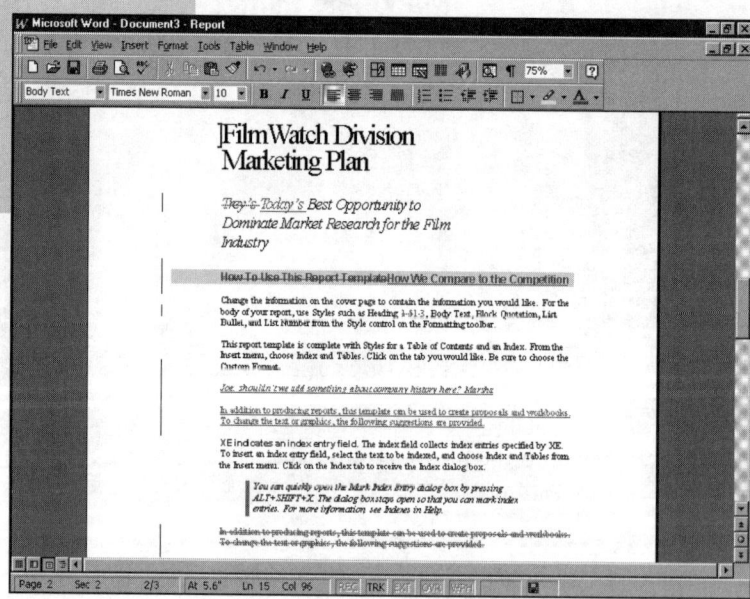

Figure 18.6
Notice the vertical lines indicating each paragraph where a change has occurred.

14. Move your insertion point over the new heading that you typed. A text box, like the one in Figure 18.7, appears.

CHAPTER 18 • WORKING IN A GROUP: A DEPARTMENT REPORT   **463**

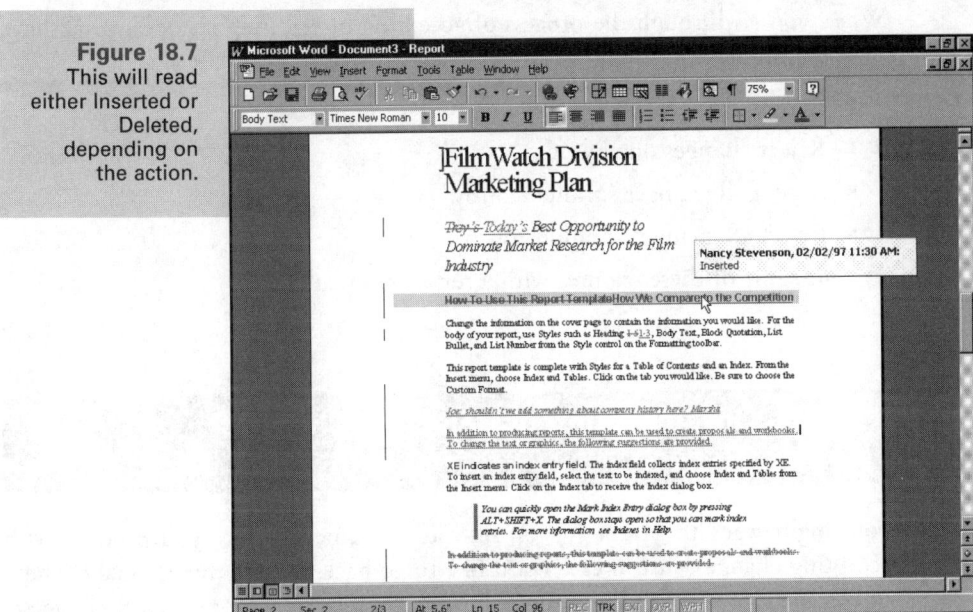

Figure 18.7
This will read either Inserted or Deleted, depending on the action.

This last feature can be a mixed blessing. No more taking credit for someone else's work: if you get your buddy to do your work for you, your boss will know it now! The name that appears here is taken from the user profile that Windows creates for you. If this is a company workstation, it may say something like `Company Computer User` here. If you really want to use this feature accurately, make sure that everyone working on the document has the correct user name associated with his or her computer and that they all use their own computers to make changes.

Accepting Revisions

When you get through the revision phase for your document and are ready to make it final, you can easily accept revisions, either one by one or all at once. After you've accepted revisions, if you leave on the revision tracking feature, any new changes will be marked. This removal of revision marks is useful if, after editing a first draft, you find that it's too full of revision marks to see what you're doing. Accept changes to date and start fresh with a clean second draft for everyone to comment on.

PART V • USING WORD WITH OTHERS

When you go through the process of accepting or rejecting changes, you'll have several options:

- Accept changes one by one
- Reject changes one by one
- Accept all changes simultaneously
- Reject all changes simultaneously

Try out some of these features with a report template.

Hands On: Accepting or Rejecting Changes to Your Report

You might want to save a version of your document before you proceed with accepting changes, just in case you'd like to go back and see the original changes or comments. When you're ready, follow these steps to accept or reject changes:

1. Choose Tools, Track Changes, Accept or Reject Changes. The dialog box shown in Figure 18.8 appears.

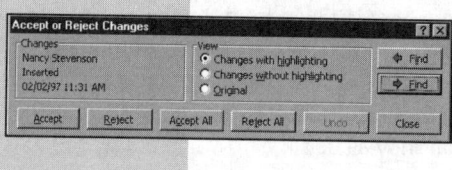

Figure 18.8
The author of the currently displayed change will be listed in this dialog box.

Tip

To help you make decisions about how changes impact the document, you can choose to look at your document with changes highlighted, look at it without highlighting (so that you can see how the document would look with all changes accepted), or look at the original version of the document. Select the option that you want by using the View control buttons.

2. Click on the second Find button. This finds the next change going forward in the document. The other Find button looks for changes going backward. The first change is highlighted, as in Figure 18.9.

3. To accept this one change, click on Accept.

CHAPTER 18 • WORKING IN A GROUP: A DEPARTMENT REPORT   465

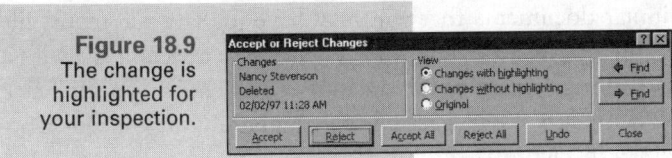

Figure 18.9
The change is highlighted for your inspection.

4. Click on the Find (forward) button. You move to the next change.
5. This time, click on Accept All. The message in Figure 18.10 appears.
6. Click on Yes to accept all changes, then use the Close button in the top-right corner to close the dialog box.

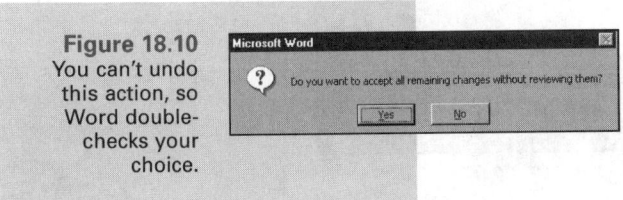

Figure 18.10
You can't undo this action, so Word double-checks your choice.

Reading through all revisions once before running the Accept or Reject Changes feature, and then simply accepting all changes, is probably easiest. Reviewing change-by-change with the dialog box on-screen, especially in lengthy documents, can be very time consuming. If you're concerned about wanting to get all the revision marks back, you can always run a document comparison between the original document and the one you've accepted changes in.

Comparing Documents

Sometimes you don't have control of a document from its inception to track changes as they occur. For example, two versions of a basic client proposal might be floating around when you start with a department, and you'd like to compare them to see how they differ. To do that, you can use the Compare Documents feature in Word. Here's how this works.

You open document A and then run the compare feature. Word asks you which document you want to compare A with. You choose document B. Anything that's different about B will be marked in A. That means that any text that's in B but not in A will be added, underlined, and in color. Any text that's not in B will be formatted with strikethrough in A.

PART V • USING WORD WITH OTHERS

Try this with two similar documents that you may have (or save the report file that you've been working on, make several changes, and save a second file with a new name). Open the edited version of the document and choose Tools, Track Changes, Compare Documents. The Select File to Compare With Current Document dialog box shown in Figure 18.11 appears.

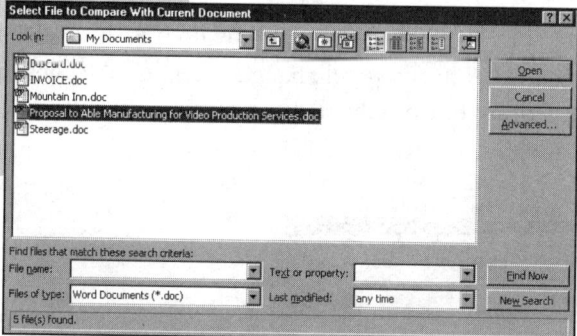

Figure 18.11
Just like other Open dialog boxes, find the file that you want here.

When you locate the original file, choose Open. All differences between the first and second document are indicated with revision marks. You can then use the Accept or Reject feature, or simply close the file without saving any changes to it.

Tip

One other feature helps with combining two documents into one. Choose Tools, Merge Documents to merge another document with one that's currently open. This doesn't compare the contents of the two documents, however; it simply places a copy of one file at the end of the first file. If you want to see the new material clearly, be sure to turn on the revision tracking feature before doing this.

Creating Document Summaries

Word has a feature that's rather intriguing, although not quite precise at this time. Called AutoSummarize, it creates a summary of key points in your document. Supposedly, the feature works by picking out sentences that Word recognizes as being relevant to the main theme of the document. What it really does is score sentences that have words that occur the most in the document (not including words such as *a*, *the*, and *and*. The more commonly used words in a sentence, the higher the score. Higher scoring sentences get included in the summary.

Chapter 18 • Working in a Group: A Department Report 467

> **Check out Chapter 4 for ways to use Word's Outline view to create overviews of document contents.**

Obviously, this isn't a foolproof system. It can, however, give you the skeleton of a document summary. One other interesting use of this feature is to see whether you've kept a consistent focus in your document. If what you consider your main topic doesn't even get called out in a summary, perhaps you should check your focus and use more consistent terminology for key concepts.

To create an AutoSummary, you'll use the dialog box shown in Figure 18.12.

You can choose to have your summary displayed one of four ways:

- Highlight Key Points shows the full document, with the summary text highlighted.
- Insert an Executive Summary places the summary text at the top of the document. You could use this as the basis of the first section of your document, often called an executive summary.
- Create a New Document tells Word to create a completely new document for the summary.
- Hide Everything But the Summary shows the summary text, but the original document is still open. A toolbar appears that will allow you to toggle back to the full document display.

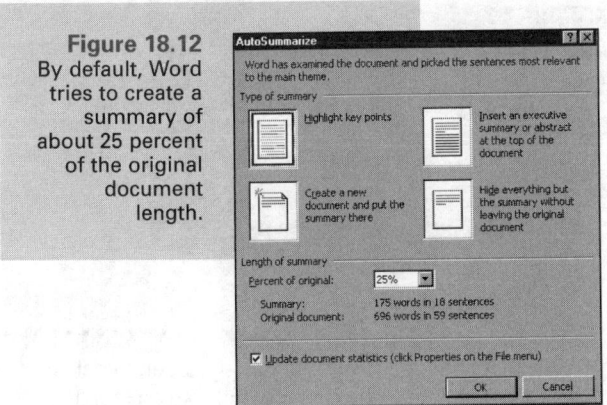

Figure 18.12
By default, Word tries to create a summary of about 25 percent of the original document length.

The Length of Summary section of this dialog box tells you that Word has created a summary that uses a certain percent of the number of words in the original. It also offers statistics about words and sentences in both the summary and original. If you'd like to add this summary to the document statistics, you can leave the Update Document Statistics check box selected.

468 PART V • USING WORD WITH OTHERS

Hands On: Displaying a Document Summary

1. Choose Tools, AutoSummarize.
2. Select one of these summary types and click on OK; you'll see something like the documents shown in Figures 18.13 and 18.14. The first shows the summary text highlighted.
3. Click on the button on the left of the AutoSummarize toolbar and you can see just the summary text, as in the second figure.

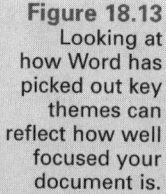

Figure 18.13
Looking at how Word has picked out key themes can reflect how well focused your document is.

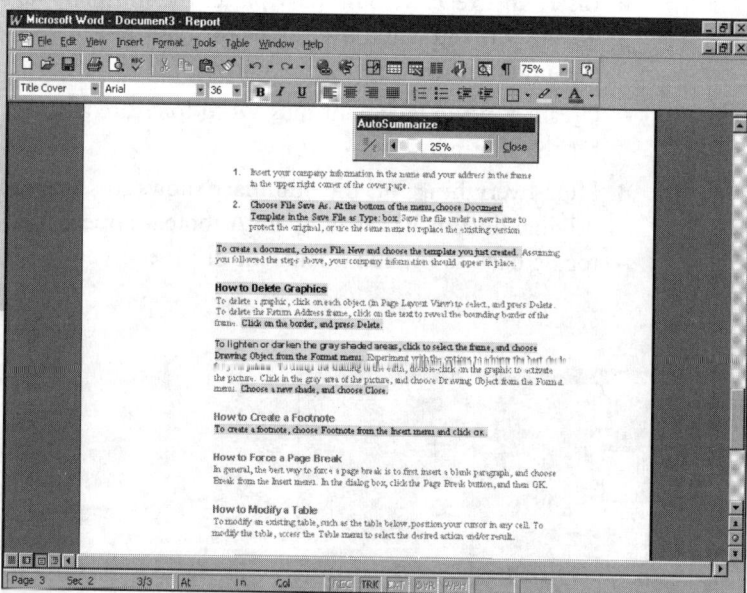

 A tool called Find All Word Forms is installed with Word. If it hasn't been installed because of a custom installation, however, AutoSummarize won't work as well. Rerun Word Setup to install it if you have problems.

Routing Documents Online

You can use Word and Microsoft Exchange (or any 32-bit MAPI e-mail program) to send documents around to your team. The Send To feature in Word allows you to create a routing slip. This routing slip can send the document to one group

Chapter 18 • Working in a Group: A Department Report 469

alias, or to each member, one after the other. You can even determine the order in which people receive the document.

Of course, this assumes that you have a network in place and that each recipient is using either Microsoft Exchange or the e-mail system. You can try this through an online service, such as the Internet, but Microsoft warns that routing documents may not work across electronic mail gateways. This feature works best within a company network or intranet.

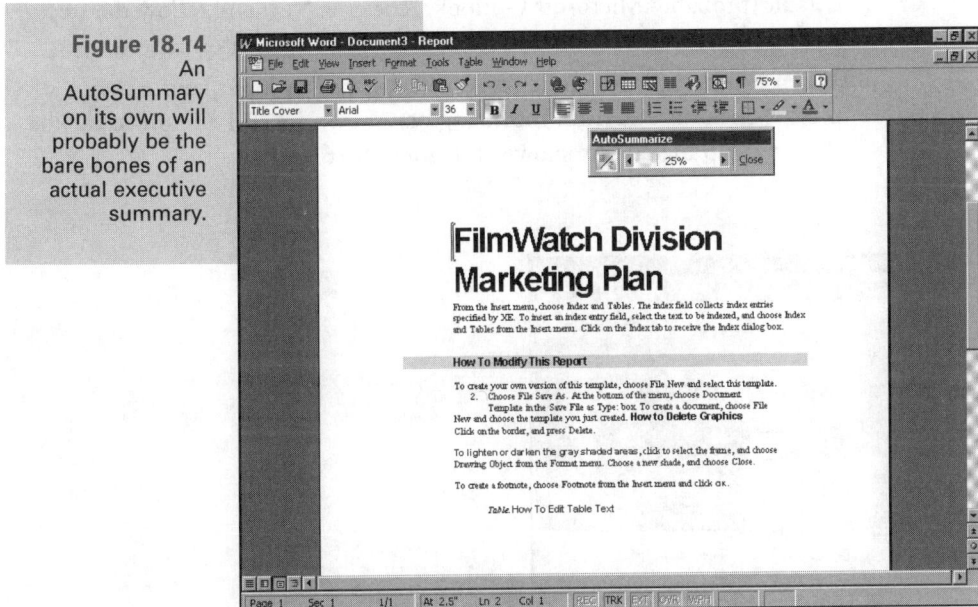

Figure 18.14
An AutoSummary on its own will probably be the bare bones of an actual executive summary.

Creating a Routing Slip

Creating a routing slip is a matter of creating the slip, which designates the order of recipients and can include a message. The first time that you do this process, you may also have to use a wizard to fill out an e-mail profile.

Hands On: Creating a Routing Slip for Your Report

1. With the report file that you've been editing open, choose File, Send To, Routing Recipient. If you haven't set up an e-mail profile in Word, you may see the Choose Profile dialog box shown in Figure 18.15.

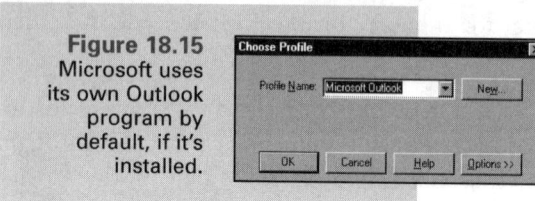

Figure 18.15 Microsoft uses its own Outlook program by default, if it's installed.

2. If you need to designate an e-mail profile other than the one shown by default (probably Microsoft Outlook), click on New and follow the steps in the wizard to enter your e-mail address and server information.

3. When you have finished the steps of the wizard to input your e-mail profile, click on OK from the dialog box shown in 18.15 to proceed. The Routing Slip dialog box shown in Figure 18.16 appears.

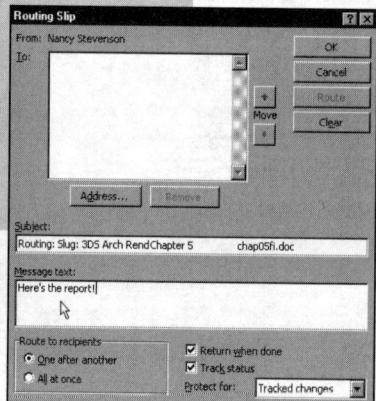

Figure 18.16 The name of the document to which the slip will be attached is listed as the Subject by default.

4. Click on Address to add recipients. A new dialog box appears; it's shown in Figure 18.17 with addressees added.

5. To add names to your recipient list, choose the source of the addresses (for example, Microsoft Outlook or other address book). A list of names in that address list appears.

CHAPTER 18 • WORKING IN A GROUP: A DEPARTMENT REPORT   **471**

If you don't have any address book on your computer and you use the wizard to set up your e-mail profile, respond Yes when the wizard asks whether you want Word to create an address book. Then you can use this dialog box to enter addresses into it.

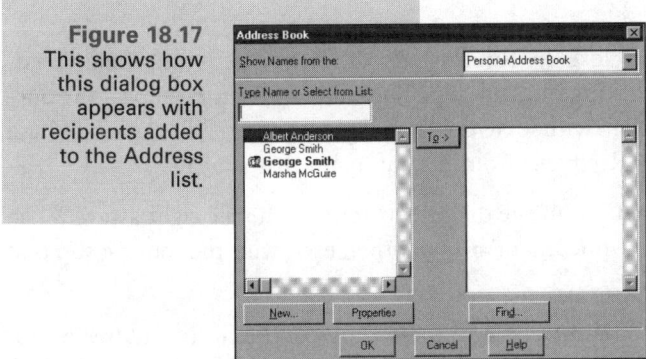

Figure 18.17
This shows how this dialog box appears with recipients added to the Address list.

6. To create a new listing in an address book, choose <u>N</u>ew and enter the person's name and address.

7. When you're done adding recipients' names, click on OK to return to the Routing Slip dialog box, which now lists recipients' names in the order that you added them (see Figure 18.18).

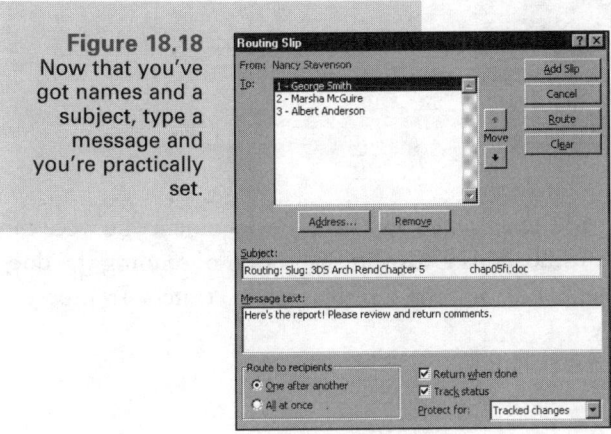

Figure 18.18
Now that you've got names and a subject, type a message and you're practically set.

PART V • USING WORD WITH OTHERS

8. If you want to change the order of recipients, select a name and use the Move arrow keys to move it in the list.

9. Type a message in the Message Text box.

10. Leave the control box for Route to Recipients set to One After Another. That way, you control sending each copy of the document.

Sending the File

At this point, you could close the Routing Slip dialog box without actually sending the document by clicking on Add Slip. This adds the routing slip to the document and lets you deal with delivery later by choosing File, Send To and choosing Next Routing Recipient from the submenu that appears.

You can also choose Route from the dialog box to send the file right away. When you do, you can send one document after another, each with the routing slip that you just created attached.

When you do choose to send the file, if there's any conflict in the addresses (for example, if you've addressed the same person twice), you might see a Check Names dialog box like the one shown in Figure 18.19.

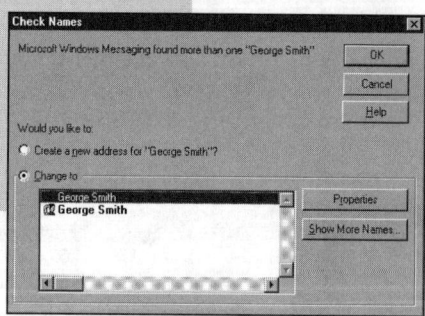

Figure 18.19
If you've duplicated entries or have a bad address, Word may ask you to verify it.

If no confusion exists about addresses, when you send the document you'll see the dialog box shown in Figure 18.20. This gives you the option of sending the document without the routing slip, or using the slip that you've created. To proceed, you simply click on OK.

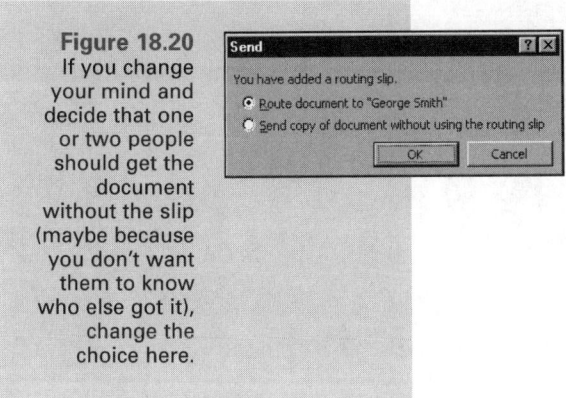

Figure 18.20
If you change your mind and decide that one or two people should get the document without the slip (maybe because you don't want them to know who else got it), change the choice here.

To send the document to the next recipient, choose File, Send To, Next Routing Recipient until you're done sending the file to all the people on your routing list.

Glossary

3-D. An effect used with pictures to add the appearance of depth (three dimensions) using shading.

A

Abstract. An executive summary of the contents of a document, generated using the AutoSummarize feature of Word.

Alignment. The arrangement of text or an object in relation to a document's margins or the edges of a cell in a table. Alignment can be left, right, centered, or justified.

Animation. A computer file that combines visual elements such as drawings in such a way as to suggest motion of the image or images.

Applet. A small software program provided with Word that allows you to perform additional operations, such as WordArt for enhanced text effects.

AutoCorrect. A feature of Word that corrects common spelling mistakes (such as *teh* for *the*) automatically.

AutoFormat. A Word feature used with tables. AutoFormat allows you to apply predefined sets of formatting to a table's text, rows, and columns.

AutoShape. A set of automated drawing shapes.

AutoText. A feature of Word that allows you to save a set of text and insert it into your document by entering a word or phrase.

Axis (pl. axes). In a graph, one of two value sets (see also *y-axis* and *x-axis*).

B

Bar chart. A type of chart that uses bars of varying lengths to represent values.

Bold. A style applied to text to make the font lines thicker.

Border. A visible line surrounding text or objects.

Break. An instruction embedded into a Word document that indicates a change, such as a Page Break to start a new page.

Bullet. A symbol that precedes an item in a list. Bullets can be any shape found in a typeface, but most commonly, bullets are solid black circles.

C

Callout. An AutoShape category used to direct a reader's attention to something using a text label.

Case. One of two forms of text, including uppercase and lowercase. Uppercase letters are also called capital letters and are used to begin the first word at the beginning of a sentence, as well as for certain proper nouns and names.

Cell. The area where a row and column in a Word table or Excel worksheet intersect.

Chart. Also called *graph*. A visual representation of numerical data.

Clip art. A ready-made drawing that can be inserted in a Word document.

Clipboard. A temporary storage area in memory where text and/or graphics are stored as you copy or move them.

Clip Gallery. A collection of clip art, pictures, and sound files that comes with Microsoft Word.

Column. A set of cells running vertically down a table or worksheet. Also a format used to display text in a newspaper-like arrangement down a page.

Contrast. The amount of black and white in a picture that can be adjusted to modify the image's seeming brightness.

Crop. A tool used to erase portions of a picture.

D

Data. Information, which can be either numerical or textual.

Data form. A place where data, such as data used in a mail merge operation, is stored in individual records.

Data series. In charts, elements that represent a set of data, such as pie segment, line, or bar.

Data source. In a Word mail merge, the information that is used to replace field codes with personalized information, such as names and addresses.

Desktop. The main area of Windows where you can open and manage files and programs.

Dialog box. A window that appears during some procedures in Word that allows you to make settings by entering text, selecting things from lists, or checking boxes or buttons.

Document Map. A feature that allows you to view and move among various levels of headings in a document in a pane displayed to the left of the document in various Word views.

Drag and drop. A method of moving text or objects by clicking on an object with a mouse, dragging it to a new location, and releasing the mouse button to drop the object into its new location.

Drop Cap. A special format applied to the initial letter of the first word in a paragraph.

E

E-mail. Electronic mail. Messages distributed and received over a computer network or system of networks, such as the Internet.

F

Fax Wizard. A Word wizard that steps you through the procedures involved in generating a fax cover sheet and faxing a document.

Field. A placeholder for corresponding data that will be automatically inserted, such as a date and time field.

Fill. To place a color or line pattern in the interior of an object, such as a square or cell of a table.

Font. A design set of letters, symbols, and numbers.

Footer. Text entered in a footer placeholder, which is then automatically placed at the bottom of each document page.

Format. To add settings for font, font style, color, and line style to text or an object.

Format Painter. A feature of Word that allows you to easily copy all formatting applied to one set of text to any other.

G

Go To. A feature of Word that allows you enter a variety of criteria, such as page number or specific text, so that Word can place that location in your document on-screen.

Gradient. A shading effect that moves from lighter to darker in such a way that it suggests a light source shining on the object containing the gradient.

Graph. Also called *chart*. A graph is a visual representation of numerical data.

Graphics. A file containing visual data, such as a line drawing, rather than text.

Graphics file format. Individual systems of storing graphics file data. Graphics file filters are required to read various graphics file formats; Word comes with several built in.

Grayscale. A process used in printing documents that utilizes shades between white and black to enhance computer graphics printouts.

Gridlines. The lines dividing rows and columns in a table.

H

Handle. Small squares that appear when you select an object that allow you to resize it. Also called a *selection handle* or *resizing handle*.

Header. Text entered in a header placeholder, which is then automatically placed at the top of each document page.

Highlight. A feature that places colored highlighting on-screen for selected text.

HTML. Hypertext Markup Language. The language used to create hypertext.

Hyperlink. Any underlined text or hyperlink object created using hypertext that a computer user can click on with a mouse, causing a different hypertext document to display.

I

Icon. A graphic representation used on toolbars to represent the various functions performed when those buttons are pressed with a mouse.

Image Control. A Word feature used to adjust the appearance of pictures relative to grayscale settings.

Indent. To set text away from a margin by a specific distance, as at the beginning of a paragraph.

Insertion point.

Internet. A globally connected system of computer networks allowing online access to various types of documents such as graphics and hypertext documents.

 **Italic**

Italic. A font style that applies a slanted effect to text.

J

Jump. Within a hypertext system, to move from one hypertext document to another using hyperlinks.

Justify. One type of alignment that spreads letters on a line so that they are spaced out between the left and right margin.

L

Label. A descriptive text element added to a chart to help the reader understand a visual element. Also refers to row or column headings.

Label (mailing). A Word document that uses preset and custom dimensions to print onto sheets of mailing labels.

Landscape. Orientation of a document so that, when printed, text runs from left to right along the longer edge of a piece of paper.

Left aligned. Text that is lined up with the left side of a tab setting or document margin, as with a set of numbers in a column.

Legend. In a chart, a feature that defines the relationship of the graphic symbols to the data elements for the reader.

Line style. Effects using width, arrows, and dashes that can be applied to a line.

M

Macro. A method of recording and playing back a series of keystrokes or commands using a software program's command language. Word uses the Visual Basic command language for macros.

Mail merge. A procedure whereby you use a form document, insert placeholders for types of data called *fields*, and merge that document with specific data to produce personalized mailings.

Main document. In a mail merge, the document, such as a form letter, to be personalized with specific data through the use of merge fields.

Margin. A border that runs around the outside of a document page, in which nothing will print.

Master Document. A feature of Word that allows you to assemble a set of subdocuments into one larger document.

Media Player. A Microsoft Windows accessory program for playing multimedia files.

O

Object. Any graphic, drawing, chart, or other file placed within a Word document.

Office Assistant. A feature of Word 97 for Windows that allows you to enter questions in natural English-language sentences.

OLE. Object Linking and Embedding. Microsoft Corporation's standards built into Windows that allows you to embed a document created in one software application into a document created in another software application. OLE also allows the establishment of a relationship (link) between the embedded data in one document to the original data.

Order. The hierarchy of placement of images on a document page relative to each other; order can make one object seem to be placed behind or in front of another object.

Orientation. A setting that designates whether a document will print with text running along the long or short side of a piece of paper.

Outline. A hierarchy of lines of text that suggests major and minor ideas. Outline View in Word is the primary view for working with outlines.

P

Page break. An instruction that can be embedded into a Word document to instruct Word to move to a new page at that point.

Page Layout. A view in Word that is commonly used for arranging objects on a page and drawing.

Page Setup. The collection of settings that relate to how the pages of your document are set up, including margins, orientation, and the size of paper that each page will print on.

Password. A word selected by a Word user to protect a document. After a document is protected, the correct password must be entered to modify that document.

Paste. To place text or an object on the Windows Clipboard in a document.

Paste Link. To place a copy of a file in a Word document while establishing a link with the original file.

Pattern. An arrangement of dots or lines that can be used to fill the center of an object.

Pie chart. A round chart type in which each pie wedge represents a value.

Portrait. An orientation that places text from left to right along the shorter side of a piece of paper.

Print Preview. A Word feature that allows you to see a preview of how your printed document will look on-screen before you print it.

Protect. To make settings so that only someone with the correct password can modify a Word document.

R

Redo. To restore an action that you have undone using the Undo command.

Revisions. Highlighting effects applied to indicate any changes in text from one version of a document to another. See also *Tracking Revisions*.

Right aligned. Text that is lined up with the right side of a tab setting or document margin, as with a set of numbers in a column.

Rotate. To move an object along a 360-degree path.

Row. A set of cells running from left to right across a table or worksheet.

Ruler. An on-screen feature provided to help you place text and objects accurately on a page.

S

Save As. To save a previously saved worksheet with a new name or properties.

Scan. To electronically record a hard copy image as a graphics file; this file can then be opened and manipulated within software such as Word.

ScreenTip. A Word Help feature that displays the name of a tool in a small box when you move your pointer over the tool.

Scrollbar. A mechanism used with a mouse for navigating around a document horizontally or vertically.

Selection bar. An invisible bar along the left side of a document; when you place your mouse pointer in it, it can be used to select a single line or multiple lines of text.

Shading. A pattern ranging between white and black that fills an object.

Shadow. A drawing effect that appears to place a shadow alongside an object.

Sort. To arrange data alphanumerically in either ascending (A–Z) or descending (Z–A) order.

Sound Recorder. A Microsoft Windows accessory program that can be used to record, edit, and play back sound files.

Spelling checker. A feature of Word that checks the spelling of words in your document against a dictionary and flags possible errors for correction.

Spike. A feature of Windows that allows you to copy several selections to a holding area (called the Spike) and paste them in a new location all at once.

Start Page. The hypertext document on the World Wide Web that will display when you first open the Web from Word.

Status Bar. An area at the bottom of Word that provides information about the document, such as what page, line, and column your pointer is currently resting in.

Style. A predefined set of formats that you can apply to text simultaneously.

Style Gallery. A collection of template files that can be individually attached to a Word document.

Symbol. A typeface that uses graphics such as circles, percent signs, or smiling faces in place of letters and numbers.

T

Tab. A setting that can be placed along the width of a line of text that allows you to quickly jump your pointer to that setting.

Table. A collection of columns and rows, forming cells at their intersection, to organize sets of data.

Template. A predefined collection of formatting and style settings on which you can base a new document.

Text box. A floating text object that is created using the Word drawing toolbar. Text can be entered into this object, which can be moved and resized, just like graphic objects.

Text wrap. This feature forces newly entered text to wrap to the next line when the insertion point reaches the right margin.

Tracking Revisions. A feature that allows you to keep a record of changes to a Word document or compare one document with another.

U

Undo. To reverse the last action performed.

Uppercase. A capital letter.

V

View. In software, various displays of documents or information that allow you to perform different tasks or see different perspectives on information; for example, the Outline view in Word.

W

Watermark. A shading effect for pictures that makes them appear to be a background impression, such as a watermark impression on fine stationary.

Web. See *World Wide Web*.

What's This? A part of the Word help system. When you select What's This?, your pointer changes to a question mark and you can click on any on-screen element to receive an explanation of that element.

Wizard. A feature that walks you through certain procedures, producing something such as a table, letter, or chart, based on answers that you give to questions and selections made in Wizard dialog boxes.

WordArt. An applet included with Word used for adding special effects to text, such as curving the text.

Word count. A tally of the number of words in a document.

World Wide Web. A hypertext system of documents transmitted and accessed over the Internet.

Wrap. See *Text wrap*.

X, Y, Z

X-axis. In a chart, the vertical value axis.

Y-axis. In a chart, the horizontal value axis.

Zoom. To modify view settings so that what you are seeing on your screen is a percentage (larger or smaller) of a document page's actual size.

Index

Symbols/Numbers
32-bit browser support, long filenames, 297

A

actions, undoing, 125, 191
Add/Remove Programs Properties dialog box, 263
address books
    data source merge document selection, 228-229
    memo recipients, 269
Align Left button
    Formatting toolbar, 58
    Standard toolbar, 300
Align Right button, Formatting toolbar, 58
alignment, text, 57-59
ALL CAPS text, 56
AltaVista, search engine, 286
America Online, 256
animated text, 340-342
announcements
    AutoCorrect example, 93-97
    multimedia, 321-345
antonyms, Thesaurus, 107
Arial Black font, 151
Arial font, 151
    Blank Document template, 43
attachments, memos, 270
AutoCorrect, 92-97
    announcement sample, 93-97
    automated lists, 62-63
    automatic document style formatting, 359-360
    capitalization exception rules, 95
    copyright symbol (c), 92
    described, 92-93
    entry creation, 96-97
    overriding, 95-96
AutoCorrect dialog box, 40, 62-63, 94-95
AutoFormat, 97-98
    simple tables, 197
AutoFormat dialog box, 359
automatic save, documents, 24
AutoShapes button, Drawing toolbar, 173-175
AutoSummarize, document summaries, 466-468
AutoSummarize toolbar, 468
AutoText, 33-36
    Spike feature, 40
    uses for, 35
AutoText toolbar, 34-35
Avery labels, 140

B

background
    document fill effects, 342-344
    patterns, Web pages, 304-305
    sounds, Web pages, 313-314, 334
Background Sound dialog box, 314
Backspace key, correcting/deleting text entry, 34
Baskerville fonts, 53
Blank Document template, 30
    Arial font, 43
    heading styles, 43
    left aligned text, 58
    memos, 50
blank lines, Enter key, 31
bmp (Windows Bitmap) filename extension, 323
Bold button, Formatting toolbar, 10, 41
bookmarks, document, 381

Borders and Shading dialog box, 153-154, 205
borders
    newsletter issue/volume numbers, 153
    photographs, 329
    table modifications, 203-206
    table row/column separators, 191-192
bottom margin, 124
Break dialog box, 114-115
brightness, photograph adjustments, 329-332
browsers
    32-bit long filename support, 297
    Internet Explorer, 23, 280
    previewing Web pages, 314-317
    Web, 280
built-in styles, 353-354
bulleted lists, 60
    custom bullet styles, 63-65
Bullets and Numbering dialog box, 63-66
Bullets button, Formatting toolbar, 60-61
bullets, Web page text, 300
business report, 179-219
buttons
    adding to toolbars, 402-404
    removing from toolbars, 406-407
    toggle, 10

C

capitalization, AutoCorrect exception rules, 95
Caption dialog box, 186, 380
captions
    numbered, 379-381
    table, 185-186
CD-ROM
    clip art, 171
    Kodak Photo CD, 322
    ValuPack folder, 373
Cell Height and Width dialog box, 201
cells
    border modifications, 205-206
    deleting from table, 188
    horizontal information alignment, 200-202
    insertion point navigation, 182
    merging, 187-188
    splitting, 188, 190-191
    tables, 47, 181
    text direction control, 299-200
    vertical information alignment, 202-203

Center button, Formatting toolbar, 58, 198, 201
Center tabs, 44
Center Vertically button, Tables and Borders toolbar, 202
Change Text Direction button, Tables and Borders toolbar, 200
character styles, described, 351-352
characters
    curly braces {}, 378
    fields, 377
    leader, 47
    minus sign (-), 16
    plus sign (+), 16
    quotation marks (""), 378
Chart Options dialog box, 215
Chart Type dialog box, 212
charts, 208-216
    cutting/pasting, 209-211
    data modifications, 213-215
    document insertion, 208-209
    Microsoft Graph program, 209-216
    modifying type, 211-212
    moving, 209-211
    sizing, 212-213
    titles, 215-216
    Web page, 314
Choose Profile dialog box, 469-470
click+drag, text selection, 37
clip art
    moving/sizing, 172-173
    newsletter addition, 171-173
    paragraph line spacing, 69
Clipboard
    cutting/copying/pasting text, 38
    spiking text, 40
clocks, system, 32-33
Close button, exiting Word, 26
codes, field, 376-384
Collapse button, Outlining toolbar, 84
Collection Letter template, 368-369
colors
    text, 57
    text boxes, 158-159
    Web page text, 302
columns
    changing number of, 166
    deleting from table, 188
    erasing borders, 191-192
    newsletters, 148, 165-170
    space redistribution, 194-195

COMMANDS   485

summing numbers in tables, 183-184
table addition, 184-185
text balance, 169-170
text box sidebar, 166
vertical line between, 169
width adjustments, 193-196
Columns dialog box, 166-167
commands
    Chart, Chart Options, 215
    Chart, Chart Type, 212
    Create Shortcut, 5
    Device, Volume Control, 337
    Edit, Clear, 309
    Edit, Find, 109,, 235
    Edit, Hyperlink, 277
    Edit, Paste Special, 218
    Edit, Paste Special, Paste Link, 378
    Edit, Repeat Format Drawing Object, 159
    Edit, Select All, 36-37
    Edit, Undo, 125
    ellipses (...) characters, 410
    File, Close, 26
    File, New, 6, 30, 146, 269, 372, 439, 459
    File, Page Setup, 123, 126
    File, Print, 136, 419
    File, Print Preview, 134
    File, Properties, 303, 366
    File, Save, 24, 296
    File, Save As, 26, 367
    File, Save As File, 289
    File, Save as HTML, 292, 318, 334
    File, Send To, 257, 278
    File, Send To, Next Routing Recipient, 473
    File, Send To, Routing Recipient, 469
    Format, AutoFormat, 359
    Format, Background, 305, 343
    Format, Borders and Shading, 153, 205
    Format, Bullets and Numbering, 64-65
    Format, Columns, 166
    Format, Font, 10, 41, 52-53, 340
    Format, Paragraph, 68
    Format, Picture, 176
    Format, Style Gallery, 361
    Format, Tabs, 46-47, 153
    Format, Text Box, 158
    Format, Text Colors, 302
    Help, Contents, 19
    Help, Microsoft on the Web, 22-23, 280-285
    Help, What's This?, 20
    Help, WordPerfect, 18
    Insert, AutoText, 33
    Insert, AutoText, AutoText, 40
    Insert, AutoText, New, 34
    Insert, Background Sound, 313
    Insert, Bookmark, 381
    Insert, Break, 114
    Insert, Caption, 186, 379
    Insert, Comment, 378
    Insert, Cross-Reference, 379, 454
    Insert, Date and Time, 32,, 378
    Insert, Field, 357-358, 378-379
    Insert, Form Field, 378
    Insert, Horizontal Line, 306
    Insert, Hyperlink, 272
    Insert, Index and Tables, 379, 452
    Insert, Object, 335
    Insert, Page Numbers, 378
    Insert, Picture, 150, 172,, 209, 311
    Insert, Picture, From File, 324
    Insert, Symbol, 386
    Insert, Text Box, 156
    menu addition, 411-413
    menus, 10-11
    Object, Edit, 337
    Start, New Office Document, 5
    Start, Open Office Document, 5
    Table, Cell Height and Width, 201
    Table, Delete Cells, 188
    Table, Delete Columns, 188
    Table, Delete Rows, 188
    Table, Formula, 183
    Table, Insert Rows, 184, 187
    Table, Select Table, 198, 202
    Table, Show Gridlines, 385
    Table, Sort, 207
    Table, Split Cells, 188
    Table, Table AutoFormat, 197
    toggles, 41, 385
    toolbar buttons versus menu commands, 10
    Tools, AutoCorrect, 62, 94, 97, 359-360
    Tools, AutoSummarize, 468
    Tools, Envelopes and Labels, 137
    Tools, Language, Thesaurus, 107
    Tools, Macro, Macros, 388
    Tools, Macro, Record New Macro, 385
    Tools, Mail Merge, 224
    Tools, Mail Merge, Create, 234
    Tools, Options, 55, 102, 426

COMMANDS

commands *(continued)*
   Tools, Spelling and Grammar, 100
   Tools, Templates and Add-Ins, 371
   Tools, Track Changes, Accept or Reject Changes, 464
   Tools, Track Changes, Compare Documents, 466
   Tools, Track Changes, Highlight Changes, 459
   View, Datasheet, 213-215
   View, Header and Footer, 115, 393
   View, Master Document, 439
   View, Normal, 352
   View, Outline, 74
   View, Ruler, 44, 69
   View, Toolbars, 35, 161, 401-402
   View, Toolbars, Customize, 402
Compare Documents, workgroup document comparisons, 465-466
Compatibility tab, Options dialog box, 430-431
complex tables, 188-196
   cell boundary addition, 191
   cell splitting, 190-191
   column space redistribution, 194-195
   column width adjustments, 193-196
   erasing row/column borders, 191-192
   horizontal cell information alignment, 200-202
   outline drawing, 189-190
   vertical cell information alignment, 202-203
components, Word environment, 9-23
CompuServe, 256
connections, worksheet information, 216-219
Contemporary fax cover sheet, 254
Contemporary Report template, 7, 459
contrast
   color saturation density, 330
   described, 330
   photograph adjustments, 329-332
Control Panel, Microsoft Fax configuration, 264-265
Copy button, Standard toolbar, 40, 182
copyright symbol, (c) AutoCorrect, 92
cover sheets
   fax, 252-253
   sending, 257-260
Create AutoText dialog box, 34
Create Data Source dialog box, 231
Create New Folder button, Save As dialog box, 25, 296
Create Shortcut command, 5
Create Subdocument button, Master Document View toolbar, 442, 448
criteria, searches, 108

Crop tool, Picture toolbar, 326
cropping, versus resizing photographs, 326-327
cross reference, Master document insertion, 453-455
Cross-reference dialog box, 454-455
curly braces {} characters, field characters, 378
cursors, I beam (insertion point), 30
Custom Dictionaries dialog box, 105-106
custom menus, creation, 420-423
custom toolbars, creating, 408-410
Custom.dic file, 105
Customize Bulleted List dialog box, 64
Customize dialog box, 389, 402
Customize Keyboard dialog box, 394-395
Cut button, Standard toolbar, 182

D

Data Form dialog box, 232-235
data source merge documents, 222
   creation, 229-232
   editing, 234-235
   existing, 233-234
   Personal Address Book data, 228-229
   record deletion, 235
   record viewing, 234
data, chart modifications, 213-215
Datasheet
   Microsoft Graph, 209
   modifying chart data, 213-215
Date and Time dialog box, 32
date field, form letter insertion, 357
dates
   document insertion, 32-33
   formats, 32-33
   newsletters, 153
   updating automatically, 33
Decimal tabs, 44
Decrease Indent button, Formatting toolbar, 71
Del (Delete) key, deleting selected text, 38
Delete key, deleting AutoShape/clip art images from newsletters, 175
Demote button, Outlining toolbar, 77-78
Demote to Body Text button, Outlining toolbar, 81
department report, 457-473
Desdemona font, 52
desktop, placing Word startup shortcut on, 5
Device, Volume Control command, 337

dialog boxes
    described, 6
    tabs, 6
dictionaries, custom, 105-106
Distribute Columns Evenly button, Tables and Borders toolbar, 195-196
DOC filename extension, 24
Document Map, 15-17
    collapsing/expanding headings, 16
    displaying/hiding, 15
    heading styles, 15-16
    Microsoft Intellimouse tricks, 17
    outlines, 80
Document Map button, Standard toolbar, 15, 80
document summaries, creation, 466-468
Document templates, 367-368
documents
    animated text addition, 340-342
    announcements, 93-97
    AutoFormatting, 97-98
    automatic formatting, 359-360
    automatic save, 24
    AutoText entry, 33-36
    Blank Document template, 30
    blank lines (Enter key), 31
    bookmarks, 381
    bulleted lists, 60-61, 63-65
    business reports, 179-219
    chart additions, 208-216
    copying a Web address into, 287-288
    correcting/deleting text entry with Backspace key, 34
    data source merge, 222
    date/time insertion, 32-33
    department report, 457-473
    DOC filename extension, 24
    Document1 temporary name, 5
    Document2 temporary name, 7-8
    double-spacing lines, 31
    dragging and dropping selected text, 38-39
    editing selected text, 38-40
    fax attachments, 260-262
    field code insertion, 379
    fill effects, 342-344
    first page header, 121-122
    first time save, 24-25
    folder creation when saving files, 25
    footers, 115-122
    form letters, 355-359
    going to items, 111
    grammar checking, 98-106
    headers, 115-122
    HTML, 26
    hypertext, 26
    I beam cursor (insertion point), 30
    letters, 28-47
    line numbers, 131-134
    lists, 59-67
    main merge, 222
    margins, 123-125
    Master, 435-455
    Master document insertion, 444-445
    memos, 49-71
    navigation with Document Map, 15-17
    newsletters, 144-177
    odd/even page header/footer, 121-122
    online routing, 468-473
    opening new, 6-8, 30
    outlines, 73-89
    page breaks, 115
    page settings, 122-133
    photo insertion, 322-329
    predefined text styles, 42-43
    print previewing, 14, 134-135
    printing, 136-137
    properties, 366
    readability statistics, 104
    relinking header/footer, 120-121
    renaming when saving, 26
    return letter entry, 31
    sales presentation outline, 73-89
    saving, 24-26
    scroll bar navigation, 111
    searches, 107-111
    section breaks, 114-115
    section header/footer, 119-120
    sending as e-mail, 278-279
    simple table insertion, 180-188
    sound clip insertion, 335-337
    spell checking, 98-106
    starting Word with new document, 4-5
    summaries, 466-468
    tabs, 44-47
    templates, 5-8
    text addition, 31-32
    text effects, 41-42
    text entry, 30-36
    text selection, 36-37
    text wrapping, 31

documents *(continued)*
  varying header/footer within, 118-119
  Web document conversion, 317-318
  workgroup, 457-473
  worksheet information connections, 216-219
  writing styles, 102
DOT (template) filename extension, 368
double strikethrough text, 56
double-spacing lines, 31
downloading
  Internet Explorer, 297
  Netscape Navigator, 297
  Web page information, 288-289
dpi (dots per inch), 325
dragging and dropping, selected text, 38-39
Draw Table button, Tables and Borders toolbar, 191
Drawing button, Standard toolbar, 173
drawing objects, file import, 323
Drawing toolbar, 173-175
drawings
  AutoShapes, 173-175
  freehand, 175
  printer, 128
drop-down menus, 10-11

E

e-mail
  document merge, 240-241
  routing recipients, 279
  sending documents as, 278-279
Edit Data Source button, Mail Merge toolbar, 234
Edit Hyperlink dialog box, 277-278
Edit menu, Cut/Copy/Paste commands, 40
Edit tab, Options dialog box, 427-428
Edit, Clear command, 309
Edit, Find command, 109, command, 235
Edit, Hyperlink command, 277
Edit, Paste Special command, 218
Edit, Paste Special, Paste Link command, 378
Edit, Repeat Format Drawing Object command, 159
Edit, Select All command, 36-37
Edit, Undo command, 125
Elegant fax cover sheet, 253
ellipses (...) characters, with commands, 410
emboss text, 56
enclosures, memos, 270

engrave text, 56
Enter key
  moving to next document line, 31
  new paragraph creation, 67
  starting new paragraph, 31
  versus paragraph formatting, 82
Envelope Address style, 353
Envelope Return style, 353
envelopes
  laser printer manual feed, 139
  printing, 137 139
  printing multiple, 224
Envelopes and Labels dialog box, 137-140
environment
  components, 9-23
  Document Map, 15-17
  Help system, 18-23
  menu customization options, 424
  menu modifications, 410-424
  menus, 10-11
  modifications, 399-431
  Office Assistant modifications, 424-426
  Rules of Thumb, 400
  Select Browse Object, 18
  toolbar customization options, 424
  toolbars, 8-10, 400-410
  views, 12-15
  Word option settings, 426-431
eps (Encapsulated Postscript) filename extension, 323
Eraser button, Tables and Borders toolbar, 191
Excel program, worksheet connections, 216-219
Expand button, Outlining toolbar, 84
Expand Subdocuments button, Master Document View toolbar, 445
Explorer, Word startup shortcut, 5
external fax/modem, 256

F

Favorites button, Save As dialog box, 25
fax machines, described, 253
fax template, 5@nd6
Fax Wizard
  document attachments, 260-262
  sending a fax from Word, 265
  sending fax cover page only, 257-260

fax/modems
  described, 253-256
  external, 256
  internal, 256
faxes, 251-265
  cover sheet creation, 252-253
  cover sheet templates, 252
  document attachments, 260-262
  document merge, 240-241
  output selection, 256
  sending cover page only, 257-260
field characters, curly braces {} characters, 378
Field Code (F9) key, 383
field codes, 376-384
  described, 375-376
  displaying, 377
  document insertion, 379
  entering, 378-379
  field characters, 377
  manipulation, 383-384
  numbered captions, 379-381
  numbered sequence field, 382-383
  quotation marks ("") characters, with switches, 378
  switches, 377-388
Field dialog box, 357-358, 379
fields
  as table placeholders, 184
  characters, 377
  date, 357
  form letter, 243
  form letters, 243-247
  memo headings, 269
  merge, 222
  numbered sequence, 382-383
File Locations tab, Options dialog box, 430-431
File, Close command, 26
File, New command, 6, 30, 146, 269, 372, 439, 459
File, Page Setup command, 123, 126
File, Print command, 136, 419
File, Print Preview command, 134
File, Properties command, 303, 366
File, Save As command, 26, 367
File, Save As File command, 289
File, Save as HTML command, 292, 318, 334
File, Save command, 24, 296
File, Send To command, 257, 278
File, Send To, Next Routing Recipient command, 473
File, Send To, Routing Recipient command, 469

filename extensions
  bmp (Windows Bitmap), 323
  DOC, 24
  DOT (template), 368
  eps (Encapsulated PostScript, 323
  gif (Graphics Interchange Format), 323
  jpg (Joint Photographic Experts Group), 323
  pcd (Kodak Photo CD), 323
  pcx (PC Paintbrush), 323
  tif (Tagged Image format), 323
  wmf (Windows Metafile), 323
files
  Custom.dic, 105
  drawing object import, 323
  HTML document save, 26
  naming conventions, 24
  photograph links, 324
  renaming when saving, 26
  sending, 472-473
  template, 5-8
Fill Effects dialog box, 305, 343
fill effects, multimedia documents, 342-344
filters, photograph, 322-323
Find and Replace, 108-110
Find and Replace dialog box, 109-110
Find button, Select Browse Object, 18
Find in Field dialog box, 235
Find Setup Wizard, 19
Find tab, Help system, 19
First Line indent, paragraph formatting, 69-71
folders, creating, 296-297
folders
  creating when saving documents, 25
  Letters & Faxes, 368
  Office 97, 5
  Printer, 256
  selecting when saving documents, 24
  Templates, 367-368
  ValuPack, 373
  Web page storage, 296
Font dialog box, 340-341
  previewing fonts, 52-53
  text effects, 41
fonts
  Arial, 43, 151
  Arial Black, 151
  Baskerville, 53
  described, 30

fonts *(continued)*
   Desdemona, 52
   editing type, 51-54
   Garamond, 53
   Gill Sans, 53
   Howie's Funhouse, 52
   listing available on Formatting toolbar, 52
   Map Symbols, 54
   memos, 271
   Mistral, 52
   newsletters, 150
   point size, 53
   previewing, 52-53
   sizing, 51-54
   symbol, 53, 65
   Times New Roman, 30
   Wingdings, 54
footers, 115-122
   creation, 117-118
   described, 115
   document section, 119-120
   first page, 121-122
   memos, 270
   odd/even page, 121-122
   relinking, 120-121
   varying within a document, 118-119
footnotes, going to, 111
form letters
   customizing, 243-247
   date field insertion, 357
   field additions, 243-247
   macro button fields, 358-359
   styles, 355-359
Format Picture button, Picture toolbar, 328
Format Picture dialog box, 176, 328-329
Format Text Box dialog box, 158-159
Format, AutoFormat command, 359
Format, Background command, 305, 343
Format, Borders and Shading command, 153, 205
Format, Bullets and Numbering command, 64-65
Format, Columns command, 166
Format, Font command, 10, 41, 52-53, 340
Format, Paragraph command, 68
Format, Picture command, 176
Format, Style Gallery command, 361
Format, Tabs command, 46-47, 153
Format, Text Box command, 158
Format, Text Colors command, 302
formats, date/time, 32-33

Formatting toolbar, 9
   Align Left button, 58
   Align Right button, 58
   available fonts, 52
   Bold button, 10, 41
   Bullets button, 60-61
   Center button, 58, 198, 201
   Decrease Indent button, 71
   elements, 9
   Increase Indent button, 71
   Italic button, 41
   Justify button, 58
   Numbering button, 60-61
   Style button, 42-43
   Underline button, 41
Formula dialog box, 183-184
formulas, table number sums, 183-184
freehand drawing, newsletters, 175
functions, menu bar, 11

G

gallery, Office Assistant characters, 426
Garamond fonts, 53
General tab, Options dialog box, 427
gif (Graphics Interchange Format) filename extension, 323
Gill Sans font, 53
global templates, 351
glossary, 475-481
Go To, 111
Go To button, Select Browse Object, 18
gradients, fill effects, 342
grammar check
   green lines under words, 93
   suggestion options, 100
grammar, readability statistics, 104
graphics
   clip art, 171-173
   going to, 111
   modifying on Web page, 311-313
   newsletters, 150
   paragraph line spacing, 69
   Web page addition, 310-313
   wrapping text around, 176-177
green lines, grammar corrections, 93
grids, table, 180-181
gutter margin, 124

HANDS ON **491**

H

hands on
  accepting or rejecting changes to your report, 464
  add a table of contents to your proposal, 451-453
  adding a background sound to a Web page, 313-314
  adding a border, 329
  adding a button to a toolbar, 402-404
  adding a chart title, 215
  adding a clip art image, 171-172
  adding a command to a menu, 411-413
  adding a header or footer to your document, 117
  adding a macro to a menu, 413-415
  adding a picture to a Web page, 310-311
  adding a row to the top of the table, 184-185
  adding a shortcut key to a menu item, 418-419
  adding animated text to the document, 340-342
  adding body text to the Sales Presentation, 81-83
  adding numbered lists, 60-61
  adding scrolling text, 307-309
  adding text effects to memos, 55-56
  adding text to your letter, 31-32
  adding texture to your page, 343
  adding Word Fields to customize a merge document, 243
  adding word fields to customize a merge document, 243-247
  adjusting heading levels in an outline, 77
  adjusting text font and size in a memorandum, 52-53
  aligning text vertically, 129-131
  applying styles, 42-43
  AutoFormatting the simple table, 197
  building the outline for your proposal, 440-441
  centering a table between the left and right margins, 198
  centering text horizontally in a cell, 201
  changing a menu item's hot key, 417-418
  changing the header or footer in a section, 119-120
  changing the hyperlink's text, 273
  changing the number of columns on the page, 166
  changing the text on the Web page, 300
  changing the Web page title, 303
  changing the width of a column, 193-194
  choosing an address book, 228-229
  combining subdocuments in your proposal, 448
  configuring Microsoft Fax, 264
  controlling the direction of the text for the regions, 199-200
  controlling wrapping, 176
  converting an existing Word document to a Web document, 318
  copying a Web address into a Word document, 287-288
  creating a data source, 229-232
  creating a memo with the Memo Wizard, 269-271
  creating a new AutoText entry, 33-34
  creating a routing slip for your report, 469-472
  creating a single-celled first row, 187
  creating a style by example, 364
  creating a text box, 156-157
  creating a Web page with the Web Page Wizard, 294-295
  creating templates, 367
  creating the chart of table 1, 209
  creating you own menu, 420-423
  creating your own AutoCorrect entries, 96-97
  creating your own toolbar, 408
  customizing bullet styles, 63-65
  customizing numbered lists, 65-67
  customizing spelling and grammar functions, 102
  deleting a row, 188
  displaying a document summary, 468
  displaying selected toolbars, 401-492
  displaying the Style area, 352
  displaying various levels of outline, 84-86
  drawing the outline of a table, 189-190
  editing in print preview, 134
  entering headings for an outline, 75-76
  erasing cell dividers, 191
  finding and replacing things, 109-110
  finding the perfect word with Thesaurus, 106-107
  first stage of building a main document, 224-225
  formatting a text box, 158
  formatting the newsletter's table of contents, 164-165
  indenting text in a memorandum, 70-71
  inserting a cross-reference, 454
  inserting a date, 32-33
  inserting a date field in a form letter, 357
  inserting a field code, 379
  inserting a hyperlink into a memo, 272
  inserting a line below the second heading of the Web page, 305
  inserting a numbered caption, 379-381
  inserting a numbered sequence field, 382
  inserting a photo, 324-326
  inserting a section break, 114-115
  inserting a simple table, 180-181
  inserting a table in Word by linking to an Excel workbook, 217-218

492 HANDS ON

hands on *(continued)*
   inserting an existing document into the proposal, 444-445
   inserting macro button fields, 358-359
   inserting sound clips, 335-337
   inseting AutoText with the autoText toolbar, 35-36
   installing Microsoft Fax, 263-264
   jumping to a linked document, 275
   linking text boxes, 161-162
   making the chart bigger, 213
   merging selectively, 239-240
   modifying scrolling text, 309
   modifying styles, 362-363
   modifying the border of an inside cell, 205-206
   modifying the outside border of the table, 203
   modifying the size of the graphic image on the Web page, 311-313
   moving and sizing a clip art image, 172-173
   moving buttons around, 404-405
   moving items around on a menu, 416-417
   moving the chart to the second page, 209-211
   moving the chart to the second page, 209-211
   previewing a Word Web page in a Web browser, 315
   printing a single envelope, 137-139
   providing a caption for the first table, 186
   realigning and indenting text, 300
   rearranging headings in the proposal, 446
   recording a keyboard macro, 394-395
   recording a macro, 385-386
   recording a toolbar macro, 388-393
   redistributing space across columns, 194-195
   relinking headers and footers, 120-121
   removing a button from a toolbar, 406-407
   reorganizing a sales presentation outline, 86-88
   resetting menus, 420
   resetting toolbars, 407
   resizing and cropping photos, 326-329
   resizing text and changing text color, 302-303
   running a spelling and grammar check, 100-102
   running the keyboard macro, 396
   running the macro, 388
   running the Newsletter Wizard, 146-147
   running the toolbar macro, 393
   second stage of building the main document, 235-237
   selecting text, 37
   sending only a fax cover page, 257-260
   setting paper size and orientation, 126-127
   setting paragraph spacing, 67-68
   setting up special headers, 121-122
   setting up the merge, 240-241
   setting up to be able to preview, 366
   setting/removing tabs, 45
   sharing styles between templates, 371-372
   sorting before merging, 238
   sorting the simple table to rank 1966 sales, 207
   splitting cells in a drawn table, 190
   summing columns in a table, 183
   supplying the volume and issue numbers, 152-155
   suppressing line numbers, 133
   tracking changes in a report, 459-463
   turning headings into subdocuments, 442-444
   using an existing data source document, 233-234
   using AutoCorrect in an announcement, 93-94
   using AutoShapes, 173-175
   using drag and drop to move text, 38-39
   using Master Document view, 439
   using Sound Recorder, 338-339
   using templates, 368-370
   using text effects, 41
   using WordArt for the banner text, 150-152
   using WordMail to send a Word document, 278-279
   vertically centering the information in the complex table, 202
   viewing a Web page from inside Word, 280
   viewing the chart as a line chart, 212
   working with line numbers, 132-133
   working with lists, 60
   working with selected text, 38

Hanging Indent, paragraph formatting, 69-70
Header and Footer toolbar, 115-116
   Switch Between Header and Footer button, 393
header record, merge, 222
headers, 115-122
   creation, 117-118
   described, 115
   document section, 119-120
   first page, 121-122
   memos, 270
   odd/even page, 121-122
   relinking, 120-121
   varying within a document, 118-119
heading fields, memos, 269
heading styles, 16-17
   collapsing/expanding, 16
   Document Map, 15-16
   outlines, 83
   right-click shortcut menu, 16-17
   subheadings, 16

headings
    deleting, 89
    demoting/promoting, 76-80
    Master document, 436-440
    moving in outlines, 88
    outline, 75-81
    predefined styles, 42-43
    subdocument conversion, 442-444
    tables, 185
Help
    Contents command, 19
    Microsoft on the Web command, 22-23, 280-285
    What's This? command, 20
    WordPerfect command, 18
Help system, 18-23
    content searches, 19-20
    contents and index, 19-20
    FAQs (Frequently Asked Questions), 281-283
    Find tab, 19
    Office Assistant, 20-22, 424-426
    online help, 281-283
    online support, 282-283
    QuickPick system, 19
    ScreenTips, 116
    ToolTips, 18
    What's This? help, 20
    WordPerfect Help, 18
    World Wide Web, 22-23
Help system ToolTips, 10
hidden text, displaying/printing, 55
Highlight Changes dialog box, 459-460
Horizontal Line dialog box, 306
hot keys, menu item assignments, 417-418
Howie's Funhouse font, 52
HTML (HyperText Markup Language), 292
    documents, saving files as, 26
    styles, 354
    Word 97 support, 289
hyperlinks, 267-289
    described, 267-268
    editing, 277-278
    formatting, 273-274
    jumps, 276
    memos, 272-278
    testing, 275-277
    text entry, 274
    Web site, 287-288
hypertext documents, saving files as, 26

I
I beam cursor (insertion point), 30
Image Control button, Picture toolbar, 332-333
image controls, photographs, 332-333
images
    clip art, 171-173
    deleting from newsletters, 175
    drawing, 173-175
    macro button assignment, 391-393
    modifying on Web page, 311-313
    moving/sizing, 172-173
    newsletter addition, 171-177
    Web page addition, 310-313
    wrapping text around, 176-177
Increase Font Size button, Standard toolbar, 302
Increase Indent button
    Formatting toolbar, 71
    Standard toolbar, 300
indents
    demoted outline heading, 76-77
    paragraph, 69-71
    Web page text, 300
Index and Tables dialog box, 452-453
indexes, Help system, 19-20
information, downloading, 288-289
Insert Hyperlink dialog box, 272
Insert Image dialog box, 325
Insert Merge Field button, Mail Merge toolbar, 236, 243
Insert Picture dialog box, 323
Insert Subdocument button, Master Document View toolbar, 444
Insert Subdocument dialog box, 444-445
Insert Table button, Standard toolbar, 180
Insert Word Field button, Mail Merge toolbar, 243
Insert, AutoText command, 33
Insert, AutoText, AutoText command, 40
Insert, AutoText, New command, 34
Insert, Background Sound command, 313
Insert, Bookmark command, 381
Insert, Break command, 114
Insert, Caption command, 186, 379
Insert, Comment command, 378
Insert, Cross-Reference command, 379, 454
Insert, Date and Time command, 32, command, 378
Insert, Field command, 357-358, 378-379
Insert, Form Field command, 378
Insert, Horizontal Line command, 306

Insert, Hyperlink command, 272
Insert, Index and Tables command, 379, 452
Insert, Object command, 335
Insert, Page Numbers command, 378
Insert, Picture command, 150, 172, command, 209, 311
Insert, Picture, From File command, 324
Insert, Symbol command, 386
Insert, Text Box command, 156
insertion point
  I beam cursor, 30
  table cell navigation, 182
installation
  Microsoft Fax, 263-264
  Web page authoring components, 292
internal fax/modem, 256
Internet Explorer
  adding Web page to Favorites list, 288
  downloading, 297
  selecting as browser, 23
  Web browser, 280
ISP (Internet Service Provider), 268
  publishing Web documents, 317
issue numbers, newsletters, 152-155
Italic button, Formatting toolbar, 41
items
  going to, 111
  hot key menu assignments, 417-418
  moving on menus, 416-417
  shortcut key assignment, 418-419

J

jpg (Joint Photographic Experts Group) filename extension, 323
jumps, hyperlink, 276
justification, newsletters, 149
Justify button, Formatting toolbar, 58

K

keyboards, hyperlink text selection, 273
keyboards, macros, 394-396
keys
  Backspace, 34
  Del (Delete), 38, 175
  Enter, 31, 67, 82
  F7 (Spelling and Grammar), 100
  F9 (Field Code), 383
  Shift+Tab, 182
  Tab, 182
Kodak Photo CD, 322

L

Label Options dialog box, 140
labels, printing, 139-140
landscape orientation, 126-127
laser printers, envelope manual feed, 139
layouts, Web pages, 294-295
leader characters, described, 47
Left Indent, paragraph formatting, 70
left margin, 124
Left tabs, 44
letters, 28-47
  creation, 28-47
  forms, 355-359
  return address, 31
Letters & Faxes folder, 368
levels, outline display, 84-86
line numbers, 131-134
Line Numbers dialog box, 132
line spacing, paragraphs, 67-69
lines
  blank, 31
  double-spacing, 31
  red wavy, 93
  vertical column separator, 169
  Web page separators, 305-307
links
  Excel workbook, 217-218
  newsletter text boxes, 160-162
  photographs, 324
lists, 59-67
  automating, 62-63
  bulleted, 60-61, 63-65
  customizing, 63-67
  document addition, 59
  numbered, 60-61, 65-67
Lock Document button, Master Document View toolbar, 446
long filenames, 32-bit browser support, 297
Lotus 1-2-3 program, 216-219

M

MACO labels, 140
macros, 384-396
   described, 376, 384
   form letter buttons, 358-359
   image button assignment, 391-393
   keyboard, 394-396
   menu addition, 413-415
   planning, 384-385
   previous Word version conversions, 367
   recording, 385-387
   running, 388
   running from toolbar, 393
   status bar REC symbol, 386
   stopping record, 386
   template storage, 384
   toggle command state, 385
   toolbar assignment, 388-393
Mail Merge Helper
   data source documents, 228-237
   document merges, 237-242
   main document creation, 224-228
Mail Merge Helper dialog box, 224
Mail Merge toolbar, 224-227
   Edit Data Source button, 234
   Insert Merge Field button, 236, 243
   Insert Word Field button, 243
main merge document, 222
   creation, 223-228
   existing data source document attachment, 233-234
   field additions, 235-237
   text entry, 226
Map Symbols fonts, 54
margins, 123-125
   applying to document sections, 124-125
   newsletter sections, 155
   types, 124
Master document, 435-455
   creation, 438-441
   cross reference insertion, 453-455
   described, 435-438
   heading level assignments, 436-440
   outline creation, 440-441
   printing, 449-450
   removing subdocuments, 447
   renaming subdocuments, 446-447
   subdocument arrangements, 446
   subdocument combination, 447-449
   subdocument protection, 450-451
   subdocuments, 436-438, 441-451
   table of contents addition, 451-453
   Word document insertion, 444-445
Master Document view, 14
Master Document View toolbar, 439
   Create Subdocument button, 442, 448
   Expand Subdocuments button, 445
   Insert Subdocument button, 444
   Lock Document button, 446
   Merge Subdocuments button, 448
   Subdocument button, 444
Media Player program, sound clip playback, 335-337
Memo templates, 51
Memo Wizard, 268-272
memos, 49-71
   attachments, 270
   Blank Document template, 50
   body text entry, 271
   creation, 49-71
   enclosures, 270
   font sizing, 271
   footers, 270
   headers, 270
   heading fields, 269
   hyperlink insertion, 272-273
   hyperlinks, 272-278
   lists, 59-67
   Memo Wizard creation, 268-272
   paragraph formatting, 67-71
   recipients addresses, 269
   text alignment, 57-59
   text effects, 54-57
   text font style/size, 51-54
   text formatting, 50-59
   titles, 269
   typist's initials, 270
   writer's initials, 270
menu bar, functions, 11
menus, 10-11, 410-424
   command addition, 411-413
   command selections, 10-11
   custom creation, 420-423
   customization options, 424
   hot key assignments, 417-418
   macro addition, 413-415
   modifications, 410-424
   moving items between, 416

MENUS

menus *(continued)*
   moving items on, 416-417
   resetting after modifying, 420
   shortcut key item assignment, 418-419
   submenus, 10-11
   versus toolbars, 10
Merge Subdocuments button, 448
merges
   data source creation, 228-235
   data source document, 222
   e-mail, 240-241
   fax, 240-241
   fields, 222
   form letter, 243-247
   information sorts, 237-239
   main document creation, 222-228
   record selection, 239-240
   records, 222
   setup, 240-241
   special options, 237-240
   unusual situations, 230
merging, described, 221-223
Microsoft Clip Gallery 3.0 dialog box, 172, 311
Microsoft Excel program, 181
Microsoft Exchange, online document routing, 468-473
Microsoft Fax program, 256, 263-265
   configuration, 264
   installation, 264
   sending a fax from Word, 265
Microsoft Graph program
   chart data modifications, 213-215
   chart titles, 215-216
   chart types, 212
   charts, 209-216
   moving charts, 209-211
   sizing charts, 212-213
Microsoft Intellimouse, Document Map tricks, 17
Microsoft Internet Information Server program, 317
Microsoft Network, 256, 280
Microsoft Outlook program, 470
Microsoft's Sound Recorder program, 334
MIDI sequence (Musical Instrument Digital Interface) objets, 334
minus sign (-) character, hide subheadings, Document Map, 16
misspelled words
   red wavy lines, 93
   replacing as you type, 92-97

mistakes
   AutoCorrecting, 92-97
   Backspace key correction, 34
   undoing, 191
   undoing last action, 125
Mistral font, 52
modems, fax capability, 253-256
mouse
   click+drag text selection, 37
   Ctrl+drag text copy, 40
   dragging and dropping selected text, 38-39
   Microsoft Intellimouse, 17
   table cell/row selection, 182
   table column width adjustments, 193-196
   text selection, 36-37
Move Down button, Outlining toolbar, 88
multimedia
   animated text, 340-342
   announcements, 321-345
   described, 321-322
   document fill effects, 342-344
   photographs, 322-333
   sounds, 334-339

N

Netscape Navigator, downloading, 297
New dialog box, 6-7, 459
New Folder dialog box, 296-297
New tool, Standard toolbar, 368
New Toolbar dialog box, 408
Newsletter Wizard, 20, 146-148
newsletters, 144-177
   banners, 150-155
   borders, 153
   changing number of columns, 166
   column creation, 165-170
   column text balance, 169-170
   columns, 148
   date information, 153
   deleting AutoShape/clip art images, 175
   drawing images, 173-175
   element overuse, 150
   fonts, 150
   freehand drawing, 175
   graphics, 150
   image additions, 171-177
   issue numbers, 152-155

OUTLINING TOOLBAR **497**

justification, 149
moving/sizing images, 172-173
Newsletter Wizard, 146-148
paragraph styles, 149
section margins, 155
shading elements, 150
table of contents box, 163-165
text box links, 160-162
text boxes, 155-165
vertical lines between columns, 169
volume numbers, 152-155
wrapping text around pictures, 176-177
Normal style, 350-351
Normal template, 350-351
Normal view, 5, 12
    Style area display, 352
numbered
    captions, field codes, 379-381
    lists, 60-61, 65-67
    sequence fields, document insertion, 382-383
Numbering button, Formatting toolbar, 60-61
numbers, newsletter issue/volume, 152-155

O

Object dialog box, 335
Object, Edit command, 337
objects
    going to, 111
    MIDI sequence, 334
Office 97 folder, starting Word from, 5
Office 97 ValuPack, 317
Office Assistant, 20-22
    accessing, 20, 424
    cartoon characters, 426
    changing personalities, 21
    described, 20
    modifying, 424-426
    natural language interface, 2j0
    searches, 20-22
Office Assistant button, Standard toolbar, 20
Office Assistant dialog box, 21
Office Shortcut Bar, starting Word from, 5
one-to-one relationship, text box link, 160
online help
    accessing, 281-283
    Microsoft on the Web, 22-23
Online Layout view, 12-13

online routing, documents, 468-473
online services
    America Online, 256
    CompuServe, 256
    Microsoft Network, 256, 280
online sources, templates, 6
Open Data Source dialog box, 234
Options dialog box, 426-431
    Compatibility tab, 430-431
    Edit tab, 427-428
    File Locations tab, 430-431
    General tab, 427
    Print tab, 428
    Save tab, 428-429
    spelling and grammar options, 103
    Spelling and Grammar tab, 429
    Track Changes tab, 429-430
    User Information tab, 429-430
    View tab, 427
Organizer dialog box, 371
orientation, page settings, 126-127
outdents, promoted outline heading, 76-77
outline text, 56
Outline view, 13
    displaying, 74
    heading level display, 84-86
    toolbar, 14
outlines, 73-89
    body text, 81-83
    demoting/promoting headings, 76-80
    Document Map, 80
    heading deletion, 89
    heading level display, 84-86
    heading styles, 83
    headings, 75-81
    Master document, 440-441
    paragraph formatting, 83
    reorganizing, 86-88
    sales presentation, 73-89
    table drawing, 189-190
    text formatting, 83
Outlining toolbar, 74
    Collapse button, 84
    Demote button, 77-78
    Demote to Body Text button, 81
    Expand button, 84
    Move Down button, 88
    Promote button, 77
    Show All Headings button, 84-85

Outlining toolbar *(continued)*
    Show First Line Only button, 85-86
    Show Formatting button, 85
    Show Heading 2 button, 85
Outside Border button, Tables and Borders toolbar, 203, 205

P

page alignment, tables, 198-199
page breaks, documents, 115
Page Layout view, 5, 12
page ranges, selecting for print job, 137
page settings, 122-133
    line numbers, 131-133
    margins, 123-125
    paper size/orientation, 126-127
    text alignment, 129-131
Page Setup dialog box, 121-133
pages
    going to, 111
    odd/even header/footer, 121-122
paper
    orientation settings, 126-127
    size settings, 126-127
    source settings, 127-128
Paragraph dialog box, 68
paragraph formatting, 67-71
    First Line indent, 69-71
    Hanging Indent, 69-70
    Left Indent, 70
    line spacing, 67-69
    outlines, 83
    text indents, 69-71
    versus Enter key spacing, 82
paragraph marks, text box, 157
paragraph styles, described, 351-352
paragraphs
    double-spacing lines, 31
    Enter key creation, 67
    starting with Enter key, 31
    text wrapping, 31
    Master document subdocuments, 450-451
Paste button, Standard toolbar, 40, 182
Paste Special dialog box, 218
patterns, fill effects, 342
pcd (Kodak Photo CD) filename extension, 323
pcx (PC Paintbrush) filename extension, 323

Personal Address Book, data source merge documents data, 228-229
Personal Web Server program, 317
personalities, Office Assistant, 21
phone numbers, Toast of Tampa Show Chorus, 168
photographs, 322-333
    See also pictures
    borders, 329
    brightness adjustments, 329-332
    contrast adjustments, 329-332
    cropping, 326-329
    document insertion, 322-329
    drawing object file import, 323
    file links, 324
    filters, 322-323
    image controls, 332-333
    Kodak Photo CD, 322
    negative photo CD processing, 322
    pixel resolution, 325
    resizing, 326-329
phrases, document header/footer addition, 117-118
Picture toolbar, 326
    Crop tool, 327
    Format Picture button, 328
    Image Control button, 332-333
    Reset button, 330
    tools, 326
pictures
    See also photographs
    fill effects, 342
    modifying on Web page, 311-313
    Web page addition, 310-313
    wrapping text around, 176-177
pixels, photograph resolution, 325
placeholders
    searches, 235-237
    table fields, 184
plus sign (+) character, display subheadings, Document Map, 16
points, fonts, 53
portrait orientation, 126-127
Print dialog box, 136-137, 419
Print Preview button, Standard Toolbar, 152
Print Preview toolbar, 134-135
Print Preview view, 14
Print tab, Options dialog box, 428
printer drivers, 128
Printers folder, fax output selection, 256

printers
    dpi (dots per inch), 325
    laser, 139
    paper source settings, 127-128
    selecting, 136
printing, 136-140
    envelope, 137-139
    hidden text, 55
    labels, 139-140
    Master document, 449-450
    multiple envelopes, 224
    page range selection, 137
    previewing, 134-135
    shortcut key assignment list, 419
    text colors, 57
    Web pages, 288
Professional fax cover sheet, 255
programming languages
    Visual Basic for Applications, 367
    WordBasic, 367
programs
    Excel, 181, 216-219
    Lotus 1-2-3, 216-219
    Media Player, 335-337
    Microsoft Fax, 256, 263-265
    Microsoft Graph, 209-216
    Microsoft Internet Information Server, 317
    Microsoft Outlook, 470
    Personal Web Server, 317
    QuickLink Fax, 256
    Sound Recorder, 334, 338-339
    WinFax, 256
    WordArt, 54, 150-152
    WordMail, 278-279
Promote button, Outlining toolbar, 77
Properties dialog box, 366
publishing, Web documents, 317

Q

queries, merge record selection, 239-241
Query Options dialog box, 239-241
QuickLink Fax program, 256
QuickPick system, help system index, 19
quotation mark ("") characters, field code switches, 378

R

readability statistics, Spelling and Grammar, 104
REC symbol, status bar, 386-387
recipients, memos, 269
Record Macro dialog box, 386, 389
records
    deleting, 235
    header, 222
    merge, 222
    merge selection, 239-240
    viewing, 234
red wavy lines, spelling corrections, 93
Reports tab, New dialog box, 6-7
reports
    business, 179-219
    department, 457-473
Reset button, Picture toolbar, 330
Reset Toolbar dialog box, 407
resolution
    photograph pixels, 325
    printer dpi (dots per inch), 325
return address, letters, 31
revision tracking, workgroup documents, 458-466
revisions, workgroup documents acceptance, 463-465
right margin, 124
Right tabs, 44
right-click shortcut menus
    Font dialog box, 52
    heading styles, 16-17
    Spelling check, 98
Routing Slip dialog box, 470-473
routing slips
    creation, 469-472
    online documents, 468-473
    sending files, 472-473
rows
    deleting from table, 188
    erasing borders, 191-192
    table addition, 184-185
    tables, 182
ruler
    displaying, 44
    First Line Indent, 69-71
    Hanging Indent, 69-70
    Left Indent, 70
    Tab button, 45
    tab styles, 44
    text indents, 69-71

Rules of Thumb, environment, 400
rules, AutoCorrect capitalization exceptions, 95

S

sales presentation outline, 73-89
    creation, 74-83
    using Outline view, 84-89
saturation, photograph contrast, 330
Save As dialog box, 24, 296, 367
Save As HTML dialog box, 318
Save button, Standard toolbar, 25
Save tab, Options dialog box, 428-429
ScreenTips, 424
    button functions, 116
scroll bars
    document navigation, 111
    vertical, 18
Scrolling Text dialog box, 307-309
scrolling text, Web pages, 307-309
search engines
    AltaVista, 286
    Microsoft, 285-286
    World Wide Web, 285-287
searches
    criteria, 108
    document, 107-111
    Find and Replace, 108-110
    help contents, 19-20
    Office Assistant, 20-22
    placeholders, 235-237
    World Wide Web, 285-287
section breaks, documents, 114-115
sections, newsletter margins, 155
Select Browse Object
    Find button, 18
    Go To button, 18
Select Browse Object button, vertical scroll bar, 18
selection bar, text selection 36-37
separators
    table row/column borders, 191-192
    vertical column line, 169
shading, table modifications, 203-206
shadow text, 56
Shift+Tab keys, cell table navigation, 182
shortcut keys
    Beginning of document (Ctrl+Home), 385
    Convert (Ctrl+Shift+F9), 184

    Date Field (Alt+Shift+D), 384
    Demote Heading (Shift+Tab), 77
    End of Document (Ctrl+End), 166, 385
    Field Code result (Alt+F9), 383
    Field Code view (Shift+F9), 383
    Field Code/text conversion (Ctrl+Shift+F9), 383
    Insert Spike (Ctrl+Shift+F3), 40
    Lock Field (Ctrl+F11), 384
    menu item assignment, 418-419
    Page Break (Ctrl+Enter), 115, 166
    Previous Field (Shift+F11), 383
    printing lists, 419
    Select (Click+Drag), 37
    Select All (Ctrl+A), 37
    Select Entire Hyperlink (Ctrl+Shift->), 273
    Spike (Ctrl+F3), 40
    table cell tab (Ctrl+Tab), 47
    Thesaurus (Shift+F7), 106
    Unlock Field (Ctrl+Shift+F11), 384
    What's This? (Shift+F1), 20
shortcut menus
    right-click Font dialog box, 52
    right-click Spelling check, 98
shortcuts, Word startup, 5
Show All Headings button, Outlining toolbar, 84-85
Show First Line Only button, Outlining toolbar, 85-86
Show Formatting button, Outlining toolbar, 85
Show Heading 2 button, Outlining toolbar, 85
sidebars, newsletter columns, 166
simple tables
    AutoFormatting, 197
    captions, 185-186
    cell merge, 187-188
    cell splitting, 188
    cell/row selection, 182
    cells, 181
    deleting rows/columns/cells, 188
    described, 180
    field placeholders, 184
    grids, 180-181
    headings, 185
    insertion point cell navigation, 182
    moving/copying text, 182
    number sums, 183-184
    row/column addition, 184-185
    rows, 182
    typing/editing entries, 181-183
Small Caps text, 55
Sort dialog box, 207

sorts
  merge information, 237-239
  table information, 206-208
Sound Blaster sound cards, 334
sound cards, 334
Sound Recorder program, 334, 338-339
sounds, 334-339
  document insertion, 335-337
  MIDI sequence objects, 334
  recording, 338-339
  volume controls, 337
  Web page background, 313-314, 334
sources
  templates, 6, 373
  Wizards, 373
spacing, paragraphs, 67-69
Sparkle Text effect, 341-342
Spelling and Grammar, 98-106
  custom dictionaries, 105-106
  customizing, 102-104
  readability statistics, 104
  writing styles, 102
Spelling and Grammar (F7) key, 100
Spelling and Grammar button, Standard toolbar, 10
Spelling and Grammar dialog box, 100-104
Spelling and Grammar tab, Options dialog box, 429
spelling check
  program limitations, 98-99
  red wavy lines under misspelled words, 93
  suggestion options, 99-100
Spike, Clipboard text selections, 40
spiking text, 40
Split Cells button, Table Borders toolbar, 190
Split Cells dialog box, 190-191
standard (built-in) styles, 353-354
Standard toolbar, 9
  Align Left button, 300
  Copy button, 40, 182
  Cut button, 182
  Document Map button, 15, 80
  Drawing button, 173
  elements, 9
  Increase Font Size button, 302
  Increase Indent button, 300
  Insert Table button, 180
  New tool, 368
  Office Assistant button, 20
  Office Assistant tool, 424
  Paste button, 40, 182

Print Preview button, 152
Save button, 25
Spelling and Grammar button, 10
Tables and Borders button, 189
Undo button, 191
Web Page Preview button, 315
Web Toolbar button, 10, 276
Start menu, starting Word, 4
Start
  New Office Document command, 5
  Open Office Document command, 5
status bar, REC symbol, 386-387
strikethrough text, 56
Style button, Formatting toolbar, 42-43
Style Gallery, 355, 361-365
  style creation, 364-365
  style modifications, 362-363
Style Gallery dialog box, 361
styles
  applying, 354-365
  automatic document formatting, 354, 359-360
  built-in (standard), 353-354
  bullet, 63-65
  character, 351-352
  creating by example, 364-365
  custom, 355
  described, 16, 350-352
  document writing, 102
  Envelope Address, 353
  Envelope Return, 353
  fax cover sheet, 252-253
  form letters, 355-359
  heading, 15-16, 42-43, 83
  HTML, 354
  modifying, 362-363
  Normal, 350-351
  paragraph, 351-352
  predefined text, 42-43
  sharing between templates, 371-372
  Style Gallery, 355, 361-365
  Web pages, 294-295
subdocuments
  combining, 447-449
  creation, 442-444
  heading conversion, 442-444
  Master document, 436-438, 441-451
  moving, 446
  passwords, 450-451
  protecting, 450-451

subdocuments *(continued)*
    removing, 447
    renaming, 446-447
subheadings, Document Map display, 16
submenus, 10-11
subscript text, 56
summary, document, 466-468
superscript text, 56
Switch Between Header and Footer button, Header and Footer toolbar, 393
switches, field code, 377-388
Symbol dialog box, 65, 386
symbol fonts, 53, 65
symbols
    bulleted lists, 60, 63-65
    copyright (c) AutoCorrect, 92
    REC, 386-387
synonyms, Thesaurus, 106-107
system clock, date/time document insertion, 32-33

T

Tab button, ruler, 45
Tab key
    cell table navigation, 182
    tab settings, 45
Table AutoFormat dialog box, 197
table cells, tabs, 47
table formatting, 197-206
    AutoFormatting simple table, 197
    border modifications, 203-206
    cell border modifications, 205-206
    centering tables, 198-199
    horizontal cell information alignment, 200-202
    page alignment, 198-199
    shading modifications, 203-206
    text direction control, 199-200
    vertical cell information alignment, 202-203
table of contents
    Master document addition, 451-453
    newsletters, 163-165
Table, Cell Height and Width command, 201
Table, Delete Cells command, 188
Table, Delete Columns command, 188
Table, Delete Rows command, 188
Table, Formula command, 183
Table, Insert Rows command, 184, 187
Table, Select Table command, 198, 202
Table, Show Gridlines command, 385
Table, Sort command, 207
Table, Split Cells command, 188
Table, Table AutoFormat command, 197
Tables and Borders button
    Eraser button, 191
    Standard toolbar, 189
Tables and Borders toolbar
    Center Vertically button, 202
    Change Text Direction button, 200
    Distribute Columns Evenly button, 195-196
    Draw Table, button, 191
    Outside Border button, 203, 205
    Split Cells button, 190
tables
    captions, 185-186
    cell boundary addition, 191
    cell merge, 187-188
    cell splitting, 188, 190-191
    cell/row selection, 182
    chart creation, 209
    column space redistribution, 194-195
    column width adjustments, 193-196
    complex, 188-196
    deleting rows/columns/cells, 188
    document insertion, 180-188
    erasing row/column borders, 191-192
    field placeholders, 184
    going to, 111
    grids, 180-181
    header record, 222
    headings, 185
    information sorts, 206-208
    insertion point navigation, 182
    merge field, 222
    merge record, 222
    moving/copying text, 182
    number sums, 183-184
    outline drawing, 189-190
    row/column addition, 184-185
    simple, 180-188
    typing/editing entries, 181-183
tabs, 44-47
    dialog boxes, 6
    leader characters, 47
    setting/removing, 44-47
    types, 44

Tabs dialog box, 46-47, 153
templates, 5-8, 366-372
    applying, 368-370
    Blank Document, 30, 43, 50, 58
    Collection Letter, 368-369
    Contemporary Report, 7, 459
    creation, 367-368
    described, 5-6, 252, 350-351
    Document, 367-368
    fax, 5-6
    fax cover sheet, 252
    global, 351
    macro storage, 384
    Memo, 51
    modifying, 370-372
    Normal, 350-351
    online sources, 6
    opening, 370-371
    opening as template, 7
    sources, 373
    style sharing, 371-372
Templates and Add-ins dialog box, 371
Templates folder, saving text as a template, 367-368
terms, 475-481
text
    animated, 340-342
    autoformatting as you type, 97-98
    AutoText, 33-36
    balancing between newsletter columns, 169-170
    colors, 57
    copying, 38-40
    Ctrl+drag copying, 40
    deleting, 38-40
    displaying/printing hidden, 55
    document addition, 31-32
    document entry, 30-36
    dragging and dropping, 38-39
    editing selected, 38-40
    formatting, 50-59
    grammar checking, 98-106
    hyperlink entry, 274
    indents, 69-71
    main merge document, 226
    memo body, 271
    moving, 38-40
    moving/copying in tables, 182
    newsletter banners, 150-152
    outline body, 81-83
    printing selected, 137
    replacing misspellings as you type, 92-97
    selecting, 36-37
    selecting before setting tabs, 45
    spell checking, 98-106
    spiking, 40
    text box entry, 163
    unique formatting AutoCorrect entry creation, 96
    vertical alignment, 129-131
    Web page entry/formatting, 299-304
    wrapping, 31
    wrapping around pictures, 176-177
Text Box toolbar, 161-162
text boxes
    colors, 158-159
    creation, 156-157
    formatting, 158
    linking, 160-162
    newsletters, 155-165
    one-to-one relationships, 160
    paragraph marks, 157
    sizing, 156
    text entry, 163
text formatting
    alignment, 57-59
    ALL CAPS, 56
    boldfacing, 10, 41-42, 55
    colors, 57
    double strikethrough, 56
    double-spacing lines, 31
    effects, 54-57
    emboss, 56
    engrave, 56
    hidden, 56
    italicizing, 41-42, 55
    outline, 56, 83
    paragraphs, 67-71
    predefined styles, 42-43
    shadow, 56
    sizing, 55
    Small Caps, 55-56
    special effects, 41-42
    strikethrough, 56
    subscript, 56
    superscript, 56
    underlining, 41-42
    Web page colors, 302
    Web page sizing, 302
    Web pages, 299-304
    when to use, 57

textures, fill effects, 342
Thesaurus dialog box, 106-107
tif (Tagged Image format) filename extensions, 323
Times New Roman font, 30
times
    document insertion, 32-33
    formats, 32-33
tips
    =Rand() sample text entry, 163
    adding cell boundaries to tables, 191
    adding menu commands to toolbars, 10
    adding text after chart insertion, 209
    adding Web page to Favorites list, 288
    animated text guidelines, 341
    applying text effects from font dialog box, 41
    banner print preview, 152
    built-in HTML styles, 354
    capitalization rule exceptions, Spelling and Grammar dialog box, 95
    cell text alignment, 201
    cell text centering, 201
    chart title selection handle sizing, 216
    clip art on the CD, 310
    clip art selection, 311
    closing menus, 412
    closing Office Assistant, 270
    column width adjustments, 194
    column/row table additions, 181
    combining documents, 466
    context-sensitive toolbars, 401
    converting prior Word version macros, 388
    copying templates from the Organizer dialog box, 372
    copying text, 40
    creating hyperlinks before closing Web page, 297
    creating shortcut to Word, 5
    custom shortcut key non-display, 424
    custom toolbar template assignment, 408
    customizing Office assistant, 21
    deleting clip art/AutoShape images from newsletters, 175
    delete original subdocument after renaming it, 447
    deleting scrolling text, 309
    demote/promote headings, 77
    display Font dialog box, 52
    displaying body text, 86
    displaying current time and date, 33
    displaying hidden field codes, 383
    document AutoFormat, 359
    document bookmarks, 381
    document page breaks, 115

document section breaks, 114
Drawing toolbar text box button, 156
e-mail routing recipients, 279
ellipses (...) with commands, 410
fax cover sheet information storage, 260
Find All Word Forms tool, 468
font size stated in points, 53
FTP site file saving, 318
generating an index, table of figures or table of authorities, 453
grammar check disable, 100
hidden text, printing and displaying, 55
HTML (HyperText Markup Language), 292
HTML format support, 289
hyperlink jumps, 276
hyperlinks in WordMail messages, 279
identifying user that makes revisions, 463
insertion point, 64
item captions, 380
keyboard macro key assignments, 395
locating Templates folder, 368
macro button toolbar display, 393
making multiple changes, 461
menu commands for cut/copy/paste, 40
modifying color to indicate revisions, 461
modifying Internet Explorer, 23
mouse pointer shapes, 193
moving a chart, 213
moving headings that contain subheadings and body text, 88
moving items between menus, 416
multimedia file Web sources, 324
newsletter paragraph borders, 153
newsletter section margins, 155
Normal template document opening, 368
Page Setup dialog box quick display from ruler, 124
paragraph selection when Style area is visible, 352
placeholder search, 235
printer drivers, 128
printing envelope to Exchange/Outlook address book address, 138
printing multiple envelopes, 224
printing selected text, 137
printing shortcut key assignment list, 419
recording macros with status bar REC symbol, 386
removing commands from custom menu, 423
removing shortcut key assignments, 419
reordering field names in merge list, 232
resetting picture images, 330

right-click Spelling check shortcut menu, 98
Same as Previous button, Header and Footer toolbar, 119
sample text in text boxes, 163
saving documents as HTML document, 334
saving documents before inserting hyperlinks, 271
saving subdocuments, 443
saving text as a template, 367
saving Web pages when creating, 296
scroll bar document navigation, 111
selecting and replacing text, 38
selecting fonts, 52
selecting how to view revisions in a document, 464
selecting hyperlink text with the keyboard, 273
shortcut to indenting, 71
smaller Find and Replace dialog box, 110
Spelling and Grammar options, 102-103
Spelling and Grammar writing styles, 102
splitting table cells, 188
stopping sound playback, 337
table "totals" rows, 209
table borders, 205
table column alignment, 207
table formulas, 184
table headings, 185
testing hyperlinks, 278
testing menu modifications, 413
testing modified toolbars, 403
text box column sidebar, 166
text box link creation, 160
text box paragraph marks, 157
text box repeat formatting, 159
text box sizing, 156
text, turning into a bulleted list, 64
undoing accidental section break deletions, 125
undoing mistakes, 191
unique formatting AutoCorrect text entry, 96
use WordArt to apply special effects, 54
use WordPerfect help, 18
using a wizard to create an address book, 471
viewing toolbars, 402
viewing toolbars, 404
Web page text color, 302
titles
   charts, 215-216
   memos, 269
   Web page, 303

toggles
   buttons, 10
   command, 385
   command buttons, 41
toolbars, 8-10, 400-410
   assigning macro to, 388-393
   AutoSummarize, 468
   AutoText, 34-35
   button additions, 402-404
   button arrangements, 404-405
   button removal, 406-407
   custom creation, 408-410
   customization options, 424
   customizing, 400-410
   displaying selected, 401-402
   Drawing, 173-175
   Formatting, 9
   Header and Footer, 115-116
   macro button display, 393
   Mail Merge, 224-227
   Master Document View, 439
   Outline view, 13
   Outlining, 74
   Picture, 326
   Print Preview, 134-135
   restoring to default, 407
   running macros, 393
   Standard, 9
   Text Box, 161-162
   toggle buttons, 10
   tool ToolTips, 10
   versus menus, 10
   viewing, 401-402
   Web, 275-276
Tools, AutoCorrect command, 62, 94, 97, 359-360
Tools, AutoSummarize command, 468
Tools, Envelopes and Labels command, 137
Tools, Formatting toolbar, 9
Tools, Language, Thesaurus command, 107
Tools, Macro, Macros command, 388
Tools, Macro, Record New Macro command, 385
Tools, Mail Merge command, 224
Tools, Mail Merge, Create command, 234
Tools, Options command, 55, 102, 426
Tools, Picture toolbar, 326
Tools, Spelling and Grammar command, 100
Tools, Standard toolbar, 9
Tools, Templates and Add-Ins command, 371

Tools, Tool Tips

Tools, ToolTips, 10
Tools, Track Changes, Accept or Reject Changes command, 464
Tools, Track Changes, Compare Documents command, 466
Tools, Track Changes, Highlight Changes command, 459
ToolTips, 10, 18
top margin, 124
Track Changes menu, 460
Track Changes tab, Options dialog box, 429-430
trays, printer paper, 127-128
typing mistakes
    AutoCorrecting, 92-97
    Backspace key correction, 34
typist's initials, memos, 270

U

Underline button, Formatting toolbar, 41
Undo button, Standard toolbar, 191
undoing last action, 125, 191
Up One Level button, Save As dialog box, 25
URL (Universal Resource Locator), copying into a Word document, 287-288
Use Address Book dialog box, 229
User Information tab, Options dialog box, 429-430

V

ValuPack folder
    templates, 373
    Wizards, 373
vertical
    alignment, text, 129-131
    lines, columns separators, 169
    scroll bar, Select Browse Object button, 18
View menu, selecting views from, 14
View tab, Options dialog box, 427
View, Datasheet command, 213-215
View, Header and Footer command, 115, 393
View, Master Document command, 439
View, Normal command, 352
View, Outline command, 74
View, Ruler command, 44, 69
View, Toolbars command, 35, 161, 401-402
View, Toolbars, Customize command, 402

views
    described, 12-15
    Master Document, 14, 436
    Normal, 5, 12, 352
    Online Layout, 12-13
    Outline, 13, 74-89
    Page Layout, 5, 12
    Print Preview, 14
    switching between, 14
Visual Basic for Applications language, 367
Volume Control panel, 337
volume numbers, newsletters, 152-155

W

Web address, copying into a Word document, 287-288
Web authoring features, 298-299
Web browsers
    32-bit long filename support, 297
    adding Web page to Favorites list, 288
    Internet Explorer, 280
    launching from inside Word, 280
    previewing Web pages, 314-317
Web documents
    publishing, 317
    Word document conversion, 317-318
Web Page Preview button, Standard toolbar, 315
Web Page Wizard, Web page creation, 293-295
Web pages, 291-319
    background pattern, 304-305
    background sounds, 313-314, 334
    bullets, 300
    chart additions, 314
    creation, 293-299
    design issues, 292-293
    downloading speed, 293
    graphic additions, 310-313
    graphic modifications, 311-313
    HTML (HyperText Markup Language), 292
    hyperlinks, 287-288
    indents, 300
    layouts, 294-295
    line separator insertion, 305-307
    modifying, 299-317
    previewing, 314-317
    printing, 288
    publishing, 291-319
    readability, 292-293

saving, 295-298
scrolling text, 307-309
storage folder creation, 296-297
styles, 294-295
text colors, 302
text entry, 299-304
text formatting, 299-304
text sizing, 302
titles, 303
viewing from inside Word, 280
Web authoring features, 298-299

Web sites
Azar grammar series, 99
Creative Labs, 334
fonts, 54
Internet Explorer download, 297
Microsoft, 23
Microsoft FAQ's (Frequently Asked Questions), 23
Microsoft Fax, 263
Microsoft Home Page, 283-284
Microsoft Office, 373
Microsoft online reference manual, 39
Microsoft Word templates, 6
Microsoft's Best of the Web, 284-285
Microsoft's FAQs (Frequently Asked Questions), 281-282
Microsoft's Free Stuff, 281
Microsoft's Online Support, 282-283
Microsoft's Search page, 286
Microsoft's Support Wizard, 283
Microsoft's What's New page, 281
Netscape Navigator download, 297
photography, 325
Prima Publishing's Other Books page, 287-288
Web Tutorial, 284-285

Web toolbar, 275-276
displaying/hiding, 276

Web Toolbar button
displaying/hiding on Standard toolbar, 276
Standard toolbar, 10

What's This? help, 20
WinFax program, 256
Wingdings fonts, 54
Wizards, 372-373
accessing, 372
described, 20
Fax, 257-265
Find Setup, 19
Memo Wizard, 268-272
Newsletter, 20, 146-148

sources, 373
Web Page, 293-295

wmf (Windows Metafile) filename extension, 323
Word 97
environment components, 9-23
exiting, 26
HTML format support, 289
opening a new document upon startup, 4-5
opening from Start menu, 4
shortcut creation, 5
starting, 4-5
Web authoring features, 298-299
Web browser launch, 280

WordArt Gallery dialog box, 150-151
WordArt program, 54
newsletter banner text, 150-152

WordBasic language, 376
WordMail program, 278-279
hyperlinked messages, 279
sending Word document as e-mail, 278-279

WordPerfect Help, accessing, 18
words
Find and Replace search, 108-110
grammar correction green lines, 93
misspelled red wavy line display, 93
right-click Spelling check shortcut menu, 98
Thesaurus, 106-107

workgroup documents
document comparisons, 465-466
revision acceptance, 463-465
revision tracking, 458-466
tracking changes, 458-466

World Wide Web (WWW)
HTML (hypertext) documents, 26
online Word Help, 22-23
search engines, 285-287

wrapping
text, document entries, 31
text around pictures, 176-177

writer's initials, memos, 270

# # #

The Essential Word 97 Book

Your COMMENTS
Send Us

Dear Reader:

Thank you for buying this book. In order to offer you more quality books on the topics *you* would like to see, we need your input. At Prima Publishing, we pride ourselves on timely responsiveness to our readers needs. If you'll complete and return this brief questionnaire, *we will listen!*

Name: (first) _____ (M.I.) _____ (last) _____

Company: _____ Type of business: _____

Address: _____ City: _____ State: _____ Zip: _____

Phone: _____ Fax: _____ E-mail address: _____

May we contact you for research purposes? ❏ Yes ❏ No
(If you participate in a research project, we will supply you with your choice of a book from Prima CPD)

---

❶ How would you rate this book, overall?
- ❏ Excellent
- ❏ Fair
- ❏ Very Good
- ❏ Below Average
- ❏ Good
- ❏ Poor

❷ Why did you buy this book?
- ❏ Price of book
- ❏ Content
- ❏ Author's reputation
- ❏ Prima's reputation
- ❏ CD-ROM/disk included with book
- ❏ Information highlighted on cover
- ❏ Other (Please specify): _____

❸ How did you discover this book?
- ❏ Found it on bookstore shelf
- ❏ Saw it in Prima Publishing catalog
- ❏ Recommended by store personnel
- ❏ Recommended by friend or colleague
- ❏ Saw an advertisement in: _____
- ❏ Read book review in: _____
- ❏ Saw it on Web site: _____
- ❏ Other (Please specify): _____

❹ Where did you buy this book?
- ❏ Bookstore (name) _____
- ❏ Computer Store (name) _____
- ❏ Electronics Store (name) _____
- ❏ Wholesale Club (name) _____
- ❏ Mail Order (name) _____
- ❏ Direct from Prima Publishing
- ❏ Other (please specify): _____

❺ Which computer periodicals do you read regularly? _____
_____
_____

❻ Would you like to see your name in print?

May we use your name and quote you in future Prima Publishing books or promotional materials?
❏ Yes   ❏ No

❼ Comments & Suggestions: _____
_____
_____

SAVE A STAMP

Visit our Web Site at: **http://www.primapublishing.com** and simply fill in one of our online Response Forms

8 Where do you use your computer?

Work	☐ 100%	☐ 75%	☐ 50%	☐ 25%
Home	☐ 100%	☐ 75%	☐ 50%	☐ 25%
School	☐ 100%	☐ 75%	☐ 50%	☐ 25%

Other _____

9 How do you rate your level of computer skills?

☐ Beginner
☐ Advanced
☐ Intermediate

10 What is your age?

☐ Under 18
☐ 18-24
☐ 25-29
☐ 30-39
☐ 40-49
☐ 50-59
☐ 60-over

11 I would be interested in computer books on these topics

☐ Word Processing
☐ Database:
☐ Networking
☐ Spreadsheets
☐ Desktop Publishing
☐ Web site design

Other _____

PLEASE
PLACE
STAMP
HERE

PRIMA PUBLISHING
Computer Products Division
701 Congressional Blvd., Suite 350
Carmel, IN 46032

To Order Books

Please send me the following items:

Quantity	Title	Unit Price	Total
_____	_____	$_____	$_____
_____	_____	$_____	$_____
_____	_____	$_____	$_____
_____	_____	$_____	$_____
_____	_____	$_____	$_____

Shipping and Handling depend on Subtotal.

Subtotal	Shipping/Handling
$0.00–$14.99	$3.00
$15.00–$29.99	$4.00
$30.00–$49.99	$6.00
$50.00–$99.99	$10.00
$100.00–$199.99	$13.50
$200.00+	Call for Quote

Foreign and all Priority Request orders:
Call Order Entry department
for price quote at 916/632-4400

This chart represents the total retail price of books only (before applicable discounts are taken).

Subtotal $_____
Deduct 10% when ordering 3-5 books $_____
7.25% Sales Tax (CA only) $_____
8.25% Sales Tax (TN only) $_____
5.0% Sales Tax (MD and IN only) $_____
Shipping and Handling* $_____
Total Order $_____

By Telephone: With MC or VISA, call 800-632-8676 or 916-632-4400, Mon - Fri, 8:30 - 4:30 P.S.T.

By E-mail: We're on the Web at http://www.primapublishing.com.
Send orders to: sales@primapub.com

By Mail: Just fill out the information below and send with your remittance to:

Prima Publishing
P.O. Box 1260BK
Rocklin, CA 95677

My name is _____

I live at _____

City _____ State _____ Zip _____

MC/VISA# _____ Exp _____

Check/Money Order enclosed for $_____ Payable to Prima Publishing

Daytime Telephone _____

Signature _____

Other Books from Prima Publishing, Computer Products Division

ISBN	Title	Price	Release Date
0-7615-0801-5	ActiveX	$40.00	Available Now
0-7615-0680-2	America Online Complete Handbook and Membership Kit	$24.99	Available Now
0-7615-0915-1	Building Intranets with Internet Information Server and FrontPage	$40.00	Available Now
0-7615-0417-6	CompuServe Complete Handbook and Membership Kit	$24.95	Available Now
0-7615-0849-X	Corporate Intranet Development	$45.00	Available Now
0-7615-0743-4	Create FrontPage Web Pages in a Weekend	$29.99	Available Now
0-7615-0692-6	Create Your First Web Page in a Weekend	$29.99	Available Now
0-7615-0428-1	The Essential Excel 97 Book	$24.99	Available Now
0-7615-0969-0	The Essential Office Book	$27.99	Available Now
0-7615-0695-0	The Essential Photoshop Book	$35.00	Available Now
0-7615-0752-3	The Essential Windows NT 4 Book	$27.99	Available Now
0-7615-1013-3	Hands-On Java	$40.00	Spring '97
0-7615-1046-X	Hands-On Visual Basic 5	$40.00	Spring '97
0-7615-1005-2	Internet Information Server 3 Administrator's Guide	$40.00	Available Now
0-7615-0815-5	Introduction to ABAP/4 Programming for SAP	$45.00	Available Now
0-7615-0901-1	Leveraging Visual Basic with ActiveX Controls	$45.00	Available Now
0-7615-1008-7	Microsoft Excel 97 Visual Learning Guide	$16.99	Available Now
0-7615-1162-8	Microsoft Office 97 Visual Learning Guide	$16.99	Available Now
0-7615-1007-9	Microsoft Word 97 Visual Learning Guide	$16.99	Available Now
0-7615-0690-X	Netscape Enterprise Server	$40.00	Available Now
0-7615-0691-8	Netscape FastTrack Server	$40.00	Available Now
0-7615-0852-X	Netscape Navigator 3 Complete Handbook	$24.99	Available Now
0-7615-0759-0	Professional Web Design	$40.00	Available Now
0-7615-0773-6	Programming Internet Controls	$45.00	Available Now
0-7615-0914-3	Programming ISAPI with Visual Basic 5	$40.00	Spring '97
0-7615-0780-9	Programming Web Server Applications	$40.00	Available Now
0-7615-0063-4	Researching on the Internet	$29.95	Available Now
0-7615-0686-1	Researching on the World Wide Web	$24.99	Available Now
0-7615-0769-8	VBScript Master's Handbook	$45.00	Available Now
0-7615-0684-5	VBScript Web Page Interactivity	$40.00	Available Now
0-7615-0903-8	Visual FoxPro 5 Enterprise Development	$45.00	Available Now
0-7615-0814-7	Visual J++	$35.00	Available Now
0-7615-0726-4	Webmaster's Handbook	$40.00	Available Now
0-7615-0751-5	Windows NT Server 4 Administrator's Guide	$50.00	Available Now
0-7615-1083-4	WordPerfect 8 Visual Learning Guide	$16.99	Spring '97

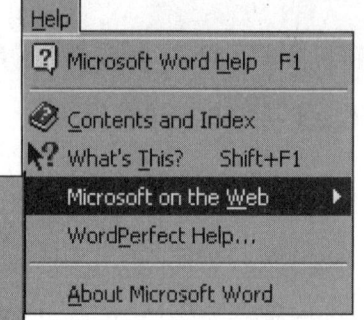
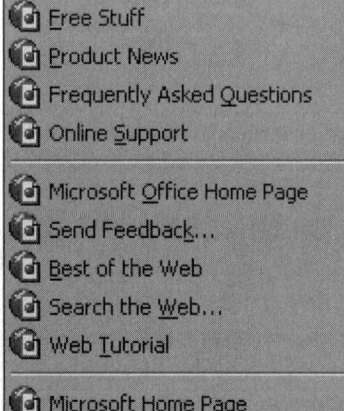

Microsoft

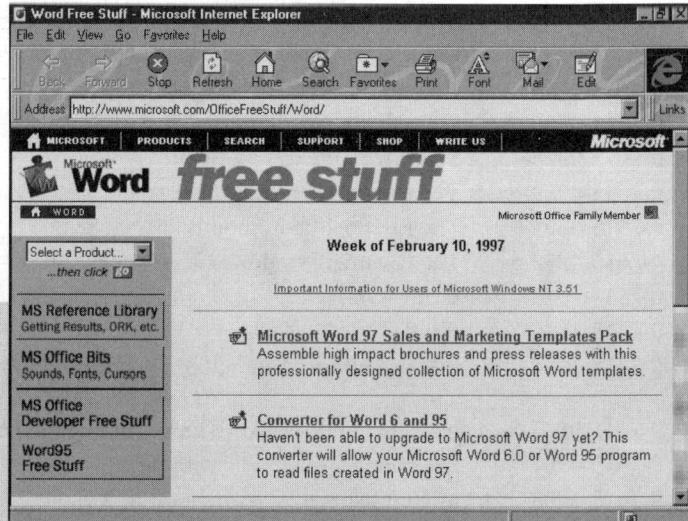

Free Stuff

- Get free multimedia files
- Receive Web publishing tools
- Find support drivers and add-ins
- Get product updates

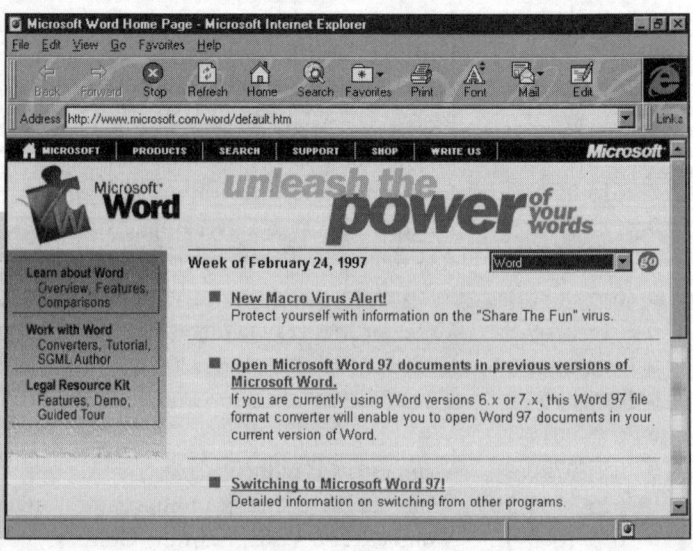

Product News

- Download virus alerts
- Get file format converters
- Read information on making the move to Word 97
- Look at the Microsoft Word 97 Brochure of features
- Obtain specialty items, such as the Legal Resource Kit